Strategic Advertising Management

Strategic Advertising Management

THIRD EDITION

LARRY PERCY

RICHARD ELLIOTT

OXFORD

UNIVERSITY PRESS

OXFORD

UNIVERSITY PRESS

Great Clarendon Street, Oxford OX2 6DP

Oxford University Press is a department of the University of Oxford.
It furthers the University's objective of excellence in research, scholarship,
and education by publishing worldwide in

Oxford New York

Auckland Cape Town Dar es Salaam Hong Kong Karachi
Kuala Lumpur Madrid Melbourne Mexico City Nairobi
New Delhi Shanghai Taipei Toronto

With offices in

Argentina Austria Brazil Chile Czech Republic France Greece
Guatemala Hungary Italy Japan Poland Portugal Singapore
South Korea Switzerland Thailand Turkey Ukraine Vietnam

Oxford is a registered trade mark of Oxford University Press
in the UK and in certain other countries

Published in the United States
by Oxford University Press Inc., New York

The moral rights of the authors have been asserted
Database right Oxford University Press (maker)

First published 2001
Second edition 2005
Third edition 2009

British Library Cataloguing in Publication Data

Data available

Library of Congress Cataloging in Publication Data

Percy, Larry.
    Strategic advertising management / Larry Percy, Richard Elliott.—3rd ed.
       p. cm.
    ISBN 978–0–19–953257–5
  1. Sales promotion. 2. Advertising—Management. 3. Strategic
planning. 4. Communication in marketing. I. Elliott, Richard H.
II. Title.
    HF5438.5.P475 2008
    659.1—dc22   2008038449

Typeset by Newgen Imaging Systems (P) Ltd., Chennai, India
Printed in Italy by
L.E.G.O. S.p.A.

ISBN 978–0–19–953257–5

10 9 8 7 6 5 4 3 2 1

■ PREFACE TO THE THIRD EDITION

Over the last ten years, since the first edition of this book, the world of advertising and marketing communication has seen significant and continuing change. It began with a downsizing of the overall business, a reorientation in the way business was handled by agencies and media companies, and now a rapidly changing media environment. While today, and for the foreseeable future, 'traditional' forms of media will still account for the bulk of media spending, there is no questioning the inroads and growth of what has come to be called the 'new media'.

While this new media offers many new options for delivering advertising and promotion messages, the key to successful communication remains effective strategic planning to identify the optimum target audience, understand how they make purchase decisions in a category in order to positively influence brand choice, find the best positioning for the brand in its marketing communication, determine the most effective communication strategy for the message, and come up with a media strategy that not only maximizes the number of target audience members reached, but importantly the appropriate media for optimizing the likelihood the message will be processed. This continues to be what this book is all about.

The strategic planning process establishes the core framework for the book, and it is the strategic orientation to everything covered that sets it apart from most other advertising texts. The strategic orientation informs discussions of the understandings managers need in order to make the decisions necessary for the effective development and delivery of the brand's message. This means understanding how advertising and promotion 'work', identifying what is necessary for effective communication. We leave it to introductory texts to talk about different types of advertising and media.

It is perhaps a good idea to again remind readers that although most of our discussion and examples are consumer oriented, this is only meant as a convenience to readers who will likely be more familiar with consumer marketing rather than business-to-business or corporate. The key point is that the principles involved are the same, regardless of the market. Individuals process messages in the same way regardless of whether that message is about a business purchase decision, the financial situation of a corporation, public service goals, or even political candidates. The strategic planning and communication principles discussed in this book apply to any attempt to persuade with marketing communication.

This third edition of the book builds upon earlier editions in a number of ways. Perhaps the most important change is a more thorough integration of promotion as a strategic consideration throughout the text. This underscores the important role consideration of promotion should play in the strategic planning process. At every point in planning the manager must ask whether some *immediate* tactical response from the market is needed, in addition to the brand's advertising. Various specific types of promotion are now considered separately, under the more usual term of sales promotion. The book also now includes:

- A new chapter dealing with the many cultural considerations needed with international advertising.
- An overview of the role different aspects of the broader communications mix plays in the overall delivery of advertising and promotional messages, including such things as personal selling, sponsorships, public relations, and trade shows.
- A more extensive discussion of new media.
- A discussion of ethics in the creation of advertising.
- Case studies relevant to each chapter, along with study questions.

As always, our thanks to all those involved in the hard work necessary in completing the new edition. This includes all those who reviewed the manuscript and our editors at OUP, with special thanks to Helen Cook who did all of the tedious work in tracking down permissions for the adverts used in the book. Special thanks too for Kristie Hutto who typed all of the changes and additions from the first author's handwritten pages, and to Hazal Huang and Natalia Yannopoulou for pulling together the cases. And finally, for the ongoing support of our wives, Mary Walton Percy and Chris Elliott.

Larry Percy
Richard Elliott
July 2008

▦ CONTENTS

LIST OF TABLES

■ LIST OF FIGURES

LIST OF ADVERTS

■ LIST OF PLATES

Overview of Advertising and Promotion

What are Advertising and Promotion?

➡ **KEY CONCEPTS**

1 The basic difference between advertising and promotion is that advertising is strategically more long term, 'turning' the consumer towards the brand by creating positive brand attitude, while promotion is more short term, focusing on immediate sales.

2 Advertising 'works' when the desired communication effect is achieved, and this must *always* include creating brand awareness and a positive brand attitude.

3 Strategies for building positive brand attitude depend upon understanding the type of purchase decision and what motivates purchase behaviour, because this will dictate the creative tactics needed.

4 While there are many criticisms of advertising, if responsibly considered and presented it will benefit the consumer and the market.

In this first chapter we will be taking a broad introductory look at just what we mean by advertising and promotion, and how they are seen in today's world. This will provide a foundation and perspective for the subject in general before we begin to look specifically at the role advertising and promotion can and do play in support of brands, and how to manage them strategically in order positively to position and build brands.

Defining Advertising and Promotion

If we look up the word 'advertise' in the *New Shorter Oxford English Dictionary* we find the following definition: 'Make an announcement in a public place; describe or present goods publicly with a view to promoting sales.' Right after that we find advertisement defined as: 'A public announcement (formerly by the town-crier, now usually in newspapers, on posters, by television, etc.).'[1]

This is certainly what most people have in mind when they think of advertising—adverts in the newspaper or magazines and commercials on radio or TV. But this really does not begin to tell us much about what advertising actually is. In fact, we are about to spend most of this book in effect defining advertising.

A better feel for what advertising is really all about may be gained by looking back to the Latin root of the word 'advertising'. It was Daniel Starch, one of the early pioneers of advertising theory in the twentieth century, who, back in the 1920s, reminded us that the Latin root for advertising is *advertere*. This roughly translates as 'to turn towards'.[2] Returning to the *New Shorter OED*, we find that the word 'advert' is colloquial for advertisement, *and* when used as a verb means 'turn towards'. This definition is more relevant, because it implies more than simply 'an announcement in a public place'. In a very real sense, advertising is meant to turn us towards a product or service by providing information or creating a positive feeling—something that goes well beyond simply calling our attention to it. Advertising is an *indirect* way of turning a potential customer towards the advertised product or service by providing information that is designed to effect a favourable impression, what we will call a positive brand attitude. This favourable brand attitude then helps place the consumer on the path towards seeking out the product or service advertised.

If advertising is meant to encourage consumers to 'turn towards' a brand, what is the function of promotion? Returning to the *New Shorter OED* we see that a promotion 'helps forward'. This definition is quite consistent with the Latin root of promotion, *promovere*. Roughly translated, this means 'move forward'.[3] Contrasting the Latin root of 'promotion', 'move forward', with the Latin root of 'advertising', 'turn towards', illustrates the fundamental difference between the traditional ideas of advertising and promotion. Advertising is aimed towards the long-term building of positive brand attitude by 'turning' the consumer towards the brand; promotion is aimed at the more short-term tactical goal of 'moving forward' brand sales now.

Advertising and Promotion within the Marketing Plan

It is important to realize that advertising and promotion are only one part of the marketing plan. Other key marketing considerations include product configuration (for example, making sure the product is offered in the right sizes, shapes, or colours), pricing structure, and distribution—what E. Jerome McCarthy has called the 'Four P's of Marketing' (Promotion, Product, Price, and Place).[4] We will be dealing with the idea of the marketing mix again in Chapter 7.

In fact, advertising and promotion are not the only elements in the 'promotion' or marketing communication section of the marketing plan. In addition to advertising and promotion, the 'promotion' component of the marketing mix also includes public relations and personal selling. We will be discussing the close strategic relationship between these central concepts in Chapter 5. This is not to suggest that there is no relationship between advertising and public relations or personal selling; of course there is, especially with industrial and corporate advertisers. However, the budgets and staff involved with personal selling and public relations traditionally tend to be separate from those of advertising and promotion.

While a simple definition of public relations is that it is 'unpaid promotion', there is a lot more to it than that, and one can take whole courses in the various aspects of public relations. For our purposes, we need to remember that the position being taken in advertising must be consistent with the story being told about the campaign through public relations. The same holds true for any collateral material used in personal selling, including catalogues, brochures, and presentations used by the sales force. An added responsibility for advertising is to help pre-sell a prospect for the salesman. To do this, the selling message must be consistent with *all* other aspects of a brand's marketing communication. We shall be looking at public relations and personal selling, along with other components of the broader communication mix, in Chapter 14.

A Closer Look at Advertising

Keeping in mind how advertising fits into a company's marketing plan, and our definition of how advertising turns a potential customer towards an advertised product or service, let us look at an example to illustrate how this definition of advertising applies. Remember, we are suggesting that advertising deals indirectly with potential action on the part of someone by providing information or creating feelings that turn them towards the product or service advertised. This will be true regardless of whether we are dealing with fast-moving consumer package goods (fmcgs) such as food or household cleaners, industrial manufacturer advertising of heavy equipment, corporate advertisers talking about their company, or non-profit organizations soliciting funds or reminding us to take better care of ourselves.

What do you think Nestlé is trying to do with its advert for Nescafé Gold Blend coffee (Advert 1.1)? What does it wish us to 'turn towards'? We can never really know exactly what an advertiser has in mind without actually reading his or her marketing plan and creative strategy. But from looking at this advert it would appear that Nestlé wants us to think about the aroma of coffee brewing, and to associate Nescafé Gold Blend coffee with this experience. It wants us to 'turn towards' the idea that Nescafé Gold Blend coffee creates this pleasant experience better than any other brand of coffee. Of course, much more

Advert 1.1 Advert for Nescafé Gold Blend coffee that illustrates a positive experience with the brand and provides a strong brand identification. NESCAFÉ, GOLD BLEND, the JAR shape and the SCOOP OF COFFEE BEANS scenery are all protected through intellectual property rights by Société des Produits Nestlé SA, Trade Mark Owners.

is *implied*. We are also asked to associate this wonderful 'golden aroma' with rich, good-tasting coffee, a truly satisfying experience, almost sensual.

The point is, this advert is not *explicitly* asking you to buy Nescafé Gold Blend coffee now, but rather is helping to create a positive feeling and attitude for the brand. This positive brand attitude is what will lead to purchase. At the same time, the other components of the marketing mix, mediated by competitive activity in the market, will all contribute to the likelihood of someone actually purchasing Nescafé Gold Blend coffee after seeing this advert. Advertising for a brand only plays a part, but, as we shall see through the course of this book, it is a very important, often critical part.

How does Advertising Work?

In a very real sense, the remainder of this book is dedicated to answering this question. But in this section we will provide a very brief introduction and overview of what is involved. Some very basic things must occur if any type of communication is to work. A person must have the opportunity to see or hear the message, must pay attention to it, understand what is being presented, and then act upon the message in the desired manner. This sequence is the same whether the message is from a parent, a boss, a friend, or an advertiser. In advertising we call these four steps the consumer response sequence, and it is covered in detail in Chapter 4.

Consider the Nescafé Gold Blend coffee advert again. What must happen for this advert to work? It ran in a women's magazine, so the first step is that potential buyers see the magazine and at least skim through it. While doing this, they must notice the advert and spend enough time with it to 'get the meaning'. They must then associate a positive feeling with the brand in response to the idea of a 'golden aroma' and think to themselves, 'I'd like to try Gold Blend.'

Realistically, of course, this is *not* likely to happen all at one go. You may glance at this advert several times without paying much attention to it. But over time, the visual imagery and headline 'Enjoy before drinking' will begin to register and be associated with the brand. As this happens, it will help to build or reinforce a positive attitude for the brand. Then one day while shopping, you see the brand on the shelf and 'remember' the positive feelings and think 'I'll give it a try.'

If someone does pay attention to a brand's advertising, we want them to 'get' something specific. Of course, each advert will have a particular message to deliver, consistent with its creative strategy. But at a more general level, the advertising must satisfy a communication objective. All advertising and marketing communication has the ability to stimulate four communication effects: need for the category, brand awareness, brand attitude, and brand purchase intention.[5]

In a very real sense, when you pay attention to advertising, all these effects could run through your mind. While we will later devote a complete chapter to them, at this point it will be helpful to understand briefly what is meant by each of the four communication effects, because communication objectives are determined by the communication effect desired.

Category need. Before any purchase decision is made, there must be at least some interest in the product category. This is true of even the most trivial purchase. If you stop to think of it, if there were no 'reason' or need for something, why would you buy it?

Brand awareness. You must be able to identify a brand in order to purchase it. There are two types of brand awareness: recognition and recall. With recognition, at the point of purchase you recognize the brand on the shelf. With recall, you must think of the brand on your own prior to purchase.

Brand attitude. Unless a product is inexpensive or trivial, brand awareness alone will not be enough to drive you to an actual purchase. For purchase to occur, you must have a favourable attitude towards the brand, even if it is only tentative. This attitude will be some combination of what you know or learn about the brand, and any feelings you associate with it.

Brand purchase intention. Someone's mind could be full of different attitudes towards various brands. And quite possibly, people may hold generally favourable attitudes towards several of these brands. Brand purchase intention refers to such thoughts as 'I think I'd like to try that' or 'I'll buy that', and these follow from favourable brand attitudes, perhaps encouraged by an incentive promotion. In fact, brand purchase intention is always the primary communication objective for promotion.

This discussion should provide you with a brief introduction to what we mean by communication effects. As you can see, the effects are simply a reflection of the process your mind is likely to go through prior to almost any purchase. Do you have a need? Are you aware of alternatives? What do you think about those alternatives? Will you buy one? Before you make any purchase you will probably need to give a positive answer to each of these questions.

While each of these four communication effects can be part of the response to any advertising or promotion, they are not all required to be a specific part of the execution. Some may be implied or already understood. Those that are not become communication objectives. The correct communication objective is critical to effective advertising and promotion. We will learn that brand awareness and brand attitude are *always* communication objectives given their importance to a brand, and that under particular circumstances either of the other two communication effects may also serve as a communication objective.

Let us return to the Nescafé Gold Blend coffee advert. This advert assumes that a category need already exists. For this advertising to work, the reader must already drink coffee. But is he or she aware of the brand? If not, the advert provides good brand name and package visibility, essential for recognition brand awareness, as we shall learn. Earlier we discussed how the advert should stimulate a positive feeling for the brand. This translates to a positive brand attitude, and could also include a positive brand purchase intention. The actual communication objective for the Nescafé Gold Blend coffee advert cannot be known for sure without seeing the original creative brief, but it appears to reflect the primary communication objectives of brand awareness and brand attitude. There is no attempt to 'sell' the category, to convince people to drink coffee, or to buy soluble coffee (often called 'instant' coffee), and there is no *specific* call to purchase action. Rather, the advert does a good job of creating an impression of a positive experience with the brand, and provides strong brand identity.

Brand Attitude Strategies

We have just pointed out that brand awareness and brand attitude are always communication objectives. Obviously, people must be aware of a brand if they are going to buy it, aware of a service if they are to avail themselves of it, aware of a company if they are going to do business with it. But the real heart of most advertising messages conveys information or communicates a feeling about the product or service being advertised. This is what comprises brand attitude.

There are four brand attitude strategies that we will be concerned with in this text, and they are covered in depth in Chapter 9. These four strategies are based upon two dimensions critical to consumer behaviour: the type of purchase decision, and the type of motivation that drives the decision.[6]

Type of purchase decision. In terms of the type of decision, we will be classifying all consumer decisions as either low involvement or high involvement.[7] When a decision is *low involvement*, it means that there is very little, if any, risk attached to the consequences of making that decision. For example, if you think you might like a new candy bar, trying it would no doubt be a low-involvement decision, because you would not really be risking much money. But when a decision requires a lot of information prior to deciding, and a great deal of conviction that you are making the right decision, it is *high involvement*. A good example here would be buying a car.

Type of motivation. We will be devoting a lot of time in this book to motivation. For now, in order to begin to understand brand attitude strategies, you need to know only that people do some things because of negative motivations (for example, to remove or avoid a problem) and some things because of positive motivations (for example, to make them 'feel good').

Since decisions in the marketplace are governed by type of decision and type of motivation, we know that development of brand attitude strategy in advertising must take this into account. As a result, brand attitude strategies in advertising will reflect one of the four combinations of decision types and motivation:

- low-involvement decisions driven by negative motivations;
- low-involvement decisions driven by positive motivations;
- high-involvement decisions driven by negative motivations;
- high-involvement decisions driven by positive motivations.[8]

Again, looking at the Nescafé Gold Blend coffee advert, what brand attitude strategy has been followed? Under most circumstances, there will probably be little risk attached to the purchase of coffee. An exception might be if you were entertaining someone very special and wanted a specific brand or blend of coffee in order to impress your guest. But in most cases, if you try a brand of coffee and do not like it, you will not have lost much. So, we can be fairly safe in assuming that coffee is a low-involvement decision. And what is likely to motivate a person to buy a particular brand of coffee? It is unlikely to be a negative motive. You may buy soluble coffee for its convenience (a negative motive), but that is a *category*, not a brand, decision. Once you have decided upon the type of coffee you want, the *brand* selected is likely to be the one you think you will most enjoy (the positive motive of sensory gratification). This Nescafé Gold Blend coffee advert is a good execution of a brand attitude strategy for a low-involvement decision driven by positive motivations.

As we shall see later, in Chapter 12, the creative tactics differ significantly for each of the four possible brand attitude strategies. If the wrong brand attitude strategy is used, the target audience will not be as likely to pay attention to the advertising or 'get' the message.

What have we learned about brand attitude strategies up to this point? We have seen that one of the jobs of advertising is to generate a communication effect, and that brand attitude is one effect that is always a communication objective. In addition, we know that, in order to create advertising that will satisfy a brand attitude communication objective, one of four fundamental brand attitude strategies must be followed. The correct brand attitude strategy will reflect the involvement in the decision by the target audience as well as the likely motivation for its choice. Once the correct brand attitude strategy is selected, the creative and media tactics required to implement that strategy will be more easily identified.

Message Appeal

Now that we have introduced the concept of brand attitude strategies, how does that relate to the appeal that should be used in creating the message? As mentioned, we shall spend a great deal of time looking specifically at creative tactics in Chapter 12, but it is also good to have a general idea about what is meant by 'persuasive appeals' in communication. Persuasion is studied by psychologists interested in attitude-change theory, and obviously what they know about persuasion informs our understanding of how advertising and other marketing communication works.

William J. McGuire, a social psychologist who taught at Yale University, is considered perhaps the foremost authority on attitude-change theory, and he has pointed out that the distinctions Aristotle made in the *Rhetoric* between logos, pathos, and ethos provide a very useful way of classifying the options available for message appeals.[9] Roughly speaking, logos appeals use logical arguments, pathos appeals address our passions, and ethos appeals deal with the credibility or attractiveness of the person delivering the message.

Logos and pathos appeals correspond closely to our brand attitude strategy ideas based upon involvement and motivation. Following Aristotle, logos appeals ask the recipient of a message to draw an inference or conclusion based upon arguments presented in the message. With low-involvement decisions when the underlying motivation is negative, where a problem is to be solved or avoided, this is exactly the appeal that is necessary. When the motive is negative and the decision is high involvement, the logos requirement—accepting as true what is presented or implied—applies. When we get to Chapter 9, you will see that we call the brand attitude strategies dealing with negative motivation *informational*, because you are providing information to help solve or avoid a problem. In essence, this means using a logos appeal.

On the other hand, a pathos appeal, as characterized by Aristotle, means a persuasive message that involves creating an appropriate *feeling* in the person receiving the message. This is exactly what we are looking for when the brand attitude strategy deals with positive motivations. We will be referring to such strategies as *transformational*, because the message appeal is meant to transform the target audience by creating an authentic emotional experience.[10]

The third message appeal suggested by Aristotle is ethos. By ethos he meant a persuasive message that relied more upon the *source* of the message than the message itself. An example in advertising would be when a popular spokesperson is used in the expectation that the target audience will be 'persuaded' to use the brand because of their endorsement (real or implied). Rosenthal made the point that ethos appeals attempt to persuade by forcing the attention of the receiver of a message on the source, while logos and pathos appeals focus on message content.[11] We consider a correct understanding of ethos to be very important when using spokespeople in advertising. This is also related to brand attitude strategy, as we shall see in our discussion of the VisCAP model of source effectiveness in Chapter 12. For example, when dealing with logical or logos appeals, *credibility* in the message source is needed, but with a pathos or emotional appeal, *attractiveness* is needed. Aristotle talked about ethos appeals in terms of tapping into someone's 'moral principles'.

A Closer Look at Promotion

When most people think about promotion, including most marketing managers, they are thinking about *sales promotion* where an incentive is usually involved. We shall be looking at this in Chapter 14. However, it is important to understand that a promotion does *not* require an incentive. All that is required is that the primary communication objective is brand purchase intention, and that the message is aimed at encouraging *immediate* action on the part of the target audience. When retailers feature a brand, or a marketer features one item from a brand's line, this will almost always be a promotion. They are featuring the brand or item in order to encourage immediate purchase.

While promotions are used tactically when there is a need to accelerate purchase or stimulate immediate trial, it is important to remember that the decision to include promotion as part of the brand's marketing communication mix is a *strategic* issue. Promotion executions must be consistent with the brand positioning in its advertising, and built upon the same key benefit. Prentice, a marketing executive in the USA talked about this years ago. He pointed out that promotions should be designed to be what he called 'consumer franchise-building', meaning they will contribute to the brand's awareness and help build positive brand attitude as well as stimulate immediate action.[12] Additionally, promotions must be coordinated with the brand's advertising so that it has had an opportunity to build sufficient awareness for the brand, and at least a tentatively favourable brand attitude, *prior* to the promotion.

As we shall see in the last chapter, when this is done successfully the overall result for the brand will be stronger than if either promotion or advertising is used alone. Always, when promotions are considered, the manager should be thinking about how a particular promotion can be an effective part of the *whole* marketing communication effort. Simmons puts this very well when he refers to the 'two great commandments of sales promotion'—it must relate directly to the objectives, and it must be compatible with the total brand proposition.[13]

Promotions are usually thought of as aimed at consumers, but in fact much more money is invested in promotion to the trade than to the consumer. There are three fundamental types of promotion: trade promotion, retail promotion, and consumer promotion.[14] We may think of a *trade promotion* as a programme of discounts or incentives to increasing distribution or merchandising collateral or incentives to help move more product; *retail promotion* as promotions offered by the retailer, and which may have originated with the brand; and *consumer promotion* as promotions offered to business-to-business customers or consumers to accelerate or reinforce the decision process.

Criticism of Advertising

Advertising seems to be everywhere. Perhaps because of this, many people are concerned with the potential impact advertising has upon society.[15] Critics of commercial advertising raise several concerns about the impact of advertising upon society, and they are worth reviewing. As society evolved over the last half of the twentieth century, so too did the criticism of advertising. The left especially adjusted its criticism. As Martin Davidson has pointed out, the Marxist critique, for example, now sees advertising as doubly culpable. Not only is it highly suspect in its own right as an image, but it is an image of something even *more* suspect, the commodity.[16]

Perhaps the most widely made criticism of advertising is that it makes people buy things they neither want nor need. We will examine this charge first.

Advertising Creates Unnecessary Desires

To begin with, by the time you have finished reading this book, you will be well aware that communicating with a target audience through advertising is very, very difficult. Even though people are bombarded with messages, they pay attention to very few of them. And even when they do pay attention, that does not mean they will actually learn anything from the advert, or be positively influenced by it. In fact, many studies have shown that not only do we not pay much, if any, attention to advertising, but we do not pay much attention to the newspapers, magazines, or television shows where the advertising runs. It is not an easy job to communicate at all with advertising. This is why advertisers go to such lengths to identify a target audience where consumers are already favourably disposed towards their product. The more philosophical question of whether advertising helps create unnecessary wants is a much more difficult question to answer. Critics of advertising feel that by its very nature advertising stimulates materialism, exaggerating the requirements of a good life. But these needs are driven by other social forces well beyond advertising. A much more serious charge is that advertising creates the desire for unattainable goals. Again, we doubt that advertising alone must shoulder this charge. This is a problem with society in general. As long as contemporary movies, magazines, and television convey this image of life, some advertising is likely to reflect those images.

Nevertheless, there are areas where the images presented in advertising can and should be realistic. Remember, in advertising you are trying to match the attributes of a product with the perceived needs of the target audience. The problem comes when achieving the perceived need is unrealistic. In the end, the best advertising should be responsible advertising.

Advertising is Misleading

The second most generally made criticism of advertising is that it is deceptive. It seems almost an article of faith that advertising is deceptive, and this has occasioned a rather general scepticism on the part of most people towards most advertising, as we shall see below. In certain cases, especially on the local level, there is no doubt that advertising can be misleading. But think for a moment about the consequences of such behaviour. If a product is misrepresented and you buy it, how likely are you ever to buy that brand again—or anything else from that company? In the long run, if advertising is deceptive, it will kill a brand.

One of the important results of advertising is the creation of brand names. Brand names bring with them almost an implied warranty of quality. Critics will argue that this image is false and that unbranded products are just as good. But are they? Is there not a social value in enhancing the benefit people perceive in a product? Research has shown that advertised brand names are felt to taste better, last longer, and so on. While advertising may have created these images, the products themselves must live up to the expectation. Davidson provides an interesting criticism here. He feels that the real problem with advertising is that it presents products in terms of values that are more important than the product itself, and this leads to a diminution of those values.[17]

The problem with the question of deception in advertising is that it is largely a subjective one. If a claim is truly deceptive, you can be sure that the competition will be quick to let government regulatory agencies know about it. In fact, long before an advert runs, attorneys for a brand will have considered it, and the censors at the media where it is to run will have taken a hard look at any claim the brand makes. Before a commercial is approved for showing on air or an advert is run in print media, it will require substantiation in terms of valid research for any major claim made for the brand.

In 1991 the European Union created the European Advertising Standards Alliance to provide a mechanism for dealing with false or misleading advertising. While it encourages self-regulation, the EU Misleading Advertising Directive requires member countries to institute powers to protect consumers against misleading claims.[18]

Although advertisers are permitted by law to make *obvious* exaggerations in their adverts, something called 'puffery' (for example, 'best ever', 'great taste'), any attempt to misrepresent the overall nature of a brand is unlikely. An interesting example of just how restrictive this can sometimes be, even to the point of absurdity, is a commercial that ran in the USA several years ago for San Georgio spaghetti. The commercial told the story of 'harvest time' at the San Georgio 'spaghetti farm' where they grow the 'best spaghetti' and featured peasant farmworkers harvesting spaghetti from spaghetti trees. The claim 'best spaghetti' was considered puffery, and was acceptable. But the advertiser was required to include a disclaimer that said 'of course you know spaghetti really doesn't grow on trees' before television networks would approve the commercial for use on air.

Responsible advertising will not be deceptive, for the simple reason that it is bad for business. But the grey area of misleading claims or images is more difficult to pin down. In the end, if the media let something slip by, it is unlikely that your competitors will.

Advertising Insults our Intelligence

The charge that advertising is often insulting to the reader's or viewer's intelligence is again one that is frequently heard, but hard to define. What is in bad taste for one segment of the population may not be so for another. There is no doubt that certain adverts will be found to be tasteless, insulting, or offensive to certain people—even large groups of people. If the advertising is seen as tasteless by the intended target audience, however, the advertising will be unlikely to communicate its intended message effectively. So once again we see that to the extent that the charge of 'insulting to my intelligence' is true, it will tend to be counter-productive for the advertiser. It is in the advertiser's best interest to provide advertising that will be well received by its target audience. This is one of the reasons you should test adverts before running them.

Advertising and the Economy

Another general area of advertising criticism revolves around the role advertising does or does not play in the economy. Classical economics, as a rule, provides very little comfort for advertising. But most marketers believe advertising does indeed make a positive contribution to the economy—if by no other way than pumping a great deal of money into the economy. For example, it was estimated that spending on advertising in the UK for the year 2004 was US $23 billion, US $18.6 billion in Germany, and US $11.9 billion in France.[19]

It is often argued that advertising drives up the cost of products, and that, without advertising, most things would cost less. This really is not the case. Of course, the cost of a product does include the cost of the advertising, but dropping the advertising would not necessarily drop the price of the product. Advertising helps increase consumption, which in its turn permits certain economies of scale that help drive *down* prices. For example, consider recent experiences with personal computers. Additionally, an argument can be made that price competition is enhanced by a broader awareness of price, which comes from advertising.

Another very real effect advertising has had on the economy is in the area of new product and new market development. Think of the enormous cost involved in the development of a new market. Without advertising it would be very difficult to generate enough sales fast enough to ensure a realistic payout. Advertising provides a rapid entrée to the consumer, and this encourages innovation on the part of companies. In the same sense advertising helps to expand existing markets, encouraging more and better products for the consumer.

We have already mentioned the idea of brand names and what their role is in today's market. From a business standpoint, a brand name is an *asset*, and is treated as one. In this sense advertising for brand names is often treated by a manufacturer as a long-term capital investment rather than an immediate cost. This is almost universally true of new product introductions. It is advertising that provides relative stability for a brand, building brand equity. There are many examples in almost any field of what happens to a company that does not protect its brand name through advertising. So, in a very real sense, advertising is one of the ways in which we are able to provide stability in our economy.

Advertising and the Consumer

There is abundant evidence in the consumer behaviour and social psychology literature that suggests that global attitudes about something will condition how specific messages related to it are received. This is a rather fancy way of saying that, if you do not like coffee, you are unlikely to be persuaded to buy a particular brand. This same principle applies to marketing communication. If someone distrusts advertising generally, he or she will be less likely to trust certain advertising messages. However, this relationship is anything but simple or easily understood.

In an interesting report, Calfee and Ringold reviewed six decades of survey data dealing with consumer attitudes towards advertising.[20] What they found was a core set of beliefs about advertising that has remained relatively constant over time and across a variety of question formats. Roughly 70 per cent of consumers feel advertising is often untruthful, seeks to persuade people to buy things they do not want, should be more strictly regulated, but nevertheless provides valuable information. In fact, despite feeling advertising is more likely to 'seek unduly to persuade' than to 'provide useful information' (when asked to choose between the two), most people tend to feel the benefits of advertising outweigh the deficits. As we remarked, this relationship is not easily understood.

A Question of Trust

One of the key relationships between a brand and its consumer is trust. Unfortunately, in many of today's markets there has been a significant erosion of this critical bond. What is, or has been, the role of advertising in this erosion? One can imagine problems here at many levels. If pricing policies (for example) have led to a certain distrust of a brand, this distrust could significantly affect consumers' perceptions of the brand's advertising. At the same time, a distrust of advertising in general impedes its credibility, and this not only reduces overall marketplace efficiencies, but acts like a cancer, attacking individual advertising messages. As Pollay and Mittal in their analysis of consumer criticism of advertising put it: 'High levels of distrust and cynicism put the professions of marketing and advertising in disrepute and *ultimately require greater advertising spending and creativity to accomplish the same ends*' (emphasis added).[21]

Should we expect this basic distrust of advertising to affect all advertising equally? No, and in fact there is some research available to help us identify types of advertising that are more or less likely to be believed. To the extent that a consumer feels a claim can be verified before purchase, consumer faith in that claim will be stronger than if it can be verified only after purchase ('5-year unconditional warranty', for example, versus 'tastes great'). Least credible are so-called credence claims, which ordinarily can never be verified ('best performance ever').

The alert reader will see that this could be at the heart of the seeming paradox that people often feel advertising is untruthful, yet find it a useful source of information. Some types of advertising are seen as more likely than others to be true. Following this reasoning, as we shall see when we get into this in more detail in Chapter 9, high-involvement brand attitude strategies (that is, those where there is a psychological or fiscal risk attached to the brand decision) should be seen as more credible than those for low-involvement brand attitude strategies. Again, some support for this has been found, but it is by no means something that occurs as a matter of course. Even if you are advertising a high-involvement product, credibility is far from guaranteed; and consumers are not sceptical of all low-involvement advertising. A lot of other things influence the perceived credibility of advertising in general, as we shall see.

Ippolito has talked about advertising's ability to create a bond, signalling product quality to the consumer. He goes so far as to suggest that this bond can enable advertisers to induce a useful level of credibility in their advertising simply by advertising heavily![22] The implication here is that, if consumers are exposed to a message repeatedly over time, they will begin to assume that it must credibly reflect experience with the product. Consumers will reason that surely the product must be doing well since they see so much advertising for it. A rather complex notion, to be sure, but if true this would be one way to induce a certain level of credibility into a brand's advertising.

In any event, there certainly are important relationships between trust and advertising credibility, and these relationships should be monitored on a continual basis. The better these relationships are understood, the greater the likelihood of maximizing credibility for one's own advertising.

Regulatory Environment

One of the findings in the Calfee and Ringold review of all that research into consumer beliefs about advertising mentioned earlier is that, when asked, some 60–70 per cent of consumers will support the idea of stronger regulation of advertising.[23] Somehow they seem to equate regulation with more credible advertising. Unfortunately, a real increase in regulation does not seem to translate into a perceived increase in advertising credibility. While increased regulation and intervention in advertising increased significantly during the 1970s in the USA, especially with the implementation of the US Federal Trade Commission (FTC)'s Advertising Substantiation Program, there was no perceived increase in advertising credibility on the part of the consumer. What is really interesting here is that, in objective terms, all the evidence suggests that actual claims made in advertising were indeed more credible after adoption of the substantiation requirements.[24]

Perhaps what we see happening here is another variation on the paradox discussed earlier. While people feel that increased regulation of advertising will make it more credible, as they become aware of the increased regulation, the very knowledge of this activity fuels scepticism. In other words, if it was not so bad, there would not be a need for this regulation. One thing is certain: in the USA, when the FTC does publicly act upon a case of false or misleading advertising, the advertiser in question will lose approximately 3 per cent of its share value in the stock market.[25] And the fall-out from an action against a particular advertiser for false or deceptive advertising increases consumer scepticism of all advertising, not just that of the advertiser accused.

Understanding Consumer Attitudes towards Advertising

Researchers have for years been surveying the public's attitudes towards advertising and have noticed no significant change in beliefs about advertising. Precisely because there is more to this than meets the eye, and its impact can significantly affect how *individual advertisers'* messages are perceived by consumers, it is important for an advertiser to have a good grasp of general consumer attitudes towards advertising. Beyond this, to the extent that someone in the business of advertising wishes truly to *understand* the business of advertising, it is critical to understand the market's perception of its 'product'. Just as it is important for an advertiser to track response to its specific advertising, it is important to track attitudes towards advertising in general. There are a number of reasons for this, and some should be evident from the paradoxes in consumer beliefs about advertising we have just discussed.

We have seen how trust can play an important role in people's beliefs about advertising, and how external factors such as regulation and publicity about 'false' advertising can influence consumers' feelings of trust. While the relationship among all these factors is far from clear, monitoring consumer trust in advertising along with things known to influence it puts advertisers in a better position to understand how their customers and prospects are likely to respond to advertising in general for their brand. As an example, what is the effect of political advertising upon how people respond to advertising for brands? There is no doubt that people seem fed up with the strident tone of political advertising, and, as an article in *Advertising Age* suggests: 'there's a growing concern that they also may be effective in turning off the public from all advertising.'[26] In that article, Sean Fitzpatrick (then a vice-chairman with McCann-Erickson Worldwide) is quoted as feeling that political advertising directly affects any advertising that is running at the same time, even to the extent of effectively blocking it out so that it is not heard. To what extent does political advertising negatively affect regular advertising? And just as important, how long does this negative carryover effect persist? Is it likely to affect some types or categories of advertising more than others, such as advertising with spokespeople or comparative ads?

Another important question to consider here is the 'universality' of consumer beliefs about advertising. In the Pollay and Mittal article mentioned earlier, they report some preliminary findings that show significant subsets or segments within the population in terms of core beliefs about advertising.[27] As one might expect from the general findings of Calfee and Ringold that 70 per cent of consumers held consistent basic beliefs about advertising, three of the four segments Pollay and Mittal identified reflected degrees of wariness. But one segment (amounting to about a third of the population) did hold positive global attitudes. This sort of segmentation raises interesting questions. Do these segments vary in size over time? Does their make-up differ over time? Do some of the wary segments react differently to external factors such as regulation, 'false' advertising publicity, product recalls, and corporate problems, or perhaps even the vast variety of new media? Is the depth of scepticism related more to some categories or types of advertising than others? These are important issues that could be dealt with tactically in a brand's advertising, given the right information.

At the end of their article, Pollay and Mittal ask the question: *What can the industry do?* They answer: 'The industry can profit from taking the public pulse every so often, utilizing a comprehensive belief inventory.'[28] For many reasons we feel strongly that a continuous reading of consumer beliefs and attitudes is superior to 'taking the pulse every so often', because of the dynamic nature of the factors that mediate those beliefs and attitudes. But, however it is measured, it does make sense to track consumer opinion of advertising in general.

CHAPTER SUMMARY

In this chapter we have defined what we mean by advertising and promotion and introduced the key concepts related to communication effects, which will be used to organize our discussions throughout the book. We have discussed some of the common criticisms of advertising and the importance of consumer attitudes towards advertising and the important role played by trust. We have emphasized the vital role of continuous research in tracking consumer attitudes to advertising in general.

QUESTIONS TO CONSIDER

1.1   What is the major difference between advertising and promotion?

1.2   What is necessary for persuasive communication to work?

1.3   Why are brand awareness and brand attitude always communication objectives?

1.4   What is the basic difference between informational and transformational brand attitude strategies?

1.5   In what ways does advertising make a positive contribution to the economy?

1.6   Do you feel there is merit to any of the traditional criticisms of advertising?

1.7   Why is it important for an advertiser to be aware of trends in public attitude toward advertising in general?

CASE STUDY 1

Johnnie Walker — A Walk Around the World

Johnnie Walker was amongst the first global brands; sold in 120 countries by 1920 and now sold in over 180. It had two products, Red Label and Black Label. It is the world's biggest scotch in terms of volume and value. Johnnie Walker's brand values were known to be international and high quality. It was not just the market leader, but perceived to be the market leader as well.

But Johnnie Walker faced problems in the late nineties. The brand had fragmented, and the products were marketed separately, with different campaigns in different places. Between 1997 and 1999 at least 27 different campaigns for Red Label and Black Label existed. Marketing was often tactical, with a short-term promotional focus. Fragmentation had dissipated brand strength in a category where brand is a critical point of differentiation. And fragmentation reflected in sales, which dropped by 9.3 per cent between 1995 and 1999. In addition, the brand was threatened by other newer, trend-setting drinks. Whisky was becoming 'Dad's drink'.

Johnnie Walker needed renovation. After researching the world's most famous global brands, Johnnie Walker found that they had two key things in common. First, they were founded on a perceived fundamental human truth that united people the world over. Second, they were able to transcend countries, culture, and language via a universally recognized icon that was symbolic of everything the brand stood for. To compete with them, Johnnie Walker needed to establish itself as an 'icon brand'.

Research studying Scotch drinkers showed that there is always difference if you look for it. Around the world Scotch drinkers are old, young, rich, and poor. It is a quiet drink by the fire, a male bonding experience, or a party drink; it's drunk neat, with water or ice, with coke, coconut water, or green tea; it's your own personal bottle kept behind the bar, or a whole bottle, lid discarded, drunk all at once with a friend after work. All of this was interesting, and important in its own way, but none of it was the fundamental insight. And it was easy to get lost in the difference. Johnnie Walker had to look for similarity.

The recurring themes in Scotch advertising are masculinity and success. Reviewing more than 300 international whisky ads revealed that other brands had spotted this. One of Johnnie Walker's biggest challenges was breaking out of a clichéd category. Research suggested that whilst previous generations defined success as material accomplishment, a new generation of men were rewriting the rules. For them life was not just about the destination; the journey was equally important. Regardless of age, life stage, or situation, every man shares the desire to move forward, to better himself in some way. This innate need to progress became the fundamental human truth that Johnnie Walker would use as the foundation of its global brand.

How could Johnnie Walker turn this insight into a powerful brand property? The answer lay in the brand's history. It was the desire to progress that had catapulted Johnnie Walker so far from humble beginnings in an 1820s Kilmarnock grocery shop, and that drove the Walker family to start global distribution in 1887. Progress had been part of Johnnie Walker's past, now it would be part of the future. The striding man, central to Johnnie Walker's advertising for over fifty years, was the strongest expression of this progress. It was originally drawn in 1908 by eminent cartoonist Tom Browne to represent the pioneering and entrepreneurial zeal of the Walker family. It carried the strength of heritage but was inherently dynamic. But part of the striding man had become passive. He was the forgotten hero of Johnnie Walker's progress story. The striding man needed a change; he was the one who forged a deep connection between the innate desire to progress and the Johnnie Walker brand. He came to the front-centre of the new brand. This meant a literal and metaphorical change in direction. He had to be striding forwards, striding into the future. He became a pro-active person who inspires progress. This was encapsulated in the simple but powerful exhortation to 'Keep Walking'.

There were two main phases. The first phase was to launch with focus and control, starting in 1999. The launch focused on 'the walk' as a fundamental expression of human progress. At this stage central control and consistency was essential in ensuring the idea was launched effectively. The same ads ran everywhere. The TV campaign was based on individual stories of personal progress; sometimes celebrities, sometimes just stories of inspirational individuals. The print featured inspiring quotes relating to walking or a journey. The campaign then evolved to lionize the striding man, showing him conquering challenges on his restless journey of progress—a pioneering media strategy amplified the message by placing the image in surprising and meaningful places, whether leaping across buildings or adjacent to relevant editorial content.

The second phase was to expand with flexibility and local sensitivity, starting from 2000. The campaign developed from 'personal walks' to many expressions of progress, tackling different brand needs. This helped local markets to embrace the campaign and mitigated the threat of 'not invented here' that can so easily dilute global campaigns. The campaign has also reinforced the pioneering element of the brand, coped with specific legislation, surprised in cluttered TV environments, exploited local relevance to gain footholds in vast markets like China, and embraced sponsorship properties, even including a responsibility message.

The two phases allowed Johnnie Walker to clearly establish the idea, capture the imagination, and constantly surprise whilst also striking a balance between global and local priorities.

The campaign has been effective at increasing volume, value, and market share:

> *'The Keep Walking campaign launched in February 2001 was a key driver of growth'*
> North America

> *'Johnnie Walker volume grew 1%, with a 24% growth in Johnnie Walker Black Label in response to the introduction of the Keep Walking campaign'*
> Spain

> *'The successful introduction of the Keep Walking campaign for Johnnie Walker led to a strong year'*
> Taiwan

Source: Diageo Annual Report, 2001

Between 1995 and 1999 sales dropped by 9.3 per cent. After the 'Keep Walking' campaign the sales volume grew 21.2 per cent and sales value grew 24 per cent between 2000 and 2004. The growth in volume and value was also reflected in its market share and price. Over the period of growth, the Johnnie Walker average price per case grew 10.7 per cent, slightly ahead of key competitors at 9.4 per cent. Besides, an additional success has been brand stretch into more premium segments. The original brief focused on Red Label and Black Label, but following 'Keep Walking', the SuperDeluxe variants grew eleven times faster than the core products.

The campaign instantly created awareness and differentiation. In every case except Thailand (awareness was at 98 per cent, 2 per cent behind Singha) 'Keep Walking' was the most salient alcohol campaign in the market. Many respondents believed the campaign was distinctive. This statement is ranked in the top 5 in every market and the level of differentiation endures five years on.

The foundation of fundamental human truth inextricably linked to a powerful brand icon means 'Keep Walking' has united the world—an icon for consumers. One of the secrets is looking for the things that unite; chase difference and you chase forever. Uniting behind a universal truth and a potent brand symbol can act as a strong consumer force. This is a powerful idea. Once you have it, control and flexibility are usefully wielded in equal measure. Although the world is a big place, with terrific richness and diversity, it is possible to find ways of bringing people together.

The 'Keep Walking' campaign has run in more than 120 countries over six years with a budget of US $40 million a year. There are two global principles that guide the advertising strategy: (1) to reinforce stature and (2) to demonstrate pioneering spirit. Thereafter, the media was managed at a local level allowing these two principles to be exploited in the most appropriate way for the local media environment. After the 'Keep Walking' campaign, Johnnie Walker's sales decline has been reversed and growth is accelerating. The scale of the challenge is just a reflection of the scale of the prize. What have we learned? That genuinely global brands and global campaigns are not only possible, but profitable.

Source: WARC, IPA Effectiveness Awards 2006, Johnnie Walker—A Walk Around the World, by Orlando Hooper-Greenhill

Edited by Hazel H. Huang

Discussion Questions

1 Discuss the advertising strategy before and after the 'Keep Walking' campaign.

2 The case described the importance of finding similarities between Scotch drinkers in order to establish an icon brand for Johnnie Walker. Discuss the meaning of similarity in global advertising. Is there any risk in pursuing similarity?

3 The 'Keep Walking' campaign had two phases: global control and local flexibility. Are they necessary for an advertising strategy?

4 Discuss the reasons why the 'Keep Walking' campaign worked successfully.

FURTHER READING

- Jef Richards and Catharine Curren, 'Oracles on "Advertising": Searching for a Definition', *Journal of Advertising*, 31/2 (Summer 2002), takes an in-depth look at trying to define 'advertising', looking first at a review of definitions in the literature, and then using a modified Delphi method to explore the issue.

- Special issues of the *Journal of Advertising Research* (Sept./Oct. 2002) and the *Journal of Advertising*, 31/3, Fall 2002) both deal with advertising and the Web, and with new media.

- A special issue of the *Journal of Consumer Psychology*, 13/1–2 (2003) deals with 'consumers in cyberspace', discussing a broad range of subjects relating to consumer behaviour and e-marketing.

- Stephanie O'Donohue, 'Living with Ambivalence: Attitudes to Advertising in Postmodern Times', *Marketing Theory*, 1/1 (Sept. 2001), provides a good review of research on the structure of attitudes to advertising, and then places it all within an interesting postmodern perspective.

NOTES

1 *The New Shorter Oxford English Dictionary* (Oxford: Clarendon Press, 1990).

2 Daniel Starch, *Principles of Advertising* (Chicago: A. W. Shaw, 1926).

3 Ibid.

4 McCarthy introduces this idea of the so-called Four P's of the marketing mix in his original text, *Basic Marketing: A Management Approach* (Homewood, Ill.: Irwin, 1960).

5 The four communication effects introduced here and discussed extensively in the text were originally described by John Rossiter and Larry Percy in *Advertising and Promotion Management* (New York: McGraw-Hill, 1987).

6 This notion of type of decision, as well as the idea of motivation, is at the heart of the Rossiter–Percy grid, originally introduced ibid., and discussed in much of the book.

7 While we talk about involvement in terms of 'risk', this is a function of the processing required, and this is reflected in traditional models of low- and high-involvement processing. Low-involvement models suggest that advertising and other forms of marketing communication cause brand awareness and a *tentative* brand attitude, but actual brand attitude is not formed until after experience with the brand. Perhaps the best example of a low-involvement model is the one advanced by A. S. C. Ehrenberg in his 'Repetitive Advertising and the Consumer', *Journal of Advertising Research*, 14 (Apr. 1974), 25–34, and 'Justifying Advertising Budgets', *Admap*, 30 (Jan. 1994), 11–13. Low-involvement models

have been called the 'weak theory' of advertising by John Phillip Jones in 'Advertising: Strong Force or Weak Force? Two Views an Ocean Apart', *International Journal of Advertising*, 9 (1990), 233–46.

The generally accepted model of high involvement is the so-called hierarchy-of-effects or H-O-E model. Here marketing communication first stimulates awareness, then affects brand attitude, which leads to brand purchase. In an interesting review of tests of the H-O-E model as applied to advertising, T. Barry and D. Howard suggest the results are 'inconclusive'. This is discussed in their paper 'A Review and Critique of the Hierarchy of Effects in Advertising', *International Journal of Advertising*, 9 (1990), 121–35. The reason the results are inconclusive, of course, is that the model applies only where high-involvement decisions operate.

8   This follows directly from the Rossiter–Percy grid referred to in n. 6.

9   McGuire often refers to these distinctions when discussing persuasive message appeals. A good summary may be found in his seminal work on attitude change, 'The Nature of Attitude and Attitude Change', in G. Lindsey and E. Aronson (eds), *The Handbook of Social Psychology*, iii (Reading, Mass.: Addison-Wesley Publishing, 1969), 136–314. Another good reference is his 'Persuasion, Persistence, and Attitude Change', in I. deSala Pool *et al.* (eds), *Handbook of Communication* (Chicago: Rand McNally, 1973), 216–52.

10   Larry Percy and John Rossiter provide a review of the psychological literature associated with logos, pathos, and ethos message appeals in their *Advertising Strategy: A Communication Theory Approach* (New York: Praeger Publishers, 1980), 102–4.

11   P. I. Rosenthal, *Concepts of Ethos and the Structure of Persuasive Speech, Speech Memographs*, 33 (1996), 114–26.

12   See R. M. Prentice, 'How to Split your Marketing Funds between Advertising and Promotion', *Advertising Age* (January 1977), 41.

13   P. Simmons, 'Sales Promotion in Marketing', in N. Hart (ed.), *The Practice of Advertising*, 4th edn. (Oxford: Butterworth Heinemann, 1995), 251.

14   Simmons makes an interesting point in his discussion of sales promotion, pointing out that promotions are also directed towards employees, either for individual performance or for group performance; see ibid.

15   A good review of many criticisms of advertising may be found in William Leiss, Stephen Klein, and Sut Jally, *Social Communication in Advertising* (London: Routledge, 1997).

16   Martin Davidson, *The Consumerist Manifesto: Advertising in Postmodern Times* (London: Routledge, 1992), 177.

17   Ibid.

18   Matti Alderson, 'Advertising: Self-Regulation and the Law', in Norman Hart (ed.), *The Practice of Advertising* (Oxford: Butterworth Heinemann, 1995), 259–72.

19   These figures were supplied by Zenith Media and reported in *Advertising Age International* (Feb. 2000).

20   John E. Calfee and Debra Jones Ringold, 'The 70% Majority: Endorsing Consumer Beliefs about Advertising', *Journal of Public Policy and Marketing*, 13 (1994), 228–30.

21   Richard W. Pollay and Banwari Mittal, 'Here's the Beef: Factors, Determinants, and Segments in Consumer Criticism of Advertising', *Journal of Marketing*, 57 (1993).

22 P. Ippolito, 'Bonding and Non-Bonding Signal of Product Quality', *Journal of Business*, 63 (1990), 41–60.

23 Calfee and Ringold, 'The 70% Majority'.

24 R. Sauer and K. Leffler, 'Did the Federal Trade Commission's Advertising Substantiation Program Promote More Credible Advertising?', *American Economic Review*, 80 (1990), 191–205.

25 Calfee and Ringold, 'The 70% Majority'.

26 Steven W. Colford, 'Fear of Being Painted with Pols' Dirty Brush', *Advertising Age* (1996).

27 Pollay and Mittal, 'Here's the Beef'.

28 Ibid. 99–114.

 Visit the Online Resource Centre that accompanies this book for additional resources to support the text: http://www.oxfordtextbooks.co.uk/orc/ percy_elliott3e/

2

Perspectives on Advertising

 KEY CONCEPTS

1 While the traditional cognitive information processing view of advertising continues to be the most viable way of thinking about advertising, there are other perspectives that can help in understanding how advertising works, and its effect upon society.

2 These other perspectives may be thought about in terms of their assumptions about the target audience and the level of explanation at which they are working.

3 These two considerations provide the axes of a 'mapping', where the different perspectives on advertising may be seen in terms of either passive individuals, passive social or cultural groups, active individuals, or active social or cultural groups.

For many years all areas of marketing research, and particularly advertising research, have been dominated by the cognitive information processing perspective. However, in this chapter we review a wide variety of alternative perspectives on how advertising works and its effects on society. Some of these approaches have emerged as explicit criticisms of advertising and are not concerned with advertising as a managerial practice, but some new approaches to visual imagery and meaning-based models, together with an understanding of cultural differences, hold great potential for developing more effective advertising strategies.

Audiences and Individuals

The practice of advertising has for a long time been the butt of attacks from some economists (for example, Galbraith[1]) and social and political theorists of the Frankfurt School (for example, Marcuse[2]). But recently sociology and anthropology have started to take consumption seriously as a central element in modern (or postmodern) culture, and together with a developing interest in semiotics, advertising is now studied from a plethora of social science perspectives. To enable us to locate these differing and complex viewpoints, we can organize them along two dimensions in relation to their assumptions about the audience (active versus passive) and to the level of explanation at which they are working (individual versus cultural) and construct a map of perspectives on advertising (see Fig. 2.1). This provides us with four sectors into which we can slot most approaches to understanding advertising and society: Sector 1: Passive Individuals; Sector 2: Passive Social/Cultural Groups; Sector 3: Active Individuals; and Sector 4: Active Social/Cultural Groups.

Sector 1: Passive Individuals

The major theoretical approaches used by marketing academics and advertising practitioners for explaining 'how advertising works' are located in this sector.

Learning Theories and Information Processing

Learning theories such as classical or Pavlovian conditioning focus on repetition and the creation of simple associations between elements (for example, a brand name becomes associated over time with a slogan), while more sophisticated approaches to learning are concerned with how advertising messages are stored in memory. These processes of storage and retrieval are the major focus of the dominant perspective in cognitive approaches to advertising, that of information processing. The approach taken in this text is an information processing approach, which assumes that the audience can be conceived of as largely passive, and managerial attention should be concerned with how individuals move through various stages in making a decision choice (see Chapter 7). While this model does not attempt to reflect the complex reality of communication, it is managerially useful in that it provides guidance for decision making that other perspectives do not.

Psycho-Dynamic Theories

Psycho-dynamic theories of advertising have a long history in both applied marketing research and critical views of advertising effects. The theories of Freud have been most

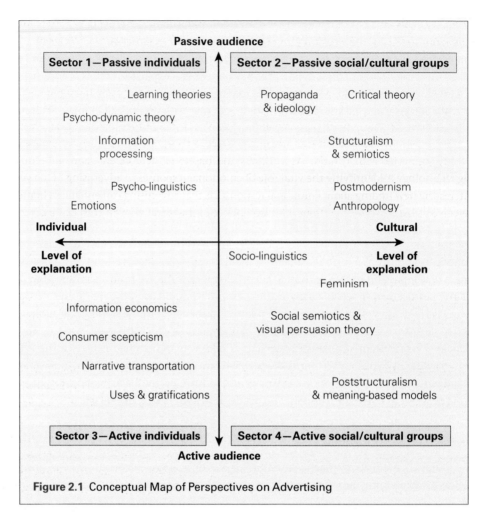

Figure 2.1 Conceptual Map of Perspectives on Advertising

popular in this regard, although Jung's ideas of symbolism and myths have also been used (and some would say abused). In the 1950s motivational research showed that the unconscious mind may play an important role in our responses to advertising,[3] while Vance Packard in his notorious book *The Hidden Persuaders* claimed that advertisers were cynically using hidden messages that were not noticeable consciously but that had an irresistible effect on our unconscious minds via such (unproven) processes as subliminal perception.[4] We shall have more to say about this when we talk about processing messages in Chapter 11.

Freudian concepts have been fused with semiotic analysis by Judith Williamson in a sophisticated and insightful analysis of advertisements that claims to have revealed a code by which advertisers can (and do) tap into our unconscious desires and achieve their desired effects on our buying behaviour.[5] If only it was that simple!

Psycho-Linguistics

Psycho-linguistics has been applied to advertisements by such people as Cook[6] and Vestergaard and Schroder,[7] who take advertisements as texts that can be studied using conventional linguistic theory. This close reading of language has largely been overtaken by the socio-linguistics approach, which falls into Sector 4, and is difficult to square with the rather crucial fact that most advertising uses visual images as well as, or instead of, language.

Emotions

The relationship between advertising, rationality, and emotion is complex and the source of much-heated debate. Certainly, the dominant approach to advertising has been cognitive, emphasizing rational processing, persuasion, and knowledge. However Ehrenberg's 'weak theory' of advertising suggests that the prime effect of advertising is to reinforce emotions already connected with a brand.[8] As we discuss in Chapter 11, neuroscience and brain imaging technology is identifying the vital role of emotional responses to advertising.[9] One very interesting new finding about emotional responses is that advertising can enhance a brand's perceived trustworthiness without prior experience of the brand or overt trust claims.[10]

Sector 2: Passive Social/Cultural Groups

Many of the most negative perspectives on advertising are located in this sector, where society is seen as being at the mercy of the power of organized capital through its vanguard weapon, which is selling the delights of consumer culture to unsuspecting dupes.

Critical Theory, Propaganda, and Ideology

An early approach was that of Raymond Williams, who posited that capitalism could function only with the help of advertising, as rational consumers would be satisfied with purely functional goods.[11] The task of advertising is to imbue products with 'magical' symbolic meaning so that we are never fully satisfied.

A seminal approach is that of the Frankfurt School, which brought a quasi-Marxist analysis to the modern phenomena of consumer society. Earlier concepts such as Gramsci's hegemony (which claimed that the masses were persuaded to accept the self-serving beliefs of the ruling classes through the power of mass communication, and thus could be used to explain why the working class would vote against its own class interest) were brought together with the concept of false needs to build a critique of the entire consumer society.[12] Marcuse describes consumers as caught within a 'happy consciousness' where their alienation and lack of freedom are balanced with their enjoyment of consumer goods, so that they are unable to escape and achieve an authentic existence.[13] In this view, advertising's role is to maintain the hegemonic dominance of consumption as the prime source of human happiness.

Advertising has been analysed by Galbraith as a very powerful form of propaganda that uses seductive imagery to form the ways in which we think about ourselves and society.[14] This view of advertising as ideology (a communication system that supports a vested interest by making the individual believe that his or her conditions are natural, and opposition unthinkable) has been applied to advertising by Goldman, who sees its effects as inescapable.[15] However, as will be discussed in Sector 4, although advertising may be the 'super-ideology' of late capitalism, its persuasive power has to be set against the countervailing effects of polysemy (adverts can have multiple possible interpretations) and oppositional cultural practices, where subcultural groups (for example, gay rights activists) resist the intended meanings of advertisers by such means as parody and distortion.[16]

Structuralism and Semiotics

A structuralist position is taken by Williamson, who maintains that advertising operates as a structure that transforms the language of objects into that of people and vice versa, and that this translation system can be broken down into its structural elements and processes.[17] Based largely on work by Barthes,[18] her approach uses semiotics to analyse sign systems where a sign (such as an advertisement) has two parts, the signifier and the signified. The signifier is a material object (such as a product) and the signified is an idea and/or an emotion (such as excitement). As an analytic system, semiotics has been widely used in discussions of advertising to unpack some of its communicative complexity, especially in relation to visual imagery.[19] But as more emphasis has been placed on the ability of active audiences to make their own interpretations of advertisements rather than just accept the semiotic codes they are presented with, semiotics has tended to be replaced by social semiotics and poststructuralism, which will be discussed in Sector 4.

Postmodernism

Writers on postmodernism have had a field day with advertising. Central to postmodern theory is the proposition that consumers no longer consume products for their material utilities but consume the symbolic meaning of those products as portrayed in their images. Products in fact become commodity-signs.[20] 'The real consumer becomes a consumer of illusions', as Debord has put it,[21] and 'the ad-dict buys images not things', in the words of Taylor and Saarinen.[22] Based on semiotic theory, postmodernism points to the uncontrollable disconnection of signifiers and signified, the 'free-floating signifiers' in contemporary consumer culture, where any sign can stand for any aspect of a product.

Advertising is the most visible manifestation of a culture bombarded with commodity-signs, a society where reality and illusion are difficult to distinguish, a society of simulations and even hyperreality that is 'more real than the real'. The phrase 'postmodern condition' depicts a society where media images dominate and construct our consciousness, where the boundary between high culture and popular culture disappears, where style dominates substance, and where, according to Strinati, 'as a result, qualities like artistic merit, integrity, seriousness, authenticity, realism, intellectual depth and strong narratives tend to be undermined'.[23] Advertising is seen as a major form of popular culture, which people consume as signs and imagery, and adverts can be seen as cultural products in their own right, consumed independently of the product being marketed.[24] As advertising increasingly uses images and references taken from other forms of popular culture such as cinema, television, and pop music, it becomes less about telling us why we should buy a product and more about associating the product with style and image, often through a parody of advertising itself.

The complex relationship between the two symbol systems of popular culture and advertising has been explicated by Fowles, who maintains they are the 'two grand domains of public art in these times', if only because of their ubiquity.[25] Many postmodern discussions of advertising are partly a celebration of 'mass culture' in opposition to the Frankfurt School's derision of the way in which the 'culture industries' (cinema, radio, magazines) were 'liquidating' high culture and deceiving the working class into accepting a consumer society and abandoning their heritage of great art. However, other themes in postmodernism seem to be very much informed by critical theory and are really just the

Frankfurt School updated for the late-twentieth-century media environment. This dialectic continues in the cultural theories discussed in Sector 4.

Anthropology

Anthropology has drawn our attention to the fact that there may be no such thing as universal human nature, all behaviour being determined by culture,[26] and that different cultures have different communication styles. De Mooij has focused on cultural differences in relation to advertising, using Hofstede's 5-D model of culture.[27] This identifies five dimensions of culture that may affect advertising communication: power distance, individualism versus collectivism, masculinity versus femininity, uncertainty avoidance, and long-term orientation. If we then add the additional cultural dimension of high versus low context, we can start to explore the complexity of communicating with people from different cultures. De Mooij points out that all models of how advertising works are culture bound. In some cultures advertising is assumed to be persuasive in nature, while in others it is assumed to be about building trust. The role of pictures versus words in carrying information and communicating meaning varies between cultures, as does the way people process information. In Chapter 6 we will discuss de Mooij's analysis of cultural differences in advertising. The overall conclusion is that, in order to maximize effectiveness, advertising must reflect local cultural assumptions and communication styles, and advertising effectiveness research must also be culture sensitive.

Sector 3: Active Individuals

In this section we look at disciplines that consider the audience for advertising as active individuals.

Information Economics

Information economics takes the view that rational consumers already know what they want and the task of advertising is simply to inform them of availability and product specifications so as to make their search behaviour efficient.[28] However, only a minority of advertising falls into this information category. The majority of advertising does not appear to carry much information at all. Rather, it conveys implicit information about the brand or company that it is advertising.

The fundamental proposition of economic theory is that the most important information that advertising conveys is primarily of commitment to a market and that consumers are active in forming inferences about the product quality of a brand from the amount of money that is spent: 'the persuasive quality arises from the fact, not the content, of advertising', as Kay puts it.[29] This seems to assert that all advertising is equally effective and content free, and that to beat the competition you need only to spend the most money. We completely reject this perspective and maintain that there is effective advertising and ineffective advertising and the managerial task is to know and manage the difference.

Uses and Gratifications Theory

A very different perspective that also sees the advertising audience as active individuals is uses and gratifications theory. This was the first attempt in communication theory to view the audience as active in its selection of content and messages from the media, and posits that much mass media use is goal directed. This approach has been applied to advertising by O'Donohoe, who separates the marketing-related uses (information, choice, consumption stimulation, image, vicarious consumption) from a wide range of non-marketing-related gratifications.[30] Some of these gratifications will be discussed in Sector 4 as they are social in nature, but some important individualistic 'things people do with advertising' include: entertainment, escapism, role models, reinforcement of attitudes and values, and ego enhancement.

People often consume advertising as an entertainment form in its own right without any direct relevance to purchase behaviour, and this may also apply to the use of advertising for escapism and fantasy. Advertising may provide consumers with role models or other personal aspirations. This is directly related to the way in which we may also use advertising as a raw material to help us make sense of the world through the social construction of reality, and thus to reinforce our attitudes and our values.[31] Advertising may also help us to sustain our sense of self-worth by keeping us in touch with what is fashionable.

Narrative Transportation

A fascinating new approach to the way that consumers may become absorbed in advertising and relate it to their lives is narrative transportation theory.[32] Narrative transportation happens when viewers of adverts become very engaged with a story, and this leads to persuasion through reduced negative cognitive responding and strong positive emotional responses.

Consumer Scepticism

Scepticism towards advertising has emerged as an important factor in advertising theory as it fundamentally changes the way consumers respond to advertising. They may dismiss arguments and generate more counter-arguments or even detach themselves from interaction with advertising messages altogether.[33] The most comprehensive account of the way scepticism influences consumer processing of persuasive communication is the persuasion knowledge model which points to consumers learning about advertisers' motives, strategies, and tactics.[34] This learning is amplified by mass media discussions of consumer culture.

Sector 4: Active Social/Cultural Groups

This sector considers a number of relatively recent applications of theory to advertising. These views take a strong social orientation and assume active participation on the part of advertising's audience.

Socio-linguistics

The socio-linguistics perspective draws on speech act theory in linguistic philosophy to emphasize the social action aspects of language, and on ethnomethodology to focus on how people use language in everyday situations to make sense of their world. It has extended the study of the use of language to include contextual aspects such as relations of class, power, and gender. The fundamental assumptions of socio-linguistics and its various forms of discourse analysis are that language is a medium oriented towards action and function, and that people use language intentionally to construct accounts or versions of the social world. Evidence for this active process of construction is said to be demonstrated by variation in language. This concept of variability is central for analysis, as discourse will vary systematically depending upon the function it is being used to perform.[35] Language performs a variety of functions in the world and does not just represent it, for, as Foucault pointed out, we are only able to think within the constraints of discourse.[36] Discourse is defined here as a system of statements that constructs an object, supports institutions, reproduces power relations, and has ideological effects. In applying this to advertising, Fairclough suggests that adverts 'help' the consumer to build a relationship with products, evoking an interpretative framework that situates both consumer and product in a 'modern lifestyle'.[37] In a study of overt sexuality in advertising, Elliott and his colleagues have suggested that, if consumers could classify overt sexuality within an interpretative framework of 'art', then this would function to legitimate positive interpretations by changing their category from sexual, which would be unacceptable, to art in which the same representation could then be given approbation. This seemed to be related to the product being given very little attention in the advertisement and therefore allowing it to be transferred from the commercial to the artistic realm where moral judgement could be suspended.[38]

Myers allows more freedom to the members of the audience in the construction of their 'position as consumers', and points to the potential for multiple interpretations of advertising.[39] We will discuss the possibilities for multiple meanings—polysemy—in more detail below when we consider poststructuralism. He also points out that adverts are not consumed alone, but depend on interactions with other people in order to make socially shared meaning.

Feminism

There is a long history of feminist analysis of advertising, almost always from a critical perspective that implicates advertising in maintaining and even enhancing aspects of male subordination of women. In an early empirical study Goffman demonstrated how many print advertisements presented woman in a subservient role to men, the men usually depicted as being above and in control of women.[40] Subsequent content analyses of female images in advertising showed a serious bias towards stereotyped sex-role portrayals of women as primarily homemakers.[41]

A particular focus for analysis has been the extent to which advertising imagery constructs women's sense of beauty, and may in fact have harmful effects on their sense of worth. Certainly, this seems to be the conclusion from a number of experiments that have shown that exposure to idealized images of women in advertising resulted in women having lower levels of satisfaction with their own attractiveness.[42] Myers suggested that women are more vulnerable to manipulation by advertising than men because their upbringing and social expectations have already been influenced towards accepting gender stereotyping.[43] However, other research has found that women are perfectly able to identify and resist unrealistic gender portrayals in advertising.[44]

Social Semiotics and Visual Persuasion Theory

The recent development of theories of social semiotics, and in particular that of the theory of visual persuasion, is an important development, as the vast majority of advertising makes potent use of visual images. Kress and van Leeuwen present an articulated theory that attempts to explain how socially meaningful images can be built into visual narrative systems.[45] In common with socio-linguistics, social semiotics assumes that language varies with social context, and also assumes that the reader of any narrative system plays an active part in its interpretation.

Messaris presented the first comprehensive theory of visual persuasion, in which he utilizes the three semiotic concepts of iconicity, indexicality, and syntactic indeterminacy and applies them to persuasive images.[46] Iconicity relates to the fact that an image not only can represent an aspect of the real world but also comes with a wealth of emotional associations that stem from each individual's unique experiences in addition to the shared influences of culture. These associations are communicated not just by visual content but also by visual form. Indexicality is particularly relevant to photographs, and relates to the fact that a photographic image can serve as documentary evidence or proof of an advert's claims because of its 'authenticity'. He maintains, contrary to the claims of Kress and van Leeuwen, that there can be no precise syntax or explicit propositional system using visual images. It is precisely this relative 'deficiency' of visual syntax that gives images such persuasive power, as not only can they escape explicit interpretation by the audience and thus say what might be slightly unacceptable if fully spelt out, but they can also evade legal and moral restrictions through implicit communication. These are very important issues in relation to advertising and persuasion.

Poststructuralism

Poststructuralism is the final perspective we shall consider here, and this develops from both the uses and gratifications approach and from postmodernism. Literary analysis of texts has increasingly seen the growth of reader-response theory, which shows how a text works with the probable knowledge, expectations, or motives of the reader and leads to multiple interpretations of meaning.[47] A basic assumption here is that advertising, like other communicative texts, is subject to polysemy: that is, it is open to multiple interpretations by the audience. A number of recent studies provide empirical evidence of advertising's polysemic status.[48]

Polysemy is a potentially fatal threat to a successful advertising campaign because it can prevent the advertiser from getting the intended meanings across to the target audience. This will pose a significant limitation to a campaign's effectiveness and consequently a brand's future success in the market. In practice (rather than in theory) the interpretation made by the reader or viewer of an advert will be limited in two crucial ways. First, polysemy is limited by the text; some texts are more polysemic than others, being more or less open texts. Secondly, readers or viewers represent a polysemic limitation in that, rather than arriving at a unique, totally idiosyncratic meaning, they will subjectively interpret the text, but the end result will be a meaning that is very similar to other individuals' subjective interpretations of the same text.

These individuals form an informal social group called an 'interpretive community'.[49] Ritson and Elliott identified several interpretative communities within a group of young people, formed around readings of advertising texts, because the proximity of their social location and cultural competencies had led them to interpret the text in a similar way and with similar semantic results.[50] Indeed several groups showed an implicit awareness of their membership in an interpretive advertising community, and used this knowledge as part of their identification with the group.

A late-twentieth-century development in advertising theory was that of meaning-based models. These see advertising not as a conduit of information but as a resource for the construction of personal, social, and culturally situated meanings where human reality is mediated. In this view, consumers construct a variety of meanings from advertising as outcomes of a personal history and subjective interests as expressed through their life themes and life projects. In one study, three brothers had very different interpretations of the same five magazine adverts, each one constructing interpretations that resonated with their subjective interests, goals, and ambitions.[51] Ritson and Elliott have extended the meaning-based approach from the individual's life world to social contexts, and have shown that advertising texts are often the source for a wide variety of social interactions in which advertising meanings are often changed, transferred, or solidified within the social contexts of everyday life.[52] This suggests an expansion of the concept of advertising context to include the social setting of the viewer alongside the textual setting of the advert. The impact that an advertising execution has on a particular audience and the uses to which it is put are partially dependent on the social context within which the viewer exists.

Implications for Advertising Strategy

The wide range of theoretical approaches to understanding how advertising works that we have discussed raises a number of issues for advertising management. Although the cognitive information processing approach used in this book is pragmatically the most useful for developing and managing advertising strategy, it tends to ignore the way people interact with advertising in their day-to-day lives. We must also remember that the audience is not usually passively absorbing our advertising messages but is actively creating meanings that make sense to them in the context of their lives and harmonize with their own experiences. To develop really effective advertising we must pay attention to the rich social and cultural environment in which people consume products, services, and advertisements, and seek to use this knowledge to build connections between individuals, social groups, and brands. Keep this in mind as we now turn our attention to the development and management of effective advertising strategy.

CHAPTER SUMMARY

This chapter has reviewed a wide range of perspectives on how advertising works and on its effects on society. To help in this complex task we have introduced two dimensions that relate to assumptions about the audience (active versus passive) and to the level of explanation (individual versus cultural), and used these dimensions to construct a conceptual map. We conclude from this analysis that the cognitive information processing approach is pragmatically the most useful for advertising management, but we must also pay attention to the broader social and cultural environment.

QUESTIONS TO CONSIDER

2.1 Why is it important to think about alternative perceptions of how advertising works?

2.2 In what ways do you see the different perspectives discussed in this chapter adding to our overall understanding of advertising?

2.3 Which of the specific alternative perspectives discussed in this chapter do you feel offers the most insight into how advertising works?

2.4 How can these different perspectives be used by managers in a practical way to ensure more effective advertising for their brand?

CASE STUDY 2

Audi—From Private to Public Prestige

In 1995 Audi UK launched an all-new range of cars, the A-series, with a new communication strategy. The brand's communications adopted an understated tone, appealing to people who weren't comfortable with the flashy nature of other prestige car marques. The commercials, 'It won't be appreciated by everyone', had made the brand discreetly or privately prestigious. This 'private prestige' had firmly positioned Audi as the choice for the more discerning driver. By 2000, Audi had built its image and sales to join the prestige car sector. This sector, defined by cars with a prestige image and a sizeable sales volume, had previously comprised BMW and Mercedes.

Despite its sales success, the brand was still only third in the market. An already impressive growth rate had to be bettered. Audi UK had a long-term goal of challenging the leader of the sector, BMW, but now it limited itself by the 'private prestige' communication strategy. Although the 'private prestige' in the minds of a discreet group of consumers was successful, the target buyers are a relatively small segment. In order to start accelerating volume growth, Audi had to appeal to a broader buying audience of all prestige car buyers.

Most prestige cars are bought for outer-directed reasons—they are status symbols that gain value as more people think highly of them. Therefore, to appeal to the 175,000 prestige car buyers, Audi had to be understood by an even broader audience, the general public. But competing with the established status symbols BMW and Mercedes for 'public prestige' would be tough. Their 'public prestige' is evident in the range of lyricists using them to denote status; from Janis Joplin ('Oh Lord, won't you buy me a Mercedes Benz') to Beenie Man ('Zim zimmer, who's got the keys to me Beamer').

Audi could not afford to continue a brand strategy of quiet confidence anymore. For prestige brands the product is the hero, and their tone is that of absolute confidence. It needed to evolve its personality to persuade the general public of its prestige. To be more publicly prestigious, Audi had to gain a more obvious and impactful presence: The brand strategy moved from 'understatement' to 'statement'; its brand personality evolved from dry, witty, and intellectual to bold, confident, and forceful. In line with the revised brand strategy, the cars supplemented their strong quality and design credentials with a sportier, more aggressive, styling. Together with the new design philosophy being implemented gradually via new versions of existing models, the launches of the dramatically designed TT and A2 helped the signs of change in the brand.

With the revised brand strategy and product design in place, the communication strategy was important to convey the brand's message to consumers, both to the general public and to the target prestige car buyers. However, research showed that the majority of the general public does not pay much attention to car advertising. Audi needed to find a way beyond advertising to engage the general public and build a sense of Audi's prestige. In Audi's case, a concept of 'brand content' might work more effectively than advertising to transform Audi's private prestige to a public one. 'Brand content' uses the gaps between the advertising; it is the placement of a brand in editorials, our day-to-day life, or our culture. Appearing in more engaging editorial space (rather than the obvious advertising space) would give the brand's message a better chance of being enthusiastically consumed by the general public; and a greater chance of becoming embedded in the public consciousness. Moreover, brand content would also make our other, more targeted, communications work more effectively. A publicly prestigious brand is likely to command greater attention from prestige car drivers. The rationale was that once brand content has established 'public prestige', prestige car buyers would pay more attention to the brand's advertising and direct activity.

With 'brand content' in position, advertising was then used to drive desirability with Audi's specific buying audience. The media target changed from upmarket men 35+ to a broader target of all prestige car buyers, including younger men and women. And it used a combination of public and prestige media to ensure the target saw Audi in both a public and prestige context (e.g. Champions League Football on Sky and Yachting World). The advertising appealed to the status-oriented prestige car buying audience. It was assumptive and bold, centring on what Audi was, not what it wasn't. Different ads dramatized different elements of the products, product features, product attitude, product inspiration. And an always used end-line, 'Vorsprung durch Technik' (advancement through technology), was still constantly used in advertising to encapsulate Audi's prestige. Finally, direct marketing was used to turn the increased appeal generated by the 'brand content' and advertising into purchase enquiries. A high proportion of the budget was spent on direct marketing because each communication piece reflected the prestige values generated through the advertising. Quality materials were deployed (e.g. leather and aluminum) and hi-tech formats (e.g. DVDs and USB sticks) were incorporated.

After the 'public prestige' campaign was put in place in 2000, the brand made strong progress against its ambitious sales objectives. The average annual growth rate in this period was 14 per cent, compared to 11 per cent in 1995–2000; volume almost doubled. The rate of volume share growth between 2000 and 2005 was more than double that of the previous period. By February 2006, it was no longer third in the sector; it managed to replace Mercedes and assume second place. It came as no surprise, therefore, to see that brand desirability started to increase in 2000 and follow a similar pattern to ad awareness.

The brand content method succeeded in making the brand more 'public'. From the start of the new campaign, Audi's share of public presence increased: mentions of the brand in the nation's press increased by 3000 per cent (1995–9 vs. 2000–5). Moreover, the nature of the brand content carried a prestige message. Audi's prestige image with the general public increased during the campaign. Audi had now risen to the hallowed ranks of musical status symbol. Audi cars were established as status symbols and buyers were more willing to spend more on them. For the UK's very own arbiters of bling, Blazin' Squad, an Audi is the very essence of status:

'And now it's all about making Gs, Travel over seas, Drinking Cris, Driving Audi TTs'

Blazin' Squad, 'How Blazin' Rolls' (July 2003)

The consistent use of 'Vorsprung durch Technik' meant that Audi's end-line became even more entrenched in the culture. In 1996, only 53 per cent of prestige car buyers were aware of the line, by 2004 84 per cent of all adults in UK were aware of it.

The increase in ad awareness was with no increase in advertising spend because of the mixture of communication methods, brand content, advertising, and direct marketing. Audi's brand content made advertising capture the attention of the target audience. Research showed that ad awareness was higher amongst those aware of the brand's public presence. Largely as a result of this, the TV ads were twice as efficient at generating branded impact as before. The number of people, per £500 spent on TV, who remembered the TV ads (and knew they were from Audi) doubled with the new campaign. It cost less money to get more people to pay attention. And an above 4 per cent rate of responses to Audi's direct marketing clearly beat industry norms (0.5–3 per cent). Direct marketing prompted people to send off or go on-line for a brochure. As a result, Audi has seen a steady growth in new visitors to audi.co.uk (+90 per cent—February 2005 to February 2006) which has outstripped the other top 25 automotive manufacturer sites (+52 per cent). Efficiencies were also gained through Audi's growing loyalty. The increase in loyalty has the beneficial effect on Audi that costs per car sold decrease, as it is cheaper to sell to an existing customer than to win a competitor's customer.

In summary, Audi successfully turned its private prestige to public. It increased its brand awareness, brand value, volume share, and value share. And all of this was done with a decrease in marketing spend per car sold.

Source: WARC, IPA Effectiveness Awards 2006, Audi—From Private to Public Prestige, by Laurence Parkes, Paul Kershaw, and Bernard Chudy

Edited by Hazel H. Huang

Discussion Questions

1 Place the campaign, 'It won't be appreciated by everyone', on the conceptual map of perspectives on advertising (p. 26) and discuss the pros and cons of the campaign strategy.

2 '...research showed that the majority of the general public does not pay much attention to car advertising.' Why did the company think brand content would work? And why did Audi still use advertising as one of its communication outlets?

3 Discuss the role of direct marketing in the campaign strategy.

4 The new campaign, public prestige, used three different communication channels: brand content, advertising, and direct marketing. Discuss their positions on the conceptual map of perspectives on adverting on p. 26.

FURTHER READING

- A special issue of *Marketing Theory*, 4(1) (2004) and a special issue of the *Journal of Advertising*, 32/1 (Spring 2003), deal with new developments in advertising theory and consumer culture, and look at a number of subjects in the light of many of the points discussed in this chapter.

- Stephen Brown, *Marketing: The Retro Revolution* (London: Sage, 2001), offers some very interesting insights into the entire area of retro-marketing, and takes a new perspective on looking at the influence of advertising's history on retro-advertising campaigns.

NOTES

1 J. K. Galbraith, *The New Industrial Society* (Harmondsworth: Penguin, 1968).

2 H. Marcuse, *One-Dimensional Man* (London: Routledge and Kegan Paul, 1964).

3 For a review of motivational research, see P. Martineau, *Motivation in Advertising* (New York: McGraw-Hill, 1957), and E. Dichter, *The Handbook of Consumer Motivation* (New York: McGraw-Hill, 1964).

4 V. Packard, *The Hidden Persuaders* (Harmondsworth: Penguin, 1957).

5 J. Williamson, *Decoding Advertisements* (London: Marion Boyars, 1978).

6 G. Cook, *The Discourse of Advertising* (London: Routledge, 1992).

7 T. Vestergaard and K. Schroder, *The Language of Advertising* (Oxford: Basil Blackwell, 1985).

8 See J. Jones, 'Advertising: Strong Force or Weak Force? Two Views an Ocean Apart', *International Journal of Advertising*, 9/3 (1990), 233–246.

9 W. Gordon, 'What Do Consumers Do Emotionally With Advertising?', *Journal of Advertising Research*, 46/1 (2006), 2–10.

10 F. Li and P. Miniard, 'On the Potential for Advertising to Facilitate Trust in the Advertised Brand', *Journal of Advertising*, 35/4 (2006), 101–112.

11 R. Williams, 'Advertising: The Magic System', in R. Williams, *Problems in Materialism and Culture* (London: Verso, 1980).

12 A. Gramsci, *The Prison Notebooks* (London: Lawrence and Wishart, 1971).

13 Marcuse, *One-Dimensional Man*.

14 Galbraith, *The New Industrial Society*.

15 See R. Goldman, *Reading Ads Socially* (London: Routledge, 1992).

16 See Richard Elliott and Mark Ritson, 'Poststructuralism and the Dialectics of Advertising: Discourse, Ideology, Resistance', in S. Brown and D. Turley (eds), *Consumer Research: Postcards from the Edge* (London: Routledge, 1997), 190–219.

17 Williamson, *Decoding Advertisements*.

18 See R. Barthes, *Mythologies* (St Albans: Paladin, 1973).

19 See e.g. G. Dyer, *Advertising as Communication* (London: Methuen, 1982); A. Wernick, *Promotional Culture: Advertising, Ideology, and Symbolic Expression* (London: Sage, 1991); and R. Goldman and S. Papson, *Sign Wars: The Cluttered Landscape of Advertising* (London: Guilford Press, 1996).

20 See J. Baudrillard, 'For a Critique of the Political Economy of the Sign', in M. Poster (ed.), *Jean Baudrillard: Selected Writings* (Cambridge: Polity Press, 1988).

21 G. Debord, *Society of the Spectacle* (Detroit: Black and Red, 1977).

22 M. Taylor and E. Saarinen, *Imagologies: Media Philosophy* (London: Routledge, 1994).

23 D. Strinati, *An Introduction to Theories of Popular Culture* (London: Routledge, 1995), 225.

24 See M. Nava, 'Consumerism Reconsidered: Buying and Power', *Cultural Studies*, 5 (1991), 157–73.

25 J. Fowles, *Advertising and Popular Culture* (Thousand Oaks, Calif.: Sage Publications, 1996).

26 See C. Geertz, *The Interpretation of Cultures* (New York: Basic Books, 1973).

27 M. de Mooij, *Global Marketing and Advertising: Understanding Cultural Paradoxes* (Thousand Oaks, Calif.: Sage Publications, 1998).

28 See e.g. P. Nelson, 'Advertising as Information', *Journal of Political Economy*, 81 (1974), 729–54.

29 J. Kay, *Foundations of Corporate Success* (Oxford: Oxford University Press, 1993).

30 S. O'Donohoe, 'Advertising Uses and Gratifications', *European Journal of Marketing*, 28/8–9 (1994), 52–75.

31 See F. Buttle, 'What Do People Do with Advertising?', *International Journal of Advertising*, 10 (1991), 95–110.

32 J. Escalas, 'Self-Referencing and Persuasion: Narrative Transportation Versus Analytical Elaboration', *Journal of Consumer Research*, 33/1 (2007), 421–429.

33 L. Nan and R. Faber, 'Advertising Theory: Reconceptualising the Building Blocks', *Marketing Theory*, 4/1–2 (2004), 7–30.

34 M. Freistad and P. Wright, 'The Persuasion Knowledge Model: How People Cope with Persuasion Attempts', *Journal of Consumer Research*, 21/1 (1994), 1–31.

35 J. Potter and M. Wetherall, *Discourse and Social Psychology: Beyond Attitudes and Behaviour* (London: Sage Publications, 1987).

36 M. Foucault, *The Archaeology of Knowledge* (London: Tavistock, 1972).

37 N. Fairclough, *Language and Power* (London: Longman, 1989).

38 R. Elliott, A. Jones, B. Benfield, and M. Barlow, 'Overt Sexuality in Advertising: A Discourse Analysis of Gender Responses', *Journal of Consumer Policy*, 18/2 (1995).

39 K. Myers, *Understains: The Sense and Seduction of Advertising* (London: Pandora, 1986).

40 E. Goffman, *Gender Advertisements* (London: Macmillan, 1979).

41 A number of studies have dealt with this issue, such as A. Courtney and T. Whipple, *Sex Role Stereotyping in Advertising* (Lexington, Mass.: Lexington Books, 1983), and S. Livingstone and G. Green, 'Television Advertisements and the Portrayal of Gender', *British Journal of Social Psychology*, 25 (1986), 149–54.

42 M. Richins, 'Social Comparison and the Idealized Images of Advertising', *Journal of Consumer Research*, 18/1 (1991), 71–91.

43 Myers, *Understains*.

44 See e.g. Elliott *et al.*, 'Overt Sexuality in Advertising'.

45 G. Kress and T. van Leeuwen, *Reading Images: The Grammar of Visual Design* (London: Routledge, 1996).

46 P. Messaris, *Visual Persuasion: The Role of Images in Advertising* (Thousand Oaks, Calif.: Sage Publications, 1997).

47 L. Scott, 'The Bridge from Text to Mind: Adapting Reader-Response Theory to Consumer Research', *Journal of Consumer Research*, 21 (1994), 461–80.

48 See e.g. the work of R. Elliott, S. Eccles, and M. Hodgson, 'Re-Coding Gender Representations: Women, Cleaning Products, and Advertising's "New Man"', *International Journal of Research in Marketing*, 10 (1993), 311–24; R. Elliott and M. Ritson, 'Practicing Existential Consumption: The Lived Meaning of Sexuality in Advertising', *Advances in Consumer Research*, 22 (1995), 740–6; and D. G. Mick and K. Buhl, 'A Meaning-Based Model of Advertising', *Journal of Consumer Research*, 19 (1992), 317–38.

49 See S. Fish, *Is there a Text in this Class? The Authority of Interpretive Communities* (Cambridge, Mass.: Harvard University Press, 1980).

50 M. Ritson and R. Elliott, 'The Social Uses of Advertising: An Ethnographic Study of Adolescent Advertising Audiences', *Journal of Consumer Research*, 26/3 (1999), 260–77.

51 Mick and Buhl, 'A Meaning-Based Model of Advertising'.

52 Ritson and Elliott, 'The Social Uses of Advertising'.

 Visit the Online Resource Centre that accompanies this book for additional resources to support the text: http://www.oxfordtextbooks.co.uk/orc/percy_elliott3e/

3

Advertising across Cultural Borders

 KEY CONCEPTS

1 There is evidence that consumer behaviour across cultures is converging in some markets, but also some suggestion that it is diverging with growing affluence.

2 The basic sources of different cultural assumptions include language, ethnicity, religion, and family organization.

3 Hofstede's dimensions of culture have been found to be useful in many studies, especially the individualism/collectivism dimension.

4 The differences between high-context versus low-context communication cultures is important for advertising using symbolic visuals.

5 A gradient of cross-cultural adaptation based on level of consumer involvement and emotion, and degree of cultural differentiation can be used to aid decisions about advertising strategies across cultures.

6 Cultural value systems can be used to segment the world into three basic clusters of countries.

The key issue in advertising across cultural borders relates to the extent to which consumers are really so alike around the world that advertisers can ignore differences and standardize their advertising behind global brands. This issue is still being keenly debated but there is evidence that there is some convergence in consumer behaviour in some markets and that guidelines can be developed to guide advertising management decisions about when and where global advertising may be appropriate and when it may not.

Convergence or Divergence

Back in 1983 Ted Levitt started the pursuit of a 'magic bullet' that would solve all the difficulties of marketing across cultures: he claimed that consumers around the world were converging on a single set of needs and wants so that all marketing from now on would just be global marketing. However, as de Mooij[1] points out, this claim in the Harvard Business Review[2] was based on the assumption that consumers made rational decisions and that they would converge on high-quality/low-priced global products rather than higher-priced customized products. This has proved to be an accurate prediction in technological product categories, e.g. computers, cameras, MP3 players, and to some extent motor cars, where brands are produced and advertised on a global basis. However, consumer behaviour in many areas instead of converging has diverged, so just as many organizations are standardizing their marketing, so consumers are demanding localized products and services. For example, Coca-Cola's CEO explaining his company's falling profits said: 'We kept standardising our practices, while local sensitivity had become essential to success.'[3] De Mooij[4] presents a convincing set of studies that demonstrate that consumer behaviour has converged in some areas but in most areas has diverged. What seems to be happening is that with increasing economic development consumption of some products, such as TV sets, telephone main lines, computers, and cars, is converging in terms of levels of ownership per thousand population, but how they are actually used at the household level differs across countries; for example see Fig. 3.1, where despite similar levels of TV ownership, the average US household watches nearly four times as much television as Swedish households. In fact, de Mooij reaches the conclusion that 'As people become more affluent their tastes diverge'.

But there is evidence to suggest that there is one particular global group with convergent tastes: the global teen market.[5] Sharing high involvement with music, media, sports, and communication, teens are seen as a global targetable group. However, the homogeneity of the group was contested by Moses,[6] who argued that not only are teens not alike worldwide, but are segmented into six value clusters that differentiate them globally and within specific countries. This large-scale study used elements of the cultural value theory of Schwartz[7] and this was also the conceptual base for another study[8] which also identified six global segments and related these to global advertising strategy and media consumption. We will discuss this study later in the chapter. But in order to understand the cultural dimensions of communication we need to analyse the basic sources of culture and different cultural assumptions, the cognitive organization of cultural values and the way these values are expressed in consumer behaviour. The fundamental elements

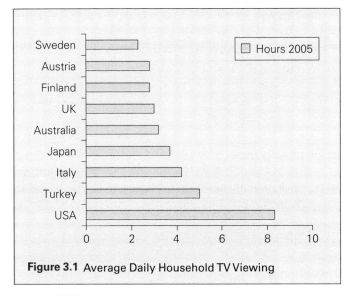

Figure 3.1 Average Daily Household TV Viewing

Source: OECD.

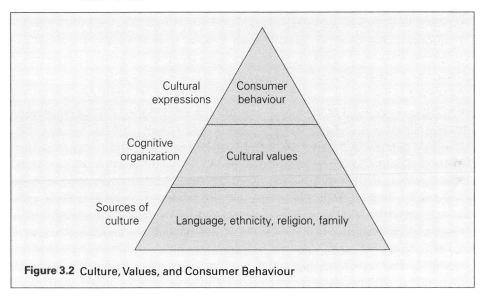

Figure 3.2 Culture, Values, and Consumer Behaviour

of language, ethnicity, religion, and family organization structure cultural value systems that are then expressed in consumer behaviour. See Fig. 3.2.

Basic Sources of Different Cultural Assumptions

The foundation for understanding the cultural dimensions of communication, as we see in Fig. 3.2, is built upon language, ethnicity, religion, and family. In many ways, they are interrelated, but at the heart is language. As language is acquired, it is influenced by the ethnicity, religion, and the family environment of a child; and once language is formed, it influences a person's understanding of their own ethnicity, religion, and family. Each of these cultural dimension building blocks is briefly discussed below.

Language

The Sapir-Whorf hypothesis of linguistic relativity claims that language creates mental categories which organize how we perceive the world and construct reality: 'the real world is to a large extent built up on the language habits of the group. No two languages are ever sufficiently similar as to be considered as representing the same reality. We see and hear and otherwise experience very largely as we do because the language habits of our community predispose certain choices of interpretation. The worlds in which different societies live are distinct worlds, not merely the same world with different labels attached.'[9] The 'strong' claim that thought depends on language is disputed by some linguists, but not by neuroscientists, who generally believe that thought is dependent upon words. The key insight ('weak' claim) that language can influence ways of thinking has considerable empirical support.[10] The idea that the availability of words structures thought has been influential in the literature of politics and oppression, for example in Orwell's *Nineteen Eighty-Four*, Newspeak has replaced standard English and thought is controlled by removing words so that what cannot be said cannot be done. In Elgin's *Native Tongue*, set in a future extreme patriarchal society, women develop a feminist language in secret in order to resist male oppression.

Somewhere between the linguistic and the novelistic and of particular relevance to advertising, Lakoff and Johnson[11] analysed the power of metaphor to frame thought, demonstrating that metaphors are vital in creating meaning and thus influencing behaviour. The essence of metaphor is understanding and experiencing one kind of thing in terms of another. They use the example of the metaphor 'Argument is war' to demonstrate that this is not just linguistic usage but has real-world consequences on how we actually argue. Lakoff[12] has applied linguistic relativity to political analysis demonstrating that metaphor can be used to deceive and persuade. The influence of language on cultural differences will be discussed later in the chapter, in particular by reference to Watzlawick's[13] communication theory and its emphasis on analogue non-verbal modalities, as well as the role of context in cross-cultural communications.

Ethnicity

The rather broad term of ethnicity relates to a process of identification with an ethnic group and is intimately bound up with the social context in which a person grows up and matures.[14] This means that ethnicity involves a wide range of factors, being intimately concerned with the symbolic activities of language, customs, representations of the past, religious beliefs, and a sense of common origin.[15] However, ethnicity may not just be imposed and there is an implication that one of the choices inherent in a postmodern culture is a choice of which ethnic group to connect to. In fact, Bouchet[16] argues that postmodern ethnicity is a lifestyle choice, particularly for second and third generation immigrants. The importance of ethnicity for marketing involves the concept of ethno-centrism: 'the universal proclivity for people to view their own group as the center of the universe...the symbols and values of one's own ethnic or national group become objects of pride and attachment, whereas symbols of other groups may become objects of contempt'.[17] We will discuss the importance of considering levels of consumer ethnocentrism in the marketing of global brands later.

Religion

One of the most powerful influences on cultural values and consumer behaviour may be a function of religious beliefs. Taboos against beef for Hindus and pork and alcohol for Muslims obviously have a major influence on consumer behaviour in many areas of the world. Islamic beliefs against charging interest on loans creates the need for specialist Islamic banking practices.

Family

The social organization of the family is closely linked with religion and varies widely around the world. In particular, the role of the extended family is pervasive in many cultures and takes many forms including the 'baradari' or joint family which is a feature of Hinduism. The centrality of family and kinship relations is a core element in the cultural assumptions underlying collectivist cultures rather than individualistic cultures and we will explore this in detail later.

Cognitive Organization and Cultural Values

The seminal work on systematic differences in cultural values is that of Hofstede,[18] who originally identified four dimensions of culture based upon thirty years of quantitative research in seventy-two countries and in twenty languages: power distance, individu-alism/collectivism, uncertainty avoidance, and masculinity/femininity. This was later updated, and a fifth dimension added; long-term orientation.[19] Hofstede's definitions for these dimensions of culture are shown in Table 3.1.

In cultures characterized by power distance, organizations tend to be hierarchical and unequally accepted. Countries that score high on power distance include France and Mexico, the USA is relatively low, and Denmark and Austria very low. Individualistic cultures tend to be task oriented, and verbal; more collectivist cultures are relationship oriented. Most Western cultures tend to be higher on individualism, Asian and Latin American cultures more collectivist. Uncertainty avoidance implies exactly what it says: people in some cultures are comfortable with a certain level of uncertainty, others hate it. Cultures that score high on the dimension include Germany and Japan, while low scoring cultures include the UK and Scandinavian countries such as Sweden and Denmark. Anglo-Saxon cultures tend to score high in terms of masculinity, and Scandinavian cultures low.

Table 3.1 Hofstede's Dimensions and Definitions

Power Distance	'the extent to which less powerful members of a society accept and expect that power is distributed unequally'
Individualism/ Collectivism	'people looking after themselves and their immediate families only versus people belonging to in-groups that look after them in exchange for loyalty'
Uncertainty Avoidance	'the extent to which people feel threatened by uncertainty and ambiguity and try to avoid these situations'
Masculinity/ Femininity	'the dominant values in a masculine society are achievement and success, the dominant values in a feminine society are caring for others and quality of life'
Long-Term Orientation	'the extent to which a society exhibits a pragmatic future-oriented perspective rather than a conventional historic or short-term point of view'

Source: Adapted from M. de Mooij, *Global Marketing and Advertising: Understanding Cultural Paradoxes* (London: Sage, 1998).

The addition of the fifth dimension, long-term orientation, resulted from research into trying to find an explanation to Asian economic success. Originally labelled Confucian Dynamism because it included values of Confucian philosophy, it includes values of family, duty, hierarchy, and long-term perspective. Those scoring high on long-term orientation tend to have a sense of perseverance, and order relationships by status; low scorers have a focus on more short-term goals related to happiness. Most Asian countries, especially those with large Chinese populations, score high on long-term orientation, and Anglo-Saxon cultures low.

High-Context versus Low-Context Communication Cultures

Hall[20] identified two different approaches to communication which he calls high context versus low context. A high-context culture is one where most of the information in a communication is either part of the context or internalized in the audience, very little is made explicit as part of the message, relying often on visuals and symbols. A low-context culture is characterized by explicit verbal messages carrying facts and data. Asian, Arab, and Mediterranean countries tend to be high-context cultures, and body language and non-verbal cues are essential to understanding the 'words' spoken. In low-context cultures such as Britain and the United States, the interpretation of spoken words is less dependent on non-verbal cues. In fact, serious misperceptions of meaning can occur when this is not taken into account. The important implications of this for advertising will be examined later, as there is evidence that advertising in high-context cultures makes much use of symbolic visuals.

This is very like Trompenaars's[21] distinction between neutral cultures where feelings are not usually shown overtly but are controlled, whereas in an affective culture verbal and non-verbal displays of thought and feelings are the norm. These cultural differences in emotional expression have obvious implications for advertising.

Hall[22] makes an interesting distinction between cultures based upon assumptions about time, which he called monochronic versus polychronic cultures. In monochronic cultures time tends to be seen as limited, structured in a sequential linear fashion, whereas in polychronic cultures time is experienced as unlimited and simultaneous.

Universal Cultural Values Systems

A theory which has gained much credence recently is that of Schwartz and Bilsky,[23] who maintain that all humans share a set of seven motivational values which are differently combined in different cultures and this has been validated across a number of countries. The seven values are shown in Fig. 3.3 and show some correlation with Hofstede's individualism/collectivism values.

This approach has been developed in a large-scale study by Chow and Amir[24] in 30 countries with a sample of over 25,000 people which identified six value dimensions which form a universal structure of values. These six values and some of their typical contents are described in Table 3.2.

The weighting of the values varies markedly between countries, for example Sweden is dominated by intimate values whereas Saudi Arabia is dominated by devout values. This is illustrated for four countries in Fig. 3.4.

Importantly, this value structure has been used to develop a value segmentation model which has been related to global brands which we will use to discuss implications for advertising management later in the chapter.

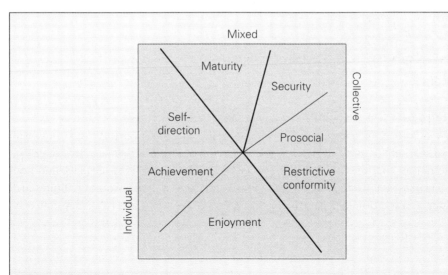

Figure 3.3 Universal Value Structure

Source: S. Schwartz and W. Bilsky, 'Toward a Theory of the Universal Content and Structure of Values: Extensions and Cross-cultural Replications', *Journal of Personality and Social Psychology*, 58/5 (1990), 878–91.

Table 3.2 Content of Universal Value Dimensions

STRIVER	FUN-SEEKER	CREATIVE	DEVOUT	INTIMATE	ALTRUIST
Power	Excitement	Beauty	Spirituality	Honesty	Preserving the environment
Status	Leisure	Fulfilling work	Tradition	Personal support	Justice
Ambition	Individuality	Self-esteem	Duty	Enduring love	Social responsibility
Material security	Pleasure	Freedom	Obedience	Authenticity	Equality
Public image	Live for today	Knowledge	Modesty	Friendship	Social tolerance

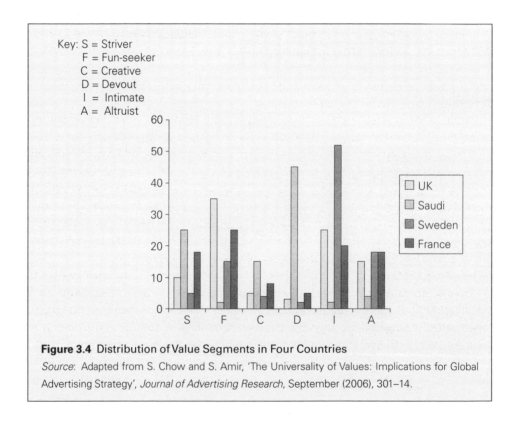

Figure 3.4 Distribution of Value Segments in Four Countries

Source: Adapted from S. Chow and S. Amir, 'The Universality of Values: Implications for Global Advertising Strategy', *Journal of Advertising Research*, September (2006), 301–14.

Cultural Differences and Values in Advertising

A number of studies have used content analysis to examine advertising executions from different cultural locations to explore the values portrayed and have compared them with elements of the theoretical value structures above. A comparison of Chinese and American

TV advertising[25] found that Chinese advertisements utilized the following cultural values more often than US advertisements: a soft-sell appeal, veneration of the elderly, group consensus, and status appeals. In contrast, the US advertisements used the following cultural values more frequently: a hard-sell appeal, individualism/independence, time orientation, product merit. This finding of Chinese advertising being more consensual and family oriented is a common one across many studies about East Asian countries. Similar findings about traditional cultural values being expressed have also been found in comparisons between Arab and American advertising.[26] Less extreme differences have been found between the USA and France and despite a shared language even between the USA and UK.[27] However, with globalized communications there are indications that traditional values are becoming less ubiquitous in some East Asian societies, for example values of modernity and individualism are becoming prevalent in advertising aimed at younger, affluent Chinese people.[28]

Cultural Values and the Effectiveness of Executional Elements

Cultural values will inform how advertising is processed, and should be reflected in the way in which the message is constructed and executed. In this section we shall be looking at some executional elements that have been shown to depend upon cultural values for effectiveness.

Appeals

Matching appeals and arguments to cultural differences on the individualism/collectivism dimension demonstrates that culturally congruent appeals are most effective.[29] Collectivism and uncertainty avoidance are highly correlated and it seems that high uncertainty avoidance leads to more positive response to loss-framed advertisements than to benefit-framed advertisements.[30] Similarly, utilitarian appeals performed better in a 'masculine' culture (USA) than did 'image' appeals but no difference was found in a 'feminine' culture (Taiwan).[31] But even within Europe, audiences react differently to appeals[32] and to representations of female beauty.[33] So we can conclude that even across culturally similar countries we must pay attention to potential differences in responses.

The role of context (high versus low) has been found to influence audience responses to direct comparative advertising, which is more persuasive in low-context cultures.[34] But 'likeability' of executional techniques and their influence on purchase intentions varied across a range of five high-context Asian countries.[35] Another consideration is the distinction between rational-digital and emotional-analogue communication made by Watzlawick,[36] who point out that digital communication (low context) carries little emotion compared to analogue (high context). The implication is that brands wishing to emphasize emotional meaning should be especially careful to identify the dominant communication style in target cultures.

Visual Factors across Cultures

Because of the limitations of language use around the world, some global brands have tried to put an emphasis on visual rather than verbal elements in their communications, and there is some evidence that this tactic may be effective as long as the emotional portrayal is perceived to be authentic.[37] However, the role of context (high versus low) has been found to affect the response to the visual components of advertising. In high-context cultures such as Japan, Korea, and China, much more use is made of symbolic visuals and celebrity models as featured characters, while low-context cultures such as the USA, UK, and Germany make more use of literal visuals.[38]

In processing colour, there appears to be both cross-cultural similarity and difference. For example blue, green, and white are liked across cultures and share similar meanings. In contrast, black and red received high 'liking' ratings yet their meanings were considerably different.[39] Visually complex advertising, such as television commercials, raises even more problems across cultures as the images used are not always universally interpreted in the same way, as viewers use culturally sited advertising knowledge and visual signs to interpret meaning.[40]

Learned, Cultural, and Biological Schemas

Up to this point we have been looking at general characteristics of culture and how they might affect advertising. But we can also look at the issue of advertising across cultural borders more specifically in terms of the knowledge and assumptions people will bring to bear on processing that advertising. In the execution of any advertising or promotion, it is important that the target audience immediately understand that the message is for them. It must quickly and easily 'resonate' with them, and the words and images used must be immediately understood in the way in which the advertiser intended. This will depend upon the schema used in processing the advertising, and in many cases that will be a function of culture.

In very broad terms, schemas represent categorical or general knowledge in a way that researchers in cognitive science found more useful than semantic networks. Kroeber-Riel[41] has suggested three levels of schema: learned, cultural, and biological. What this means is that in our memory we have some things we have learned that tend to be restricted to a particular group to which we belong (learned schema). Some memories are culturally determined, and are found in such things as the myths and arts of a culture (cultural schemas). These cultural and learned schemas are what is involved in the cultural values we have been talking about. But there are other things in memory that are there because we are human, and tend to rely upon deeply psychological responses that have a relatively strong impact upon behaviour *without* our conscious awareness (biological schemas).

This means that people may react to an image in terms of things they have learned to associate with a particular group or thing, their culture, or innate psycho-biological responses. Let us look at some examples of what we are talking about. If you are a real fan of a particular football team, certain associations or images linked to that team are likely to mean something very different to you than to others who are not fans of that team, and have not learned those same associations. We can all think of cultural stereotypes, but cultural schemas can be much more subtle. If a group of Eastern Europeans saw a crowd of people all pushing in a mass to enter the just-opened doors of a theatre, it would seem perfectly normal. But if an English group were to observe this, they would be surprised at the seemingly unruly behaviour because the English queue up under these circumstances. There is not a 'correct' behaviour here, the response will depend upon cultural schemas.

The importance of what we have been discussing up to this point in the chapter is that cultural differences indeed imply distinct cultural schemas in place in memory. It is these common understandings that bind cultures, and provide the schemas that will be used in processing advertising messages (or any type of communication for that matter). Cultural schemas reflect both genetic as well as learned factors. An interesting side bar here is the way in which we learn language. It is *strongly* informed by culture.

Words are made up of phonemes, which are the smallest distinguishable vocal utterances. Exposure to language as an infant establishes dedicated connections between auditory receptors and neurons in the auditory cortex, where each phoneme will have a specific site. Different languages are made up of different phonemes, and different numbers of phonemes. English has 43 phonemes, but Hawaiian has only 15. This is significant because after a phoneme site is established (and this will be before age 1), people become functionally *deaf* to sounds not found in their native language.

Certain words in English, for example, cannot be 'heard', and so not processed, by the Japanese because certain phonemes in those English words are not found in Japanese. With hard work it can be learned, but it is not easy. So, there are not only basic cultural differences to account for in terms of the knowledge and assumptions that make up a cultural schema, but for broadcast advertising certain words may not even be 'heard' because of the phonemes involved in particular languages.

Whenever you are not certain that your target audience share a common learned or cultural schema, or when using a multinational campaign across many cultures, the message should tap into biological schemas. This means using words and images that are associated in memory at a limbic level, universally understood because they are part of our evolutionary development as humans. These images should also tap into primary emotions, also universal across cultures.

Basically, these are reactions that in some way relate to latent survival responses. This is why almost everyone reacts to an infant with a warm, nurturing feeling, and with alarm to the high-pitched cry of a baby. Some very fascinating work by Jay Appleton[42] deals with this same idea. He has developed something he calls Prospect and Refuge Theory that suggests we respond to our environment in terms of both prospect and refuge. When humans first wandered the plains, they needed to be able to see out to the horizon (prospect). This provided a sense of opportunity as well as ample warning of danger. Humans also needed a place to hide for security (refuge). Appleton argues that we still respond to our environment in these same ways, a response based upon biological schemas, and recent empirical studies support him.

The implication of this work is significant. When people are looking at advertising, they are *unconsciously* reacting to the visual environment depicted. If we want the target audience to feel secure, the visual image should be consistent with refuge; if the target audience is to feel a sense of opportunity, the image should be consistent with prospect. To be effective, advertising must be consistent with commonly shared learning or the cultural values of the target audience; or it must reflect a biological schema that is universally understood.

Brand Perceptions across Cultures

Just as we have seen that cultural values inform how advertising will be processed, culture will also be a factor in how brands are perceived. In this section we shall be looking at some key characteristics of brands that are culture dependent.

Credibility

The credibility of brands is a key factor in the information economics view of brand equity and this has been found to be consistently important in choice across a range of cultures.[43] However, the positive effect of brand credibility on choice is greater for consumers who rate high on collectivism (increasing perceptions of quality) or uncertainty avoidance (decreasing perceptions of risk).

Brand Personality

The basic approach is that human personality traits come to be associated with a brand and Aaker[44] demonstrated that five major factors summarized the traits that consumers attributed to a wide range of brands: sincerity, excitement, competence, sophistication, and ruggedness. Obviously, advertising is a major source of brand personality perceptions. Subsequent work has shown that personal meanings of brands vary across cultures. Indeed it has been shown that there are important boundary conditions for the generalizability of Aaker's brand personality model, as when applied across different cultures, the five factors of brand personality have to be revised. In Japan and Spain, only three of the factors transferred from the USA,[45] and similar results were found in Russia.[46]

Perceived Brand Globalness

There is some evidence that brands that have a 'global image' may gain some advantage through perceptions of prestige and product quality.[47] However the effect is weaker for ethnocentric consumers. 'Globalness' can also be applied to positioning strategy in advertising in emerging global markets, where it can be differentiated from local consumer culture positioning and foreign consumer culture positioning. It has been found to apply to meaningful percentages in TV advertisements across seven countries on three continents.[48]

  As globalization of marketplaces increases, the tension between global and local cultural influences impacts on brand perceptions and consumer behaviour. This tension can be expected to differentially affect product categories. For example, in food and beverages ethnocentrism may have its strongest influence, while in luxury goods and electronics acculturation to global consumer culture may be most powerful.[49] See Fig. 3.5.

  When a brand integrates the foreign with the local to create a new culturally rooted product, this has been called creolization.[50] This goes beyond the so-called glocal brand, which merely adapts some parts of its marketing mix in a particular geographic region,

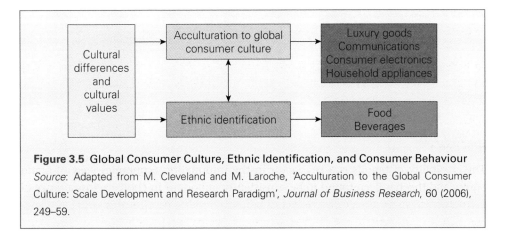

Figure 3.5 Global Consumer Culture, Ethnic Identification, and Consumer Behaviour

Source: Adapted from M. Cleveland and M. Laroche, 'Acculturation to the Global Consumer Culture: Scale Development and Research Paradigm', *Journal of Business Research*, 60 (2006), 249–59.

and 'may fuse the outer elements of the foreign with the local to give birth to crossover products, images, or identities'.

Perceived Brand Localness

A brand's perceived localness creates unique values for the consumer because it enhances the brand's relevance and acceptability to the local market.[51] By retaining its own local identity and culture it can 'out-localize' global brands by developing symbolic meanings of authenticity. Local brands across major European countries show higher levels of awareness, trust, and reliability than do international or global brands.[52]

Some Implications for Advertising Management

The major implication of the cultural factors we have discussed in this chapter is that advertising strategies can be located on a gradient of adaptation depending on the level of consumer involvement and emotional arousal in the product category, and the degree of cultural differentiation in the target marketplace. See Fig. 3.6.

We can take the basic structural components of the Rossiter–Percy grid, of level of involvement and positive or negative motivation (this is covered in detail in Chapter 9), and combine them with an evaluation of just how much cultural differentiation exists between the source culture (often US/European) and the target culture. At low levels of cultural differentiation and in product/market categories with low consumer involvement and emotional arousal, we can assume that a global campaign will be relatively effective, but as we ascend the gradient we can maintain most of our global strategy but may have to adapt our advertising to some local conditions and therefore our strategy should be 'glocal'. However, further up the gradient we have the opportunity to work with consumers' culturally rooted interpretations to co-create a creolized version of a global strategy which makes full use of emotional responses (see Chapter 11). At the head of the gradient where cultural differentiation is at its peak, an essentially local brand and advertising strategy is required for optimum effectiveness.

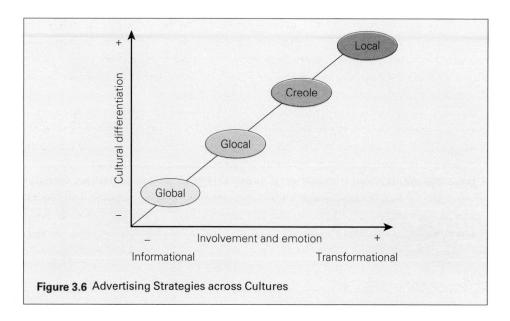

Figure 3.6 Advertising Strategies across Cultures

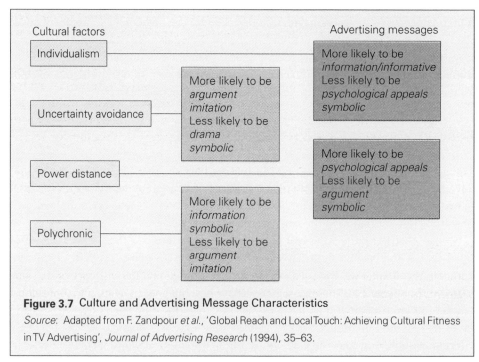

Figure 3.7 Culture and Advertising Message Characteristics

Source: Adapted from F. Zandpour *et al.*, 'Global Reach and Local Touch: Achieving Cultural Fitness in TV Advertising', *Journal of Advertising Research* (1994), 35–63.

Culture and Advertising Message Characteristics

Some general guidelines for advertising creative strategy can be drawn from cultural theory. For example, Zandpour and his colleagues[53] have linked four cultural characteristics with appeals used in advertising messages. This has been summarized in Fig. 3.7.

In highly *individualistic* cultures, advertising should be more likely to include information, and less likely to make use of psychological appeals or symbolic language and images. If what they call *uncertainty avoidance* dominates a culture, advertising appeals should be more likely to utilize arguments or imitation, and less likely to use drama, or symbolic language or images. Where *power distance* is the primary cultural factor, psychological appeals will be more likely to be used, and argument and symbolic language and images less likely. Finally, when the dominant cultural factor in a market is *polychronic*, advertising is more likely to be informative and to use symbolic languages and imagery. Here advertising messages would be less likely to use argument or imitation.

Looked at another way, information is more likely to be used in advertising messages when individualism or polychronic is the dominant cultural factor, argument and imitation where uncertainty avoidance dominates; psychological appeals with power distance; and symbolic language and images where polychronic is the dominant cultural factor. In fact, this is the only place where you are likely to find symbolic messages because they are unlikely with any other cultural characteristic.

Cultural Perspectives on the Self and Advertising

The role of the self has been located within the Western individualist tradition versus the Confucian collectivist tradition and related to the consumption of luxuries by Wong and Ahuvia,[54] and this has important implications for brand strategy and advertising for high-involvement brands in many East and South Asian countries. In particular, it suggests that while luxury brands in the West may be acquired primarily by the self and for the self, in Eastern Confucian culture they are often acquired through gift exchange. It also suggest that the symbolic meaning of a brand in the West may be used to express self-image, in the East it may be used to locate the individual in a social hierarchy. See Fig. 3.8.

It is clear that the same product can have very different meanings in different cultures so that advertising for symbolic brands should be based on their cultural value and local consumption practices.

Global Value Segments and Advertising

Earlier in the chapter we discussed universal value systems and the existence of six value segments (see Table 3.2). These six segments have been mapped in relation to some global brands and two underlying dimensions emerged: Self-direction versus Conformity and Hedonism versus Prosocial. See Fig. 3.9.

According to Chow and Amir[55] there are perhaps only three basic clusters of countries: a modern and hedonistic cluster dominated by Striver and Fun-seeker ideals (USA, UK, Canada, Australia, Germany), a more traditional and conformist cluster but still high on striving (China, India, and South-East Asia), and a third cluster which tends to be more prosocial and altruistic (Sweden, Japan, Argentina). Locating a target country within these clusters can point to the dominant values and therefore appropriate advertising strategies.

Western individualistic tradition	Marketing implications	E. Asian Confucian tradition
	Focus on the goods as	
	Source of pleasure · · · · · · · · · · Publicly visible	
– Independent self	*Luxuries acquired often*	– Interdependent self
– Group & society exist to meet needs of individual	By self for self · · · · · · Through gift exchanges	– Individual conforms to group & society
– Hierarchy is suspect	*Product choice often reflects* Individual taste · · · · · · · · · · · · Social norms	– Hierarchy is legitimate
– Individuals should be judged on their own merits	*Symbolic goods often* Express one's self · · · · · · Locate individual in hierarchy	– It is legitimate to judge individuals by their lineage
	Brands are Potentially misleading indicators of quality · · · · · · Important indicators of quality	

Figure 3.8 Conspicuous Consumption and Consumer Societies

Source: Adapted from N. Wong and A. Ahuvia, *Psychology and Marketing*, 15/5 (1998), 423–41. Reprinted by permission of John Wiley and Sons, Inc.

CHAPTER SUMMARY

It should be obvious by now that cultural differences are not reducible to simple rules. The best we can provide are guidelines, which point to some key issues when thinking about advertising across cultural borders. We have suggested that global advertising may be appropriate in some limited situations, but there will always be a tension between efficiency and effectiveness. Unfortunately our state of knowledge of advertising across cultural borders is rather limited, but the best advertising is always likely to be rooted in 'truths' about consumers which are context dependent and draw on shared cultural understandings and common experiences. When there is any doubt, or if you know that cultural differences will likely interfere with how a message will be processed, tapping into biological schemas can enable you to develop multinational campaigns that will avoid these problems.

QUESTIONS TO CONSIDER

3.1 How might differences in ethnicity, religion, and family organization affect the marketing of financial services?

3.2 As traditionally collective societies become more wealthy through globalization, might this lead to a change towards individualism? What might be the implications for advertising strategy?

3.3 Identify two creolized brands in your cultural location and consider how they have combined elements of the foreign with the local. Has this been carried through to their advertising strategy?

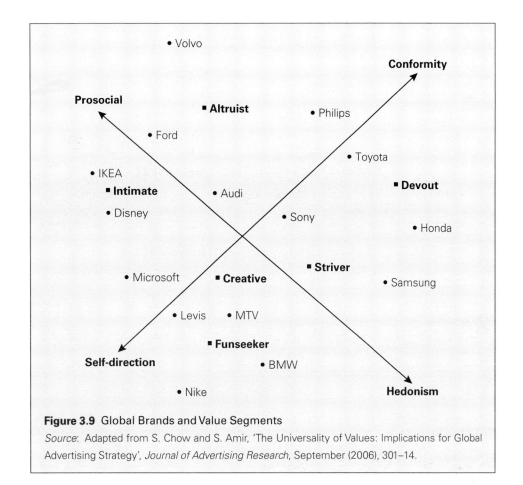

Figure 3.9 Global Brands and Value Segments

Source: Adapted from S. Chow and S. Amir, 'The Universality of Values: Implications for Global Advertising Strategy', *Journal of Advertising Research*, September (2006), 301–14.

3.4 What are the implications for developing creative strategy in a polychronic versus a monochronic society?

3.5 What product categories are most likely to be affected by ethnocentrism? Why?

3.6 How might local brands of food and drink in your cultural location develop and communicate symbols of authenticity?

3.7 How might the advertising for a luxury brand in East Asia reflect cultural values?

CASE STUDY 3

Sprite — Freedom from Thirst: A Darwinian Route to Global Success

In early 2005 Sprite had many different campaigns and creative strategies globally. The challenge was to identify ideas that could cross borders between countries where market situations, brand equities, communications histories, and more importantly local cultures varied widely. This campaign was originally designed to only cross borders within Asia. However it was soon recognized that it would have potential to work broadly. Hindsight was indicating there was so much variation between the Asian markets that an idea which had potential to work *across* Asia, would inevitably have potential to work *beyond* Asia. Therefore we started the planning process with two initial considerations.

Market contexts: we needed an idea with enough scale and simplicity to make an impact in widely differing Asian market contexts.

Consumer contexts: although the markets varied widely, the target audiences had something in common.

We were looking to bring new, younger users to the brand; from teens to young adults depending on the market. We were talking to the suburbs of Shanghai, to rural Indonesia, to the malls of downtown Delhi. The question was simple, but daunting: how could a single creative idea possibly lead young people from such diverse backgrounds to get into Sprite? This was made tougher by the fact that often the most effective approaches to getting young people into a brand are culturally specific—quirky humour, taking the piss, risky metaphors, amusing use of celebrities etc., and approaches like these often take a great deal of finessing to travel between widely different cultures. We wanted something more flexible, with a big footprint.

With this in mind, we decided to put the experience of *drinking* Sprite front and centre. The creative idea was to dramatize this experience, to make our target audience *feel* what it's like to drink a Sprite—and to do this in a context that would have resonance across a great swathe of young people around the world. This is how we expressed it in the creative brief: *'We want people to feel the refreshing sensation of Sprite. As a product, a clear cold assault on thirst. As a brand, a blast of fresh air: unpretentious, contemporary, fun.'* The idea that Sprite can 'free' you from thirst seemed to tap into a deeper insight—and one that stemmed from the shared context of youth in very different countries. In markets as far-flung as Mexico, Thailand, China, and Ireland, young people feel a very similar mixture of pressures: physical and psychological tension resulting from the pressure of societal expectations and a desire to *make it* and *do well*. For our target audience, therefore, Sprite can be a refreshing moment of release.

Markets running Freedom From Thirst campaign grew at 4.6 per cent—an additional 14 million case sales. In fact, growth was 17.3 per cent—an additional 52.7 million case sales. This implies that Freedom From Thirst markets delivered 38.7 million case sales over and above the growth that might have been expected. A strong indication of the effectiveness and flexibility of the 'Freedom From Thirst' idea is the fact that it spread far beyond its original scope. Although it was conceived as a campaign to run across a small number of Asian markets, by the end of 2005 it was adopted by 28 markets in five continents, including some highly developed markets. Furthermore in 2006 Coca-Cola expects that 38 markets will run the campaign. These include markets which were not previously planning any advertising support for Sprite, but recognize the potential of the campaign to build volume. This was a campaign that generated confidence and momentum.

Looking at key markets which invested the most in media during the campaign, and for which brand and advertising tracking data were available, it is obvious that 'Freedom From Thirst' delivered results in a range of circumstances. As follows, we look at mainly volume targets and year-on-year growth for these markets.

CHINA: The Carbonated Soft Drinks market in China is growing at almost 20 per cent a year. The challenge was to exceed this. Thus Coca-Cola set aggressive volume targets, which were substantially exceeded. If we look at year-on-year volume growth, we can see that Sprite succeeded in beating category growth in China. Year-on-year volume sales are 25.7 per cent ahead, compared to total CSD volume growth in China of 19.8 per cent year on year. The main message of our campaign was that Sprite is a refreshing moment of release. So, we were also pleased to note that the number of people agreeing that Sprite 'is very refreshing' increased from **24 per cent** in Jan '05 to a peak of **41.9 per cent**—a gain of **17.9 points**.

TURKEY: The biggest challenge for Turkey was to grow volume in the face of a major re-launch by Sprite's principal competitor (and market leader) Fruko, which was repositioning its brand with strong media support and promotional activities. Not only did Sprite succeed in fighting off competitors in the Lemon-Lime CSD sector, but its growth outstripped the entire CSD category. Year-on-year volume sales are 58.3 per cent ahead, compared to category growth of 18.1 per cent year on year. Thus, Turkey's volume growth outstripped the category by an impressive **40.2 per cent**. Again, the central idea of the ad seemed to be resonating: the number of people agreeing that Sprite 'is very refreshing' increased dramatically—from **0.9 per cent** in Jan '05 to a peak of **7.2 per cent**—a gain of **6.3 points**.

AUSTRALIA: We wanted to develop a campaign that was flexible enough to be used to support a range of different marketing objectives. In Australia, this took the shape of a new variant launch: Sprite Zero, a no-calorie version of Sprite launched to extend the franchise of the brand. The marketing challenge for 'Freedom From Thirst' was therefore to support this product launch, whilst at the same time building the equity of the Sprite brand. The volume targets set by Coke accounted for the uplift that might be naturally expected from a new variant launch. Even so, these targets were exceeded by 15 per cent. Year-on-year growth was also impressive—8.3 per cent ahead of the previous year, compared to a *decline* in total CSD volume of—2.9 per cent year-on-year. Thus, Australia's year on year volume growth for Sprite beat a declining category by **11.2 points**. Australia had also set a target for Spontaneous Brand Awareness of **65 per cent**, and the campaign achieved **79 per cent**.

THAILAND: In Thailand, the Carbonated Soft Drinks market is heavily dominated by colas, which have very high levels of awareness. Historically, Sprite hasn't been top-of-mind when people walk into a convenience store. Building Spontaneous Brand Awareness and saliency for the brand were therefore the biggest marketing challenges for Sprite in Thailand. Hitting the volume target in a highly competitive market, was a challenge—so we were pleased to learn that Thailand was **10 per cent ahead** of target, even before the year end. Year on year for the period of Feb '05 to Oct '05, Thailand's volume sales are 5 per cent ahead. Thailand set a target for Spontaneous Brand Awareness of **65 per cent**, and the campaign achieved **76 per cent**, which is 9 points over target. We were also pleased to note that the number of people agreeing that Sprite 'is very refreshing' increased significantly—from 4.2 per cent in Jan '05 to a peak of 24.6 per cent—a gain of **20.4 points**.

We've established that 2005 was a very good year for markets running the 'Freedom From Thirst' campaign. Can we though be sure that our campaign was responsible for this? To do that, we need to eliminate other potential factors that could be driving growth such as, distribution, price, promotional activity, media spend, and product changes.

- **Distribution**: We have compared changes in distribution across markets that were running 'Freedom From Thirst' and against the control group of markets running other campaigns. We can discount distribution as a major factor.
- **Media Spend:** In fact, media spend for Sprite *fell* across the board in 2005—both in markets running 'Freedom From Thirst', and in markets running other campaigns.
- **Promotional Activities:** An ongoing level of promotional activity is present in all markets—in particular, tactical retail promotions and sampling. For the soft drinks category, promotional activity is business-as-usual. During the period that the 'Freedom From Thirst' campaign was running, there were no significant departures from this level of business-as-usual promotions.
- **Price**: Coca-Cola assured us that there were no significant changes in the relative price of Sprite which would explain the strong performance of those countries running the 'Freedom From Thirst' campaign. We are therefore able to exclude price as a factor.

- **Product:** There were changes to the product made in both markets that ran 'Freedom From Thirst', and those that didn't. These changes include the launch of a new format and size (Turkey), and the launch of the low-calorie variant Sprite Zero (Australia). However we don't believe that these launches undermine the case for effectiveness of the 'Freedom From Thirst' campaign, because there have been similar product changes in markets that did not run the campaign and yet these markets did not present growth. For example the launch of new formats in the US has not managed to staunch the decline in Sprite volumes.

In conclusion, once upon a time, Coca-Cola would impose globally created campaigns upon local markets. Then most campaigns were created entirely at a local level. Now Coca-Cola is entering a new phase where strong ideas are allowed to gather their own momentum. 'Freedom From Thirst' was created to run across some Asian markets in 2005, and will run in 38 markets in five continents in 2006. This organic, 'survival of the fittest' approach has shown its worth as a way of developing campaigns that are both effective and efficient.

Source: WARC, IPA Effectiveness Awards, 2006, Sprite—Freedom from Thirst: a Darwinian Route to Global Success, by John Shaw & Jon Miller

Edited by Natalia Yannopoulou

Discussion Questions

1 What would be the best way for the competition to react to such an internationally successful advertising campaign?

2 What are the benefits and challenges for Sprite for following a global advertising campaign for the long term?

3 What could be a proposed future advertising campaign for Sprite for the above mentioned markets?

4 Does the product category affect the selection of a global or local advertising campaign? Draw on previous examples that you might know.

FURTHER READING

- M. de Mooij, *Consumer Behavior and Culture: Consequences for Global Marketing and Advertising* (London: Sage Publications, 2003) widens the analysis from advertising to a wide range of consumer behaviours across world markets.

- F. Trompenaars and P. Woolliams, *Marketing across Cultures* (Oxford: Capstone Press, 2004) explores cross-cultural implications for other aspects of marketing management.

- S. Craig and S. Douglas, *International Marketing Research* (Chichester: John Wiley, 2005) gives detailed guidance on carrying out advertising research across cultures and methods for increasing validity.

NOTES

1 See M. de Mooij, 'Convergence and Divergence in Consumer Behaviour: Implications for Global Advertising', *International Journal of Advertising*, 22 (2003), 183–202.

2 See T. Levitt, 'The Globalization of Markets', *Harvard Business Review*, May–June (1983), 2–11.

3   *Financial Times*, 27 March 2000.

4   See de Mooij, 'Conveyance and Divergence in Consumer Behaviour', 1.

5   See C. Walker, 'Genworld: The New Generation of Global Youth', *Admap*, 476 (2006), 15–19.

6   E. Moses, *The $100 Billion Allowance: Accessing the Global Teen Market* (Chichester: John Wiley, 2000).

7   S. Schwartz and W. Bilsky, 'Toward a Theory of the Universal Content and Structure of Values: Extensions and Cross-cultural Replications', *Journal of Personality and Social Psychology*, 58/5 (1990), 878–91.

8   See S. Chow and S. Amir, 'The Universality of Values: Implications for Global Advertising Strategy', *Journal of Advertising Research*, September (2006), 301–14.

9   E. Sapir, 'The Status of Linguistics as a Science', *Language*, 5 (1929), 207–14.

10   See K. Au, 'Making Sense of Differences: Language, Culture and Social Reality', in S. H. Ng *et al.* (eds), *Language Matters: Communication, Culture and Identity* (Hong Kong: CU Press, 2004).

11   G. Lakoff and M. Johnson, *Metaphors We Live By* (Chicago: University of Chicago Press, 1980).

12   G. Lakoff, *Moral Politics* (Chicago: University of Chicago Press, 1996).

13   P. Watzlawick *et al.*, *Pragmatics of Human Communication* (New York: Norton 1967).

14   See A. Epstein, *Ethos and Identity* (Chicago: Aldene, 1978).

15   See J. Costa and G. Bamossy, 'Ethnicity, Nationalism and Cultural Identity', in J. Costa and G. Bamossy (eds), *Marketing in a Multicultural World* (London: Sage, 1995).

16   D. Bouchet, 'Marketing and the Redefinition of Ethnicity', in J. Costa and G. Bamossy (eds), *Marketing in a Multicultural World* (London: Sage, 1995).

17   See T. Shimp and S. Sharma, 'Consumer Ethnocentrism: Construction and Validation of the CETSCALE', *Journal of Marketing Research*, 24 (1987), 280–9.

18   See G. H. Hofstede, *Culture's Consequences: International Differences in Work-Related Values* (Beverly Hills, Calif.: Sage, 1984), 32–3.

19   The updated version of Hofstede's dimensions are in his *Cultures and Organizations: Software of the Mind* (New York: McGraw-Hill, 1991), and his dimensions are fully discussed in an advertising context by Marieke de Mooij in her *Global Marketing and Advertising: Understanding Cultural Paradoxes* (London: Sage, 1998), 72–88.

20   E. Hall, *Beyond Culture* (New York: Doubleday, 1976).

21   F. Trompenaars and C. Hampden-Turner, *Riding the Waves of Culture* (Maidenhead: McGraw-Hill, 1997).

22   See Hall, *Beyond Culture*, 20.

23   See Schwartz and Bilsky, 'Toward a Theory of the Universal Content and Structure of Values', 7.

24   See Chow and Amir, 'The Universability of Values', 8.

25   See C. Lin, 'Cultural Values Reflected in Chinese and American Television Advertising', *Journal of Advertising*, 30/4 (2001), 83–94.

26   See M. Kalliny and L. Gentry, 'Cultural Values Reflected in Arab and American Television Advertising', *Journal of Current Issues and Research in Advertising*, 29/1 (2007), 15–32.

27 See Z. Caillat, and B. Mueller, 'The Influence of Culture on American and British Advertising', *Journal of Advertising Research*, May/June (1996), 79–88.

28 See J. Zhang and S. Shavitt, 'Cultural Values in Advertisements to the Chinese X-Generation', *Journal of Advertising*, 32/1 (2003), 23–33.

29 See L. Teng and M. Laroche, 'Interactive Effects of Appeals, Arguments, and Competition across North American and Chinese Cultures', *Journal of International Marketing*, 14/4 (2006), 11–128.

30 See J. Readon, C. Miller, B. Foubert, I. Vida, and L. Rybina, 'Antismoking Messages for the International Teenage Segment: The Effectiveness of Message Valence and Intensity across Different Cultures', *Journal of International Marketing*, 14/3 (2006), 115–38.

31 See C. Chang, 'Cultural Masculinity/Femininity Influences on Advertising Appeals', *Journal of Advertising Research*, September (2006), 315–23.

32 See U. Orth, H. Koening, and Z. Firbasova, *European Journal of Marketing*, 41/3 (2007), 27–348.

33 See R. Bjerke and R. Polegato, 'How Well Do Advertising Images of Health and Beauty Travel across Cultures? A Self Concept Perspective', *Psychology and Marketing*, 23/10 (2006), 865–84.

34 See A. Shao, Y. Bao, and E. Gray, 'Comparative Advertising Effectiveness: A Cross-cultural Study', *Journal of Current Issues and Research in Advertising*, 26/2 (2004), 67–80.

35 See K. Fam and R. Grohs, 'Cultural Values and Effective Executional Techniques in Advertising', *International Marketing Review*, 24/5 (2007), 519–38.

36 See Watzlawick *et al.*, *Pragmatics of Human Communication*, 13.

37 See C. Young, 'The Visual Language of Global Advertising', *Admap* (2003), 438.

38 See D. An, 'Advertising Visuals in Global Brands' Local Websites', *International Journal of Advertising*, 26/3 (2007), 303–32.

39 See T. Madden, K. Hewett, and M. Roth, 'Managing Images in Different Cultures: A Cross National Study of Colour Meanings and Preferences', *Journal of International Marketing*, 8/4 (2000), 90–107.

40 See S. Bulmer and M. Buchanan-Oliver, 'Advertising across Cultures: Interpretations of Visually Complex Advertising', *Journal of Current Issues and Research in Advertising*, 28/1 (2006), 57–70.

41 The work of Kroeber-Riel represents perhaps the most productive research into understanding the effects of visual imagery in advertising. Unfortunately, much of his work is not available in English, including his important book on pictorial communication, *Buldkommunikation* (Munich: Vahlen, 1993). However, an introduction to his ideas on emotional elements in advertising can be found in W. Kroeber-Riel, 'Non-verbal Measurements of Emotional Advertising Effects', in J. Olson and W. K. Sentis (eds), *Advertising and Consumer Psychology*, iii (New York: Praege, 1986).

42 See Jay Appleton, *The Symbolism of Habitat: An Interpretation of Landscape in Art* (Seattle: University of Washington Press, 1990), and *The Experience of Landscape*, rev. edn. (Chichester: John Wiley and Sons, 1996).

43 See T. Edrem, J. Swait, and A. Valenzuea, 'Brands as Signals: A Cross-Country Validation Study', *Journal of Marketing*, 70 (2006), 34–49.

44 J. Aaker, 'Dimensions of Brand Personality', *Journal of Marketing Research*, 34 (1997), 347–56.

45 See J. Aaker, V. Benet-Martinez, and J. Garolera, 'Consumption Symbols as Carriers of Culture: A Study of Japanese and Spanish Brand Personality Constructs', *Journal of Personality and Social Psychology*, 81/3 (2001), 492–508.

46 See M. Supphellen and K. Grønhaug, 'Building Foreign Brand Personalities in Russia: The Moderating Effect of Consumer Ethnocentrism', *International Journal of Advertising*, 22 (2003), 203–26.

47 See J. Steenkamp, R. Batra, and D. Alden, 'How Perceived Brand Globalness Creates Brand Value', *Journal of International Business Studies*, 34 (2001), 53–65.

48 See D. Alden, J. Steenkamp, and R. Batra, 'Brand Positioning through Advertising in Asia, North America and Europe: The Role of Global Consumer Culture', *Journal of Marketing*, 63 (1999), 75–87.

49 M. Cleveland and M. Laroche, 'Acculturation to the Global Consumer Culture: Scale Development and Research Paradigm', *Journal of Business Research*, 60 (2006), 249–59.

50 See K. Hung, S. Li, and R. Belk, 'Glocal Understandings: Female Readers' Perceptions of the New Woman in Chinese Advertising', *Journal of International Business Studies*, 38 (2007), 1034–51.

51 G. Ger, 'Localizing in the Global Village: Local Firms Competing in Global Markets', *California Management Review*, 41/4 (1999), 64–83.

52 See I. Schuiling and J. Kapferer, 'Real Differences between Local and International Brands: Strategic Implications for International Marketers', *Journal of International Marketing*, 12/4 (2004), 97–112.

53 F. Zandpour *et al.*, 'Global Reach and Local Touch: Achieving Cultural Fitness in TV Advertising', *Journal of Advertising Research* (1994), 35–63.

54 N. Wong and A. Ahuvia, 'Personal Taste and Family Face: Luxury Consumption in Confucian and Western Societies', *Psychology and Marketing*, 15/5 (1998), 423–41.

55 See Chow and Amir, 'The University of Values', 8.

 Visit the Online Resource Centre that accompanies this book for additional resources to support the text: http://www.oxfordtextbooks.co.uk/orc/ percy_elliott3e/

Planning Considerations

A critical point in understanding this sort of hierarchical model (that is, one where each step is necessary, and must occur in the order presented) is that it reflects *compounding probabilities*. Let us suppose McGuire is correct in his assessment that six behavioural steps are required for a persuasive message to be successful. If that is the case, the probability of someone actually going out and buying a product as the result of an advertising message would be:

$$P(p) \times P(a) \times P(c) \times P(y) \times P(r) \times P(b)$$

where: $P(p)$ = probability of being presented the message,
$P(a)$ = probability of paying attention to the message,
$P(c)$ = probability of comprehending the message,
$P(y)$ = probability of yielding to the message,
$P(r)$ = probability of retaining the intention,
$P(b)$ = probability of behaving.

Given a rather optimistic likelihood of 50 per cent of a target audience responding positively to each of the six behavioural steps, the overall probability of an actual purchase would be less than 2 per cent ($0.50 \times 0.50 \times 0.50 \times 0.50 \times 0.50 \times 0.50 = 0.0156$). What this arithmetic exercise underscores is the very difficult job one is confronted with when trying to communicate effectively. Everything must work, and, even when it does, you cannot expect to see great changes in consumer behaviour as a direct result of advertising or promotion.

While McGuire's model was designed to explain how communication 'works' from a psychological standpoint, clearly it closely parallels what we know must happen if advertising and promotion are to work. For advertising and promotion to be effective, we must have exposure to the message, processing of the message, the correct communication effect, and target audience action.

Responding to Advertising and Promotion

The very first step that is necessary in order for advertising or promotion to be successful is for the prospective consumer to be *exposed* to the message. This means that it must be placed somewhere that the prospective buyer can see, read, or hear it, as appropriate. The opportunity for exposure to the message takes place through media of one kind or another. Exposure alone, however, is not sufficient. The prospective buyer must next *process* (respond to) one or more elements in the advertising or promotion if it is to have an effect. Processing of the message consists of immediate responses to the various elements in the advert or promotion (the words and pictures). First must come attention, then learning; and in some cases, as we shall see in later chapters, acceptance. Emotional responses will also be a part of processing.

The immediate responses to advertising and promotion must lead to a more permanent response; and, importantly, this permanent response must be associated with the brand or whatever other subject may be the object of the message, such as a company's image or a particular service. These more permanent, brand-connected responses are the *communication effects* that were introduced in Chapter 1: the two universally necessary communication effects of brand awareness and brand attitude, plus category need and brand purchase intention.

If the advertising or promotion message has been correctly processed, the resulting communication effect associated with the brand will lead to a particular response when a member of the target audience decides whether or not to take *action* as a result of the message, such as purchasing the brand. More broadly, this is called buyer behaviour, although in an advertising context we are generally seeking a response from a particular segment of the market that is known as the target audience. For example, if you are the manager of a company that manufactures concrete paving blocks, you might want to use advertising specifically 'targeted' to architects and builders whom you want to consider using your pavers in their designs and buildings.

Exposure corresponds to McGuire's presentation step; *processing* encompasses both the attention and comprehension steps of McGuire's model; *communication effects* encompass both the yielding and retention steps; and *target audience action* corresponds to McGuire's behaviour step (see Table 4.1).

As McGuire has remarked, these sequences are just common sense. Our extension of his work also makes good common sense in understanding advertising and promotion. If you do not see the advertising or promotion, it has no opportunity of working. If you do not process the message, there can be no effects; or if you process the message incorrectly, you do not achieve the desired effect. If the correct communication effect and response both follow, then target audience action will result. While Rossiter and Percy provide an interesting argument for referring to these four essential steps as a 'buyer response sequence',[2] we like to think of them as *communication* response steps.

Following through an actual example of what we mean here should help you see why these four steps are necessary for advertising or promotion to be successful. Exposure, processing, communication effects, and target audience action are steps you yourself go through when buying a product as a result of having seen or heard some advertising or promotion for it, even if you do not associate the behaviour with the advertising or promotion. Let us think about a campaign for Nescafé coffee.

Table 4.1 How the Communication Response Sequence Compares with McGuire's Information Processing Paradigm

Communication Response Sequence	Information Processing Paradigm
Exposure	Presented
Processing	Attention
	Comprehend
Communication Effects	Yield
	Retain
Target Audience Action	Behave

Exposure. Assuming you watch TV even occasionally, you have probably been *exposed* to one or more commercials for Nescafé. The Nestlé Company runs a fairly heavy TV media campaign for this brand, along with print advertising and promotion.

Processing. If you were exposed to the advertising, sooner or later you probably paid attention to at least some parts of at least one of the commercials, or saw one of the print adverts. In other words, you *processed* the Nescafé advertising in some fashion, even if it was simply noting the brand name.

Communication effects. If you have learned the brand name 'Nescafé' from the advertising, and remembered what the brand's package looks like, you have responded to one of the core *communication effects*, brand awareness. If you have also formed an opinion for or against Nescafé, you have responded to the second core communication effect, brand attitude. Brand awareness plus a favourable brand attitude will largely determine whether or not you have actually tried the brand.

Target audience action. The ultimate target audience *action* for Nescafé is purchase. If you have purchased Nescafé, then the advertising has no doubt influenced you positively through the first three steps, leading to a positive behavioural response.

But, as we have already discussed, advertising is rarely responsible for purchase in and of itself. The rest of the marketing mix must contribute too: product performance, such as the coffee's taste (especially important for repeat purchase following trial of the brand); price, assuming the price is competitive with other coffee brands; distribution, assuming you can find the brand where you shop; and other forms of promotion, such as coupons or favourable comments from your friends. But the advertising undoubtedly has played a large part, especially if you were not previously aware of the brand.

Repetition and Response to Advertising and Promotion

Advertising in most cases must repeatedly influence this process in order to initiate trial and maintain repeated purchases of a brand, or encourage response to a promotion. The one exception to this repetition or 'recycling' of the four steps is direct response advertising. With direct response advertising (which is a special case of promotion because the objective is immediately to action), the target audience goes through the sequence once, then terminates with action in the form of a single purchase. However, as you might imagine, most advertising tasks require repetition. For example, you may have had a number of opportunities to be exposed to advertising for a brand before you finally paid attention and processed the message sufficiently for the communication effects (probably brand awareness and brand attitude) to work and be strong enough for you actually to try a brand for the first time.

After you have purchased a brand for the first time, the advertiser obviously wants you to purchase it again and become a regular user. This generally requires repeated exposure to the advertising. You now have direct experience with the brand, which will affect your exposure, processing, and communication effects the next time around. This is especially true of brand attitude, which is now being influenced by experience. If you liked the product, positive brand attitudes can develop or be reinforced. But if you disliked it, this negative experience would probably prevent positive processing of future messages, leading to negative communication effects such as declining brand awareness and a change to a negative brand attitude. While, in an ideal world, one could hope that after sufficient numbers of people have formed positive brand attitudes, continued advertising would be unnecessary, this ideal is rarely reached. Not many brands can survive without advertising for any extended period. Communication effects become weaker or are interfered with by advertising and promotion for competing brands. Once this happens, the advertiser must begin again, creating new advertising that must be exposed to the target audience, then working through the full sequence.

To summarize, there are four steps in a communication response sequence that must be satisfied before advertising and promotion can be successful. First, the target audience must be *exposed* to the advertising. Next, they must *process* the information. After processing, there must be a *communication effect*. Finally, the target audience must take *action*. If any one of these steps is not influenced positively by the advertising or promotion, and reinforced over time, the advertising simply will not work. And if the advertising or promotion does not work here, it obviously cannot contribute to sales and market share, or to profit. All four steps in the sequence must be successfully accomplished if sales, market share, and profit are to increase.

Planning Overview

Careful planning is critical to the success of any venture, and understanding what processes are involved obviously leads to better plans. It is important to understand that overall advertising and promotion planning must correspond to what it takes for advertising and promotion to be successful—the four steps we have just reviewed. After a company sets profit objectives, which are based upon a certain level of sales or market share, a marketing plan lays out how marketing communication efforts will help meet those objectives (*action* sought by the target audience) and the marketing communication plan what the best message for the brand will be (*communication effects* needed) to maximize those marketing efforts. From the marketing communication plan the company and its advertising agency are able to develop a positioning and creative strategy to execute that message (to ensure *processing* of the message), and finally a media strategy (to ensure *exposure* to the message) to deliver the message.

Interestingly, you will notice that, after the marketing objectives have been set, the *planning* sequence is the reverse of the sequence needed for advertising and promotion to be successful.[3] A marketer must begin by thinking of the action to be taken by the target audience. Next, they must consider the communication effects needed from the advertising or promotion to help facilitate that action. Then they must be concerned with how the message will be processed in order to ensure those effects, and finally where to place the advertising and promotion to optimize the likelihood of reaching the target audience (see Table 4.2). Each of these planning stages is discussed next.

Table 4.2 Planning Sequence versus Communication Response Sequence

Planning Sequence		Communication Response Sequence
Stage One	Target Audience Action	Step Four
Stage Two	Communication Effects	Step Three
Stage Three	Processing	Step Two
Stage Four	Exposure	Step One

Stage One: Objectives for Target Audience Action

Once the overall marketing objectives are set, the manager must decide where, from among all the people in a market, the brand can expect to find the greatest likelihood of brand trial and usage. This will form the core of the target audience for advertising and promotion. This group of people, however, will not be particularly easy to identify, at least if we are looking for the best group possible. What we want are people who will respond to the advertising and promotion because they recognize something in it that connects, in their mind, the attributes of the advertised product with particular benefits that satisfy the reason or reasons why they are interested in products from that particular category in the first place. We will be spending a lot more time with this notion in Chapters 6 and 11.

Depending upon the actual target audience chosen, the action desired will usually be trial for the brand or repeat purchase. For non-users of the brand, the behavioural objective would quite naturally be trial. But for those who have tried the product, we would want to encourage continued or more frequent repeat purchase of the brand. This issue will be dealt with in much more detail in Chapter 6.

Stage Two: Communication Effects

Advertising and promotion work only if they can stimulate a communication effect that will lead to action. The manager, in this second stage of planning, must determine how to position the brand in the communication and which communication effects need to be established in the mind of the target audience in order to cause it to take action. Once the manager has determined the appropriate communication effects, they become communication *objectives* for the advertising and promotion. Those communication objectives are selected from options within the four basic communication effects already introduced: category need, brand awareness, brand attitude, and brand purchase intention. Chapter 9 will cover this subject in depth.

Returning to our Nescafé example, when the brand was first launched, the brand manager probably set a number of communication objectives for Nescafé advertising and promotion.

1. Since Nescafé was the original 'freeze-dried' version of soluble coffee (or 'instant'), the introductory advertising probably tried to stimulate interest in the soluble category as a whole, since Nescafé would benefit from an increase in primary demand for soluble coffee (category need).

2. Potential consumers of Nescafé would also need to learn the new product's name, and learn to recognize the product on the supermarket shelf (brand awareness).

3. Further, before trying Nescafé, potential new consumers would have to develop at least a tentatively favourable opinion of the brand (brand attitude), perhaps by positioning it against the belief that freeze drying improves the taste of soluble coffee.

4. Also, a definite intention to try it at the first opportunity would no doubt be a likely advertising communication objective (brand purchase intention), along with a promotion to increase the likelihood of following through on the intention.

Stage Three: Processing

Once the communication objectives for a campaign have been determined, the next step in planning is to devise (if in an advertising agency) or approve (if the advertiser) a creative strategy that will achieve the communication objectives. This involves designing specific advertising and promotions that not only meet the communication objective set in the marketing plan, but also maximize its likelihood of then being *processed* by the target audience in the intended manner to produce the desired communication effects. Since it is impossible to know beforehand if a new advert or promotion will accomplish these very important goals, that advert or promotion should be tested.

We shall be dealing with these issues of positioning in Chapter 8, setting communication strategy in Chapter 9, processing in Chapter 11, and creative tactics in Chapter 12.

At this point it is important to understand that there are many possible ways to position a brand in marketing communication and to achieve a particular communication effect (that is, one of our four effects: category need, brand awareness, brand attitude, or brand purchase intentions) in order to facilitate processing of the message. Let us return to our Nescafé example. If brand attitude was the primary communication objective, Nescafé's advertising agency may have proposed positioning the brand on the freeze-dried attribute and its taste advantage. Or, the focus could have been on the same freeze-dried attribute, but its emphasis directed towards 'fresh' as a benefit. Either of these positionings (or many others) could probably have been capable of delivering the required communication objective. We would hope that the actual positioning and communication strategy that was pursued was chosen over other alternatives because it was tested among a sample of the target audience and found to work better at stimulating the desired communication response.

Stage Four: Exposure

The last step in the planning sequence requires the manager to decide how best to expose the advertising to the target audience that has been selected. This fourth and final planning stage centres on media strategy. In this stage there are two main decisions to be made: media selection, or *where* to reach the target audience most efficiently; and media scheduling, or *how often* the target audience must be reached in order to produce the intended communication response and ultimate action.

The agency for Nescafé, for example, had to select and then schedule the media for the brand. The Nestlé Company, which markets Nescafé, does most of its consumer advertising on television, so this was likely the primary medium selected for the introduction of Nescafé. Additionally, no doubt other back-up or secondary media were used, such as print advertising and coupon inserts in newspapers.

The second media strategy decision, media scheduling, is a lot more complicated. How many times would the Nescafé advertising need to be exposed to the non-user in order to entice him or her to try the brand? And once tried, assuming a favourable opinion of the product, how often, between typical coffee purchase occasions, would the continuing advertising have to be seen or heard in order to keep the consumer aware of and interested in the brand? These problems concern the effective exposure of a brand's advertising. Of course, much more would have gone into this decision, and we will be covering some of it in Chapter 10.

Once all these strategic media decisions have been taken, they must be made operational within the budget available. As we shall see in Chapter 15, this is not always as simple a job as one might think. Frequently the optimum media plan is too expensive, and trade-offs in the schedule must be made.

The Advantage of Sequential Planning

There is no doubt that the planning process in advertising is complex and often difficult. So far we have talked generally about the planning process in terms of four stages that roughly parallel (in reverse) the four communication response steps required for advertising or promotion to be successful. At each stage the manager is confronted with any number of questions that require answers, and decisions that must be made. Just as we saw with the communication response sequence, where the likelihood of success is a series of compounding probabilities, the four stages in developing advertising plans also encounter compounding probabilities. To be truly successful, the plans made at each stage must be as correct as possible, for each shortcoming will be enlarged or compounded at a subsequent stage in the planning process.

But there is a difference. With the four steps of exposure, processing, communication effects, and action, we have seen that for an advertising message to be successful overall *each* step must be achieved in order. In a sense, each step either succeeds or it does not. When one step fails the entire process fails, and the advertising is unsuccessful. For example, if the target audience does not see or hear the advertising, *nothing else will happen*. There will be no processing, no communication effect, no buyer behaviour to lead to sales or profit (at least as a result of advertising). Likewise, if there is exposure, but no processing (or no correct processing) of the message, nothing else will follow.

The planning process, on the other hand, enjoys the benefits of *sequential planning*. If the strategic decision made at a given stage does not work, this does not invalidate the

Table 4.3 Relating the Communication Response Sequence to the Five-Step Strategic Planning Process

Five-Step Strategic Planning Process	Communication Response Sequence
Step One: Select Target Audience Step Two: Understand Target Audience Decision Making	Target Audience Action
Step Three: Determine Best Positioning Step Four: Develop Communication Strategy	Communication Effects, Processing
Step Five: Set Media Strategy	Exposure

decisions made at other stages (assuming, of course, that they were sound in the first place). Unsuccessful strategies need only be replaced by others that are better designed to meet the objectives set out in the marketing and overall communication plan. Unlike the four steps of the communication response sequence, a failure at one stage does not mean the entire process has necessarily failed.

In the next chapter we will be introducing a five-step strategic planning process that will enable the manager successfully to achieve the desired communication response sequence. Table 4.3 illustrates how this five-step strategic planning process relates to the communication response sequence. To understand what target audience action makes the most sense within the parameters of the marketing plan, we must first select an appropriate target audience and then gain an understanding of how it makes purchase and usage decisions in the category. The desired communication effect follows from positioning the brand in a way that will build positive brand attitude, and developing a communication strategy that reflects that positioning and the appropriate brand attitude strategy. This will optimize the likelihood that the message will be processed. Finally, setting media strategy consistent with the communication strategy will increase the likelihood of exposure and processing.

Let us look at this question a little more closely. Before communication planning can begin, the most critical decision that must be made is: what is our marketing objective, and what will the role of advertising and promotion be in meeting that objective. It is the marketing objective that guides the planner in making decisions regarding target audience selection at the initial stage of the planning process. If the wrong target audience is selected, this does not invalidate the marketing objectives, but it *will* invalidate any subsequent decisions that are based upon the target audience chosen. For example, if the marketing plan calls for increasing secondary demand for a brand (in other words, more usage from existing customers rather than attracting new users), a reasonable target audience might be made up of brand loyals. But what if brand loyals, assumed to be the easiest to influence, already buy what they see as their limit? This would not mean that the underlying strategy of generating secondary demand for the product is wrong. A change to brand-switchers as the target audience may be all that is needed. If brand-switchers bought more of our advertised brand than that of the competitors', our sales would increase at our competitors' expense without running into problems with the consumer's self-imposed limit. Consumers would still be buying the same amount, but they would be buying more of our brand. Similarly, the target audience selected will directly affect the communication strategy, because of its particular behaviour and attitudes. If the wrong communication strategy is chosen, this would not mean the target audience strategy was wrong. Advertising based upon the wrong communication strategy is unlikely to satisfy the goals of the marketing plan, but this would not be the fault of the target audience selected. In the same way, the media strategy developed will be set based upon the target audience and communication strategy. Each stage is sequential, guiding the decisions made at the next stage. But a mistake made at one stage does not affect the *planning* that has gone before.

So, while both the communication response sequence and the strategic planning process are hierarchical (remember, that is where one step must precede another), because of the starting point for the four-step communication response sequence, there are no alternatives to the successful execution of the desired response at each step in the sequence. On the other hand, there is room for adjustment in the planning process.

Relating Objectives and Goals to the Communication Response Sequence

In the marketing plan certain objectives will be set for the brand, and the manager must be able to relate these brand objectives to his or her advertising and promotion planning. On the face of it, there are certain obvious reasons for this. With clearly stated objectives, it is possible to coordinate advertising and promotion programmes with the plans of other company units. For example, financial planning and production plans should be matched with the advertising expectations of the brand. If we know our product sells significantly better at certain times of the year, advertising strategy will be geared to those peak selling periods. In terms of cash flow for the company, more money will be required during these periods for marketing expenses, as well as for raw materials and perhaps labour as well. Production will need to plan for greater manufacturing demands for the brand in terms of raw materials, labour, and time. With written objectives, all the managers involved will know what the demands upon the company will be at any given time.

These written objectives are important for the advertising agency as well. If everyone working on an account—account service, creative, media, planning—knows what the advertiser's objectives are for the brand, there is less opportunity for misunderstandings between the agency and the client advertiser, or between groups within the agency. A third advantage to having written objectives is that they provide something against which both the advertiser and the agency can evaluate the brand's performance.

A distinction often made in marketing management, and an important distinction, is the difference between *objectives* and *goals*. In the broadest sense, objectives define the general ends sought by the company while goals are objectives that have very specific definition. For example, a reasonable objective for a brand might be generally to increase share among a particular target market, while a goal would be specifically to increase share from 15 to 18 per cent in the next year. Generally speaking, most companies will have specific goals of one sort or another when they put together their marketing plan. After all, without some estimate of likely sales, not only will it be difficult to determine what money will be available for marketing expenditures, but the company will not be able to plan effectively for things such as production schedules, raw material acquisition, and so on. If only the vague objective of increasing sales has been adopted, it should be clear that important planning decisions will be very difficult, if not impossible, to formulate.

Having said all this, we must ask ourselves if it is also important to set goals rather than objectives for advertising as well. The answer is that 'it depends'. The reason it depends is that for advertising to be effective it must successfully negotiate each of the four steps in the communication response sequence, and each step makes different demands in terms of planning. Additionally, rarely are we considering the effect of a single advertisement or commercial. We will be much more likely to be considering a campaign made up of several adverts, as well as other marketing communication. In fact, we can actually look at this question of goals versus objectives for each of the four steps we have been talking about as depending upon whether we are considering a single ad, or an entire campaign. Let us now examine whether or not goals or objectives are more appropriate for each of the steps (see Table 4.4).

Exposure. The first step is exposure and here it makes sense to set *goals* for an individual ad, but only objectives for a campaign. Why? Think about what we are attempting to do in this first step. We have been given a target audience definition, and, as we plan for and buy media, we estimate that a particular advert that is a part of the plan will reach a certain percentage of the target audience. Goals for this percentage can and should be set. But over the course of the entire media planning period, many adverts will run, and run in different media and various media vehicles (for example, a specific programme or magazine). As a result, more broadly based objectives are made, such as maximizing reach or frequency. We will learn more about these important terms in Chapter 10. For now, simply put, *reach* means the percentage of the target audience likely to be exposed to a message, and *frequency* the number of times these people will have the opportunity to be exposed.

Table 4.4 Setting Goals and Objectives relative to the Communication Response Sequence for Individual Adverts versus Campaigns

	Setting Goals	Setting Objectives
Exposure	Adverts	Campaign
Processing	Adverts	Campaign
Communication Effects	Campaign	Adverts
Target Audience Action	Campaign	Adverts

Processing. At the second step, we again find that it is appropriate to set goals for an individual advert, and objectives for a campaign. The reason here is that, while we can set goals for message processing, for example that 45 per cent of our target audience should learn the brand's primary benefit as a result of the advertising, it would be much more difficult to think of specific goals for an entire campaign. Remember, promotion and other types of marketing communication may be involved in the campaign. Instead, more broadly based objectives make sense here, like increasing overall attention to our advertising as a whole.

Communication effects. At the third step goals should be set for the overall campaign rather than any specific advert within the campaign. An appropriate goal for communication effects might be to raise overall favourable attitude to our brand from 4.0 to 4.5 on a 5-point attitude scale (where 5 means very favourable). Communication effects are meant to result from a campaign, not from a single advert or commercial within the campaign. Objectives for a single advert might be something like helping to increase positive brand attitude.

Action. To complete the four steps, goals should be set for target audience action only at the campaign level, and not for any single advert within the campaign. For example, a goal for the campaign might be to increase usage of our brand from 50 per cent to 56 per cent, while the objective for each advert is to contribute to this goal. However, individual goals should be set for specific promotions.

To summarize our discussion of goals and objectives as related to the communication response sequence, we have seen that objectives are set at every level of planning, but goals are set only where they make sense and can be measured. This means goals are set for an individual advert's contribution to exposure and message processing, and for a campaign when considering communication effects and target audience action.

CHAPTER SUMMARY

This chapter has introduced the communication response sequence of four behavioural steps that are required for advertising to be successful: exposure, processing, communication effects, and action. We have then compared these steps to the sequential stages of strategic planning and emphasized the importance of relating brand objectives and goals to the buyer response sequence.

QUESTIONS TO CONSIDER

4.1 Why is it so important to understand McGuire's information processing paradigm?

4.2 How does the communication response sequence help the manager better understand what is needed for effective strategic planning in communication?

4.3 What are the major benefits of sequential planning?

4.4 What is the role of the marketing plan in strategic planning for advertising and other marketing communication?

4.5 Why is it important to understand the difference between goals and objectives in strategic planning for advertising and other marketing communication?

CASE STUDY 4

Felix—Continuity Saved the Cat

Until the 1980s, Whiskas dominated the UK cat food market. Its strength was supported by a hefty £11m annual advertising investment. Whiskas created a formula which set the norms for cat food advertising. The standard script showed a perfect housewife with a perfect cat followed by a scientist explaining the nutritional value of the product. It was all very rational and focused around the cat as an animal rather than a friend or pet. For over a decade, this proved a successful formula. By 1988, Whiskas' 53 per cent market share left its six remaining competitors scrambling for the leftovers.

By contrast, in 1988, Felix was an undifferentiated brand with merely 5 per cent market share. Felix was relaunched with an extended range of flavours, new packaging, and, for the first time in the brand's history, a £250,000 budget for advertising. Felix conducted market research, which revealed that the stolid, perfect cats represented in Whiskas' ads were unrecognizable to many cat owners. Their cats were naughty, cheeky, and demanding. They loved their cats not because they were well groomed bundles of fluff but because they had fun-loving and mischievous personalities. Felix decided to take advantage of this critical insight. So the black and white animated cat called Felix was born. He was scruffy and designed to remind owners of their cat at home. If the animated Felix liked Felix cat food, then the chances were their cats would, too. Indeed, 'Cats like Felix like Felix.' There were no clichéd lines about meatiness, nutrients, and goodness. The ads broke every established rule of cat food advertising set by Whiskas.

It worked. Within just twelve months, Felix rocketed from the bottom of the market to become the third largest brand in the market. By 1992, Felix was the second fastest-growing brand in any grocery category and the second biggest brand in the market. The winning formula was to tap into people's real relationships with their cats. This campaign was successful not just in the UK, but globally. By 1999, Felix was tussling with Whiskas for market leadership.

Whiskas relaunched in response to this ever-growing Felix threat. They repackaged, dispensed with the men in white coats, and rolled out a succession of new campaigns. Try as they might, Whiskas' ever-changing advertising campaigns failed to engage cat owners. Their market share kept slipping away. But in 1997, Whiskas reached a turning point. The turning point did not come through its advertising strategy but through a new product: a 100g single serve foil pouch, with just enough food for one meal. Single serve formats offer benefits over the standard 400g 'multi-serve' cans for both owner and cat. For the cat, the main benefit is taste; for owners, there are no half-eaten cans of cat food creating a bad smell in the kitchen or the fridge. In 2001 Whiskas tried to broaden the appeal of the pouch by directly addressing price perceptions with advertising. This move extended the appeal of the pouch to a more mainstream audience.

What did Felix do? Adspend was cut back and transferred to increased spend on tactical promotions to boost volume. But the promotions did not work. Felix kept losing market share. Whiskas kept growing at Felix's expense. Until May 2002, Felix was finally ready to launch its own new pouch. In product, packaging and price it went head-to-head with Whiskas.

The pouch was new territory for the Felix brand. It was a new product, in a new sector, with a higher price. It was to be followed by other new premium products. These new launches would

Plate I Birds Eye

This Birds Eye advert is a very good example of a category leader using a category benefit to build overall demand for the brand through category growth. Reproduced with kind permission © Birds Eye.

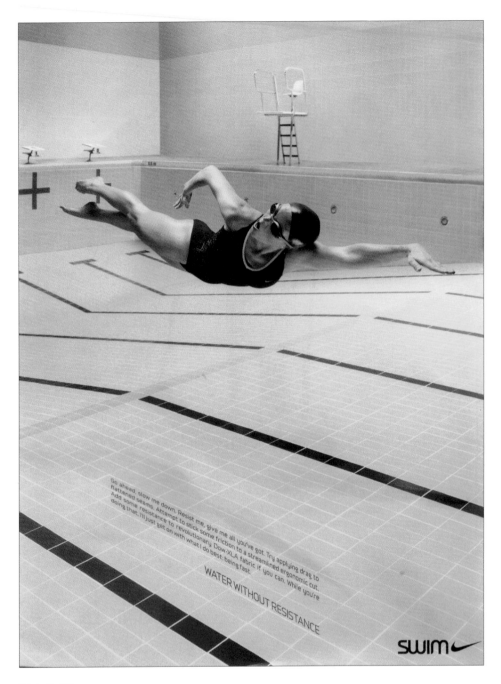

Go ahead, slow me down. Resist me, give me all you've got. Try applying drag to flattened seams. Attempt to stick some friction to a streamlined ergonomic cut. Add some resistance to revolutionary Dow-XLA fabric if you can. While you're doing that, I'll just get on with what I do best, being fast.

WATER WITHOUT RESISTANCE

SWIM

Plate II Nike

Here we see the benefit for Nike's Swim brand shown in the extreme, an excellent example of the appropriate creative tactic for a low involvement decision. Reproduced with kind permission © Nike.

Nu kan du barbere dig hvor som helst

Philips Bodygroom. Helkrops-barberingssystem til mænd. Vi introducerer den første helkrops-trimmer og shaver fra Philips. Den er genopladelig og vandtæt, så du kan bruge den under bruseren, og takket være den hypoallergente skærfolie er den også ideel til sensitiv hud. Det er den sikre og nemme måde at barbere og trimme alt fra halsen og ned: bryst, ryg, ben, armhuler, balder… eksotisk frugt?

www.philips.com/bodygroom

PHILIPS
sense and simplicity

Plate III Philips Bodygroom

This advert for Philips Bodygroom provides a very good example of how to believably illustrate a primary benefit for a high involvement decision. Philips Bodyroom advert, 2007, created by DDB. Reproduced with kind permission.

Plate IV Really Wild Clothing

Here is a good example of where a product and retailer are basically the same, and the execution delivers strong brand awareness as well as positive images for both the store and Really Wild's clothing. Reproduced with kind permission © Really Wild Clothing.

dictate the brand's future success. In addition, Felix started to doubt its Felix the cat. It had a long-running campaign, but it did not carry any product news before. Research was also telling Felix the same thing—adding to the momentum for change. New concepts were created featuring a different version of Felix. He stood on two legs and was dressed as a posh waiter who served posh new Felix food from a pouch. But the result from pre-testing was disappointing:

> *'He's not my Felix!'*
> *'It's quite cute, but it's not the Felix I know.'*
> *'Please don't change it, no, no…'*
> *'Oh, no, no, they mustn't change it…I love that cat!'*
> *'It doesn't feel right.'*

Source: Added Value, and DDB qualitative research

Felix buyers were unhappy by the threat posed to their long time friend. Their enduring relationship with the Felix cat in the ads mirrored the relationship they had with their own cats. It turned out that what Felix had thought was its weakness—the long-running campaign—was, in fact, its greatest strength.

Felix decided that the long-running campaign could and should be adapted to launch the pouch and other new products, so the good old Felix cat was kept. There was one other significant benefit to keeping the Felix of old. Research revealed that although families were by far the biggest sector of cat food buyers, they still were not buying single serve pouches. Despite Whiskas' attempts to address price perceptions, they still perceived pouches as extravagant and not for people like them. Felix could change this. The new campaign linked Felix the cat with insights about why the new pouch was appealing to cats.

The Felix pouch launched in May 2002, supported by media targeted at cat food buying families. Felix sponsored *You've Been Framed*, a family-oriented TV comedy show that matched Felix's target and perfectly complemented the brand's personality. This campaign included other media as well. Felix's below-the-line agency, Geronimo, created the 'World of Felix', offering loyal Felix buyers Felixy goodies to strengthen their connection with the brand. Felix's online agency, JPMH, created Felix screensavers and games. In 2004, the Felix campaign added more new products. Felix added a new product to its range called 'As Good As It Looks'. It had meat shaped to look more like 'real' human food. Priced at £0.38 above the standard pouch, it was for people prepared to spend a bit more on their cats. This new premium pouch was supported by outdoor and TV advertising that targeted more affluent cat owners.

The new products and the advertising managed to reverse the fortunes of the Felix brand. The TV programme sponsorship proved very effective: reaching approximately 81 per cent of housewives with children, frequently and throughout the year. Buying the same amount of airtime in the form of advertising around the programme would have cost on average three times more than the sponsorship. In 2002, with its new pouch and renewed investment in advertising, the Felix brand saw an immediate uplift in sales in the single serve category. This brought the brand's market share almost back to parity with Whiskas, competing for top position in the market again. Cat owners developed a relationship with Felix the cat in the advertising. This strengthened their relationship with Felix the brand. Impressions of the Felix brand overall have improved significantly over the life of the campaign. As Felix's customers have become more loyal and less price sensitive, it has been able to increase price without losing market share. In fact Felix's prices relative to the market have increased; it is now the most expensive mainstream brand in the market. As the long-running campaign reinforced this relationship, loyalty levels also improved, overtaking Whiskas in 2004. Felix surpassed Whiskas in both single serve volume and value.

All of this has been achieved, despite Felix's pouch entering the market five years late, it had no obvious product superiority, had no price advantages, faced increased competition (not just from Whiskas, but also from supermarket own-label products), and was consistently outspent by its key competitor, Whiskas (the gap between the Whiskas and Felix adspends was between £4 million and £5 million annually).

With a spend of a mere £2.5m per year over 16 years, the Felix campaign transformed a minor brand into a mainstream brand with sales of over £138m a year. Felix's long-running campaign, a key drive of ad efficiency, was rooted in owners' relationships with their cats, not product messages. While Felix bravely stuck with its long-running campaign, adapting to accommodate new products, Whiskas succumbed to the temptation of continual disruption. Year after year the Whiskas campaign chopped and changed. They had dancing, animated mice, a charity appeal for cats who are fed tinned food, ads to attract the attention of cats, grannies enticing cats away with pouches, 90 per cent of cats prefer Whiskas in pouches, a trendy young urbanite in his New York apartment, and a purring cat in a family home. Whiskas was one crazy, mixed up cat. It is likely that Whiskas' confused communications strategy inadvertently reinforced the enduring relationship between the Felix cat and cat owners. Felix has successfully proved the effectiveness of long-running campaigns.

Source: WARC, Best Read & Silver, IPA Effectiveness Awards 2006, Felix—Continuity Saved the Cat, by Georgia Challis, Barry Lustig, Julia Wood, Les Binet, and Sarah Carter

The Felix name and logo is produced by the kind permission of Société des Produits Nestlé S.A.

Edited by Hazel H. Huang

Discussion Questions

1 When facing the threat from the Whiskas pouch, Felix cut its adspend and transferred to price-off promotions to boost volume. But reducing the price did not increase the market share in return. Why?

2 Please discuss the differences of the target audience between Whiskas' classic advertising of the 80s and the Felix the cat campaign.

3 What is the role of a long-running campaign in a strategic advertising planning? What are the potential risks of a long-running campaign in advertising?

4 Applying McGuire's information processing paradigm, discuss Felix's long-running campaign.

FURTHER READING

- The idea of consumers taking more control of the communication environment through the interactive nature of available information, while not obviating how consumers will respond to that information, nevertheless places it potentially in a different perspective. This idea is argued, for example, in Don Schultz and Beth Barnes, *Strategic Brand Communications Campaigns* (Lincolnwood, Ill.: NTC Business Books, 1999).

- Leslie de Chernatony, *From Brand Vision to Brand Evaluation* (Oxford: Butterworth Heinemann, 2001), offers a broad perspective of how the manager can take a brand's vision and build a stronger brand, providing a broader context for the issues discussed in this chapter.

NOTES

1 Perhaps the definitive work on attitude-change theory is McGuire's original essay, 'The Nature of Attitudes and Attitude Change', in G. Lindsey and E. Aronson (eds), *The Handbook of Social Psychology* (Reading, Mass.: Addison-Wesley Publishing, 1969), iii. 136–314. This work and others of McGuire's are reviewed in terms of their implications for advertising by L. Percy and J. R. Rossiter in *Advertising Strategy: A Communication Theory Approach* (New York: Praeger, 1980).

2 J. R. Rossiter and L. Percy, *Advertising Communication and Promotion Management*, 2nd edn. (New York: McGraw-Hill, 1997).

3 This is something originally pointed out by J. R. Rossiter and L. Percy, in *Advertising and Promotion Management* (New York: McGraw-Hill, 1987).

 Visit the Online Resource Centre that accompanies this book for additional resources to support the text: http://www.oxfordtextbooks.co.uk/orc/percy_elliott3e/

5

The Strategic Planning Process

 KEY CONCEPTS

1 Before the manager can begin the strategic planning process it is essential first to review the marketing plan, in general, and advertising in particular, because marketing communication must be consistent with, and support, the overall marketing plan.

2 The strategic planning process itself follows five steps: identifying the target, determining how the target behaves in the category, looking at the best way to position the brand in the communication, developing a communication strategy, and then setting a media strategy for how best to deliver the message to the target audience.

3 At the heart of this process is an understanding of brand awareness and brand attitude strategy.

The actual strategic planning process, as you might imagine, is much more specific than the general planning sequence we introduced in the previous chapter. While that provided a good way of relating planning overall with the communication response sequence, a good strategic plan must go further. What must we do in order to link the target audience to our marketing objectives? How do we actually decide upon the appropriate communication effects? What determines the optimum creative strategy? What do we need to know in order to deliver our message effectively?

In this chapter we will be considering five specific steps a manager should take in developing a strategic plan for a brand's marketing communication. Then, in the next part of the book we will devote a chapter to each of these five areas as we explore in detail the important issues involved at each step. Before discussing these steps in more detail, we will want to consider some of the things managers should be looking for in the marketing plan.

Review the Marketing Plan First

All marketing communication must be consistent with, and in support of, the overall marketing plan. Before a manager even begins to think about specific communication issues, it is important to review the marketing plan. Once this review is completed, it is then helpful to outline briefly 'what we know' about the market and the specific marketing objectives and goals for the brand. This sort of information often has a significant bearing upon what it is that we will want to communicate to the target audience, and it provides important background information for those charged with creating the message.

There are at least five key areas where the manager will want information *before* beginning the strategic planning process for marketing communication. Each of these five areas is discussed briefly below, and outlined in Table 5.1.

Product Description

What are you marketing? This may seem too obvious to think about, but that is precisely the point. While it may be obvious to the manager, it may not be quite so obvious to the

Table 5.1 Marketing Background Issues in Strategic Planning

Key Areas	Issues
Product Description	What are you marketing?
Market Assessment	What is your overall assessment of the market where you compete?
Source of Business	Where do you expect business to come from?
Competitive Evaluation	What is your competition and how does it position itself?
Marketing Objectives	What are the marketing objectives for the brand?

target market. Think carefully, and write out a description of the product or service to be advertised or promoted in such a way that someone totally unfamiliar with it will understand exactly what it is. This description will then serve as background for the creative staff who will be charged with executing the brand's marketing communication.

Market Assessment

What is your overall assessment of the market in which you compete? It is important that your source of information here is absolutely up to date. The background information in the marketing plan could be as much as a year old. Be certain that nothing has happened in the market that could possibly 'date' this information. What is needed here is information about the market that might influence the potential success of the brand. How are brands performing relative to category performance? Where does the market seem to be heading? Are there potential innovations or new entries on the horizon? This is also a good time to review any recent market research that has been conducted for the brand. It is important here to provide enough information to convey a good sense of the market, but only those things likely to have a real impact upon a brand's performance should be included.

Source of Business

Where do you expect business to come from? It is necessary here to consider both potential customers as well as competitors. Do we expect to increase our share of business by attracting new customers to the category, or by attracting users of other brands (a trial action objective); or are we looking to increase usage by our existing customers (a repeat purchase action objective)? What is there about the purchase behaviour of potential customers that we need to know? To what extent does our brand compete with products or services *outside* its category?

Competitive Evaluation

What is the competition and how does it position itself? It is essential to have an accurate understanding of just who the competition is in the *minds of the consumers*. Does the competitive set change depending upon how the product is used? What are the creative strategies of the competition? It is a good idea to include examples of competitive marketing communication to illustrate the benefits they emphasize and their executional approach. As we shall see in Chapter 13, advertising and promotion must be unique, with their own consistent 'look and feel'. What media tactics are used by competitors? How do they employ advertising and promotion options? We need to have a good understanding of the environment created by our competitors' marketing communication.

Marketing Objectives

What are the marketing objectives for the brand? Here you want to include not only brand marketing objectives, but specific market share or sales goals as well. Usually, these numbers will be available in the marketing plan. If not, you must work them out for the brand. What we want is an estimate of what will happen if our marketing communication programme is successful. This is critical for determining the marketing communication budget.

It is strongly recommended that the manager prepare a briefing document that summarizes each of these key marketing issues. With this review as background, it is time to begin the strategic planning process.

Implement the Five-Step Strategic Planning Process

As we have seen, the strategic planning process begins with a review of the marketing plan and a determination of what constitutes the target market. While the consumer or customer is ultimately at the heart of any marketing communication programme, there may be many more people involved whom it will be necessary to consider in our planning. Deciding with whom we must communicate is obviously the first step in communication, so the strategic planning process begins there. While a company's marketing plan will have identified (or should have!) the general target market, the manager must know a lot more about the dynamic at work in the marketplace as people make decisions to buy or use products and services.

Step One in an effective strategic planning process is where the target audience is selected, consistent with the overall marketing strategy. In *Step Two* an understanding must be gained of how the target audience makes decisions in the category. The next two steps begin to address specific communication issues. In *Step Three* the best positioning for the brand within its marketing communication is established. *Step Four* is where the communication strategy is developed. Media strategy is set in *Step Five* by considering how best to accomplish the communication tasks required using available marketing communication options, and selecting the specific advertising or promotion media for delivering the message. Table 5.2 summarizes the five-step strategic planning process. Next, we shall discuss in more detail each step of the process.

Table 5.2 The Five-Step Strategic Planning Process

Review the Marketing Plan and:	
Step One	Select the target audience based upon the overall marketing strategy
Step Two	Understand how the target audience makes decisions in the category
Step Three	Determine the best positioning for the brand within its marketing communication
Step Four	Develop a communication strategy based upon the communication objective selected
Step Five	Set media strategy to deliver the message and satisfy the communication objectives

- Where are sales or usage to come from?
- What is known about the target audience?
- Where does the trade fit?

Figure 5.1 Key Target Audience Questions

Step One: Select the Target Audience

Consistent with what we saw in the previous chapter, the first task is to decide upon the target audience. Whom we select must be consistent with the brand's marketing objectives. If part of the marketing strategy is to build the category, this means a trial action objective and looking for new users. If the marketing strategy is to increase usage, this means a repeat-purchase action objective and focusing upon existing users. In the next chapter we will deal with the issue of target audience in depth. But for our purposes here as we outline the strategic planning process, we will consider three questions that should be addressed in the planning process (see Fig. 5.1).

Where are Sales or Usage to Come from?

In the review of the marketing plan we looked at the question of where business is expected to come from. Now we must decide if our primary emphasis should be users or non-users of our brand. While we obviously want a broadly based business, realistically it is either a trial or a repeat purchase target audience objective that will best satisfy a brand's *marketing* objectives. Communication strategy will differ significantly, depending upon which of these target audience action objectives is used.

A trial action objective means a non-user-based target audience, a repeat purchase objective a user-based target audience. But, as we shall see in the next chapter, there are further distinctions to be made within each of these groups. With a trial action objective, are we interested in new *category* users, or people already in the category but not using our brand? With a repeat purchase action objective, are we interested primarily in those loyal to our brand or those who use our brand along with other brands in the category?

In this first step of the strategic planning process the manager should be thinking about the relationship between trial and repeat purchase action objectives and which user groups to target.

What is Known about the Target Audience?

Once the appropriate user groups have been determined, the manager must build a profile of them. Too often this profile includes only demographic characteristics—for example, 'women, 25–45, with children'. This is not nearly enough. Even when so-called psychographic or lifestyle descriptions are included, descriptions like 'outgoing with an interest in cultural activities', this is not enough. These descriptions are useful, but not often sufficiently discriminating. For marketing communication to be effective it is important also to know those target audience attitudinal and behavioural patterns that are relevant to a brand's marketing communication and media strategies. This means knowing what the proposed target audience's category behaviour is now, or is likely to be in response to our campaign; and how their underlying brand attitudes and motivations affect choices.

Where does the Trade Fit in?

The manager must never lose sight of the fact that the trade is almost always a part of our target audience. It is easy to fall into the trap of thinking only about consumers when considering a target audience. But our strategic planning requires a *total* look at the marketing communication task, and when advertising and promotion to the trade are used they must be integrated with advertising and promotion to the consumer. Even if the message is different (as is likely), the 'look and feel', the theme, must be consistent with the overall creative umbrella. Why this is so important will be evident when we talk about the five decision roles in the next section. It would not be unusual for the trade to be either an 'initiator' or an 'influencer' in a brand decision, especially for high-ticket consumer goods or in business-to-business marketing.

Step Two: Understand Target Audience Decision Making

Once the target audience has been selected, we must next gain an understanding of how that target audience goes about making purchase decisions in the category. This is important, because if you are to affect the purchase decision positively and increase the likelihood of your brand being selected, you must understand what is involved in the making of that decision. As we shall see in Chapter 7, quite a lot may be involved. Who is involved in making the decision? How do they go about it? Where can advertising and promotions or other marketing communication influence the process?

To begin with, those who study consumer behaviour remind us that in a decision to buy or use a product or service a number of people may be involved, and they may play different roles in that decision process. In Chapter 7 we will introduce a decision grid that helps focus the manager's thinking on the various roles people may play in the decision to buy and use a brand. Basically, there are five possible roles involved:

- *initiators* who propose purchase or usage;
- *influencers* who recommend (or discourage) purchase or usage;
- *deciders* who make the actual choice;
- *purchasers* who make the actual purchase;
- *users* who use the product or service.

One person may play all five roles in the decision process, or others may be involved, playing one or more roles. It is critical to understand who is involved and what roles they are playing. When we address the members of our target audience we are talking to them as individuals, but as *individuals in a role*.

Once we have an understanding of those involved in the decision and the roles they play, we must then develop a model of how consumers actually make a purchase decision. This involves determining the stages the target audience goes through in choosing, purchasing, and using a brand. Looking at consumer decision making provides a dynamic view of the process that a target audience is likely to go through in making a decision to buy or use a product or service. It provides valuable insight into the likely motives driving behaviour. Understanding *why* people do what they do is critical in establishing an appropriate brand attitude strategy (which we develop as part of Step Four in the strategic planning process), and the brand attitude strategy is at the heart of successful advertising and promotion, as it is with *any* marketing communication. Additionally, identifying the various people involved in the purchase or usage decision, along with the roles they play, helps target messages more effectively to the appropriate audiences in their appropriate roles.

Using this consumer decision making model, the manager is in a position to determine how best to influence the decision process positively in order to maximize the opportunity for your brand to be chosen. With this model in hand, a manager will know where in the decision process it is most important to communicate with the target audience, and the type of message that will be required.

Step Three: Determine the Best Positioning

The third step in the strategic planning process is to determine how best to position the brand. While the basic brand positioning will no doubt already be established (except for new products), the strategic planning process must address the particular *communication* positioning that will be adopted for a brand. The manager must decide whether we want to link the brand in the target audience's mind to the category need in which it already sees it competing, or *re*position the brand by linking it to another category need where the brand will have a stronger competitive advantage. In such cases the repositioning rarely involves a drastic change, but rather a switch to another branch or level of the way the overall product category is partitioned in the mind of the target audience.

We shall spend a great deal of time in Chapter 8 discussing the importance of understanding how markets are partitioned. To give you an idea of what we mean by partitioning, think about snacks. What comes to mind? Is it a packet of crisps, say, or a candy bar? Clearly both are snacks, but would you position a candy bar against crisps? Unlikely. Candy bars are a different type of snack, and likely to satisfy a different category need. We might imagine the overall snack category dividing (that is, partitioning) into savory versus sweet snacks. Sweet snacks might then be seen as splitting into baked snacks like biscuits or pastries versus confections like candy. Candy bars, then, following our example, would be in the confection category, and positioned against the category need associated with it.

But even within the candy bar category itself there may also be different types of bars that offer various positioning options against more specific category needs. For example, there could be 'luxury' bars to satisfy an exotic indulgence, like Inca in France; or basic chocolate bars, like those marketed by Cadbury, to satisfy a need for just chocolate; or filled bars, like Lila Parse in Germany. The issue of how the category need is defined for our brand is a critical decision in the strategic planning process.

In addition to establishing the category definition in order to identify the market where the brand or service will compete, positioning also requires us to look for a differential advantage for our brand. How will the brand be presented to the target audience? What benefit does the brand offer, or what benefit could it be seen as offering, that gives the brand a unique advantage over its competition?

As we shall see in Chapter 8, this will require a thorough knowledge of a target audience's basic attitude towards the brand and its major competitors. What do people believe about the brands in the category? What is important to them, and which brands deliver on these important considerations? The answers to these questions are critical for successfully positioning a brand, and must be addressed as part of the strategic planning process.

Step Four: Develop a Communication Strategy

In developing a communication strategy the manager must first establish communication objectives by selecting the desired communication effects. This is taking the first step in addressing what we want marketing communication to say about our brand in order to motivate the target audience to take whatever action is required.

Communication Effects

Communication objectives are quite simply the communication *effects* for which we are looking. In Chapter 1 four communication effects were briefly introduced: category need, brand awareness, brand attitude, and brand purchase intention. It is from this set of possible communication effects that we draw our communication objectives.[1]

We will be dealing with these in depth later in Chapter 9. Here we shall look only briefly at how each of the four communication effects is likely to translate into communication objectives.

Category Need

It does not make much sense to try and market a brand if there is no perceived need for the product. Most of the time this is not an issue. But for innovative new products, for example, until there is awareness of *the new product as such*, it is almost impossible to create interest in a brand of that new product. Before there were TVs or home computers or CD players, there was really no 'need' in the market for such products. When they were developed, it was necessary to establish the 'need' by introducing the product category itself to the public. Once people understand what this new product category is all about, it is possible to talk about brands.

This does *not* mean that the brand should not be mentioned at the same time as the product category is being introduced into the market. What it means is that, when category need is a communication objective, it is first necessary to emphasize in the initial marketing communication what this new product category is all about in order to create interest in the category, while also positioning the brand to satisfy this new 'need'.

Category need may also be a communication objective where demand in a category seems to be slackening. This can happen, for example, when something goes out of fashion for a period of time. If this should occur, it may be necessary to *remind* people of a latent category need. This is a particularly appropriate strategy for market share leaders, who should reap the benefit of any renewed interest in a category.

The Birds Eye advert shown in Plate I offers a very good example of a category leader using a *category* benefit in order to strengthen demand for the category, in this case frozen food. They are reminding people of a frozen food benefit by pointing out that each year 30 per cent of fresh food is thrown away, but frozen food is not: 'it would just be thrown in the freezer'. By making people aware of this, it should help increase sales of frozen food, and with the increased category demand, increased sales of the Birds Eye brand. Again, this makes sense for Birds Eye because of their doormat position in the category.

Brand Awareness

Creating or reinforcing brand awareness is *always* a communication objective, regardless of what type of marketing communication you may be using in a campaign. While this is an obvious point for advertising, it is also true for everything from promotion to packaging. Without this essential link between the message and the brand, there is no chance for effective marketing communication.

Brand Attitude

Like brand awareness, creating or developing brand attitude is *always* a communication objective for every type of marketing communication used in a campaign. Brand attitude strategy is at the heart of developing a communication strategy for advertising and all other forms of marketing communication. Brand attitude itself, as a communication effect and objective, is a complex issue that we will be covering in some depth in Chapter 9.

While brand attitude strategy is a function of how involved a person is in the decision to purchase or use a product or service, along with what motivates them, the brand attitude itself relates more specifically to the brand. It may be thought of as a summary of what a person knows and feels about a brand, providing the link between the brand and the motive to buy or use it.

Brand Purchase Intention

Too often managers feel that the most important, perhaps the only, objective for marketing communication is to generate sales or usage of their product or service. While this is almost always a *marketing* objective, it is not often a primary communication objective. Of course we want our marketing communication to help contribute to an intention to buy or use the brand, but this is rarely the primary objective. Without brand awareness and brand attitude there can be no brand purchase intention.

Brand purchase becomes a *primary* communication objective (always along with brand awareness and brand attitude) when the principal thrust of the message is to 'act now'. As a result, it is always the primary communication objective for promotion, but not often for advertising. Because promotion's role in the overall marketing communication for a brand is to accelerate purchase, most promotions will include an incentive to encourage immediate action. The six basic types of incentive promotion for consumers are: coupons, refunds and rebates, sampling, loyalty and loading devices, sweepstakes and contests, and premiums. These will be discussed in some detail later in Chapter 14.

Regardless of the types of marketing communications that make up a campaign, whether traditional advertising or promotion, direct marketing, store signs, or even packaging, all have the potential to create any of the four communication effects we have just discussed.

But, as we shall learn in later chapters, some types of marketing communications are better suited than others to creating these effects. As a result, the choice of communication objectives will *directly* affect the choice of which type of advertising or promotion is to be used. The communication objective will also affect the media choice, both traditional media and new media such as the Internet and SMS messaging.

Brand Awareness and Brand Attitude Strategy

In the development of a communication strategy for a brand's marketing communication, getting the brand awareness and brand attitude strategy right is critical. Step Two in the strategic planning process helps the manager determine if the purchase decision follows from recognition or recall of the brand, if there is perceived risk in making the brand choice, and whether positive or negative motives are driving behaviour in the category. It is these determinations that will inform brand awareness and brand attitude strategy.

What is the Brand Awareness Strategy?

As we briefly mentioned earlier, there are at least two types of brand awareness that the manager must consider: recognition and recall. Brand awareness strategy deals with getting this right. *Recognition* brand awareness is when someone 'sees' the brand at the point of purchase and is reminded of a need for it. *Recall* brand awareness occurs when someone has a need and must 'remember' the brand as something that will satisfy that need. There are important strategic and tactical issues that must be considered in relation to the type of brand awareness, as we shall see later in the book, depending upon whether recognition or recall is central to how products or services are chosen.

What is the Brand Attitude Strategy?

The answer to this question follows from an understanding of the four quadrants detailed in the Rossiter–Percy grid.[2] This concept was briefly introduced in the first chapter, and will be covered in depth in Chapters 9 and 12. As part of their grid, Rossiter and Percy suggest that brand attitude strategy is a function of the two fundamental considerations we introduced in the first chapter: (1) whether there is low or high involvement with the purchase or use decision, based primarily upon the target audience's perceived risk (either in fiscal or psychological terms); (2) whether the underlying motivation that drives behaviour in the category is positive or negative. Combining these two considerations produces the four brand attitude strategy quadrants of the grid: low involvement with negative motives; low involvement with positive motives; high involvement with negative motives; and high involvement with positive motives.

Understanding these constructs is critical for identifying the appropriate brand attitude strategy, which in turn is critical for creative strategy. That is why we shall spend so much time on this issue later in the book. At this point, all we need is an initial understanding of its importance and where it fits in the strategic planning process.

The creative tactics that maximize the likelihood of an effective message are directly linked to the brand attitude strategy that follows from the appropriate quadrant defined by the Rossiter–Percy grid. These tactics differ significantly for each quadrant. Strategies associated with negative motives require *information* to help solve or avoid a problem, while those associated with positive motives must help *transform* the consumer—for example, by gratifying a want by meeting a need for social approval. As you might imagine, the creative message needed for brand attitude strategies associated with negative motives will be quite different from those associated with positive motives. For the informational strategies, the focus will probably be on benefits associated with the brand, while for transformational strategies the focus will generally be centred around the emotions associated with attitudes towards the category or brand.

This will all become much clearer in Chapters 9 and 12. For now, the contrast between Adverts 5.1*a* and 5.1*b* should help illustrate the point. The advert for Flash (5.1*a*) deals with an informational strategy, and you can see the benefit emphasis is on specific claims: 'they clean', 'they kill germs', 'they go on working for up to 12 hours'. The advert for Jordans Luxury Muesli (5.1*b*) reflects a transformational strategy, and you can see that the benefit focus is more 'emotional', utilizing a strong visual that projects a very positive feeling, with the copy in the headline reinforcing the overall sense of luxury contentment.

Creative tactics also differ as a function of involvement. Because involvement is defined in terms of risk, when there is low involvement it is not necessary for the target audience to be really convinced before buying. If people make a mistake, they have not suffered much of a loss. On the other hand, when involvement is high, the potential buyer does not want to make a mistake. In this case the target audience must be convinced by the marketing communication before buying. Consider how much an advert would need to

(a)

(b)

Advert 5.1 An example of the contrast between the benefit emphasis of an informational strategy, seen in the Flash advert (5.1*a*), and the more 'emotional' focus of a transformational strategy, seen in the advert for Jordans Luxury Muesli (5.1*b*). Flash: courtesy Procter and Gamble. Jordans: reproduced with kind permission © Jordans.

convince you that a new snack was 'great-tasting' or that a new personal computer was the 'best yet' before you would think of buying. Before buying the computer you would certainly want to know more, but you would probably be willing to take a chance on buying the new snack based only on the feeling that it might be something you would like.

The advert for Nike's Swim brand shown in Plate II is an excellent example of what we are talking about for a low involvement decision. The strong image presents the benefit of low resistance in the extreme: 'water without resistance'. Is it really that good? Because there is little risk involved, you can try and see. The advert for Philips Bodygroom shown in Plate III offers a very good example of how to believably present a brand's primary benefit for a high involvement decision. No words are really necessary. If the product can remove the 'fuzz' from the delicate skin of a fruit with no nicks or cuts, it should do the same for you. Comfort, effectiveness, and no cuts are all believably implied by this image, and reflect what people will be looking for in a product like this.

What we have are four potential brand attitude strategies based upon involvement and motivation: low- versus high-involvement informational strategies and low- versus high-involvement transformational strategies. The quadrant that best reflects the decision process of the target audience is what determines the brand attitude strategy.

Promotion Strategy

When creating brand purchase intention is a communication objective, the manager must decide if promotion should be part of the communication strategy for the brand. We have noted that brand purchase intention is rarely an objective for advertising. While advertising is meant to contribute to the target audience forming a positive intention to buy a brand, in most cases this follows from the positive brand attitude formed as a result of the advertising.

If brand purchase intention is an objective, the key to whether or not a promotion should be part of the overall communication strategy is whether that intention is to be acted upon immediately. If so, a specific promotion strategy must be developed as a part of the overall communication strategy for the brand, and brand purchase intention will become the *primary* communication objective for the promotion.

When we first talked about promotion in Chapter 1, we identified three basic types: consumer, retail, and trade. If promotion is to be part of the brand communication strategy, a promotion strategy must be part of the strategic planning process, and one or all of these basic promotion types could be involved. Consumer and retail promotions are more likely to be involved when dealing with consumer markets; and retail and trade promotions when dealing with business-to-business markets. Customers are the target for promotion in business-to-business markets, but as with consumers they are aimed at *individuals*. There will always be exceptions, of course, but this is a good rule-of-thumb.

Consumer Promotions

Consumers will not make a distinction between trade promotions delivered at retail outlets, retail promotions, and consumer promotions. In fact, consumers are not likely to make a distinction between promotions and advertising. They tend to think of all marketing communications as 'advertising'. In an interesting study, 1,000 consumers were asked what they would call a wide variety of different forms of marketing communication, and they answered advertising to over 100 of them. This included clearly incentive promotions such as coupons and sweepstakes, games, and contests, as well as non-incentive promotion-like messages such as bill inserts, information brochures, and window displays in stores.[3] If they see a special display in the store or have a coupon or see a price special, they are not concerned with whether it was the brand or the retailer that was responsible.

But, from the brand's perspective, there is a world of difference. Consumer promotions are initiated by the brand, not the retailer, and the brand controls the content. Even though consumers may think about promotions as 'advertising', they tend to have a pretty good idea about how often brands offer incentive promotion.[4] This is important to the brand, because it will affect consumer buying strategy for the brand in the light of the perception of the brand's availability on promotion. So, even if marketing managers do not have control over retail promotions that include their brand, it is essential that they have knowledge of them and include that knowledge in their promotion strategy.

Retail Promotion

When people think of retail promotions, the first things that probably come to mind are newspaper, food, or pharmacy adverts. But, of course, almost any retailer can use promotion, and car dealers, mass merchandisers, shoe stores, and even banks frequently do. Retail promotions are also found in local magazines and even on local radio and television. Retailers may carry out traditional advertising as well, and we must not confuse the two. If a retailer is talking about something related to the store or image, this is *not* retail promotion.

You may be wondering why we are treating retail promotions separately from trade promotions when retailers are a major part of the trade. It is because retailers form a very specific subset of the trade, one that has direct contact with the end consumer. Other aspects of the trade, such as brokers or wholesale distributors, do not as a rule deal directly with consumers. As a result, the effects of promotion to non-retail trade may or may not be passed on to the consumer through retailers.

We have just pointed out that a brand may not have control over how a retailer will use a particular promotion. A very interesting study has shown that the objective for many retail promotions is not simply to attract shoppers to a store, but to move product off the shelf, in effect reducing inventory costs.[5] This strategy may not always be consistent with the strategy behind a promotion offered to retailers. This can be a real problem for a marketer. In trying to integrate all the elements of a brand's marketing communication, retail promotion can be a wild card. Later in Chapter 14 we will be looking at channels marketing, which is an attempt by marketers to gain better control over retail promotion, and better integration with advertising and other brand marketing communication, all an important part of the strategic planning process.

An important consideration with retail promotions is that they are independent of a brand's marketing strategy. While the brand would like to coordinate retail promotions with its own marketing and communication strategy (as we will see when we discuss channels marketing), the reality is that retail promotions are offered *independently* of the pricing policy or other trade or consumer promotions offered by the brand. Often a retailer's promotion strategy is geared more to competitive activity than to anything else. It is very important during this stage of the planning process to have as good an understanding as possible of the likely use of promotion for the brand by the retailer.

There will be cases, of course, when the retailer and the brand will be the same. In such cases, the retailer will develop both an advertising and promotion strategy. The promotion for Really Wild Clothing Company shown in Plate IV provides a good example where the product and retailer are basically the same. The execution does a good job of delivering retailer brand awareness, and with a strong and appropriate visual image it helps build positive attitudes not only for their clothing, but also for the image of their retail store. The visual clearly contributes to a positive emotional response, important for transformational brand attitude strategy. If this were all there was to the execution, it would be considered a good advert. But look at the copy: 'contact us at our flagship store', 'visit us at our new on-line shop', and a special offer of a Really Wild T-shirt for ordering on-line. Clearly these are all promotion-like messages designed to encourage immediate action, including the offer of a premium. This is what makes this a promotion.

Trade Promotion

Trade promotion takes up a significant proportion of most marketing communication budgets. Whether the promotion directly affects pricing or indirectly affects volume through merchandising material, the trade views trade promotions from the manufacturer as a way to move more money to its bottom line. Most trade promotions do this directly through a price-related promotion of one kind or another. These can include such things as direct price-off reductions from invoices, agreements to buy back any unsold product, and at the retail level slotting allowances.

Slotting fees are a fee to stock new items, and have become a cost of doing business for fmcg brands. The reasoning is that, with an ever-increasing demand to handle new products and line extensions, and given the high failure rate, the trade feels it needs help in dealing with the cash flow and overhead involved. While there is certainly some truth to this, it is estimated that as much as 70 per cent of slotting fees go directly to the bottom line and not to defraying cost. With the general trend of retailers to merge into larger chains, slotting fees are expected to be applied to products other than fmcgs.[6]

If a consumer or business-to-business marketer is offering a discount on its price to the trade, the trade has the option of retaining all or part of the discount, sending it to its bottom line. To the extent that any of the trade discount is passed on to the retailer or directly to the consumer, these trade promotions are still expected to increase volume, also leading to larger profits for the trade. This is also the reasoning behind the trade's interest in merchandising promotion. Here the brand will supply collateral material such as in-store banners, special end-aisle displays, or sales incentive premiums for target sales goals. Of course, the brand is looking for something in return: such things as better stocking and shelf positioning (for example, more package 'facings' and at a more desirable height on the shelf),[7] counter displays, and other opportunities for better exposure.

In many markets the distribution channels, especially mass retailers, have become so powerful that, even when trade promotions are given, there is no guarantee the trade will offer anything in return. It is important to remember that the brand's goals and the trade's goals are not necessarily the same. The trade profits from category sales. It does not particularly care which brands are stocked as long as it maintains or increases its margins. The marketer, of course, is vitally interested in its *brand* whether consumer or business-to-business.

This underscores a very important point. Too often trade promotions (and retail and consumer promotions as well) are seen only as a way to buy share or sales in order to satisfy an immediate, short-term sales goal. True, promotion is a short-term *tactic*, but it must be seen within a larger marketing communication *strategy* for the brand. As we shall see in the final chapter, this means integrating trade promotions with all other promotion and advertising activity.

To go beyond the obvious, trade promotions should be designed to improve relations with the trade in order to gain and hold new distribution, to build inventory with the trade, or to obtain trade cooperation and merchandising support.

Step Five: Set a Media Strategy

In this fifth step of the strategic planning process, the manager must select the best communication options to deliver the message executions.[8] This is the first step in determining media selection, and one of the most important things the manager will need to think about at this point is the different relative strengths of advertising and promotion in satisfying the four possible communication objectives. (Remember from our earlier discussion of advertising and promotion that from a practical standpoint we are talking about marketing communication options only in terms of advertising and promotion, while nevertheless realizing that every type of marketing communication should be evaluated in the planning process.)

Basically, both advertising and promotion should have a significant effect upon brand awareness; the primary strength of advertising is brand attitude, while the primary strength of promotion is brand purchase intention, and neither advertising nor promotion can have much of a direct effect upon category need. The relative strength of traditional advertising versus promotion will be covered in more detail in Chapter 15.

After this basic consideration of how best to integrate advertising and promotion communication options in the marketing communication programme for the brand, specific media are considered in terms of the communication objectives. As we shall see in Chapter 10, for the media choice to be effective it must be consistent with the communication objectives, especially for brand awareness and brand attitude strategies. For example, we know that for recognition brand attitude strategies the product must be shown as it will be seen at the point-of-purchase. This means that radio is not an option.

Setting media strategy requires a careful consideration of the processing requirements of the message, and the selection of communication options that will help facilitate that processing. You will remember from the previous chapter how important this is. If the target audience does not effectively process the message, there can be no target audience action.

Direct Marketing

We are including direct marketing here as a part of setting a media strategy because it is at this step in the strategic planning process that the manager should consider whether or not to use direct marketing as part of the brand's marketing communication. We shall go into some detail now rather than later in the media chapter because the consideration of direct marketing is strategic; do we want to use it or not?

Direct marketing is really a bit of a hybrid, being both a form of marketing as well as a way of delivering an advertising or promotion message. If direct marketing is to be used, it is essential that the message involved be consistent with the overall positioning and communication strategy of the brand, and integrated appropriately. To many marketing managers, direct marketing simply means direct mail. Although direct mail is the most popular medium for direct marketing (telemarketing is a close second[9]), it is only one of many. Direct marketing is a very specific *means* of marketing communication, and may include elements of both advertising and promotion, although historically it is thought of more in terms of promotion.

So what exactly is direct marketing? According to the Direct Marketing Association in the USA, direct marketing is:

An accountable system of marketing which uses one or more communications media to effect response. It is an interactive process where responses from or about buyers are recorded in a database for building profiles of potential customers and providing valuable marketing information for more efficient targeting.

The really important parts of this definition are two interrelated terms: 'interactive process' and 'database'. We shall deal with them in more detail later when we talk about the database in direct marketing, but first we will take a more general look at direct marketing.

Implicit in the DMA's definition of direct marketing is that it is an *ongoing* process. While direct marketing may be used tactically, it must be a part of a brand's longer-term strategic marketing communication planning. This is underscored when you consider the cost of delivering an effective direct marketing programme. As an executive of a major direct marketing company has pointed out, it is hard for marketing managers to adjust to spending as much as *25 times more* per response than they are used to paying for responses to other marketing communication programmes.[10] For example, direct mail has been shown to be a very cost-effective method for direct marketing, but it is still difficult for marketing managers to budget so much more than they are accustomed to paying for other media on a cost-per-thousand-exposure basis. It must be remembered that effective direct marketing builds a foundation for the future, and will more than pay for itself.

There are several fundamental strategic differences between direct marketing and more traditional forms of marketing communication such as advertising. The most important of these is that, rather than trying to influence brand purchase intentions over multiple exposures, direct marketing usually relies upon a single exposure to generate a response. Whether the desired response is to place an order, to call for more information, or to visit a dealer, the target audience is expected to *do it now*. Target audiences are much more tightly targeted with direct marketing than with traditional advertising. You address the target audience in a more precise way about its particular needs, and never in the third person. Another difference is the way in which distribution is treated. With direct marketing, distribution itself can become a benefit claim, as in 'not available in stores'. In a very real way, direct marketing media are used *as the marketplace*, in contrast to advertising,

Table 5.3 Fundamental Strategic Differences between Direct Marketing and Advertising

	Direct Marketing	Advertising
Exposure	Single exposure	Multiple exposure
Action	Immediate	Eventual
Target Audience	Tightly targeted	Widely targeted
Distribution	Media is the marketplace	Distribution defines the marketplace

- Does direct marketing make sense given the brand's communication objectives?
- Is there a good database available for the target audience?
- How will you deliver the message?

Figure 5.2 Questions Managers Must Ask when Considering Direct Marketing

where distribution is used to define the marketplace. These differences are summarized in Table 5.3.

Using Direct Marketing

In considering direct marketing as part of an integrated marketing communication programme, there are three questions the manager must ask (see Fig. 5.2). First, does direct marketing make any sense given the brand's communication objectives? We have just reviewed a number of strategic differences between advertising and direct marketing. Obviously, if you are addressing a mass audience, direct marketing is not likely to be as effective as other means of marketing communication. Also, given the tactical nature of direct marketing, brand purchase intention is the most appropriate communication objective. If brand attitude is the primary objective (remember it is *always* an objective, along with brand awareness, even if something else is the primary objective), direct marketing is likely to be less effective than other means of marketing communication.

If direct marketing does make sense for a brand's marketing communication programme, the next question is whether or not a good database for the target audience is available. If the brand has used direct marketing in the past, then an updated database should be available. If not, you must be able to acquire or build a target list before you can even think about developing a direct marketing programme. This suggests that, even if direct marketing is not currently a part of a brand's marketing communication efforts, it will still make sense to develop a database for possible future use. The importance of a good list for direct marketing cannot be understated. Studies have shown that the quality of a list accounts for some 40 per cent of the effectiveness of a direct marketing campaign,

- Direct Mail
- Telemarketing
- Mass Media
- Interactive

Figure 5.3 Four Basic Types of Direct Marketing Media

equal to the 40 per cent attributed to the headline of the message (the remainder of the message accounts for the other 20 per cent).[11] We shall look more closely at databases later in the chapter.

If direct marketing makes sense for the brand and you have a good database, the final question to ask is how you will deliver the message. There are four basic direct marketing media available: direct mail, telemarketing, mass media, and interactive media. Generally only one of these four media will be used for a particular direct marketing programme. An exception would be if various segments of the target audience are more easily reached with one medium than another. Each of these four basic types of direct marketing media is now reviewed (see Fig. 5.3).

Direct Mail

We have already noted that direct mail is the most popular direct marketing medium. This stems in large part from its ability to target an audience effectively while providing broad latitude for creative options in delivering the message. Direct mail can be used to deliver almost any type of message, and through a wide variety of means: everything from flyers and brochures to videos or CD-ROMs for computers.

Telemarketing

While a close second to direct mail, telemarketing does not offer the same flexibility in delivering a message. What it does offer is the ability actively to converse with the consumer. This has the advantage of immediate feedback, which can be used to adjust and more finely tune a message. This interaction also enables effective telemarketing callers to deal with concerns and questions from target audience members as they come up. This, of course, requires well-trained people making the telephone calls. When we think of telemarketing, we generally think of what is known as *outbound* telemarketing, where the marketer initiates the calls, as opposed to *inbound* telemarketing, where the marketer answers calls from the target audience that have been generated by such things as toll-free numbers. A real disadvantage with telemarketing is the inability to use visual material.

Mass Media

Any mass medium could be used for direct marketing; the difference is in *how* it is used. Direct marketing is looking for the ability to target the market tightly, and to optimize *immediate response*. In the past television was rarely used in direct marketing. However, with the increasing potential for better targeting with specialized cable channels, along with the ability to run longer commercials (up to two minutes or longer) on cable, direct marketing is finding a use for television. Another growing phenomenon on cable television is the so-called infomercial. This is basically a direct marketing pitch for a product lasting as long as thirty minutes, and made to look like regular programming. Infomercials are a growing trend, even among well-known brands, and are expected to continue.[12] In fact, there is a 24-hour cable channel in the USA that shows nothing but infomercials! Radio, as you might imagine, is not often considered for direct marketing. The obvious reason is the difficulty in generating an immediate response. Yet radio does have the advantage of tight targeting, and radio messages can be produced and aired quickly when necessary. If you can overcome the passive nature of radio with a good creative execution, radio can be effective.

Of the four principal mass media, the newspaper is probably the one used most often for direct marketing. It offers a brand the ability to insert a message of almost any length, from a single page to multi-page brochures complete with order blanks and return envelopes for posting, and it can be printed on almost any paper stock, not just newsprint. With newspapers you can also tightly control the timing of the delivery. The disadvantage is the lack of specific targeting ability beyond geographic areas, and the shrinking base of newspaper readership. Magazines offer just the opposite. They provide a highly targeted audience but lack the ability to control the timing as tightly. Magazines do not appear as frequently as newspapers, and require much longer lead times for delivering the inserts.

Interactive

Although they do not play a large part yet in direct marketing, interactive media are sure to be an increasingly important part of direct marketing in the future. The pace of new technology almost guarantees it. Yet, without knowing what technological advances may bring, managers should be cautious about how large a role interactive media are likely to play, not only in direct marketing, but in traditional advertising as well. These media are perfect for immediate response, but difficult to control delivery of the message.

Today, CD-ROM catalogues are available for Internet shopping by those with CD-ROM-equipped computers. Almost anyone with a computer will have access to the Internet, and many big-name brands now use the Internet for direct marketing. The biggest problem for direct marketing on the Internet is how to target your market tightly enough, and creatively, and how to persuade them to respond now. As one Web catalogue executive has said, encouraging people to look through a catalogue on the Internet is not the problem, but 'getting them to buy is hard because they might not be direct response buyers'.[13]

Databases

The definition by the Direct Marketing Association suggests that having a sound contact database lies at the heart of direct marketing. It is important to understand, however, that, although a database is necessary for direct marketing, databases can be and are used in a number of other ways in marketing (often referred to as 'database marketing'). In other words, just because you are using a database does not mean you are necessarily engaged in direct marketing. It is also important to understand that a database is not just another name for a mailing list. In direct marketing a database provides much more than a name and address. There will be details of past and current purchase behaviour and other information about each person in the database that help better target consumers with appropriate messages. Using databases in direct marketing is also a dynamic process. Every time it is used, the database is updated and re-evaluated. Obviously, the most effective databases are computer driven, although direct marketing used paper files on consumers for a long time before computers became so accessible and cost-effective.

To build an effective database you must begin with *a list*. A brand can develop its own list, or buy or rent one to get started. But a good list is not enough. It must be fully *analysed* in order best to understand how to use it most effectively. What part of the list will be most appropriate for a particular direct marketing campaign? What does the list tell you about the consumer that might influence the nature of the direct marketing effort? Once the list has been analysed, the appropriate part is used in implementing the programme. Then, *analyse the results*. Remember one of the key parts of the definition of direct marketing is *accountability*. How effective was the information in the database in generating a response? Is there any information within the database that might help explain any unexpected response (whether good or bad)? Finally, after the results of the direct marketing programme have been analysed, use that information to *update* the information in the database. This is a perfect opportunity to track those who do not respond to a particular type of message, as well as response rates and patterns. These steps for building a strong database are summarized in Fig. 5.4. In following them, a brand is always building its database.

Databases are essential for direct marketing, but they are also strategically useful in identifying opportunities for direct marketing. A good database helps identify consumers who make multiple or repeat purchases. By looking at purchase patterns, if you see that purchase cycles are short, using direct marketing may not be cost-effective. On the other hand, if the purchase cycle is too long, it may not pay to use direct marketing, because too few people may be in the market at any one time. Of course, if it made cost sense, you could certainly target those who *should* be in the market, based upon their past behaviour. Analysing the database in this way enables the manager to do a cost analysis relative to the likelihood of a response given known purchase behaviour. It also permits direct marketing efforts as a defensive move against competitors' promotions when you can predict times your customers are most likely to be in the market. Finally, by its very nature, a good database provides background information that might suggest opportunities for direct marketing to specific segments or market niches.

Disadvantages of Direct Marketing

There is no question that the growth of direct marketing has been fuelled by advances in technology, especially computer-driven systems and software. But there are some

---

- Develop a good list for the target market
- Fully analyse the list before using it
- Analyse the results after using the list
- Use the analysis to update the database

Figure 5.4 Steps for Building a Strong Database

disadvantages that should be considered. The first is the image of some direct marketing media. Remember, consumers do not distinguish one type of marketing communication from another. Marketing managers may call a direct mail campaign a promotion, or it may be direct marketing, but the consumer is more likely to see any such mailing as 'junk mail'. The image of telemarketing is even worse. Those on the Internet are likely to see unsolicited email from a brand as an unwanted intervention by 'spammers' (indiscriminate senders of email). We have also pointed out that direct marketing can be expensive compared to other forms of marketing communication. Still, when carefully considered and planned, direct marketing can be an important and effective part of a brand's marketing communication effort.

CHAPTER SUMMARY

We have now introduced the five decision steps in the strategic planning process: select the target audience, understand target audience decision making, determine the best positioning, develop a communication strategy, and set the media strategy. We have explored each stage at the preliminary level and the following chapters will discuss each stage in depth. We have considered how the Rossiter–Percy grid can be used to guide brand attitude strategy and creative tactics, and the role of promotion strategy was introduced. Direct marketing was introduced, because whether or not to use direct marketing should be part of the overall strategic planning.

QUESTIONS TO CONSIDER

5.1 Why is each of the five steps in the strategic planning process needed, and why must they be considered in this order?

5.2 How should the roles people play in a purchase or usage decision influence a manager's thinking about a strategic plan for a brand's advertising and other marketing communication?

5.3 Why is it important to understand the difference between recognition and recall brand awareness?

5.4 When are sales likely to be a specific objective for advertising messages?

5.5 Why is an understanding of consumer decision making critical for an effective brand attitude strategy?

5.6 How do involvement and motivation affect brand attitude strategy?

5.7 When should promotion be considered as part of the communication strategy?

5.8 What must the manager consider when matching media options with communication objectives?

5.9 How can direct marketing contribute to a brand's marketing communications?

5.10 Find an example of direct marketing that does not involve a promotion.

Royal Mail—How Advertising Can Reposition an Entire Industry

For 350 years Royal Mail, the mail carrier in the UK, was nearly the only communications medium, for all intents and purposes a virtual monopoly. This monopoly has no pricing power, no ability to increase distribution, and limited ability to improve product. Indeed, Royal Mail cannot change the price of stamps to make mail more attractive, introduce new 'products' without regulatory approval, nor open outlets wherever they please.

Royal Mail makes money from providing mail services to businesses and consumers. Consumer revenue consists mainly of postage stamps, Special Delivery fees, and sundry mail components like collectible stamps. Business revenues range from bulk mail postage fees, courier services, and private mail solutions (e.g. delivering company mail internally). While Royal Mail's image evokes smiling postmen delivering birthday cards to grandmothers at home, it is business mail that drives Royal Mail's future. It accounts for about 80 per cent of total company revenues. It is also the fastest growing mail sector because of the growing direct marketing tactics.

However, new technologies have appeared to challenge Royal Mail's communications stranglehold. With the digital age serious communication alternatives emerged that significantly challenge the mail business: email and mobile phones posed the first credible threat to 'physical mail'. First, email not only carries words; it incorporates pictures, sounds, or video and allows you to record that the message was received, read, and by whom. Second, with digital signatures, email documents have a legally binding status, allowing email to replace the physical mailing of a contract. Lastly, other digital communications technologies offer an instant response capability (e.g. instant messaging and text messaging). These new technologies have started changing some people's communications habits. The challenge was to determine how the technology age affected Royal Mail's business.

A scenario planning exercise was performed to examine the impact of the new technologies. Four potential scenarios emerged:

- Scenario 1—Pure Digital: people start rejecting legacy solutions like mail and embrace new technologies like email and texting.
- Scenario 2—Return To 'Yesteryear': people become tired of novelty and return to the more 'authentic' and personal letter writing.
- Scenario 3—Tuning Out: people become overwhelmed by increasing communications demands on their time and significantly reduce their communications activity.
- Scenario 4—Communications Deluge: digital communications act as a catalyst (e.g. email quickly expands one's global contacts), triggering an increased need to communicate through all media, including mail and its competitors.

Clearly, the fourth scenario is the best option from Royal Mail's perspective, as it would have the biggest impact on business growth, while scenarios 1 and 3 would be disastrous. Thus, the challenges became: can advertising have a sustainable long-term transformational effect on the business? Can advertising effectively influence the scenario outcome?

The first task was to retain Royal Mail's leading role in the evolving communications landscape. To achieve this, Royal Mail had to pre-empt possible changes in consumer and business attitudes towards mail as a communications solution; it had to defend mail against the emergence of potentially substitutive technologies and to defend it differently in two markets, consumer and business segments. The consumer campaign would position Royal Mail as the only genuine vehicle for important messages, while the business campaign would position mail as a competitive business tool.

Consumer campaign was featured to change fundamental attitudes towards mail. Two successive campaigns were launched. 'I Saw This And Thought Of You' (1996–2001) was designed to encourage consumers to send more mail to one another by demonstrating that mail is more personal and impactful, as it is the only way to include a tangible object with your message. And then, 'Nothing Gets Through Like A Letter' (April–November 2001) was launched. It used emotionally loaded situations (a break-up, moving away to school) to show mail as the most likely medium to get through to the recipient.

As for the business campaign, it was designed to get more businesses to consider mail as a marketing and CRM medium. Indeed, while most businesses use mail, it is often at the bottom of the 'media hierarchy'. Typical business decision makers tend to put TV, press, and outdoor ahead of mail as a way to attract customers. The business campaign needed to turn around the perception of mail in terms of attracting customers. As a result, the business campaign leveraged a central branding platform—Royal Mail's Real Network. Royal Mail has a communications network of postmen and vans. More importantly, it offers an information network and communications solutions designed to help businesses do their jobs more effectively than other media. It positioned Royal Mail as a key enabler of UK business.

The first campaign called 'Target' (March–November 2001) aimed to make the network visible and positioned mail as a universal, communications channel for marketing. The second campaign called 'Elton John Packets' (October 2001–January 2002) aimed to make the network valuable and stressed Royal Mail's role as the enabler of ebusiness, helping two-thirds of UK websites deliver goods and strengthen customer relationships. The strategy continues with the new 'Special Delivery' campaign and the final campaign, 'Brand Reveal'. The final campaign aimed to make the Royal Mail network essential.

But one thing to note was that attitudes toward mail are ingrained in long-standing childhood and cultural experiences, so the change would be slow and both campaigns required heavy long-term investment to pay off. The campaign period was between 1999 and 2002. The campaign results showed that the impact of adspend on profitability was significant. The return of investment was as high as 379 per cent. Though running separate campaigns to the consumer and business sectors, Royal Mail saw an emerging communications ecology. Royal Mail's consumer advertising had a material impact not only on consumer mail volume but also on business mail, and vice versa. Indeed, there is a virtuous cycle. If home consumers feel more positively predisposed to mail, the advertisers who want to market to them are more likely to use mail to reach them.

On a consumer social mail level, the advertising campaign was successful. It was successful in creating a relevant message that made mail and Royal Mail more appealing. Research also showed that the advertising campaign reminded consumers of the uses of mail. Mail is not mail anymore; mail can evoke the deep, long forgotten emotion residing in each individual.

The three business campaigns successfully positioned Royal Mail as the only communications network with the scale to reach any customer target. Post tracking showed significant positive differences in attitudes towards mail as a business tool. The brand values were featured as intelligent, modern, future looking, essential, and confident. Thus, 'Target' successfully positioned mail as an appropriate medium for business communications, an effective CRM tool, and a growth in the intent to use mail for marketing purposes.

While usage of communications technologies (Internet, mobile phones) continues to explode, mail usage has stopped decreasing among home users since Royal Mail started its advertising campaigns. Research has indicated that countries with high communications technology penetration (e.g. Internet, mobile phones, etc.) experience a higher degree of mail substitution than countries with low penetration. The fact reflected the emergence of Scenario 1—Pure Digital, a disaster to the mail industry globally. But if the UK had behaved like the average high penetration country, it would have shown a 3 per cent decrease in mail volume from 1996 to 2000; instead, mail volume increased by 16 per cent. This is further evidence that the campaign shielded the UK market and Royal Mail from the technology threat.

Advertising can have an immediate impact on business on the basis of financial, strategic, and attitudinal perspectives even with a regulated monopoly without pricing and distribution power or new product development freedom, like Royal Mail. This case demonstrates that advertising has a sustainable long-term impact to transform perceptions of an industry over the long term.

Source: WARC, IPA Effectiveness Awards 2002, Royal Mail—How Advertising Can Reposition an Entire Industry, by Nick KojeyStrauss, Becky Taylor Wilkinson

Edited by Hazel H. Huang

Discussion Questions

1   What is the role of the scenario exercise performed by Royal Mail in the strategic planning process?

2   Why did Royal Mail need to communicate to consumer and business sectors separately?

3   What are the differences in the strategic planning process between targeting consumers and business customers?

4   The case information did not include the media strategy. How would you implement the media strategy? What differences would there be in your media strategies between those targeting the general public and those targeting business customers?

FURTHER READING

- In an interesting article, 'Academic Marketing Knowledge and Marketing Managers', *Marketing Theory*, 2/4 (Dec. 2002), 355–62, Berend Wierenga argues that the manager brings a great deal of knowledge and experience to planning and decision making, beyond the academic understanding of marketing knowledge.

- Michael Podsedly, 'Lessons from the Tech Collapse', *Journal of Business Forecasting*, 21 (Spring 2002), argues that traditional planning tools may be ineffective, and that a reluctance to accept a change contributed to the collapse of the technology sector.

- Jerry Wind and Vijay Mahajan, *Convergence Marketing* (Upper Saddle River, NJ: Prentice Hall, 2002), offer a very broad view of planning that argues against old views, looking at the consumer as a hybrid dealing with new technologies but being driven by age-old desires and motivations.

NOTES

1   John Rossiter and Larry Percy first introduced this idea of establishing communication objectives from the expected effects of communication in *Advertising and Promotion Management* (New York: McGraw-Hill, 1987).

2   The Rossiter–Percy grid was originally presented in *Advertising and Promotion Management*, and subsequently summarized in more detail in J. R. Rossiter, L. Percy, and R. J. Donovan, 'A Better Advertising Planning Grid', *Journal of Advertising Research*, 32/5 (1991), 11–21.

3   D. Schultz, 'What is Direct Marketing?', *Journal of Direct Marketing*, 9/2 (1995), 5–9.

4   See A. Krishna, F. S. Currin, and R. W. Shoemaker, 'Consumer Perceptions of Promotional Activity', *Journal of Marketing*, 55 (1991), 14–16.

5   See R. C. Blattberg, G. D. Eppen, and J. Lieberman, 'A Theoretical an Empirical Evaluation of Price Deals for Consumer Nondurables', *Journal of Marketing*, 45/1 (1981), 116–29.

6   See A. R. Rae and H. Mahi, 'The Price of Launching a New Product: Empirical Evidence of Factors   Affecting the Relative Magnitude of Slotting Allowances', *Marketing Science*, 22/2 (2003), 246–68.

7   The advantages of positioning a package on the shelf eye level were demonstrated in a study conducted by *Progressive Grocer,* and is discussed by J. R. Rossiter and L. Percy in *Advertising Communication and Promotion Management* (New York: McGraw Hill, 1997), 356.

8   Rossiter and Percy devote a great deal of their discussion of media selection in *Advertising Communication and Promotion Management* (New York: McGraw-Hill, 1997) to the need for a proper correspondence between communication objectives and the specific vehicles needed to deliver such an objective.

9   Latest data reported for the UK by the Direct Marketing Association (in 1996) listed direct mail expenditures at £1,459,000 versus £1,305,000 for telemarketing.

10   See J. W. Pickholz, 'From the Practitioners', *Journal of Direct Marketing*, 8/2 (1994).

11   See B. Lamons, 'Creativity is Important to Direct Marketing Too', *Marketing News*, 7 Dec. 1992, 10.

12   See K. Cleland, 'More Advertisers Put Infomercials in their Plans', *Ad Age*, 18 Sept. 1995, 50.

13   See C. Miller, 'Marketers Find it Hip to be on the Internet', *Marketing News*, 27 Feb. 1995, 2.

 Visit the Online Resource Centre that accompanies this book for additional resources to support the text: http://www.oxfordtextbooks.co.uk/orc/ percy_elliott3e/

Developing the Strategic Plan

Chapter 6 — | Selecting the Target Audience | — Identify target audience and establish trial vs. repeat purchase target *audience action objectives*

⇩

Chapter 7 — | Understanding Target Audience Decision Making | — *Determine level of involvement* and *motivation* to guide communication strategy, and identify where media can effectively reach the target audience

⇩

Chapter 8 — | Determining the Best Positioning | — *Link brand to category need* to guide brand awareness strategy, and *link brand to benefit* to guide brand attitude strategy

⇩

Chapter 9 — | Developing a Communication Strategy | — Establish communication objectives and determine *recall vs. recognition* brand awareness strategy, and brand attitude strategy in terms of *involvement* and *motivation*

⇩

Chapter 10 — | Setting a Media Strategy | — Identify media options, in terms of specific *brand awareness and brand attitude* strategy

6

Selecting the Target Audience

In this and the next four chapters we will be laying the foundation for effective advertising and other marketing communication by determining what is necessary in order to implement the strategic planning process. The first thing the manager must do is select the appropriate target audience, which will be a function of the brand purchase objective laid out in the marketing plan. This, in turn, will have implications for both communication and promotion strategy, as we see below.

Implementing the Strategic Planning Process

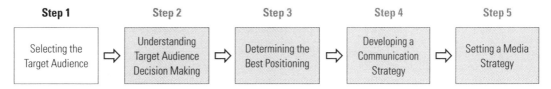

Step 1	Step 2	Step 3	Step 4	Step 5
Selecting the Target Audience	Understanding Target Audience Decision Making	Determining the Best Positioning	Developing a Communication Strategy	Setting a Media Strategy

---

STEP 1 SELECT THE TARGET AUDIENCE

Target Audience Action Objective		Objective for Communication Strategy	Options for Promotion Strategy
Repeat Purchase	⟶ User	• Strengthen existing brand attitude	• Loyalty and loading devices • Premiums • Sweepstakes, games, contests
Trial	⟶ Non-users	• Generate brand awareness • Encourage a more favourable brand attitude	• Coupons • Refunds and rebates • Sampling

> **➤ KEY CONCEPTS**
>
> **1** The most practical way of looking at target audience selection is in relation to buyer behaviour because it is easily measured, but the real key is brand loyalty.
>
> **2** Brand loyalty is a reflection of awareness, attitudes, and behaviour.
>
> **3** There are many other ways to describe a target audience, and these profiles are helpful in creative development, but not for selection.
>
> **4** The fundamental distinction made in marketing plans between brand users and non-users is directly related to the target audience action objectives of trial and repeat purchase.
>
> **5** Overall, attitude is the most important thing to understand about a target audience.

As we saw in the previous chapter, the first step in the strategic planning process for marketing communication (or for *any* advertising or promotion programme) is to select the appropriate target audience. The marketing plan establishes marketing goals and defines the target market. From this target market it is necessary to identify the specific target audience required for a particular marketing communication programme. If we are advertising, are we more interested in attracting new users or encouraging existing users to buy or use more often? If we are running a promotion campaign, is it to reward loyal customers or to attract new users?

Selecting the appropriate target audience is not as easy as it may seem. From the examples above, a simple distinction between customers and non-customers may seem to suffice. But this is *not* enough. Much more definition is required. For example, what if someone is a customer only because he or she has not yet found something he or she likes better? Or what if someone is a customer because he or she simply would not think of using any other brand? Obviously it will be important to understand just what type of customers (and non-customers) comprise the market if the manager is to make intelligent target audience decisions.

Target Audience Groupings

There are a number of different ways to think about target audience groups. Gerrit Antonides and W. Fred van Raaij take a broad view of target audience groups, describing them in terms of three levels: general, domain specific, and brand specific.[1]

At the *general level* they consider target audience groups in terms of descriptive characteristics such as standard demographics (for example, age, income, geographic location), lifestyle variables (for example, active in sports, travel), and psychographics (for example, outgoing, risk-taking).

At the *domain-specific level* target audience groups are described in terms of those characteristics associated with a product or product category. This would include such things as category usage behaviour (for example, eat a lot of frozen food, own three cars), attitudes towards the product category (for example, vitamins are a waste of money), and how decisions are made in the category (for example, a need is aroused in the product category, a set of brands is considered, one is selected, purchased, and used).

At the *brand-specific level* they describe target audience groupings in terms of such things as brand loyalty (buys one brand in the category all the time, or at least most of the time), beliefs about the brand (for example, Brand A has more cleaning power than Brand B), and brand buying intentions (for example, will buy Brand A if it is on special, otherwise will buy Brand B).

In effect Antonides and van Raaij look at possible target audience groupings in terms of their overall descriptive characteristics, how they behave generally in the product category, and how they behave towards specific brands. Rossiter and Percy, on the other hand, discuss target audience groupings primarily in terms of their brand purchasing behaviours.[2] They suggest a brand could potentially be purchased by any of five buyer groups: *brand loyals*, who regularly buy your brand in the category; *favourable brand-switchers*, who buy your brand but also buy competitor brands; *other-brand-switchers*, who buy more than one competitor brand, but not your brand; *other-brand loyals*, who regularly buy a competitor brand; and a fifth group of *new category users*, who are entering the category for the first time or re-entering after a long time.

This idea of looking at a target audience in terms of purchasing behaviour is a reflection of brand loyalty. Brand loyalty, of course, means regular purchase of the brand, and that is generally assumed to follow from a positive attitude toward the brand. This positive attitude, over time, leads to a certain 'immunization' to competitive advertising and promotion. This idea of positive attitudes leading to resistance to competitive marketing communication follows from McGuire's notion of inoculation theory.[3] Initial counter-arguing to a brand's message, after trial and usage, will tend to be adopted as a defence against competitive communication much in the way a small inoculation of a flu virus stimulates resistance to the flu.

In addition to brand attitude, brand awareness will also figure in purchase behaviour, and as a result, brand loyalty. This may seem obvious, because if you are not aware of a brand you will not be looking to purchase it. But as we shall see as we look more deeply into this below, there is more to it. As Rossiter and Percy have suggested, brand loyalty is an awareness-attitude-behaviour concept.[4]

The Antonides and van Raaij classifications of target audience groupings offer the manager a general-to-specific way of profiling potential target groups. However, this classification screen does not really help the manager *select* an optimum target audience. In this regard the Rossiter–Percy notion of looking at brand purchase behaviour is more helpful. In fact, it makes a great deal of intuitive sense. It is a logical refinement of the basic customer versus non-customer division of the target market.

Obviously, a brand will want to retain consumers who are loyal to it and reinforce that loyalty. This is the hard core of any business. Those who buy a brand along with the occasional competitor brand, however, probably make up the bulk of any business. Here it is necessary to retain these customers and try to encourage less usage of other brands. As we shall see later in this chapter, the objective with these two groups is *repeat purchase*.

If we are looking for new customers, those who buy more than one other brand, but not ours, probably offer the best potential. Since they already buy more than one brand, it should be possible to persuade them to include our brand (either in addition to, or in place of, one of the brands they now buy). The most difficult prospect would be those who tend to be loyal to a competitor brand. But those who do not use the category will not be easy to attract as new customers either. In addition to persuading them to buy your brand you must also persuade them to enter the category in the first place. Again, as we shall see later, the objective for these non-users of your brand is *trial*.

This division of target audience potential into repeat purchase versus trial behaviour is reflected in the five Rossiter and Percy buyer behaviour groups. A repeat purchase object-ive means selecting a target audience from among brand loyals and what they call favour-able brand-switchers. A trial objective will mean selecting a target audience from among what they refer to as other-brand-switchers, other brand loyals, and new category users. But beyond this obvious distinction, brand awareness and brand attitude will be playing an important role.

Those loyal to a brand should have the highest awareness and most positive attitudes toward the brand, although as we shall see in the next section, this does not necessarily always follow. A brand's most loyal buyers will always be of critical importance to any brand, but if driving up repeat purchase is the objective, they may not be the best target for increasing business. The manager must understand their attitudes toward the brand *and the category*. Brand loyals must be more than just happy with the brand, if increasing their usage is part of the strategy. They must be amenable to using more. However, with some categories, it would make very little sense to even try and increase usage. Think about categories such as toothpaste or cold remedies. We would need to encourage brush-ing more, or hope for the target to have more colds.

The bulk of any brand franchise, and where to look for increasing brand usage, is among what Rossiter and Percy called favourable brand-switchers, those who buy our brand, but also buy others as well. Here awareness should be strong, but it must be *maintained* because if the salience for the brand slips, the greater will be the likelihood those other brands will be purchased. Understanding this group's attitude toward the brand is import-ant in order to help the manager assess the extent to which these switchers (or some seg-ment of them) have the potential for increasing their purchase of the brand, and perhaps becoming brand loyals. It will also be important for the manager to understand the extent to which their sustaining behaviour is driven by incentive promotions.

When considering a trial strategy for increasing business, the manager must first know what the awareness and brand attitudes are among non-users. Other-brand-switchers' behaviour, those who switch among brands but do not include our brand, argues well for considering them when looking to add new users because they already switch among several brands. But what if they are not aware of our brand; or hold neutral or even nega-tive attitudes toward our brand; or see the brand as too expensive? Any of these awareness or attitude states would effect the potential cost of persuading them to try the brand. The manager must understand the level of awareness and brand attitude among potential triers in developing the communication strategy and its cost.

Those loyal to a competitive brand will have the least potential as new triers because of the strong positive attitude they hold for that brand. As discussed above, this will tend to 'immunize' them to our advertising and promotion. On the other hand, suppose those

Table 6.1 Awareness and Attitude Considerations for Potential Target Audience Buyer Groups

Buyer Group	Awareness and Attitude Considerations
Users	
Brand loyals	• Highest awareness • Most positive brand attitude, likely to immunize against competitive message
Favourable brand-switchers	• Awareness should be high, but must be measured • Positive brand attitude, but only moderate preference
Non-users	
Other brand switchers	• May or may not be aware • Attitude likely to be neutral or positive
Other brand loyals	• May or may not be aware • Strong positive attitude for loyal brand likely will immunize against our message
New category users	• Both brand awareness and attitude less important than *category* awareness and attitude

attitudes are not strongly held? Suppose they are not aware of our brand, and only consider the brand they are 'loyal' to as the best of the available alternatives? As we shall see in the next section, brand loyalty as measured behaviourally, without an understanding of brand attitude, will not paint the whole picture.

Those potential triers with no experience, or no recent experience in the category, the group Rossiter and Percy described as new category users, may or may not offer potential for a brand. The key here is not so much brand awareness and attitude, but *category* awareness and attitude. Both must be strong to consider this group as part of the target audience when trial is an objective. There are reasons these people have not been using products in the category, and the manager must understand those reasons before deciding if they offer any potential.

In earlier chapters we talked about the importance of brand awareness and brand attitude to effective marketing communication strategy. Here we have seen that it is also an important component of target audience selection. Both help identify and define brand loyalty, especially brand attitude, *and* attitude toward the category (see Table 6.1). In the next section we take a closer look at this relationship between a person's attitudes and their loyalty to a brand.

Loyalty in Target Audience Selection

In recent years the notion of loyalty has become a big issue in marketing. When thinking about brand loyalty, it is important to understand the *degree* of loyalty, both to our brand and to competitors. As we have been discussing it, loyalty refers to a tendency to purchase a brand based upon awareness of it and some level of preference based upon the consumer's attitude toward the brand. Being loyal to a brand does not necessarily mean buying only one brand. It means buying the brand or brands one *prefers*.[5] Many brand loyals do prefer to buy a single brand in a category; but others may be loyal to two or three brands. This does not make them 'switchers' in the way in which we have discussed them. Brand loyals have strong preferences for the brand or brands they buy in a category while switchers only have moderate preferences for the brands they switch among. Again, it is a matter of attitude.

A number of models have been proposed that seek to identify 'loyal' consumers. Perhaps the most familiar is the so-called 'conversion model'.[6] This model looks at consumer attitudes towards brands in a category as well as their involvement with the category. It analyses consumer attitudes on four key dimensions: interest in competitive alternatives, overall satisfaction, category involvement, and intensity or ambivalence. On the basis of a 'black-box' analysis,[7] consumers are assigned to one of four groups based upon their 'vulnerability' to switching brands: the more vulnerable, the less loyal.

We would like to introduce our own loyalty 'model' based upon how involved a person is with the category and how satisfied he or she is with a current brand. As discussed briefly in Chapter 1, involvement is a key dimension for defining brand attitude strategy for advertising and promotion. It is also a key dimension in determining brand loyalty. How much 'risk' does a consumer see in switching brands? Obviously, for most fmcgs there will be very little perceived risk in switching brands. But for more durable goods and for purchases and services such as banking and healthcare, there can be a good deal of perceived risk. If the perceived risk in switching is low, people *may* be open to switching brands; if the perceived risk is high, even if people are open to the idea of switching, it may be seen as too much trouble. If consumers are very satisfied with the brand they use, they will be less likely to switch; if they are unsatisfied, they will be more open to switch.

If we combine these two dimensions of perceived risk in switching and satisfaction, we can look at the target market in terms of four loyalty-related potential target audience groupings (see Fig. 6.1). The four loyalty groupings are defined as:

- *loyal*: highly satisfied with their brand and unlikely to switch;
- *vulnerable*: satisfied with their brand, but little perceived risk in switching;
- *frustrated*: not satisfied with their brand, but feel the risk is greater than the potential gain in switching;
- *switchable*: neither satisfied with their brand nor inhibited from switching.

This model offers more than simply looking at brand purchase behaviours, in that people who regularly buy a brand may be loyal *or* frustrated. If they are frustrated, the manager must find out why and address the problem in order to retain them as customers and build brand equity. On the other side, someone who regularly buys a competitor's brand may also be either loyal or frustrated. Those who are frustrated obviously offer more potential for trying our brand if we can overcome the perceived risk in switching. Looking at consumers who buy more than one brand in a category (for example, Rossiter and Percy's

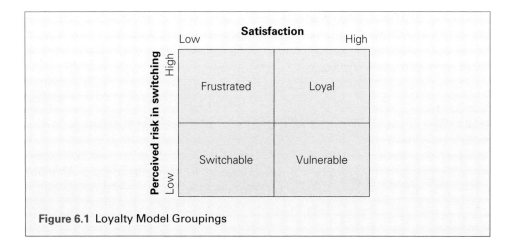

Figure 6.1 Loyalty Model Groupings

favourable brand-switchers and other-brand-switchers), we see that they can be either switchable *or* vulnerable. Those who buy our brand along with others in the category may or may not be satisfied with our brand. They may see *all* brands as merely adequate, and be open to something better. For our switchable customers it will be necessary to build a more positive brand attitude; for our vulnerable customers, we will want to reinforce the already favourable brand attitude, strengthening brand equity to reduce the likelihood of their using other brands. Switchable competitive brand users should be open to trying our brand, given the right message. They already use more than one brand, but are not particularly happy with any of them. Our competitors' vulnerables, on the other hand, will be a tougher sell. They do use multiple brands, but are generally satisfied with them. To attract these switchers we must convince them they should also be using our brand.

It might help at this point to think about this idea of brand loyalty with regard to some of your own brand purchase behaviour. Think about some of the things you buy. Do you regularly use the same brand of toothpaste or shampoo? What about candy or snacks? If you do, how open would you be to trying other brands? For most people, they *really* like only a few brands they use, and are not likely to try others in those categories even with a substantial promotional inducement. In fact, for personal use products such as toothpaste and shampoo about 40 to 50 per cent of all customers are loyal to a single brand.[8] Those are the brands that have what is known as strong *brand equity* for those consumers. But the vast majority of brands people use are bought more out of habit than from a strong commitment to the brand.[9] This is why it is so important to look beyond brand purchase behaviour and also to determine the degree of loyalty to a brand.

Cost Implications in Selecting a Target Audience

When the manager selects a specific target audience, it is not enough simply to look at the projected market share or revenue potential. Equally important is the *cost* of gaining these new customers (a trial objective) or of increasing usage (a repeat purchase objective).[10] If the objective is to gain new users for a brand, the cost will be greater than protecting or building on current business. The cost of attracting potential users who are not new to the category will be substantial, but going after regular users of a competitor brand will be even more expensive.

In selecting a target audience, a manager must be consistent with the marketing plan, but he or she must also approach selection with an eye on the return on investment (ROI). Next, we discuss the cost implications of selecting a target audience on the basis of brand loyalty.

Cost Implications and Brand Loyalty

Except in very rare circumstances, you should consider a prospective group as a target audience only if the expected return outweighs the cost. The manager must give this matter careful attention. At a very basic level, it will cost less to maintain your business than to build on it, and to build on it than to attract new business. In selecting the target audience to satisfy the marketing objective for the brand, the manager must consider the *value* of successfully reaching the appropriate target audience group. What is the potential increase in business relative to the cost of the advertising and promotion required to secure it? We will now consider the relative cost effectiveness of the brand loyalty groups following from our model for existing and potential customers.

Loyal

Our brand's loyal customers are relatively inexpensive to maintain at their current level of use. They are quite satisfied with our brand and are not interested in switching. All we really must do is remind them of their positive attitude towards the brand, reinforcing brand equity. But if we want to *increase* their usage, that could be expensive because it means changing an already established and satisfactory behaviour pattern.

Those loyal to other brands are for all practical purposes beyond the reach of a competitor brand, ours included. They are not disposed to switching brands, and, even if they were, the perceived risk is too great. What could we offer? If we literally gave the product away, assuming they would even try it, the likelihood that they would then go on and actually purchase our brand is very low. They simply do not have a sufficiently positive motivation to try our brand. On the other hand, if our brand has a significant *demonstrable* difference such that an immediate positive brand attitude would result from trying it, perhaps it would be worth the cost of giving the product away in a large-scale sampling promotion. But the price would be high, and would need to be carefully looked at in terms of ROI. Generally speaking, this could be a consideration only for fmcgs. Higher-priced products and those with longer purchase cycles would present too high a cost *and* risk.

Vulnerable

Our brand's vulnerable customers have a generally positive brand attitude, but do not see us as necessarily better than some other brands in the category. Maintaining this positive brand attitude is relatively inexpensive, but to retain or increase their usage of our brand will cost more because of the pressure of competing messages and promotions from other brands. Remember, they see no risk in switching even though they are happy with our brand.

Vulnerable competitor brand users who do not include our brand among those they buy, because they are generally satisfied with the brands they are currently using, will tend to be somewhat costly to attract. What keeps them from being very costly is their disposition to switch among different brands in the category. Unless they have tried and rejected our brand, in which case they will be very costly to reach, the cost of addressing the vulnerable competitor brand users relative to our own vulnerable users should only be moderately higher. We need to build a positive brand attitude in their mind for our brand, and provide an incentive for trial.

Frustrated

Because our frustrated users are not satisfied with our brand, even though they regularly use it, maintaining their current level of usage should be relatively inexpensive since they are reluctant to switch (for whatever perceived risk). But our goal should be to build a more positive brand attitude to increase brand equity and satisfaction. This will be more costly. Frustrated competitor brand users are not happy with the brand they regularly use, but because they perceive some risk in switching, it will be somewhat expensive to get them to overcome this sense of risk. Either marketing or advertising and promotion should be aimed as much at the barriers to switching as at building a positive attitude towards our brand.

Switchable

Our own switchable customers will be somewhat expensive to deal with as a potential target audience. Even though they are currently using our brand, they are not particularly satisfied with it, and they are already using other brands as well. This means they will be receptive to effective advertising and promotion for other brands, especially those they already use. This makes our task that much more difficult. A considerable effort must be made to build a more positive brand attitude (as with our frustrated users). It will cost even more if we want to increase their usage of our brand.

The cost of attracting competitor brand switchables should be roughly the same as reaching our own, assuming they have not tried and rejected us. While they do not now buy our brand, they are not particularly happy with the ones they do use; and they are disposed to using multiple brands. In both cases it will be necessary to build a more positive attitude in their minds for our brand.

These cost implications associated with selecting target audiences based upon brand loyalty are summarized in Table 6.2. While we believe that brand loyalty is the best way of looking at target audience optimization, we also understand that there are certain practical limitations. Unlike brand buyer groups, where there is plenty of syndicated research available tying brand behaviour to media behaviour (for example, the Target Group Index (TGI)[11]), brand loyalty groups must be determined through basic research conducted by the company. However, the increased effectiveness of the concept of brand loyalty groups over that of brand buyer groups is worth this extra effort.

Table 6.2 Relative Cost Associated with Brand Loyalty Target Audience Selection

Loyalty Grouping	Cost to Protect or Build Users	Cost to Attract Non-users
Loyal	Low	Very high
Vulnerable	Low-moderate	Moderate-high
Frustrated	Moderate	Moderate
Switchable	Moderate-high	Moderate-high

Profiling a Target Audience

Whether you are dealing with brand loyalty groupings or brand buyer groupings, it is usually helpful to have a more detailed understanding of the target audience selected. This means looking at your target audience in terms of those characteristics that Antonides and van Raaij describe as 'general-level' characteristics.[12] They consider general-level characteristics as more or less permanent characteristics of people, and classify them as either objective or subjective. *Objective characteristics* are things like age, education, income, and place of residence—what are known as demographics and geographics. *Subjective characteristics* are things like lifestyle, personality, and values—what are known as psychographics. Next we shall take a closer look at these general-level characteristics.

Demographics

Demographics are perhaps the best known and most familiar of all target audience descriptions. Because they are objective characteristics, they are not only easy to identify, but conceptually it is quite easy to think about them. If you market laundry soap powder, it is only natural to think in terms of women, especially women with families, as your target audience. But this does *not* describe a target *audience*. Are you really interested in all women with families? Hardly, since some are loyal to other brands, and others use liquid laundry detergents. It is certainly true that some products or services suggest a very specific demographic group as a target. Toys are for families with young children, baby products for mothers with infants, retirement services for older adults, and Ferraris for people with high incomes. The advert shown in Plate V for Senior Railcard from National Rail offers a good example of an advert specifically targeted to a particular target market segment, in this case those 60 or older. The imagery suggests travel, and the benefit is simple and clear: save money on rail travel. The benefit of saving '1/3 on most Standard and First Class rail fares throughout Britain' should be particularly attractive to this target segment.

But these are demographic characteristics that define a *target market*, not a target audience. This is a very important distinction. It may make sense to define a target market in terms of particular demographic characteristics, but then, *within* that demographic, we must select the target audience in terms of brand loyalty or brand buyer groupings.

Once the target audience has been selected, additional demographics (or geographic or psychographic characteristics) may be looked at in order further to refine the target audience for a particular campaign. Cosmetics may be targeted at women (the target market), but, once the appropriate brand loyalty or brand buyer groupings are used to select the target audience, it would not be unusual for a particular campaign to target younger or older women—not all younger or older women, but younger or older women within the appropriate brand loyalty or brand buyer groupings.

One of the major reasons demographics are inappropriate as primary criteria for selecting a target audience is the large amount of individual variation that can exist within a particular demographic. For example, one of the most popular misuses of demographics is with socio-economic classification. This is an attempt to group individuals in terms of their supposed 'social class', related to occupation and education or income. Antonides and van Raaij have defined social class as a 'summary of people's ranking in society with respect to profession and education'.[13] But there are potential pitfalls with such a classification.

Perhaps the most fundamental error is the assumption that all members of a particular class behave in the same way and hold the same basic attitudes about a product or service they use. This is rarely, if ever, the case. In a very interesting study conducted by Nestlé, a group of upper-middle-class shoppers, all with substantial six-figure incomes, were questioned about their use of higher-priced frozen foods. All used frozen foods, but some refused to consider the somewhat more expensive brands. When asked why, they answered that they couldn't afford to *indulge* themselves because of large, pressing expenses such as school fees or dental braces for children. When it was pointed out that the actual difference in price was very small, and in terms of the frozen food they bought would amount to no more than a Euro/dollar or two per month, this simply did not matter. They could easily afford the money. But because of the 'luxury' image of these higher-priced frozen foods, this group of wealthy people felt they could not 'indulge' themselves, even though they could well afford it.

At an even more fundamental level, demographics can be misleading when used to profile a target audience. Someone with a high income may have a lot of expenses, while a retired couple with a lower income may nevertheless have significant disposable income. Age, in many ways, is less a matter of actual years than a state of mind. As Robert East has stated so well, 'demographic factors are only loosely connected to the attitudes, beliefs and opportunities that more directly control behaviour'.[14]

Demographics can be useful, but the manager must be very careful how they are used. They should *never* be used as the primary selection criteria for a target audience, but they can often prove helpful in profiling the brand loyalty or brand buyer groupings for particular campaigns.

Geographics

It is always important to understand the geographics of your target audience. But, as we noted with demographics, this is generally a part of the *target market* descriptions. Are we looking at a multi-country marketing programme, or a programme restricted to a particular country or small group of countries, or are we dealing with a regional or local product or service? Geographics can clearly help define the target market, but they can also be useful in better defining a target audience. Because of regional preferences or attitudes (more about this when we discuss culture below), campaigns may be targeted for particular geographic areas. If so, this becomes part of the target audience definition for that campaign. Geographics, then, can help define a target market area, and can be used (if needed) to help narrow down the *location* of the target audience as defined by brand loyalty or brand buyer groupings. But, just as we saw with demographics, they should *never* be used as primary selection criteria for a target audience. Do we really think that just because people live in a certain area they hold identical attitudes towards, and preferences for, particular products or brands? Of course not. Unfortunately, this is the underlying assumption of something called 'geodemographics'.

Geodemographics

By combining geographic information with demographic information, markets can be described in terms of geodemographics. One of the best-known geodemographic systems in Europe is offered by Acorn (which is an acronym of A Classification Of Residential Neighbourhoods).[15] Acorn classifies residential neighbourhoods on the basis of postal codes, with certain demographics (usually income or social class) in common.

The assumption here is that people who live in a particular neighbourhood will have similar buyer behaviour patterns. While Acorn does include demographic profiles in its database, this underlying assumption is wrong. There is simply no reason to believe that people living in similar neighbourhoods are going to be loyal to the same brands, or will be more or less vulnerable or frustrated in a particular product category.

What has made geodemographic systems like Acorn (and other systems such as Mosaic and Pinpoint) so popular is that they make it very easy to target direct mail on the basis of postal codes. But the manager must ask, just what is being targeted? Once a target audience has been defined in terms of brand loyalty or brand buyer groups, *if* a correlation is found between the target audience and geodemographic classifications, fine. However, geodemographics should never be the sole or even primary criterion for selecting a target audience.

Psychographics

The word 'psychographics' first entered the vocabulary of advertising in the late 1950s following the introduction of a new technique for studying consumer behaviour called *motivational research*. The father of this technique was a psychologist, Ernest Dichter. The idea behind motivational research was to conduct a number of in-depth personal interviews with consumers in order to discover why they behave as they do in the market. Dichter suggested from one of his studies, for example, that men buy convertibles as a surrogate mistress, reflecting the sublimated desire of the purchaser for the lifestyle of a roué.[16] You can see why creative people in advertising loved this sort of thing.

In the twenty-first century psychographic or lifestyle variables, while still used as a subjective classification, reflect a broad assessment of non-product-related characteristics that could influence purchase- or usage-related behaviour. Psychographics give you a picture of a person's lifestyle by looking at such things as his or her general attitudes, interests, and opinions (often referred to as AIO). Some general examples of psychographics would be someone's attitude towards sports or fitness, willingness to take risks, traditional versus modern taste, concern with the environment, political opinions, concern with fashion, and innovativeness.

You can see how knowing such things about a target audience would help in better understanding them, but, as with the more objective demographic and geographic characteristics, they cannot define the target audience. The primary use of psychographic information is in helping to guide creative development of the message, and possibly in helping to select specific media vehicles that reflect a particular lifestyle.

One UK advert for a Ford Explorer (Advert 6.1) clearly reflects a 'lifestyle' dimension. It depicts a young, upscale family that enjoys spending time outdoors. But the fact that a Ford Explorer 'fits' this lifestyle does not mean that this lifestyle should define the target audience. There are many people who enjoy an outdoor lifestyle yet have no interest in a sports utility vehicle (that is, they are not in the category), or, if they are interested, may be interested in a different size (for example, the Mercedes M-Class) or have a loyalty to another brand (for example, a Land Rover). So, while lifestyle can help target a *message*, as is well illustrated in the Ford Explorer advert, the message must be for those *within* the appropriate brand loyalty or brand buyer grouping who have that lifestyle.

Advert 6.1 An example of how an advert can reflect the lifestyle of its target audience, increasing the likelihood of its being processed. Reproduced with kind permission © Ford Motor Co.

Another difficulty with trying to classify people in terms of lifestyle is that it is generally not stable across product categories. At a very general level there tends to be some commonality, but not at the specific level. For example, someone who has a keen interest in outdoor activities may not be interested in some specific outdoor activity.

Social Class

Back in our discussion of demographics we spent some time talking about social class. Practically speaking, it is a demographic variable, but many marketers also consider it a lifestyle variable. As Rossiter and Percy have put it, although social class is measured by *combining demographics*, it functions as a *lifestyle* variable.[17] The assumption is that people in different social classes are likely to have different lifestyles. One of the more popular European classifications of social class is provided by the Joint Industry Committee for National Readership Surveys. It classifies people into six groups: (A) Upper Middle Class, (B) Middle Class, (C1) Lower Middle Class, (C2) Skilled Working Class, (D) Working Class, and (E) those at the lowest levels of subsistence.

Even though Antonides and van Raaij feel that social class is an important determinant of consumer behaviour,[18] as we pointed out in our earlier discussion, and while there may be a certain *implied* relationship between social class and consumer behaviour, it is more likely to be at the target market, not target audience, level. We may be targeting the upper middle class or middle class for designer clothing, but for our brand marketing communication strategy we must understand the appropriate brand loyalty or brand buyer groupings from the social classes in order to pinpoint the target audience. As Fill has reminded us, relying upon social class can be misleading and prone to excessive generalization.[19]

Values

Another popular lifestyle measure is centred around 'values'. But again, assuming we can find a good summary measure of someone's values, while this may be useful in profiling a target audience or in trying to explain behaviour at a general level, it has more utility in the development of creative *execution* than it does for communication strategy. There are a number of value classification systems used by advertisers, but we would recommend *extreme* caution with all of them.

Perhaps the best-known such value system is VALS, introduced in the late 1970s (VALS-1) and revised in the late 1980s (VALS-2) by SRI International in the USA. VALS-2 classifies people into eight groups based upon two dimensions: 'resources' (things like education, skills, and income) and 'self-orientation'. The names of the eight resulting groups are meant to suggest the 'most important value' to that group: Strugglers, Believers, Fulfilleds, Strivers, Achievers, Makers, Experiencers, and Actualizers. Of course, rather detailed descriptions are available for each of these groups.[20]

One of the many problems with VALS has been its inability to be applied across countries—not just, say, between the USA and Thailand, but between more homogeneous-seeming countries in Europe such as Sweden and Germany. Another problem stems from the fact that a person can belong to only one group. This is always a problem with any rigid system that aims at too much generality.

Another values system is marketed by Synergy Brand Values in the UK and Europe. Their system is based upon Maslow's hierarchy of needs. It utilizes the dimensions of 'inner-directed', 'outer-directed', and 'sustenance-driven' to classify people into seven groups: Self-explorers, Experimentalists, Conspicuous Consumers, Belongers, Survivors, Social Resisters, and the Aimless. These groups vary in size from the Aimless at 6 per cent of the population to Survivors at 23 per cent.

These social value groups, however, have the same problems as those discussed above for VALS, as well as the fact that they are based upon Maslow's work. We are in agreement with the many authors cited by Landy[21] who feel that Maslow's theory is of more historical than functional value, and conclude that there is really no evidence to support the high regard in which his theory seems to be held by many marketers.

Culture

Another important lifestyle characteristic is culture, a subject covered in some detail in Chapter 3. We have chosen to consider culture as a lifestyle variable rather than a demographic or geographic variable because the idea of 'culture' is not necessarily fixed. To say that someone is from England or France or Germany is not the same thing as saying he or she is English, French, or German. Antonides and van Raaij have defined culture as 'the entirety of societal knowledge, norms and values', very much as they define lifestyle as 'the entire set of values, interests, opinions and behaviour of consumers'.[22]

Culture is clearly related to how people behave, and for that reason is an important target audience profile variable. But additionally, in Europe as elsewhere in the world, how people look at or understand advertising messages is heavily influenced by their culture. In fact, as de Mooij has pointed out, the advertising 'style' of different European countries clearly reflects the cultural values of that country (see Table 6.3). There seems little doubt that culture conditions perceptions, and this influences how people respond to advertising.[23] A cultural assessment of your target audience provides a very important profile variable, and is essential for multi-country or global advertising.

Personality

Personality is definitely not something ever to consider as a primary characteristic by which to select a target audience—and personality characteristics do not help determine a target market. Then why consider personality as a profile variable? Its importance as a target audience profile variable comes from the effect that personality characteristics have on how advertising and promotion messages are *processed*. This is especially true of the *verbal content* of marketing communication.

Generally, when we think of personality we are thinking about *personality traits*. These are the more or less permanent characteristics of personality that lead people to respond to life in a basically predictable fashion. In the psychological literature, of all the possible mediators of persuasion in communication, personality traits have probably been studied more than any other. But we must also be aware of *personality states*. As Rossiter and Percy have pointed out, a personality state is actually something of a contradiction, since personality is an *enduring* predisposition whereas a 'state' is only temporary.[24] Nevertheless,

Table 6.3 How European Advertising Style Reflects Cultural Values

Britain	• Reflects a highly individualistic society • Ads show individuals or couples (large groups are rare) • Much use of direct address • Strong focus on humour • Only European country where class differences are recognized in advertising
Germany	• Reflects the need for structure, directness, and facts • Characterized by the need for structure and explicit language to avoid ambiguity
Italy	• Reflects a collectivist culture • Drama and theatre, with strong role differentiation reflected in depiction of males and females
Spain	• Reflects collectivist culture, but takes into account individualistic claims • As a result, less direct than advertising style of Northern Europe • Use of visual metaphors
France	• Reflects a need to be different • A propensity for the theatrical and the bizarre • Sensual and erotic style
Netherlands	• Strongly reflects the levelling attitude induced by a feminine culture • Softer, more entertaining advertising • Hype is not appreciated, nor are pushy presenters
Sweden	• A very feminine culture • Men are shown doing the work in the home • Entertainment is frequently used, often within a context of disrespect for authority

Source: Adapted from Marieke de Mooij, *Global Marketing and Advertising: Understanding Cultural Paradoxes* (Thousand Oaks, Calif.: Sage, 1998). Reprinted by permission of Sage.

as we all know, in certain circumstances we may exhibit personality traits that are not usual for us—for example, undue anxiety during times of stress.

Personality Traits

We mentioned that personality traits are one of the most widely studied variables affecting persuasion in communication. Interestingly, the results of all these studies often produce quite opposite-seeming conclusions. These contradictions mean that you must be very careful when looking at personality traits and their probable effects on how a target audience will process advertising.[25] Three personality traits that particularly influence how advertising messages are processed are self-esteem, intelligence, and introversion/extroversion.

Self-esteem is perhaps the most widely studied personality trait, at least in relation to how susceptible someone might be to a persuasive message. It also illustrates how careful you must be when considering a personality trait in relation to marketing communication. When a message is *simple*, the higher someone's self-esteem, the less likely he or she is to be persuaded; the lower the self-esteem, the more likely. But when the message is more *complex* or specific, the higher someone's self-esteem, the *more* likely he or she is to be persuaded; and the lower the self-esteem, the less likely.

The difficulty, of course, is how to know if your target audience has high or low self-esteem. Once the appropriate brand loyalty or brand buyer groupings have identified your target audience, a random sample of the target could be given a brief personality inventory to complete. If it is found that they are more likely to have high (or low) self-esteem, your message execution should take that into account. Testing a sample of the target audience is actually the only way for a manager to determine if a personality trait should be considered as a target audience profile variable.

Intelligence is a highly relevant personality trait for advertising, again in terms of the target audience's ability to deal with the complexity of a message. It should make intuitive sense that a more intelligent person will be better able to deal with a complex message, and this is true. Additionally, especially for high-involvement advertising, a more intelligent person should require fewer repetitions to learn the message. Remember that we are talking about the personality trait of raw intelligence here, *not* a surrogate such as education. If the manager is concerned that intelligence could significantly affect the message delivery needed for the brand, perhaps because there is a complicated story to tell, a random sample of the target audience should be given an IQ test of some kind.

Something else to be considered here has been suggested by Rossiter and Percy. When advertising or other marketing communication is *written* in English (or the audio in radio or television is in English), people whose first language is not English should be thought of as 'less intelligent' as far as processing the message is concerned. It is not that they have lower IQs. They are simply not as competent in English as a native speaker. This means that English-language advertising running in continental Europe (or *any* other non-English-speaking country) should avoid complex messages, and the copy should be kept simple.[26]

Introversion/extroversion is one of the few personality traits that is in fact strongly correlated with actual behaviour and attitudes. For example, extroverts have been shown to like novelty and change, even while being realistic and practical in their attitudes. They are adventure seeking, more likely to use tobacco, and more likely to drink coffee and alcohol. Introverts, on the other hand, value privacy and close friendships, and tend to be anxious in social situations.[27]

You can see how knowledge of people as introverts or extroverts could make a difference in how you communicate with them. A number of English psychologists have done extensive work with introversion/extroversion, and the implications of this work offer some interesting insights on how we look at advertising (as pointed out by Rossiter and Percy[28]). Informational appeals (those addressing a negative purchase motive) should be more effective with introverts, while the more outgoing extrovert should be more responsive to appeals addressing positive motives like social approval.[29]

The population is roughly split in terms of whether introversion or extroversion is the dominant trait (with a slight edge to extroverts). But because of the more obvious attitudinal and behavioural associations of this personality trait, for many product categories there is a good likelihood of the target market or target audience being dominated by either introverts or extroverts. Again, a simple testing of a random sample of the target audience with a version of Eysenck's Introversion/Extroversion Scale can alert the manager to the possible relevancy of I/E as a target audience profile variable. The Eysenck scales have been found to be the most useful measure of I/E, and they have considerable equivalence across age groups and cultures.[30]

Personality States

We pointed out earlier that a personality state is really nothing more than a temporary activation of a personality characteristic that is not enduring for that individual. Since it actually operates like a trait when it is activated, we can think of it in much the same way. This means that it can have an important effect upon how the verbal content of communication is processed. As an example, let us look at *anxiety*, a personality characteristic that is often aroused by outside stimulation, acting on a personality state. If you are planning to drive to the French Alps for a skiing holiday and the day you leave the weather report forecasts heavy snow en route, this could very well raise your anxiety level. What is happening is that the anxiety state is 'warning' you to consider avoiding the storm because it is thought to be potentially threatening. This is really what anxiety is all about, a state that warns you to avoid a future situation.

How might anxiety as a personality state affect the processing of advertising? Anxiety can interfere with the likelihood or the length of time that people pay attention to your message; and, even if they do pay attention, anxiety can interfere with comprehension. If what you see or read in an advert raises your anxiety level, you simply tune it out, either actually by turning away or leaving the room, or mentally. This is something that often happens with some of the more gruesome public service advertising against drug and alcohol abuse. But it can also occur with insurance company or car tyre advertising that depicts bad accidents, or healthcare advertising showing realistic emergency treatment. We do not want to leave the impression that anxiety is always a problem. In fact, if the message makes you anxious, but you still pay attention, you are actually *more* likely to be persuaded. The trick is to make sure the creative execution does not go too far and raise anxiety so high that it interferes with attention. Unlike personality traits, a personality state cannot be measured with a series of scales unless the target audience has been aroused and is experiencing that state. Because advertising itself can occasion a personality state, it is important to pre-test your advertising. You want to be sure that a personality characteristic like anxiety does not arouse a state that will interfere with the processing of the message. On the other hand, you may hope to arouse a particular personality state, such as a warm, nurturing feeling. Pre-testing can help determine if the advertising is activating either desirable or undesirable personality states.

Unfortunately, it is difficult if not impossible to anticipate generally when a particular personality state is likely to be aroused in your target audience. In fact, the likelihood of a *common* personality state being present at one time among a significant portion of any target audience is negligible. While there are a few predictable situations that tend to

Just one trip and a Railcard could pay for itself.

(Imagine how much you could save in a year.)

60 or over? Buy a Senior Railcard for £20, and you'll save ¹/₃ on most Standard and First Class rail fares throughout Britain. So, if you make one journey normally costing £60, or a couple of shorter trips, you will have covered the cost of your card, just like that.

- New! Buy online at www.senior-railcard.co.uk
- Pick up a leaflet at your nearest staffed train station
- Or call 08457 48 49 50 for your local Train Company number

National Rail

Senior Railcard

Craik Jones
WATSON MITCHELL VOELKEL

APPROVED BY	INITIALS	SIGNATURE
Production		
Art Director		
Copywriter		
Client Service		

Plate V Senior Railcard

This advert for Senior Railcard provides a good example of an advert targeted to a specific target market segment. Advertisement supplied by the Association of Train Operating Companies.

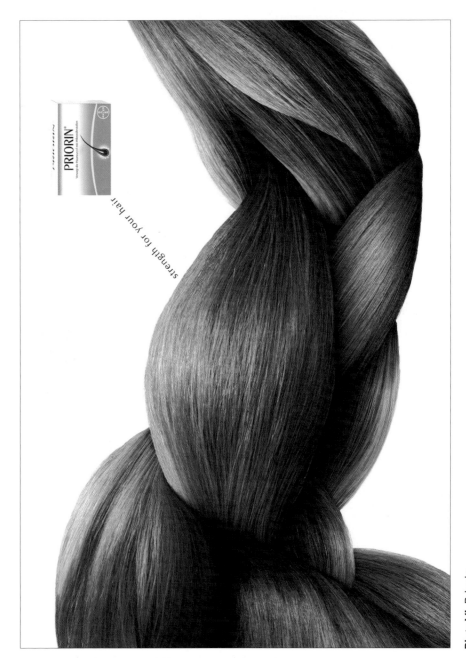

Plate VI Priorin

This advert for Priorin is a great example of a low involvement informational benefit delivered through the visual communicating in this case 'strength for your hair'. Reproduced with kind permission © Priorin / JWT.

Plate VII Surf™

An excellent example of a low involvement informational strategy where the benefit is presented in a humorous and extreme way. Reproduced with kind permission © Unilever UK. Surf is a registered trade mark.

Plate VIII Kinder Bueno

Here we have a good example of a low involvement, transformational strategy, where the emotional authenticity felt in the pleasure and contentment of the woman receiving a massage is nicely linked to the brand. Kinder Bueno 'A little bit of what you fancy' 2007 Press Campaign. Client: Ferrero; Agency: Audacity, London.

arouse some personality states (for example, when a target audience might be tired), the manager's concern should be with the potential of the advertising itself, along with the context within which it is delivered, to arouse a personality state.

Personality and its Relationship with Advertising

Figure 6.2 provides a simplified idea of how personality traits and states can affect or be affected by advertising and other marketing communication. People's prior experience and their attitudes will always affect how a message is processed, and we will spend a lot of time dealing with this in later chapters.

As we have seen, personality traits, because they are enduring characteristics, can influence how someone processes a message. For example, if people whose personality reflects a high level of nurturance (a personality trait that suggests a desire to look after and care for people) see an advertisement for a product positioned as helping you take better care of your family, their naturally high level of nurturance should mean they will pay more attention to the advertising and there will be a greater likelihood of them responding positively to the message.

Personality states, because they are temporary, can influence message processing in two ways. If some outside event has aroused a personality characteristic, this could influence how a message is processed at that time, or the message itself could arouse that state. Continuing with our nurturance example, while someone may not naturally exhibit a high degree of nurturance, we all occasionally experience it as a state. Think about how you feel when you see a baby, or even a puppy. Suppose you have just watched a particularly heart-warming programme on television and have a warm, contented feeling. This could certainly affect how you process any advertising within the programme or immediately after. On the other hand, a particularly 'warm and fuzzy' advertisement could itself stimulate a temporary warm feeling that could influence how you process the message. In order to account for the effects of personality in your target audience, it makes sense to test a sample of the brand loyalty or brand buyer groups selected as your target audience *if* you feel a particular personality trait might have either a positive or a negative effect upon how they process your message. Recall the examples we discussed in the section on personality traits. To address personality states, the manager must pay attention to the

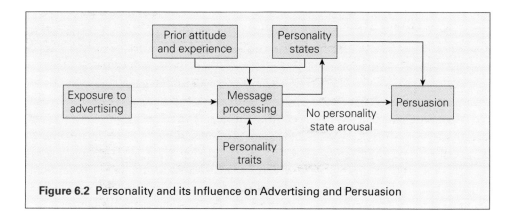

Figure 6.2 Personality and its Influence on Advertising and Persuasion

context where advertising or other marketing communication is likely to be seen—for example, in a situation comedy, on a bus poster, or at a sporting event. Additionally, if a personality characteristic could potentially be aroused by the message—for example, positively by a very 'warm and fuzzy' execution or negatively by a 'frightening' message— check for these effects when pre-testing the advertising.

Segmentation

This is a good place to talk about segmentation. Segmentation is a powerful tool for understanding a market and helping to optimize targeting, but we will not spend a great deal of time discussing it in this book. Why not, if it is so important? The reason is that the primary use of segmentation is in defining a target *market*, not a target audience. As noted earlier, this is an important distinction, and one not often made.

Any good marketing or consumer behaviour text will have a chapter on market segmentation (and it should). We like Fill's definition of market segmentation as 'the division of a mass market into distinct groups which have common characteristics, needs, and similar responses to marketing action'.[31] Although this definition is in a marketing communication text, it is in a chapter on *marketing strategy*. This is where market segmentation belongs, in discussions of marketing strategy.

Having said this, segmentation does have a place in better defining a target audience. When we talked about loyalty groups as the best way to select a target audience, we pointed out that this is because loyalty reflects the target market's *attitude* towards the category and its brands. Segmentation relevant to marketing communication must be based upon attitude. Attitudes bear directly upon communication strategy because it is attitude that determines how someone is likely to respond to a message, and how he or she behaves. It is easy to become confused because all the target audience variables we have just discussed can and are used as *market* segmentation variables. But, as we have continually pointed out, knowing that someone is young or old, lives in the country or the town, is outgoing, likes sports, or travels a lot is simply not good enough to identify a target audience. It may help you to understand the target audience better, but it will not define it. How segmentation should be used in the development of marketing and communication strategy is illustrated in Fig. 6.3. Traditional market segmentation looks at the entire market, using as a basis for segmentation any and all relevant variables. These could very well be demographics, geographics, or psychographics, what Rothschild has called 'enduring variables' that do not change across product categories, or they could be what he has called 'dynamic variables' such as usage or benefits.[32] It is of course also possible to use attitudes for market segmentation as well.

But once we have set our marketing strategy and selected the target market, we must then identify the target audience. Here the only correct segmentation variable is attitude.[33] We are looking for groups of people in the target market who hold relatively similar attitudes towards category usage and brands within the category. Our primary concern is to identify brand loyalty groups, but it is also important to know how the target market segments generally in terms of other relevant attitudes if we are to optimize communication strategy. Our target audience 'segments' have common attitudes in terms of their brand loyalty, but is what they are looking for, say, in terms of benefits the same?

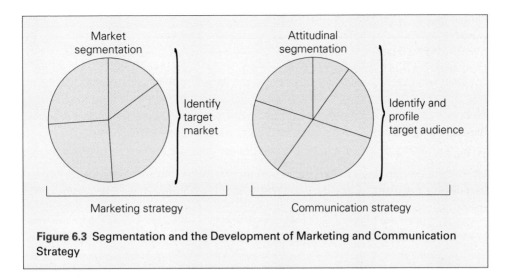

Figure 6.3 Segmentation and the Development of Marketing and Communication Strategy

This is why a communication-based and loyalty attitudinal segmentation is so desirable. Without it, the manager must select the target audience only in terms of brand buying behaviour. While it is easy to select a target audience in this way because brand purchase data is readily available (for example, from the TGI), to develop the most effective communication strategy and creative executions an understanding of our target audience's category and brand attitudes is essential. It is not enough simply to understand purchase behaviour.

The target audience, whether identified from brand loyalty or brand buyer groupings, is selected to satisfy the objectives of the marketing strategy. But to *communicate* effectively with the target audience, the manager must fully understand what fundamental attitude segments they reflect. This, along with appropriate demographic, geographic, and psychographic profile variables, enables the manager to put together an effective communication strategy, as well as helping in media selection.

Target Audience and Strategy

Once the target audience has been selected and profiled, it remains to link the target audience with the marketing strategy and that with the communication strategy. Indeed, the selection of the target market and then the target audience will have followed from the marketing objectives set out in the marketing plan. What we are more concerned with are the specifics of the *behavioural* objectives associated with the target audience that should result from our marketing communication, the target audience action we talked about in the communication response sequence. The selection of the target audience will have determined whether we are looking principally at customers or non-customers (or perhaps both), and this in turn will determine whether the target audience action objective is *trial* or *repeat purchase* or use.[34] All this should be spelled out in the marketing plan, but must now become a part of our strategic communication planning.

Target Audience Links to Marketing Strategy

The marketing objectives as detailed in the marketing plan will generally specify whether concentrating on new customers or on repeat business is to be the principal path for building or maintaining the brand. If a market is growing, the marketing manager is usually looking for new customers. In a more stable market, maintaining share or increasing business is more likely to come from current customers, or from both new and existing customers if the objective is to increase business. For example, with fmcg products about 60 per cent of sales growth comes from attracting new customers who continue to purchase, and 40 per cent from encouraging existing customers to buy more.[35] These marketing objectives clearly help specify the target audience at a macro-level—will it be primarily customers or non-customers?

We need to keep this in mind when planning our communication strategy. If the target audience is made up primarily of customers, the action objective will be repeat purchase or use; if the target audience is primarily non-customers, the action objective will be trial. This distinction will hold regardless of whether we are talking about a consumer, business, or trade target audience. Typical examples of trial and repeat purchase objectives linked to a marketing strategy are offered below.

Consumer target audience. The types of trial behaviour sought from consumers include such things as encouraging people to try a brand if it is an fmcg, or to take the first step towards considering higher-involvement, higher-risk purchases. This could be anything from making a phone call to request information to visiting a dealer. When the action objective is repeat purchase, we may be looking for our customers to continue purchasing at the same rate (especially those loyal to the brand), to increase the number of units they buy at a time, or to buy our product more often.

Business target audience. These same general action objectives apply to business-to-business marketing. When we are looking for new customers, the specific trial behaviours desired could include such things as enquiries about a new product, requests for a demonstration or feasibility study, or asking to see a sales rep. If we are looking to customers for repeat business, just as with consumers we may want them to maintain their current level of business, increase the number of units they buy at a time, or use our product more often.

Trade target audience. In addition to consumer and business markets, many companies must also market to their trade—the wholesalers or retailers that carry or distribute their products. If you are looking for new trade outlets, this corresponds to a trial action objective. If you are trying to get the trade to maintain premium shelf space or display, or to move more of your brand, this corresponds to a repeat purchase action objective.

Target Audience Links to Communication Strategy

The target audience links to marketing strategy address the fundamental distinction between customers and non-customers, and relate that distinction to the behavioural objectives of trial and repeat purchase. Now we must also consider this same distinction within the context of communication strategy for both advertising and promotions. As you might suppose, the communication strategy that drives trial will be different from that driving repeat purchase. In Chapter 9 we will see that coupons, refunds and rebates,

Table 6.4 Target Audience Action Objectives and Groupings

Target Audience Action Objectives	Brand Buyer Groupings	Corresponding Brand Loyalty Groupings
Non-users	NCU	None
Trial objective	OBL	L
	OBS	F/V/S
Users	BL	L
Repeat-purchase objective	BS	F/V/S

NCU: New category users; OBL: Other brand loyals; OBS: Other-brand-switchers; BL: Brand loyals; BS: Brand-switchers; L: Loyal; F: Frustrated; V: Vulnerable; S: Switchable.

and sampling work best for trial while loyalty and loading devices, sweepstakes, games and contests, and premiums work best for repeat purchase objectives.

While a target audience based only upon brand buyer groupings already accounts for the distinction between customers and non-customers, brand loyalty groups do not. Both brand users and non-users (with the exception of those not category users at present) can fall within one of the four brand loyalty groupings, and the target audience action objective will vary accordingly. This distinction is summarized in Table 6.4.

Throughout this chapter we have been underscoring the importance of *attitude* in selecting and understanding the target audience. Brand loyalty groupings, and at heart even brand buyer groupings, result from an individual's attitude towards the category and its brands. We have pointed out several times that brand attitude (along with brand awareness) is *always* a communication objective. It should be no surprise that the attitude of the target audience towards the brands in the category will be instrumental in formulating the overall communication strategy.

At a very basic level, we can see how the attitudes towards a brand that underlie the brand loyalty groupings will influence strategy. When loyals are part of a target audience, it will be essential at least to maintain their already high positive brand attitude. Frustrated and switchable consumers, because of their lower satisfaction with a brand, will require the building of a more favourable brand attitude. Vulnerables, even though they are generally satisfied with a brand, need to have their brand attitude strengthened, because there are no real barriers to switching.

Practically, however, we must deal with brand loyalty groups for both customers and non-customers. Obviously, those loyal to our brand must be treated differently from those loyal to competitor brands. While the general brand attitudes will hold for our customers in the target audience, when the target audience includes non-customers as well, the attitudinal assumptions will be different. It is unlikely that those loyal to a competitive brand will be in our target audience, but, if they are, it will be necessary to modify their brand attitude, changing it if negative. For frustrated non-customers, we need to increase positive attitudes towards our brand (they are currently unsatisfied with the brands they are using), but also to address their barriers to switching. With switchable non-customers, it will be important to build or increase positive brand attitude, while for the vulnerable we must modify their attitudes, or change them if negative.

CHAPTER SUMMARY

In this chapter we have explored in depth issues concerning decisions relating to the target audience. We have emphasized the key importance of considering aspects of brand loyalty and have introduced a model that focuses on the role of perceived risk and levels of satisfaction to yield four loyalty groups: loyal, vulnerable, frustrated, and switchable. We have explained how these loyalty groupings can be used to optimize target audiences. We have discussed the problems with simple demographic segmentation approaches and suggested that the only correct segmentation variable is attitude.

QUESTIONS TO CONSIDER

6.1   What is the best way to select a target audience?

6.2   In what way should brand loyalty play a part in target audience selection?

6.3   How would you distinguish between a target market and a target audience?

6.4   Why should demographic factors never be used as the primary criteria in target audience selection?

6.5   How should the manager use audience characteristics such as demographics, psychographics, or lifestyle when considering a target audience?

6.6   Why is it important to distinguish between customers and non-customers when planning communication strategy?

CASE STUDY 6

Eurostar—How Mr JetSet Made Eurostar Mean Business

Eurostar was launched in 1994. It is a unique rail product, which connects the UK with France and Belgium. Following a period of steady growth between 1994 and 2000, Eurostar declined in terms of volume and revenue. The reasons for this decline included increasing consumer demand for choice of destination, the rise of low-cost airlines, the effects of terrorism and war, and some Eurostar-specific issues such as bad weather, strikes, and an ageing product.

   The successful relaunch of Eurostar in the UK in 2003 was built on significant product improvement and the 'Fly Eurostar' marketing campaign. Significant volume and revenue growth was achieved by converting travellers from planes to Eurostar and by growing the leisure market. 'Fly Eurostar' provided a good platform for the leisure market. But while leisure travel is largely discretionary and so can be stimulated, business travel is not, resulting in a relatively static business market on those routes. The relatively low business market share of Eurostar in the UK on both routes suggested significant room for improvement. With the average business ticket worth four times a leisure ticket, growth in the business share would be highly profitable. This, and the rather different nature of business travel choices, led to the development of a dedicated campaign to convert more business travellers to Eurostar.

The short-haul business travel market London–Paris and London–Brussels is characterized by ferocious competition. Eurostar faced low-price pressure from low-cost airlines on one hand. On the other hand, it faced BA, a trusted and respected brand with a strong heritage in business, with an adspend of £26.8 million in 2003 on business travellers. In addition to competition, Eurostar needed to deal with the influence of Travel Management Companies (TMCs), which provide holistic travel solutions for the majority of UK companies. In 2003 54 per cent of all Eurostar business ticket sales were distributed through TMCs. Other critical factors included the reduced short-haul business class travel following the New York World Trade Centre attack of 2001 and strong incentives to stay loyal to existing modes of transport (Frequent Flyer Programmes).

To improve Eurostar's competitiveness, the business fare structure had been fundamentally altered in 2003 to increase accessibility for and appeal to the business audience; punctuality had risen dramatically to record levels; the journey time (less than 2 hours 40 mins) had been seen as competitive with airlines. After the relaunch and the 'Fly Eurostar' campaign, business volumes and revenues were already rising. Eurostar now enjoyed parity with or rational advantage over its rivals on convenience, lack of hassle, flexibility, and best use of time.

Despite all this, market analysis and qualitative research indicated that there remained a significant core of stubborn business travellers for whom flying to Paris or Brussels remained an integral part of their business regime. While those more naturally predisposed to Eurostar were switching, there remained significant barriers for others.

There was evidence of a much lower emotional connection with Eurostar than with airline travel among flyers.

'In business travel [Eurostar] is seen as basic and functional.'

Source: Hall & Partners Qualitative Pricing Research

Long-haul business creates a powerful 'halo' effect.

*'[Business travellers] tend to judge Eurostar negatively against their best
long-haul experiences . . .—limo, massages, fast-track, loyalty schemes, business
lounge for networking.'*

Source: Hall & Partners Europe Brand Proposition Research

In-depth individual qualitative interviews were conducted among two key audiences: Eurostar converts/loyalists and frequent flyers. The interviews with the Eurostar converts and loyalists found that they were less prone to self-identity as 'business people', preferring to see themselves as people who travelled for business. They endorsed the view that Eurostar offered them the option to work while they travelled and allowed their real self (not a stressed business person) to emerge at the point of departure. However, some frequent flyers believed that flying proved how successful they had become in business. For them it was a badge of status. They therefore rejected making the same journey by train even though it would have enabled them to be more productive or even enjoy their journey. The critical insight was the dissonance between perception of status and reality of experience for the business flyer. Communications would have to highlight this and contrast it with the positive benefits of Eurostar if it was to win them over. Once the emotional barrier to switching had been overcome, the Eurostar experience would do the rest and convert usage into loyalty.

Business travel advertising as a category is characterized by an overwhelming number of conventional stereotypes and familiar clichés. It was decided that the most effective route would be to break with these conventions and confront the business flyer's state of denial head on. The creative route was an illustrated comic character called Mr JetSet: the embodiment of a stereotypical businessman for whom travel to Paris or Brussels always equals flying—the ultimate in status. Armed with his catchphrase 'I came by plane you know', he is willing to sacrifice comfort and productivity just to stick to what he knows. The use of a cartoon character was a bold, disruptive approach but ideal to achieve cut-through on a limited budget. The humour enabled Eurostar to communicate a few 'home truths' to the ingrained flyer without alienating them or making them feel defensive. The campaign worked by 'de-positioning' flying in an engaging and relevant way. There were two phases to the campaign. The first was the self-explanatory 'Introduction to Mr JetSet'; the second was entitled 'Stupidity and Solution', where the emotional and rational benefits of Eurostar were introduced. Total spend on the Mr JetSet campaign between 10 September 2004 and 23 March 2005 was £1.36m.

The overall Eurostar picture—leisure + business—delivered increased sales volume during the campaign period between September 2004 and March 2005. As intended by the Mr JetSet campaign, the sales volume of the Eurostar 'business' volume showed sharp growth. The incremental net revenue to Eurostar was £5.7m in the campaign period alone. Moreover, the combined incremental net revenue in business travel to Eurostar during the campaign period and the following three-month expected 'lag' period is £10.3m. Together with leisure travel, total incremental net revenue to Eurostar during the campaign period and 'lag' period from business and leisure tickets is £11.2m. This data only shows the period up to June 2005. Given the long carryover effects, the campaign will continue to deliver revenue for a much longer period. A rough estimate of the overall payback of Mr JetSet on the Paris route for business tickets alone will be £21.2m, after subtracting the campaign media and production spend, £1.4m, and the cost of handling additional passengers. If the Brussels route is included, which accounts for 30 per cent of total business revenues for Eurostar, the estimate is £27.6m.

Impact on the business traveller from the campaign was obvious not just on the sale values, but on the awareness of Eurostar and its campaign. The effect among the core business flyers whose behaviour and attitudes were specifically targeted by the campaign was significant. By March 2005 all key measures of brand consideration and advocacy had increased. The campaign was appreciated by both business people and other key audience, including TMCs and business travel agencies.

> 'It made Eurostar look like a serious and simple alternative without using the same storylines of the airline adverts.'

Business Development Manager—The Walt Disney Company Ltd

> 'Great campaign, different to any I had seen before in business travel and a refreshing change from the usual corporate "stiff collar" advertising in our sector.'

Marketing Manager—Fleet Street Travel

Yet Mr JetSet achieved far more than a financial return. Critical objectives of brand health and share growth were also delivered. Core business flyers have been challenged to reconsider their ingrained habits and there is evidence of a change in attitudes. Eurostar had the confidence in its ability to attract business flyers. Mr JetSet—the most unlikely of anti-heroes—has made Eurostar mean business.

Source: WARC, IPA Effectiveness Awards 2006, Eurostar—How Mr JetSet Made Eurostar Mean Business, Authors unknown

Edited by Hazel H. Huang

Discussion Questions

1 What is the target market and target audience in Eurostar's case?

2 To target business travellers, what factors do we need to take into consideration?

3 Why did Mr JetSet, a comic character, work successfully on targeting businessmen?

4 How did the loyalty model groupings shift before and after the 'Fly Eurostar' and Mr JetSet campaigns?

FURTHER READING

- Two articles in the September 2002 number of *Marketing Theory* offer interesting insights into understanding potential target audiences. Ronald Hill, 'Consumer Culture and the Culture of Poverty: Implications for Marketing Theory and Practice' (pp. 273–94), deals with the role of marketing in the lives of the poor; and Rob Lawson and Jonah Todd, 'Consumer Lifestyles: A Social Stratification Perspective' (pp. 295–308), argues that lifestyle dimensions should be looked at from Weber's social stratification approach to status rather than psychographics.

- Mohan Dutta-Bergman and William Wells, 'The Values and Lifestyles of Idiocentrics and Allocentrics in an Individualist Culture: A Descriptive Approach', *Journal of Consumer Psychology*, 12/3 (2002), 231–42, looks at the growing cross-culture interest in the effects of individualism-collectivism on preference for advertising appeals.

- In 'Convergence and Divergence in Consumer Behaviour: Implications for Global Advertising', *International Journal of Advertising*, 22/2 (2003), 183–202, Marieke de Mooij questions the prevailing assumption of convergence in consumer behaviour, and argues rather for evidence of divergence and its consequences for international brand management and global advertising.

NOTES

1 Gerat Antonides and W. Fred van Raaij talk about target groups in their book *Consumer Behaviour: A European Perspective* (Chichester: John Wiley and Sons, 1998). Interestingly, the subject does not come up until quite near the end of the book in a section on market segmentation.

2 J. R. Rossiter and L. Percy, *Advertising Communication and Promotion Management* (New York: McGraw-Hill, 1997).

3 As discussed by William J. McGuire in his seminal work, the second edition of *The Handbook of Social Psychology*, vol. iii, ed. Gardner Lindzey and Elliot Arusan (Reading, Mass.: Addison-Wesley Publishing Co., 1969), 263–4. The innoculation approach to resistance was originally suggested by Janis in the 1950s, and was then developed by McGuire and his colleagues, as well as Tannenbaum and his group.

4 See Rossiter and Percy, *Advertising Communication and Promotion Management*, 58.

5 The importance of the degree of preference in identifying brand loyals even when loyal to two of the brands, from switchers is discussed by John Rossiter and Steve Bellman in *Marketing Communication: Theory and Application* (Frenchs Forest: Pearson Education Australia, 2005), 83–4.

6   A number of research institutes in Europe and the USA have developed versions of a 'conversion model' to help identify customer loyalty. Charles Moore of Taylor Nelson Sofres-UK discusses their model in 'Linking Market Research Techniques to Database Marketing to Assist Customer Retention', in *The eXperts Report on… Database Marketing and Integrated Marketing Communications* (New York: Advertising Research Foundation, 1998), 11–16. A more technical discussion may be found in J. Hofmeyer, 'The Conversion Model: A New Foundation for Strategic Planning in Marketing', unpub. paper presented at the 3rd EMAC/ESOMAR symposium, 'New Ways in Marketing and Marketing Research'.

7   Because conversion models developed by research institutes are considered proprietary to those institutes, *how* the model is applied is not revealed. As a general rule we do not approve of using such 'black-box' models because you have no way of evaluating how valid the model may be.

8   These findings are reported from a Roper survey discussed in an article by H. Charpa, 'Ripe Old Age', *Advertising Age*, 13 May 2002, 16.

9   This reflects something John Howard, one of the founders of the study of consumer behaviour, referred to as 'routinized response behaviour'. He considers this the simplest of three stages of consumer behaviour (the other two are 'limited problem solving' and 'extensive problem solving'). This subject is explored in some depth in his book *Consumer Behaviour: Application of Theory* (New York: McGraw-Hill, 1977).

10 Rossiter and Percy discuss this in *Advertising Communication and Promotion Management*, 61–2, in terms of 'leverage', and offer an equation for measuring the return on investment in advertising or promotion expenditure.

11 A good discussion of the Target Group Index (TGI) may be found in P. R. Smith, *Marketing Communication: An Integrated Approach*, 2nd edn. (London: Kogan Page, 1998), 124–5. Basically, the TGI compiles information on brand usage for a wide range of consumer products, and relates that behaviour to the usage, demographic, and media behaviour of the buyer.

12 Antonides and van Raaij, *Consumer Behaviour: A European Perspective*, 548.

13 Ibid. 29. D. K. Oliver, in his book *Marketing Today*, 3rd edn. (Hemel Hempstead: Prentice Hall, 1990), has suggested that the advertising industry was one of the first to combine and use demographic data in terms of socio-economic variables.

14 Robert East, *Consumer Behaviour: Advances and Applications in Marketing* (Hemel Hempstead: Prentice Hall, 1997), 237.

15 Good discussions of Acorn can be found in Chris Fill, *Marketing Communications: Framework, Theories, and Application* (London: Prentice Hall, 1995), 70, and Smith, *Marketing Communication*, 126.

16 See William M. Weilbacken, *Advertising* (New York: Macmillan, 1979), 477.

17 Rossiter and Percy, *Advertising Communication and Promotion Management*, 96. In their discussion of social class, Rossiter and Percy point out how important social class is to retailers. There is a strong positive correlation between the quality image of a store and the social class of its customers, confirmed in a study by J. P. Dickson and D. L. MacLachlan, 'Social Distance and Shopping Behaviour', *Journal of the Academy of Marketing Science*, 18 (1990), 153–61.

18 Antonides and van Raaij, *Consumer Behaviour: A European Perspective*, 30.

19   In his discussion of socio-economic groups in the UK, Chris Fill provides a good argument for the careful use of social class variables: see Fill, *Marketing Communications*, 69.

20   Information about VALS may be found at their web-site, SRIC-BI/VALS.

21   F. J. Landy, *Psychology and Work Behavior* (Pacific Grove, Calif.: Brooks-Cole, 1989).

22   Antonides and van Raaij, *Consumer Behaviour: A European Perspective*, 39, 377.

23   A good review of the importance of cultural considerations for effective advertising is found in Marieke de Mooij, *Global Marketing and Advertising: Understanding Cultural Paradoxes* (Thousand Oaks, Calif.: Sage, 1998).

24   Rossiter and Percy, *Advertising Communication and Promotion Management*, 98.

25   Perhaps the best attempt to explain the often conflicting research in this area is offered by McGuire's theory of personality-persuasibility relationships: see his 'Personality and Susceptibility to Social Influences', in G. F. Borgoatta and W. W. Lambert (eds), *Handbook of Personality Theory and Research* (Chicago: Rand McNally, 1968), 1130–87. In this work he describes five postulates that underlie the complex relationships found in personality trait research: a mediational principle, a compensation principle, a situational-weighting principle, a confounding principle, and an interactive principle.

26   Rossiter and Percy, *Advertising Communication and Promotion Management*, 97.

27   See L. W. Morris, *Extroversion and Introversion: An International Perspective* (New York: Halsted Press, 1979).

28   See Rossiter and Percy, *Advertising Communication and Promotion Management*, 97–8.

29   Much of this work can be found in H. J. Eysenck (ed.), *A Model for Personality* (Berlin: Springer-Verlag, 1981).

30   See A. Handel, 'Personality Factors among Adolescent Boys', *Psychological Reports*, 39 (1976), 435–45.

31   Fill, *Marketing Communications*, 68.

32   M. Rothschild, *Marketing Communications* (Lexington, Mass.: D. C. Heath, 1987).

33   The importance of segmenting target markets in terms of attitude for developing a communication strategy that identifies target audiences was pointed out as long ago as the mid-1970s by Larry Percy in a still frequently cited article, 'How Market Segmentation Guides Advertising Strategy', *Journal of Advertising Research*, 16/5 (1976).

34   While the fundamental behavioural objectives are trial and repeat purchase or use, Rossiter and Percy, in *Advertising Communication and Promotion Management*, 63, point out that there are 'finer gradations' based upon behavioural considerations such as occurrence, rate of purchase, amount purchased, timing, and persistence.

35   See A. L. Baldinger, E. Blair, and R. Echambadi, 'Why Brands Grow', *Journal of Advertising Research*, 42/1 (2002), 7–14.

 Visit the Online Resource Centre that accompanies this book for additional resources to support the text: http://www.oxfordtextbooks.co.uk/orc/percy_elliott3e/

7

Understanding Target Audience Decision Making

After selecting the target audience, the manager must now gain an understanding of how the target audience goes about making purchase decisions in the category. This involves establishing who is likely to participate in the decision and the roles they play in the process, and developing a Behavioural Sequence Model (BSM) that identifies the likely stages the target audience goes through in making a purchase decision. Once constructed, the model provides important insights into positioning, communication, and media strategy.

Implementing the Strategic Planning Process

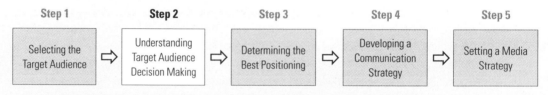

Step 1	Step 2	Step 3	Step 4	Step 5
Selecting the Target Audience	Understanding Target Audience Decision Making	Determining the Best Positioning	Developing a Communication Strategy	Setting a Media Strategy

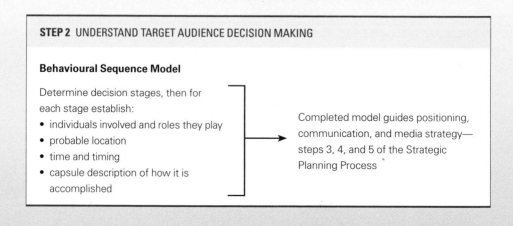

STEP 2 UNDERSTAND TARGET AUDIENCE DECISION MAKING

Behavioural Sequence Model

Determine decision stages, then for each stage establish:
- individuals involved and roles they play
- probable location
- time and timing
- capsule description of how it is accomplished

Completed model guides positioning, communication, and media strategy—steps 3, 4, and 5 of the Strategic Planning Process

➡ **KEY CONCEPTS**

1 It is important to understand not only who is participating in a purchase decision, but the *roles* they play in the decision process, which may be as an initiator of the process, an influencer, decider, purchaser, or user.

2 A person may play all the roles in a purchase decision or participate only in some; and advertising must address people in terms of the role(s) they play, not just as individuals.

3 The key to understanding how the target audience makes purchase decisions is to develop a Behavioural Sequence Model (BSM) to determine the various stages they go through, from when a need for the product first occurs until they have selected, purchased, and used a particular brand.

4 Then establish who is involved at each stage and the roles they play, where each stage occurs, the timing, and how each stage in the decision process occurs, which will help guide positioning, communication, and media strategy.

The importance of understanding how consumers behave in a category before attempting to develop marketing and communication strategies may seem obvious to us today. Yet, oddly enough, the formal study of consumer behaviour as such is a relatively recent phenomenon. It was not until the 1960s that consumer behaviour became an academic field of study in its own right, and the first textbooks on the subject were written. From the very beginning, however, researchers and academics have noted the important link between understanding how consumers behave and creating effective marketing and communication strategies.[1]

Also from the earliest days of the study of consumer behaviour as a discipline, those working in the area have been interested in modelling how consumers behave, and have included in these models the important link between how consumers deal with information and how that influences the way they go about making decisions.[2] In Antonides and van Raaij's book on consumer behaviour from a European perspective,[3] the authors devote an entire chapter to the consumer decision process, and one to situation and behaviour. People who study consumer behaviour know how important it is to understand how consumers go about making decisions to buy products or utilize services, and it is *equally* important to the study of the management of advertising and other marketing communication.

It has been suggested that theories of decision making behaviour fall into two categories: behavioural processes and cognitive processes.[4] Most people involved in the study of consumer behaviour think about decision making as a cognitive process, with a few notable exceptions such as Gordon Foxall. The behavioural sequence model we will be discussing in depth later on in this chapter, despite using the term 'behavioural', is squarely in the tradition of cognitive notions of decision making.

Proponents of the behavioural process in decision making do not believe it is possible to even discuss what is going on in a consumer's mind, let alone base a theory upon it. For them, we must rely upon analysis of observations or self-reports of actual behaviour. This idea is informed by Skinner's theory of operant behaviourism.[5] Foxall has advanced this idea in recent years, arguing that insight into behaviour follows from an examination of the environment surrounding the behaviour of interest, both past and present.[6]

Those who advocate a behaviourist approach to understanding consumer decision making feel that the job of marketing communication is to stimulate the correct environmental cues. For example, messages that relate a brand's benefit specifically to the positive consequence of using it or the negative consequence of not using the brand.

Those who look at consumer decision making in terms of a cognitive process look at it in terms of how the mind is processing information when making a decision.[7] Most of the early models of consumer decision making were built upon this idea, while also looking at it as a *process*. In other words, one was interested in understanding, in modelling, what went on in the consumer's mind during a series of steps or stages that are involved in reaching a decision.

The processes outlined in these models range from the rather straightforward representation offered by Howard to much more involved models. Howard identified three potential processes in consumer decision making: routinized response behaviour, limited problem solving, and extensive problem solving.[8] These have been adopted by Solomon as a 'continuum of buying decision behaviour', reflecting (as he puts it) the amount of effort that goes into the decision each time it is made.[9] More complicated models have grown out of the early Howard and Sheth model to multicomponent models such as that offered by Engel and his colleagues.[10] These are very extensive models, but basically outline a series of stages associated with some identification of need, information search and evaluation, purchase, and post-purchase evaluation.

While it is beyond the scope of this book to undertake an in-depth study of consumer decision making,[11] it is none the less important for the manager to have a way of looking at how people in his or her target market are likely to go about making decisions to buy or use products or services. A very practical tool that can help managers deal with this issue is the Behavioural Sequence Model (BSM) first introduced by Rossiter and Percy in 1987.[12] The BSM is strongly rooted in previous cognitive process models of buyer behaviour, but it deals much more specifically with the decision *process*, and how that process is likely to be affected by marketing communication. In this chapter we will look at the foundation of the BSM, and at how this can be used to help guide the development of marketing communication strategy.

Decision Participants

As we begin to consider the decision process consumers use to reach buying decisions, the first question we must ask ourselves is who is involved in that decision. Quite often there is more than one person, even when the decision involves only a fast-moving consumer good (fmcg) such as snacks or toothpaste. The key of course is understanding not just who is participating in the decision, but the *role* each participant plays in the process.

Table 7.1 Probable Communication Objectives for Decision Roles

Role in Decision	Communication Objective
Initiator	Brand awareness, initial brand attitude
Influencer	Brand attitude
Decider	Brand attitude and brand purchase intention
Purchaser	Brand purchase intention
User	Brand attitude

There are five potential roles for participants to play in the decisions leading up to the purchase and use of a product or service, as noted in Chapter 5 (Table 7.1):

• as the *initiator* who suggests the purchase;
• as an *influencer* who recommends or discourages purchase;
• as the *decider* who makes the actual choice;
• as the *purchaser* who does the actual purchasing;
• as the *user* who consumes or uses the product or service.

The reason it is so important for the manager to understand this idea of roles in the decision process is that advertising and other marketing communication is aimed not just at individuals, but at *individuals in a role*.

Effective marketing communication matches a message with the role (or roles) an individual plays. When we are trying to arouse interest in a product, we are talking to the consumer in his or her role as an initiator. We want him or her to initiate the process that will lead to purchase or usage of our product or service. This could be the same message that is also used to address the consumer in his or her role as an influencer, but it need not be. For example, what if you were introducing a new product, especially a new product when there was no awareness of or experience with the category (think of when iPods were introduced)? All your effort initially may be required simply to raise awareness of and stimulate curiosity in the new product. Later messages will begin to build more substantial understanding of the product, addressing consumers in their role as influencers and deciders.

We also need to keep in mind that influencers may exist well outside the immediate circle of a consumer's family or acquaintances. What if we are advertising a holiday resort? Clearly we will want to make people aware of our great resort and spark an interest (initiating the decision process) as well as begin to influence them positively to consider us as a holiday destination. But at the same time, we will also want to be talking with travel agents, encouraging them to influence their clients to consider our resort. This will surely be a different message from the one directed to consumers. Basically, no matter how many participants may be involved in a decision process, we want to be sure that initiators are aware of our product and positively inclined to suggest considering it (either to themselves or to others), and that influencers have reasons to recommend it (again either to themselves or to others).

In appealing to the consumer's role as decider, advertising and other marketing communication must stimulate a positive *intention* to buy or use the product. In later chapters we will discuss in some detail how consumers' perception of personal risk in buying or using a product is related to how they form intentions. Risk may be defined in terms of fiscal risk because a lot of money is involved, or psychological risk because of personal or social involvement associated with the product. If consumers perceive risk in a purchase, they will obviously want to be more convinced they are making the right choice in buying or using a particular product or service. When there is this perceived risk, the decision is described as *high involvement* and when there is little perceived risk present, the decision is *low involvement*. We have already introduced this idea, and the distinction will be taken up again in Chapter 9, when we talk about brand attitude strategies, and in Chapter 11, when we talk about processing. The reason we are reintroducing the subject here is that it is important to see that it will require more commitment from a consumer in the role of decider when the product choice decision is high involvement than where it is low involvement. This will have clear implications for strategic message development.

For most low-involvement purchase decisions, the decider will be a single person. With high-involvement purchase decisions, the decider may be a single person; or for large household purchases, a couple; or for certain major business decisions, a group. Once the decider makes the decision, the person in the role of purchaser actually buys the product or secures the services. It is important to remember that the decider and the purchaser may not be the same person. The significance of this means, especially for low-involvement purchases where there is little or no risk involved, that there is a final opportunity to influence the actual purchase at the point of purchase with some form of marketing communication such as a special promotion or point-of-sale message.

The last role played in the decision process is that of user. You may be wondering why using the product or service is considered as part of the decision process. If the product or service was never to be used again, or nothing else made or offered by that company likely to be bought, perhaps usage would not be a part of the process. But, as we know, for most products or services a marketer is looking to encourage *repeat* purchase or usage. This means that in a real sense the user role is really the first step towards repeat purchase.

Roles and Message Objective

Before we proceed further with our discussion of the roles participants play in a decision process, this is a good point to introduce the issue of how *what* you say in your marketing communication is related to *whom* you say it to, in terms of the roles they play. We have already suggested that the message needed to stimulate awareness for an initiator may be different from the message needed for other roles. We will, of course, be dealing at great length with the subject of creative strategy later on in this book, but it is important to understand at this point that messages need to accomplish different things depending upon where you are and what role you are playing in the decision process.

Under some circumstances, the same message may be appropriate regardless of role. This is especially true for low-involvement purchase decisions. For most fmcgs you can think of, communicating brand awareness and positive brand attitude will accommodate all five roles, whether played by a single consumer or by multiple individuals. The initiator, influencer, and decider must be aware of the brand, and have at least a tentatively favourable attitude towards it. This will in turn lead to at least an initial positive intention to try, which is required of the decider and the purchaser. Continued awareness and a favourable attitude maintains a positive intention to repurchase, which is the goal for a user. Because more people are likely to be involved in a high-involvement purchase decision, even though the role may require the same type of message, the *nature* of the role being played may require a different message. Consider the example of potential influencers in a holiday resort destination decision. The potential traveller and his or her friends or others who may play a role as an initiator or influencer will probably require a different message from travel agents in their role as initiators or influencers. The communication objective is the same: raise brand awareness and build a positive brand attitude for the resort. However, the specific messages directed to the consumer are likely to be different from those directed to the travel agent.

Beyond this difference, with high-involvement decisions, because there is risk, deciders must be *convinced* of their choice prior to a purchase. It is unlikely that a single advertisement for a high-involvement purchase will be able to build the brand awareness and positive brand attitude sufficient to satisfy the initiator and influencer, and also be able to ensure a positive intention to buy. You may see a great commercial for staying at a resort in the Alps and think that it might be a really great place for a holiday. But it is unlikely that you would pick up the phone and book without first learning a lot more about the resort. A specific message keyed to the person in the decider role is almost always required when dealing with high-involvement decisions.

A good example of this may be found when we consider the decision to buy a new car. Research into how people go about making a buying decision for a car suggests that it is at least a two-stage process.[13] In the first stage potential buyers must *like* the car. They must see themselves behind the wheel, and feel that this particular vehicle reflects how they want to be seen by the world. This is the 'image' part of the decision, and reflects the positive motives associated with buying a car. Once this is satisfied and potential buyers are comfortable with the *idea* of owning a particular vehicle, in the second stage they must satisfy themselves that the car meets their more *functional* criteria (mileage, service record, features, and so on), reflecting the negative motivations associated with buying a car. (This very important idea of motivation is critical to our view of communication strategy, as we have already suggested.) In our terms, one message is necessary to reach potential new car buyers first in their roles as initiator and influencer (and later as user); a very different, more fact-filled message or messages will be required for them in their roles as decider and purchaser.

Decision Participant Grid (DPG)

As you can now see, it is very important to look at the *roles* people play in the decision process leading to the purchase and use of a product or service. There may be only one

Role in decision	Target audience	
	Consumer	Provider
Initiator		
Influencer		
Decider		
Purchaser		
User		

Figure 7.1 Decision Participant Grid

person involved, playing all the roles in the decision; or, for higher-involvement purchases, a number of different people playing different or multiple roles. To help focus the manager's thinking on all those who might be involved and the roles they are likely to play, it is useful to complete a Decision Participant Grid (Fig. 7.1).[14] For each of the five roles, think about which members of your immediate target market might be likely to be involved. The key, of course, is to see that your potential target audience for marketing communication messages could be wider than simply the person buying the product. Initially you will want to think as broadly as possible. Later, you can refine the list of possible participants. At this point it is not necessary for the grid to be precise.

You will also notice that, in addition to consumers, there is a column for *providers*. This is to remind us that, for many decisions, especially high-involvement ones, various parts of the trade could be involved in the process. In one of our earlier examples, we saw how travel agents could play a role as initiator or influencer, as illustrated in Fig. 7.2. Often salespeople can play a role in the decision. You will want to account for these possibilities where members of the trade are dealing directly with the consumer during the decision process.

To help understand how the DPG enables managers to stimulate and organize their thinking, let us consider some examples. Perhaps the simplest case is where a single individual is likely to play all the roles in a decision. Suppose it is late afternoon, and a student has a fifteen-minute break between lectures. The student thinks to herself, 'I need a snack (initiator). What do I want, some chocolate or a salty snack (influencer)? I know, a Mars bar (decider).' She goes to a vending machine in the lounge, buys the Mars bar (purchaser), and eats it (user).

You may be wondering why in the world you would need the discipline of a DPG for such a simple case. To begin with, this scenario would be only one of many possible snack scenarios if you were the maker of Mars bars. But even if you could assume that for nearly all relevant confection scenarios one individual would play all the decision roles, it would still be a good idea to *think about the roles* in filling out a DPG. Earlier in this

Role in decision	Target audience	
	Consumer	Provider
Initiator	Self, friends, family	Travel agent
Influencer	Self, friends, family	Travel agent, resorts, and other destinations
Decider	Self, companion	
Purchaser	Self, companion	Travel agent
User	Self, companion, family	

Figure 7.2 Decision Participant Grid for a Holiday

chapter we talked about how different messages may be necessary to deal effectively with various roles a consumer may play. Suppose you were introducing a new candy bar. You would almost certainly want to use more than one message, keyed to different roles, even though all the decision roles are played by the same person.

We know, for example, that television advertising is probably the best way to introduce a new candy bar, raising awareness and stimulating interest; important for initiator, influencer, and decider roles. But how likely is it that people seeing an advertisement for our new candy bar will drop everything they are doing and dash out to the shops to find one? Unlikely. What they will do is form a positive intention to try one, and put it out of their mind. For that reason, it makes a lot of sense to offer in-store promotions or use shelf-talkers (those signs or pads sometimes found on the product shelf in stores) to *remind* the consumers of their intention to try the new candy bar (in their role as purchaser). If you were marketing Mars bars and knew a competitor was introducing a new candy bar, you might want to do something to interfere with their message at the point of purchase. By taking time to think through a DPG the manager is forced to focus upon the roles in the decision process and what implications there may be for marketing communication, even in the simplest case where one person plays all five roles.

Let us look at another case that on the surface may seem quite simple, but where a lot more could be going on. In most families the mother is the principal shopper. Continuing our snack scenario, let us suppose that a young child in the family has just seen a commercial on television for the new candy bar we have been talking about and asks the mother to buy some next time she shops (initiator). The father overhears this, and seconds the request, saying he would also like to try it (influencer). The mother agrees (decider), and makes a note to look for the new candy bar next time she is in the shops. On her next trip, there it is, *but* next to the display is a special offer for the candy bar she usually buys.

Too good a deal to pass up; she buys the regular bars (purchaser). At home, she promises to buy the new bars next time, and the family continues to eat the old favourite (users). The same product, but with different people playing multiple roles.

What these examples illustrate is that the underlying communication strategy for the brand will follow from the roles various participants play in the decision. The first scenario assumes that marketing communication is targeted at immediate individual consumption, the second that it is aimed at consumption out of in-home inventory. Can the same message or messages accommodate both strategies? Perhaps, but at this point, in considering the roles being played by the target market, we are not setting communication strategy. What we are doing is considering all those who might be involved in the decision, and whom we may need to address with the marketing communication.

Both these examples illustrate why advertising alone, especially for a new product, may not be sufficient even for very simple decisions where one person plays all, or all the principal, roles. Advertising does a good job of generating awareness of a brand and creating interest in it. But, unfortunately, most consumer packaged goods products are purchased out of habit, without much thought being given to the product.[15] This is an issue we will examine in some detail later on in Chapter 9 when we talk about brand awareness. While advertising builds interest in a brand, it is often necessary to utilize other means of marketing communication, such as promotion or in-store merchandising where the actual purchase is made, if you want to *change* a consumer's usual, routine purchase behaviour.

Developing a Model of Target Audience Decision Making

Up to this point we have concentrated our attention upon those who participate in the decision to buy or use a product or service. Now it is time to see how these participants in the decision and the roles they play relate to the decision process itself. We shall do this by looking at what we have been talking about in relation to the BSM. This model utilizes a grid format that requires you first to identify the probable *stages* involved in making a decision, and then for each stage in the process determine: *who* is involved; *where* that stage in the decision is likely to occur; *when* each stage occurs in relation to the other decision stages; and *how* that stage is likely to occur. The result is a detailed flow chart that identifies where potential members of the target market are likely to be making decisions and taking actions that lead to actual purchase and use of a product or service.

The objective of any model of consumer decision making is to provide a useful format to help managers begin to think of where in the target audience's decision process marketing communication may be expected to influence brand choice. Once the model has been developed, it helps the manager to identify specific targeting objectives. It is surprisingly easy to construct a decision-making model like the BSM, utilizing what those involved with a brand know about their market. As the manager works through the model, if 'gaps' in the understanding of the brand are uncovered, it will be necessary to conduct whatever research is required in order to feel comfortable that the model does indeed accurately reflect how consumers are making choices in the brand's category.

	Decision Stage			
	Need arousal	Brand consideration	Purchase	Usage
Individuals involved and decision roles				
Where stage is likely to occur				
Timing of stage				
How stage is likely to occur				

Figure 7.3 Generic Consumer Decision-Making Model

While it is important that a target audience decision making model be developed specifically for a particular product category, utilizing the decision stages most likely to be operating for that category, a generic model can be helpful in initiating the process. The generic model shown in Fig. 7.3 illustrates how four general decision stages are combined, with the decision roles involved at each stage, where each stage is likely to occur, the timing for each stage, and how each stage is likely to happen. Each of the components of the model will now be discussed.

Decision Stages

From as long ago as the beginnings of consumer behaviour theory the idea of 'stages' of a consumer's decision process has been central to notions of how consumers make choices.[16] Complete models of consumer behaviour have almost always included some stepwise component dealing with the decision model as we have mentioned earlier. While these models can often be very intimidating, they do acknowledge the necessity of understanding the consumer's decision process, and the stages in the decision, in order to understand consumer behaviour.

Perhaps the most widely known and most enduring of these general models is the one originally offered by Engel and his colleagues in the 1960s. In a recent version of their model we find a five-stage decision process component composed of: need recognition, search, alternative evaluation, purchasing, and outgoings.[17] The similarity of this to our set of decision stages in the generic model is not accidental. Some such 'flow' of thought and action is at the heart of any consumer purchase behaviour, and this is what we want to capture with a target audience decision making model.

However, the important point to understand is that the exact words we use are not the important thing. What is important is that the manager begin to think about how consumers make decisions in the category, and at what points in this process advertising and other marketing communication can influence what brand is chosen. While the decision stages in the generic model are useful, and can generally be adapted to almost any product category, it is best to develop *specific* decision stages that more closely reflect how you understand decisions to be made in a brand's category. Some decisions may be quite simple, others more complicated. The decision stages for most fmcg products among brand loyals is simply need arousal—purchase—usage. For example, if you have a favourite candy bar that you regularly buy, when you want a candy bar (need arousal), you will probably seek out your favourite brand and buy it (purchase), then eat it on the spot (usage).

But, returning to our earlier resort holiday example, the decision stages involved there are likely to be much more involved. Something will get you thinking about your next holiday, and you will begin to look into various alternatives. You will evaluate the options, and decide where you would like to go. Then you will need to check on availabilities and see if you can schedule the trip. You make the arrangements, go on the trip, and hopefully enjoy yourself, then 'relive' the experience afterward with pictures and discussions with friends.

The decision stages in this resort example are much more descriptive than those in the generic model, but they still reflect the basic generic stages. Starting to think about a holiday is need arousal; looking into and evaluating places to go is brand consideration; checking into availability and scheduling the trip is purchase; and going on the trip and 'reliving' it is usage. Modifications of the generic stages to fit specific circumstances enhances the utility of the model. The whole idea is to capture the essence of the decision process in order to facilitate marketing communication planning. Even though we are only at the first step in constructing the model (admittedly the most important), already we can see how laying out the decision stages can help pinpoint opportunities for affecting choice outcomes with advertising and other marketing communications.

Continuing with our holiday example, if we are the marketing manager for a resort on the southern coast of France, we will want to be sure potential guests are aware of us so that we come to mind when they begin to think about a holiday and look into various alternatives. In later chapters we will discuss the importance of building this link between what we call category need (going on a holiday in this case) and brand awareness (our resort). We will want to be sure potential guests have the information they need about our resort to evaluate it favourably. This could mean print advertising in appropriate magazines or direct mail brochures, as well as collateral material for travel agents. To facilitate the decision in our favour, perhaps we will want to offer some sort of incentive (especially at off-peak times of the year). At the resort itself, we will want to remind the guests of what a great choice they have made. The resort will, of course, need to meet the guests' expectations, but in many ways marketing communication can help reinforce this positive experience. Once guests have returned home, follow-up direct mail and general advertising can continue to reinforce the experience, building a stronger brand attitude, and increasing intentions to return. It should now be clear that managers must do more than simply decide they want to advertise and perhaps run the odd promotion or two. Marketing communication must be considered in the light of how it is most likely to influence consumers positively as they are going through the process of making decisions. A good understanding of the decision stages is a key element in strategic marketing communication planning.

Low Involvement versus High Involvement

The alert reader has no doubt already noticed that the distinction we made earlier in this chapter between low-involvement and high-involvement decisions is also related to the complexity of the decision stages associated with a particular product category. The reason is directly related to the fact that, with low-involvement decisions, because there is relatively little risk involved in the choice, consumers really do not need to be *convinced* they are making the best choice. With high-involvement decisions, because there is risk attached to the choice, consumers will want to be more certain they are in fact making the best possible choices.

If we consider our generic model, what this means is that, for low-involvement decisions, at the brand consideration stage there will not be a great deal of serious thinking going on. Using our candy bar example again, once need is aroused, the consumer will look for something to purchase and eat. At the time of need arousal, a brand may come to mind ('I think I'll get a Mars bar'), or it may just be a general category need ('I think I'll get a candy bar'). At the point of purchase the consumer sees what is available and makes a choice from a set of already known favourites. Perhaps there is a new candy bar there that the consumer then remembers seeing an advertisement for and thinks 'I might like that, I'll give it a try.' Because there is very little risk in this decision, at the brand consideration stage it is unlikely that the consumer in this case will postpone trial of the new candy bar until she looks into things more, perhaps seeking out friends who have tried it and asking for their opinion.

In consumer behaviour language, there is not a lot of 'information search and evaluation' required for low-involvement decisions. As a result, the decision stages tend to be less involved, even if there are several of them. This becomes evident as we look at the likely decision stages for two typical low-involvement choices: laundry detergent and casual eating out.

- *Laundry detergent* notice getting low—shop—select brand—purchase—use
- *Casual eating out* need arousal—decide what in 'mood' for—decide on restaurant from that type—go to restaurant—eat

Contrast this with high-involvement decisions. Since consumers want to be confident they are making the best choice, there will be a corresponding 'information search and evaluation' to help ensure this. This means, in terms of our generic model, much more attention at the brand consideration stage. Suppose you have just bought your first house and with the onset of warm weather begin to notice a lot of bugs. You need an exterminator, but who? You will find out who is supposed to be good, and check them out. What is their reputation? Do they offer a guarantee and if so how long? What do they cost? After convincing yourself that one of them is likely to do the best job, they are engaged. You evaluate the job and decide whether to continue to use their service.

Let us consider another high-involvement decision, this time a business-to-business decision. Suppose you manufacture plumbing fixtures that are distributed through wholesale plumbing distributors. How do these wholesalers decide what fixtures and brands they will stock? A possible set of decision stages might begin with the wholesalers keeping an eye out for better fixtures to maintain an edge over competitors. This would lead to knowledge about any new lines or items they might wish to stock. Once the wholesalers' interest is aroused, the fixtures that caught their eye would be compared with what is currently stocked, and assessed against potential demand. If this evaluation of the potential for the product is positive, contact will be made with the manufacturer and there will be a second evaluation, this time in terms of the business arrangement. If the deal with the manufacturer is acceptable, the fixture will be ordered. Once stocked, sales and product reaction will be monitored, and if positive, the fixture will be reordered. Notice in this example that because the wholesaler is in effect the consumer for the fixture manufacturer, the decision stages and BSM are developed around how the wholesaler makes a vendor choice.

It should be quite clear that more attention is given brand consideration, and often purchase and usage, in high-involvement decisions, and our decision stages must reflect this. The decision stages for the two high-involvement examples just discussed might be thought of as follows:

- *Exterminator service* need arousal—identify services—evaluate services—decide on service—contact and schedule service—evaluate results—decide whether to retain service
- *Wholesale plumbing distributor stocking* monitor manufacturer and wholesale competitors—identify items to evaluate—evaluate items—contact vendor—evaluate vendor—order and stock item—evaluate sales performance—reorder

Table 7.2 summarizes the various decision stages we have been discussing. As you review them, think about the decision stages in relation to the four decision stages in the generic model. You will see that, while the generic model certainly could be used in each case, when you custom-fit the decision stages for a specific product category or situation, you have a much better feel for where advertising and other marketing communication will be likely to have a positive effect upon the outcome of the purchase or usage decision.

Table 7.2 Decision Stage Examples

Laundry Detergent	Notice getting low—shop—select brand—purchase—use
Casual Eating Out	Need arousal—decide what in 'mood' for—decide on restaurant from that type—go to restaurant—eat
Exterminator Service	Need arousal—identify services—evaluate services—decide on service—contact and schedule service—evaluate results—decide whether to retain service
Wholesale Plumbing Distributor Stocking	Monitor manufacturer and wholesale competitors—identify items to evaluate—evaluate items—contact vendor—evaluate vendor—order and stock item—evaluate sales performance—reorder

Decision Roles

Once we have identified what the likely decision stages are for consumers making choices in a category, we must identify everyone who might play a part in the decision process, and the role or roles they play at *each decision stage*. This is really the first step in determining the target audience for marketing communication. We have already looked at the roles people can play in the decision process. Now we must determine where in the process specific individuals are likely to be involved.

This brings up a very important point. We are looking at *individuals*. In the marketing literature and in the talk of marketing managers today much is made of the notion of 'group decisions'. Important business decisions are rarely made by a single person; important household decisions are made jointly by husbands and wives. While this is certainly true, what we must be concerned with in developing advertising and other marketing communication strategy is the individual and the role he or she is playing in the decision. Advertising and other forms of marketing communication do not influence groups; they influence individuals in their role as part of the group making the decision. Constructing a target audience decision-making model enables the manager to see that many people may be involved in a decision, as we saw earlier, but as individuals in a role.

Let us return to the example of a resort holiday discussed earlier and the DPG in Fig. 7.2 to see how this analysis of decision roles fits into the model. From our earlier discussion, the decision stages for a holiday trip might be seen as:

- *Holiday trip* need arousal—identify possible holidays—evaluate options—choose holiday—book holiday—take holiday—post-holiday evaluation

According to the DPG, what individuals are likely to be involved at the need arousal stage and in what roles? Because those playing a role as *initiator* get the process started, they are the ones most likely to be involved at this stage. This would include the potential traveller, other family members or friends, and travel agents. All of these people, this time in their role as *influencer*, could be involved in identifying possible holidays and helping to evaluate options. Then the potential traveller and companion (if there is one) in their role as *decider* will both play a part in choosing the holiday, and either they or a travel agent as the *purchaser* will book the holiday. Everyone who goes on the holiday plays a role as *user*, as well as an *influencer* in post-holiday evaluations.

Where the Decision Stage is Likely to Occur

An important key to effective marketing communication is to identify in the decision process where a message of some kind might make a positive contribution. The better we understand where those opportunities lie, the better our media planning. We need to know where members of our target audience (which at this point is potentially *everyone* involved in the decision process) are likely to be making decisions. These locations are fairly easy to generate, and can range from a single location to many locations spread over a considerable period of time. The important thing is to *think* about likely locations for each stage consumers go through when making a brand choice.

The lower involvement the decision, the more concentrated the decision process is likely to be. Generally this will be somewhere prior to purchase where awareness and initial attitudes are formed, then at the point of purchase and time of use. This is most likely to be simply at home and in the store. There are always exceptions, of course. You could be shopping and someone could give you a sample of a new snack. You taste it and really like it, see it on a special rack at the check-out, buy one, and eat it on your way out of the store. Everything occurred in the store, but this would *not* reflect the probable location for all decision stages in all snack choices. Do consider exceptions, for possible specifically targeted marketing communication. But in thinking about where decision stages are likely to occur, think more broadly.

Let us continue with our holiday trip example. Where is need arousal likely to take place? For the potential traveller, it could occur at home, while visiting friends (who perhaps are just back from a holiday), or at a travel agency. It could even occur almost serendipitously when the potential traveller sees a poster on the underground or at the train station. *Already media planning possibilities should occur to you.* Broadcast advertising to the home, newspaper advertisements for the commuter, banners and collateral at travel agencies, posters on or near transportation. This is the sort of thinking a consumer decision-making model is designed to encourage.

People might identify possible holidays in any of the places that need arousal occurs, as well as evaluate them there, although they are most likely to evaluate potential destinations at home or with a travel agent. From home or at a travel agent is also where the holiday is most likely to be booked. The holiday itself, of course, occurs at the destination, while the post-holiday evaluation could occur almost anywhere they are reminded of it.

Identifying opportunities for advertising and other marketing communication is, as we have said, a key to implementing a marketing communication programme effectively. Careful attention to where each decision stage in a consumer decision model is likely to occur can be a big help.

Timing of the Decision Stage

Understanding the timing of the decision stages is also very important for media planning, especially for when to schedule media. The timing of most decisions may seem too obvious to occasion much concern. But it can make a critical difference to many products. The timing of most holiday decisions is generally not much more than a few months, unless it is for a very special trip. But what if you are a cruise line? By the time someone is normally at the stage of evaluating options, it is generally too late to book a cruise. This means that a cruise advertiser must do something to stimulate need arousal at a much earlier date relative to when people generally start thinking about holiday travel in order to allow for the longer advance booking generally required for a cruise. In this case, knowing the timing of a holiday decision will alert the cruise line manager to the fact that it will be necessary to design messages and schedule media to initiate holiday thinking much earlier among potential travellers.

The timing of a decision can also often play a critical role even in low-involvement decisions. Suppose you are a food company that markets dessert products. You might not think timing would play much of a role in the dessert decision. But, while it does not in terms of purchasing dessert products, it is vital to when the decision to *serve* is made. We know from research that the decision stages for desserts are as follows:

- *Dessert decision* need arousal—purchase for inventory—decide to serve—choose dessert from inventory—serve and eat

Before moving on, notice that the decision stages include more than the simple low-involvement model of need arousal—purchase—usage. Given the nature of this decision, the *usage* stage is more complicated than normal for an fmcg. Working through a consumer decision-making model alerts the manager to special situations such as this that can significantly affect marketing and communication strategies.

The critical timing concern here occurs at the decision-to-serve stage. This stage, for all but special-occasion meals that are planned ahead, occurs *after the meal*. This means the product must be ready to eat once the meal is finished and the question is asked: 'What's for dessert?' At this point, it is too late to bake a cake. It is also too late for a product like Jell-O.

Jell-O is a gelatin dessert product that is very popular in the United States, especially among children: when asked if Jell-O would have been a good choice for dessert at yesterday's evening meal, almost everyone will say 'yes'. Unfortunately, when the decision to serve is made, Jell-O is a box of granular crystals. To be ready to serve, the box of Jell-O crystals must be dissolved in hot water and left in the refrigerator for some time to set before the dessert is ready to eat. Because the decision of what to serve for dessert is made after the meal, Jell-O is not an option. Knowledge of the timing of the decision, however, led to an advertising campaign called 'early morning reminder to serve'. In this campaign messages were placed in early morning in-home media reminding people they will want Jell-O for dessert that evening, so why not prepare it now while the hot water is at hand for coffee and tea?

Here is an example where the decision itself appears rather simple and straightforward, but where understanding the *timing* of the decision had a significant impact upon increasing usage of the product.

How the Decision Stage is Likely to Occur

The final step in developing a target audience decision-making model is to consider what is going on at each of the decision stages. In thinking about how each stage happens you are taking one of the first steps towards establishing a *positioning* strategy for your advertising and other marketing communication. The 'how' is your best description of what is happening at each stage of the decision process. What happens to stimulate a perceived need for the product? How is the target market going to behave? Where are consumers likely to find information about brands (if they need it)? What goes on when actually making a purchase? How is the product actually used? Answers to questions like these complete the model.

To finish our example of the decision to take a holiday trip, let us look at how each of the stages in that process is likely to happen. *Need arousal* will occur when the potential travellers are talking with friends about their recent holiday, when they see advertising for

	Decision Stage						
	Need arousal	Identify possible holidays	Evaluate options	Choose holiday	Book holiday	Take holiday	Post holiday evaluation
Individuals involved and decision roles	Self, friends, family as **initiators** and **influences** Travel agent as **initiator**	Self, friends, family as **influences** Travel agent, resorts and other destinations as **influences**	Self, companion as **decider** Travel agent as **influence**	Self, companion as **decider**	Self, companion as **purchaser** Travel agent as **purchaser**	Self, companion	Self, companion
Where stage is likely to occur	Home, friends, travel agency	Home, friends, travel agency	Home, travel agency	Home, travel agency	Home, travel agency	Destination	Almost anywhere
Timing of stage	2–4 months before holiday	Immediately after need arousal	Over 2–4 weeks following need arousal	Within 4 weeks of need arousal	Within 1 week of choice	2–3 months after booking	After holiday
How stage is likely to occur	Friends talk, see adverts, at travel agency	Talk with friends, family, see adverts, visit travel agency	Call or write to destinations, see adverts, talk with friends, family	Compare costs, what is offered, when available	Call destination, travel agent, Internet	Travel to destination, experience at destination	Tell friends, relatives of experience, reminded when see adverts

Figure 7.4 Target Audience Behavioural Sequence Model for a Major Holiday Trip

a holiday destination, or perhaps when they are visiting a travel agent. They will *identify possible holidays* at the time their interest is piqued during need arousal, and in the period immediately following, by asking friends or family members, paying more attention to advertising on television and in the newspapers and magazines, and perhaps by visiting a travel agent.

In *evaluating options* the potential travellers might ask for specific information from destinations identified in the previous stage, talk about places with friends or family who have been there or know people who have, or ask the advice of a travel agent.

In *choosing the holiday destination* they will no doubt pick the place that best offers what is most important to them for this trip. We mentioned earlier the importance of this 'how' step to positioning strategy for marketing communication. If our example is a good approximation of the actual decision stages and what is involved in making a holiday trip decision (and it is based upon proprietary research conducted by one of the authors), then we can see the importance of *other people* in the evaluation and selection of a holiday destination. Other people will also serve as sources of information to form the basis of beliefs that will help shape the potential travellers' attitudes towards the various destinations under consideration. This insight is critical to the formulation of a communication positioning strategy, as we shall see when we deal with positioning in Chapter 8.

To *book the holiday*, the potential travellers will either call the destination and make their own arrangements or use a travel agent. They will *take the holiday* by travelling to the destination and experiencing what is there. *Post-holiday evaluation* will actually begin as soon as they leave, and reoccur when they talk about the trip with family and friends, when they occasionally just think about the trip and relive the experience, and when they are reminded of the trip by seeing advertising for their holiday site.

This illustrates what forms the foundation of a target audience decision-making model like Rossiter and Percy's BSM, and you can see how it can provide a very detailed look at a target audience in terms of how they actually go about deciding to buy or use a product or service. Figure 7.4 summarizes a BSM for a holiday trip, which we have been using as an example. As you review this example, notice how it offers a *dynamic* view of the target market and suggests opportunities for delivering targeted messages to different people who may be involved in affecting the outcome of the decision.

CHAPTER SUMMARY

In this chapter we have examined consumer behaviour in depth by utilizing a target audience decision-making model. We have identified the five roles that participants may play in the decision process and linked this to message objectives. To aid in the analysis process we have introduced the Decision Participant Grid and illustrated its use. We then went on to analyse the stages of consumer decision making and related this to high- versus low-involvement decisions based on perceived risk, and within the context of the BSM. We considered the importance of when the stages occur and their timing, and how each stage is likely to happen. We then saw how this information might be used to identify opportunities for targeted messages to different people at different stages of the decision process.

QUESTIONS TO CONSIDER

7.1 Why is it important to understand the roles people play in a purchase or usage decision?

7.2 When might the manager use the same message regardless of the role involved?

7.3 Why is it also important to consider the roles providers may play in a purchase or usage decision?

7.4 Why do consumers seek more information when making a high-involvement purchase decision than when making a low-involvement decision?

7.5 How does advertising influence 'group decisions'?

7.6 In what ways can the behavioural sequence model help the manager make better strategic decisions?

CASE STUDY 7

Seeds of Change—How Seeds of Change Sharply Increased Sales by Using Branded Content to Create a 'Foodie Fan Club'

By the start of the 21st century, all major food manufacturers recognized that the UK organic market had long-term growth potential. The UK organic food market was booming, with a growth rate at 40 per cent during 2000, significantly higher than other food categories. Growth was apparently being driven by the expansion of the UK's 'foodies'—consumers willing to pay a premium for food on aspirational, ethical, or quality grounds. A range of new organic food added further fuel to the fire.

Masterfoods launched its first and only organic brand, 'Seeds of Change' (SOC), into the UK market in late 1999. SOC was a newly bought brand from a New Mexico farm; nobody in the UK had ever heard of it. Masterfoods' long-term ambition was to secure a slice of the initially small organic market and then watch the value of that slice grow with the category. But despite their long-term ambition for SOC, the brand had to quickly prove that it could generate sales efficiently. The new brand was to compete in four premium food lines: pasta, Italian and 'ethnic' wet cooking sauce (WCS), cereal bars, and soups.

Between 1999 and 2003, SOC's communications strategy was conventional. Advertising talked of the brand's 100 per cent organic credentials, communicating more about what was not in the food than what was. Copy of this type of advertising was familiar—'As nature intended'. The artwork consisted of 'organic-porn' with pious imagery of the natural world alongside glossy product shots. Meanwhile, the brand built a media plan around well-targeted but essentially conventional channels. During 2003, for example, the brand made its appearances in a number of 'foodie' titles (*Good Housekeeping* et al.) and a brief series around Channel 4's *River Cottage*.

During late 2003, TNS segmentation had identified a concentration of potential heavy buyers called 'Everyday Foodies' that lived in London. 'Everyday Foodies' accounted for just 6 per cent of UK households but 40 per cent of all premium Wet Cooking Sauce (WCS) volume sales. Since 50 per cent of SOC's value sales came through WCS, they offered serious potential. Importantly, the segmentation also offered a critical insight into their attitudes and behaviour: 'Everyday Foodies' bought any premium brands because of *tasting* great. At the start of 2004, SOC decided to invest its media budget in a 'hit and run' on London's Everyday Foodies with a poster campaign across the Tube network. 70 per cent of the budget would be invested in May alone, hitting 90 per cent of all Londoners. SOC developed an advertising idea that made fun of such organic conventions in order to talk about taste. The end-line read 'The Only Thing That's Far Out Is The Taste'; long copy told stories of why SOC's ingredients *tasted* great; and headlines joked 'Our pasta sauce was carefully crafted in a kitchen, not a commune' and 'We're always taking trips. Usually to Italy to buy capers and tomatoes.' Despite 2004's reduced media spend, and after a flat performance in 2003, SOC's sales climbed 18 per cent to £6.7m. Furthermore, evidence suggested that it was the heavy buyers that accounted for the growth of SOC.

With still limited marketing support, the task for communications and penetration was to remain within a niche, a niche that included a fan club of heavy buyers who can grow the brand. SOC decided to focus on the value of SOC's heavy buyers with a strategy that went beyond 2004's advertising-led 'hit and run'. SOC needed to find potential heavy buyers more *precisely*, hold a conversation with them for *longer* and engage them more *deeply*. The axiom, 'more precisely, longer, deeper', became the strategic touchstone. TNS's 'Everyday Foodies' might have been a relevant target audience of potential heavy buyers. However, the most effective way to connect the SOC brand with them 'more precisely, longer, deeper' would be to connect through their richer interests beyond the grocery aisle.

In order to connect with these interests 'more precisely, longer, deeper', it was necessary to know where the heavy buyers consumed organic food. Qualitative research revealed that food, itself, was valuable cultural currency—it enriched cultural interests like art and travel, not just stomachs. SOC aimed to connect with its Cultural Creatives, through their cultural interests, by being the food brand that helped them share their 'foodie memories'. As a result of this research SOC targeted a segment of potential heavy buyers, called 'Cultural Creatives', defined by their cultural interests and shopping habits. The potential targets were ABC1 adults aged 25–54 years old who agreed with at least six of the eight statements: (1) I consider myself to be a creative person, (2) I like to pursue a life of challenge, novelty, and change, (3) I consider myself interested in the arts, (4) I am interested in other cultures, (5) I appreciate good food, (6) I prefer to take holidays off the beaten track, (7) I would never think of taking a package holiday, and (8) It is important that a company acts ethically.

To connect to its Cultural Creatives through their cultural interests, the creative idea of sharing 'foodie memories' via photos was born. It was to develop a foodie's photography competition with a content partner from the 'cultural' national weekend press. First, the selection of the content partner was critical. It had to be capable of reaching SOC's Cultural Creatives and it had to have a brand heritage that was in line with that of SOC's. *Observer Food Monthly* (*OFM*), the UK's most read food supplement, has a readership of 1.2m foodies. It is considered to be the UK's most influential foodie voice. Most important of all, its brand essence, 'life lived through a food lens', was consistent with SOC's philosophy on food's cultural value. For these reasons, *OFM* was chosen to be the content partner.

The activity was named 'Feed Your Imagination'—share with us life's great food moments. It was a competition with a £10,000 winner's prize. From May to October 2005, the press of this activity was circulated to the potential audience. Positive editorial and columnist coverage about this competition also had an effect, with advertising support in major newspapers (e.g. *The Observer*, *The Guardian*), magazines (e.g. *Practical Photography* magazine), and news letters (e.g. the weekly *Guardian* email). In addition, a dedicated 'Feed Your Imagination' micro-site within *The Observer* website was established to draw interests of potential targets and to update the participants. To increase the interest and 'buzz' levels, the judges were the leading critics, chefs, and photographers, including Martin Parr, Nigel Slater, Harry Borden, and Robin Derrick. A two-week exhibition for the 36 finalists at London's Oxo Tower Gallery was also held. At the same time, traditional advertising was used to communicate to a broader audience. The advertising focus remained the same as in 2004, 'The Only Thing That's Far Out Is The Taste', but changed to the much more relevant 'cultural' national weekend press, with updated ingredient stories.

The 'Feed Your Imagination' coverage and press advertising as a media plan demonstrated that SOC connected potential heavy buyers 'more precisely, longer, deeper'. 'Feed Your Imagination' reached a smaller total audience; however, when combined with press advertising, the brand connected with a greater number of more relevant people. Moreover, it connected with an audience whose interests matched Cultural Creatives'. The exposed audience enjoyed a strong interest in photography, exhibitions and galleries, home cooking, and eating out—stronger even than *The Observer*'s broader audience. And a significant proportion of the exposed audience claimed to purchase premium brands. As a result of the campaign, the communications reached 2 million Cultural Creatives, generating 55 per cent coverage, opposed to 2004's communications with 20 per cent coverage.

The content-led strategy was demonstrated to be successful because the photography competition generated massive participation and interest amongst Cultural Creatives. SOC originally aimed to match *The Observer*'s Hodge Award's 500 entries—a highly prestigious photography competition with twenty years of history and publicity. But 'Feed Your Imagination' beat this tenfold with over 5,000 entries, making it the UK's largest photography competition. The competition also generated massive interest beyond these participants. The Oxo Tower Gallery, just large enough to hold 36 photographs, received a staggering 9,949 visitors over two weeks, approximately 750 people per day. Furthermore, 82.1 per cent of visitors to the 'Feed Your Imagination' micro-site expressed an interest in visiting the exhibition. Comments in the gallery visitors' book signalled the strength of brand's positive engagement. Of 155 comments left, 152 were positive, including many that played back the exact same insight about the role of food in Cultural Creative's lives.

> 'Thank you for reminding us that food is culture'
> 'I love the communion of food in our lives. It's a universal item, a universal language'
> 'Very imaginative. Lovely photos from all over the world.'

During 2005 SOC's sales increased sharply; the growth rate was 50 per cent. Prior to the 'Feed Your Imagination' campaign, the growth rate was 0 per cent in 2003 and 18 per cent in 2004. The source of this sales growth was in line with SOC's strategy, from the target audience of heavy buyers. With a similar size within the UK households that consume organic food, the campaign drove the value share of SOC's heavy buyers from 12 per cent in 2004 to 64.1 per cent in 2005. And the number of SOC's heavy buyers doubled in 2005.

The 'Feed Your Imagination' campaign generated an uplift in the SOC brand perception and quality perception amongst the audience exposed to the competition. SOC WCS loyalty increased 25 per cent, making SOC the most loyally supported WCS brand and above the premium leader Lloyd Grossman and non-premium leader Dolmio. This loyalty increase came from the growth of 'exclusive loyals' (100 per cent loyalty) and 'high loyals' (>50 per cent loyalty) as the size of both groups grew 28 per cent. The improved brand attitudes also increased the repeat purchase rate, from 7 per cent to 39.4 per cent.

After flat sales in 2003, 2004's 'hit and run' appeared to find some success. Still, the strategy was conventional and SOC wanted to prove that communications could work harder—at a similar adspend. During 2005, in a world moving from passive audiences and active interruptions to one where the media can be 'a conversation', SOC went beyond convention and developed a content-led 'connections idea' that enabled the brand to hold its very own, engaging conversation. For this, the SOC brand was richly rewarded by a growing foodie fan club that rapidly accelerated the brand's growth.

Source: WARC, IPA Effectiveness Awards 2006, Seeds of Change—How Seeds of Change Sharply Increased Sales by Using Branded Content to Create a 'Foodie Fan Club', Authors unknown

Edited by Hazel H. Huang

Discussion Questions

1 How would you divide the organic food market?

2 Considering the issue of involvement, how differently do you think heavy buyers and light buyers of organic food consider brand choices?

3 How did the campaign influence heavy buyers and transform the brand consideration into purchase?

4 What are the differences between traditional advertising and the 'Feed Your Image' campaign? Why was the campaign successful, though reaching a smaller audience?

FURTHER READING

- For a different perspective on consumer decision making and behaviour, Gordon Foxall talks about an interpretative approach in 'Foundations of Consumer Behaviour Analysis', *Marketing Theory*, 1/2 (Dec. 2001), 165–200.

- For a more extensive discussion, see his book with Ronald Goldsmith and Stephen Brown, *Consumer Psychology for Marketing*, 2nd edn. (London: International Thomson Business Press, 1998).

NOTES

1 One of the first textbooks in the field of consumer behaviour was Francesco M. Nicosia, *Consumer Decision Process: Marketing and Advertising Implications* (Englewood Cliffs, NJ: Prentice Hall, 1966).

2 One of the first and most comprehensive models of consumer behaviour is found in John A. Howard and Jagdish N. Sheth, *The Theory of Buyer Behavior* (New York: John Wiley and Sons, 1969).

3 Gerrit Antonides and W. Fred van Raaij, *Consumer Behaviour: A European Perspective* (Chichester: John Wiley and Sons, 1998).

4 See D. Pickton and A. Broderick, *Integrated Marketing Communication*, 2nd edn. (Harlow: Prentice Hall, 2005), 70.

5 For an introduction to behaviourism, see the father of behaviourism B. F. Skinner's *The Behaviour of Organisms* (New York: Century, 1938).

6 In the 1990s Gordon Foxall argued for a behavioural approach to understanding consumer decision making. See G. R. Foxall, *Consumer Psychology in Behavioural Perspective* (London: Routledge, 1990) and 'Situated Consumer Behaviour: A Behavioural Interpretation of Purchase and Consumption', in R. W. Belk (ed.), *Research in Consumer Behaviour* (Greenwich, Conn.: JAI Press), 5.

7 See H. Assael, *Consumer Behaviour and Marketing Action*, 5th edn. (Ohio: South Western College Publishing, 1995).

8   John Howard dedicated a book for exploring these three consumer decision-making processes, *Consumer Behaviour: An Application of Theory* (New York: McGraw-Hill, 1997).

9   While not referencing Howard's work, Soloman and his colleagues specifically describe his three decision-making processes (although in the text rewording routinized response behaviour to habitual decision making) in N. Soloman, G. Bamossy, and Søren Askegaard, *Consumer Behaviour: A European Perspective* (New York: Prentice Hall Europe, 2002), 237.

10 Now in its 10th edition, the most recent example of Engel's model may be found in R. D. Blackwell, R. W. Miniard, and J. F. Engel's *Consumer Behaviour* (Cincinnati: South-Western, 2005).

11 There are a number of recent books on consumer behaviour from many different perspectives, in addition to the Antonides and van Raaij book. Examples include: Robert East, *Consumer Behaviours: Advances and Applications in Marketing* (London: Prentice Hall, 1997); Frank R. Kardes, *Consumer Behaviour and Management Decision Making* (Reading, Mass.: Addison-Wesley, 1999); Solomon, Bamossy, and Askegaard, *Consumer Behaviour: A European Perspective*.

12 In J. R. Rossiter and L. Percy, *Advertising and Promotion Management* (New York: McGraw-Hill, 1987), and subsequently expanded in their *Advertising Communication and Promotion Management* (2nd edn., New York: McGraw-Hill, 1997), as well as in L. Percy, *Strategies for Implementing Integrated Marketing Communication* (Lincolnwood, Ill.: NTC Business Press, 1997).

13 Two-stage choice models can differ significantly from the more usual single-stage choice models. A good review of this issue is found in Dennis Gensch, 'A Two-Stage Disaggregate Attribute Choice Model', *Marketing Science*, 6/3 (1987).

14 This idea of a Decision Participant Grid was first introduced in L. Percy, *Strategies for Implementing Integrated Marketing Communication* (Lincolnwood, Ill.: NTC Business Press, 1997).

15 See John Howard's notion of routinized response behaviour in *Consumer Behaviour: An Application of Theory*.

16 In *Consumer Behaviour*, Howard, one of the fathers of consumer behaviour theory, dealt with the idea of stages in the consumer decision process, integrating how managers, psychologists, and economists view them. This discussion marked an extension of his original work with Jag Sheth (see n. 2).

17 This model was first introduced in J. F. Engel, D. T. Kollat, and R. D. Blackwell, *Consumer Behavior* (New York: Holt, Rinehart and Winston, 1968), and is remarkably similar to the Howard and Sheth model (see n. 2). Authors of consumer behaviour textbooks continue to include this model or a close variation in their books. For example, East, *Consumer Behaviours*, includes the most recent version of the Engel *et al.* model. While not completely immune to criticism, principally because of its cognitive nature (see especially A. S. C. Ehrenberg, *Repeat Buying: Theory and Applications*, 2nd edn. (London: Charles Griffin and Co., 1988)), this general model of consumer behaviour has proved to be remarkably long-lived.

 Visit the Online Resource Centre that accompanies this book for additional resources to support the text: http://www.oxfordtextbooks.co.uk/orc/percy_elliott3e/

8

Determining the Best Positioning

With an understanding of how the target audience makes decisions in the category, the manager is now able to address the issue of how best to position the brand within its advertising and other marketing communication. The target audience decision-making model helped identify the likely connection between category need and the brand, along with benefits associated with the brand. Now it is time to consider positioning the brand, specifically addressing the question 'What *is* it?', in order to drive brand awareness effectively, and then the question 'What does it *offer*?', to select the benefit or benefits that will best position the brand, and determine the best way to focus upon that benefit consistent with purchase motivation. Effective positioning will ensure optimum delivery of the two core communication objectives of brand awareness and brand attitude, as we see below.

Implementing the Strategic Planning Process

Step 1	Step 2	**Step 3**	Step 4	Step 5
Selecting the Target Audience	Understanding Target Audience Decision Making	Determining the Best Positioning	Developing a Communication Strategy	Setting a Media Strategy

---

STEP 3 DETERMINE THE BEST POSITIONING

General Model of Positioning

Addresses two critical questions about the brand:

What *is* it?	Answer provides the link between brand and category need	Establishes brand awareness
What does it *offer*?	Answer provides the link between brand and benefit	Establishes brand attitude

---

KEY CONCEPTS

1 Positioning strategy for advertising and other marketing communication begins with the marketing plan.

2 Understanding how the market where your brand competes is defined *by consumers* is essential for framing positioning strategy.

3 After identifying the market where a brand competes, it is necessary to determine the best way to present your brand in communication in order to gain a differential advantage over your competition.

4 This requires determining how to present the brand with regard to the product category and relative to competitive brands; selecting a brand benefit to talk about that is important to the target audience, that it believes the brand delivers, and that it believes your brand delivers better than other brands; and then focus upon that benefit in a way that is consistent with the motivation driving behaviour in the category.

Interestingly, most marketing scholars seem to have a rather consistent definition of positioning. In David Jobber's marketing principles book, he has defined positioning as 'the choice of: target market, *where* we want to compete; [and] differential advantage, *how* we wish to compete' (emphasis in original).[1] Compare this with the very similar definition offered by Hooley and Saunders in the preface to their book on competitive positioning, where they describe the two central issues in marketing strategy formulation: 'The identification of target market or markets, the customers that the organization will seek to serve', and 'The creation of a differential advantage, or competitive edge, that will enable the organization to serve the target market more effectively than the competitor.'[2] And Peter Doyle in *Marketing Management and Strategy* says: 'Positioning strategy is the choice of target market segments, which determine where the business competes, and the choice of differential advantage, which dictates how it competes.'[3]

There would seem to be a consensus that 'positioning' entails identifying and defining the market where you compete, and then seeking a differential advantage. In this chapter we shall look at how to define markets, and then the best way to identify the benefit that will provide a brand with a differential advantage over competitors.

Overall, positioning strategy is generally outlined in the marketing plan, and takes into account all aspects of the marketing mix. While a full discussion of this is well beyond the scope of this book,[4] it would be a good idea, before we get specifically into positioning strategy, to look at just where marketing communication does fit within the marketing mix.

Marketing Mix

To begin with, just what do we mean by the 'marketing mix'? Generally speaking, when people talk about the marketing mix, they are referring to those marketing variables that the marketer controls, and that are used to achieve a company's overall marketing objectives. While there are certainly a great many variables that could be considered here, most people classify them into the four groups popularized by McCarthy that we mentioned in Chapter 1: Promotion, Product, Price, and Place—the so-called four Ps of marketing. The key here is that the marketing mix deals with *controllable* variables.

A company certainly decides what product it will manufacture. Clearly it should make a product that corresponds to consumer demand in the category, but it is really up to the company to determine what it will offer. Accordingly, price points are decided upon by the company. Again, while competition within the category will influence pricing strategy, in the end it is really up to the company to decide the prices for its products. Place, McCarthy's 'P' for distribution, is also a marketing variable clearly under the control of the company. Of course the company cannot simply 'wish' for distribution and achieve it. But to the extent that the company's sales force is effective in gaining and holding distribution, the delivery of the product to the consumer is determined by the company.

This brings us to the final 'P', promotion. McCarthy uses the word 'promotion' in a very generic way: advertising, promotion, public relations, and sales-force selling. Most marketers would agree that, in addition to promotion and advertising, personal selling and public relations are also included in the promotion component. Personal selling, while it may account for more actual expenditure from the marketing budget at many companies, is generally a more specialized marketing function and is outside the scope of advertising and marketing communication planning. Nevertheless, as we shall see in Chapter 14, it cannot be ignored completely. It is important that the overall positioning and key benefits of the brand's advertising and promotion also be reflected in personal selling.

The overall emphasis a company places upon personal selling versus advertising and promotion differs markedly from one type of business to another. As you might guess, industrial marketers are more likely to feel that personal selling and trade promotion are more important to their business than advertising, so they concentrate their marketing monies in that area. Companies that manufacture consumer durable goods (heavy appliances, cars, and so forth) place about equal emphasis upon advertising and promotion, and personal selling. Consumer package goods companies, of course, rely very heavily upon advertising and promotion in marketing their products.

Public relations, on the other hand, is similar in many ways to advertising in that it bring a message to the market about the brand, and in many cases should be coordinated with advertising strategy. But public relations is implemented in different ways from advertising. The most obvious difference is that much of public relations is 'free' in the sense that the company does not pay to have stories appear in the media. It does, of course, pay public relations specialists to create the stories and attempt to gain exposure for them. There is a great deal to understand about public relations, and we discuss some of the implications for a brand's marketing communication in Chapter 14.

In this book, we are really interested only in advertising and promotion. But for a company, all their marketing communication strategies must be coordinated so that expenditure on advertising is reinforced by the money spent on promotion, public relations, and sales; money spent on promotion reinforces advertising, public relations, and sales, etc.

Positioning and the Marketing Mix

McCarthy's broader view of 'promotion' is only one part of the marketing mix, and traditional advertising and promotion only one part of that. Nevertheless, all components of the marketing mix must be understood if effective *marketing plans* are to be developed. How does a company go about determining the strategy that will ultimately affect advertising and other marketing communication planning? Simply put, it must gain as complete an understanding of its market as possible. This means knowing how competitors are positioned, and what benefits consumers are seeking in the market. From this information a marketing plan is developed. Perhaps an illustration here will help us see just how a company must look at all aspects of the marketing mix before setting a strategic direction. Suppose the brand space shown in Fig. 8.1 reflects the major competitive brands of DVD players in the marketplace, with their relative market shares reflected by the size of their circles.

What this tells us is that, of the five leading brands, most consumers tend to see them as differing primarily along two dimensions: price and number of features. The alert reader will immediately see that these two dimensions reflect two components of the marketing mix: price and product. Of course, this need not be the case. Consumers could just as easily compare DVD players along other product attribute dimensions, such as European-made versus made in the Pacific Rim, or DVD only versus DVD plus VCR. But, as an example, we will look at how price and features might drive strategy.

What we have here is a market where the brand share leader A is seen to be mid-priced, with some features but not a lot. Brand B and Brand C have roughly equal shares, but Brand B is seen as having more features with a higher price, while Brand C is lower priced with fewer features. Brand D has the smallest share, and is seen as somewhat expensive

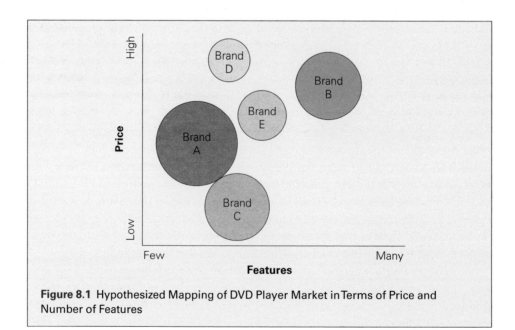

Figure 8.1 Hypothesized Mapping of DVD Player Market in Terms of Price and Number of Features

with few features. Brand E—let us say this is our brand—is the fourth largest and seen as having relatively few features, and a moderate price.

Given these general relationships among the brands in the market, where should Brand E position itself to optimize sales? Practically speaking, it should try to move more to the centre and compete with Brand A, or move toward Brand C's pricing in an effort to attract more buyers. But why should consumers be interested in either new position? There are already products satisfying those segments of the market. Nevertheless, with the proper marketing and communication efforts, along with product modifications, this could be a valid course.

Another course would be to attempt to move alone into the lower right quadrant with a lower-priced DVD player that offers a lot of features. If possible, this would be ideal, because there are no competitors offering such a product. Of course, there may be good reasons why this quadrant is unoccupied. Brand E's marketing managers must ask themselves whether or not it is possible to manufacture a DVD player with a number of features, but still at a low cost. Perhaps the company could put up with lower profit margins, or perhaps the company's research and development could come up with product or manufacturing innovations that would save costs.

In any event, you should by now see that one cannot simply decide upon a positioning for a brand without taking into consideration all the components in the marketing mix. In this brief example we have seen that price is dependent upon the cost of the features that will be built into the product, and is also perhaps a function of persuading the trade to accept lower margins on the brand (place, or distribution).

Suppose R & D tell marketing that they have achieved a breakthrough that permits them to include all the features currently available with Brand B, while still maintaining the existing cost structure. Good news indeed for the brand manager, but his positioning options with respect to the marketing mix are still open. For example, one strategy might indeed be price related, communicating that the brand now offers many new features at the same price. But another strategy could be to upgrade the brand's image by pursuing a quality-feature strategy at higher price points. This would make a lot of sense, since our brand could now offer more features than Brand A at the same price as A, or the same features as Brand B, but at a lower price (while maintaining a higher price than Brand A). Either of these latter two strategies would also permit larger margins at the retail level, pleasing the distribution chain, while at the same time increasing the unit profit for the company.

Although marketing communication is only one part of the marketing mix, all four components interact and must be considered as you begin to think about positioning and communication strategy. Overall, you can think of the marketing mix as providing consumer value. By this we mean that the marketing mix should be construed so as to offer a set of benefits to the consumer, benefits the consumers will relate to their underlying motivations to behave. Of the four components of the marketing mix, the product or service must provide attributes that are seen as offering particular benefits to the consumer; price must be seen within the context of a price-value relationship; place or distribution must provide convenient access to the product as well as positive store image; and finally promotion will alert the consumer to these potential benefits. These points

Table 8.1 Consumer Benefits related to the Four Components of the Marketing Mix

Product	Must provide attributes that are seen as offering particular benefits to the consumer
Price	Must be seen within the context of a price–value relationship
Place	Must provide convenient access to the product as well as a positive store image
Promotion	Will alert the consumer to potential benefits

are summarized in Table 8.1, and this relationship between what the product offers, the benefits perceived by the consumers, and their motivation to respond will be explored in greater depth in later chapters. In fact, it is this relationship that advertising, and other forms of marketing communication, must forge if it is to be successful.

Identifying and Defining the Market

As the definitions of positioning offered earlier make clear, one of the most important considerations in the development of a positioning strategy is exactly how you are defining the market where you are competing. This may sound like a very simple question. After all, if you are selling beer, your market is made up of all the brands of beer that are sold along with yours in a particular area, right? Well, this is not necessarily true. For example, what if you were marketing a lower-calorie beer like Amstel Light? You might have a 10 per cent share of the European beer market; or you might be thought of as having a 35 per cent share of the lower-calorie beer market; or even a 3 per cent share of the 'light alcoholic beverage' market, which would include wine and other speciality light alcoholic products as well. To establish what category we are dealing with—which will define the important communication effect of category need—requires us to define the market in which our brand competes.

We can see by the Amstel Light example that defining your market is not necessarily a straightforward issue. The actual basis for what defines the true market for a brand is how *consumers* see a group of products or brands competing for the same usage situation. If the majority of consumers regard a group of brands as being close substitutes for each other, or as purchase alternatives, then this group of brands defines the market.

The reason we are so very much concerned about knowing the true definition of a market is that without it the strategic direction for the brand, especially in terms of market share objectives, could well be misleading. If the strategic direction is wrong, you can bet the communication strategy will also be wrong, because it will be based upon a misleading definition of the market.

You may be thinking that the best way to define a market is surely to look for the biggest possible segment, and in a sense you would be right. It is certainly more desirable to have a large share of a big market than of a small market, or at times even a smaller share of a big market than a big share of a smaller market. But this is not the point. It does not matter how *we* define the market. The market actually defines itself by how *consumers see the market*. The way in which consumers look at a market will determine how they behave, and for us to develop effective advertising and marketing communication strategy we must understand why and how consumers behave as they do.

Another important reason to understand how markets are defined is that it permits you to make more effective positioning decisions for new products. To the extent that a company positions a new product or brand within the same market as other products sold by that same company, it encourages cannibalization. ('Cannibalization' is a term used in marketing to describe a situation where the introduction of a new product takes sales away from existing products the company sells rather than adding incremental new sales.) Again, this could have significant implications for marketing communication.

Let us consider the case of Nestlé, which for many years marketed a frozen pizza product that was made with French bread rather than a traditional pizza crust. First introduced in the USA under the Stouffer brand name, it was then marketed in Europe and the Pacific Rim under the Findas brand. This French bread pizza soon became one of the leading frozen pizzas. But a real question arises as to whether or not the consumer saw this product as just another frozen pizza, or as a different pizza-like product. You may feel that it really does not matter as long as it has strong sales. But Nestlé obviously considered its product as competing in the frozen pizza market, because it referred to it in its advertising as 'Findas Pizza' and not 'Findas French Bread Pizza'.

However, in 1988 Stouffer's introduced in the USA a new round frozen pizza similar to other traditional frozen pizzas. At that time, the only frozen pizza Stouffer's and Findas marketed was the French bread product, which, as we have noted, was referred to in its advertising simply as Stouffer's or Findas Pizza. The brands had an obvious problem: how to position both products to maximize overall market share. This should help you begin really to appreciate the importance of good market definitions. What should the brands have done? Reposition the French bread product for a French bread frozen pizza market, or position it simply as one of two types of frozen pizza that the brands offer? The first position assumes that the consumer looks at French bread pizza products as a different market from traditional round frozen pizzas, but there was no evidence of this. The second position assumes that the consumer looks at all frozen pizza products, regardless of form, as a single market, and would welcome a line extension from Nestlé. The implication for advertising would obviously be different, depending upon how consumers define the market. Nestlé introduced the product under the Stouffer's and Findas brands, but was not successful. The market did not see the need for a 'second' pizza from Nestlé. Perhaps the best way would have been to introduce the round pizza under a new brand name. The problem was that Nestlé did not have a clear understanding of how consumers defined the market where French bread pizza competed.

Ways to Define Markets

Perhaps the most traditional way of describing markets is simply to look at a broad category and then break it down by whatever characteristics of the product make sense. For example, traditionally the beer market is seen as divided first into regular versus lower alcohol or lower calorie, then price brands, then regular, premium, super-premium, imported, and micro-brewed brands. The interesting thing here is that, while those who brew and market beer look at the category in this way, consumers are less precise. In fact, if you were to ask the ordinary beer drinker to classify brands such as Becks, Budweiser, Heineken, or Miller, they would call them regular beers, but these are classified as premium or imported beers (depending upon where you are in the world) by the industry.

Other ways to describe markets a priori include defining them in terms of their channels of distribution. For example, especially with industrial products, those sold directly through a manufacturer will be seen as different from those sold through a jobber or distributor. Consumer package goods are often looked at as national brands versus private label, or advertised versus unadvertised brands.

The point in presenting these traditional ways in which markets are described is to show that they tend to reflect a product-oriented approach to marketing more than a consumer-oriented approach. Not only are such non-consumer-oriented approaches to market definition likely to lead to less effective advertising and marketing communication strategy, but they can also interfere with effective overall marketing. An interesting case in point was the forced divestiture of Clorox (a brand of laundry and household bleach) by Procter and Gamble. Some years ago one of the issues raised in support of the antitrust action was the high share of the bleach market controlled by Clorox. Unfortunately for Procter & Gamble, Clorox's market share was defined only in terms of liquid bleach: the definition excluded dry bleaches from consideration. If dry bleaches had been included in defining the category, its overall market share would have been significantly smaller and unlikely to have attracted the interest of government regulators.

Cross-elasticity

A rather interesting, if somewhat abstract, way of thinking about defining markets considers the cross-elasticities between products. As you might imagine, this is a method that has been proposed by economists and is price related. It is not unusual for economists to propose various schemes for dealing with consumer behaviour that are based upon the utilities of time and price. Practically speaking, however, such schemes tend to mask more than illuminate what is going on in the market. Nevertheless, it is useful at least to be aware of some of these ideas.

The notion of using price cross-elasticity to define markets is rooted in the idea that cross-elasticity of price between two products or brands is directly proportional to the shift in sales for one brand as a result of a change in price for another. In other words, to the extent that an increase in the price of one brand brings about an increase in the sales of a second brand, they may be considered substitutable, and therefore part of the same market.

As we have suggested, this is certainly plausible, but rather difficult to measure accurately in the market. Perhaps now that scanning data is widely available, shifts in sales as a function of price changes will be easier to detect. But, even if such shifts in market share are reliably measured, there remains the question of controlling for all other variables in the market, especially advertising and other marketing communication.

Perceived Similarity

A much more understandable way of looking at markets is in terms of how similar consumers perceive the brands in a particular category to be. Measures of similarity can range from the very simple to the quite complex. For example, consumers can simply be asked to list all the products they use for a particular task or in a particular situation. Those products felt to be appropriate for the same usage situation could be thought of as similar, and hence defining a market. For example, in household cleaning consumers may feel that such diverse products as ammonia and soap are appropriate products to clean a worktop. If so, one could certainly say that they help to define the market for worktop cleaners.

However, while a simple method like this does define a market in a certain way, and it certainly is consumer based, it does not offer a very precise definition. All this method provides is an aggregate definition of the market, without really telling us how the consumer makes fundamental judgements in the market, and it is these fundamental judgements that are important in formulating advertising strategy. That said, it should be noted that this simple idea of perceived similarity is nonetheless the foundation of category need, which is essential to positioning brands in marketing communication, as we shall see later in this chapter.

A somewhat more advanced version of this simple model permits the consumer to group together products or brands in terms of their perceived relative similarity. There are a number of statistical methods available to deal with this question, and they are usually referred to as perceptual mapping procedures.[5] What these techniques do is take a set of similarity judgements and map them in such a way that those brands that are considered similar to each other end up close together while those that are further apart are seen as less alike.

Let us consider the mapping shown in Fig. 8.2. This represents the actual results of a study where consumers were asked to rank-order all the pairs of brands studied from the two they felt were most alike through to the pair they felt were least alike. While we need not get into the actual way this is done, the results when mapped place those brands close together on the map that consumers see as most alike, and those that are not seen as alike are placed far apart. In this example we can see that brands such as Sanka, Nescafé, and Nescafé Decaffeinated are seen as unique, whereas other brands—Folgers, Maxwell House, and Taster's Choice regular and Decaffeinated—are seen as alike.

This is a particularly interesting example, because both caffeinated and decaffeinated soluble (or 'instant') coffee brands are included. If consumers initially defined the soluble coffee market by types, we would expect that the caffeinated brands would be mapped separately from the decaffeinated brands. But, as we can see, while Sanka and Nescafé Decaffeinated are indeed separate from the caffeinated brands, Taster's Choice regular and Decaffeinated are mapped together, indicating that consumers see them as quite similar. Additionally, Brim (a decaffeinated brand) is also mapped near the regular brands. It is simply not clear from this example how consumers are defining the soluble coffee market.

All we can say about the soluble coffee market based upon this similarities mapping is that Folgers, Maxwell House, Taster's Choice, Taster's Choice Decaffeinated, and

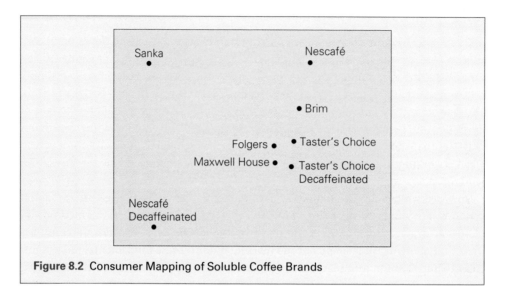

Figure 8.2 Consumer Mapping of Soluble Coffee Brands

Brim—two decaffeinated and three caffeinated brands—are seen as similar, and all these brands are seen as quite different from Nescafé, Sanka, and Nescafé Decaffeinated. While there are methods available to help us determine just why consumers feel these similarities exist, this mapping itself does not offer a very clear understanding of how consumers define this market.

Even though this method is an improvement over the simple aggregate method of looking at similarities in terms of, say, usage, since it does permit us to identify submarkets, it still is not quite as useful as defining markets *hierarchically*, which we shall look at next. The problem is that we still do not know whether, for example, the critical classification is made first in terms of type or of brand. Actually, these mappings have much more value in defining the relationship among products or brands than in defining markets.

Hierarchical Market Definition

We encountered the idea of a hierarchical process in our discussion of the four-step response sequence. You will recall that we talked about the compounding problem, where what comes before determines what comes later. One way to look at how consumers define markets is to look at the order in which they consider characteristics of a product in the decisions they make.[6] In marketing terminology this is often referred to as *partitioning* a market.

The idea of partitioning follows from classical categorization theory in psychology, which posits that all 'concepts' are organized in memory according to some hierarchy,[7] working from the more abstract down to the more specific. Even though neuropsychologists no longer feel this is how constructs are actually established in memory, *markets* are partitioned by consumers in terms of some sort of hierarchical system, and this structure informs how brand decisions are made. In fact, when making a product or brand choice, consumers will always have 'partitioned' the category.

The thinking that underlies a hierarchical definition of a market is that an overall product category (such as beverages, deodorants, cars, and so on) can be divided and then

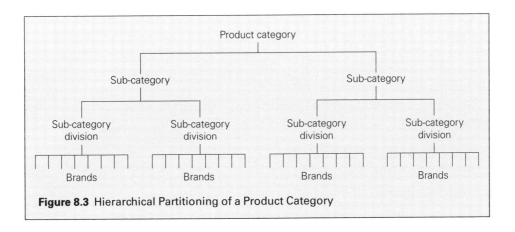

Figure 8.3 Hierarchical Partitioning of a Product Category

subdivided several times into subcategories that define narrower markets, and which will tend to end when consumers make their actual choice. Several things are implied in this notion of partitioning markets about the way consumers behave. First of all, as we proceed down the hierarchy, we assume that consumers see different brands in the market as more and more alike, and hence that they are more substitutable. Then, assuming consumers see brands as more and more alike, they will be increasingly more willing to switch among brands. This idea is illustrated in Fig. 8.3. You can see that advertising and other marketing communication must be able to deal with this tendency of consumers to view brands as more or less alike as they move down the partitioning hierarchy. It must correctly position the category need in relation to the appropriate decision level in the hierarchy, and work to create a unique positioning for a brand against the competition. This should become clearer soon, when we illustrate hypothetical executions of partitioning hierarchies for the drinks category.

Bases for Partitions

When consumers are asked to describe how products in a category differ, they do not make a hierarchical distinction, but they do tend to talk about brands and products in terms of four general characteristics:

- *Type of product*: for example, in frozen foods there are full dinners versus just main dishes, main dishes versus side dishes, main meals versus breakfast, and so on.

- *End benefit*: for example, aspirin could be taken to ease pain or to help prevent a heart attack, or you could buy an expensive Scotch because you like the taste or because you want to impress your friends.

- *Usage situation*: the end benefit that you are seeking in a product may vary as a function of when or how the product is used—for example 'instant' or soluble coffee only for breakfast, but ground roast for when you have friends over.

- *Brand name*: finally, the brand itself implies many things and could be a key factor in defining markets; for example, we can all think of brands we consider 'quality' brands versus 'price' brands.

Notice some important things about these characteristics. They could all be used to describe the same product or brand, but the *order* in which they are used by consumers in arriving at a choice is what will determine how consumers define markets. You should be able to see how each factor, depending on which is the final arbiter of choice, will suggest different advertising strategies to deal with it.

Thinking in terms of these four characteristics, if we were to define the coffee market, we would want answers from consumers to questions like these:

• What kind of a product is coffee?

• Why do you drink coffee?

• When do you drink coffee?

• What are the differences among various brands of coffee?

Answers to questions like these begin to explain how consumers see the coffee market, and helps the marketing manager define the market strategically the way consumers themselves do.

If you were the marketing manager for a coffee brand, how do you think the market structure would be defined? This is actually a more complicated question than you might imagine. If you consider simply what coffee 'is', it is something people drink. Fig. 8.4 suggests a reasonable product-based hierarchical partition of the drinks market. If this is an accurate representation (and research suggests it is), then at the product level coffee competes with non-alcoholic, hot drinks. But this is really much too simple, and is actually misleading.

When you ask consumers to talk about coffee, addressing questions like those above, they do talk about it in terms of product characteristics, especially ground roast versus

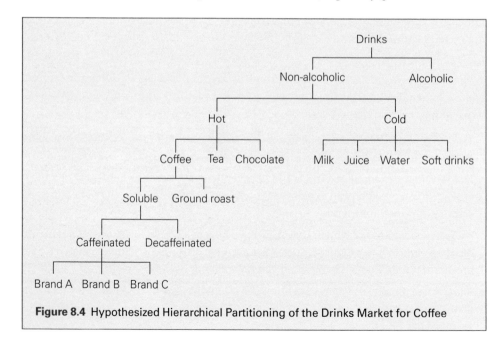

Figure 8.4 Hypothesized Hierarchical Partitioning of the Drinks Market for Coffee

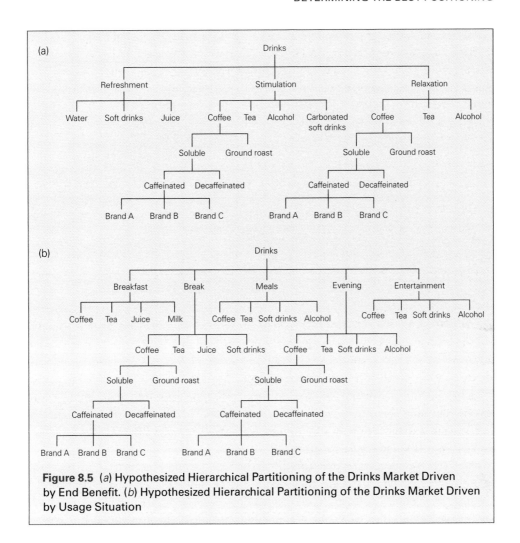

Figure 8.5 (*a*) Hypothesized Hierarchical Partitioning of the Drinks Market Driven by End Benefit. (*b*) Hypothesized Hierarchical Partitioning of the Drinks Market Driven by Usage Situation

'instant' (i.e. soluble). But they are *much* more lively when discussing coffee in terms of end benefits and usage situations.[8] Figures 8.5*a* and 8.5*b* illustrate how we might imagine the drinks market partitioned along these lines.

From these partitionings we can see that the market strategy should be aimed at positioning coffee against the end benefits of stimulation and relaxation, or against situational usage. Interestingly, the end benefits partitioning suggests that coffee should be thought of as competing more with alcoholic beverages than with soft drinks. While some perceptions overlap in the consumer's mind, coffee has more in common with tea and alcoholic beverages, and it is not seen as refreshing. Clearly the advertising and marketing communication strategy suggested by this market definition will be very different from that suggested by the product-based positioning. An interesting use of mappings in conjunction with hierarchical descriptions has been offered by Urban and Hauser.[9] In the method they suggest, you begin with a hierarchical approach, but you define the

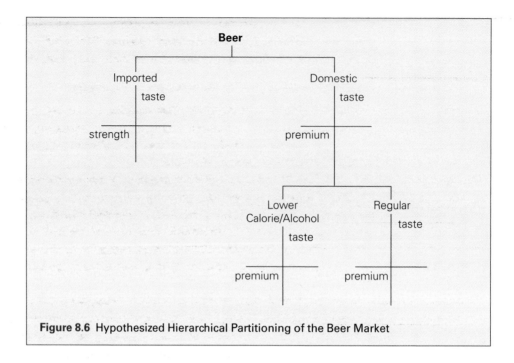

Figure 8.6 Hypothesized Hierarchical Partitioning of the Beer Market

branches not only in terms of the physical attributes or characteristics of the product, but also by consumer perception. Perceptions are modelled by a map for each branch of the tree generated by the hierarchical definition. Figure 8.6 illustrates a hypothetical application of this method to the beer market.

What Fig. 8.6 suggests is that consumers first define the beer market in terms of imported versus domestic beers, then define the domestic market in terms of lower-calorie, low-alcohol, 'lite beers' versus regular, full-calorie beers. Then, within these hierarchical definitions they see brands along taste versus premium dimensions. If this were a true representation of the beer market (remember, it is only a hypothetical example), it would suggest that for domestic beers it would be important to understand that, since consumers make primary distinctions between 'lite' and full-calorie beers, advertising strategy must also take this into account. Specifically, separate campaigns would be necessary for, say, Amstel and Amstel Light. If both types of beer were mentioned in the same advert, as some brewers have done, consumers could be a bit confused because they see these as two distinctly different products.

On the other hand, again assuming our hypothetical example, with imported beers consumers may not distinguish between lower-calorie and full-calorie beers. This would mean that advertisers of imported beers might only be concerned with identifying their brand as imported. How the notion of greater European unity may change ideas of 'imported' beer remains to be seen. The perceptual map of the imported beer market suggests that consumers evaluate *imported* beers in terms of taste and strength.

In summary, you should now see that a consumer-driven definition of markets is essential for the development of effective advertising strategy. Also, the most desirable technique for looking at how consumers define markets is some variation of a hierarchical partitioning.

Seeking a Differential Advantage

Up to this point we have looked very broadly at how various components of the marketing mix influence the overall market positioning of a brand, and how markets are defined. Now it is time to look more specifically at how a brand is to be positioned *within* the market definition. In a sense, up to now we have been dealing with the first half of the positioning definitions introduced at the start of the chapter: *identifying the market where you compete*. This is what helps pinpoint the *category* where the brand competes, and frames something we have been calling category need.[10]

Category need defines why the target audience wants the product or service offered by the market. A category, at its basic level, is what people think of spontaneously when asked: 'What is this?' When asked this question, people tend to respond in such terms as beer, coffee, soft drink, or perhaps a brand name. They do *not* talk in terms like 'a beverage', although they may very well describe something like this as 'something to drink'. You can see that people tend to think about categories, and as a result category needs, well down the hierarchical market definition.

For consumers, brands exist to satisfy a need, and it is this 'need' that defines the category for them. It does not matter what or how a marketer defines the category for their brand, what is important is how the consumer defines it, and that will be in terms of satisfying a particular need.[11] We will be dealing a lot more with this idea of category need in later chapters because it is an important communication effect to consider when setting marketing communication strategy.

What we want to do now is turn our attention to the second half of the positioning definition: *seeking a differential advantage*. This is where we must identify the optimal way of presenting our brand in advertising and other marketing communication.

Initial Positioning Decisions

Managers should always take a fresh look at the brand's positioning in the development of a marketing communication plan. Markets change, competitor positionings change, and what the consumer is looking for in the product could change. As we look more specifically now at positioning a product or service for marketing communication, there are two decisions the manager must make: how should the brand be positioned with regard to the product category; and whether the brand's position in relation to other brands should be in terms of product users or the product itself. In order to make these decisions, we must begin by asking two questions about the brand: what *is* it, and what does it *offer*? Answers to these questions are critical because they are linked to the two universal communication objectives of brand awareness and brand attitude.

The answer to the question 'what is it?' connects the brand to category need, sometimes referred to as the brand's *market* position. There are two ways this can be done.

A brand can be positioned in relation to the product category or category need either *centrally* or *differentially*. To be centrally positioned a brand must be able to deliver on all the main benefits of the category. In effect, it will be positioned as the *best* brand in the category. Because a centrally positioned brand more or less defines the category, it should be limited to brands with a strong market position. Often, this is the first really successful brand in a category. Think of brands such as Xerox and Hoover; they *literally* define their categories. Xerox *means* copying ('Xerox that for me please'); Hoover *means* vacuuming ('Hoover that rug, it's a mess').

This idea of centrally positioned brands reflects what some in psychology have called 'prototypes', something that helps people quickly and accurately identify things (such as a brand).[12] In fact, one could think of brands like Xerox as an archetype which helped define future copiers. In psychology, some theories define a prototype as an abstract representation in memory, others as a concrete representation.[13] Yet a third theory posits that people create an abstract idea of what the typical product in a category would be, and then associate it with a specific brand.[14]

While some people have suggested that it is possible for a 'me-too' brand to adopt a central positioning if the people can in fact *objectively* determine that, compared with the leading brand, it can equally deliver the category's primary benefit, and do it at a lower price, this is not easy to do.[15] Store brands often adopt this strategy, offering the same benefits as the category leader, but at a lower price, and almost always using the same positioning as the market leader.[16] However, it will usually only be a brand seen as a strong market leader that should be centrally positioned. And, with a centrally positioned brand, it is important that the perception of it doing the best job in delivering the primary category benefit be constantly confirmed.

In all other areas, which means for most brands, a differentiated positioning strategy is called for. We already know the answer to the question 'what does it offer?' for a centrally positioned brand. It will be the primary category benefit. But, for a differentiated positioning, we must look for another benefit the brand offers, different from the primary category benefit that helps position the market leader centrally. Creating a distinct positioning is what helps differentiate a brand from the estimated 10,000 brands the average adult has represented in memory.[17] Identifying the best benefit to differentiate your brand from the market leader and other competitors is what we will be taking up later in the section on selecting the appropriate benefit.

We have looked at the 'what is it?' and 'what does it offer' questions in order to help decide how the brand should be positioned with regard to the product category. Now the manager must consider a second decision, whether the positioning strategy should place the brand, relative to its competition, in terms of the user or of the product itself. This decision follows consideration of whether the brand should be centrally or differentially positioned because either may be implemented via a user or a product-benefit orientation.

User-Oriented Position

While both user- and product-benefit-oriented positioning strategies (covered next) make use of brand benefits in the message, with user-oriented positionings the message is specifically addressing the user; the *user* is the focus, not the product. User-oriented positionings make sense when a brand is marketed to a specific segment, satisfying their particular needs. But this does not necessarily mean that a brand positioned towards the user is appropriate only for that specific target audience, only that it is positioned that way. For example, a performance wear brand advertised for the 'serious runner' or Scotch for the 'discerning drinker' would be examples of a user-oriented positioning, because a strategic decision has been made specifically to position the brand to a particular segment of the market.

Another case where a user-oriented positioning should be considered is when the underlying purchase motivation in the category is social appeal. We will be dealing with this issue of motivation in more detail shortly, because benefit selection and focus should always be related to the appropriate purchase motivation. For now, we need only know that social approval is a positive motive that reflects purchase decisions made because the user is looking for social rewards through personal recognition in using the brand.

When most people in a brand's target audience are driven by social approval in their brand selection in that category, a user-oriented positioning makes sense. By focusing on the users you are reminding them of how good *they* will feel in using, and importantly displaying, your brand. This is why brands of luxury cars and high fashion often employ user-oriented positionings. But you can also choose to tap into an otherwise latent social approval motive. Most people, for example, do not buy peanut butter for social approval, but Procter & Gamble has for many years utilized a user-oriented positioning for its Jif brand. It focuses upon a mother's (and recently also a father's) nurturing feelings for their children, positioning Jif 'for mothers who really care'.

Product-Benefit-Oriented Positioning

Addressing a specific segment or when the underlying purchase motive is social approval are the two circumstances where the manager may *consider* using a user-oriented positioning. But this is only one option. In either case one could instead choose to use a product-benefit-oriented positioning.

While a manager must always consider whether or not a user-oriented positioning is appropriate, in the majority of cases a product-benefit-oriented positioning should be used (Table 8.2). With a product-benefit-oriented positioning the product is the hero of the positioning, and the positioning will be defined by specific benefits related to the product, not the user. In a product-benefit-oriented positioning, *product characteristics* are the message; in a user-oriented positioning, *user characteristics* are the message.

Table 8.2 Options for Positioning Brand relative to Competitors

User-Oriented Positioning	• When marketing to specific segment
	• When social approval is primary purchase motivation
Product-Benefit-Oriented Positioning	• In all other cases

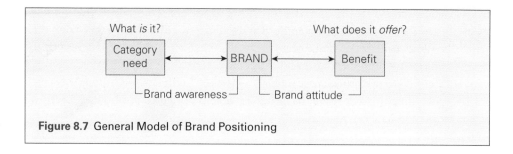

Figure 8.7 General Model of Brand Positioning

In this first step towards positioning a brand we have addressed the initial decisions a manager must make: how do we position the brand with regard to the product category; and, relative to other brands, should we use a user-oriented or a product-benefit-oriented positioning. In effect, these decisions determine how the brand will be positioned in terms of its brand awareness and brand attitude communication objectives. We can think of this in terms of a general model of positioning, as shown in Fig. 8.7. The 'what *is* it?' question helps us link the brand to the need in the mind of the target audience, and the 'what does it *offer*?' question helps us associate a relevant benefit to the brand in the minds of the target audience, which enables us to build a positive brand attitude. Even if a user-oriented positioning is adopted, the 'user as hero' *becomes* the benefit as users are positioned within the context of a product benefit (for example, implied in the Jif positioning 'for mothers who really care' is that a caring mother wants only the 'best'). But how do we determine that benefit? We take this up in the next section.

Selecting the Appropriate Benefit

Now that we have a broad understanding of where to locate the brand within the overall positioning framework of the product category and brand benefits, the manager must determine what benefit (or benefits) to emphasize in the positioning. What we want to do is select those benefits that will best distinguish our brand from competitors in a way that is important to the target audience. Ideally, these benefits will reflect the underlying motivation that drives purchase behaviour because they are at the heart of brand attitude communication strategy. What we want to do is be able to 'tap into' the purchase motivation via the benefit presented in the advert or other marketing communication. The difficult question, however, is what benefit should be emphasized in order to get the job done.

We will be looking for a benefit that is *important* to our target audience in influencing purchase, one that our target audience believes (or can be persuaded to believe) our brand can *deliver*, and one that the target audience believes (or, again, can be persuaded to believe) our brand can deliver *better* than other brands (Fig. 8.8).[18] This is what we are looking for, but finding it is not easy. One way is to explore the basic, underlying attitudinal structure used by the target audience in evaluating brands. Perhaps the best way of doing this is to use a multi-attribute model based upon Fishbein's notion of expectancy value.[19]

> - It is *important* to the target audience
> - The brand can *deliver* it
> - It can be delivered *better* than other brands
>
> **Figure 8.8** Considerations in Selecting Benefits for Marketing Communication

The Expectancy-Value Model of Attitude

What this model suggests is that a person's attitude towards an object (A_o) is the sum of all the things they believe about it (b_i), weighted by how important each of those things are to them (a_i). Mathematically, this is expressed as:

$$A_o = \sum_{i=1}^{n} a_i b_i$$

where : A_o = attitude towards the object,

a_i = importance of belief, and

b_i = belief about the object.

Do not be put off by the mathematical equation, because this is really not very complicated. Think about chocolate bars. Using the model, how would you determine someone's attitude towards, say, Snickers? What the model says is that a person's attitude towards something, Snickers in this case, will be the sum of its perceived characteristics and how important they are to what *motivates* that person to buy a chocolate bar.

What are some of the characteristics of chocolate bars? The obvious attributes are ingredients such as chocolate, caramel, and peanuts, but the characteristics of a chocolate bar will also include more intangible ones such as 'provides energy', 'is an inexpensive snack', and 'is an indulgence'. While there are clearly more characteristics than these, we will work with this set to see how we can learn something about people's attitudes towards Snickers.

Look at Table 8.3. This hypothetical example shows that people feel that chocolate and a sense of indulgence are essential to a chocolate bar; that caramel, peanuts, and being an inexpensive snack, while desirable, are not essential; and that it really is not important that a chocolate bar provides energy. Their perception of Snickers is that it really delivers chocolate and peanuts, and it is seen as an inexpensive snack, but it does only an OK job in providing caramel and energy, and as an indulgence. Computing an expectancy-value measure of Snickers' brand attitude, using the appropriate numbers and following the model, yields 19.

So what does 19 mean? By itself, very little. The important thing here is to look at *how* the attitude is determined. We can see that for the chocolate bar attribute most important to people, chocolate, Snickers is seen to do a very good job delivering the benefit. It also delivers well on peanuts, but peanuts are less essential in a chocolate bar. Caramel is desirable but not essential in a chocolate bar, and Snickers does an OK job on this attribute.

Table 8.3 Expectancy-Value Model of Attitude for a Chocolate Bar

	Importance Weight (a_i)	Beliefs (b_i)	Benefit ($a_i \times b_i$)
Chocolate	3	3	9
Caramel	1	1	1
Peanuts	1	3	3
Provides energy	0	1	0
Inexpensive snack	1	3	3
Indulgence	3	1	3
$A_o = \sum_{i=1}^{6} a_i b_i =$			19
	3 = Essential	3 = Definitely delivers	
	1 = Desirable	1 = Does OK	
	0 = Of no importance	0 = Does not deliver	

Looking at the more benefit-oriented characteristics, Snickers is seen as definitely an inexpensive snack, which is desirable, but not essential. People believe Snickers does an OK job in providing energy, even though that is not important. But in terms of being seen as an indulgence, which is essential for a chocolate bar (in our example), Snickers is seen only as OK.

Positioning with the Expectancy-Value Model

If the expectancy-value attitude does not mean much on its own, then why compute it? The reason is that it provides an important *relative* feel for what people's attitudes are likely to be, depending upon how they perceive a brand. This is why the model is so important for positioning.

The strength of people's attitudes towards Snickers in this example is that it is seen as having everything important in a chocolate bar, except for only doing an OK job as an indulgence. But suppose that among chocolate lovers the beliefs about chocolate and caramel were reversed? If that were how chocolate lovers saw Snickers, it would mean it was seen as doing only an OK job on the two things most important to them in a chocolate bar—chocolate and being an indulgence.

In the first example, where Snickers is seen by the general population as really delivering on the chocolate attribute, the overall attitude score is 19; in this second example, where it does only an OK job on chocolate among chocolate lovers while really delivering on caramel, the overall attitude score is only 13. If the first example reflected general attitudes towards Snickers in the market while the second reflected the attitude of chocolate lovers towards Snickers, how would we need to position Snickers to attract the chocolate lover?

Looking only at the attitude scores, we know that attitudes towards Snickers in the general population are much more favourable than they are among chocolate lovers: 19 versus 13. But even more importantly, as we look at the beliefs and their weightings, we know that the reason for this less favourable attitude among chocolate lovers is their perception that Snickers is more about caramel and peanuts than it is about chocolate. This suggests that, if Snickers is to attract chocolate lovers, it must be positioned more strongly against that benefit. Since we know (again in our hypothetical example) that in a chocolate bar chocolate is more important than caramel or peanuts, taking a strong chocolate positioning would reinforce the already held beliefs of the general population while building this perception among chocolate lovers.

Let us take this idea one step further and look at hypothetical beliefs about two chocolate bar brands, Snickers and Cadbury. Assume that consumer attitudes toward these brands are the results of the weighted beliefs shown in Table 8.4. These figures suggest that the overall attitudes towards Snickers and Cadbury, as measured by an expectancy-value model, are roughly equal, although the edge goes to Cadbury.

If you were the brand manager for Snickers, what would you do to position the brand more strongly against Cadbury? The two most important benefits are chocolate and

Table 8.4 Comparative Expectancy-Value Model of Attitude for Two Chocolate Bars

	Importance Weight (a_i)	Beliefs (b_i)	
		Snickers	Cadbury
Chocolate	3	3	3
Caramel	1	1	0
Peanuts	1	3	0
Provides energy	0	1	1
Inexpensive snack	1	3	3
Indulgence	3	1	3
$A_0 = \sum_{i=1}^{6} a_i b_i =$		19	21
	3 = Essential	3 = Definitely delivers	
	1 = Desirable	1 = Does OK	
	0 = Of no importance	0 = Does not deliver	

indulgence. Cadbury delivers both, while Snickers lags behind on the indulgence bene-fit. In other words, Snickers does not deliver as well as Cadbury on this important bene-fit; Cadbury does it better. One way for Snickers to build a more positive brand attitude would be to position itself more as an indulgence. If it were to succeed, its overall attitude score would jump to 25, better than Cadbury at 21. Another option would be to *drive down* the importance of indulgence, while playing up the 'extra' taste of caramel and peanuts. If the importance weighting of indulgence were to drop from essential to desir-able, Snickers would enjoy a slight edge in overall attitude (17 versus 15). Add to this a heightened awareness among candy bar buyers that Snickers really delivers on caramel, and the advantage becomes even stronger (19 versus 15).

We must remember that in these examples the numbers have been made up in order to illustrate the points, and also that there could be many other important benefits we have not considered. But the important thing to understand is that you can use an expectancy-value model to identify the importance of benefits to your target audience, the degree to which it perceives that you and your competitors can deliver those benefits, and which benefits one brand is seen to deliver better than its competitors.

In using the model, include those benefits seen by the target audience as being import-ant or potentially important, and have the target audience evaluate your brand and two or three key competitors. Remember that this exercise must be done for the *appropriate target audience*, not the population at large (unless, of course, that happens to be the tar-get audience). As you work out the numbers, it will be possible to evaluate positioning options in terms of:

- reinforcing or building a uniqueness for your brand on important benefits;
- capitalizing upon competitive weaknesses on important benefits;
- emphasizing important benefits your brand delivers better than others;
- increasing the importance of benefits your brand delivers better than others (if not already seen as essential);
- decreasing the importance of benefits your brand does not deliver better than others.

Benefit Focus

One final consideration in benefit positioning is how to focus on or emphasize the benefit in marketing communication. At this point we need to look more closely at what is meant by a benefit. Up until now, we have been talking about benefits in a rather general way. But in order correctly to understand benefit focus we need to 'deconstruct' benefits, and look at what it is about a product or brand that someone is likely to see as a benefit.

A benefit may be experienced in different ways: an objective *attribute* of a product (anti-bacterial, no calories) might be seen by some as a benefit; a subjective claim or *characteristic* of a product (easy to use, tastes great) might be seen as a benefit; or an *emotion* (excitement, relief) could be experienced as a benefit. In effect, a benefit might be thought of in terms of what you *want* from a product, and you may find that in terms of what a brand *has* (attribute), what you *experience* with a brand (characteristic), or what you *feel* (emotion). This is summarized in Table 8.5. How we focus on the benefit will depend upon what

Table 8.5 Different Aspects of a Benefit

Attribute	An *objective* component of a product (anti-bacterial, no calories)
Characteristic	A *subjective* claim about a product (easy to use, tastes great)
Emotion	A *feeling* associated with the product (excitement, relief)

aspect of the benefit is involved, and upon the motivation associated with purchase in the brand's category. This will depend upon the motivation associated with purchase in a category. As we shall discuss in the next chapter, brand attitude communication strategy depends upon understanding the correct underlying purchase motivation. We shall defer a detailed discussion of this to then. For now, we need know only that some advertising and marketing communication strategies are based primarily on providing 'information', others on addressing 'feelings'. When the motive is negative, information in some form is provided in order to address a problem of some kind: how do I get my clothes looking better, what is the best washer, what can I take for real pain? When the motivation is positive, messages must address the target audience's 'feelings' in some way: I want a car everyone will notice, I want to indulge myself, and so on.

The way the brand positioning in a message addresses the benefit should reflect this fundamental distinction between purchase motivations. When the motive is negative and the advertising and other marketing communication is basically providing information, the emphasis should be *directly* on the benefit. You can draw attention to the benefit by simply focusing on an attribute of the product. But, this is really effective only when dealing with an 'expert' target audience. Experts are those people who are only looking objectively at a product, evaluating its specific characteristics. They will infer the benefit from the 'data'. The attribute (or attributes) will tell them if the product is likely to solve their problem. Otherwise, when dealing with negative emotions you want to focus on the benefit by drawing attention directly to a subjective characteristic the target audience is looking for in the product (as identified in the benefit selection process), using objective attributes to support a subjective characteristic or claim (the subjective characteristic again having been identified in the benefit selection process), or indirectly by focusing upon a negative emotion that is dispelled by the subjective characteristic or claim associated with the brand (see Table 8.6).

Let us look at a few examples of how some advertisers have used various benefit focus reflecting negative and positive motives (all of which are presented in Table 8.7). Kira St Johns Wort uses a straight attribute focus (**a**), dealing with the negative motive of incomplete satisfaction: 'Kira St. Johns Wort tablets contain 900 micrograms of Hypericin.' Dove Summer Glow body lotion uses a direct, simple headline implying a subjective characteristic of the brand (**c**): 'Basking in the glow.' To support its claims of being the best facial skincare product (a subjective characteristic) Nivea Visage Beauty Boost relies upon the fact that it is the 'best facial skincare product in a poll of over 12 thousand consumers.' (**a** → **c**). For women who have a problem with their lipstick fading (**e⁻**), Max Factor Lipfinity

Table 8.6 Benefit Focus Options

Negative motivation	• Draw attention to an attribute or attributes (**a**) if dealing with an expert target audience
	• Draw attention directly to a subjective characteristic of the brand (**c**)
	• Use an attribute to support a subjective characteristic of the brand (**a** → **c**)
	• Dispel a negative emotion or problems with a subjective characteristic associated with the brand (**e⁻** → **c**)
Positive motivation	• Use a subjective characteristic to draw attention to the emotional consequences of using the brand (**c** → **e⁺**)
	• Simply deliver an emotion (**e⁺**)

Table 8.7 Examples of Benefit Emphasis in Positioning

Motivation	Benefit Focus	Example
Negative	Attribute only (**a**)	'Contain 900 micrograms of Hypericin'
	Subjective characteristic without support (**c**)	'Basking in the glow'
	Attribute supports the subjective characteristic (**a** → **c**)	'Best facial skincare product in a poll of over 12 thousand consumers'
	Negative emotion resolved by subjective characteristic of brand (**e⁻** → **c**)	'Is your lipstick still on … sexy lips 100% guaranteed all night'
Positive	Subjective characteristic leads to emotion (**c** → **e⁺**)	'Memories: the most valuable commodity known to man'
	Pure emotion (**e⁺**)	'Live in Italian'

asks 'Is your lipstick still on?' and goes on to 'solve' that problem with the claim 'sexy lips 100% guaranteed all night'. Here we have a negative emotion occasioned by lipstick that doesn't last removed by the long-lasting characteristic of Lipfinity (e⁻→c).

When the motive is positive and the advertising and other marketing communication is addressing the target audience's 'feelings', the emphasis should be on the *emotional consequences* of the benefit. This can be accomplished in two ways. You can draw attention to the emotional consequences of using the brand through a claim about a subjective characteristic (c→e⁺), or simply deliver the positive emotion (e⁺). A Mercedes-Benz advert creates a strong visual feeling of serenity, and uses the claim 'Memories: the most valuable commodity known to man' to stimulate a position emotional response, linked then to the brand (c→e⁺). An example of pure emotion (e⁺) is offered by Pellegrini, with an illustration of a young couple, the male on a motor scooter and the woman leaning out of the window of a small car on a cobbled street and the statement beneath, 'Live in Italian.' Here the focus is entirely on the emotional consequences of using the brand.

The correct benefit focus in positioning a brand through advertising and other marketing communication is essential to maximizing a brand's position within its market.

Effective Positioning

We now have the tools a manager needs to position a brand effectively in advertising and other marketing communication. Initially, two positioning decisions are made. First, how should the brand be positioned with regard to the product category? Here a central positioning is chosen if the brand is a strong market leader; otherwise, in almost all cases a differential positioning will be used. Secondly, how should the brand be positioned with regard to competitive brands? Here, a user-oriented positioning may be used if the brand is being marketed to a specific segment of the category, or if the underlying motivation for purchase is social approval; otherwise, a product-benefit-oriented positioning will be used. These two decisions are critical for correctly establishing the link between the brand and category need for effective brand awareness, and the link between the brand and its benefit to build and sustain positive brand attitude (as reflected in the general model of brand positioning; see again Fig. 8.7).

Once you have made these initial decisions, the appropriate benefit to use in positioning the brand must be selected. You are looking for a benefit that is important to the target audience, that the target audience believes (or can be persuaded to believe) the brand

Step 1	Make initial positioning decisions
	• With regard to the product category, choose
	   – *central versus differentiated*
	• With regard to other brands, choose
	   – *user versus product* orientation

Step 2	Select appropriate benefits
	• Identify the benefits that
	   – are *important* to the target audience
	   – the brand can *deliver*
	   – can be delivered *better* than other brands

Step 3	Use correct benefit focus
	• When the purchase motivation is positive,
	   – emphasis is on the *emotional consequences*
	• When the purchase motivation is negative,
	   – focus directly on the *benefits*

Figure 8.9 The Three Steps to Effective Brand Positioning

can deliver, and ideally one that the brand can be seen to deliver better than competitors. Having selected the benefit to use, the correct benefit focus in the message will be a function of whether the underlying motivation driving purchase behaviour for the target audience is positive or negative. If the motivation is positive, the emphasis must be on the emotional consequences of the benefit; if it is negative, the emphasis or focus will be directly on the benefit. This procedure for effective positioning of a brand is summarized in Fig. 8.9.

CHAPTER SUMMARY

We have now considered in detail how positioning strategy can be developed, and have empha-sized the importance of market definition in this process. After discussing the market mapping approaches, we suggested that hierarchical market partitioning offers a number of advantages for the development of positioning strategy, and that this can be used in conjunction with data on con-sumer perceptions. We next looked at how to seek a differential advantage by considering how to position the brand in the product category, and whether it should be positioned in relation to other brands in terms of the user or the product itself. We then introduced the expectancy-value model of attitude as a tool to investigate underlying attitude structures and explained how it provides guid-ance on the relative importance and delivery of benefits to the target audience. We then went on to discuss how to emphasize benefits depending on the underlying motivation for purchase.

QUESTIONS TO CONSIDER

8.1 What is meant by positioning?

8.2 How do you determine the best basis for defining a market?

8.3 In what ways can using hierarchical positioning help the manager in developing advertising?

8.4 What is the difference between a central versus a differentiated positioning, and why is it important?

8.5 What are the key questions a manager must ask when first developing a positioning strategy?

8.6 How can the expectancy-value model of attitude help in positioning a brand?

8.7 What should the manager be looking for in selecting the best benefit to focus upon in positioning a brand in advertising?

8.8 What are the important considerations needed for getting the benefit focus right in advertising and other marketing communication?

CASE STUDY 8

Maybelline: Maybe She's Born with It. Maybe It's Maybelline.

In the US mass cosmetics category, Maybelline had long been number three. Then, in the late 1990s, it climbed to number two, passing Revlon, which slipped during a time of corporate strife.

The aim of the 1999/2000 campaign was to wrest the top position in the mass market from the perennial leader, Cover Girl. Cover Girl was a Procter & Gamble brand, with all of P&G's power driving it. For Maybelline to capture leadership in the category would demand gains in sales and market share and, most importantly, a major change in brand imagery.

Maybelline had long been perceived as cheap, garish, tacky—even dime-store. Even with continual upgrades in product and packaging for more than a decade, this perception had changed very little. In fact, L'Oréal, which had been Maybelline's corporate parent since 1995, didn't think all that well of it. Compared to L'Oréal's department-store brand, Lancôme, and the company's other premium-at-mass brands, the lower-priced-brand Maybelline was the poor stepsister. Furthermore, the environment was becoming more and more competitive. Cover Girl and Revlon were not the only front-runners. As recently as mid-1999, the packaged-goods powerhouse Johnson & Johnson had introduced the Neutrogena brand. At the same time, P&G had flexed its massive marketing muscle by bringing out Oil of Olay. And smaller players were on the sidelines, eager to grow by targeting younger consumers with such teen brands as Wet-n-Wild and Jane, both owned by the beauty giant, Estée Lauder.

After reviewing the competitors and itself, Maybelline set two goals. First, Maybelline needed to broaden the product area it had focused. The brand's historical strength was in Eyes. In this segment, Maybelline already dominated. It enjoyed a heritage of innovation in mascara, where its Great Lash had been the leader for almost thirty years. Maintaining the brand's historical strength in Eyes was not enough to obtain the position of the market leader. It had to include more product areas and it decided to focus on Face (i.e. foundation) and Colour (i.e. Lip and Nail). Strengthening the brand's Face and Colour businesses could bring significant potential growth for Maybelline. Success in the Face segment would give Maybelline a competitive advantage over Cover Girl, which had been the best-seller since the 1960s. And success in the Colour segment would give Maybelline a competitive advantage over Revlon, whose lipsticks and nail polish had led the Colour segment since the 1950s. Strengthening its position in Face and Colour could enhance the brand's credentials in beauty and fashion. Thus, the aim was to keep the position in the Eyes segment while improving the brand's position in Face and Colour. Second, the focus of the brand's target audience is women. The target was immense: all ages, all ethnicities, and all women. But a concerted effort had to be made against teens and those 18 to 24. This age group was seen as trend setting and opinion leading in beauty, style, and fashion. As 'beauty influentials', their vote for Maybelline almost guaranteed an aura of coolness and desirability for the brand. The aim was therefore to increase the brand's penetration, especially among teens and women 18 to 24.

To accord the brand's particular target, women aged 18–24, the products advertised must address their patterns of use and the needs of their skin types. And advertising had to appear in their media in a voice that spoke to them. Age was a specific descriptive of the target. Research showed that younger women have fun with the colour and playful nature of cosmetics. But most of them don't know much about how to apply and use them, so they gravitate to the easy-to-use: lip and nail colour, mascara, and non-liquid foundation that serves three purposes—as base, powder, and concealer. At the same time, the young women are in a learning mode. They want substantive information on products. But when it comes to complicated regimes on make-up, they are like older women: they have neither the time nor the energy to deal with them. In the midst of complex lives, a woman's appearance is only one facet of how they define themselves. Their purchase decisions, even in such an image-driven category as cosmetics, are based not on emotion but on reason.

Therefore, the creative strategy focused on positioning Maybelline as a lifestyle cosmetic brand. The rationale was that it offers products that fit seamlessly into today's demanding lives.

Advertising would tap into relevant issues concerning lifestyle, addressing the various needs of the brand's broad target audience, as it delivered functional information about the product. Specifically, the advertising would concentrate on key products that were appropriate for younger women. One was the new Express 3-in-1 Stick Makeup, which fulfilled several functions: base, powder, and concealer. In addition, it was so easy to use that it was foolproof. Another was also new: Full n Soft Mascara, the first mascara that magnified lashes while leaving them soft and pliant.

How to demonstrate these products and talk about them? Today's young women find celebrities such as singers and actresses, who are considered 'cool' because they are 'do-ers' rather than just 'lookers', more relevant than traditional models. The celebrities' multidimensional lives, their talents and achievements, outshine mere appearance. Therefore, the creative strategy recognized that Maybelline had to find the right celebrity 'face' that would make younger women aspire to the brand, attracting them to products that, given the targets' lifestyles and stage of life, made sense. That celebrity was actress Sarah Michelle Gellar. Younger women admired her for her movie roles and hit television show, *Buffy the Vampire Slayer*. Wrapping her performance message in aspirational imagery, she could give Maybelline a desperately needed coolness quotient. And the tagline, 'Maybe she's born with it. Maybe it's Maybelline', was developed to extend the coolness from the celebrity to Maybelline.

Colour is seasonal. In line with the product's nature, advertising was brought to support Maybelline's Colour Businesses: Face and Eyes. In the key fashion months, both spring and fall, advertising for Express Makeup (Face) and for Full n Soft Mascara (Eyes) was supplemented with strong stories on shades that could be found across several products (in the Colour segment). Along with the media plan came several special programmes. First, the introduction of Sarah Michelle Gellar as the new 'face' of Maybelline, along with several new products, all included in a comprehensive public-relations programme that ranged from extensive publicity (e.g. 'The Maybelline 5' selection activity, to select a representative group of five young women) to special events (e.g. Sponsorships, In-store activity).

The strategy was simple: schedule such a pervasive media presence that, at a budget of US $100 million, younger women could not ignore Maybelline; it was an expenditure that could drive Maybelline to dominate the category. And the vehicles included TV, print, and Internet because of their ability to do two things: deliver younger viewers and give the brand the 'cool' environment that was so desired. National TV took the bulk of the spending. The mix combined network programming: WB, for its teen orientation; such syndicated shows as 'Access Hollywood', to give the brand 'sizzle'; such hip cable networks as MTV, VH1, and E!, to skew the message right to younger women. And print included *Glamour*, *Cosmopolitan*, and *Seventeen* for their broad reach, plus such books as *Style* and *Teen People* for their ability to build some buzz. The role of the Internet in the media mix was to help the campaign extend its reach among younger women. To drive traffic to www.Maybelline.com, banner advertising was placed on numbers of cutting-edge sites skewed to younger women.

The results confirmed that Maybelline succeeded in gaining all its campaign objectives. In dollar volume, Maybelline became the No. 1 cosmetics brand in the US mass market, gaining category leadership in October 1999, and still holding that position in April 2000. With category growth rising some 5 per cent, Maybelline growth was 11 per cent. The results also showed that the objectives of each product area were achieved. While volume for the total foundation category rose 15 per cent, Maybelline foundation grew by 20 per cent. And in the total Face segment (foundation, powder, blush, and concealer), the category went up 10 per cent while Maybelline rose 17 per cent. In Colour (Lip and Nail), total volume for the category showed no increase. Maybelline's flagship Moisture Whip Lipcolor gained 26 per cent, obviously at the expense of other competitors. And with the nail colour category worse than flat overall—it was down 6 per cent. But Maybelline's Ultimate Finish Nail Color dollar share went up 24 per cent. As for the Eyes area, Maybelline's total volume (mascara, eye shadow, and eyeliner) rose 16 per cent, while the category grew only 6 per cent. With mascara alone, Maybelline volume climbed 19 per cent, against category growth of 4 per cent.

The campaign successfully reached young women as planned. Overall penetration among teens rose 20 per cent in 2000 versus 1997. And the penetration increase was between 12 per cent in mascara and 58 per cent in foundation. Moreover, younger women found the advertising compelling and strongly associated Sarah Michelle Gellar, the Maybelline Face, with Maybelline. Among teens, persuasion by the Express 3-in-1 Makeup commercial (titled 'My Life') was 47 per cent, 135 per cent above the 20 per cent norm. For the Full n Soft commercial (titled 'Mascara Love'), persuasion among teens was 60 per cent, 150 per cent above the 24 per cent norm. In addition, Maybelline enjoyed substantial gains in image, enhancing brand awareness and perceptions. Among women aged 14 to 24, top-of-mind awareness rose 33 per cent from February to November 1999. And brand perceptions improved significantly in all key dimensions. The range of the percentage increase in the key dimensions were between 52 per cent (Appropriate for evening and special occasions) and 210 per cent (Comes in attractive packaging).

Altogether, with a clear positioning, the campaign was effective. It improved brand perceptions and introduced new products into the highly competitive cosmetics market. More importantly, it leveraged a specific age group to take the brand to position number one.

Since 1968, the Effie Awards have been honouring the most significant achievement in marketing communications: ideas that work. Today, Effie celebrates marketing communications effectiveness worldwide with the annual World Effie Festival, the Global Effie, the Euro Effie, the Asia Pacific Effie and more than 35 national Effie programmes (www.effie.org).

Source: WARC, EFFIE Awards 2001, Maybelline: Maybe She's Born With It. Maybe It's Maybelline, Authors unknown

Edited by Hazel H. Huang

Discussion Questions

1 How did Maybelline divide the cosmetics market? How would you divide it differently?

2 What are the differences between Maybelline's old and new positioning?

3 What are the pros and cons for Maybelline to position itself head-to-head against its major competitors?

4 Why did Maybelline use almost all kinds of media (TV, print, the Internet, In-store display, etc.) to run the campaign?

FURTHER READING

- In a book that has significant implications for positioning, *[re]inventing the brand* (London: Kogan Page, 2001), Jean-Noël Kapferer asks the question, can top brands survive the new market realities?

- And, from a totally different perspective, Stephen Brown argues in his *Free Gift Inside!!* (Chichester: Capstone, 2003) that in positioning brands it is time to forget about the consumer.

NOTES

1   David Jobber, *Principles and Practice of Marketing* (New York: McGraw-Hill, 1998), 193.

2   Graham Hooley and John Saunders, *Competitive Positioning: The Key to Market Success* (London: Prentice Hall, 1993), p. xi.

3   Peter Doyle, *Marketing Management and Strategy* (London: Prentice Hall, 1994), 79.

4   A discussion of the marketing plan may be found in any number of marketing textbooks, and is covered in detail by W. A. Cohen in his book *The Marketing Plan*, 2nd edn. (New York: John Wiley and Sons, 1998).

5   Perceptual mapping was developed in the late 1960s at Bell Laboratories in the USA. One of the best books on the subject is still Paul Green and Vilhala Rao, *Applied Multidimensional Scaling: A Comparison of Approaches and Algorithms* (New York: Holt, Rinehart and Winston, 1972).

6   See J. R. Bettman, *An Information Processing Theory of Consumer Choice* (Reading, Mass.: Addison-Wesley, 1979).

7   See G. Franzen and M. Bouwman, *The Mental World of Brands* (Henley-on-Thames: World Advertising Research Center, 2001), 232.

8   This finding comes from research conducted by Larry Percy for a major multinational coffee company. The company was so disturbed to learn that its traditional view of the market, based upon a product definition, was wrong that it refused to complete the project.

9   Glen Urban and John Hauser, *Design and Marketing of New Products* (Englewood Cliffs, NJ: Prentice Hall, 1980).

10 In *Advertising Communication and Promotion Management* (New York: McGraw-Hill 1997), J. R. Rossiter and L. Percy discuss the first half of this definition in terms of product location—how a brand can be located within the product category with either a central or a differentiated position. Simply put, a central location requires the brand to be positioned to deliver all those benefits associated with the category (generally a positioning for market leaders), while a differentiated location means finding a unique or differentiated positioning. Generally speaking, most brands should pursue a differentiated positioning.

11 In a pioneering study by B. Loken and J. Ward on the determinants of brand typicality we see the basis of this idea of category need and its relationship to market definition, 'Alternative Approaches to Understanding the Determinants of Typicality', *Journal of Consumer Research*, 17/2 (1990), 111–26.

12 Franzen and Bouwman, *Mental World of Brands*, 234.

13 These definitions are discussed in D. L. Medin and M. M. Schaffer, 'A Context Theory of Classification Learning', *Psychological Review*, 85 (1978) 207–38.

14 The dual idea of both abstraction and concreteness in developing a prototype is discussed in N. Cantor and J. F. Kihlstrom, 'Social Intelligence and Cognitive Assessment of Personality', in R. S. Wyer and T. K. Sroll (eds.), *Advances in Social Cognition*, vol.ii (Hillsdale, NJ: Lawrence Erlbaum Associates, 1984).

15 For a more detailed consideration of a model that deals with this point, see Rossiter and Percy's discussion of what they call an I–D–U (Importance, Delivery, Uniqueness) model of benefit emphasis in *Advertising Communication and Promotion Management*.

16 See S. Sayman, S. J. Huch, and J. S. Raju, 'Positioning of Store Brands', *Marketing Science*, 21/4 (2002), 378–97.

17 While only an estimate, this figure reported in W. Gordon and S. Ford-Hutchinson, 'Brains and Brands: Re-thinking the Answers', *Admap*, January (2002) 47–50, suggests the difficulty involved in positioning a brand to 'stand out.'

18 See G. S. Carpenter and K. Nakamoto, 'Consumer Preference Formation and Pioneering Advantage', *Journal of Marketing Research*, 26/3 (1989), 285–98, for some examples.

19 While it can be argued that Harry Triandis actually developed the idea of an expectancy-value model of attitude, Martin Fishbein is generally credited with its development. See M. Fishbein and I. Ajzen, *Belief, Attitude, Intention, and Behavior: An Introduction to Theory and Research* (Reading, Mass.: Addison-Wesley, 1975).

 Visit the Online Resource Centre that accompanies this book for additional resources to support the text: http://www.oxfordtextbooks.co.uk/orc/percy_elliott3e/

9

Developing a Communication Strategy

The positioning strategy has helped establish how the manager should address the two core communication objectives of brand awareness and brand attitude. Now it is time to establish communication objectives and the specific brand awareness and brand attitude strategies that reflect what was learned about how the target audience makes decisions in the category. Depending upon how awareness is used to identify the brand for purchase, a recognition or recall brand awareness strategy will be required; and the level of involvement with the purchase decision along with the motivation driving category behaviour will determine the brand attitude strategy, as we see below.

Implementing the Strategic Planning Process

Step 1	Step 2	Step 3	**Step 4**	Step 5
Selecting the Target Audience	Understanding Target Audience Decision Making	Determining the Best Positioning	Developing a Communication Strategy	Setting a Media Strategy

---

STEP 4 DEVELOP A COMMUNICATION STRATEGY

Brand Awareness

Target audience *recognizes* brand at point of purchase and remembers need

Requires *recognition* brand awareness strategy

Need occurs and target audience must *recall* brands that satisfy need

Requires *recall* brand awareness strategy

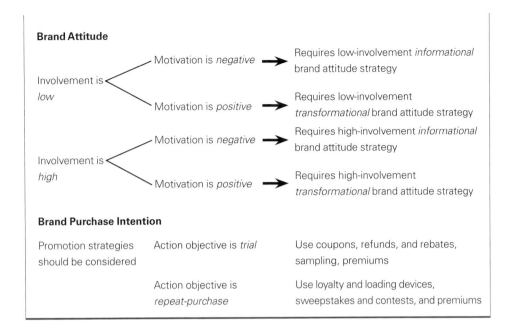

Brand Attitude

Involvement is *low*
- Motivation is *negative* ➡ Requires low-involvement *informational* brand attitude strategy
- Motivation is *positive* ➡ Requires low-involvement *transformational* brand attitude strategy

Involvement is *high*
- Motivation is *negative* ➡ Requires high-involvement *informational* brand attitude strategy
- Motivation is *positive* ➡ Requires high-involvement *transformational* brand attitude strategy

Brand Purchase Intention

Promotion strategies should be considered	Action objective is *trial*	Use coupons, refunds, and rebates, sampling, premiums
	Action objective is *repeat-purchase*	Use loyalty and loading devices, sweepstakes and contests, and premiums

➡ KEY CONCEPTS

1 Communication objectives are determined by which of four communication effects are needed: category need, brand awareness, brand attitude, brand purchase intention.

2 While any of the four communication effects may be a communication objective depending upon the situation, brand awareness and brand attitude are *always* communication objectives.

3 Brand awareness strategy is determined by whether a brand at the point of purchase reminds the target audience of a need for purchase (recognition brand awareness) or whether the brand must come to mind when the need occurs (recall brand awareness).

4 Brand attitude strategy depends upon whether the level of perceived risk in a purchase is seen as low or high and whether the underlying motivation driving behaviour in the category is seen as negative or positive (the Rossiter–Percy grid).

5 Promotion strategy is considered when brand purchase intention is a communication objective, and specific incentive promotions are linked to trial versus repeat purchase action objectives.

We are now going to deal with communication strategy, and the first thing we must consider as we address this issue is the development of communication objectives. We have been through our initial planning stages—selecting a target audience, developing a model of consumer decision making, and positioning our brand. Now it is time to decide how to put together our message. Clearly, before we can create advertising or other marketing communication executions we must have an overall communication strategy, and this begins with setting communication objectives.

In this chapter we will be looking at how to go about selecting communication objectives, with a special emphasis on brand awareness and brand attitude, which are *always* communication objectives, and how brand purchase intention triggers consideration of promotion. Chapter 11 will take this a step further and look at how understanding the way people process messages can lead to more effective communication, and then in Chapter 12 we will look specifically at creative tactics.

Setting Communication Objectives

We have already briefly introduced four communication effects discussed in the work of Rossiter and Percy, and it will be from these effects that the manager will select the brand's communication objectives: category need, brand awareness, brand attitude, and brand purchase intention.[1] In this section we will see how and when each of these effects may become an objective for advertising and other marketing communication (see Table 9.1)

Category Need

Category need refers to the target audience's feeling that it would like a particular product or service in order to satisfy a specific need. It is important to remember here that category need is a *perception*, and therefore it can be established by the advertiser. By successfully establishing a belief in the minds of the target audience that links the product category and a felt need, the advertiser can stimulate *primary demand* for the product category. Category need is the communication effect that causes primary demand. But note that category need, and the primary demand it can stimulate in the marketplace, applies to *all brands* in the category. To stimulate secondary or selective demand, the advertiser must also influence brand-level communication effects such as brand awareness, brand attitude, and brand purchase intention.

Table 9.1 Potential Communication Objectives

Category Need	An objective only when it is necessary to remind the target of his or her need for the category or when you must sell the target audience the need
Brand Awareness	Always an objective in order to enable the target audience to identify the brand in enough detail to purchase or use the brand
Brand Attitude	Also always an objective because there must be some other reason to select one brand over another
Brand Purchase Intention	Not often a specific objective for advertising except when brand attitude is positive and a 'reason to buy' now is required, but always an objective for promotion

Because different consumers may be looking for different things in a product, category need can be seen differently, given the particular perceived needs of various segments of the target market. As an example, with the introduction of DVDs, people needed first to be informed about this new category, and interest in DVDs had to be stimulated. However, interest in DVDs can very easily be different among various consumer groups. One group may be interested because it is always interested in being first with anything new. A second group may be drawn to DVDs because of their better picture quality. A third may become interested later because it cannot find videos any more. Category need in each case will be stimulated by different perceptions, and hence can require different communication strategies.

How do you decide when category need should be a communication objective? Category need must be present at full strength before purchase of a brand within that category can occur. In other words, the potential consumer must be in the market for the product (category). Category need is not very often required as a communication objective, because most brands are marketed in categories where the perceived need is well established. But when circumstances dictate it, it is absolutely essential. There are two cases when category need must be a communication objective: when it is necessary to remind the target audience of its need for products in the category, or when you must sell the target audience the need for the category.

Reminding the Consumer of the Category Need

The first situation in which category need becomes a communication objective is when you must remind the prospective consumer of a latent or forgotten (but previously established) category need. Campbell's soup in the USA provides a perfect example of reminding prospective buyers of the category need. Since the 1980s, whenever sales have begun to soften, Campbell's has run a campaign built around the category benefit 'soup is good food'. By reminding the consumer of the category need, eating soup because it is good food, Campbell's is able to renew interest in serving soup. It is able to support such a campaign because it dominates the category. As interest in soup increases, so do sales of the Campbell brand.

Usually, however, reminding the target audience of a category need applies to product categories that are infrequently purchased, such as pain remedies. It also applies to one-time-purchase products that are infrequently used, at least in the opinion of the advertiser. Traveller's cheques are another good case where it is important to remind people of the category need because of infrequent use. Category need reminder campaigns can generally be achieved without devoting a lot of copy specifically to the category need. The purpose is merely to re-establish a previously held need. There is plenty of opportunity to address the brand. This is in sharp contrast to when it is necessary to sell a category need.

Selling the Category Need

When a category need has not yet been established in the minds of the target audience, the advertising campaign, often with promotional support, must sell the need. Selling category need is a communication objective for all new products and also for established products aimed at new users. If the target audience has not bought within the category before, advertising must include selling the category need as a communication objective. While it is easy to see that new product categories obviously must be sold to the consumer, you should also see how it is important to sell the category to anyone who has not yet purchased products in the category. This is why advertising always relies upon category need as an *effect* in communication, but selling category need becomes an objective only when the target audience is made up of people who have no experience with the category.

In order to sell the category to someone new to it, the content of the advertising requires the selling of *category* benefits in addition to brand benefits. Selling the category involves creating, in the potential consumer's mind, *category communication effects*. As a result, just as we have brand communication effects, we will have category awareness, category attitude, and category purchase intention. When selling category need, these category-level communication effects must be addressed *in addition to* brand-level communication effects. This is not an easy job, and almost impossible within a single execution. It requires a campaign.

Category awareness, category attitude, and category purchase intention, which must be addressed when selling the category, are no different conceptually from their brand counterparts—brand awareness, brand attitude, and brand purchase intention. But they are separate communication objectives, which must be decided along with brand-level communication objectives.

Brand Awareness

Brand awareness is the target audience's ability to identify a brand within a category in sufficient detail to purchase or use it. There are at least two ways in which to identify a brand. You can either *recognize* the brand or you can *recall* it. As we shall see below, this is a very important distinction to understand when setting brand awareness objectives.

The reason we say that the brand must be identified in sufficient detail is that brand awareness does *not* always require identification of the brand *name*. For the consumer, brand awareness may be stimulated by a familiar package or an even more general stimulus such as colour. For years in the UK, before tobacco advertising was banned, Silk Cut cigarette advertising did not use the brand name in its adverts. Rather, they always featured a piece of purple silk, with a cut somewhere. Of course, this was possible only because the association of the purple silk with a cut and the brand name was built over many years before the name was removed from its advertising (something we will be dealing with in Chapter 13 when we talk about consistency). Identifications such as these still enable brand response, even though no brand name is mentioned.

You may not even need to remember beforehand the brand name or be able to describe the package or colour. Instead, brand awareness may occur through simply recognizing it at the point of purchase. When a package is recognized in a supermarket (for example, the red stripe over a picture of the Yorkshire countryside on packages of Yorkshire Tea) or when a fast-food restaurant sign is recognized on a trip (for example, McDonald's golden arches), brand awareness does not require brand recall.

We have already seen that at the product category level consumers will not buy unless there is a perceived category need. At the brand level, consumers *cannot* buy unless they are first made aware of the brand. As a result, brand awareness must always be considered first, before any other communication effect.

Recognition or Recall: An Essential Difference

Brand awareness is widely misunderstood even by the most experienced people in advertising. The difficulty relates to the essential difference between recognition and recall, a difference that is fundamentally important to advertising and all other forms of marketing communication.[2] Brand recognition and brand recall are two fundamentally different types of brand awareness, as we have pointed out in earlier chapters. The difference depends upon which communication effect occurs first in the consumer's mind: the need for the product (that is, category need) or seeing the brand in the store (that is, brand awareness). *Recognition* brand awareness is when the awareness of the brand reminds you of the category need. *Recall* brand awareness is when the category need occurs and you must remember brands that will satisfy that need.

Brand Attitude

Just as with brand awareness, positive brand attitude must always be a communication objective. If there is no brand attitude present among the target audience, there is very little likelihood they will want to purchase the product. Why? If you think about it, for most product categories most people are aware of more than one brand. Unless we believe that brand choices are made randomly from among the brands people are aware of, there must be something about the brands that lead a person to purchase one rather than another. That something is a brand attitude.

   The study of attitudes is really based in psychology, but those who work in the area of consumer behaviour have adapted various theories of attitude as to why people behave as they do. It is from this body of knowledge that we borrow our definition of attitude. We look at brand attitude as the understanding a person has in terms of how he or she evaluates a particular brand and its ability to satisfy what the consumer is looking for in the product. Because of the importance of brand attitude to effective communication, we will explore it in more depth later in this chapter.

Brand Purchase Intention

Brand purchase intention is the communication response that relates to the target audience's *decision* to purchase a brand or use a service. It refers not to the actual behaviour of buying the brand or using the service, but only to the *intention*. The target audience, as a result of processing an advert or promotion, says to him or herself: 'I think I'll try that brand' or 'I want to pick that up again next time I shop.' Remember, in the communication response sequence, the final step *after* communication effect is actual behaviour. All marketing communication can do, if correctly processed, is generate either a low-level curiosity to try (with low-involvement product decisions) or a definite intention to buy (for a high-involvement product decision).

   We should also take note here of the potential ways in which brand purchase intention may be influenced by advertising. It may not always be the same person who both intends to buy as a result of the advertising and actually makes the purchase, as we saw when we discussed the roles people play in the decision process. A common example of this would be advertising to children for such things as toys or breakfast cereals. The advertising may be aimed at children in their roles as initiator and influencer, stimulating a brand purchase intention for some child-oriented breakfast cereal, but the mother will actually buy the product. You can surely imagine other cases where the intention to purchase is really only a recommendation or proposal to someone else who will actually make the purchase decision. Nevertheless, for our purposes we will consider all this under the communication objective of brand purchase intention.

In those situations where the strategy is to build or reinforce an image for a brand, and there is very little risk involved in the purchase decision, brand purchase intention will almost surely be delayed, and therefore should *not* be considered as a communication objective. This situation occurs with products such as beer and soft drinks, certain well-established food products, and other generally inexpensive, routinely purchased packaged-goods products.

Let us illustrate what we mean here. If you see an advertisement for ice cream or beer or soft drinks, it is unlikely that you will say to yourself that you are going to go out and immediately buy that brand. What is more likely is that after you have seen the advertising a few times you will begin to feel good about the brand and begin to identify with it. Then if you are passing the ice cream section of the store, or see the advertised brand of beer or soft drink when shopping, you will remember the feeling and then, at the *point of purchase*, decide to buy.

Contrast this with other advertising you are familiar with, where there is 'information' provided. Advertising for such things as cold remedies, for example, provides you with a 'reason to buy' right then, if you are suffering from a cold or cough: 'relieves sore throat pain' or 'helps you sleep'. You learn the information and form a tentative decision to try the brand because of what you have learned about it. In cases like this, brand purchase intention can be a communication objective.

Brand purchase intention is not often a communication objective for advertising, but it is *always* the primary communication objective for promotion. In developing a brand's communication strategy, the manager will use promotion when it is necessary to accelerate brand purchase intention to immediate action. While a promotion does not necessarily require an incentive to encourage that action, most do.

Brand Awareness and Brand Attitude Strategy

How do you decide which awareness response and which aspect of brand attitude should form the basis for a brand's communication objectives? We have seen that both brand awareness and brand attitude are *always* communication objectives. But with brand awareness, should it be recognition or recall? How do we look at the various aspects of brand attitude in developing an optimum communication strategy? In this section we will look into these questions as we take a more in-depth look at brand awareness and brand attitude strategy.

Brand Awareness Strategy

There are three possible ways for brand awareness to be used as a communication objective. As we have seen, brand awareness may be executed as brand recognition or brand recall, or in certain cases both may be appropriate. As noted in our discussion of positioning, the link between the category need and the brand is what brand awareness is all about. In effect, this is how advertising and other marketing communication 'brand' the product. Unfortunately, failure to brand effectively in advertising is an all too common problem. As a result, it is critical to effective branding in marketing communication that the creative tactics used are appropriate to the type of brand awareness most likely to be involved in the brand choice decision. The behavioural sequence model, because it identifies how, when, and where a brand choice is made, helps the manager identify how the brand is used in the decision, whether *primarily* when seen at the time of purchase (for brand recognition awareness) or when linked to the need for the product when that need occurs (for brand recall). Specific creative tactics for recognition and recall brand awareness strategies will be discussed in Chapter 12.

There is an important point to understand here. When we refer to a brand recall objective for advertising, we do not mean recall of the actual advertising. The reason we point this out is that many advertisers try to test their advertising with day-after recall experiments where people are called the day after a commercial has run on television and asked if they remember seeing it. Our concern is with *brand* recall, regardless of whether or not the consumer can remember the advertising.[3] And, importantly, recall of the brand in response to the need.

When we have decided that brand recall should be the communication objective, advertising should repeat the name as often as possible, linked with the category need. With television, the name should be not only heard often, but seen as well. In radio, of course, the name can only be heard, and in print adverts only seen. But the critical point is that the brand is always *linked to the need*, so that, when the need occurs in 'real life', our brand will come to mind.

Encoding Specificity

This reflects an important principle of memory first talked about by the psychologist Endell Tulving called *encoding specificity*.[4] What this suggests is that to retrieve something successfully from memory there must be a match between the information encoded at the time of learning and the information available when it is retrieved from memory. This means that, for a brand to be recalled when the appropriate need occurs, it must have been encoded in memory linked to that need; and *in that order*. Because the need occurs first, and we must search our memory for an appropriate brand, the presentation in advertising should be need first, satisfied by our brand.

The retrieval cue available when the purchase or usage decision is made is the need, so that is the order in which we will want the target audience to learn the association between the need and the brand. And because this is not easy, this category need-brand association should be repeated within the advertising. One way to help facilitate learning this need-followed-by-brand link is to personalize the association between the need and the brand, for example by using personal pronouns such as *me*, *you*, and *I*. This is very well illustrated in the promotion for Warner Breaks shown in Advert 9.1. When the need for a break

This is an invitation to 'why not?' and 'let's have another go'.

This is an invitation to laugh until it hurts.

This is an invitation to enjoy a bottle and not just a glass.

This is an invitation to show the real you.

This is an invitation to make friends with the Azaleas.

This is an invitation to surprise yourself.

This is an invitation to do nothing, but have fun.

This is an invitation to get lost in the music.

This is an invitation to have a fuss made of you.

This is an invitation to do exactly as you please.

This is an invitation to 'a nice bit of peace and quiet'.

This is an invitation to make new friends.

This is an invitation to just sit back and enjoy the show.

This is an invitation to a good ol' boogie.

This is an invitation to try something completely new.

This is an invitation to a world away from home.

This is an invitation to take the break you fully deserve.

This is an invitation to let yourself go.

Advert 9.1 This promotion for Warner Breaks is a very good illustration of personalizing copy to facilitate learning. Reproduced with kind permission © Warner Leisure Hotels.

occurs, *you* are personally invited by Warner Breaks to satisfy that need at one of their thirteen Old Hotels and resorts. This personalization is reinforced throughout the copy.

The encoding specificity principle is also at work with brand recognition awareness. It is why advertising must present the brand as it will be confronted when purchased, within an easily recognized category need. By ensuring that the brand-category need link

Brand recognition	Brand recall
Brand awareness → Category need	Category need → Brand awareness
Memory retrieved *at* the point of purchase	Memory retrieved *prior* to purchase

Figure 9.1 Brand Awareness and Encoding Specificity

is learned *in that order* for brand recognition awareness, being confronted with the package or brand name at the time of purchase will act as a retrieval cue, reminding the buyer of the need for the product. This is illustrated in Fig. 9.1.

Brand Recognition and Brand Recall

Occasionally both brand recognition and brand recall should be considered as communication objectives. However, this is a very difficult objective to effect since it requires two different types of creative execution tactics, and may also require different media (since, for example, radio is unable to communicate visual recognition).

None the less, there are two circumstances where it may be appropriate to set a dual communication objective of brand recognition and recall. The first situation is where your target audience is generally made up of two major segments, one of which makes its brand choice prior to shopping, the other at the point of purchase. We should understand, however, that this is a very rare occurrence.

The second case where a dual brand awareness communication objective may be called for is when the average member of the target audience finds him or herself frequently in both decision-making situations. This case is far more common than the first, but it too is not likely to occur often. An example of what we mean here would be the brand choice for liquor. Frequently the potential buyer of vodka, say, will recognize a brand name like Absolut at the store when shopping and be reminded of a need to buy, a situation calling for a brand recognition communication objective. When this same consumer is in a bar or restaurant and orders a martini, if the waiter asks whether any particular vodka is preferred, it will be necessary to remember the brand name, a situation calling for a brand recall communication objective.

Brand Attitude Strategy

Again, brand attitude will always be a communication objective. There are several possible specific communication objectives related to brand attitude. Depending upon what beliefs the target audience holds for a brand, the brand attitude options are to: create, increase, maintain, modify, or change its brand attitude. We can see that, without a prior knowledge of the target audience's brand attitude, the manager will not know which option will be best for the brand. So the first step is *always* to understand fully the attitudes of the target audience towards both the category in general and the specific brands that the target audience feels compete in that category.[5]

We need to *create* a brand attitude for new category users or when introducing a new brand. It is hard to imagine any other case where someone in the market has no attitude at all towards a brand, always assuming he or she is aware of it. When we find that our target audience has a moderately favourable brand attitude, the brand attitude communication objective will be to *increase* the already favourable brand attitude. Almost anyone who at least occasionally buys a brand will hold at least a moderately favourable attitude towards it. Even new category users may have formed some tentatively positive or negative attitudes about a brand. For example, young mothers have probably begun to form brand attitudes for baby food some time before actually having their babies. In such cases, if we find our target audience has at least some positive brand attitude, we will want to try to increase it.

If we find that the majority of the target audience already has a strong positive attitude towards a brand, the brand attitude communication objective will be to *maintain* that already favourable attitude. This is often the case in more mature markets, where a large proportion of a brand's users tend to be relatively loyal.

The alert reader may wonder here how this idea squares with that part of our brand attitude definition that points out that brand attitude is *relative*. In a sense it is true that one is probably always trying to increase brand attitude. But in a case where the competitive environment is stable and your brand has a generally loyal customer base and a dominant share, maintaining that strong brand attitude is a proper objective. However, the advertiser must always be alert to positive shifts in competitive brand attitude that could signal a shift in the brand attitude objective for its brand.

What we mean by *modifying* a brand attitude is basically to reposition a brand. In a sense, what you are trying to do is increase the potential target market by appealing to a different motivation or reason for seeking certain benefits in the brand. A good recent example of this is the way in which many diet control products have been repositioned from strictly 'diet-oriented' products to products that are good for 'watching' your weight, and then repositioned again as products that are more 'healthy' for you. This type of change in brand attitude was recognized when Findas introduced Lean Cuisine, and positioned it as a product for watching weight rather than dieting to lose weight.

While almost any target audience could potentially be seen as appropriate for a modified brand attitude if the advertiser sees changes in the marketplace that demand this sort of action, modifying brand attitude can also be useful as a communication objective when it does not appear feasible to increase brand attitude. Examples here are the way in which Arm & Hammer baking soda modified brand attitude in suggesting to consumers that they should use a box of Arm & Hammer in the refrigerator to absorb odours, and how Vaseline Care extended its usage through repositioning as a lip balm.

It is necessary to *change* brand attitude when a significant proportion of your target audience holds a negative attitude towards the brand. Regardless of the number of positive beliefs a consumer may hold towards a brand, if there is a significant negative belief it will in almost all cases 'overrule' the positive beliefs. Choosing to change brand attitude as a communication objective involves removing the negative link between the brand and the reason why a consumer purchases the product. If this link is not removed, regardless of what your advertising may say about a brand, the consumer will still be likely to think: 'Yes, that may be true, but...'. It is essential to remove the reasons for this 'but'.

Look at Advert 9.2 for the Volkswagen Polo L. In the mid-1990s Volkswagen significantly reduced their prices in the UK, yet the image of Volkswagen as unaffordable persisted. People felt Volkswagen made quality cars (positive belief), but also felt they were expensive (negative belief). The creative challenge was to change the negative aspect of brand attitude while retaining the positive. This is always a tricky job when you are dealing with a price-quality interaction, but it is well handled in this advert, which ran in London Underground stations as part of a larger campaign. The obvious humour in the association with Underground 'danger' warnings helps attract and hold attention as the eye is visually drawn to the price and then on to the tag line, 'Surprisingly ordinary prices'. The advert deals with the negative belief in a humorous way, stimulating generally positive feelings, without challenging or jeopardizing the quality image.

We cannot minimize the potential danger to a message if negative attitudes remain with the target audience; nor can we minimize the difficulty in changing a negative brand attitude. In fact, it may come to the point where it is simply not feasible even to try to change the attitude, and we must eliminate those people from our target audience.

We should remember that different segments of the potential target audience may hold different initial attitudes towards a brand, and as a result the advertiser may need to isolate those segments that are most likely to respond to the brand. Some brand attitude objectives will be easier to achieve, and, if the manager can match those objectives with segments in the market that offer a reasonable likelihood of responding to the brand's message, it will in effect be maximizing advertising and marketing objectives for the brand.

Characteristics of Brand Attitude

There are four important characteristics about brand attitude that we need to understand. They are: what the consumer wants now from the brand, what he or she knows and feels about the brand, the beliefs that make up that knowledge, and the relativity of brand attitude (see Fig. 9.2).

Brand attitude depends upon what the potential buyer wants *now* from the brand. This is really the motivation that drives someone to behave in a certain way. We will spend more time talking about this later, but for now we need realize only that it is essential to know why someone is motivated to make a purchase or utilize a service in a brand's category. It also stands to reason that, if consumers' motivation changes, they may also re-evaluate the brands in the category. With a different motivation other things about a brand could become important, changing the consumers' evaluation of the brand.

Most people studying consumer behaviour see brand attitude as made up of two components: what someone knows about a brand and what he or she feels about a brand. Psychologists often refer to these two components as cognitions (beliefs) and affect (feelings). We will learn more about these two components below. While some psychologists also include a behavioural (conative) component when talking about attitudes, this is generally not considered a part of brand attitude in consumer behaviour, but a separate idea.

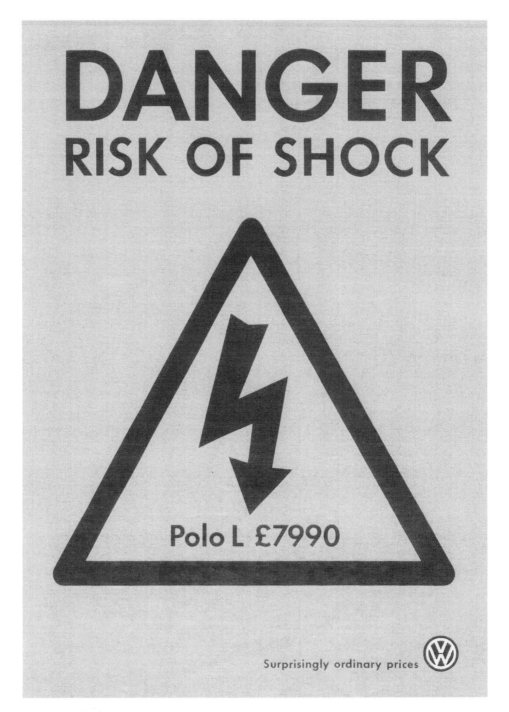

Advert 9.2 This advert for the VW Polo L provides a good example of how humour can be used in helping change a negative perception without jeopardizing a quality image. Reproduced with kind permission © Volkswagen.

- Brand attitude depends upon what the target audience wants now from the product
- Brand attitude is made up of what someone 'knows' about a product and what they 'feel' about a brand
- What someone 'knows' is usually made up of a number of different beliefs
- Brand attitude is a relative concept

Figure 9.2 Important Characteristics of Brand Attitude

What someone knows about a brand, the cognitive component, could be made up of several different beliefs. As we relate these beliefs to advertising, we will be concerned with the benefits associated with these beliefs. A person's brand attitude will be made up of these benefit beliefs, weighted by their importance (as we saw in the previous chapter when we discussed the expectancy-value model of attitude).

Finally, brand attitude is a *relative* concept. In almost any product category, a number of brands will probably satisfy a consumer's motivation in purchasing or using a product. But, given the associations consumers draw between the brand and its supporting beliefs, one brand will usually end up being seen as relatively better than the others in meeting their motivation to buy.

We will now look at each of these points in more detail. As mentioned above, once we begin to relate all this to specific examples, you will understand its importance to advertising and why a good understanding of brand attitude is necessary to a good understanding of how advertising works.

Brand Attitude and Motivation
We pointed out above that brand attitude is related to the underlying reasons behind why people behave—what we know as *motivation*. Also, we pointed out that brand attitude could change if the associated motivation changed. As a matter of fact, while this is certainly a straightforward and commonsense notion, you would be surprised at how many managers ignore these connections when setting communication strategy. Too often advertisers will rely upon brand information that is not linked to a motivation. For example, simply to ask people why they think a particular brand is best may completely overlook situational motivations. What results is very general information about attitudes that may be practically meaningless.

Consider for a minute what goes through your own mind when you think about purchasing such diverse items as calculators and beer. All calculators have certain basic functions, but beyond that what you are looking for in a calculator might be related to a specific area of interest—for example, financial functions or math functions. From this simple example we can imagine a number of possible segments. (Think about how partitioning a market, as discussed in the last chapter, applies here.) Originally, all you may want is a basic calculator—you may be motivated simply to avoid the problem of doing all those arithmetic calculations by hand (like balancing your chequebook!). Later, you may be motivated by different reasons, and want a calculator more suited to your new role as an economics student. A brand that was fine originally no longer measures up. Brand attitude has changed. We need to know what motivation we are dealing with if we are to advertise effectively, in this case, a calculator.

Now let us consider beer. If you are out with your friends after playing a ball game, you are probably ordering a beer because you are thirsty. As we will learn later, this would be in response to a positive, sensory gratification motivation. But what if you were having lunch with a prospective employer and were asked if you would like a beer? The brand choice here would probably be motivated by a desire to 'look good', a different positive motivation: 'social approval'. Chances are that the brand you choose in these two situations would be different, because the motivation in each situation is different. In the first situation, almost any beer you like might be appropriate, but in the second situation, you would want a beer like Grolsch. If so, the advertising for these brands would need to reflect these different underlying motivations.

Cognitive and Affective Components of Brand Attitude

The cognitive and affective components of brand attitude reflect what someone 'knows' about a product, their beliefs, and the feelings associated with a brand. As mentioned earlier, some psychologists talk about behavioural intention or conation as part of a definition of attitude.[6] However, along with most people working in the area of consumer behaviour, we believe that a two-component view is probably more useful. This does not mean we ignore behavioural intent (it is, after all, one of our communication effects), only that we do not find it critical to defining brand attitude. There is interesting support for this idea from the neuroscience literature, where we learn that the brain receives and handles cognitive and affective inputs in a parallel fashion.[7]

Let us now see how the cognitive and affective components of brand attitude fit together to form an *overall* brand attitude. Our definition of brand attitude is how someone evaluates a brand with respect to its perceived ability to satisfy what he or she is looking for in the product—in other words, the appropriate motivations. The cognitive and affective components of brand attitude relate to this perceived ability to satisfy and the underlying motivation to behave.

In the previous chapter we looked at the expectancy-value model in determining overall attitude towards a brand for purposes of positioning. We were dealing with these same two components. Now we are taking this idea one step further and relating it to *motivation*. This next step is essential for brand attitude strategy.

The *cognitive or belief* component represents the existence and strength of the perceived linkage between the brand and the underlying motivation. In other words, it represents the perceived ability of the brand to satisfy the motivation. This belief or perception guides or directs the consumer towards a particular brand. The *affect or feeling* component is generated by the motivation itself. Whether this belief is or is not important depends upon the motivation to buy or use a product or service. Since the motivation must be relevant *at the time*, the motivation is experienced as an emotional or felt deviation from the consumer's current state. This feeling energizes the target audience to choose a brand.

Beliefs as Benefits in the Cognitive Component

It would be very unusual indeed for an advertiser to try to build brand attitude directly by referring specifically to why the consumer wants a brand. In fact, most of the time people do not really know what motivations underlie their behaviour, or at any rate do not really give it much thought. If you are hungry and want a snack, do you say to yourself 'I want something to remove my feeling of hunger'? Not likely. This negative problem-removal motive is certainly what leads you to think about a snack, but that is a *category* decision. Once you have decided on a snack, if you are at home you are much more likely to say to yourself, 'What do I have around that's not too filling?' or 'What's in the house that tastes good?' These are the benefits that people think about when they are looking for *brands* in a category that can be related to their underlying motivations. In this case, the motivation will be *positive*: you are looking for something to enjoy.

Advertising especially, but other marketing communication as well, including promotion, must communicate the benefits of the brand to the target audience. An advert must take specific attributes, characteristics, or emotions and link them to a brand in such a way that it is seen as *uniquely* satisfying their motive.

Brand Attitude as a Relative Concept

While it is certainly possible to think about brand attitude in terms of the brand's perceived ability to meet absolutely what the potential buyer is looking for in a product, it makes a lot more sense to think about brand attitude as *relative*. There is rarely a brand that offers exactly what every individual buyer is looking for. Almost always there are other brands out there trying to beat you in meeting what potential buyers want. Even when a company has a virtual monopoly of a category, it should adopt a relative stance towards brand attitude. You never know when stronger competition may arrive. This makes sense when we remember that, even in product categories where there is one dominant brand, the target audience will still have other brands to choose from. In almost all product categories, brand attitude communication effects will stimulate *relatively* more positive feeling about the brand.

Importance of Involvement and Motivation

We have talked off and on throughout this book about *involvement* and *motivation*. This is because they are the critical elements affecting purchase and usage behaviour, and as such must be taken into account when creating advertising and other marketing communication. In terms of involvement, we need to know whether or not the target audience sees any risk in the decision to buy or use a product or service. This perceived risk can be seen in either fiscal or psychological terms, and is dependent upon the target audience.

For most of us, the purchase of a new car carries with it a substantial financial risk. We do not want to make a mistake, so we will do a lot of work to be as certain as possible that we are making the right choice. But what about rock stars or seriously wealthy investment bankers? They could see a new car on the road, perhaps a Ferrari, and simply call up a dealer and order one. If they do not like it after a month or so, they will just trade it in and buy something new.

So you can see that perceived risk must be determined *for the target audience*. While perceived risk in terms of money might be more or less correlated with financial circumstance, psychological risk is open to a much greater likelihood of individual differences. What is absolutely required dress for one group of teenagers, another group of teenagers would not be seen wearing. What one cohort or culture sees as a status brand may not be seen as such for another.

The reason this idea of involvement is so important, as we shall see in Chapter 11, is that, in processing a message, when involvement is low and there is little if any risk involved, you do not really need to believe the message is true. If the advertising merely excites your curiosity or interest, something Maloney calls 'curious disbelief', that will be enough.[8] On the other hand, when the decision is high involvement and fiscal or psychological risk is involved, you must accept the message as true before you will consider the brand.

A more detailed model of involvement and processing that has had a great deal of influence is the Elaborative Likelihood Model (ELM) developed by Petty and Cacioppo in the early 1980s.[9] In their model they look at involvement in terms of something they refer to as central versus peripheral processing.

The central route deals with attention to the actual content of the message. Here the four-step communication response sequence, as we have called it, is essential. To form a brand attitude via the central route of processing requires message comprehension, learning, and retention. The peripheral route, on the other hand, associates positive or negative cues with the brand as a result of the execution or message without engaging in any extensive benefit-related thinking. Here, a positive (or even negative) brand attitude can result simply from affective cues in the execution. This could include almost anything, such as liking the spokesperson or liking the actors used in the advertising, or the humour; or even a more limbic-based response to some element in the execution.[10]

To summarize what we have been saying about the importance of motivation, if we do not know *why* someone wants to purchase a product or use a service, we will not be able to identify effectively the appropriate brand attitude and associated benefits. And, if we cannot identify these, we will not be able to come up with tactically optimal creative executions.

Fundamentally, motivation can be divided into negative versus positive motives (although some psychologists argue that all motivation is negative). Please remember that when psychologists talk about 'negative' motives they do not mean 'bad'. What they mean is that the motivation is negatively originated. You have a headache (problem) and you want relief (solution); you do not want to worry about getting a flat tyre (problem avoidance). Negative motives generally concern solving or avoiding problems. Positive motives generally involve seeking more personal satisfaction.

A good way to illustrate why it is so important to understand whether the underlying motivation driving behaviour is positive or negative is to look at the calorie-controlled food category. What exactly motivates people to watch their weight? Research into this question has shown that women are positively motivated to watch their weight while men are negatively motivated. A woman will see an attractive woman and think 'I would like to look like that...I'd better watch my weight.' Men don't react that way at all. They are more likely to respond to seeing someone overweight and out of breath from climbing stairs and think 'I don't want to get like that...I'd better watch my weight.' You should certainly be able to see that the same creative execution cannot be used for both men and women. Their basic motivations to watch their weight require different appeals. Women are driven by the positive motive of 'looking good' (sensory gratification or social approval), while men are driven by the negative motive of problem avoidance.

The Rossiter–Percy Grid

Given the importance of involvement and motivation in understanding how and why purchase decisions are made, Rossiter and Percy have suggested integrating these two dimensions into a strategic grid.[11] It is a logical extension of the important implications derived from the psychology literature in learning and persuasion on the role of involvement and motivation in the processing of messages and how people behave.

To begin with, as we have already seen in our discussion of involvement, there is a critical difference in what is required successfully to process a message dealing with a low- versus a high-involvement purchase decision. With low-involvement decisions, to initiate a positive brand attitude the target audience needs only to pay attention to the message and learn something positive about the brand. That should be enough to form an intention to try, and with trial, to build brand attitude. On the other hand, with high-involvement decisions the target audience must not only pay attention and learn something from the message; it must also accept or believe what is said in order to begin to build a positive brand attitude that will lead to purchase. Understanding the level of involvement is critical to building positive brand attitude because it affects the processing requirements for the advertising's message.

With motivation, we have seen how important it is to understand what motivates purchase and usage decisions for effective benefit selection and focus in positioning; and hence for building brand attitude (the link between the brand and the benefit). Also, motivation is linked to emotion, which plays a very important role in the processing of a message (as we will discuss in Chapter 11). To address positive versus negative motivations properly requires significantly different creative tactics.

Basically, when you are dealing with positive motives, you are creating a mood, and when you are dealing with negative motives, you are providing information to help address a perceived (or potential) problem. In their model, Rossiter and Percy refer to brand attitude strategies when motives are positive as *transformational* (transforming your mood) and when motives are negative as *informational*.

Others in the past have attempted to deal with criteria they feel are important to communication strategy by proposing various grids to help identify types of marketing communication. Perhaps the best-known example is the so-called FCB grid introduced back in the 1960s.[12] Unfortunately, while many texts and even some practitioners continue to refer to it, the FCB grid has a number of problems.[13] Among other concerns, it does not distinguish between product-category choice and brand choice. Also, their 'think-feel'

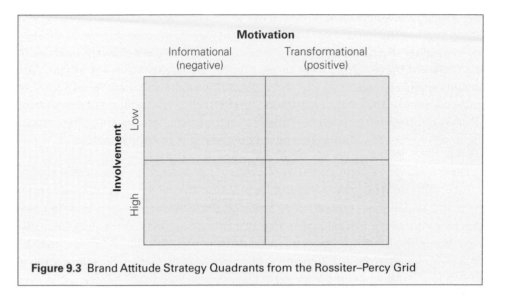

Figure 9.3 Brand Attitude Strategy Quadrants from the Rossiter–Percy Grid

dimension is rather superficially conceptualized, making the mistake of many in assuming only positive emotions or feelings when *negative* feelings must also be accounted for.

The Rossiter–Percy grid begins with the distinction between recall and recognition awareness, reminding the manager that, whatever the brand attitude strategy, it must be associated with the correct brand awareness strategy. But the real strength of the Rossiter–Percy grid in planning is that it helps focus the manager's thinking about a product or service in terms of the *target audience's* involvement with the choice decision and the motivation that drives its behaviour. This in turn alerts the manager to specific *tactical* requirements for creative execution (see Fig. 9.3).

Implementing a Low-Involvement Informational Brand Attitude Strategy

Low-involvement informational brand attitude strategies deal with low-risk purchase decisions driven by negative motivations. Because the motivation is to solve or avoid a problem in some way, we must supply information about the brand, in terms of the benefit, that will resolve the problem and provide 'relief' through the brand. In order to implement this the message should be concerned with benefit claim support and how it is resolved. The obvious format to accomplish this is to present the problem first, 'solved' by the brand. This is virtually every Procter & Gamble advert you have ever seen. 'How did those clothes get so dirty!' (the problem). 'Tide cleans even the dirtiest clothes' (the brand solves the problem).

An effective creative tactic to use with low-involvement informational advertising is to present the benefit claim in the extreme. This is possible because there is little or no risk involved in the purchase, so you do not need to actually believe the claim is true, only that it might be true. Look at the advert for Priorin shown in Plate VI. Here is a great example of a low-involvement informational strategy where the benefit of 'strength for your hair' is presented visually in a simple, yet extreme way. Strength is clearly implied by the flexed 'muscle', which is easily recognized as hair. Additionally, for the recognition brand awareness objective the package is clearly presented to facilitate recognition in the store.

Interestingly, it is not necessary to 'like' low-involvement informational advertising. The important thing is that the benefit is clearly communicated, even in the extreme. In one of the most successful campaigns ever, Procter & Gamble's Charmin toilet tissue for years featured an obnoxious store clerk named 'Mr Wipple'. He was always lurking around corners, while shoppers tried to avoid him so they could 'squeeze the Charmin' because it was so soft (the benefit). But every time they tried, he would stick his head around the aisle and call out: 'Ladies, please don't squeeze the Charmin.'[14]

Everyone hated the commercials, but the brand soon became the category leader. Why? The benefit of 'softness' was being clearly and dramatically demonstrated. When people were shopping in the toilet tissue aisle and saw the Charmin package (the recognition reminding them of the need), they did not think: 'Oh, Charmin. They have that awful TV commercial, I'm not buying that!' No, they were wondering if it really was that soft. Because it is a low-involvement decision, one with little or no risk, they gave it a try. This does not mean that you should go out of your way to produce advertising people do not like, only that liking the advertising, at least when dealing with negative motivations, is not required.[15]

The Charmin example, in fact, illustrates each of the important considerations involved in implementing low-involvement informational brand attitude strategies. First of all, it uses a problem-solution format. The problem here is *implied*: toilet tissue that is not soft. Charmin is the solution; it is 'squeezably soft'. Secondly, you do not need to like the execution, and the target audience did not. Thirdly, keep it simple, using a single benefit or a group of benefits that reinforce each other. For Charmin, the benefit is clear: softness. And, finally, the benefit claim is stated in the extreme.

Implementing a Low-Involvement Transformational Brand Attitude Strategy

With low-involvement transformational brand attitude strategies we are again dealing with a low-risk purchase decision, but the motivation is positive, based upon a 'reward' for using the product. Unlike when dealing with informational strategies, here the key is in the emotional portrayal of the benefit in order to arouse the correct emotional response; not in providing information. The advertising must 'ring true'. Beyond anything else, low-involvement transformational advertising must suggest *emotional authenticity*. The target audience must simply look at it and see it as 'real'. We put this in inverted commas because we do not mean it must be literally real. What must happen is the target audience must see itself emotionally in the role of using the products: 'That ice cream bar looks so good I want one right now!' You can just *feel* how good it tastes by looking at the execution.

A good example of what we are talking about may be seen in two very similar outdoor poster campaigns that ran in Sweden, one for milk and one for ice cream. Two examples from each campaign are shown in Adverts 9.3 and 9.4. Which of these looks most appetizing to you? Overall recognition for the milk campaign was 55 per cent versus only 20 per cent for the ice cream campaign.[16] The images used in the milk campaign are clearly more 'real' in the sense of exciting interest in 'drinking one now'. They are simply

Advert 9.3 Here we have two posters from a campaign in Sweden promoting milk that stimulated strong recognition.

Source: Åke Wissing & Co., Clear Channel Outdoor, and Mejerrerna.

more attractive. As a result, they were more likely to have been fully processed and stored in the memory, available to be remembered later on a shopping trip.

In effect, the benefit is *in the execution*. For this reason, when dealing with positively motivated behaviour the target audience must like the advertising, because it is the execution itself that elicits the emotion, not the information in the message. This is often difficult for advertisers to accept. There is a strong temptation to include a more tangible benefit when advertising a low-involvement product purchased from positive motives, a kind of benefit that would be more appropriate when dealing with negative motivations.

An example of what we are talking about is illustrated in a test conducted in Sweden of two Toblerone commercials using Åke Wissing & Co.'s Ad Box technique, a procedure for pre-testing advertising. Toblerone is a chocolate bar, a perfect example of a low-involvement product where you need to address a positive purchase motive, sensory gratification. A good commercial was produced creating a positive emotional experience, but there was some question as to whether the good feeling created by the commercial would be enough to drive purchase intent. A second version of the commercial was produced, identical to the first except for the ending, where an incentive was added: 'You can now buy Toblerone for the normal price, but you get 10 per cent more chocolate.' In other words, the original advertisement was turned into a *promotion* using a loading device (a bigger bar for the same money).

Frames from the two commercials are shown in Advert 9.5 on pp 214–215 illustrating the different endings. Results of the test showed that the original advertising version consistently outperformed the promotion version, including buying interest—65 per cent

Advert 9.4 These posters from a campaign promoting ice cream in Sweden, very similar to the adverts in 9.3, did not generate strong recognition.

Source: Åke Wissing & Co., Clear Channel Outdoor, and Glace-Bolaget.

versus 55 per cent (see Fig. 9.4). This brings up another important issue. A promotion, while it must be consistent with the brand's advertising, must be created in its own right. Too often managers think all that is needed for a promotion is to add an incentive of some kind (frequently a coupon or price-off announcement) to an existing advert or commercial. As this example shows, one message may interfere with the other. This is all too likely when dealing with positive motives in advertising because a promotion incentive will almost always be addressing a negative motive unless carefully positioned.

While all advertising executions should be unique to the brand, it is doubly critical for transformationally driven strategies. An advert may provide an effective and authentic emotional portrayal, but, if it is not firmly linked to the brand, it goes for naught. For this reason, a strong visual device, unique to the brand, can be effective when it is used consistently over time (something we deal with later on in Chapter 13). The visual component of the advertising should trigger an appropriate positive emotional association from the target audience's non-declarative emotional memory (that part of our memory, out of consciousness, where emotional memory is stored), which over time becomes linked to the brand (more about how this works is discussed in Chapter 11).

Implementing a High-Involvement Informational Brand Attitude Strategy

High-involvement informational brand attitude strategies deal with purchase decisions where there is a perceived risk involved in buying because of cost or psychological considerations; and where the motivation to buy or use the product is negative. Just as with low-involvement informational brand attitude strategies, because there is a problem to

Advert 9.5 (here and opposite) The same commercial, but with two different endings, the first reflecting a positive emotional experience, the second a specific product attribute. The first version significantly outperformed the second, as we would expect for a low-involvement product where purchase is driven by positive motives.
Source: Åke Wissing & Co., Clear Channel Outdoor, and Mejerrerna. TOBLERONE is a registered trademark of Kraft foods.

be solved, information must be provided. But because of the risk attached to the decision, *more* information must be provided. Remember, the target audience must be convinced. To ensure this happens, it is absolutely critical that the target audience's existing attitude be understood and taken into consideration: attitudes towards the brand (if they exist) and attitudes associated with the product and product category.

The reason it is necessary to understand the target audience's attitudes towards the brand is obvious. The more negative the brand attitude, the more difficult it will be for someone to accept anything the brand has to say. Of course, in most cases people with stray negative attitudes towards a brand would not be in the target audience. But people with moderately unfavourable attitudes, or those just indifferent to the brand, could very well be targets. If the moderately negative attitude is not firmly held, perhaps because of a perception related to an important category benefit ('They just don't last'), because of a general 'sense' that it is not one of the better brands in the category, or because of something heard about the brand, a well-positioned message that utilizes an important, believable benefit could help overcome this moderately negative initial attitude.

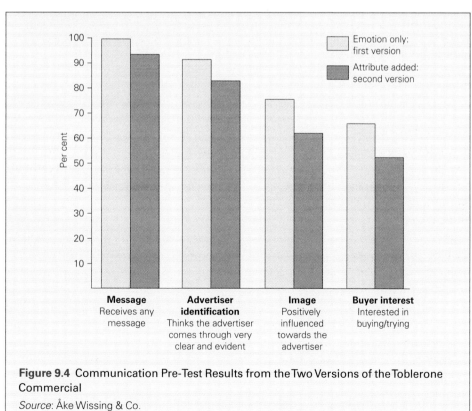

Figure 9.4 Communication Pre-Test Results from the Two Versions of the Toblerone Commercial

Source: Åke Wissing & Co.

Many people in the target audience may have only a vague understanding of the brand and as a result may not really have formed much of an attitude towards it. But if they are familiar with it, and in the absence of any other contrary information, simply because they have never considered it, at an implicit level of memory they are as likely as not to hold a mildly positive attitude towards the brand.[17] Others may have a good 'feeling' about the brand, even if they know very little about it, for many of the same reasons people may hold somewhat negative attitudes towards the brand. Again, a well-positioned message based upon an important, believable benefit could begin the process of building a more positive brand attitude. Those who already hold strong positive attitudes towards the brand will generally have a good understanding of the brand. Their positive brand attitude will be the result of favourable evaluations of what they attribute to the brand. (Remember the expectancy-value model of attitude?) The point is, we need to know what these initial attitudes are before we can begin to think about how to approach the message.

But understanding the target audience's attitudes towards the brand is not enough. We are trying to *persuade* people to consider our brand for a high-risk purchase. So, regardless of their initial *brand* attitude (with the exception of brand loyals who already have a strong positive brand attitude reflecting positive evaluations of the brand's benefit), we must also know what is important to them *in the product*, and how well or likely they are to think the brand can deliver.

Why? Again, it is because the message must be accepted as true. Because it is a high-involvement decision, much more cognitive activity will be involved in processing the message. Assuming the target audience pays attention, it will take the information provided in the message and integrate it with its existing knowledge base in the conscious or declarative memory. These associations in memory will create new thoughts about the brand in relation to the links formed in memory between existing beliefs, and the new information.[18] These new thoughts will be favourable or unfavourable towards the brand relative to the information already in memory. This is why understanding the target audience's existing attitudes towards the product and category are so important. Without this understanding, it will be difficult if not impossible to effectively develop advertising that is likely to build or reinforce a positive brand attitude.

Since understanding the target audience's attitude is so important to pitching the message at an acceptable level, does this mean one can talk only about things the target audience already believes? Can we not 'stretch' those attitudes to make them more favourable? The answer is yes, we can, but we must be very careful not to go too far. That, of course, begs the question, how far can we go before the target audience will simply reject what we are saying. The answer comes from early work in attitude-change theory that addressed this very issue. In Sherif and Hovland's assimilation-contrast theory, they identified an area of 'indifference' that falls between those things a person can readily accept and those they reject outright.[19] The key to implementing high-involvement informational brand strategy successfully is to know where the 'latitude of rejection' begins beyond the latitude of indifference, and not to cross the line. This answer will come from good research into the target audience's attitude towards the category, product, and brand.

While the target audience must believe the message, as was the case with low-involvement informational brand attitude strategies, it does not need to like the advertising itself.

Learning is simply not dependent upon liking the advertising, even in the high-involve-ment case.[20] If the benefits presented in the message are convincing, how they are pre-sented will not matter—assuming, of course, that it is the 'style' of the advertising that is not liked, not the fact that the audience cannot understand it. As mentioned earlier, however, this does not mean that you should go out of your way to create advertising the target audience does not like, only that its 'liking' it need not be a concern.

Implementing a High-Involvement Transformational Brand Attitude Strategy

High-involvement transformational strategies deal with purchase decisions that involve risk, and that are made to satisfy an underlying positive motivation. This means that, again, because of the perceived risk involved with the purchase, the message must be accepted as true. And, while the underlying motivation driving the decision is positive, because the decision involves some level of fiscal or psychological risk, there may sometimes be a need to provide information to help overcome potential problems associated with that risk.

Just as in the low-involvement transformational case, the critical concern is *emotional authenticity,* but at the high-involvement level, the target audience must also *person-ally* identify with the brand as it is portrayed in the execution and the benefit is in the execution. The target audience wants the product in order to *feel* the thrill of driving a new sports car or the sense of glamour that goes with wearing high fashion clothes. The execution must arouse those feelings.

Because of this, the target audience must 'like' the advertising. But, that liking must go beyond simply liking the execution itself. The liking must be *product and brand* based. Because it is a high-involvement decision, in processing the message the target audience must really believe that the brand, as portrayed in the advertising, is the one that will sat-isfy the sensory gratification or social approval motivation underlying its need. The brand must be portrayed in such a way that it elicits from non-declarative emotional memory the correct emotions, the *feelings* the target audience wants to experience in using the product. (How this happens will be discussed in Chapter 11.)

The advert for Ford's Puma shown in Advert 9.6, provides a good example of what we are talking about here. The execution places the target audience in the driver's seat, pro-viding a very specific image with which to identify. Fans of old Steve McQueen movies like *Bullet* will immediately recognize the look-alike behind the wheel, triggering strong emotional associations. But this 'recognition' is not necessary for the advert to work. There is a strong emotional feeling associated with the driver that will resonate with those looking for that experience with a motor car.

Reviewing Brand Awareness and Brand Attitude Strategy

A good way to appreciate what goes into the effective implementation of brand awareness and brand attitude strategy is to compare good executions of adverts for each of the four quadrants of the Rossiter–Percy Grid. Such examples may be seen in Plates VII to X. First, look at the advert for Surf detergent in Plate VII. It provides an excellent execution of low-involvement informational advertising. The benefit is presented in the extreme, and in a humorous way. Are clothes cleaned with Surf detergent really so 'irresistibly clean' that people will snatch them right off you? Hardly, but the point is made. And when the

Advert 9.6 A good example of placing the target audience in the action to personally identify with the benefit.

brand is seen in the shop (and note the strong package presentation, facilitating recognition brand awareness), you are likely to remember the advert *and* importantly the benefit of irresistibly clean clothes. Could it really be that good? Since this is a low-involvement decision with little risk, why not give it a try. This is a well-done advert.

Contrast this with the advert for Kinder Bueno in Plate VIII. The difference is immediately felt. Here we have an appetizing look at the chocolate bar stimulating positive associations in memory, which are reinforced as the eye carries down to the contented woman receiving a massage, with the message 'A little bit of what you fancy.' The emotional authenticity is real, communicating a sense of pleasure and contentment that will be associated in memory with the brand. The package is well presented for easy recognition at the point-of-purchase, so that when seen in the store it will trigger the good feeling and desire you felt when you saw the advert, leading to purchase.

Looking at the high involvement quadrants from the grid, the Panasonic advert in Plate IX provides a really good example of high-involvement informational brand attitude, and recall brand awareness, strategy. In terms of brand attitude strategy, the visual is strong and vivid, consistent with the benefit, and most importantly, believable. It implies the intensity and clarity to be found in the Viera HD plasma television. The image attracts your attention and draws you into the copy, which reinforces the benefit. While always difficult to accomplish in print, the recognition brand recall strategy is well executed. The 'need' for a better television experience is presented first via the visual, then linked to the brand. This link is then repeated in the copy, again in the correct need-brand sequence, with 'Enjoy wildlife as nature intended' (the need) followed by 'thanks to Panasonic' (the brand). When in the market for a new HD television to enjoy a more vivid picture, because this need has been linked to Panasonic, in the need-brand order, it should come immediately to mind as the way to 'solve' that problem.

Finally, the Australia advert in Plate X offers a great example of a high-involvement transformational advert. The visual image is likely to elicit a strong positive emotional response from anyone interested in a possible holiday in Australia. They will immediately identify with the image and the 'feeling': Wow!, would I like to be there. The appropriately sparse copy reinforces this feeling with 'So where the bloody hell are you?' The easily recognized Sydney Opera House clearly identifies the 'brand', which will follow immediately upon the strong positive emotion that is elicited by the image. The way this works will be addressed in our discussion of emotion in Chapter 11. Again, this is the necessary need-brand order for recall brand awareness. The feeling of Wow! is immediately followed by a conscious association with Australia. When the time comes to consider an exciting holiday, Australia will come to mind for consideration. That positive feeling generated from the advert is the benefit, and will encourage looking into a trip to Australia.

Corporate Image Advertising

This is a good place to consider corporate image advertising. Like all advertising, both brand awareness and brand attitude must be communication objectives (the brand here, of course, is the company). Obviously, corporations want their name to be *recognized*, hence recognition brand awareness strategies are called for. In terms of brand attitude, the primary objective is to build and sustain overall positive attitude towards the company. In effect, companies want people to 'like' them.

What brand attitude strategy, then, should be used? In almost all cases, corporate image advertising should follow a *transformational* brand attitude strategy.

Consider this for a minute. We know that transformational brand attitude strategies are needed when dealing with positive motives. What motive is involved here? There is obviously no *direct* purchase or usage decision involved, but in a sense there is a decision to consider the company. If someone pays attention to the advertising, is it to solve a problem? In the absence of any immediate concrete action being considered by the target audience, the answer is no. Rather, if people pay attention to the advertising, it is probably because they wish to *learn* something about the company, and what they learn will inform their attitude towards the company. Learning in order simply to acquire knowledge is almost always positively motivated, and this indicates a transformational brand attitude strategy.

The difficult question is whether we are dealing with a low- or high-involvement decision. What is the 'risk' of making a bad decision about the company based upon what is learned from the corporate image advertising? This will depend a lot upon the specific target audience, and how or if people eventually act upon their feelings associated with the company. If the objective is to foster 'goodwill', building or maintaining a positive attitude towards the company, then a low-involvement transformational strategy will be all that is needed. Often after bad publicity, a company may wish to restore positive feelings among the population at large or among specific target groups. If the effect of the negative publicity was slight, again a low-involvement transformational strategy should work.

But what if the damage done to the company's image is serious? If that occurs, attitudes towards the company may have been seriously affected, and as a result for corporate image advertising to be effective the target audience will need to be *convinced* by the message. This means a high-involvement transformational strategy. There are many other situations where a high-involvement transformational brand attitude strategy would be needed. As an investor, you may 'like' a company, but you will also want to understand more about it; you need to feel convinced it might be a good company in which to invest. We are not talking about the actual investment decision here, which would involve negative motivations, but the 'feeling' an investor has about a company prior to seriously considering it as an investment.

Suppose the target audience is people working in government, in regulatory agencies. From the corporation's perspective, it will want them to have the strongest possible positive attitudes towards the company, and not just a general 'liking', because, if it does become involved in any actions with a regulatory agency, it will want to be starting from a positive association in memory, not an indifferent or even moderately positive association; and certainly not from a negative one.

Corporate image advertising will almost always utilize a transformational brand attitude strategy, and usually a high-involvement transformational strategy, because, in the long term the target audience must *accept* the message that this is a 'good' company. Corporate *image* advertising is not aimed at specific decisions on the part of a target audience. Of course, corporations also advertise in order to influence particular decisions: for example, to specifically influence investors to buy or analysts to recommend a stock or bond issue; or to specifically get a government agency to look favourably on something the company wishes to do. In such cases, the appropriate brand attitude strategy will be the one that reflects the risk and motivation involved in the particular decision being addressed, just as with any other brand advertising.

Promotion Strategy

Promotion must be considered as part of the communication strategy when brand purchase intention is a communication objective. While brand purchase intention may be a communication objective for advertising, as we have seen, that is rarely the case. In those situations where it is necessary to accelerate purchase intention to immediate action, promotion becomes a part of the communication strategy. This may be a part of the initial strategic planning process; however, the need for a promotion may also occur during a campaign for tactical reasons. For example, a competitor may be about to introduce a new version of their product and you might want to encourage accelerated purchase of your brand to remove your favourable brand-switchers from the market just prior to the introduction; or, you may find sales weak because of some unforeseen circumstance in the market. In either event, the execution of the promotion, its visual imagery and message, must be consistent with the brand's advertising.

We have defined promotion generally as that part of a brand's marketing communication strategy dealing with the more short-term tactical goal of immediate action. While this is certainly a useful definition, there is more to consider. For example one important consideration is time. When consumer decision-making models were introduced in Chapter 7, we saw how important it is to understand the timing of various stages in the decision process. Just as with advertising, one needs to integrate the use of promotion techniques in relation to the target audience's decision process. Some promotions may be more helpful early in the decision process, prior to purchase or use of a service, others more appropriate at the point of purchase, still others after purchase or even during usage. When considering traditional promotion tactics, it must be considered as part of the overall marketing communication effort. Promotion is used when you want to speed up the decision process, but should never be considered in isolation. As pointed out earlier, most promotions involve an incentive, and are known as sales promotion.

Sales promotions may be broadly classified as either *immediate* or *delayed*.[21] This idea of immediate versus delayed promotions is closely associated with the two target audience action objectives of trial and repeat purchase, which we introduced when we were discussing target audience buyer groups in Chapter 6.

Almost any promotion should help generate trial or encourage repeat purchase. For example, while loyalty programmes are clearly designed to encourage and promote repeat purchase of and loyalty to a brand, if the loyalty programme is seen by non-users as particularly attractive, it could also encourage trial. Equally, while coupons are effective in attracting trial, they also encourage repeat purchase by existing customers by effectively reducing the price.

When we speak of a type of promotion being more oriented towards trial or repeat purchase, what we are talking about are general strengths (Table 9.2). If we look at the six basic types of consumer sales promotions, for example, coupons, sampling, and refunds are strong candidates for trial, while sweepstakes and loyalty promotions are best suited to repeat purchase. Premiums are a little more difficult to place because they can really be effective for either objective. An appropriately chosen premium could have a strong appeal to other-brand-switchers, providing just the incentive to get them to try our brand along with the others they use. Say someone switches among two or three brands of condiments, but not your brand. Offering a recipe booklet as a premium with the purchase of any of your condiments could provide the necessary incentive to give your

Table 9.2 Strengths of the Six Basic Consumer Sales Promotion Techniques in Terms of Trial and Repeat Purchase

Trial Strength	Repeat Purchase Strength
Coupons	Loyalty and loading devices
Refunds and rebates	Sweepstakes, games, and contests
Sampling	Premiums
Premiums	

brand a try. On the other hand, especially for more durable products with longer pur-chase cycles, a well-targeted premium could indeed get previous buyers to purchase again now. This would be particularly appropriate for those in the target audience just beginning to think about perhaps replacing, say, an appliance that is showing some age. There is no real need yet, but they are thinking about it. An attractive premium could very well get them to act now.

Strategically, repeat purchase sales promotion techniques are used for more targeted, short-term objectives. Unlike trial promotions, which are designed to attract new custom-ers to the brand, repeat purchase premiums are used to affect the *timing* of purchases by brand users. You want your customers either to buy now, effectively removing them from the market in the short term to avoid switching, or to buy continually with little or no switching.

CHAPTER SUMMARY

In this chapter we have discussed the development of communication strategy, based on the four communication objectives of category need, brand awareness, brand attitude, and brand purchase intention. We have emphasized the important distinction between recognition brand awareness and recall brand awareness, and the implications for creative and media strategies. The critical importance of involvement and motivation was highlighted and related to the process-ing of messages. We then looked at how these important considerations influence brand attitude strategy in the context of the Rossiter–Percy grid, and outlined the principles involved in imple-menting brand attitude strategy. Finally, we discussed the role of promotion in communication, and its relation to trial and repeat purchase objectives.

QUESTIONS TO CONSIDER

9.1 Under what circumstances should the manager consider including category need as a communication objective?

9.2 When should brand purchase intention be considered as a specific communication objective?

9.3 What are the important considerations the manager must use in setting the brand awareness strategy?

9.4 Why is it important to think about brand attitude as a relative concept?

9.5 In what ways are involvement and motivation involved in driving brand attitude strategy?

9.6 What are the key strategic differences between informational and transformational strategies?

9.7 How should the manager look at corporate advertising in terms of communication strategy?

9.8 Why are some incentive promotions more appropriate for trial action objectives and others for repeat purchase action objectives?

Plate IX Panasonic

High involvement informational strategies require believability, and this Panasonic advert offers a good example of a believably presented benefit. © Panasonic UK Ltd.

Plate X Tourism Australia

With high involvement transformational strategies a strong, emotional response is needed with which the target must personally identify, and this advert for Australia is a great example for anyone considering a holiday in Australia. Reproduced with kind permission ©Tourism Australia.

Plate XI Anthisan

This advert for Anthisan PLUS is a very good example of using words and pictures to attract and hold attention. Reproduced with kind permission © Anthisan PLUS.

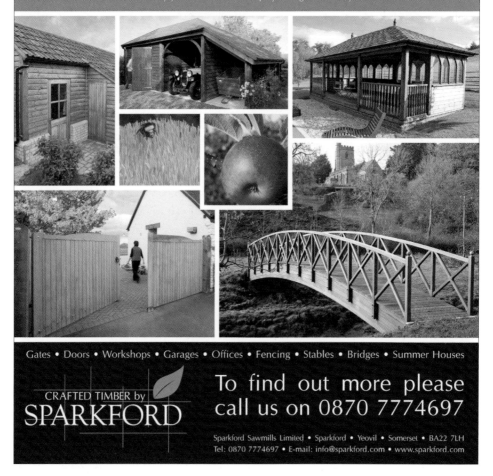

Plate XII Sparkford

This advert for Sparkford is a very good example of using a series of illustrations to convey a number of ways the product is 'in use'. Reproduced with kind permission © Sparkford.

Waste Awareness

Think of the last thing in the world you find yourself thinking about. Or would ever find interesting. Think of the last thing in the world you would bring up with friends at a party or in conversation as an ice-breaker. Now think of an ad campaign that takes this non-issue and transforms it into a big issue; positions it as top of mind, socially important, and persuades you to act differently with it and towards it. It's Rubbish. Or more specifically, it's the Waste Awareness campaign commissioned by the Environment and Heritage Service (EHS) in Northern Ireland (NI) in partnership with the Department of Environment, Heritage and Local Government (DEHLG) in the Republic of Ireland (ROI). This All-Island activity followed two separate and recent waste awareness campaigns in the North and South of Ireland, both of which used shock imagery and stark messages to force a reaction from the public. But this new campaign was up against a tougher challenge. What was new? What would capture the imagination? What would shake inertia and make people continue to care?

The 'Change Will Do You Good' campaign was exceptional in its achievements:

- 84 per cent awareness levels and 72 per cent of respondents reported a behaviour change.
- An increase in overall recycling rates in the months of the campaign.
- The Irish Direct Marketing Association reported that they received twelve times more calls than on an average day during the campaign as a result of 'prevent waste/say no to junk mail' messaging.

The theme of the campaign was 'Transformations', taking what was considered rubbish and demonstrating that it could be useful. It's not rubbish. It's Gold.

The European Union Council Directive 1999/31/EC of 26 April 1999 on the landfill of waste has set targets for each member state to improve waste recovery and reduce waste going to landfill. Northern Ireland and Ireland were in recent years playing catch-up to their European cousins. The marketing objectives of the project were to reduce the volume of waste going to landfill and increase the recycling of waste materials in the cross-border area, and to encourage entrepreneurs in identifying opportunities in materials reprocessing from recycled products and encourage business development. The cross-border area is of particular importance for sustainable waste management programmes across the island of Ireland because:

- It is disadvantaged by increased costs and distance to markets due to its location
- There is potential to locate a network of waste management and reprocessing facilities which takes advantage of economies of scale
- The area suffers from the pressures of illegal dumping.

Previously, EHS and DEHLG had separately commissioned *LyleBailie* to develop awareness-raising communications campaigns, and the strategy utilized before was shock. Both campaigns had dramatized the consequences of not addressing the waste issue, followed by information messages on how and what to recycle. The achievements of the campaigns are indisputable but in essence, 'Wake Up To Waste' and 'Race Against Waste' started at zero—even the smallest change would have been an improvement.

This time achieving change would be tougher. The challenge of the new cross-border waste awareness brief was how to achieve yet a further increase in attitudes, behaviours, and actual recycling rates when the previous campaigns had achieved such a remarkable spike in understanding and activity. Quite simply, how could we possibly make people involve themselves even more in something they were just coming to grips with and inherently don't want to do?

Our research showed that once we persuaded people to do a few simple things, like glass bottle or newspaper recycling, they could be persuaded to do more. We further identified that as people engaged with waste management, the more questions were generated about the detail of recycling. For this campaign, we took each major waste issue at home and at work and drilled down into more detail than before, involving the target audiences in more waste action under the creative banner of 'The Change Will Do You Good'. The new strategy allowed the campaign to innovate a response to an emerging question: 'is all this recycling worth my effort?' This issue was worsened in the case of the twelve border counties by negative publicity surrounding illegal dumping in that area.

The new campaign would be energetic, entertaining, and would communicate:

- Very specific details of how to recycle properly
- The first national waste prevention message
- The metamorphosis of waste into a transformed resource, recycled plastic into fleeces

This new thinking was designed to answer the real questions arising from previous campaigns and to progress the target to greater and deeper involvement in active recycling by proving that it all is worthwhile and by showing that today's waste is tomorrow's resource. Furthermore, by demonstrating a range of waste 'transformations', the campaign engaged businesses with the 'muck-to brass' potential of several waste streams.

The campaign was based around the drill-down detail demonstrating 'How To' reduce, reuse, and recycle waste, followed by a visual transformation showing the outcome of each action. The transformation was designed to empower people at work and at home with the feeling that their personal involvement is worthwhile and beneficial. This metamorphosis served to dramatize the message that one person's waste is another's resource. The creative vehicle was the music track 'The Change Will Do You Good' by Sheryl Crowe—a contemporary, high-energy track that served to drive the call-to-action through all the broadcast TV and radio communications, limited to the explicit benefits dramatized in the transformations. At the heart of the creative device were two celebrity spokespeople—one from the North, one from the South, one male, one female, using ping-pong dialogue to convey each specific message. Our celebrities were Diarmuid Gavin the Celebrity Gardener, and Olivia Nash a Northern Irish actress and comedienne. Through great performances and good direction they conveyed popular empathy.

Through a series of six TV edits featuring home and work contexts both in the vision and dialogue, the campaign isolated specific messages based on: Glass Bottles and Jars, Plastic Bottles, Cans, Paper, Composting, Prevention (of unsolicited, unaddressed mail).

The core elements in this creative approach were designed to optimize impact, recall, and viewability of the cross-border message:

- The music track by Sheryl Crowe packaged all the benefits of Race Against Waste under the thought 'the change will do you good'. This tried and tested technique for optimizing recall and populist buy-in worked well for the campaign.
- The transformation idea demonstrated how 'the change will do you good'—and why it is worthwhile to join the Race Against Waste or Wake Up to Waste!
- The two celebrities, balancing North and South, increased the talkability of the campaigns while making the more mundane information in the drill-down 'How To' scenes more enjoyable and interesting to watch.

The Campaign ran from 14 September to 30 November 2005 and the total spend was £1,184,968.55. For this campaign the crucial medium was television. Reaching all target audiences, television's unique 'show and tell' quality was deployed to empower and stimulate the widest mix of targets—at home, work, farmers, shoppers, entrepreneurs, business decision makers, educators, retailers, manufacturers, local authorities, and so on. Radio and Regional Press were used as local support media, with Regional Press identified as having a role in communicating with and attracting new entrepreneurs. Trade Press (with an upweight in Agricultural titles) was used as an important medium for reaching business decision makers. The 15–34 audience was targeted through cinema advertising, and our business targets through on-line marketing. The cornerstone of our communication channel to businesses was an all-day Business Workshop event. The aim was to initiate a multi-stakeholder dialogue, building knowledge and understanding of the opportunities which exist for enterprise and new business creation as well as highlighting the economic benefits for business addressing their own waste management practices. This was achieved through a mix of presentations, video presentations from Reprocessors, and breakout sessions that focused on key issues relating to business opportunities and development.

In sum the results of the campaign were: 84 per cent awareness, 95 per cent understood the message, 31 per cent increase in the number of respondents who had been exposed to any publicity about waste, 90 per cent 'makes me think', 88 per cent were influenced by the campaign, 88 per cent were favourable, 72 per cent reported a behaviour change, 74 per cent learnt something new. Also

- Overall recycling rates: 7.8 per cent increase from August to September
- A Workshop Evaluation was also completed. The attendance exceeded expectations.
- 94 per cent of respondents indicated positively that the workshop was important
- 92 per cent of respondents indicating positively that the workshop had been beneficial
- 92 per cent of respondents would consider new partnerships in developing their business.

Source: WARC, IPA Effectiveness Awards 2005, Waste Awareness

Edited by Natalia Yannopoulou

Discussion Questions

1   Evaluate the communications strategy of this campaign for the increase of brand awareness.

2   What made the campaign so successful and resulted in such attitude change?

3   Propose suitable communication strategies that would increase brand awareness depending on different product categories.

4   What would make a marketing campaign achieve long-term brand awareness?

FURTHER READING

- For a theoretical discussion of the important difference in the *direction* of learning brand awareness in relation to category need, see D. L. Nelson, C. L. McEvoy, and L. Pointer, 'Spreading Activation or Spooky Action at a Distance?', *Journal of Experimental Psychology: Learning, Memory, and Cognition*, 29/1 (2003), 47–52.

- An important aspect of the difference in high- versus low-involvement processing is that there is a greater likelihood that the benefit claims made in high-involvement processing will interact, as pointed out by Stijn van Osselaer and Chris Janiszewski in 'Two Ways of Learning Brand Associations', *Journal of Consumer Research*, 28/2 (Sept. 2001), 202–23.

- In 'Emotional Contagion Effects on Product Attitudes', *Journal of Consumer Research*, 28/2 (Sept. 2001), 199–201, Daniel Howard and Charles Gengler deal with the influence of perceived emotion in a source on brand or product attitudes.

NOTES

1   The four communication effects discussed here, and their use as communication objectives, follow from the work of John Rossiter and Larry Percy, first introduced in *Advertising and Promotion Management* (New York: McGraw-Hill, 1987). This book also talks about a fifth communication effect, something Rossiter and Percy call purchase facilitation, to account for situations where the advertiser may need to address issues arising from problems with other components of the marketing mix.

2   This very important distinction was first made in Rossiter and Percy, *Advertising and Promotion Management*.

3   Measures of *advertising* recall are not valid predictors of advertising effectiveness. The most that can be said of day-after recall (DAR) measures is that they *might* provide some indication of attention to an advert. What is important is that the *brand* is remembered. Even published studies by leading DAR companies have never shown advertising recall to be a valid measure of effectiveness.
     See e.g. M. H. Blair, 'An Empirical Investigation of Advertising Wearin and Wearout', *Journal of Advertising Research*, 28/6 (1988), 45–50, and P. R. Klein and M. Tainter, 'Copy Research Validation: The Advertiser's Perspective', *Journal of Advertising Research*, 23/5 (1983), 9–17.

4   The principle of encoding specificity is explained in E. Tulving, *Elements of Episodic Memory* (Oxford: Oxford University Press, 1983).

5   To understand fully the attitudes of your target audience, it will be necessary to conduct *primary* research. There is really no alternative to measuring your target audience's perceptions of your brand and competitors, and general category attitudes.

6   See M. Fishbein and I. Ajzen, *Belief, Attitude, Intention, and Behavior: An Introduction to Theory and Research* (Reading, Mass.: Addison-Wesley, 1975).

7   See Steven P. R. Rose, *The Making of Memory* (London: Bantam Books, 1993).

8   See J. C. Maloney, 'Curiosity versus Disbelief in Advertising', *Journal of Advertising Research*, 2/2 (1962), 2–8.

9   See R. E. Petty and J. T. Cacioppo, 'Central and Peripheral Routes to Persuasion: Application to Advertising', in L. Percy and A. G. Woodside, *Advertising and Consumer Psychology* (Lexington, Mass.: Lexington Books, 1983), 3–24.

10 Limbic-based responses emanate from the palaeomammalian mind and are unconsciously stimulated. An example would be the warm feeling you have when you see a small baby. For a discussion of how such responses can influence advertising processing, see L. Percy, 'An Introduction to the Theory of Symbolism of Habitat and its Implication for Consumer Behavior and Marketing Communication', in Flemming Hansen (ed.), *European Advances in Consumer Research* (Provo, Ut.: Association for Consumer Research, various years), ii. 19–28. For a more detailed medical discussion, see Paul D. MacLean, *The Triune Brain in Evolution: Role in Paleocerebral Functions* (New York: Plenum Press, 1990).

11   See J. R. Rossiter and L. Percy, *Advertising Communication and Promotion Management*, 2nd edn. (New York: McGraw-Hill, 1997).

12   See R. Vaughn, 'How Advertising Works: A Planning Model', *Journal of Advertising Research*, 20/5 (1980), 27–33.

13   See J. R. Rossiter, L. Percy, and R. J. Donovan, 'A Better Advertising Planning Grid', *Journal of Advertising Research*, 30/5 (1991), 11–21.

14   In 2002 Charmin attempted to bring back the original Mr Whipple, but it did not work. The problem, of course, was that he was no longer recognizable as *the* Mr Whipple; he was much older, and looked it. Also, a very large part of the target audience did not have memories of the original campaign, and could not readily associate him with the 'soft' benefit that always triggered the 'please don't squeeze the Charmin' admonition.

15   Despite a large number of studies in the 1980s to the contrary, an excellent study by Marty Lautman and Larry Percy clearly demonstrated that ad-liking is appropriate only for transformational brand attitude strategies ('Cognitive and Affective Responses in Attribute-Based versus End-Benefit Oriented Advertising', in T. C. Kinnear (ed.), *Advances in Consumer Research*, xi (Ann Arbor: Association for Consumer Research, 1984). The problem of the studies advocating the need for ad-liking for advertising effectiveness is that these studies (e.g. the most frequently cited paper by Mitchel and Olsen, 'Are Product Attribute Beliefs the Only Mediator of Advertising Effects in Brand Attitudes?' *Journal of Marketing Research*, 18 (1987), 318–32) utilized adverts that dealt with low-involvement *transformational* brand attitude strategies. No one tested adverts using informational brand attitude strategy.

16   These results are reported from research conducted by ISI Wissing in Sweden.

17   This is similar to Tulving's notion of mere exposure, which we discuss in Chapter 11.

18   We will be spending a great deal of time on this subject in Chapter 11 where we talk about learning and memory. In that chapter we will show how neural networks overlap, incorporating new information with existing knowledge and assumptions to build new knowledge.

19   This notion of Sheriff and Hovland is outlined in *Social Judgment* (New Haven: Yale University Press, 1961), and has been discussed within an advertising context by Larry Percy and John Rossiter in *Advertising Strategy: A Communication Theory Approach* (New York: Praeger Publishers, 1980).

20   A really good study demonstrating the irrelevance of liking an advert for influencing a high-involvement informational purchase decision is found in L. Percy and M. R. Lautmen, 'Creative Strategy, Consumer Decision Goals, and Attitude toward the Ad and Advertised Brand', in J. Olson and K. Sentic (eds), *Advertising and Consumer Psychology*, iii (New York: Praeger Publishers, 1986), 55–73.

21   See Peter Simmons, 'Sales Promotion in Marketing', in N. Hart (ed.), *The Practice of Advertising*, 4th edn. (Oxford: Butterworth-Heinemann, 1995), 256, and Larry Percy, *Strategies for Implementing Integrated Marketing Communication* (Lincolnwood, Ill.: NTC Business Books, 1997), 96.

 Visit the Online Resource Centre that accompanies this book for additional resources to support the text: http://www.oxfordtextbooks.co.uk/orc/ percy_elliott3e/

Setting a Media Strategy

Once the communication strategy is set, the manager is in a position to set a media strategy. The media selected must be consistent with what is required to process the message successfully, and this will differ depending upon the brand awareness and brand attitude strategy needed for the brand, as we see below.

Implementing the Strategic Planning Process

Step 1	Step 2	Step 3	Step 4	Step 5
Selecting the Target Audience	Understanding Target Audience Decision Making	Determining the Best Positioning	Developing a Communication Strategy	Setting a Media Strategy

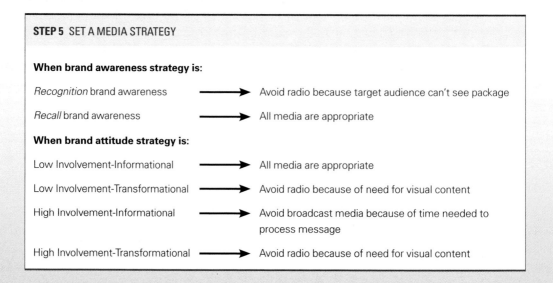

STEP 5 SET A MEDIA STRATEGY

When brand awareness strategy is:

Recognition brand awareness ⟶ Avoid radio because target audience can't see package

Recall brand awareness ⟶ All media are appropriate

When brand attitude strategy is:

Low Involvement-Informational ⟶ All media are appropriate

Low Involvement-Transformational ⟶ Avoid radio because of need for visual content

High Involvement-Informational ⟶ Avoid broadcast media because of time needed to process message

High Involvement-Transformational ⟶ Avoid radio because of need for visual content

> **KEY CONCEPTS**
>
> 1 Media selection decisions are becoming more complex as the number of message delivery options increases, especially in the area of new media.
>
> 2 Media must be selected based upon communication objectives, with special attention to the processing requirement of brand awareness and brand attitude strategy.
>
> 3 Direct matching of media to buyer or attitude of groups is much more efficient than demographic matching.
>
> 4 New media are presenting both opportunities and challenges for delivering messages, but the strategic use of new media, like any media, must conform to the processing requirements of the communication strategy.

We have made the point at various stages of this book that the decisions relating to media are of major importance. In this chapter we review the strategic factors that affect decisions regarding media selection. To a large extent the decisions relating to media scheduling are at the tactical level and are now largely handled by specialist media-buying agencies who have each developed very sophisticated suites of computer programs, such as Zenith Media's Zoom systems. They are, therefore, not dealt with here in any detail. Interested readers should consult the specialist media planning literature, such as Rossiter and Danaher or Sissors and Baumber.[1]

The Turbulent Media Environment

Beginning in the 1980s, there has been an ever increasing number of media channels, accompanied by a fragmentation and segmentation of audiences. In the UK in 1982 there was one commercial TV station; in 1999 there were more than 100. Over the same period commercial radio has grown from 28 stations to more than 200, consumer magazines from 1,300 to 2,600 plus, and business magazines from 2,000 to 5,400 plus.[2] And, of course, there are the new media (dealt with in some detail later in the chapter), CD-ROMs, and other screen-based channels, and the bewildering variety of ambient media such as petrol pump handles, postcards, shopping trolleys, litter bins, and bus tickets.

As a result, media selection decisions have become far more complex and have led to the growth of specialist media agencies that are used by many major advertisers instead of their advertising agency's media departments. In a parallel move, some of Europe's largest advertisers, including Procter & Gamble, BT, and Unilever, have put media planning at the heart of their communication strategy. For example, 'communication channel planning' has been made mandatory across all Unilever's worldwide businesses, where after setting brand priorities and objectives, media channel recommendations are agreed before a communication plan and subsequent creative briefs.[3] It is against this turbulent and fast-changing background that we will examine how media strategy can be guided by the communication strategy concepts developed in previous chapters.

Table 10.1 Key Media Concepts

Reach	The percentage of the target audience exposed to an advertisement in a given time period
Frequency	The number of times an individual member of the target audience is exposed to an advertisement in a given time period
Opportunities to See (OTS)	The cumulative exposures achieved in a given time period, usually used in media planning in place of frequency
Gross Rating Points (GRPs)	A summary statistic for the achievement of a media plan, calculated by multiplying reach by frequency
Effective Frequency	A hypothetical construct that attempts to estimate the number of OTS required to have an effect in the target audience

The Media Trade-off Trinity

Before we go any further, it is important to define some of the specialist terminology used in relation to media (see Table 10.1).

Reach is the percentage of the target audience that is exposed to an advertisement in a given time period, usually four weeks. *Frequency* is the number of times an individual member of the target audience is exposed to a particular media vehicle in a given time period. *Opportunities to see* (OTS) refers to the cumulative exposures achieved in a given time period and is usually used instead of frequency in media planning. *Gross Rating Points* (GRPs) is a summary statistic for the achievement of a media plan and is calculated by multiplying reach by frequency. The word 'gross' indicates the problems with this statistic, as a media plan that achieves, say, 180 GRPs could be achieved by reaching 90 per cent of the target audience with an OTS of 2, or by reaching 45 per cent of the audience with an OTS of 4.

Effective frequency is a hypothetical construct that attempts to estimate the number of OTS that are required to have an effect on the target audience. Despite extensive econometric modelling and some highly exaggerated claims, there is no general answer to this question. One obvious problem is the widespread assumption that all advertising executions are equal. This is, of course, nonsense. As Millward Brown has demonstrated through tracking studies of hundreds of brands around the world, a good advert can be at least three times as effective as the average for a category, and over ten times as effective as the worst.[4] Some media auditing studies have shown a variation in the effect of advertising on sales due solely to creative execution of 10 to 1.

There are also a few terms associated with how advertising is scheduled that it is good to know. One very popular way of scheduling media is to be in the market for two or three weeks, then out for a few weeks before returning. This is known as *flighting*. Another practice is where advertising appears heavily a few times a year between long periods of no advertising. This is referred to as *bursts*. When advertising runs more or less continuously, this is known as *continuity scheduling*.

Reach versus Frequency

At the heart of media strategy is the fact that there is never enough money to achieve very high reach and very high frequency for a very long period of time. Hence media strategy involves decisions between three elements that trade off frequency for coverage or vice versa, and whether to have a heavy weight of advertising for a shorter time period or less weight for longer. A media plan must deal with these three basic variables: reach, frequency, and timing. The ideal media plan, of course, would enable you to reach everyone in your target audience as often as necessary to ensure a positive response to your message. But you never have this luxury, because it would require an all-but-unlimited budget. The reality of set budgets requires careful trade-offs between how many members of your target audience you can successfully reach, how many times you reach them, and when. While the timing of a schedule is an important consideration, the key is the trade-off between reach and frequency. This is a critical strategic issue.

A strategic emphasis on reach means spending the advertising and marketing communication budget in a number of different media, and a number of different vehicles, in order to reach as many members of the target audience as possible. By utilizing a number of different media you help ensure that people who do not use certain media are none the less reached. Some people watch a lot of television, some very little; others read a lot of magazines, some none at all; many people do not read newspapers at all. If reaching as many members of the target audience as possible is your goal, it will require using many different media, and then, for each medium, a number of different vehicles (for example, different types of television and radio programmes, and several different magazines).

When you emphasize reach, frequency suffers. If your emphasis is on frequency, you want to make sure that members of the target audience are exposed to your message a number of times. As we shall see below, higher frequency is important for recall brand awareness and for brand attitude strategies that deal with positive motives.

So how do you optimize media strategy in terms of reach and frequency? The key is something known as *minimum effective frequency*. Minimum effective frequency is the point at which we can reasonably expect that our advertising will begin to work, the point where the target audience will have had enough opportunity to process the message successfully. If the frequency is below this minimum level, the likelihood is that the advertising will not work at all. Computing the minimum effective frequency needed for a particular campaign is not easy, but there are models available for estimating it.[5] A good point to remember is that it is better to ensure you communicate successfully with at least some of your target audience so they are disposed to buy than to reach a lot of your target audience without being able to communicate successfully. In the trade-off between reach and frequency, it is better to err on the side of frequency.

Selecting Media

Just as we have already noted for creative strategy, a media strategy depends upon your communication objectives. In order to ensure that the media selected to deliver the message are compatible with the communication objective, there are at least three important points for the manager to consider: visual content, the time available to process the message, and the frequency potential. Visual content is essential for recognition brand awareness, because you must be able to present the brand as it will be seen at the point of purchase. It is also important for transformational brand attitude strategies because of the need to facilitate emotional authenticity.

The time available to process a message is important for high-involvement informational brand attitude strategies because of the need for acceptance of the message. The ability to deliver high frequency is important for recall brand awareness as well as for low-involvement transformational brand attitude strategies. Here there is a need for several exposures in order to build the link in memory between the category need and brand for recall brand awareness, and to build the emotional association with the brand for low-involvement transformational brand attitude strategies. Because brand awareness and brand attitude are always communication objectives, they largely determine media selection. Table 10.2 details how a number of primary media rate on these three characteristics. We will now look at some of the implications of this for media selection decisions associated with brand awareness and brand attitude strategies in a bit more detail.

Table 10.2 Media Ratings on Essential Media Selection Characteristics

	Visual Content	Time to Process Message	Frequency
Television	Yes	Short	High
Radio	No	Short	High
Newspapers	Limitations	Long	High
Magazines	Yes	Long	Limitations
Posters	Yes	Long	Limitations
Internet	Yes	Long	High
Direct Mail	Yes	Long	Low

Source: Adapted from J. R. Rossiter and L. Percy, *Advertising Communication and Promotion Management* (New York: McGraw-Hill, 1997).

Brand Awareness Strategies

The difference between brand recognition and brand recall has important implications for media selection. Brand recognition requires an emphasis on the visual representation of the pack or logo, while brand recall puts the emphasis on frequency to build an association between the brand name and category need. This difference of emphasis, for example, would lead to the conclusion that radio is unsuitable for brand recognition, but offers cost-efficient high-frequency repetition. Let us look at what this means for other media.

Brand Recognition

When brand recognition is our communication objective, we are looking for good visual content, not much time should be required for processing, and low frequency will do. If we look at Table 10.2, we see that television, magazines, posters, the Internet, and direct mail could be considered. Radio is out because you cannot see the package, and, while newspapers might be a possibility, we must be sure that good colour reproduction can be counted on.

Brand Recall

If brand recall is our communication objective, our biggest concern is with frequency. Good repetition of the linkage of category need and brand name is necessary, and this requires high frequency. Looking again at Table 10.2, we see that television, radio, newspapers, and the Internet offer the potential for high frequency. Magazines and direct mail have obvious frequency limitations. Posters have a potential frequency limitation because they are stationary media (unless, of course, they are on a bus or train, which will have their own frequency limitations).

Brand Attitude Strategies

The importance for brand attitude strategy of correct media selection focus based upon the three characteristics of visual content, processing time, and frequency will be discussed in detail in Chapter 15. What we want to do here is look at which media make sense for specific brand attitude communication objectives as defined by the Rossiter–Percy Grid. Each of the four basic brand attitude strategies is reviewed next. You will recall from previous chapters that brand attitude strategies reflect low versus high involvement in the purchase decision process and whether the underlying motivations driving the use of products or services in the category are positive or negative.

Low-Involvement, Informational Strategy

Brand attitude communication objectives that reflect a low-involvement brand decision coupled with negative motivation can be addressed by almost any medium. It is perhaps the easiest communication objective to deal with in terms of media selection. There is no strong visual requirement, only a brief processing time is needed, and high frequency is not necessary because the benefits used in adverts following this type of brand attitude strategy must be learned in one or two exposures if it is to be effective. This is why almost any medium can be selected. A possible exception would be if the benefit must be *demonstrated*, in which case the medium selected must be capable of presenting the demonstration.

Low-Involvement, Transformational Strategy

With a brand attitude strategy for a low-involvement brand decision when the underlying motivation is positive, *good visual content* is critical. Although only a brief processing time is required, a relatively high frequency is necessary because of a generally slower brand attitude development. Here television is the ideal medium. All the other primary media, with the exception of the Internet, are a potential problem because of processing time or frequency limitations. The exception here is radio, but it must be excluded because it lacks visual content. We should point out, however, that highly creative radio can sometimes overcome this problem if it can really make you 'see' the product.

High-Involvement, Informational Strategy

Because brand attitude strategies that involve high-involvement brand decisions and negative motives require a longer processing time for the more extensive information content necessary to convince the target audience, media selection emphasis is likely to be on print-oriented media. And, since frequency is not an issue, again because the benefits must be accepted in one or two exposures, almost any print medium will do (including the Internet).

High-Involvement, Transformational Strategy

As with low-involvement strategies associated with positive motivations, visual content is critical. The key difference here is that there is no need for high frequency. You may think this strange, since we pointed out that brand attitude builds slowly in the low-involvement choice situation. The reason for this seeming contradiction is that most low-involvement/transformational brand attitude strategies involve fast-moving consumer goods with a relatively *short purchase cycle*. This means there is not a lot of time for the advertising to work. With high-involvement brand decisions we are usually dealing with brand decisions for products with much longer purchase cycles. This is what permits a relatively lower rate of frequency. Of the primary media we have been considering in Table 10.2, television and most print media could be selected. Newspapers have the potential colour limitation we discussed earlier. Radio would not be appropriate.

A caveat should be noted here. Even though we are dealing with positive motives, because the brand decision is high involvement, eventually it might be necessary to provide a certain amount of detailed information. When that is the case, processing time will need to be considered in your media selection.

Brand Awareness and Brand Attitude Strategies

Taking all these considerations into account, we can classify particular media as appropriate or not for the core communication objectives, in some cases subject to potential limitations. These options are summarized in Table 10.3.

Table 10.3 Media Selection Options to Satisfy Brand Awareness and Brand Attitude Communication Objectives

	Brand Awareness Recognition	Brand Awareness Recall	Low Involvement		High Involvement	
			Infor-mational	Transform-ational	Infor-mational	Transform-ational
Television	Yes	Yes	Yes	Yes	No	Yes
Radio	No	Yes	Yes	No	No	No
Newspapers	Limitations	Yes	Yes	Limitations	Yes	Limitations
Magazines	Yes	Limitations	Yes	Limitations	Yes	Yes
Posters	Yes	Limitations	Yes	Limitations	Limitations	Yes
Internet	Yes	Yes	Yes	Yes	Yes	Yes
Direct Mail	Yes	Limitations	Yes	Limitations	Yes	Yes

Source: Adapted from J. R. Rossiter and L. Percy, *Advertising Communication and Promotion Management* (New York: McGraw-Hill, 1997).

An important point to remember in media selection is that an attempt must be made to accommodate *all* your communication objectives. This means that, at the very least, the media selected must meet *both* brand awareness *and* brand attitude strategies. When recognition is the brand awareness communication objective, because all the primary media are acceptable, selection will be driven solely on the basis of the brand attitude strategy. But when brand recall is the communication objective, you must be careful to consider the requirements for both brand recall and the brand attitude strategy in your media selection. The only medium that works regardless of the strategy is the Internet. In every other case you must check for compatibility between the two communication objectives involved, and look carefully at potential limitations.

Even if a medium cannot achieve total compatibility between these two objectives, it might still be worth using; but it should not be the *primary* media selection. For example, television is a perfect medium for driving up awareness of any kind. Even though it is not really suitable for high-involvement brand decisions when the motivation is negative, it could certainly be used to generate recall brand awareness, as long as another, more appropriate medium carries the primary informational message with sufficient time for processing.

Demographic versus Direct Matching

Up to this point we have been talking about media types. Now we need to consider how to select specific media vehicles within types—for example, a particular television programme or magazine. Despite the many shortcomings of this method, media vehicles are often selected by 'matching' demographics. Demographic matching is the practice of defining a target audience in terms of specific demographic characteristics, then 'matching' that demographic profile with the demographic profile of a media vehicle's audience. This method is popular with media planners because data on the demographics (and other variables such as 'lifestyle') of audiences for television and radio programmes, and readers of newspapers and magazines, are readily available, and there are computer programs for putting together media schedules based upon optimizing these demographic 'matches'.

But there is a fundamental flaw in all of this, and that is why we have placed the word match in inverted commas. Suppose usage for our brand is 10 per cent in the overall population. This means the likelihood of finding a user randomly would be one in ten. Now suppose you selected a target audience of women, 18–49 years of age, with incomes over 15,000 euros a year, because this group has a significantly higher concentration of brand users (if we have a repeat purchase target audience action objective) or potential triers (if a trial target audience objective) than the general population.

Obviously, the odds of locating a user will be much greater if we can find media that reach this group. But it is not that simple. There is no reason to believe brand usage is evenly distributed among all media that have this profile. Some women in this demographic group may read *Elle* because they are interested in high fashion; others may read *Country Life*. If we are marketing country casual clothes, what is the likelihood our brand users read *Elle*?

If we really wanted to increase the odds of finding a brand user, why not find media that brand users read or watch? This is *direct matching*. It may require directly surveying your market to measure its media habits, but in most cases it will be worth the effort directly to identify the media habits of those who are attitudinally and behaviourally consistent with your target audience. As we have already pointed out in our discussion of target audience selection in Chapter 6, while demographic profiles provide useful diagnostic information, they should not be the basis of target audience selection.

Scheduling Media

One of the more vexing questions in developing effective media strategies is how to schedule media. Earlier we defined three basic types of scheduling: flighting, bursts, and continuity. While these basic types do indeed define the *structure* of most media scheduled, the actual scheduling itself is a much more difficult issue. There is seemingly an almost infinite number of circumstances that could have an effect upon how to optimize your media schedule. What is the purchase cycle for the category? Are sales seasonal? If so, do we want to break the pattern? How do competitors schedule their advertising? What creative units are to be used (for example, 15-second versus 30-second versus 60-second commercials, or half-page versus full-page versus two-page spreads in magazines)? How many different creative executions are being used? How difficult is it to reach the target audience? Is the target audience segmented? If so, how? You should be getting the idea.

There are, of course, many models available to help the media planner put together a good media schedule. But most media models, by their very nature, make general assumptions and tend to average. It is virtually impossible for any one model to take into account all the many variables involved. This has led to a number of rules of thumb among media planners. But again, because every brand's situation is different, and often changes from campaign to campaign, following well-known formulas may not lead to the most effective schedule.

Does this mean the task of developing an effective media schedule is all but hopeless? Not at all. What it means is that each schedule must be carefully assessed, and assessed for *each* media plan developed. How to go about this task is quite beyond the scope of this book, but there are a number of good books that deal with scheduling in depth. One book in particular offers a great deal of insight into this problem: Simon Broadbent's *When to Advertise*.[6] Broadbent has had a significant influence on media issues, especially in the UK. What we like about his approach is that he defines a *process* to determine when to advertise. He suggests that to schedule media effectively you must look at what you need to pay for the media, when you most want it to have an effect, and how you think the advertising will work. You can see how these points address the kind of issues raised by the many questions associated with trying to optimize a media schedule. There is nothing at all easy about how you go about implementing this process, but he offers a framework for addressing the problem. The important point is that it acknowledges the fact that effective media scheduling depends upon the 'particular circumstances; there is no single solution'.[7]

Target Audience Factors and Brand Ecology

In Chapter 6 we discussed at length the issues of target audience selection and suggested that brand loyalty segmentation based on attitude is the most effective method for developing communication strategy. While the customer's relationship with the brand is an essential element in communication planning and usually has to be based on primary market research, a relatively new approach to media selection also uses the customer's relationship with the media as an input into media selection. Syndicated audience research services provide a wealth of quantitative data about media use. The Target Group Index (TGI) in the UK also provides usage data on 4,000 brands in 500 product categories, cross-referenced to usage of print media and TV. In addition, it provides some basic attitudinal data as well as standard demographics. Major media also supply extensive syndicated audience data. In the UK the Broadcasters' Audience Research Board (BARB) provides TV viewing behaviour on a continuous basis, showing audience figures per programme on the major terrestrial and satellite channels. Rich data on over 250 newspaper and magazine titles in the UK are provided by the National Readership Survey (NRS), and similar data are provided for radio by Radio Joint Audience Research (RAJAR). Similar services are available in other countries. These syndicated audience data sources are the basis of all the major media planning systems, and are also utilized within the most sophisticated proprietary media systems such as Zenith Media's ZOOM Excalibur, which models effective frequency levels against marketing and media factors.

However, the fragmentation of the media landscape has led to the emergence of a new active media consumer, who can choose from a huge portfolio of media to construct a 'personal media network' using an increasing array of technology and information actively to edit his or her own media environment.[8] The opportunity in this fragmentation of audiences is that it offers the possibility of going beyond simple demographics to understand the relationship smaller audiences have with their chosen media, and to develop an understanding of consumer 'brand ecology'.

Brand ecology considers not just the attitudinal, emotional, and behavioural aspects of brand consumption, but explores how this brand-related behaviour integrates with wider social and cultural experience in the lifeworld of the active consumer. As we pointed out in Chapter 6, demographics and lifestyle analyses are not stable predictors of consumer behaviour across categories, and, as media choice explodes, multi-TV households become the norm, and technological aids such as the Electronic Programme Guide (EPG) proliferate, the media are responding with ever more focused offerings that can be built into a consumer's personal media schedule.

The close relationship between consumers and their personal media architecture is at least as important as any brand-consumer relationship, because it is from our trusted media that we construct our view of the world, gain enjoyment, entertainment, stimulation, and information. A deep understanding of the consumer-media relationship can also be the prompt for great creative work, as it informs the creative brief with a three-dimensional picture of the target audience. As Henny has put it: 'Find out what makes them laugh. What makes them cry. What they think about current affairs, what books they read, what music they prefer, and if there are any other cultural things they are into because then I can rip those off for the creative execution.'[9]

Understanding Brand–Consumer–Media Relationships

The starting point for exploring media aspects of brand ecology is the wealth of industry audience data described above. Interrogating these data can set out the parameters of media usage, related to attitudinal and lifestyle dimensions; but for developing really effective media strategy we require information on the emotional aspects of media consumption, its social and cultural context, and the meaning it carries in consumers' lives. In an era of money-rich but time-poor people working ever-longer hours, media consumption often involves active choice behaviour between competing alternatives, and this choice behaviour is itself driven by attitudes and emotions to the various media and how its consumption integrates with other individual and social activity.

Consumers have media imperatives, such as a 'must-view' appointment with an episode of a soap opera, or a 'must-read' appointment with a heavyweight Sunday newspaper. Increasingly the same consumer can consume a paradoxical range of media, often in a different mindset at different times of the day or week. One TV consumer may switch from low-involvement consumption of US comedies, to high-involvement consumption of a high-brow arts programme, to high-involvement consumption of a football match, all on the same evening.

In order to match our brand attitude strategy with media consumption we need to know how and why people are consuming the media, not just that they are in the same room as the TV. The *who* question of media consumption has a very complex answer once we recognize the variety of consumption modes within the same person's media architecture. Some media are often consumed alone—print media, for example—while some depend on company for satisfying experience—for example, TV comedies. But consuming media in a social setting may itself vary greatly depending on the composition of the group and the social rules and expectations that apply. The relationship with a medium may involve high levels of trust, respect, affection, and personal and family history. Alternatively it may involve distrust, lack of respect, an absence of any emotional connection, and little history.

We need to be able to profile the members of our target audience on these and other emotional, social, and cultural factors and be able to relate them to their brand relationships in order to maximize our ability to make appropriate media choices. This investment in researching our target group's media consumption is a vital step towards developing effective media strategy, as 'traditional data is simply too broad and too shallow to yield the detailed insights which can inspire imaginative media solutions'.[10]

Evaluating the Efficiency of Media Strategy

The demand for greater media accountability continues to grow,[11] and we now consider briefly some important approaches to evaluating the efficiency of media strategy. As will be discussed in Chapter 13, continuous tracking studies make a major contribution to evaluating the effectiveness of creative strategies, and they also have an important role to play in assessing media strategy in combination with creative content against communication objectives. However, the method of choice for evaluating media efficiency is 'media auditing'. A major media auditing operator is the Media Audits Group, which operates in sixty countries and provides media audit services for over 300 clients on $3 billion adspend. Media auditing operates by comparing a specific advertiser's media expenditure with that of a very large data pool containing actual prices paid for media supplied by clients and then advising on buying efficiency. This comparison of price paid for media against the pool average gives powerful information to advertisers and allows them to put pressure on their media-buying agency to lower costs. Using econometric models, a number of media auditors offer advice on such issues as media weighting, frequency rates, weighting between media, and regional effects.

The New Media

In recent years, technology has provided new ways of delivering both advertising and promotion messages. The Internet has offered both new opportunities as well as challenges to marketers; and recently mobile marketing has begun to have an impact. We will be looking at both of these areas, always keeping in mind that as you read this section much of what we are talking about may have been overtaken by new advancements. The important point, however, is that *strategically* the way media, including new media, is selected will follow the same processing considerations discussed earlier regardless of advances in technology. Technological advances will likely only effect efficiency.

One consequence of the rapidly changing media environment is the challenge it poses for media planning and placement agencies. Many now have dedicated staff whose job it is to follow the changes occurring and work on adapting their research methods to deal with how consumers are using the new media alternatives. Another change has been occasioned by the rapid diversification of many large media companies who now offer a wide range of outlets. These can include everything from traditional media vehicles to web-sites, podcasts, and mobile platforms.[12]

Internet

Global spending on Internet advertising in 2005 was some US $18 billion, up over 28 per cent from the previous year, accounting for about 5 per cent of overall spending on advertising.[13] Some estimates suggest that by the year 2015 spending could reach US $150 billion.[14] At the same time, the cost of Internet advertising has risen significantly (anywhere from 19 per cent on sports sites to 30 per cent on health sites).[15] One consequence of bigger brands moving onto the Web and driving up cost has been that smaller long-term users are being driven out.

Something that may challenge this growth, as well as affect Internet advertising, is an EU law that took effect in July 2003 requiring *non*-EU companies to collect value-added tax on fees paid for Internet services, as well as products downloaded by customers over the Internet (for example, music, videos, and software).[16] As a result, for example, Europeans using eBay will have to pay VAT, and EU sellers will have to pay VAT on the fee they pay eBay to list their products. This is obviously an administrative nightmare for larger companies, but could be a deterrent to smaller business.

Even though the Internet is incredibly wide based, the top fifty web-sites account for almost all the money spent on Internet advertising, with most of it concentrated with AOL, Google, MSN, and Yahoo. This is because these are the most visited sites, and as with all media cost is a function of audience size. In 2005, daily visits ranged from 2.9 million at Google to 4.0 million at Yahoo.[17]

Still, even these very large web-sites had not proved immune from economic downturns. In late 2007 and early 2008, Internet advertising was found to be more vulnerable than expected to a general slowdown in the economy. Sites such as Google experienced a significant decline in advertising revenue.[18]

In 2003 Google introduced free e-mail, and coordinated advert exposure to incoming messages. For example, someone receiving an e-mail from a friend asking if they would like to go out for Chinese food would see an advert for a Chinese restaurant near them next to the message.[19] Advertisers are charged each time someone clicks on the advert. An on-line auction is held among potential advertisers for the right to have their advert appear when certain key words are present in a search query or e-mail. Google is also testing the idea of offering more diversified advertising, putting them in direct competition with newspaper and on-line classified advertising.

One of the positive values of Internet advertising, in addition to its ability to reach very specific target audiences, is the ability to assess its impact on a daily basis by measuring the number of times someone clicks on an advert, opens, or downloads it. This encourages enormous flexibility in execution because of the opportunity to test and make modifications on very short turnaround. More recently, Internet and on-line advertising companies are gaining better tools for targeting display adverts to specific groups of users. Yahoo and Microsoft, for example, use Web users' search habits and pages visited to pick which adverts to show when those people visit their own or partner web-sites. A technique called behavioural targeting observes and analyses on-line activities of Internet users, keeping tabs on every web-site visited.[20]

On-line Video

In 2007, on-line video became the fastest-growing category of Internet advertising spending.[21] This growth has been spurred by user dislike of pop-up adverts[22] and preroles (where the user is forced to watch the advertising before viewing the video clip).[23] While it is projected to continue growing over the next few years, there is no real consensus on what works and what does not. Some marketers are using graphics that slide over the bottom of the screen without interrupting the video clip, variously known as overlays, bugs, or trackers, or using advertising graphics that surround the screen, called 'player skins'. The viewer can then click on the graphic to pause the clip and see more information from the advertiser.

Advertising is now being shown alongside user-generated videos on sites such as YouTube. They offer a semitransparent advert that appears on the bottom 20 per cent of the video, appearing 15 seconds after the start of the video and disappearing 10 seconds later if the viewer does not click on it. If the viewer chooses to watch the advert, the main video pauses until the commercial stops. In a test before introducing the system, it was found that 75 per cent of viewers watched the entire advert, a 5 to 10 times greater click-through rate than standard display advertising on web-sites.[24]

While on-line marketing is growing rapidly, even the largest social-media sites such as YouTube and Facebook have failed to meet their own advertising revenue forecasts. Part of the problem is thought to be a reliance on more static advertising options such as banner adverts or homepage video adverts. One advert to get around this problem is exemplified by the introduction of Toyota's 2009 Corolla sedan. They worked with YouTube on a campaign that created a new site exclusively for Toyota called 'Best in Test' where YouTube identified up-and-coming comedy videos to feature on the site.[25]

Social networking services such as Bebo.com and MySpace are capitalizing on the popularity of on-line video by creating original Web series to attract advertising. This is in contrast to mere traditional web-sites such as Yahoo and AOL that are cutting back on original programming. This could be a function of the still relatively small payback involved. While production costs for such original programming is inexpensive (about US $1,000 per minute to film versus, say television production at US $50,000 or more), advertisers pay only about US $400,000 for a six-month sponsorship.[26]

Widgets

Widgets are small computer programs that enable people to incorporate professional looking content on their personal Web pages. As of this writing, widgets are the only way an advertiser can get inside MySpace pages. Advertisers are beginning to use widget-based content as a way of reaching young people with their message, and encouraging them to visit their web-site. Many marketers see this as the next generation of Internet marketing. Reebok created a widget that enabled users to display customized RBK shoes for others to evaluate.[27]

A study of 9–17-year-olds in the USA found that while these young people do not like banner adverts, there was a willingness to accept bits of marketing messages on their personal Web page if they were seen as useful or entertaining. While spending on social network web-sites is not much now, it is expected to grow significantly over the next few years.[28]

Other Applications

There are many other ways in which the Internet is being used to deliver on-line advertising and promotion. Advertising messages are being included as a part of video games. Adverts on on-line radio enable listeners to click on a box at the station's web-site which directs them to the brand's web-site. Advertisers are creating entertainment programming specifically for the Web that weaves a product endorsement into the storyline; and perhaps the ultimate in product placement gives the viewer of a video the ability to stop and click to purchase the clothing worn by the actors.

Cutting-edge streaming video is being used by some advertisers, in effect mini-movies that feature the brand. At BMWfilms.com, which is separate from BMW's home page, they offer short streamed films that have been produced by well-known directors, and using well-known actors.[29]

Promotions too are delivered via the Internet. Specific sites exist solely to provide incentive promotions for brands. Fatwallet.com sends out early morning e-mails alerting people of on-line specials. Sites like GottaDeal.com feature information about mail-in rebates, and sites such as CouponMountain.com and CouponCraze.com enable users to print coupons for both store and on-line retailers.

Current predictions for Internet advertising are that direct mail will be the most heavily affected traditional media channel. On-line will also increasingly take spend from outdoor and radio advertising, and will begin to dent press advertising, but is not expected to have much impact on TV advertising over the next four years.[30]

Apart from a relatively high cost relative to other media, an important implication of the Internet for developing media strategy is the question of control of brand messages. Orthodox media strategy aims to control the different channels and methods through which the brand can target the consumer. However, with the rapid enabling of consumer networks of contacts and peers, brand messages are becoming increasingly uncontrollable, which means that official brand messages are becoming increasingly unimportant compared to the unsanctioned 'word of mouse' within a particular brand or anti-brand community.[31] The interactive and uncontrollable nature of the Internet raises serious issues for media strategy, and suggests that in the future we will have to engage consumers in dialogue rather than monologue format and attempt to invite customers to participate in 'conversations' rather than being passive targets for messages. So once again we return to the need for in-depth understanding of consumer behaviour as the driver for all strategy, and in the next chapter we turn to examining how consumers process messages.

Mobile Marketing

The use of advertising on mobile phones began in the early 2000s in Scandinavian and Asian countries, but it was several years later before it entered Europe and the USA, where there was a feeling consumers would not like the idea. But by the mid-2000s major networks in the UK (e.g. Vodafone Group) and in the USA (e.g. Sprint, Nextel, and Verizon) were offering advertising on their wireless networks.[32] Newer cell phones have facilitated this, being much more like small computers.

While such mobile advertising is dominated by text messages, in 2007 some European carriers began offering video commercials. One of the UK's largest networks, 3, a unit of Hutchison Whampia, was offering free information and entertainment video clips paid for by the advertising.[33]

The appeal of mobile advertising to marketers is the ability to tightly target messages to an audience that has given permission to receive it (at least in most cases). Additionally, they are better able to control the message environment, better time the exposure of the message, and better track exposure. It also provides a good opportunity for developing a database to better target messages, and to be available for more traditional direct marketing. A good database is essential for good mobile marketing because it must be driven by consumer data,[34] as with direct marketing.

Coupons are even being made available on cell phones. Consumers may sign up on-line or by sending a text message to a mobile marketing company (e.g. Cellfine in the USA) that provides coupons from client retailers. They collect personal information such as birth data and geographic area, which enables retailers to more tightly target whom they send coupons.[35] In another unique application, outdoor posters and billboards have the ability to electronically beam messages to cell phones.

CHAPTER SUMMARY

This chapter has introduced some of the specific concepts and terminology used in relation to media. We began by pointing out some of the key issues of reach versus frequency. We then related media selection decisions to communication objectives, especially the brand attitude objectives based on involvement and motivation. We considered media scheduling decisions and then went on to discuss the concept of brand ecology and the importance of understanding the consumer's emotional relationship with various media. Lastly, we discussed the new media, with special attention to the Internet, and mobile marketing and the implications for media strategy of the interactivity and uncontrollability factors related to brand messages.

QUESTIONS TO CONSIDER

10.1 What must the manager consider in developing an effective media schedule?

10.2 What are the media implications associated with brand awareness strategy?

10.3 What are the media implications associated with brand attitude strategy?

10.4   What is meant by brand ecology, and how does it affect media strategy?

10.5   How is the Internet similar or different from other media in terms of media strategy?

10.6   In what way are the new media likely to affect media planning and strategy in the future?

CASE STUDY 10

Story Selling: How LEGO Told a Story and Sold a Toy

The Bionicle story started with the dilemma of a changing market. The LEGO Company's product range (Slizer 1st and RoboRiders 2nd generation product lines) during the mid-1990s for children of 7–12 years was characterized as having a definite focus on the constructional element of the toys. In 1997, the Company set up a project group that would examine the possibility of developing a product that would appeal to more physically active boys who have a shorter attention span and have less time to play. The aim of the new LEGO products was to be relevant for a greater number of older boys (7–12-year-olds) and in doing so extend the length of time that these children stayed with the LEGO brand. Moreover there was a strong belief that the success of the new products could be increased by introducing a storytelling element. The idea was to create an ongoing epic story in which the LEGO products could act as the lead characters. New chapters could be introduced each year supporting new products launches but under the same brand/story umbrella. Storytelling strategy believed to have the following effects:

- inject emotional value, thereby increase the perceived value and purchase intent.
- a very wide appeal among children across cultural boundaries as good against evil is a universal theme in the imaginations of boys.
- create a long-term emotional bond for boys in the target group.
- increase the relevance among older boys.
- increase the size of LEGO's target group.
- encourage the boys to collect more products/characters in the 'story'.
- LEGO could capitalize on the continuing story development.

The inspiration for the name of the new product range came from the underlying theme for the story, which would be a 'biological chronicle'. The concept was named Bionicle. The next question, however, was more difficult: 'How do we tell the story and create authenticity around it when we have neither a movie, nor a TV series nor a book to work from?' The answer to this demanded an innovative execution of the communication and the development of an integrated marketing campaign. The challenges however of communicating this story of a strange and mystical universe, legends, heroes, and a mission against evil would be enormous. It was a story so rich in detail and too complex to be explained with a 30-second commercial and traditional shop marketing material. Therefore the communications objectives put forward were the following:

- create understanding of and involvement in the story
- make Bionicle and LEGO cool and relevant to the 7–12-year-old target group
- promote the collecting of Bionicle products and develop a long-term fan base
- develop Bionicle into an intellectual property (IP), which could be tied in with other strong brands and could benefit other business areas.

Since movies create emotional attachment, images, and an entire world that children can relate to, developing a movie-like execution of the story, as well as using movie advertising media, would appeal to the target group. The movie execution style would also give the story validity, by packaging in a style that felt authentic to the target group. Executing the 'movie' idea took place through a five-point strategy:

1. *Create a Simple and Compelling Entrance to the Story*

2. *Expose the Target Group to a Broad Mix of Media*

A main theme of the communication strategy was to use as wide a range of media as possible in order to expose the children to the story in several different ways. Each one of the media that was chosen would carry a different part of the story depending upon time and the individual medium's storytelling ability. Most importantly, a differentiation was made between 'single-message media' and 'story-carrying media'. In order to create awareness of the concept, it was necessary to use a range of mass media (single message media) to communicate a coherent basic theme. These media would work in the same way that ads for a movie work, by communicating the simple introduction to the story. For the first time LEGO used outdoor posters and cinema ads.

In order to communicate the story in more detail, three main media were identified that could handle carrying the story: a web-site, a CD-ROM and comics. These and other story-carrying media would work like the 'movie' itself by delivering various elements of the story. In this way, a dynamic media mosaic was created to tie the two main levels of media together and thereby tell the story. The different media would work together to create the complete story, while the target group would constantly be exposed to new pieces of the mosaic or story all the time. As it wasn't possible to control in which order the children would come into contact with these pieces, it was important that each piece of the story could stand by itself, and be understood and appreciated by the target group independently. At the same time, the children could only get a full picture of the story by going to the different media. This encouraged them to seek out different parts of the media mosaic—in other words, the media mosaic was designed to make the kids become story collectors. One other essential part of the multifaceted communication strategy was the 'peer-to-peer marketing', that is to get the children to actively pass on the story themselves.

3. *Quality, Compelling Graphics*

When communicating with children, the success of a story or product depends heavily upon how visually 'cool' it is. So rather than merely telling the story or promoting the 'movie' through text, a range of story pictures were developed. Each picture had to tell a story by itself and relate a different part of the overall story, which the children could then relate further, leading to the creation of their own stories. The strategy of launching a visually movie-like story was accomplished in several ways. Posters, movie trailers, and story pictures were made to look like something from a feature film. To support this idea, it was decided from the start to create the entire Bionicle universe in 3D. The popularity of 3D in the film industry and among children is huge, with films like *Toy Story*, *Shrek*, and *Monsters, Inc.* achieving massive success. But, above all, 3D was chosen because it would allow the characters to be constructed in animated form, bringing the entire Bionicle universe to life and strengthening the overall visual experience. The combination of attractive media and the movie-like execution of the media strategy would be highly effective in creating coolness, awareness, and involvement.

All media rated 'cool' and exciting: 'Coolness is definitely not an issue for Bionicle', Millward Brown, 2002. The Millward Brown research also showed recall of the TV and cinema advertising was strong and was linked to the message and the brand. Many of the children thought that the cinema ad was a movie.

4. *Reveal the Story over different Time Phases*

Just as with movies, in order to ensure that the children stay involved with Bionicle over a longer period of time, the whole story was released not all at once, but in phases. Again inspired by movie trailers, Bionicle would begin with a teaser phase to arouse the curiosity of the target group. This would get children, including boys who normally didn't buy LEGO products, involved with the Bionicle story first, before the physical products were launched. At the launch of the true products, the next step was revealed, and so on. On the bionicle.com website, new chapters of the story came out each month through an on-line adventure game. The purpose of this was to keep the children's interest throughout the entire year and in the longer term.

5. *Use Partners*

The new marketing strategy, focused on telling the story through the movie-like media mosaic, offered a new role for potential global partners. Instead of being a part of the product launch they could become an active part of an intellectual property (IP) and play a more dynamic, long-term role. There was a large amount of interest shown by potential partners from the very beginning. Nestlé, McDonald's, Universal Music, Upperdeck (trading cards), Nintendo, along with an array of local partners, were among those finally chosen. The decision was made to let all global partners take an integrated role in the story. For example, McDonald's was allowed to launch six new characters in the story as part of its partnership with Bionicle. This new partnership strategy also ensured that the Bionicle campaign would be supplemented with several other media, which would carry the story forwards and add new elements to it. Finally, the partnership strategy contributed to a relevant awareness where children could find further pieces of the story.

Long-term Momentum

As one of the key aims for the whole marketing strategy was to create a lasting marketing success that would stretch over a period of years, it is important to note the successes of Bionicle since its launch year. Following the launch in 2001, the marketing strategy had given children high expectations of the year to come. And these expectations were met with the launch of twelve new products—all of which were integrated into the next chapter of the Bionicle saga.

Source: WARC, IPA Effectiveness Awards, Story Selling: How LEGO Told a Story and Sold a Toy, by Jeppe Fonnesbaek and Morten Melbye Andersen

Edited by Natalia Yannopoulou

Discussion Questions

1 What are the benefits for the Lego brand for selecting this marketing approach?
2 What would be a proposed marketing strategy and media strategy in particular for the coming years?
3 What are the challenges of this marketing approach for the long term?
4 Could you propose an alternative marketing/media strategy for the launch of the Bionicle product?

FURTHER READING

- Media scheduling is discussed from two planning perspectives in Hugh Cannon, John Leckenby, and Avey Abernathy, 'Beyond Effective Imagery: Evaluating Media Schedules Using Frequency Value

Planning', *Journal of Advertising Research* (Nov./Dec. 2002), 33–47; and in Erwin Ephron and Colin McDonald, 'Media Scheduling and Carry-over Effects: Is Adstock a Useful Planning Tool?', *Journal of Advertising Research* (July/Aug. 2002), 66–70.

- An extensive examination of media effects from a theoretical standpoint may be found in *Media Effects: Advances in Theory and Research*, 2nd edn., eds Jennings Bryant and Dolf Zillman (Mahwah, NJ: Lawrence Erlbaum Associates, 2002).

- Philip Napoli, *Audience Economics: Media Institution and the Audience Marketplace* (New York: Columbia University Press, 2003), offers a critical discussion about the way audience understandings are used in 'selling' media, including the Internet, and the potential problems involved.

- Sally McMillan, Jang-Sun Hwang, and Guiohk Lee talk about the need to adjust to the specific demands of the Web, just as media planners did when there was a shift to broadcast media, in 'Effects of Structural and Perceptual Factors on Attitudes toward the Website', *Journal of Advertising Research* (Dec. 2003), 400–9.

NOTES

1   Perhaps still the best book available for anyone really interested in media strategy is still John R. Rossiter and Peter J. Danaher, *Advanced Media Planning* (Norwell, Mass.: Kluwer Academic Publishers, 1998), which comes with its own disc containing all the models discussed. Another good book is the latest edition of J. Sissors and L. Baumber, *Advertising Media Planning*, 5th edn. (Lincolnwood, Ill.: NTC Business Books, 2002).

2   A. Tillery, 'The Strategic Importance of Media', in L. Butterfield (ed.), *Excellence in Advertising* (Oxford: Butterworth Heinemann, 1999).

3   A. Rutherford, 'Managing the Media', *Uniview Magazine* (1999).

4   *The Millward Brown Link Tests* (London: Millward Brown Ltd., 1997).

5   This issue of minimum effective frequency is discussed in some depth in J. R. Rossiter and L. Percy, *Advertising Communication and Promotion Management* (New York: McGraw-Hill, 1997).

6   Simon Broadbent, *When to Advertise* (Henley-on-Thames: Admap Publications, 1999). See also the books cited in n. 1.

7   Broadbent, *When to Advertise*, 102.

8   See Tillery, 'The Strategic Importance of Media'.

9   G. Henny, 'Creative Briefing: The Creative Perspective', in Butterfield (ed.), *Excellence in Advertising*.

10   G. Michaelides, 'Street Wise', *Admap* (May 2000), 27.

11   J. Billet and I. Fermoi, 'The Agenda of Media Accountability', *Admap* (June 2000), 33–5.

12   See P. Andruss, 'Taming media overload', *The Wall Street Journal* (1 September 2007), 21.

13   A. O. Patrick, 'Technology boosts outdoor ads as competition becomes fierce', *The Wall Street Journal* (28 August 2006), A1.

14   R. A. Guth, 'New Microsoft service will rely on online ads', *The Wall Street Journal* (2 November 2005), B2.

15   J. E. Vascellaro, 'Web advertisers find offline ads can pay off too', *The Wall Street Journal* (25 May 2006), B1.

16 This potential problem was discussed in the 20 October 2003 issue of *The Wall Street Journal* in an article by Matthew Newman (p. R5).

17 J. Angwin and K. J. Delaner, 'Top web sites build up ad backlog', *The Wall Street Journal* (16 November 2005), B1.

18 K. J. Delany, 'On the Web, signs of a click recession', *The Wall Street Journal* (27 February 2008), B3.

19 A description of Google's text adverts based upon key words in their user's e-mail is discussed in K. Delaney's Advertising column in the 6 April 2004 issue of *The Wall Street Journal* (p. B1), along with the issue of privacy.

20 These and other techniques for customizing adverts to particular targets are discussed in K. J. Delaney and E. Steel, 'Firm mines offline data to target online ads', *The Wall Street Journal* (17 October 2007), B1.

21 E. Steel, 'Web's niche TV program with sponsors', *The Wall Street Journal* (28 August 2007), B8.

22 K. Oser, 'Money, mayhem to be first with pop-ups', *Advertising Age* (28 June 2004), 51.

23 K. J. Delaney and E. Steel, 'Are skins, Bugs or tickets the Holy Grail of Web advertising?', *The Wall Street Journal* (13 August 2007), B1.

24 See E. Steel, 'YouTube to start selling ads in videos', *The Wall Street Journal* (22 August 2007), B3.

25 E. Steel, 'Toyota makes sharp turn on the Web', *The Wall Street Journal* (7 March 2008), B3.

26 J. E. Vascellaro, 'Video's new friends', *The Wall Street Journal* (28 February 2008), B1.

27 E. Steel, 'Web-page clocks and other "widgets" anchor new Internet strategy', *The Wall Street Journal* (21 November 2006), B4.

28 E. Steel, 'Young surfers spurn banner ads, embrace "widgets" ', *The Wall Street Journal* (2 July 2007), B3.

29 G. Silberer and J. F. Engelhardt, 'Streaming Media: A New Way of Online Advertising', in *Advertising and Communication*, proceedings of the 4th International Conference on Research in Advertising (Saarbrucken: Saarland University, 2005), 254–9.

30 Fletcher Research website, <http//:www.fletch.co.uk>.

31 Happy Dog website, <http//:www.happydog.co.uk>.

32 See L. Yuan and C. Buyan-Low, 'Coming soon to cell phone screens—more ads than ever', *The Wall Street Journal* (16 August 2006), B1.

33 A. O. Patrick, 'TV ads find spot on tiny screen', *The Wall Street Journal* (5 July 2007), B4.

34 J. W. Peltier, J. A. Schibrowsky, and D. Schultz, 'Interactive Integrated Marketing Communication Combining the Power of IMC, New Media, and Database Marketing', *International Journal of Advertising*, 22 (2003), 93–115.

35 See S. King, 'Coupons gain new market on cell phones', *The Wall Street Journal* (11 September 2007), B8.

 Visit the Online Resource Centre that accompanies this book for additional resources to support the text: http://www.oxfordtextbooks.co.uk/orc/percy_elliott3e/

Making it Work

11

Processing the Message

 KEY CONCEPTS

1 There are four concerns in message processing: attention, learning, acceptance, and emotion. Attention and learning are necessary for all messages, and acceptance for high-involvement brand attitude strategies; emotion facilitates all message processing.

2 Attention may be either conscious or unconscious, and in advertising this distinction is often discussed in terms of reflexive versus selective attention.

3 Learning involves memory, and at a conscious level this means declarative or explicit memory, and at an unconscious level implicit memory. This distinction is tied to the idea of top-down (conscious) processing versus bottom-up (unconscious) processing.

4 The very nature of how memory 'works' can often lead to problems in processing or retrieving memories of an advertising message.

5 Emotions associated with memories are stored in the amygdala and are activated when exposed to a message, framing how the message will be processed.

Processing a message is clearly critical to successful advertising communication, as we discussed in Chapter 4 when we introduced the idea of a communication response sequence. Processing is much more than an abstraction. While it does reflect what must go on in a person's head as he or she is exposed to advertising and other marketing communication, at the same time it also suggests what we must include in the execution if it is to be correctly processed. Once we understand what goes into processing, we will be in a better position to understand why and how various creative strategies and tactics are used in order to satisfy particular communication objectives.

What do we Mean by Processing?

For our purposes, we define processing as that which goes on in a person's mind when he or she is exposed to an advert or any form of marketing communication *in response to it*. This would include all people's reactions when they are actively *or passively* looking at or listening to an advert, as well as after the exposure if they are still thinking about it. These reactions can quite literally be anything, as long as they are in response to the communication itself. For example, look at Advert 11.1, which appeared in a British women's magazine.

What are you now thinking about as you look at this advert? Whatever it may be, it reflects your processing of the advertising. You may be thinking 'That looks interesting' or 'I wish I could float like that.' Perhaps you are thinking 'I didn't think any washing machine was easy to unload.' You may even be thinking 'I don't need a washing machine.' All these responses represent processing the advertising.

There are four main processing responses that we are concerned with when people are exposed to advertising and other marketing communication:

- *attention* to the advertising itself;
- *learning* something from the advertising;
- *acceptance* of or belief in what the advertising says;
- *emotion* that is elicited by the advertising.

We shall briefly introduce each of these processing responses, and then delve much further into them.

Attention. Before anything else can occur, you must first pay attention to the advertising. In Chapter 4 when we introduced exposure, the first step in our communication response sequence, we pointed out that exposure was an opportunity to see the advertising. But until you pay attention to the advertising, you have not begun to process it. Exposure is necessary or you do not have the opportunity to process the message. Once you are aware of the advertising, you have paid attention to it and begun processing. This is true even if you go no further than identify it as, say, an advert and not part of the programme you are watching, at which point you leave the room to get a snack.

Learning. Once you have paid attention to the advertising, you are in a position to learn something as a result of what is presented in the execution. In a sense, all you are doing

Advert 11.1 Whatever you are thinking about as you look at this advert reflects what and how you are processing the advert. Reproduced with kind permission ©Whirlpool.

is acquainting yourself with the content of the advertising. Returning to the Whirlpool advert, assuming you have looked at it in the magazine (and therefore paid attention to it), you probably learned that it is an advert for a washing machine. You may have even gone further and found that it also talks about how easy it is to unload.

The advert also says 'it's not magic, it's Whirlpool'. If you read that, in terms of processing this would also be something you learn. Yet an important point must be made here. You will have learned that the advert claims it is easy to unload, but you may not necessarily believe it. Believing what the advertising says constitutes acceptance, and that is a separate processing response.

Acceptance. If you have learned something from advertising, you are then in a position to accept or reject it. The entire thrust of the various elements in advertising, both words and pictures, is to present the brand in the most positive way possible. Whirlpool quite literally wants you to believe its machines are easy to unload. Interestingly, while the claim is made in the copy, the major impact comes from the visual. So, if your reaction when first seeing the advert was 'That looks easy', you have personally accepted the message as true. In terms of processing, you paid attention to the advert, learned from the pictures, copy, or both, and, from what you learned, accepted the fact that the machines must be easy to unload. In other words, if this was your reaction to this advert, this was how you processed the advertising. When we discuss this in more detail below, we will see that it is not always necessary to accept the message for advertising to be effective.

Emotion. Beyond everything we have just talked about, there is a fourth response to advertising that mediates both learning and acceptance. This is the emotional response you have to advertising once you have paid attention. Emotional responses are something that just happen, actually a response of the autonomic nervous system. At its simplest level, you like something or you don't. For example, if your reaction to the Whirlpool advert was a positive sense of 'floating', or simply a pleasant response to the flowing illustration, you were reacting emotionally to the visual elements in the execution. These emotional responses will help energize or stimulate learning and acceptance responses.

An important point to understand here is that, when we talk about processing advertising, we are not referring to some general or overall process. What in fact goes on is that each of the elements in the advertising has the ability to communicate, and therefore has the opportunity to be processed. Depending upon the medium, everything from the pictures to the spoken word, from the written word to music, can contribute to the overall communication of the message. Each of these components may be processed, and if they are successfully processed, they will follow the sequence described above: attention followed by learning and, if necessary, acceptance; and all this will be facilitated by emotion.

If an advert is to be truly effective, the processing of each important component of the advert must be successful if the overall communication objective is to be reached. If recognition is the brand awareness communication objective, then the *package* must be processed, or, for verbal recognition awareness, the brand name. For recall awareness, the category need and brand name must be processed together, and in that order linked together in memory. In terms of awareness, whether recognition or recall, the brand name should be clearly communicated.

Brand attitude in many cases relies heavily upon visual components, and this is almost always the case in television adverts. While the copy can and does contribute to brand attitude, the real communication potential is more often conveyed by the visual representations. An interesting test of this for television commercials is to view it with the

Table 11.1 Processing Necessary for Achieving Communication Objectives

Communication Objective	Attention	Learning	Acceptance	Emotion
Category Need	Yes	Yes	Yes	No
Brand Awareness	Yes	Yes	No	No
Brand Attitude				
Low-Involvement	Yes	Yes	No	Yes
High-Involvement	Yes	Yes	Yes	Yes
Brand Purchase Intention	Yes	Yes	Yes	Yes

sound off and see what the visuals alone communicate. But it should go without saying that the visual and verbal components should reinforce each other in what they communicate.

Now that we have a feeling for what we mean by processing in advertising, it is time to take a closer look at each of the four main processing responses and how they facilitate achieving our communication objectives (see Table 11.1). First, we will address attention, learning, and acceptance.

Attention

As we have already mentioned, attention is necessary before any other processing can occur. This should be obvious. If you have not paid any attention to something, how can you learn or accept what has been said? But what exactly *is* attention? The concept of attention implies that somehow we focus a 'mental spotlight' on some activity in our external environment or internally on a memory or something we are thinking about. This 'spotlight' could be conscious—for example, when you scan your memory for a name; or it could be unconscious and you are not aware of it. After a rather uneven history in psychology, researchers in both cognitive science and neuroscience have returned to the position first introduced 100 years ago by William James: 'Everyone knows what attention is. It is the taking possession by the mind, in clear and vivid form, of one out of what seems several simultaneously possible objects or trains of thought.'[1]

Over the last fifty years a number of theories of attention have been offered, the strongest being Broadbent's filter theory.[2] In effect filter theory suggests that we have the ability to block or weaken any message coming to the brand from our sense organs, meaning that the content of working memory is filtered by attention. Attention is a complex process that enables us to better understand and manage what is going on around us, and to control how information is processed.[3]

Unconscious versus conscious attention is a function of automatic versus conscious processing. Psychologists understand that certain behaviour can be performed with little if any focused attention (for example, skimming through a magazine). Such behaviour is directed by *automatic processing*, processing of information that occurs without conscious awareness; and, importantly, without interfering with other activity going on at the same time. If you are riding your bicycle and someone steps out in front of you, you will 'automatically' apply the brakes. This occurs because of something called 'bottom-up' processing, where the information processing relies almost exclusively on the information gathered from what is happening in your environment. Someone stepped out in front of you.

On the other hand, conscious processing does require focused attention, and relies upon something called 'top-down' processing. Top-down processing uses information that is already in your memory. If you are riding your bicycle down a street and are looking for a particular address, this would be an example of top-down processing. To find the address you must consciously focus attention on the street numbers, looking for the address you have in memory. We will return to this idea of top-down versus bottom-up processing later in the chapter.[4]

One explanation for why we consciously pay attention to some things and not others is offered by Kahneman.[5] He suggests that we have a limited capacity to perform mental activity, so that at any one point in time that capacity must be allocated among the many alternatives at hand to process. Since one aspect of attention is the amount of effort that will be required to 'pay attention', the effort directed at a particular task will reflect the level of attention required. If the task is routine, little attentional focus will be used. If you are looking for something, however, attention must be focused.

Reflexive Attention

When thinking about advertising, this distinction between unconscious versus conscious attention is often discussed in terms of reflexive versus selective attention; and sometimes mistakenly as low- versus high-involvement processing. Reflexive attention is initiated every time there is a change in your environment, and it is a wholly involuntary reaction. For example, when a commercial comes on TV, even if you were only half attending to the programme, the switch in programming from the show to the commercial will cause you to notice the commercial. If you then jumped up to run to the kitchen in order to get something to eat because of the commercial break, it is because the change in the stimulus (in this case the TV programming) involuntarily attracted your attention. The same thing occurs each time you turn a page in a magazine. Even if you are only skimming the magazine, each time the page turns your attention will involuntarily be drawn to the page. If there is an advert on the page, you will process it at least far enough to identify it as such, and in most cases choose not to spend time actually reading it. This is automatic, bottom-up processing. Unconscious attention is being paid to the things in your immediate environment.

Unfortunately, this reflexive attention does not last very long. If the stimulus is visual, such as the beginning of a TV commercial or a page turned in a magazine, reflexive attention lasts only about one-tenth of a second,[6] and if the stimulus is a word that your eye fixates upon or that you hear spoken, the reflexive attention will be only about three-tenths of a second.[7] Only if something in that brief period of attention *holds* your attention will you actually spend time with the advert.

This might be a good place to answer a question that may have come to mind as you read this material on reflexive attention: the question of subliminal perception. We do not intend to spend a great deal of time on this issue because, quite frankly, it is not a significant consideration in either the execution or the processing of advertising. The popular perception of the subliminal effects (*sic*) of advertising dates back to the 1950s when the words 'Drink Coca-Cola' and 'Eat popcorn' were said to have been flashed subliminally on the screen of a movie theatre, stimulating a rush to the concession stand. In fact, it never happened. In the 1970s the man behind it all (James Vicarey) admitted he made it all up in order to promote his consultancy business.[8]

Even if some advertisers were to include subliminal cues in their advertising (and there really is no evidence that they do), it would have little if any influence. In some studies conducted by Moore,[9] it was shown that, even when such cues were purposely included in an advert, it had no significant effect on the advertising's ability to communicate or persuade.[10] An extensive search of the literature in this area in the early 1990s came up with over 200 studies that failed to find any subliminal effects upon behaviour.[11]

Subliminal messages do have the potential to create a feeling of familiarity with a product that has been seen before.[12] Basically this is what is known in psychology as a priming effect, but such priming has no effect upon consumer choice. It would only work if the choice was between two unfamiliar brands. In that case, the unconsciously 'primed' brand would seem more familiar, and as a result more likely to be selected.

Selective Attention

Selective attention, on the other hand, occurs when you voluntarily pay attention to advertising. This could occur, for example, if you see an advert for a laptop computer when you are actively thinking about buying one. This is top-down, conscious processing. You would first reflexively attend to the advertising, and, assuming there is enough there to link the advert to your category need for a new laptop, you will probably pay further attention to the advertising. This is no guarantee that you will read or listen to the entire advert, but you will certainly spend more than a fraction of a second with the advertising. In such cases, attention must be maintained with a good execution.

From this discussion you should now appreciate that we pay conscious attention to some things and unconscious attention to others. But why is it that we do not seem to pay attention to certain things, even very important things? How often has something been brought to your attention and you cannot imagine how you missed it? One explanation is that our visual system must be filtering out some information, even if it is neurologically retaining it at an unconscious level.

In a classic experiment on inattention, Simons and Chabris showed a group who volunteered for the study a film clip of people tossing a basketball back and forth to each other. The participants in the study were asked to count the number of passes. After about 45 seconds a person in the film wearing a gorilla suit walked directly across the display and exited on the other side 5 seconds later. This was not a brief exposure, yet unbelievably over 70 per cent of those participating in the study did not see the gorilla! When shown the film clip again and asked to look for the gorilla, they easily saw it.[13]

Neurologically, it seems that activity in the frontal-parietal network simply filters out some information when your attention is focused on something else. Things that would otherwise be obvious are suppressed. This has clear implications for advertising and other marketing communication. If the execution draws attention to one thing, it could very well be to the exclusion of other information. In effect, inattention to something is a necessary fall-out from the focusing of attention on other specific information.

How do we Maintain Attention?

The key to maintaining attention to an advert lies in the elements used in the execution, as we shall see in Chapter 12. While these can vary, depending upon the communication effects involved, let us take a brief look at the manner in which they relate to our two primary communication effects: brand awareness and brand attitude. Remember that all advertising must achieve these two responses, and, in fact, they are always communication objectives.

Brand Awareness

As you might suspect, it does not require a great deal of processing to effect positive brand awareness. In fact, once we have achieved exposure to the advertising and at least reflexive attention, one strategy that can be used to continue stimulating reflexive attention is to utilize something a bit different either visually or verbally within the execution itself. Another way of maintaining reflexive interest is with unexpectedly positioned ads. For example, you could use the equivalent of a full-page advert in a magazine horizontally run as two consecutive half-page spaces. Because we are so used to seeing advertising as same-page executions, reflexive attention should be maintained here as the mind tries to figure out what is going on. The same principle is sometimes used with broadcast advertising when a commercial is continued after a station break or other commercials. Specific creative tactics to help maintain awareness are discussed in the next chapter.

Brand Attitude

In our discussion of brand attitude as a communication objective in Chapter 9, we learned that brand attitude must be associated with the motivation that drives target audience behaviour in the category. Since attention is the first, and necessary, step in processing an advertising message, it is especially important in initiating the desired brand attitude. However, this is much more complex than the attention response associated with brand awareness. What we find with attention and brand attitude is that target audiences will be likely to attend *selectively* to advertising *only* if the message in the advert relates to their *current* motivation in the category. Here are a few examples to help clarify what we mean. At the extreme, if you are a man there is probably very little likelihood that you would selectively attend to a cosmetic advert for a new eye shadow. You would have no motivation to respond in this category. On the other hand, women could be motivated to respond to an advert for men's cosmetics, because they may want to encourage a friend or spouse to purchase or use the product. At a more general level, if you do not have a baby, you are unlikely to attend selectively to advertising for baby food, or if you do not

Advert 11.2 This poster for Mack, a low-price, self-serve petrol brand in Sweden, illustrates the effect of selective attention. Recognition of the advertising ranged from 25 per cent among those who buy at full-serve petrol stations to 60 per cent among self-serve, low-price petrol buyers. Source: Åke Wissing & Co. and Clear Channel Sverige AB.

have a problem with athlete's foot, you will not attend to advertising for an athlete's foot remedy.

In each of these examples, you would pay reflexive attention, enough to let you know you were not interested in the category, and hence have no interest in further processing the advert. However, if you were actively seeking information in this category, once reflexive attention has oriented you to the content of the advertising, your selective attention would be activated as you related the subject of the advertising to your current category motivation.

Advert 11.2 is a poster for BP's MACK brand of low-price, self-service garages in Denmark. In a research study measuring recognition of the advertising we find clear evidence of selective attention. Among people who buy from full-service garages, only 25 per cent remember seeing the advert, while 35 per cent of those who buy from self-service garages recognize the advert. Among those who buy low-price petrol, 60 per cent remember the advert, and among current customers 72 per cent.

The underlying motivation to respond here has a great deal of significance for how likely you are to attend selectively to the advertising. If the underlying motivation is *negative*, unless the problem involved is current or likely to recur, there really is not much likelihood that you will attend to the attitudinal content of the advertising. On the other hand, if the motivation is *positive*, there is a greater likelihood that you will. After all, who does not like to see a really sensuous dessert or a 'glamorous' image? It simply makes you feel good. Now this does not mean you will necessarily respond positively to the advert's message, only that you will be more likely to attend selectively to the message because of its positive reinforcement.

Of course, a well-executed advert will have the ability not only to attract attention, but to hold it as well. What we want to happen is for *something* to be learned, even if only at a sub-cognitive level. Reflexive attention alone provides enough time at least to impress the brand name and a positive association with the brand *if* the execution embodies this in a clear fashion. Then, the more unique the execution, the greater the selective attention. Advertising cannot assume the target audience will pay attention. We must assume it probably will not, and so ensure we communicate something, if only during the reflexive attention span.

You should now have a pretty clear understanding of what we mean by paying attention to advertising. It is the first step in the processing sequence, but in and of itself is not sufficient to effect the desired communication response. For advertising to be effective it must also stimulate a learning response, and, in the case of high-involvement purchase decisions, an acceptance as well. As we have just seen, London Transport did a good job in gaining attention *and* stimulating learning. In the next two sections we will explore the processing responses of learning and acceptance.

Learning

The second processing response necessary for effective communication is *learning*. What exactly do we mean by learning? This may seem obvious, but it is important to understand just exactly what is involved in learning and memory. Fundamentally, when we are talking about learning we are referring to rote learning. This is a passive repetition before new memories for the learned response are retained.[14] This is one of the reasons consistency in message and execution is so important.

At its most basic level, learning occurs at the level of neurons. Changing the strength of synaptic connections, how neurons 'talk' to each other, is the basis for learning. Figure 11.1 illustrates the basic parts of a neuron and its surrounding glia. Information moves from one end of a neuron to another electrically as a single dendritic spine is electrically excited. With repeated stimulation (for example, the input of new information from an advert), an action potential is triggered and flies down the axon. Restimulating that same spine after a period of time, even after several weeks, will cause a 'potentiated' electrical response known as long-term potentiation (LTP).[15]

It is this long-term potentiation that influences long-term memory and declarative (or explicit memory), but it does not influence short-term working memory or procedural

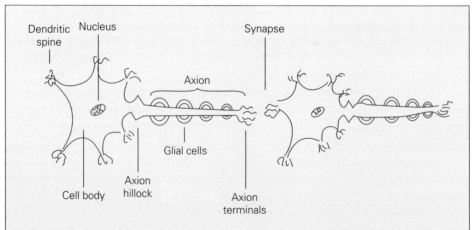

Figure 11.1 Basic Parts of a Neuron and the Surrounding Glia, and the Relationship between Neurons

memory. We will have more to say about memory shortly. We might imagine reading an advert and exciting an appropriate neuron, and later on seeing it again and initiating an LTP, adding the information from the advertising to our memory—a very simplistic analogy, but it does describe more or less what happens.

Learning is the process of making certain neural pathways work more quickly than they did before. This is a relatively recent idea, although the foundation goes back over 100 years to Cajal's 'neuron doctrine'.[16] Earlier neurologists believed that when something new was learned a new neuron or a synapse was formed. But we now understand that learning *strengthens* the functioning of pre-existing synapses, and only very occasionally is a new synapse developed.

You may be wondering why we are looking so closely at the neurology involved in learning and memory. It is because, if we understand what is involved at the most basic level, we can begin to appreciate how we 'learn' from advertising; and how important our existing knowledge is in processing advertising. If we pay attention to an advert, and continue to process it, we will 'learn' something. But we will *not* necessarily be creating 'new' knowledge or memories. The information we are learning will be processed in terms of already existing knowledge in memory. We are not filling a 'hole' or adding a unique bit of information to memory. We will be tapping into existing synapses.

To be effective, advertising must be easily associated in memory with the appropriate neural configuration in order to ensure proper learning. To facilitate this, the execution should be unique to the brand. Otherwise, there is every possibility it will be 'learned' in association with another brand for which an appropriate neural structure is already in place. The execution should also be consistent over time in terms of its 'look and feel' in order to reinforce learning (a subject we will be covering in depth later in Chapter 13).

How we learn as individuals is a function of the way layers of neurons overlap and form networks. We do not all necessarily 'learn' the same thing from the same advert. It all depends upon how our neural networks are 'wired', and this can differ from individual to individual. Neural networks are a series of neurons that form a network that interacts when it partially overlaps with another network. This is a complex process. Memory works by tapping into the neural network necessary to find the information you are trying to remember. We all 'know' different things because the overlapping projections of networks differ among individuals. Still, we have a lot more in common, in terms of a particular subject, than we differ—always assuming we are 'learning' the same thing.[17]

To illustrate what is at work here, look at Fig. 11.2. Imagine that among your memories from a course on nineteenth-century Impressionism you have a number of neural networks reflecting what you learned. As the figure shows, you have knowledge about Monet, Van Gogh, and Gauguin. Perhaps you attended a series of lectures, one on each artist. But you have also 'learned' about Impressionism as your neural networks overlapped. At the point at which the networks containing information about the artists overlap we find our knowledge about Impressionism. Again, this is an oversimplification, but it suggests how we incorporate existing knowledge as we 'learn'.[18]

Consider an analogy with advertising and marketing. It would be fair to say that our knowledge of a product category will be made up of (among other things) our knowledge of the brands in that category. Figure 11.3 illustrates how that might 'look' in memory. We

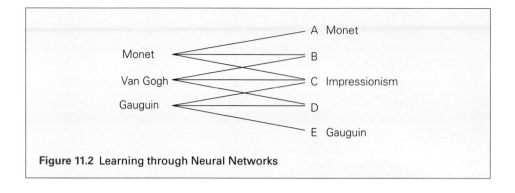

Figure 11.2 Learning through Neural Networks

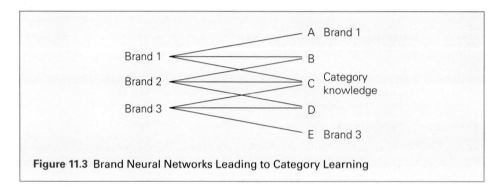

Figure 11.3 Brand Neural Networks Leading to Category Learning

have neural networks associated with various brands, and they overlap in various ways, one of which helps define our understanding of the category. Again, much more is obviously involved, but this does offer insight into how we learn.

Now that we have an understanding of what is involved with learning we will take a look at how this facilitates brand awareness and brand attitude.

Brand Awareness and Learning

If you stop to think of it, learning a brand name is very much like learning new words in a foreign language. Suppose you were studying German and were introduced to the word *schwarz*. Your attention is drawn to the word, and you form a verbal and visual image of the word in your mind. If this is all you did, you should at least be able to recognize the word if you saw or heard it again, and identify it as a German word. In this case you are associating the word with the category 'German words'. As we all know, this will not get you very far on a German test. You will also need to learn the meaning of the word.

In order to become aware of a brand such that you are able either to recognize it or to recall it when the time comes to make a decision to buy, you must learn the association between the category and the brand. You will remember that we spent a great deal of time on this point in Chapter 9. The category cue is critical, and will actually determine how likely it is that your brand will be chosen in various purchase situations.

Brand Recognition

When the brand awareness objective is recognition, what learning is required? From what we already know about brand recognition, when it is an objective, advertising should feature the package as it will be seen at the point of purchase. The target audience must learn what the package looks like so that it will recognize the package on the shelf; it should see a fast-food chain while driving, and think: 'I need that' or 'I'm hungry, so let's stop.' This is precisely what the learning response is for a brand recognition communication objective. You recognize the brand and associate it with the correct category need.

Brand Recall

Brand recall is a more difficult communication objective to achieve than brand recognition, because the learning process is more involved. If the members of a family decide to go out for dinner, they are not very likely simply to go out and drive around until they recognize some place where they would like to stop. They are going to make their destination decision before they start out. For a restaurant to be considered, the target audience must learn to associate the brand name with the category need. When the need does occur, wanting to eat out at a particular type of restaurant, we want the advertised restaurant to come to mind.

Brand Attitude and Learning

You will recall from our earlier discussions that brand attitude responses are a function of the type of decision involved and whether the underlying motive to behave is positive or negative. The type of decision has important implications for brand attitude learning.

Low Involvement

With low-involvement decisions, really all that is required is rather simple rote learning of the benefit associated with the brand. The target audience is aware of what the product is because it has just associated the brand with the category. Now the question is: so what? The benefit expressed in the advertising should answer that question. In effect what is going on here is that, while the target audience is processing the message, it will learn the connection between the brand and the benefit claimed for the brand, along with the *degree* of that connection.

High Involvement

This will not be the case with high-involvement decisions. The key to high-involvement decisions is *acceptance*, which we will be discussing next. But high-involvement learning is tied into acceptance. With low-involvement learning you can be effective if the target audience only tentatively learns a positive benefit, but with high-involvement learning there is usually more than one simple benefit involved.

Acceptance

Acceptance in processing is when the target audience *personally agrees* with something it has learned from one of the components in the advertising. Acceptance is required only for *high-involvement* decisions. With low-involvement decisions, learning is sufficient processing to generate purchase interest because there is little if any risk involved. But with high-involvement decisions, because of the need to be sure of your decision prior to purchase, the message (or at least a significant part of it) must be accepted as true.

Cognitive Responses in Processing

Now that we have a general idea of what we mean by acceptance in the processing of advertising, we need to take a closer look at what is involved when the target audience actually does accept the message of an advert. The key to this explanation is something psychologists call *cognitive responses*. In its simplest form, a cognitive response is the activity that occurs in your mind when you are confronted with something new. Think of what occurs to you when you are introduced to someone for the first time. Before that person says a word, your mind is already forming opinions. The way the person looks or is dressed provides visual impressions that you associate with various images. You may or may not like what you see, given previous experiences. If you are at a formal party, and this new person is dressed very casually, you may think: 'What a slob.' This would be a cognitive response that occurs because in your mind you expect people to dress according to circumstance, and those who do not, at least in your experience, leave something to be desired. Because of your existing beliefs, the contrast of what you expect and what you see generates negative images of this person. This is another example of top-down processing.

The same thing occurs when you look at advertising. You bring to the advertising a certain set of beliefs and expectations related to the product category or brand, and you process the images and information in the advertising within that context. As you think about what you see or read, you will be generating a number of thoughts or feelings stimulated by the advertising, at least at the conscious level. This is an important distinction that we will be discussing in the next section. To the extent that these thoughts or images, these cognitive responses, are generally positive, they will help generate a positive brand attitude. If the cognitive responses tend to be more negative, a negative brand attitude will result.

Cognitive response theory assumes that you will generally try to make sense out of what is going on around you. As you are exposed to new information, from advertising or any other source, you will tend to compare it with what you already know and feel, utilizing what is known as declarative, or sometimes explicit, memory. Thinking specifically about advertising, this suggests that, if you are really paying attention to the advertising, and the advertising is for something you might be highly involved with, you are going to be very interested in what the advertising is saying. On the other hand, if the advertising is for something that does not require much consideration on your part during the purchase decision, you may or may not become actively involved with the message.

What this tells us is that, when you are *highly involved* with a purchase decision, for advertising to be effective you *must generate* positive cognitive responses towards the brand. If your purchase decision is *low involvement*, active cognitive responses, while desirable, are *not necessary*. You should now see that active cognitive responses are necessary for acceptance when someone is processing advertising. This is what occurs when someone is consciously processing the images and claims generated by advertising, and it is essential for products with high-involvement purchase decisions.

Learning and Memory

Since learning involves memory, it is important to have at least a basic understanding of the different forms of memory. You may be surprised to learn that our understanding of the different types of memory today is a relatively recent development. Psychologists have long understood that there was a difference between what they thought of as 'short-term' versus 'long-term' memory. But today psychologists no longer regard short-term memory as a temporary holding state on the way to long-term memory as they did in the past. Rather, what was thought of as short-term memory is now understood to be how we store information while attending to it, or processing it. Braddeley and Hitch in the 1990s introduced the term *working memory* to emphasize this point.[19]

It was not until the 1980s that neuropsychologists came to the realization that memory itself, what was thought of as long-term memory, comes in different forms: declarative memory and procedural memory. *Declarative memory* is what we are able to talk about, or, as it has been described, 'what we know we know'. *Procedural memory* is what is involved in the development of motor skills, such as playing the piano or riding a bicycle.

There are two fundamental features of declarative memory that we should understand. First, it is composed of a combination of 'event-based' memories known as *episodic memory* and of 'fact-based' memories known as *semantic memory*.[20] These two components combine to form declarative memory. We acquire declarative memory through everyday experiences. For example, experience with a specific brand will go into building episodic memory for the brand, and our ability to retain and recall it will be mediated by the hippocampus (a very old part of the brain situated in the temporal lobe, and critical to memory). But this experience with the brand will also be integrated with our general knowledge of the category and of products like these that have been acquired over time by linking experiences that 'share' information (recall our discussion of overlapping neural networks). This is our semantic memory, also mediated by the hippocampus. As we accumulate 'facts' about a brand by integrating new information (for example, from advertising) with our existing general knowledge (basically how we learn, as we have seen), we will also be building episodic memories through actual experience with the brand. Together, these semantic and episodic memories combine to form declarative memory—what we know about the brand.

The second fundamental feature of declarative memory is that it is available to conscious recollection and we can talk about it. This means that declarative memories for both episodic and semantic information are special because a person can access and express these memories and use them to solve problems by making inferences from them. This is how we would make judgements about a new brand extension. We have access to appropriate memories of our relevant experiences and knowledge, and use these memories to help form our judgements about the new product.

Procedural memory, on the other hand, is acquired unconsciously. As a result, it is typically revealed only by indirect measures of memory, and is thought to be stored independently of the temporal lobe where declarative memory seems to live. We use procedural memory to facilitate routine behaviour where there is no need to compare different memories. Whether or not we can influence procedural memory with advertising is a difficult question, with no ready answer.

Another way of looking at the difference between conscious and unconscious memory is explicit versus implicit memory. While not exactly the same as the declarative versus procedural memory distinction, *explicit memory* is basically the same as declarative memory. It involves the deliberate, conscious remembering of something: what adverts have you seen for pension funds? *Implicit memory* refers to the influence of recent experiences on behaviour even when you are not aware that you are using your memory. Use of language is a good example. You are not really conscious of the fact that you are 'recalling' the name of a new brand from memory when talking about it. Unlike procedural memory, it is possible that implicit memory is involved in the processing of some advertising. Incidental exposure to advertising, if it is processed beyond working memory, could perhaps have an effect even if someone is not aware or conscious of having seen the advertising.[21]

We understand this from the work of Zajonc and his colleagues on something they called the *mere exposure* effect.[22] In a series of studies they found that merely exposing people to things like words or pictures of faces will lead to a preference for those items later, even if they are not explicitly remembered. For example, if someone is given a group of pictures of people's faces to look through, then later shown a second group of pictures, some of which are from the original set, when asked which pictures they prefer there is a decided preference for those they were exposed to in the first group. This happened even when the people were not conscious of the exposure because they were presented very quickly. This is another example of priming, which we mentioned earlier in our discussion of subliminal images.

Recall that when we were talking about attention we introduced the notion of top-down versus bottom-up processing. As it happens, this informs the difference between implicit and explicit memory and how information in memory is processed. Implicit information is perceived in the same way it is received, without the need for any manipulation of the content at a higher, conscious cognitive level. This is *bottom-up processing*. Explicit memory, however, depends upon taking information and reorganizing it, integrating the information with existing information in memory in order to store it properly. This is *top-down processing*.

The way in which information is initially processed will affect how it is recalled and used. Because people have a passive role in encoding implicit memory, it is very difficult to recall the memory. But if someone is primed by a feature of the original information source, it will be readily recalled. Advertising that is only passively attended to will result in no conscious memory of it because it will be encoded in implicit memory. Nonetheless, if some aspect of the advert is exposed later, it could be recognized. What this means is that, when a purchase is driven by *recognition awareness*, even passive or unconscious processing of an advert might be effective if there is a strong representation of the package as it will be confronted at the point of purchase. The package should be recognized from implicit memory of the advertising.

On the other hand, because you play an active role in the processing of explicit information, all the internal cues used in processing it may be used to activate recall of the information. If you see an advert and integrate it with existing knowledge of the brand, perhaps your belief that it is a high-quality product, when thinking of the category and cued with 'high quality' you will recall the brand. You should see that explicit memory will be necessary for recall awareness, because an association between the category need and the brand is required, and this will result from active processing of the links. It is also necessary for conscious learning that is used in decision making.

This top-down, bottom-up processing distinction also helps explain why we often 'see' things that are not there. Knowledge and assumptions, our explicit, declarative memory, add a great deal to how we interpret what we see. Vision is not always directly related to the retinal image. 'Seeing' an object involves general rules and knowledge about objects based upon previous experience: top-down processing (see Fig. 11.4). In a wonderful painting by Degas of a woman and man sitting at a table in a café we simply do not notice that the table does not have legs. We all know that tables have legs and do not float in the air, so we assume they are there.

When creating advertising and other marketing communication, it is important to keep this in mind. Not that anyone is likely to use an illustration of a table without legs, but it is not unusual to see adverts that rely upon visual puns. Unfortunately, unless the pun is obvious, there is every chance that the mind will 'correct' the image. If the message requires the receiver to understand the pun, but top-down processing corrects the error, the message will be lost. In fact, all visual images in advertising should be clearly understood. Anything too subtle runs the very real risk of not being understood the way it was intended. Remember, in a very real sense we see what we know.

Perhaps one more point will help underscore this idea. If you think about it, any retinal image could represent an infinite number of possibilities, yet we generally 'see' only

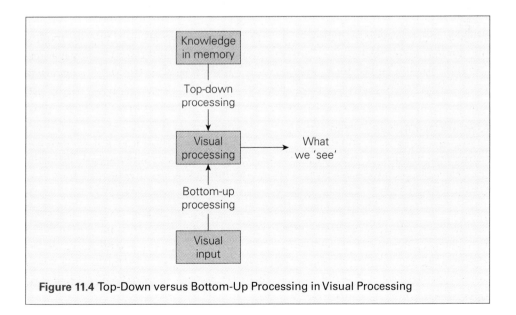

Figure 11.4 Top-Down versus Bottom-Up Processing in Visual Processing

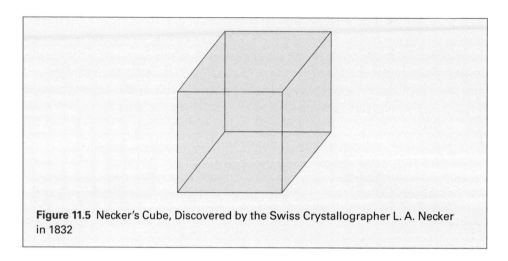

Figure 11.5 Necker's Cube, Discovered by the Swiss Crystallographer L. A. Necker in 1832

one. Why? Because we have learned to associate that image with something specific, and that information is stored in memory. But there are exceptions, when we cannot make up our minds. Necker's cube (see Fig. 11.5) and other 'optical illusions' are examples of this ambiguity.[23] With no clear evidence, we entertain two roughly equal, but different, interpretations of the depth perspective. Does the cube recede or does it project outward? The image on the retina does not change (bottom-up processing), but we cannot decide upon what we 'see' because our experience tells us either option is correct (top-down processing). What this tells us is that every act of perception, even something as simple as looking at the drawing of a cube, let alone something as complex as an advert, involves an act of judgement based upon our experience or prior knowledge.

At this point you may be wondering why we have spent so much time on what may seem to be very abstract or theoretical discussions of neuropsychology. The reason is that we must be aware that how we process and store information from advertising will depend upon what part of our memory is involved. Understanding how memory works informs how one must deal with advertising executions to ensure the most effective processing of it. The strategic implications of what we have been talking about are summarized in Table 11.2.

Memory Distortions and Forgetting

Just because advertising has been processed and information stored in the memory does not mean that the memory actually reflects what was in the advertising, or that it will be readily available when needed. Things get distorted in memory, and we 'forget' things. This is a result of what Schacter has called memory 'imperfections', and he has identified seven potential problems with memory that he has intriguingly called 'The Seven Sins of Memory': absent-mindedness, misattribution, suggestibility, bias, blocking, transience, and persistence.[24] Each of these potential problems can impact on advertising effectiveness because each can distort processing or retrieval of an advertising message (see Table 11.3).

Table 11.2 Strategic Implications related to Memory Types

Unconscious Memory	
Procedural Memory	**Implicit Memory**
• Facilitates routine behaviour	• Unconscious influence of recent experiences • *Not* integrated with other memories
Implication: unlikely to be effected by advertising	*Implication*: only likely to influence recognition awareness
Conscious Memory	
Declarative Memory	**Explicit Memory**
• Made up of semantic and episodic memory • Advertising may contribute to semantic memory, adding to general knowledge of category and brands • Episodic memory reflects experience with the category and brands	• Deliberate, conscious awareness • Integrated with existing memories at conscious level • Integrates new information from advertising with existing knowledge
Implication: what is learned from advertising will *always* be integrated with our experience	*Implication*: contributes to our understanding of brands via learning from advertising

Table 11.3 The Seven Sins of Memory

Absent-Mindedness	Results from not paying proper attention to something
Misattribution	Remembering something, but attributing it to the wrong source
Suggestibility	Attributing something from an outside source to a personal experience
Bias	When current beliefs and feelings distort the processing of new information
Blocking	When appropriate retrieval cues are in place, but the association is just not made
Transience	Natural shift over time from specific recollection to more general descriptions
Persistence	Remembering something you would like to forget

Most of these problems result from how we learn the information in advertising, how we encode or integrate the information from the advertising with what we already have in memory. Absent-mindedness comes from not paying proper attention to something, so that it is overlooked when we need to retrieve it. This is more likely to occur for more routine experiences, like exposure to advertising, where there is simply no compelling reason carefully to process the message. Misattribution and suggestibility occur when we remember something, but attribute it to the wrong source. In advertising this can occur when the message does not bond in memory with the brand because it is too similar to information already in a memory associated with something else, or because we link it to a previous personal experience unrelated to the brand. Bias occurs when our current beliefs and feelings distort how we interpret what we see in advertising.

We all are very familiar with the problem of blocking. This is what is going on when you recognize someone, but cannot remember his or her name. The appropriate retrieval cue is in place, but the association is just not made. The problem stems from people's names being isolated in memory from any conceptual knowledge of them. Recall from our discussion of how we learn that neural networks are built upon existing knowledge. When we meet someone, we rarely have an appropriate neural network in place to link the person's name to it. This makes it very difficult to find it when we need it. This can be a real problem with brand names, and especially abstract brand names or the names of new brands, if there is not a strong association made in the brand's advertising with the appropriate category need.

In Chapter 12, we will talk about creative tactics that can help minimize these potential problems with memory.

The remaining memory problems, transience and persistence, reflect simple forgetting or the persistent memory of something you want to forget. Persistence is unlikely to be a problem with advertising. Not forgetting an advertising message will not be seen as a problem by the advertiser! But we certainly do not want people to forget something positive about a brand from its advertising. What seems to happen in memory is a natural shift from specific recollections of things to more general descriptions of what is learned. This is why in advertising recall studies people are likely to recall general ideas from advertising rather than specific details.

Emotion

Up to this point we have talked about processing in terms of its traditional role in information processing, as discussed in Chapter 4 in relation to the communication response sequence. Some element within an advert—the picture or illustration, headline, copy-points (ideally *all* the elements working together)—must first of all be attended to and something must be learned from it. Then, unless you are dealing only with brand awareness or low-involvement brand attitude effects, if that learning is to communicate anything, it must be accepted as true. But the context within which this processing is occurring will also elicit a response: an *emotional* response. The advertising itself will trigger certain emotional responses, and in certain cases this emotional response will mediate what is learned and whether or how a particular point is accepted.[25]

(a)

(b)

Advert 11.3 While both of these images show children, the image in 11.3*a* elicits a stronger emotional response than that in 11.3*b*. Courtesy Åke Wissing & Co.

Look at the two images shown in Advert 11.3. What reaction do you have to these two images? Both are from adverts for a brand of washing powder. We know that emotional authenticity is not necessary for low-involvement informational advertising, but, regardless of the brand attitude strategy, we do want to elicit the correct emotional response. The benefit of 'soft' is reinforced in Advert 11.3*a* by a positive emotional response to the child. This does not occur with the image of a mother and child in Advert 11.3*b*.

Why is that? There is nothing warm or nurturing about this image, nothing to suggest a 'loving' mother, one who makes sure her children enjoy the benefit of clean, soft clothes. There is nothing sincere in the mother's expression, and in fact she is not even looking directly at the child. As a result, there is nothing there to stimulate a positive emotional response. This is reflected in research on the two adverts, which found the execution using the image in 11.3*a* generated a 55 per cent positive response to the advert versus 40 per cent for the advert using the image shown in 11.3*b*; and 50 per cent buying interest for 11.3*a* versus 30 per cent for 11.3*b*. These adverts were from the same campaign, for the same brand, but the emotional response to Advert 11.3*a* led to a much more positive processing of the message.[26]

What exactly is meant by the term 'emotion'? We certainly all experience 'feelings' that we think of as emotions, and in many cases they are. But there is much, much more to it. Concepts of emotion reflect a number of things, but perhaps the most important, and the one that seems best to account for how we understand emotions from both a psychological and a neurological perspective, is something called *affect programme theory*.[27]

In its modern form, affect programme theory deals with a specific range of emotions that correspond to Damasio's discussion of the six primary emotions: surprise, anger, fear, disgust, sadness, and joy.[28] It has been suggested that the affect programme itself is a coordinated set of changes that we experience, and that constitute an emotional response; what we 'know' or experience as surprise, anger, fear, and so on.[29] It is also understood that these emotions, or perhaps more correctly emotional responses, are basic to all humans.[30]

These primary emotional states are phylogenetically ancient, informationally encapsulated reflex-like responses that appear to be unrelated to culture.[31] They are localized in the limbic system, a system that was in place in humans before we evolved language and our present way of thinking.[32] This is one of the reasons why visual representations in advertising are so critical. Emotions are quickly and easily triggered by visual stimuli. We are also most likely to experience emotions in others visually, through their expression and body language; but also their voice. In fact, emotional responses are characterized by four classes of physical changes: facial expression, musculoskeletal changes such as flinching, expressive vocal changes, and changes within the autonomic nervous system such as adrenalin release and heart rate change.[33] With the exception of changes in the autonomic nervous system, advertising has the ability to *reflect* these emotional responses.

How facial expressions, body language, and voice changes are handled in advertising executions will be important in eliciting the desired emotional response; and critical to the emotional authenticity of transformational brand attitude strategies. Other people's emotions do have an influence upon our own emotions, and this includes the emotions expressed by people in advertising. Their emotions will be 'felt' by the viewer, and experienced by them. This is known as *embodiment*, and results from exposure to facial expression, body language, and prosody (tone of voice).[34] The most important cue in assessing another's emotion is their facial expression,[35] and it is the eyebrows that are most expressive of negative emotion and the mouth positive emotion.[36] This means that in advertising, to encourage a position emotion in the target audience, those shown in the advertising should be smiling; and this must be a true smile, not forced. This is not easy to do, even for experienced actors, because a truly felt positive emotion will occasion an involuntary response of facial muscles. One can, of course, consciously smile, but that activates a different neural system, and will not be 'felt' as a true smile.[37] Real smiles, those occasioned by an involuntary response to a truly felt positive emotion, are known as Duchenne smiles after the 19th-century anatomist who first wrote about this.[38]

A perhaps subtle point, but one worth understanding, is that our *perception* of other people's emotions is processed in the right hemisphere, in the right temporal cortex area of the brain. This means that the dominant visual input will come from the left field of vision. While this is obviously not a 'rule', if the image of a specific emotion is important to the message, the individuals expressing that emotion in an advert should be on the left side of the page or screen to optimize visual processing through the left field of vision.

While the basic emotions comprising the affect programme are fundamental to all humans, Damasio believes that *secondary* emotions and what he calls background emotions (emotions such as embarrassment, guilt, or tension) are acquired, and are triggered by things that people have come to associate with that emotion through experience.[39] They are aspects of higher cognition and as a result could differ as a function of the role culture plays in psychological development. The emotions associated with experience, whether culturally based or simply the memory of that experience, are part of our non-declarative emotional memory. In the creation of advertising and other marketing communication it is important to know what these emotional associations are in memory. In Western cultures, for example, there is a strong connection between guilt and responsibility. Other cultures also have secondary emotions that resemble our concept of guilt, but they lack this connection to responsibility.

Russell has offered an interesting variation on Damasio's distinction between primary and secondary emotions, describing them as Type 1 and Type 2 emotions.[40] The important point is that Russell feels Type 2 emotions do not require a person to consciously acknowledge experiencing the emotion while one actually is thinking about Type 2 emotions as they occur. For example, one may be angry or happy without thinking 'I'm angry' or 'I'm happy'. But if you feel empathy with someone, you will be conscious of the fact. This could have important consequences in processing advertising and promotion messages because if Type 1 emotions are associated in memory with a brand it could automatically motivate approach or avoidance behaviour.[41] If you 'love' a brand you will unconsciously be drawn to it and messages about it; if you 'hate' a brand, you will unconsciously avoid it and any messages about it. If this notion of Russell's is in fact true, it would act like an instinct.[42]

How we experience emotional responses is complex but coordinated. They occur very rapidly after exposure to the stimulus that elicited the response, and its onset is typically involuntary; and they unfold *without conscious direction*. This is very important in understanding how emotion works in mediating the way advertising is processed. The affect programme system creates brief, highly stereotypical emotional reactions that have only limited involvement with the cognitive processes that control longer-term action. To give you an idea of what this means, suppose you are walking home late on a dark night and decide to take a short cut down a dark alley. It is really dark in the alley, and about halfway down you hear a loud noise. Even before you are consciously aware of that noise, you will have experienced an emotional response. Your heart rate will have risen and adrenalin will have been released into your system; all *before* you are actually aware of the noise. This is part of our innate emotional response to a potentially life-threatening situation. The body is being prepared for 'flight or fight' even before we can rationally evaluate the situation. As we become consciously alert, we may notice a cat jumping down from a skip, and we relax.

Even though our emotions, especially primary emotions, have limited involvement in actual cognitive processing controlling long-term action, they nonetheless will be strongly integrated into the cognitive processes leading to long-term planned action. In other words, emotional responses 'frame' our conscious cognitive processing. In advertising, if the emotional response elicited is consistent with experiences associated with using the product, any positive emotions activated on behalf of the brand by an advert should help reinforce brand purchase intentions made as a result of that advertising.

How does this work? Damasio has pointed out that emotion is a cognitive *process* that actually leads to logical thinking.[43] He argues that the mechanisms of reasoning are significantly influenced by both conscious and unconscious signals from the neural networks associated with emotion. We all acquire emotional memories that are related to our experiences with different things, and these feelings are unconscious and independent of any conscious, declarative memory that we might have of those same things. These emotional memories are stored in the amygdala in something known as non-declarative (that is, unconscious) emotional memory. We discussed declarative and procedural memory when we talked about learning. Emotional memory is the third element of what the neuroscientist Eichenbaum has referred to as the three major 'memory systems'.[44]

When we are confronted with something that stimulates a memory, the unconscious emotional component of that memory will be activated as well as our conscious associations. In fact, the unconscious emotional memory stored in the amygdala will *precede* into conscious working memory any conscious, hippocampus-dependent (that area of the temporal lobe involved) explicit memories, as we begin to process new information. This means that, if an advert activates memories, either of a positive experience with the brand, or positive memories associated with the imagery in the advertising, the non-declarative emotional memory associated with these memories will immediately and unconsciously enter into our active processing of the advertising. We can see how this happens in Fig. 11.6. Emotion and cognition are intimately related, and are probably controlled by overlapping neural systems.[45]

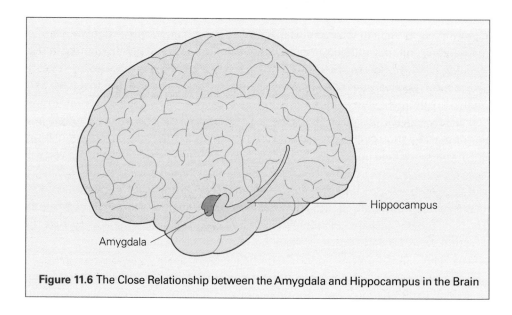

Figure 11.6 The Close Relationship between the Amygdala and Hippocampus in the Brain

Eichenbaum relates a personal experience that perfectly illustrates what happens here. He had entered a lift alone on the ground floor, and when it reached the first floor it stopped and a number of people stepped in. The first was a young woman who stood just in front of him. He immediately noticed that she was wearing perfume, and it was a vaguely familiar scent. Over the next few seconds he began experiencing a strong feeling of both familiarity and, as he described it, 'a sort of innocent sense of happiness'. He found himself emotionally transported back to the 'feeling' of high school. Within seconds he began to remember classmates he had not thought about in years. At last he fully recognized the scent, one that had been very popular among teenage girls in the early Sixties when he was at school—Shalimar.

The specific memories he had were, as he put it, 'run-of-the-mill declarative memories'. But that initial feeling of happiness and 'high-schoolness' was an example of emotional memory, one evoked by a past association, and here is the key point, 'even before the conscious recollection of the experience that provoked it'. The emotional memory framed his conscious memories. In the same way, non-declarative emotional memories elicited by advertising will help frame conscious memories of the brand, and how we process the advertising.

Before we leave this, there is an important point to be made. While positive emotional memories can certainly initiate positive processing, they do not have the ability to override conscious considerations. If the brand or advertising imagery evokes positive memories, but there is something in the message that is not liked, the conscious, cognitive processing will take precedent. Recall our example of the noise in a dark alleyway. Once the association of the noise and the cat has been made, the original intense primary emotional response will no longer control your actions.

Processing Internet Advertising

Back in the first chapter when we talked briefly about Internet advertising, we pointed out that basically it is processed like any other advert, with one difference. That difference was occasioned by the structure of Internet adverts. Look at an example of a banner advert for homestore.com (Advert 11.4); everything we have been talking about in this chapter regarding how advertising is processed will apply to this advert.

First of all, someone must pay attention to the advert, then learn that you can find everything for the home at homestore.com. Because this is a banner advert on the

Advert 11.4 Everything we have discussed about how advertising is processed applies to Internet banner adverts like this one for homestore.com. Reproduced with kind permission © homestore.com.

Internet, you do not really need to *accept* that in fact you will find everything for the home at homestore.com *to look further*. Clicking on the banner is a low-involvement decision, unlike actually visiting a retail furniture outlet. Finally, the copy headline will stimulate an emotional response that the advertiser hopes will facilitate the processing of the message. Specifically, the 'everything' should stimulate curiosity or even excitement, encouraging the viewer to click on the banner.

But, because there is more to this advert's structure, there must be additional processing. Rossiter and Bellman have introduced the idea of a micro- and macro-structure of advertising.[46] They suggest that, while all advertising shares a common micro-structure, which they define as the links between content variables, the real difference between Internet adverts and other forms of advertising is caused by macro-structure if you click on the banner. They mean by this, roughly speaking, the association and link within the advertising's content between pages in the Internet advert. In other words, because of the macro-structure of Internet advertising, people must 'navigate through the Web ad' (in their words), and they are free to navigate in any way they choose. Their path will reflect what Rossiter and Bellman call a self-constructed Web ad schema, and this may *not* be the path the advertiser would prefer they follow.

As they go on to point out, the macro-structure of a television or radio commercial is usually automatic, and it is obvious with collateral advertising such as brochures and direct response adverts. But with Internet advertising the (advertiser's) preferred processing route is neither automatic nor evident. What this means is a potential loss of control for the advertiser. This would be particularly true for the emotional responses associated with processing. Perhaps the most obvious example would be the result of any difficulty or frustration encountered in trying to navigate successfully through a site.

Overall, what we have talked about in this chapter, as well as what we will discuss in the next chapter, apply to Internet advertising, especially its micro-structure. What you need to be concerned about, however, is facilitating and controlling (if possible) the processing of the macro-structure. This will be very difficult, because individual users of the Internet will be developing their own Web ad schema, or ways of navigating Internet adverts.

CHAPTER SUMMARY

In this chapter we have focused on the ways that consumers process messages, and how knowledge about this can be used to develop creative strategy and tactics. We introduced the four basic processing responses of attention, learning, acceptance, and emotion, and then discussed in detail how each response can be used to facilitate the achievement of communication objectives. We explored the different levels of processing associated with different levels of involvement, and the key role of acceptance in high-involvement decisions and its link with cognitive responses with particular attention to learning and memory. We then considered the vital role of emotion in relation to advertising and how emotion mediates processing. Then we saw how all this applies to processing Internet adverts.

11.1 Why is it important to understand how advertising is processed?

11.2 What are the different aspects of attention and how might they affect the way in which an advert is processed?

11.3 In what ways is memory involved in learning?

11.4 Does it matter if advertising is processed consciously or unconsciously?

11.5 What aspects of memory are involved in conscious versus unconscious processing?

11.6 How can memory interfere with the successful processing of advertising?

11.7 What role does emotion play in message processing?

CASE STUDY 11

Le Lait—'Deux C'est Mieux'

This is about a decision to abandon a five-year campaign that had captured Quebecers' hearts, in favour of a new direction. Great as the previous campaign was, with brilliant tracking results, it had not stemmed the long-term decline in milk consumption. Given that this decline is almost universal, what could be done? The decline was turned around—with consumption growing 3 per cent in Year 1 and a further 1.5 per cent in the first six months of Year 2. After years of decline, this is outstanding. In Year 1 it translates to an extra $12.6 million at wholesale, 3.9 times the marketing expenditure.

Milk is an essential part of growing up. It has 98 per cent household penetration, and massive sales—28 per cent of all beverage dollar sales are milk. It is a staple in virtually every household. But milk's image of healthy, wholesome, goodness is so entrenched that people forget its role as a refreshing drink. Milk faces its greatest challenge from demographics. Consumption plummets as people age. Its share of all beverages is as high as 32.6 per cent among 0–5 year olds in Quebec, but this drops to just 6.9 per cent by age 30. Choice increases exponentially, starting with teens (water, juices, carbonated soft drinks), then college age (alcohol), then adulthood—where tea and especially coffee are added.

In Quebec the ageing population exacerbates the issue. Even if per capita consumption within each age cohort stayed the same, overall consumption would still drop 3.5 per cent between 2000 and 2005. This demographic erosion is compounded by all the activity with soft drinks, alcoholic beverages, fruit juices, bottled water, and the like. In 2002, cold beverages (Beer, CSDs, Juices, Water and Milk) spent $40.8 million on advertising in Quebec, and $122.8 million in the balance of Canada. This gave Milk a 10.3 per cent and 11.8 per cent share of voice respectively—compared to its 28 per cent sales importance. This is just one factor. Equally or more important is massive in-store merchandising, price-featuring and display. An ACNielsen 2003 study illustrates the discrepancy between milk and other beverages:

- Milk occupied only 5 per cent of linear feet devoted to beverages, while accounting for 28 per cent of beverage dollar sales.
- Milk had only 3 per cent of sales at special pricing, compared to 68 per cent for CSDs, 28 per cent for other beverages, and 33 per cent for all beverages.
- Milk averaged $1.13 a litre, compared to $0.75 for all beverages (ex-alcoholic).
- Milk got only 1 per cent of trade weighted co-op support.

These factors have led to declining per capita consumption averaging just over 1 per cent a year for the past 15 years.

Our objective was therefore to turn the decline around. But how do you do this? Many approaches had been tried—both rational and emotional. A highly emotional campaign launched in 1988—'La Campagne blanche'—leveraged the wholesomeness of milk, evoking the nostalgia of childhood. Simple white graphics and classic French songs gave a sense of milk's purity. Tracking scores broke all records for likeability, comprehension, and brand linkage. And the campaign became a part of Quebecois culture, with a CD of the songs becoming a number 1 hit. However, the campaign did not change *behaviour.* When it was launched in 1988 milk consumption was at 92.2 litres/capita. By 2003 it was at 84.8. This raised the difficult question: if a powerful campaign like 'La Campagne blanche' could not stem the tide, then what could?

The answer was simple. We decided to focus on stimulating consumption. But this was a sea change from 'La Campagne blanche', and it presented a conundrum. Would we be tampering with the emotional connection we had built? Since the emotional connection was very strong, we decided that we had the licence to launch a much more frontal assault. The challenge was to make the consumer actively select milk, rather than just passively consume it out of habit. So we simply told them that 'two glasses of milk are better than one'. The secret to salesmanship is getting prospects to agree with you early on. Our target was the 18–29 group, and they were already consuming a glass a day. So it was reasonable to ask them to extend this. Put another way, 'La Campagne blanche' had reinforced all the values of milk. So who could argue with the idea that 'if one is good, two is better'?

Execution

Creative: a) Year 1: September 2003–spring 2004

We could have developed a hard-hitting campaign based on rational arguments. But we knew that with healthy products, a father-knows-best approach is counter-productive. We had to entice rather than sell. So we chose a completely opposite course. For the Fall 2003 launch we used a mix of TV, radio, and print. The initial television spots featured characters in, can we say, unusual situations: a Fortune 500 President is playing with dolls. A wife is caught casually in bed with another man. A boyfriend savours his feminine side by wearing his girlfriend's shoes. But what astonishes the people who catch our protagonists in the act? Not the act itself, but the fact that they are drinking their second glass of milk! The protagonists deliver this message in a most understated way—as if it is the most natural thing in the world. The signature 'Un verre de lait c'est bien, mais deux c'est mieux,' is then the call to action. Good radio is about theatre of the mind. We created this in the style of a sports announcer calling the action as a person gets one glass of milk, then raising the tempo as they get a second glass—simple, energetic, impactful work. Print delivered the nutritional message, showing it as the stuff of teeth and bones. Without saying it, we were implying the benefit of calcium. In January–March 2004, we decided to focus even more on the slogan. In TV we did 'Tennis' and 'Enfants', where two people are clearly doing better than one. 'Un verre de lait c'est bien, mais deux c'est mieux' was on their tee-shirts, in the centre of the action. Newspaper had a simple layout consistent with the TV and again carried the nutritional message.

b) Year 2: fall 2004–spring 2005

Strong business results from Year 1, supported by tracking research, showed that we were on track. The slogan was magical, but we kept looking for fresher ways to embed it into the Quebecois vernacular. We found the answer in the 'V' sign. The peace or victory sign could powerfully deliver the message of two glasses of milk a day. This mnemonic was bang on target and could become a simple and cost-efficient way to remind Quebecers to drink two glasses a day:

- It stood for victory and had a real sense of energy. It was a strong emotional way to deliver a traditional message. But this was clearly not your traditional milk.
- It would allow us to deliver daily frequency in a more visually impactful and cost efficient way than radio.

So we moved forward with TV, large posters, bus shelters, and newspapers.

The idea for TV and print was simple. People posed with the V sign—some new, some real, and some from history. TV was a montage set to a powerful music track. Based on this, we also created a CD contest for the younger generation through Musique Plus. The station played the track while launching a CD. We freshened winter 2005 print by using charming cartoon-like executions and created executions around Christmas, Easter, etc.

Media Strategy and Plan: a) Year 1: September 2003–spring 2004

For the new campaign TV again formed the primary medium. At the same time we needed high frequency—ideally daily—since we were trying to change daily habits with a budget of $1.2million for fall 2003. A base of :30 TV at roughly equal weights to prior years, but in :30s (vs. :60s and :30s before). Funds saved, with funds traditionally spent in print, now went to 250–450 weekly GRP's in radio.

This gave us 9 weeks of coverage from mid-September 2003 until November 17, when we took a hiatus to avoid Christmas. Most importantly it increased frequency.

We continued the campaign from mid-January 2004 to early March, but now substituted newspaper for radio. This allowed us to deliver nutritional messages. Spend was $774K, vs. $954K the prior year.

b) Year 2: fall 2004–spring 2005

Recognizing the Year 1 success the Fédération des producteurs de lait du Québec increased the Fall 04 budget from $1.2 million in 2003 to $1.6 million in 2004. TV remained at traditional levels. But with the 'V' sign, we wanted to surround the customer—so we used large vertical posters, transit shelters, backlits, wild postings, street corner columns, and daily newspapers to hit them at home, on the way to and from work and at play. The result was 60 per cent print & outdoor / 40 per cent TV, the opposite of our traditional mix, but justified by the increased 'V' impact.

The long-term decline turned around, solely due to the successful advertising campaign. The growth in Year 1 equates to an incremental 16 million litres, $18 million at retail, and $12.6 million at wholesale.

Source: Le Lait—Deux C'est Mieux', Canadian Congress of Advertising Canadian Advertising Success Stories, 2005

Edited by Natalia Yannopoulou

Discussion Questions

1 Taking under consideration that most brand-building advertising focuses on benefits, why do you think that this campaign that focused on consumption had such positive results?

2 How would you comment on the execution of the advertising campaign?

3 What could be a creative idea for their future campaign?

4 What alternative creative idea could you propose for the same product for a country of your selection?

FURTHER READING

- A number of recent articles in the *Journal of Consumer Research* have dealt with specific processing issues. A psycho-linguistic model of bilingual concept organization is extended to the processing of advertising in David Luna and Laura Peracchin, 'Moderators of Language Effects in Advertising to Bilinguals: A Psycholinguistic Approach', *JCR* (Sept. 2001), 284–95; repetition of stimulus features in facilitating processing is discussed in Christie Nordhielm, 'The Influence of Level of Processing on Advertising Repetition effects', *JCR* (Dec. 2002), 371–82; studies dealing with factors that interact with stimulus spacing to facilitate memory for repeated information are reviewed in Chris Janiszewski, Hayden Noel, and Alan Sawyer, 'A Meta-Analysis of the Spacing Effect in Verbal Learning: Implications for Research on Advertising Repetition and Consumer Memory', *JCR* (June 2003), 138–49; the relationship between brand familiarity and wearout for both television and Internet adverts is examined in Margaret Campbell and Kevin Keller, 'Brand Familiarity and Advertising Repetition Effects', *JCR* (Sept. 2003), 292–304; and the detrimental effects of adverts with similar visual elements on memory for information in adverts is reported in Anand Kuman and Shanker Krishnan, 'Memory Interference in Advertising: A Replication and Extension', *JCR* (Mar. 2004), 602–11.

- A solid overview of the neurology involved in learning and memory is to be found in J. David Sweatt, *Mechanisms of Memory* (Amsterdam: Elsevier, 2003).

NOTES

1 It was the emergence of cognitive science that led to a re-evaluation of the behavioural view that such cognitive concepts as attention and consciousness were not necessary to explain behaviour, and a return to James's position from the late 1800s. See Bryan Kolb and Ian Q. Whishaw, *The Fundamentals of Human Neuropsychology*, 5th edn. (New York: Worth Publishers, 2003), 577, 578; and the original work of William James, *The Principles of Psychology* (New York: Holt, 1890).

2 See D. Broadbent, *Perception and Communication* (London: Pergamon, 1958).

3 A good brief explanation of this may be found in R. L. Gregory's *The Oxford Companion to the Mind*, 2nd edn. (Oxford: Oxford University Press, 2004).

4 For a discussion of top-down versus bottom-up processing, see Kolb and Whishaw, *The Fundamentals of Neuropsychology*, 579; and with special reference to visual processing, Richard L. Gregory, *Eye and Brain*, 5th edn. (Princeton: Princeton University Press, 1997).

5 Our perceptual systems can overheat, creating what D. Kahneman has called a 'bottleneck' in processing in his book *Attention and Effort* (Englewood Cliffs, NJ: Prentice Hall, 1973).

6 See I. Bredeman, J. C. Rabinowitz, A. L. Glass, and E. W. Stacy, 'On the Information Extracted from a Glance at a Scene', *Journal of Experimental Psychology*, 103 (1974), 597–600.

7 See G. R. Loftus, 'Tachistoscopic Simulations of Exposure Fixation on Pictures', *Journal of Experimental Psychology: Human Learning and Memory*, 7 (1981), 369–76.

8 This story and a very good discussion of subliminal advertising may be found in Max Sutherland's May 2007 on-line column at <http://www.sutherlandsurvey.com>.

9 Although the idea of 'subliminal persuasion' has been widely sensationalized, especially by Wilson Key in his book *Subliminal Seduction* (Englewood Cliffs, NJ: Prentice Hall, 1974), Timothy Moore has convincingly demonstrated that, even if advertisers utilized subliminal cues in creative executions, they would not affect brand choice. See T. E. Moore, 'Subliminal Advertising: What You See is What You Get', *Journal of Marketing*, 46 (Spring 1982), 38–47.

10 For a review of how subliminal sexual imagery may in fact stimulate *sexual* arousal, see W. J. Roth and H. S. Mosatche, 'A Projective Assessment of the Effects of Freudian Sexual Symbolism in Liquor Advertisements', *Psychological Report*, 56/1 (1985), 183–8. While Moore's work (see n. 4) shows that subliminal cues generally are not effective in advertising, what the Roth and Mosatche study suggests is that subliminal sexual imagery might have an effect in the specific case where a purely emotion-laden benefit focus is appropriate.

11 See A. Pratkanis and E. Aronson, *Age of Propaganda* (New York: W. H. Freeman, 1991), 201.

12 More on this may be found in G.V. Johar, D. Maheswaran, and L. A. Peracchio, 'MAPping the Frontiers: Theoretical Advances in Consumer Research on Memory, Affect, and Persuasion', *Journal of Consumer Research,* 33 (2006), 139–49.

13 This experiment is reported in D. J. Simons and C. F. Chabris, 'Gorillas in our Midst: Sustained Inattentional Blindness for Dynamic Events', *Perception*, 28 (1999), 1059–74. A shortened version of this experiment may be downloaded from <http://www.wjh.harvard.edu/~viscog/lab/demos.html>.

14 See E. Langer, A. Blank, and B. Chanowitz, 'The Mindlessness of Ostensibly Thoughtful Action: The Role of "Placebic" Information in Interpersonal Interaction', *Journal of Personality and Social Psychology*, 36/6 (1978), 635–42.

15 LTP is discussed at great length in Howard Eichenbaum, *The Cognitive Neuroscience of Memory* (Oxford: Oxford University Press, 2002), not only in terms of the cellular and molecular basis of learning for those interested in the neurobiology involved, but also, in an *understandable* way, in terms of memory.

16 Ramer y Cajal won the Nobel Prize for his observations that each nerve cell was contained within a membrane and was separate altogether in contact with other cells. For a review of his ideas, see Eichenbaum, *The Cognitive Neuroscience*, 7–9.

17 See the chapters on memory in Kolb and Whishaw, *Fundamentals of Neuropsychology*, 447–52.

18 The work of Hubel Wiesel (discussed by James W. Kalat in his book *Biological Psychology*, 8th edn. (Belmont, Calif.: Wadsworth/Thomson Learning, 2004)) provides this framework for understanding the pattern of activity in neural networks. It is also related to the idea of relational memory theory that suggests a memory space in which memories are connected by their common elements. For a discussion of this, see Eichenbaum, *The Cognitive Neuroscience*, 127.

19 See A. D. Braddeley and G. J. Hitch, 'Developments in the Concept of Working Memory', *Neuropsychology*, 8 (1994), 485–93. This definition of working memory should not be confused with an earlier use of the term by David Olton, who was talking about the role of the hippocampus in learning and memory when the solution of a problem requires memory for a particular recent event.

20 This distinction between episodic and semantic memory was first introduced by Tulving in 1972. For a more recent discussion, see E. Tulving, 'Episodic Memory: From Mind to Brain', *Annual Review of Psychology*, 53 (2002), 1–25.

21 For a good and easily understood discussion of these differences in types of memory, see the chapter on 'The Biology of Learning and Memory' in Kalat, *Biological Psychology*, 391–4.

22 We should point out that the mere exposure effect is most likely to occur when exposure time is very brief, less than one second. This means that it is unlikely to be a factor for

normal exposure to advertising, but only when someone is skimming a magazine or glancing at a poster, or when the radio or television is on but unattended. See R. B. Zajunce 'Attitudinal Effects of Mere Exposure', *Journal of Personality and Social Psychology Monograph*, 9/2, pt. 2 (1968), 1–27.

23 Necker's cube was discovered by a Swiss crystallographer, L. A. Necker, in 1832, while he was drawing rhomboid crystals seen with a microscope.

24 See Daniel L. Schacter, *The Seven Sins of Memory* (Boston: Houghlin Mifflin Company, 2001).

25 Emotion in advertising is not only misunderstood, but often ignored. K. Fletcher, in *A Glittering Haze* (Henley-on-Thames: NTC, 1992), points out that, when practitioners talk about advertising, they are more likely to talk in terms of information than any emotional contribution.

26 The research results are from a proprietary study conducted by Åke Wissing & Co.

27 The central idea of affect programme theory is that emotional responses are complex, coordinated, and automated, and has been extensively discussed by Ekman and his colleagues in terms of how they are experienced (for example, in Paul Ekman and W. V. Friesen, 'A New Pan-Cultural Facial Expression of Emotion', *Motivation and Emotion*, 10/2 (1986), 1159–68. Paul Griffiths places the entire affect programme in perspective in *What Emotions Really Are* (Chicago: University of Chicago Press, 1997), 77–9.

28 These primary emotions are discussed by Damasio in *The Feeling of What Happens* (San Diego, Calif.: Harcourt, 1999), 50–1.

29 See Griffiths, *What Emotions Really Are*, 20.

30 See ibid.

31 See Damasio, *The Feeling of What Happens*, 21.

32 The limbic system was first described by Paul MacLean in 1949. For a good discussion, see Eichenbaum, *The Cognitive Neuroscience of Memory*, 264–5.

33 These physiological responses are pointed out by Paul Griffith, *What Emotions Really Are*, 29–30.

34 A good discussion of this notion of embodiment may be found in P. M. Niedenthal, L. W. Barsalou, F. Riz, and S. Krauth-Gruber, 'Embodiment in the Acquisition and Use of Emotion Knowledge', in L. F. Barnett, P. M. Niedenthal, and P. Winkleman (eds), *Emotion and Consciousness* (New York: The Guilford Press, 2005), 21–50.

35 See B. de Geldner, 'Nonconscious Emotions: New Findings and Perspectives on Nonconscious Facial Expression and its Voice and Whole Body Context', in Barnett, Niedenthal, and Winkleman, *Emotion and Consciousness*, 123–49.

36 A number of studies related to how eyebrows and the mouth express emotion are reported in D. Linquist and A. Öhman, 'Caught by the Evil Eye: Nonconscious Information Processing, Emotion, and Attention to Facial Stimuli', in Barnett, Niedenthal, and Winkleman, *Emotion and Consciousness*, 97–122.

37 See A. J. Fridland, *Human Facial Expression: An Evolutionary View* (New York: Academic Press, 1994).

38 The implications of this and emotion in general for advertising is discussed by L. Percy in 'Unconscious Processing of Advertising and its Effects upon Attitude and Behaviour', in

S. Diehl and R. Terlutter (eds), *International Advertising and Communication* (Wiesbaden: Deutschen-Universitäts-Verlag, 2006) 110–21.

39 See A. R. Damasio, *Descartes' Error: Emotion, Reason, and the Human Brain* (New York: Grosset/Putnam, 1994).

40 See J. A. Russell, 'Core Affect and the Psychological Construction of Emotion', *Psychological Review* 110/1 (2003), 145–72.

41 See M. Chen and J. A. Bargh, 'Consequences of Automatic Evaluation: Immediate Behavioural Predispositions to Approach or Avoid the Stimulus', *Personality and Social Psychology Bulletin*, 25/2 (1999), 215–24.

42 John Rossiter and Steve Bellman offer a number of examples of how this idea of Type 1 and Type 2 emotions can be seen in the advertising of major companies, in their book *Marketing Communication: Theory and Practice* (French Forest, NSW: Pearson Education Australia, 2005) 55–6.

43 See Damasio, *Descartes' Error: Emotion, Reason, and the Human Brain*.

44 See Eichenbaum, *The Cognitive Neuroscience of Memory*, 200.

45 As Bryan Kolb and Ian Whishaw point out (*The Fundamentals of Neuropsychology*, 542), this principle of a rational relation between emotion and cognition being controlled by overlapping neural systems is found in all major theories of emotion, especially Damasio's somatic marker hypothesis, Le Doux's cognitive-social interaction theory, and Gainotti's asymmetry theory.

46 John R. Rossiter and Steven Bellman, 'A Proposed Model for Explaining and Measuring Web Ad Effectiveness', *Journal of Current Issues and Research in Advertising*, 21/1 (Spring 1999), 13–31.

 Visit the Online Resource Centre that accompanies this book for additional resources to support the text: http://www.oxfordtextbooks.co.uk/orc/percy_elliott3e/

12

Creative Tactics

 KEY CONCEPTS

1 There are a number of general creative tactics based upon how the mind processes words and pictures that will help increase attention and learning.

2 There are also specific creative tactics that can be used to help minimize the 'imperfections' of memory and help increase memory for advertising messages.

3 Creative tactics for brand awareness strategies must take into account the differences between recognition and recall brand awareness objectives.

4 When dealing with informational brand attitude strategies the key creative tactic is how the benefit claim support is presented and the key creative tactic for transformational brand attitude strategies is the emotional portrayal.

Up to this point we have been concerned with communication strategy, and our focus has been on '*what* to say' in advertising and other forms of marketing communication. In this chapter we will turn our attention to '*how* to say it'. Creative tactics deal with the ways in which words and pictures are used in marketing communication to deliver the message. As we shall see, this is a much more involved issue than it might appear on the surface, because meaning in communication is dependent upon many things beyond the obvious content of the message. For example, the semantic and grammatical structure of copy can have a significant effect upon how well a message will be understood, as well as the way in which visual illustrations are presented.

The reason it is so important to understand this sort of thing is that the easier we make it for our target audience to process and understand our message, the more likely we are to achieve the desired communication effect. You will remember that in Chapter 4 we talked about a communication response sequence and McGuire's notion of compound probabilities. After exposure, the next step in the response sequence is *processing*. The more people who *correctly* process the message, the greater the number of people likely to make a positive response to the message. We talked more about processing in the previous chapter. After someone has paid attention to an advert or other marketing communication, it is then necessary for him or her to *learn* what we wish to communicate, and, when dealing with high-involvement decisions, to *accept* the message as well (what McGuire calls 'yielding').

In this chapter we will be discussing a number of general principles concerning how to use words and pictures to optimize attention and learning. It is important to remember as we discuss these principles that they are not immutable laws. They represent the results of research in the areas of psycho-linguistics and visual imagery, and we know that, when they are followed, the likelihood of attention and learning increases. But this is not to say that they must be followed in all circumstances for advertising to be effective. Adverts are made up of a rich combination of words and pictures, and their creative use can sometimes produce interactions between and among the words and pictures that 'override' a particular principle.

The principles hold generally, and should always be a starting point, but they should not be used out-of-hand to dismiss a creative idea. However, when not following one of these principles it is *essential* to test the creative in order to be sure it is effective even though it is not following a particular linguistic or imagery principle. After we have discussed these general principles, we will be looking more specifically at the creative tactics needed to effect the correct brand awareness and brand attitude communication objectives.

Tactics for Attention

When we consider what creative tactics can help maximize attention, particularly *initial* attention, we must be concerned not only with how the advertising or other marketing communication is put together, but also the effect of the creative unit chosen. Creative units are such things as the size of a print advert (for example, full page, half page, two-page spread) or the length of a radio or television commercial (for example, 15, 30, or 60 seconds). In many ways the creative unit is important in media planning, but first and foremost it is a *tactical creative* decision. The creative unit must be considered in terms of the best way to deliver the message, not to satisfy a media plan.

In fact, long ago Rossiter showed that as much as half the variation among print adverts, in terms of their ability to attract and hold attention, is accounted for by the advertising's *structure*. It is a print advert's length, size, and pattern layout, *not* its message content, that has the greatest effect upon attention.[1]

Creative Units and Attention

The most important factor in terms of creative units for generating attention in radio and television advertising is the length of the commercial. Attention to both radio and television commercials is directly related to length. Longer commercials stimulate greater attention than shorter ones, but the relationship is not proportional. For example, while a 60-second commercial will gain more attention than a 30-second commercial, the increase in attention is only about 20 per cent, not double; and, while a 15-second commercial attracts less attention than a 30-second commercial, it will generate about 80 per cent of the attention of a 30-second commercial, not merely half.[2]

Maintaining interest in television commercials, that is *holding* attention, requires a different presentation pattern for informational versus transformational executions. With informational commercials, we want to stimulate immediate interest in the 'problem' as presented, followed by a brief pause in the action as the brand's identity is established, then building to a peak again as the 'solution' via the brand is established. With transformational executions, we want the interest to build throughout the commercial, peaking at the end with strong brand identity. This follows the idea of human evaluative conditioning, which underlies how transformational advertising tends to work.[3]

This same rule of thumb also applies to print advertising. Larger ads tend to attract more attention than smaller ads, but not proportionately. Table 12.1 demonstrates this general rule for newspaper and magazine adverts.[4]

Table 12.1 Advert Size and Attention

Advert Size	Attention Index	
	Consumer and Business Magazine Adverts	Newspaper Adverts
2 Pages	1.3	1.2
1 Page	1.0	1.0
1/2 Page	0.7	0.7
1/4 Page	—	0.5

Source: Adapted from J. R. Rossiter and L. Percy, *Advertising Communication and Promotion Management* (New York: McGraw-Hill, 1997).

Word and Picture Influence on Attention

The key to attention in print-based marketing communication is the words chosen and the illustration; with broadcast communication it is the initial audio (words or music); and with television or the Internet, the visuals. The reality of advertising and most other marketing communication is that people simply are not inclined to pay attention. Why should they? It is the job of good advertising to draw attention to itself, and in so doing communicate quickly at the very least a good positive brand attitude, and *resonate* with the target audience. Good strategy helps increase the likelihood of resonance, but the appropriate creative tactics help ensure it. What we mean by resonance is a recognition by the target audience that a particular advert is talking to it about something with which it is concerned. If you are not in the target audience, the advertising is unlikely to resonate, but it should leave a positive feeling for the brand. All this must occur during the attentional response.

In order to maximize the likelihood of gaining attention, marketing communication must pay careful attention to the ways in which the words in a headline or sub-head and in the initial audio of broadcast advertising are used, and how the visuals and video are presented. In this section we will review some of the things we know about how words and pictures can help attract attention (see Table 12.2).

Attention and Words

In a very insightful analysis of words in advertising, Greg Myers has pointed out that 'when there are many ads competing for the audience's attention, there is an enormous pressure on finding patterns of language that are unusual or memorable'.[5] He goes on to suggest that one of the simplest ways to call attention to words in marketing communication, at least with the printed word, is to use unexpected letters. This can be accomplished, for example, by using infrequently encountered letters, such as *q*, *x*, or *z* (think of brands such as Exxon or Oxo), or by deliberately altering the spelling of words (Smooooth!).

You are no doubt familiar with the logo for French Connection UK. The FCUK logo attracts and holds attention because of the unexpectedness of what is first 'seen', and

Table 12.2 How to Use Words and Pictures to Gain Attention

Words	• Use unexpected words or infrequently used letters such as Q, X, or Z
	• Vary emphasis or stress of certain words in headlines or audio content, or use them in unexpected ways
	• Keep headlines to fewer than 7–8 words
Pictures	• Use larger pictures
	• Use colour
	• Keep visual cuts in commercials to fewer than 20 per 30-second advert
	• Use pictures that hold attention for at least 2 seconds

then the realization that it is not what the mind originally understood the word to be. While still somewhat controversial, it is a very good example of using something unexpected to gain attention.

Another way to draw attention to advertising is to vary the emphasis or stress of certain words in a headline or in the audio content of commercials, or to use them in unexpected ways. Our ear is accustomed to hearing things in a particular way, and when it confronts something unexpected, we pay attention. For example, in normal conversation we are not likely to emphasize conjunctions such as *or* and *and*. But, if the emphasis is placed on a conjunction, it is likely to attract your attention because you are not used to hearing this. Consider this line from a Baxter's soup advert:

What makes Baxters soup is what makes it

Now, suppose you heard the line as follows (or even saw it printed this way as a headline):

What makes Baxters soup IS what makes it

The unexpected emphasis on *is* draws attention not only to the line, but also to the *relationship* between 'What makes Baxters soup' and its ingredients, 'what makes it'.

Headline Length

Another aspect of how words can influence attention to printed marketing communication is the *length* of the headline. Psychologists have found that when the number of words in a sentence or phrase is less than seven or eight, all that is required to understand what is there is simply exposure.[6] You do not really need to *read* the words to know what they say, only to *see* them. Look at this headline:

REVEAL A FRESH FROM THE SPA GLOW EVERY TIME YOU CLEANSE

If you only glance at this headline, all you really 'see' is a block of words, perhaps picking out one or two. Most people looking at this briefly will 'see' only the words *reveal*, *fresh*, and perhaps *spa glow*. To get any meaning from this headline you must *read* it. Now, look at this headline:

Unlock your smile

Just glancing at this conveys the full content. It is not necessary to 'read' it to understand what it says. This is because the mind processes text not one word at a time, but in sets as you read.

This means that, when you turn the page of a newspaper or magazine, the reflexive attention you automatically pay briefly to the new page to decide whether or not there is anything there worth paying particular attention to is sufficient to comprehend a headline if it is short enough. This is especially important for poster and outdoor adverts. To work, they must be able to communicate at a glance.

Look at the two adverts below for Mack. Advert 12.1*a* is the same as Advert 11.2, already discussed in the previous chapter in connection with the topic of selective attention. This campaign was recognized by over half the people in its Swedish market. But what

(a)

(b)

Advert 12.1 The addition of the promotion in advert 12.1*b* over the base poster shown in advert 12.1*a* significantly reduced the likelihood of the advertising being processed.

Source: Åke Wissing & Co and Clear Channel Sverige AB.

happens when a promotion banner is added in Advert 12.1*b*? Recognition for this promotion is only 20 per cent. Why? The problem is that, even though the new promotion copy in the banner is only a few words, and should be easily processed, it is fighting the words under it. As a result, people recognize the look and feel of the overall campaign, and so recognize it as a Mack advert. But, they do not process the new information about the special price. In effect, they simply do not 'see' the promotion banner, as we discussed in Chapter 11 when talking about seeing what we expect to see (top-down processing).

Attention and Pictures

As you might imagine, pictures play a more important role in gaining attention than do words. This is especially true of print advertising.[7] In fact, the average time spent looking at a magazine advert is about 1.65 seconds, and 70 per cent of that time is spent with the picture.[8] Without an effective picture to attract readers' attention and draw them to the text, it is unlikely the advertising will work. The size of the picture and the use of colour can significantly affect the ability of a print advert to attract attention. In terms of picture size, the larger the image, the more effective it will be. There is an old rule of thumb in advertising that recognition of print adverts increases roughly with the square root of the size of the picture. In other words, if you increase the size of the picture in an advert four times, attention will double. While this holds for all print adverts, with high-involvement executions, in addition to one dominant focal point, there should be a short headline designed to engage the reader's attention and make them want to read the advert.

Table 12.3 Colour and Attention

Colour	Attention Index	
	Consumer and Business Magazine Adverts	**Newspaper Adverts**
Four-Colour	1.0	1.8
Two-Colour	0.8	1.5
Black and White	0.7	1.0

Source: Adapted from J. R. Rossiter and L. Percy, *Advertising Communication and Promotion Management* (New York: McGraw-Hill, 1997).

Regarding the use of colour, in both magazines and newspapers full colour draws more attention than two-colour, and two-colour more attention than black-and-white. While it is sometimes argued that using black-and-white adverts in a magazine where all the other advertising is in colour will attract more attention because it will stand out, there is no real proof that this is the case. Table 12.3 summarizes the probable difference in attention to an advert in both magazines and newspapers in terms of colour. For magazine adverts, attention to a black-and-white advert is likely to be about 30 per cent less than to a standard four-colour advert, and 20 per cent less than to a two-colour advert. With newspapers, the use of two colours tends to increase attention 50 per cent over a standard black-and-white advert; and the use of four colours 80 per cent. While these estimates may be somewhat overstated for all-colour, there is still no question that colour will be significantly more effective. Again, this argues against the notion of using a black-and-white advert to stand out in an otherwise all-colour newspaper format.

Pictures, of course, dominate almost all television commercials. In terms of attention, an important consideration is the pacing of the scenes in the commercial. There has been a great deal of talk in recent years about the so-called MTV generation, and how young audiences are used to, and demand, rather frantic, fast-cut editing of visual content. Unfortunately, when the average scene time drops, so too does attention. In fact, at an 'MTV rate' of twenty or more cuts per thirty-second commercial, the attention loss is about 17 per cent. And, even more interestingly, the loss of attention is an even *greater* 25 per cent among that very 18–34-year-old MTV generation.[9]

Before leaving the subject of pictures and attention, it is important to understand that it is not enough to look for pictures that will attract attention; pictures must *hold* attention. A number of psychological experiments have shown that pictures are recognized and remembered best if they can hold the reader's attention for at least two seconds.[10] This helps explain why attention to television commercials drops when cuts in the visual come too rapidly. Remember too that attention is only the first step in the processing of marketing communication. Attention means very little in and of itself if it does not lead to fuller processing of the message *for the target audience*.

Look at the advert for Anthisan PLUS (Plate XI). This is a really excellent example of much of what we have been talking about. The picture is large, and uses the novelty of the spray container as a flying insect to *attract* attention, and the obvious link to the product category to *hold* attention. The headline, 'FLYING DOCTOR', uses words in a unique and unexpected way, tied directly to the picture. It is short, and easily processed with the picture and brand name at a glance. The sub-head, 'FAST, ANAESTHETIC STING RELIEF', is also easily understood without reading as the eye moves down the page. A brief exposure to this ad, even if simply flipping through the pages of a magazine, will attract attention and communicate the intended benefit of sting relief with Anthisan PLUS. This is a *very* good example of using words and pictures to attract and hold attention.

Attention and Music

Music is frequently a part of broadcast advertising, and in general, does seem to have a positive effect upon attention. But not just any music will do. One should be careful to ensure there is congruity between both the execution,[11] and if a radio commercial, the station's format. At the same time, popular songs should generally be avoided, unless the words to the song are not easily remembered. Otherwise, the target audience will be more likely to sing the words of the song to themselves rather than rehearse the brand name and key benefit.[12]

Music can also have a significant effect upon sales in a retail setting. There have been several studies that have shown that appropriate music will have a positive influence on sales. In one study, the tempo of the music played in a supermarket was varied between an 'easy listening' tempo of 60 beats per minute and a 'rock' tempo of 120 beats per minute. Sales were 38 per cent higher with the 60 bpm tempo![13] One possible reason for this could be that 60 bpm is the heartrate of the average person. Another study has shown that the content of music as well as tempo can influence sales.[14]

Tactics for Learning

We know that, for any marketing communication to be successful, once someone has been exposed to it and has paid attention, he or she must fully process the message if the marketer is to achieve the desired communication effect. William J. McGuire, perhaps the foremost expert on attitude change theory, about whom we talked when we discussed the communication response sequence in Chapter 4, once remarked about communicating with advertising that it is not enough to lead a horse to water, you must push his head under to get him to drink.[15] Anything we can do to help make it easier for our target audience to process our message makes it more likely it will be correctly understood, and more likely we will achieve the desired communication effect.

The words and pictures we use obviously play the most important role in delivering the message, but *how* we use them can provide a real plus. A great deal of research has been done in this area, especially by psycho-linguists and psychologists working in visual imagery, providing insight into the ways in which words and pictures can be used to facilitate learning. As we know, learning is essential for all marketing communication. In this section we will review a number of specific ways in which to use words and pictures to increase the likelihood that our target audience will learn what we want them to from our advertising or other marketing communication.

Words and Learning

It may seem almost too obvious to suggest that you must pay attention to what you say in advertising copy if it is to be understood. While this is certainly true, less obvious is the effect the way in which words are used may have on how they are understood. The often complex relationship between the linguistic construction of copy and the way the mind deals with it in processing the message is known as psycho-linguistics.

We talked in a previous section about using words in unexpected ways to help attract attention. While this will certainly help gain attention, unfortunately the use of unfamiliar words in copy can get in the way of learning. There are literally dozens of studies that have shown that using familiar words in familiar ways helps learning.[16] This illustrates a problem McGuire identified long ago. Often the things that help attract attention in communication are the very things that get in the way of comprehension or acceptance of the message.[17] What this means for us is that, while we may want to use an unfamiliar word or use words in an unexpected way as part of a headline to gain attention, we do not want this in the sub-heads or copy, where learning is the objective.

Concrete, High-Imagery Words

One interesting concept in psycho-linguistics that has a direct bearing upon copy in marketing communication, especially in advertising, is the notion of the 'concreteness' of the words used. Concrete words are generally described as those that refer to objects, persons, places, or things that can be experienced by the senses; those that do not are called abstract. Concrete words are more effective than abstract words in communicating ideas, and are better remembered. Think back to the headline of the Anthisan PLUS advert: 'FLYING DOCTOR' in Plate XI. This is a good example of a concrete headline.

The reason concrete words help with learning is that they tend to arouse mental images quickly and easily.[18] While it is certainly not impossible, strictly speaking, for more abstract words to evoke visual images, it is a lot less likely. Consider the following headlines taken from adverts in a UK women's magazine:

Because it really matters
For skin this soft
Some days matter

Which of these headlines bring a visual image to mind? Most likely only 'For skin this soft'. This is concrete, while the others are more abstract. You can 'see' or imagine soft skin, but it is more difficult to focus upon a specific image for 'Because it really matters' or 'Some days matter'. Imagery value is important in facilitating easier communication and learning.[19]

Using Negatives

Overall, people are much more likely to make favourable rather than unfavourable judgements. As a result, in every language, for example, there are far more favourable than unfavourable adjectives. Additionally, a lot of research has shown that negative words or constructs are difficult to process, and should be avoided in communication. To understand the meaning of negative words or constructions requires a two-step process. You must recognize the negative for what it is, then 'reverse' the meaning. As a result, there is a chance someone may misunderstand or overlook the negative while processing the message.

Consider this headline from a cruise line advert: 'This is not a normal day'. What the mind must do is consider first what is a 'normal day', then negate it—assuming the eye picked up *not*, and didn't skim over it. You may be thinking to yourself that this is making a lot out of very little. After all, who is likely to misunderstand? Not many, we would hope, but some will. It depends upon the focus.

In an interesting study dealing with just this issue, it was found that, when two claims are made and one is stated in the negative, misunderstanding is greater when the negative claim is second.[20] People were asked to read one of the following headlines, and decide whether taste or calories was the main emphasis (and to the advertiser, the answer was taste):

It's the taste that counts, not just the calories
It's not just the calories, it's the taste that counts

The number of people correctly saying 'taste' was only 77 per cent in the first example versus 85 per cent in the second. This is because the negative claim in the second example is not necessary to process the claim correctly, but it must be processed in the first example. Again, you may be thinking this is not much of a difference, but remember we need to ensure that the maximum number of people make it through the communication response sequence.

What do you make of this sub-head from a deodorant advert?

No, not the twit pressing the nozzle

Here we have an odd example of two negatives where one is *not* meant to negate the other. The juxtaposition of the two makes it quite easy to misunderstand the sentence as 'Yes, the twit pressing the nozzle', if you are just glancing at the copy and not reading it. What do you make of this headline from a Shell advert, 'Say No To No'? In fact, negative constructions are not often used in marketing communication, and for good reason. Why ask your target audience to go to the extra effort and time of dealing with the two steps needed to process negative constructions correctly?

Using Puns

Puns are a way of playing with meaning, and puns are often found in advertising. This is especially true of advertising in the UK, where both visual and verbal puns are often found in abundance. Look at these advert headlines from a single issue of a UK women's magazine:

> For a healthy diet—this Paper needs Fibre too!
> Anything less simply won't wash
> Have a shower with everything on
> Big cheeses on the board watch out
> When soap and water are out of reach

Without knowing the product being advertised, what do these headlines tell you? Even with the full advert in front of you, they require a lot of work, and that is the problem. Does it help you to know that these headlines advertise, respectively, the use of raw material in the paper industry, bathroom accessories, showers, cream cheese, and hand-cleaning gel? Perhaps a little, but not much.

Puns do require more work to process,[21] and, as we have said over and over in this chapter, our job is to make it *easier*, not harder, for the target audience to process our message. This is what facilitates learning. At the root of most puns are homonyms, words that have the same spelling or sound, but different meanings. (Did you know that the word 'taste' has some thirty-two meanings in *Webster's Unabridged Dictionary*?) Does this mean we should never use puns? No, but if used the meaning must be obvious, and reinforce the benefit. Ultra Chloraseptic's advert for their anaesthetic throat spray does get it right with the headline 'Don't be a sucker…Spray.' The word 'sucker' is appropriate both in its meaning of not being a 'fool' and not using hard candy-like throat medication.

Sentence Structure

The issue of how sentences are put together has a real impact upon how easy it will be to process marketing communication, and the likelihood that correct learning will occur. Unfortunately, it is beyond the scope of this book to go very deeply into this, because it is a very complex area. In fact, many of those who have studied it find it a very complicated subject with which to deal.[22]

It is important that we understand that there can be difficulties when sentence structure becomes more complicated, even with such a seemingly simple thing as where a clause is placed. To avoid potential problems, keep things *simple*. For example, we know that it is much easier to process and understand active than passive sentences. Researchers have found that passive sentences take longer to process correctly, and the likelihood of understanding passive sentences tends to be lower.

Let's look at this sub-headline:

A fluoride supplement should be taken by children living in non-fluoride water areas

This is written in the passive voice. The grammatical subject is actually the psychological object. In effect, the passive construction has reversed the order in which words are usually encountered. We know that human memory is affected greatly by the order in which words are encountered. What if this were written in the active voice?

Children living in non-fluoride water areas should take a fluoride supplement

While the meaning of both sentences is the same, the active construction will be easier to process. In addition, the main focus of the sentence, 'children living in non-fluoride water areas', is encountered first, and that will provide the desired cue in memory for fluoride supplements. If you were living in a non-fluoride water area and had children, which of these sentences would be most likely to catch your eye if you were flipping through a magazine containing this advert? You are much more likely to pay attention to something about your children than something about fluoride supplements, and that is how we want learning and memory to occur. We want the parent to learn 'my children need a fluoride supplement', *not* 'fluoride supplements are for my children'.

The form of a sentence itself can also aid message processing. Myers provides the example of the following Mars bar slogan:

A Mars® a Day Helps You Work Rest and Play

He points out that this slogan will be memorable primarily because it draws attention to its *focus*. It establishes a rhythm, and it rhymes 'play' with 'day'. Also, of course, it echoes the old saying that 'An apple a day keeps the doctor away.'[23]

Another possible way sentences can help facilitate processing of a message is by suggesting a personal, face-to-face interaction between the reader or viewer and the advertising. When you use such things as questions or strong declarative statements, you imply a certain sense of one person talking to another.[24] Look at the following headlines:

Help replace the moisture your day takes away
Love cheddar?
What could be causing my headaches?
Hold that look!
Which one's for you?

Each of these headlines engages you in an almost personal conversation because of their use of a personal question or declarative statement. This sense of personal address will help facilitate processing (even though several of these headlines have more words in them than one would like).

Pictures and Learning

While the old adage of a picture being worth a thousand words may not be literally true, there is certainly a well-understood superiority of pictures over words in learning.[25] In fact, with most print advertising some 70 per cent of the looking at the advert is directed to the picture. One of the reasons for this superiority of pictures over words is the way in which people interact with pictures. As we have just noted, one of the ways words can be used to help facilitate learning is by using strong declarative sentences or questions, because this tends to engage the reader. Pictures automatically engage the reader or viewer, but in a different way.

When we read a sentence or listen to dialogue our mind tends to provide an answer or response in words. Pictures, on the other hand, have the ability to provoke a much more elaborate response. Myers offers a good example of this. You would no doubt be very sceptical if you read or heard a claim that a particular brand of soap could make anyone beautiful. But if this same claim was *implied* by a picture of a beautiful woman holding the soap, you would be a lot less sceptical.[26] Additional support for the superiority of pictures over words comes from work by Bryce and Yalch.[27] They showed that information conveyed visually is significantly better learned than the same information content conveyed in the audio. As we look at any picture, a relationship is established between the viewer and the image. This goes for any visual image, from adverts to great works of art. There will be something about the picture that draws us to it. Depending upon the image itself, we will imagine ourselves as either *part* of what is shown in the picture, or *outside* observing what is there. The space between the viewer and the actual picture is something Shearman has called *liminal space*, and it becomes in many ways an extension of the picture itself.[28] Why should we be concerned with such a seemingly abstract notion as the space in front of a picture? Because in certain cases we will want our target audience to feel it is present and a part of the situation depicted in the advertising, while in other cases we will want it to feel it is outside the situation. The execution of the illustration or visuals in the advertising will dictate how the viewer will feel, and this applies not only to print advertising, but also to television.[29]

Myers offers an interesting observation along these lines. He reminds us that pictures provide a point of view in much the same way as pronouns do in language. When there are people in advertising, their positions and where they are looking is important to how we respond. Pictures can also suggest prior or future action, as well as context for evaluation.[30] Getting all this consistent with the message is critical to effective processing. Myers also makes an interesting point about the gaze of principal figures in advertising. He suggests that more often you will find women in advertising looking out at the reader or viewer while male figures are more likely to 'keep to their own business'.[31] This observation may be anecdotal, but it is interestingly consistent with the pop-psychology idea that women are more concerned with bonding when communicating with people while men are more concerned with establishing dominance.

Next, we will turn our attention to five areas where we know there are direct relationships between the picture and learning: the size of the picture, the use of colour, showing the product with users or in use, high-imagery pictures, and word-picture interaction.

Picture Size

We have already talked about how larger pictures tend to attract more attention. It also seems that, the larger the picture, the more visual images the mind will generate, and this, in turn, leads to better learning.[32] Research has shown that picture size has a positive impact on beliefs and brand attitude. In fact, it would seem that, the larger the picture, the more favourable your attitude towards the advertised product.[33]

There is only one print advertising situation where picture size is not important: direct-response advertising with long copy. With direct-response advertising, memory is not a significant factor, because the target audience is expected to respond immediately. Also, since a lot of direct-response advertising involves high-involvement product decisions, a great deal of information is needed to convince the reader to make a decision 'right now'. Consequently, there is a necessary trade-off between the space needed for a larger picture and that needed for more detailed copy. But, in all other cases, the larger the picture, the better.

Colour versus Black and White

Just as with picture size, we saw earlier that colour positively influences the gaining of attention. But colour also has a significant effect upon processing generally. Some years ago two psychologists in the research laboratories of Xerox Corporation demonstrated that the principal effect of colour in communication is motivation.[34] If all you need to do is communicate information, black-and-white pictures could be enough. This means you should *never* use black-and-white pictures with advertising addressing positive motives. However, with informational advertising, black and white can be quite effective.

Product and User

People are more likely to learn something from advertising if they can make a familiar association with its content. This is known as *associative learning*, and is aided by pictures that show the product being used in some way rather than leaving it up to the reader or viewer to infer interaction between the product and the user or how the product is used.[35] The importance of interactive pictures or visuals is underscored when we consider the motivation underlying behaviour. People often buy status goods or other products because they suggest a particular image with which they wish to be associated, as we saw when we discussed positive motives and transformational advertising. On the other hand, when you are dealing with negative motives and informational advertising, a product or brand must be seen as suitable for solving or avoiding a problem. Showing users interacting with a product, or seeing a product in use, helps connect the product with the motive to purchase or use.

While it is quite common to find these types of interactions in television advertising, they are much less common in print. Too often we see a picture of a user or endorser next to, but not using, the product; or the context for usage is discussed in the copy, but not shown visually. It is important in print adverts as well as in television to show the brand being used. Look at the Sparkford advert shown in Plate XII. It provides a very good example of how a series of pictures within a print advert can provide a real sense of 'whatever you're looking for...' in crafted timber products. The product is clearly being presented 'in use', and strongly connected to the motivation of solving a problem, associated with a range of potential needs.

High-Imagery Pictures

We saw earlier that concrete, high-imagery words help facilitate learning. The same is true of concrete or high-imagery pictures. More concrete, higher-imagery pictures are those that tend to arouse *other* mental images quickly and easily. They are more realistic than abstract, low-imagery pictures. These realistic pictures are probably superior for learning for at least two reasons. First of all, people can relate more to concrete representations than to abstract ones. This in turn is probably a function of their *imagery* value, regardless of their specific content. Secondly, because of something psychologists call *dual coding*, people can more easily attach a verbal label to realistic visuals. Older children and adults automatically assign verbal labels to all but the most complex and novel pictures, and thus 'double-code' them in their minds as both picture *and* words.[36] For example, if you were to see a picture of an apple, you would encode not only the image of the apple in your mind, but also the label 'apple'.

Many television ads use animation, and often you see cartoons or drawings in print adverts. This can in fact be very realistic because of its simplified rendering of its subject. Using this technique can basically 'strip' its subject to its essential denotative characters, making them very concrete.[37]

Word–Picture Interaction

In a very interesting study it was found that learning is significantly increased if the eye confronts a *picture–word* rather than a *word–picture* sequence.[38] This may seem to imply that you should always place the headline in an advert towards the bottom of the page so that the picture will be easily seen first, but this is not necessary. The eye is generally drawn initially to an illustration, so an effective use of the picture relative to the headline will ensure that it is seen first, regardless of where the headline is placed. Look at the advert for Fairy non-biological detergent (shown in Plate XIII). There is no question that the eye goes first to the picture, then to the headline at the top of the page. Even though the headline is positioned first, its size relative to the picture means the eye is drawn first to the picture. What happens is that, when the picture is seen first, it tends to draw the reader into the advert to maximize communication, and, as a result, facilitates learning. This same point also applies to television. Important spoken copy-points or printed 'supers' should either be *preceded* by an appropriate visual introduction or introduced simultaneously.

The advert for Colron Refined Danish Oil in Plate XIV offers a very good example of each of the points just discussed for using pictures to help facilitate learning. In terms of Shearman's idea of liminal space, appropriately you are meant to be 'outside' of the action, observing the loveseat that was polished with the product. The picture is large, and dominates the page (without filling it); and its unique imagery encourages visual elaboration to wood furniture of your own. The use of colour is especially well done, drawing attention to the wood. Even though this is an informational driven decision, the effective use of colour within the white space reinforces the benefit. The product is also shown 'in use', resulting in the 'beautiful wood sheen lustre' on the loveseat. As mentioned above, it uses a high-imagery picture, and the eye moves first to the picture, and then the copy. This is an excellent example of how a strong and compelling visual image can be used to quickly and easily communicate a benefit, and link it to the brand.

Tables 12.2 and 12.4 summarize how words and pictures are used to maximize attention to, and the learning of, marketing communication.

Minimizing Problems with Memory

In the last chapter we spent a good deal of time talking about memory, and discussed a number of problems inherent in how memory works that can interfere with successful remembering. However, because we are aware of these problems, there are a number of creative tactics that can be utilized to help minimize them.

Perhaps the most important tactical consideration is to ensure there is a *unique* brand–benefit link established to avoid misattribution of the message to another brand. To help

Table 12.4 How to Use Words and Pictures to Help Learning

Words	• Use familiar words
	• Use concrete, high-imagery words
	• Avoid negatives
	• Be careful with puns
	• Keep sentences simple
	• Avoid passive sentences
	• Suggest a personal interaction with the advertising
Pictures	• Be certain picture is consistent with intention for viewer to be included as observer
	• The larger the picture, the better
	• Use colour unless you only need to provide information
	• Show product being used or with user
	• Use high-imagery, concrete pictures or illustrations
	• Use pictures so that they are seen before words

get around absent-mindedness, use distinctive cues not likely to be associated with other long-term memories, and ensure a consistent 'look and feel' over time to encourage familiarity (a subject we will cover in more detail in Chapter 13). Look at the adverts in 12.2. They represent over a decade of advertising for H&M in Sweden. There is no doubt that the brand 'owns' this imagery, and that it is familiar to the target audience. This is an excellent example of a consistent look and feel over time. Consistently, well over half of the target market recognizes the advertising.[39] Other retailers in the market over the years attempted to copy this look, unsuccessfully. Why? As we learned in Chapter 11 when we talked about memory problems, the 'me-too' adverts were misattributed to H&M.

Also, to help avoid problems with absent-mindedness, establish links in memory to the appropriate category need. Make sure those links are well integrated with *obvious* associations to the category need to avoid blocking, as well as to tie the brand to appropriate emotions. Making sure the message is carefully integrated with how the brand is understood will help avoid transience, as will encouraging elaboration by the target audience of points they are interested in remembering. Using personal references, especially to positive memories, and implying current positive brand attitudes are of long standing, are ways to help capitalize upon memory bias.[40] These tactics are summarized in Table 12.5.

Brand Awareness and Brand Attitude Creative Tactics

Throughout this book we have discussed the importance of brand awareness and brand attitude as communication objectives for all marketing communication. In the previous chapter we specifically addressed this issue. Because of the nature of recognition versus

Advert 12.2 These poster adverts for H&M in Sweden over the years provide an excellent example of consistency in the look and feel of a campaign.

Source: Åke Wissing & Co. and Clear Channel Sverige AB.

Table 12.5 Creative Tactics for Minimizing Memory Problems

Minimizing Misattribution	• Create a unique brand-benefit claim link
Minimizing Absent-Mindedness	• Establish links in memory to appropriate category need • Use distinctive cues not likely to be associated with other long-term memories • Ensure a consistent 'look and feel' over time to encourage familiarity
Minimizing Blocking	• Make sure the link to category need is well integrated with *obvious* associations
Minimizing Transience	• Ensure message is carefully integrated with how brand is understood • Encourage elaboration of points the target audience is interested in remembering
Minimizing Bias	• Imply positive brand attitudes are of long standing • Use personal references, especially to positive memories

recall brand awareness and the differences in the four strategic brand attitude quadrants of the Rossiter–Percy grid, certain specific creative tactics are needed to ensure you will achieve these communication objectives.

Brand Awareness Creative Tactics

The number one task of brand awareness is to associate the *brand* with category need in the target audience's mind. As we have seen, brand awareness as a communication objective is more than simply being aware of the brand. The brand must be linked to the appropriate need in the target audience's mind when that need occurs. But before that can happen, marketing communication, and advertising in particular, must first be seen as 'belonging' to your brand. This is the only way the message can be associated with the brand. This may seem almost childishly obvious, but how often have you thought about a particular advert, perhaps because it was entertaining or unique in some way, but been unable to remember the brand being advertised?

Only after you are sure the message is firmly linked with the brand are you ready to address the issue of recognition versus recall brand awareness. You will remember from the previous chapter that the appropriate brand awareness objective is dependent upon the *choice situation*. When and how the brand choice is made dictates a recognition or recall brand awareness strategy, and what is needed to implement each strategy differs, as we discussed.

Recognition Brand Awareness

When the brand choice is activated at the point of purchase, such as when shopping at a supermarket or pharmacy, recognizing the brand in the store will remind the shopper of a need. This means that in advertising the creative execution must show the package as it will be seen at the point of purchase, and the category need must be obvious. Some advertisers for fmcgs actually create an advert that quite literally looks like the package. Even though there is some brief copy, the overall impression is one of the package itself as it will be encountered at the point of purchase.

Recall Brand Awareness

When the target audience must think of the brand prior to the point of purchase, the brand awareness objective is recall. A need occurs, and you must think of brands that might possibly meet that need. This means the creative execution must *clearly* link the need to the brand, *in that order*, and *repeat* the association. It also helps to personalize the association between the need and the brand. This is very easy to accomplish in radio and television advertising, but it is also needed in print when recall brand awareness is necessary.

These creative tactics for implementing brand awareness strategy are summarized in Table 12.6.

Brand Attitude Creative Tactics

The creative tactics needed for brand awareness help link the brand to the need. The creative tactics for brand attitude help *persuade* the target audience that your brand is the best alternative for satisfying the need.[41] In our discussions of brand attitude we referred to the expectancy-value model of attitude, where attitude towards an object (a brand in our case) is made up of what you believe about it weighted by the emotional importance attached to those beliefs, combined to form your overall attitude towards the brand. These same two considerations, beliefs and emotions, structure the creative tactics to be used to maximize brand attitude. Remember from our discussion in Chapter 9 of brand

Table 12.6 Brand Awareness Creative Tactics

Recognition	• Package must be shown as seen at the point of purchase
	• Category need must be obvious
Recall	• Category need must be clearly likened to the brand, and in that order
	• Repeat the association
	• Personalize the association between the need and the brand

Source: Adapted from J. R. Rossiter and L. Percy, *Advertising Communication and Promotion Management* (New York: McGraw-Hill, 1997).

attitude strategy that when dealing with informational brand attitude strategies we must be primarily concerned with the information being provided; when dealing with transformational brand strategies we must be primarily concerned with the emotion portrayed in the advertising.

Informational Brand Attitude

With informational brand attitude strategies, the key is how the *benefit claim support* is presented. When the decision is low involvement, you want to use a simple problem solution presentation of one or possibly two benefits. Since the decision is low involvement, use *extreme* benefit claims, such as:

No other gel works like it

Keeping skin amazing

Why? Because the message does not need to be accepted as literally true. All that is necessary is what Maloney years ago called 'curious disbelief'.[42] There is little risk involved in the choice decision, so you can exaggerate the benefit in order to tempt the audience to purchase. It is not necessary that you really believe a pain relief gel will literally work better than any other gel or that a moisturizer will really give you 'amazing' skin. You need feel only that the products *might* provide those benefits. If they do not meet your expectations, you simply do not repurchase.

But when you are dealing with a high-involvement decision, you should *not* overclaim, but keep the claim at an acceptable upper level. The benefit claims must be believable because the message must be accepted. The following benefit claims appeared in an advert for a washing machine:

load capacity that's 50% bigger than most

extra large door and a tilted drum for easy learning

specialized duvet cycle will cut out those trips to local dry cleaners

To be successful, the target audience must accept these claims as basically true. They are certainly pitched at an upper level of believability, especially the claim about cutting out trips to the cleaners. Because a cooker is a high-risk purchase, for someone to consider this brand, he or she must believe the substance of these claims.

Really this means that, to ensure a *convincing* presentation of the benefit claims, it is essential to understand what the target audience's attitudes are towards the products in the category and the brands within the category. Following our example, does the target audience believe it is possible for a washing machine to clean duvets? What about this brand? What is its reputation for reliability? For the benefit claims to be effective with high-involvement informational advertising, they must be within an acceptable range of believability among the target audience.

If you can actually deliver on a benefit, but the target audience finds it too far beyond its latitude of acceptance to believe, consider using a refutational strategy. With refutational advertising, the message begins by acknowledging the target audience does not believe the benefit claim, but then goes on to provide evidence to 'refute' or counter its disbelief. By acknowledging that people do not accept your claim, you begin by having them agree with you rather than immediately reject the message. This then gives you an opportunity to build your case. Once it has been made, repeat the benefit claim firmly.[43]

In all cases, with informational brand attitude strategies, the creative presentation of the benefit should follow an **a** → **c** or **e⁻** → **c** benefit focus (objective attribute supports a subjective claim for the brand or a negative emotion associated with a problem is resolved by a subjective characteristic associated with the brand). Looking back at the Whirlpool advert in the previous chapter (Advert 11.1), which reflects a high-involvement informational brand attitude strategy, we see an **a** → **c** benefit focus. 'The biggest door opening in the market' (a) is why it claims to be 'easier to unload' (c). The advert for Fairy laundry detergent (Plate XIII), which reflects a low-involvement informational brand attitude strategy, uses an **e⁻** → c benefit focus. The negative feelings that are associated with 'prickly' clothes (e⁻) are resolved by Fairy's 'soft' claim (c). In the low-involvement case only, a simple presentation of the benefit as a subjective characteristic of the product may also be considered as a benefit focus (c), as we see in the Anthisan PLUS advert (Plate XI): 'Fast, anaesthetic sting relief'.

The benefit should be presented in such a way that it is instantly clear what the benefit is when it is a claim about a subjective characteristic of the brand (c); that the connection is easily understood when an attribute of the product is offered in support of a claim about a subjective characteristic (**a** → **c**); or that when a claim about a subjective characteristic of the product is easily seen as resolving a negative emotional state associated with the product category (**e⁻** → **c**).

The creative tactics for informational brand attitude strategies are summarized in Fig. 12.1.

Transformational Brand Attitude

The key creative tactic for transformational brand attitude strategies is the emotional portrayal. With transformational strategies, the feelings evoked by the advertising are often the only brand benefit. As a result, it is absolutely essential that the creative execution be *unique* to the brand. Additionally, the target audience must like the advertising. Unlike advertising for informational strategies, where it is not really necessary actually to like the advertising *per se* because the execution embodies the benefit, in transformational advertising you must like the advertising to like the brand.[44]

In a vivid example of this, the actual identity and taste of beer in the USA are created quite literally by the advertising! In a very interesting study, beer-drinkers were asked to taste and evaluate a number of beers ranging from lower-calorie Miller Lite to premium beers like Budweiser, all the way through malt liquors and Guinness Stout. When the results of these taste evaluations were analysed, the 'lighter' beers were separated from the 'heavier' beers like malt liquor and stout. Also, the 'regular' beers were distinguished from the more 'premium' beers. The tastes of these beers were positioned just as their advertising presented them. However, a matched set of beer-drinkers went through the same exercise, but tasted the beers blind, not knowing what brands they were testing. When their taste evaluations were analysed, with the exception of the stout, *all the beers* were seen as tasting alike. Clearly, the 'taste' of these beers was defined by the emotional portrayal of the brands in their advertising.[45]

Key is the Benefit Claim Support

- Present problem first, resolved by brand
- Use only one or possibly two benefit claims for **low-involvement** decisions
- Present benefit claims in the extreme for **low-involvement** decisions
- Be careful not to overclaim for **high-involvement** decisions, staying within the target audience's acceptable level of attitude toward the category, product, and brand
- Consider a refutational approach if the brand can deliver the benefit but the target audience does not believe it
- Ensure that the execution elicits an emotional sequence that first associates the problem with some level of fear or anxiety, and then a sense of relief as the brand provides the solution
- Utilize an $a \rightarrow c$ or $e^- \rightarrow c$ benefit focus; or for **low-involvement** decisions a simple presentation as **c**, a subjective characteristic of the brand

Figure 12.1 Creative Tactics for Informational Brand Attitude Strategies

Because this idea of a correct emotional portrayal is so important to transformational advertising, we will take a closer look at just what this means. When you look at a good advert for perfume or fashion, you want to *imagine yourself* as being similar to the person in the advert. If you can see yourself (or your imagined self) in the advertising, the emotional portrayal is authentic and that feeling you get becomes the benefit for the brand.

But how would this work for something more generic? One way is to move up the emotional scale, linking the brand to how the consumer uses the product in an emotionally compelling way. One of the very best examples of the effective use of this tactic was the long-running series of commercials in UK for Oxo.[46] Oxo is a flavouring cube used in cooking. The Oxo commercials featured a typical family preparing and eating dinner, talking in a truly realistic way about things families do talk about: what is cooking, what went on at school, personal troubles, things that happened that day. The key to the success of this campaign was the emotional authenticity inherent in the creative execution. These were 'real' people, acting like real people. The family was seen as behaving in a natural and not exaggerated manner, at a meal where the brand is part of the meal being prepared. When an execution is seen as real and relevant, a warm emotional response to the advertising *and* brand results.

This response to the meal and its preparation, where Oxo is a part, becomes the brand's benefit. When the homemaker is shopping and sees the brand on the shelf, it will remind her of the warm feeling experienced when she saw the advertising, and this becomes the reason for purchase. This is not to suggest that she actually feels there is a cause and effect. It means only that the brand will be a catalyst, occasioning a positive feeling, and this can be reason enough to buy in an otherwise very generic product category.

Making sure the people shown in adverts dealing with transformational brand attitude strategies are seen as real people and not as actors is critical. This was key to the Oxo success.

Emotional authenticity is required for both low- and high-involvement transformational brand attitude strategies. In the high-involvement case, the emotional authenticity should be tailored to the lifestyle group to which the target audience belongs or to which it aspires. This will help the target audience *personally* identify with the emotional portrayal, a necessary condition because of the risk involved in the decisions. With high-involvement transformational strategies, because of the risk involved it may be necessary to provide some more tangible information to help facilitate acceptance of the message, as we discussed back in Chapter 9 when considering strategies for implementing high-involvement transformational strategies. When doing this it is often useful to overclaim a bit, but you must be careful not to go too far.

With transformational strategies, generally a strong visual component is critical, and that visual imagery must be unique to the brand. The emotional portrayal of the *brand* is part of the imagery created by the execution, so if it is seen as too much like the images associated with other brands, the target audience could feel it was able to enjoy the same benefit with any of these brands. This is often a problem with car advertising, high fashion advertising, and expensive cosmetics. Adverts for many of the brands in these categories are very similar. They may do a good job evoking a strong and appropriate emotional portrayal of the brand, but they all look alike. This means they are offering the user the identical benefit.

With transformational brand attitude strategies the creative presentation of the benefit should follow either a $c \rightarrow e^+$ or e^+ brand benefit focus (subjective characteristic of the brand elicits positive emotion or purely a positive emotion). Looking back at the Nescafé Gold Blend coffee advert in the first chapter (Advert 1.1), which reflects a low-involvement transformational brand attitude strategy, there is a $c \rightarrow e^+$ focus on the benefit. The 'golden aroma' (c) will put you in a state of pure bliss (e^+). The advert for Heal's (Plate XV) is pure emotion (e^+). Owning something from Heal's will quite literally make you feel 'Head over Heals' (e^+). Because transformational brand attitude strategies depend upon a positive emotional end state, the benefit focus in the creative execution must lead the target audience directly to the appropriate emotional response. These creative tactics for transformational brand attitude strategies are summarized in Fig. 12.2.

The advert for Heal's in many ways provides a good summary of what we have been talking about in this chapter. The creative tactics all work together, and facilitate both the processing and the acceptance of the message. The visual and verbal elements work together, reflecting the appropriate use of words and pictures we talked about early in the chapter. Both the surprisingly inverted headlines, and the congruence between the brand, Heal's, and the visual imagery of a 'dog' at heel, helps attract and hold attention. The advert illustrates the tactics needed for a successful high-involvement, transformational brand attitude strategy. It is emotionally authentic and the target audience can personally identify with the imagery. The 'attitude' portrayed is real. You can imagine yourself in the picture (if you see yourself as part of the target audience). Everything here works well towards building a positive brand attitude.

Brand Attitude Creative Tactics and Emotion

In Chapter 11 we learned that emotion helps mediate the way in which advertising is processed. We discussed the important role emotion, especially non-declarative emotional memory, plays in 'framing' how we think about a message. Another important

---

Key is the Emotional Portrayal

- Creative execution must be unique to the brand, employing a strong visual component
- The target audience must like the advertising
- The emotional portrayal must seem authentic, eliciting a strong positive emotional response consistent with the motivation involved
- Some information may be needed for high-involvement decisions
- Utilize a **c** → **e⁺** or **e⁺** benefit focus leading directly to the appropriate emotional response

Figure 12.2 Creative Tactics for Transformational Brand Attitude Strategies

---

aspect of the role of emotion is to ensure that the correct *sequence* of emotional response is elicited by advertising. For most situations in life we experience an ongoing series of emotional reactions, and good advertising executions will reflect this by eliciting a dynamic sequence of emotions that parallel what is experienced in using the advertised product.

In effect, advertising should elicit emotions that will not only encourage a positive affective response to the message, but also be consistent with the emotions that are associated with the underlying purchase motivation (see Table 12.7). Perhaps an example here will help make the point. Why do people buy pain relievers or washing powder? They are negatively motivated to 'solve' the problem of a headache or dirty clothes. If you have a headache, you are probably feeling annoyed, and want to experience relief. This emotional sequence should be reflected in advertising for a pain reliever. The initial imagery in the execution should make you 'feel' the pain, reminding you of the problem; then you should experience the relief that comes with using the brand and eliminating the headache.

The theoretical basis for this comes from the work of Mower, who took a very simple dual position related to unlearned emotional states that motivate people, the fundamental relationship between pleasure and pain.[47] For Mower, when we sense danger, fear is elicited, and, as the danger subsides, relief. If we are feeling safe, we experience hope, but if we lose that sense of safety, we are disappointed. This is related to motivation in that fear and disappointment elicit what psychologists call avoidance behaviour while relief and hope drive approach behaviours. Hammond built upon this work, suggesting that hope and fear lead to what he called 'excitatory' behaviour while relief and disappointment are 'inhibitory'.[48] You should see how this fits with the distinction we have been making between positively and negatively motivated behaviour, and its relationship to brand attitude strategy.

All this has a direct bearing upon creating advertising. Emotions are linked to motivations. With informational brand attitude strategies for negative motivations, the advertising should portray a negative emotion first to underscore the problem to be solved or avoided, then move to a more neutral or mildly positive emotion associated with the brand as solution. Insurance advertising, for example, which deals with a negative

Table 12.7 Relationships Linking Emotion to Motivation in Advertising

Informational Brand Attitude Strategy	
Negative Motive	*Emotional Sequence*
Problem Solution	Mild Anxiety → Relief
Problem Avoidance	Fear → Relaxation
Incomplete Satisfaction	Disappointment → Hope
Transformational Brand Attitude Strategy	
Positive Motive	*Emotional Sequence*
Sensory Gratification	Dull (neutral) → Joy
Social Approval	Apprehension → Flattered
	Ashamed → Proud

Source: Adapted from J. R. Rossiter and L. Percy, *Advertising Communication and Promotion Management* (New York: McGraw-Hill, 1997).

problem-avoidance motive, should first raise a sense of fear (What will your family do if you should suddenly die?), then resolve that fear, 'inhibit' it in Hammond's words, creating a feeling of relaxation as a result of purchasing a life insurance policy.[49]

Look again at Plate XIII, the advert for Fairy laundry detergent. This is a perfect example of what we are talking about. The execution reflects an informational brand attitude strategy addressing a problem-solution motivation: 'The problem is most Non-Bios can leave your baby's clothes feeling a bit scratchy.' The imagery of the unhappy baby with the 'prickly' clothes elicits a feeling of mild anxiety. But, with Fairy, you solve that problem and sense the relief. Note too the correct $e^- \to c$ benefit focus. The problem is resolved by the 'soft' brand.

With transformational brand attitude strategies for positive motivations the emotional emphasis is on the positive end state that results from using the brand. In transformational advertising, the 'before' emotion is often assumed rather than shown or described, but could proceed from a mildly negative or neutral state. This is likely to be the case when dealing with social approval. (Think how your friends will feel when you serve them our reserve cognac.) But the important point when dealing with transformational brand attitude strategies is that the advertising leaves the reader or viewer with a strong positive emotional response.

The advert for Indian Ocean outdoor furniture shown in Plate XVI offers a very good example of how this works. What really makes this advert effective in shifting your emotional state from neutral or even 'dull' to a strong positive emotional response is personalizing the headline, which is then reinforced by the visual. As you imagine yourself in the picture along with the furniture, you experience a positive emotion. Another subtle, yet effective, point is that when you 'put yourself in the picture' you are looking out at the horizon over water. This reflects something Jay Appleton has talked about as Prospect and Refuge theory (see Chapter 3). In this theory, the horizon represents opportunity, and this is felt unconsciously at the limbic level where emotional memories are thought to be stored. This adds to the positive emotional response to the advert.

Notice how this idea of an emotional shift in the execution is consistent with the benefit focus when emotion is used as a benefit. With informational brand attitude strategies, when emotion is part of the benefit, the benefit focus is $e^- \rightarrow c$, when a negative emotion is resolved by the benefit associated with the brand. When using a transformational brand attitude strategy, emotion is always involved in the benefit, either $c \rightarrow e^+$ or simply e^+.

VisCAP

Psychologists have long studied what it is about a person who presents a message (what they call a 'source') that influences how well it is received. For example, someone dressed in a white lab coat will be more convincing when talking about health problems than the same person dressed more casually. The first attempt to synthesize this work and apply it to advertising and other marketing communication was the VisCAP model of source effectiveness, introduced by Percy and Rossiter in 1980.[50] VisCAP is an acronym for visibility, credibility, attractiveness, and power, the main source characteristics in communication.

The source of a message in marketing communication can be anything from a person delivering a message, such as a friend, doctor, or salesperson (word-of-mouth marketing communication), to the medium through which the message is delivered. Think about an advert in a magazine. The type of magazine, the environment in which the reader finds the advert, can affect how you respond to the advertising. An advert for running shoes in *Runner's World* could be received very differently from the same advert in a general magazine. A source here is the magazine itself. The brand being advertised is itself a source of information, based upon the image it has in the mind of the target audience. But what we are concerned with here are the source effects communicated by people or characters that appear in advertising to present the benefit claim.

People or characters in advertising span a range from celebrity endorsers to experts to cartoon characters to actors playing (or actual) ordinary people. What you must consider in the selection of the people or characters to be used in advertising is how a particular person or character will affect the processing of the message. To facilitate processing, they should be selected in such a way that their personal characteristics are consistent with the communication objective. There are specific source characteristics that are best suited to specific communication objectives, and these are described by the VisCAP model.

The four components of the model are defined as follows:

- *Visibility* is how well known or recognizable the person or character is from public exposure.

- *Credibility* has two components: expertise, perceived knowledge of the source concerning what is being advertised, and objectivity, the perceived sincerity or trustworthiness in communicating what the source knows.

- *Attractiveness* also has two components: likeability of the source, and the perceived similarity of the source to the target audience.

- *Power* is source's perceived ability to instil compliance on the part of the target audience.

The way these source characteristics match up with communication objectives is rather straightforward. *Visibility* helps facilitate brand awareness, especially if a celebrity is used. But with a celebrity you must be very careful that attention to the celebrity does not overpower the brand. Awareness of the celebrity must be *transferred* to the brand. Also, when using a celebrity you must remember that you are always subject to possible changes in their popularity. This is especially true for sports celebrities. Certain long-running characters or cartoons can achieve high levels of visibility, and this will continually be associated with the brand.

The source characteristic that helps facilitate informational brand attitude communication objectives is *credibility*. You need to have perceived expertise in a source for both low- and high-involvement informational strategies, but objectivity in the source is needed only for high-involvement informational strategies. Why? Remember, you do not really need to accept a benefit claim as literally true with low-involvement informational advertising, but it must be believed and accepted as true with high-involvement informational advertising.

With transformational advertising, you want the source to be *attractive*. Here, *likeability* is the important source characteristic for low-involvement transformational advertising and *similarity* for high-involvement transformational advertising. Remember that one of the differences in creative tactics for low- versus high-involvement transformational advertising is the need for the target audience to identify personally with the high-involvement advertising. That is why perceived similarity to the source is important. This does not mean that the source must be seen as acting like members of the target audience, but it should be seen as similar to what they imagine or want themselves to be.

Power is not often a factor in advertising or marketing communication, because it is not easy to imagine how someone in an advert can reward or punish the target audience. One possible exception is with certain fear appeals. Another might be when '9 out of 10 doctors' recommend a certain behaviour for a particular problem. If you feel you might have that problem and do not follow the recommendation of the advertising, you might feel your doctor could 'punish' you if you must see him. To the extent that power might operate, it will help facilitate the communication objective of brand purchase intention.

The VisCAP model is summarized in Table 12.8.

Table 12.8 VisCAP Model of Characteristics to Look for in Matching People or Characters to Communication Objectives

Communication Objective	Characteristic to Look for	
Brand Awareness	**Visibility**	How recognizable is the person or character?
Informational Brand Attitude	**Credibility**	
Low and High Involvement	Expertise	Person or character's perceived knowledge of the product category
High Involvement	Expertise and Objectivity	Sincerity or trustworthiness of person or character in talking about the product category
Transformational Brand Attitude	**Attractiveness**	
Low Involvement	Likeability	Person or character is seen as personable or attractive
High Involvement	Similarity	Target audience sees person or character as similar to them
Brand Purchase Intention	**Power**	Perceived ability of the person or character to instil compliance with the message

Source: Adapted from J. R. Rossiter and L. Percy, *Advertising Communication and Promotion Management* (New York: McGraw-Hill, 1997).

CHAPTER SUMMARY

This chapter first considered general principles of how to use words and pictures to optimize attention and message processing. We then went on to focus on specific creative tactics related to brand awareness and brand attitude communication objectives. We introduced the concept of the creative unit, and explained its use in generating and holding attention in various media. We considered various ways of using words and pictures to enhance processing, especially the role of high levels of imagery. We emphasized the different creative tactics required for informational versus transformational brand attitude strategies, and particularly the role of emotional authenticity in transformational strategies. Lastly, the VisCAP model was introduced, outlining the characteristics to look for in a source in order to optimize effectiveness.

12.1 How can the insights gained from the fields of psycho-linguistics and visual imagery help create more effective advertising?

12.2 What can be done to minimize the effects of memory malfunctions on processing advertising?

12.3 What is the fundamental difference in the creative tactics for recognition versus recall brand awareness strategies?

12.4 What are the key differences between the creative tactics for informational versus transformational brand attitude strategies?

12.5 In what way can creative tactics be used to elicit specific emotions?

12.6 What is the relationship between motivation and emotion in advertising, and why is it important to understand?

12.7 In what way does the VisCAP model help creatives in the development of advertising?

CASE STUDY 12

Maryland Cookies

Heinz Tomato Soup. Kellogg's Corn Flakes. Robinson's Barley Water. Maryland Cookies. There are some brands that are so familiar, so trusted, so much a part of the furniture, that you've got to work damned hard to make people see them in a new light.

Maryland Cookies were launched in the UK, in 1956. It appears that the new baking technology allowing chocolate to be 'built into' the biscuit caused a great deal of excitement—this really was a whole new taste and mouth feel experience. The brand continued to be popular down the years, growing to be the 24th largest biscuit brand in the UK, with a sales value of around 10m and more than one in five households claiming to buy them at least once a year. At the point at which Horizon biscuits (formerly Premier Brands) acquired the brand from Lyons in the early 1990s, it was apparent that Maryland was in danger of becoming marginalized in the consumer's mind. The biscuit market was becoming a rather exciting place to be, with all kinds of new textures, flavours, and brand concepts being introduced on a monthly basis, the premium nature of which was supported by quite substantial media spend. At the other end of the sector, own-label's share, as elsewhere in the grocery market, had burgeoned, so that by the mid-1990s own-label products enjoyed a sterling share of 35 per cent of the sweet biscuit market. Maryland found itself in the classic grocery dilemma. On the one hand, it was unable to compete single-mindedly on price against own-label and other budget brands. On the other hand, it was equally unrealistic to expect the brand to generate the same level of consumer interest enjoyed by the more esoteric market entrants, and hence justify the premium required to generate a competitive level of promotional funds. Horizon's response to this difficult marketing conundrum had been a series of ad hoc price promotions and BOGOFs. Although the marketing team was aware that this might, in the long term, erode the brand's value, it was difficult to see another way forward. By 1999, forecasts suggested that the brand's total volume sales for the year could fall by as much as 15–20 per cent if some kind of powerful remedial action were not taken.

Horizon's smart response was to focus on new product development and, on a planned launch programme of new yummy variants to complement the traditional 'choc'n nut'. One of the more popular, in consumer research, turned out to be the replacement of chocolate chips with chewy toffee fudge pieces, and the decision was made to focus on this new variant as the spearhead for the marketing programme. Two central challenges that emerged were the following:

- We had a total marketing budget of 390,000 for a national product launch (the brand's sales profile was fairly flat regionally), in an extremely competitive sector.
- In light of the above, we knew that the multiples' embracing of the new variant was not assured. The biscuit section of your local supermarket is a busy and congested place; facings are scarce and at a premium. We had to provide a set of tools for the sales force and, ultimately, compelling reasons for the trade to stock the new product.

We knew we had to be realistic. We knew that the marketing budget, at face value, was unlikely to secure the levels of distribution and consumer awareness that a successful launch required. We had to do something different. Our objectives were twofold:

- Create an excitement around the launch that would galvanize the trade.
- Generate as much free publicity as possible.

If Benetton and FCUK could do it, why couldn't we? In reality, of course, it was not quite that simple because Maryland is a very different brand from those 'enfants terribles' of the marketing world. Benetton and FCUK are high-profile, high-fashion items, with pretty funky consumers. Sex and controversy sells to that market. Maryland, by contrast, was a lovable, family brand with fairly conservative values and consumers. Any activity deliberately designed to provoke and to create a stir would have to be carefully handled to avoid a conflict with those values.

In addition to our two main objectives, and in line with the very real need for brand consistency, what we were looking for was something relevant to the product i.e. something which dramatized the new variant's key point of difference fudgie bits. They really were Unbelieveably Fudgie Objects. UFOs. UFOs which, during three weeks in mid-September 1999, would 'crash land' in spectacular fashion, all across the nation.

- The showcase: a 40-foot wide Maryland Cookie had apparently crashed into Trafalgar Square. The UFO was promptly cordoned off with plastic tape, marked 'Caution. Unbelievably Fudgie Objects'.
- 35 12-foot wide cookies had, overnight, crashed into various landmarks in 15 cities; Blackpool Tower looked particularly spectacular.
- 2,000 2-foot wide cookies had rained down on high-traffic streets in the same 15 cities. On average 150 cookies per street.
- The crash-landed areas were peopled by 'the end is near' walking sandwich boards, with cookies apparently embedded into carriers' backs.
- A1 posters appeared on walls, fences, and other public spaces featuring giant cookies which had crashed into famous buildings around the world: the Taj Mahal, the Eiffel tower, the Statue of Liberty, Big Ben.

Trade Sell-In: We achieved our first objective. In the period following the campaign the 'Fudgie' variant achieved just under 65 per cent distribution in the grocery sector. Gareth Edwards, Sales Director of Horizon Biscuits at the time, acknowledged the effect the 'UFO' campaign had on the sell-in. 'It met the brief. We needed something dramatically different to say to the buyers if we were to convince them that this wasn't just another new line the "UFO" campaign helped us to give the sell-in some real drama. And because we lost no distribution for the existing variants, the net result was a much bigger facing for the Maryland brand as a whole.' Moreover, a 'hype video' sales tool was used by the sales force to prolong the impact of the campaign to key individuals in the trade.

PR coverage: Objective no. 2 was also met. Media coverage of the event was gratifyingly widespread. As well as a one-minute slot on TFI Friday, and similar on the Zoe Ball breakfast show on Radio One. In sum, the campaign achieved over 60 million impacts in national media alone. The campaign really came into its own, however, at a regional level where it was featured in just about all the main regional and local media in those cities where it ran. We have been told that it is impossible to track those regional impacts in the same way as the national media; suffice to say that we believe we probably achieved a higher overall level of impacts at regional level, than at national. If that assumption is correct, then the free publicity we generated overall would have resulted in more than 120 million impacts. To achieve that level through traditional press advertising would have cost, we estimate, between 1.4m and 1.8m.

Sales: it worked. Crucially though, the real success of the campaign was that sales of 'Fudgies' did not appear to cannibalize sales elsewhere in the range: on the contrary, total sales of Maryland Cookies went up over the same period by substantially more that the 'incremental' sales of 'Fudgies'. The impact of the campaign was to raise the profile of the brand as a whole. Perhaps more tellingly, total sales of Maryland outstripped the rest of its sector and all of its key competitors, boosting brand share by nearly 10 per cent.

However, the most gratifying aspect of the campaign, was the longer-term impetus it appears to have given the brand. The internal effect in the company was to demonstrate the potential reward of moving from a price-promotion to a new product development strategy. Since the 'Fudgies' campaign, Horizon have launched a 'Jammy bits' Maryland Cookies and a 'Toffee Apple' variant and more delicious variants will follow. The mid-term sales effect of this new strategy was a steady increase in brand share from the 'Fudgies' campaign through to October 2000, despite a gradual increase in price relative to the competition. As a result brand share increased by 14 per cent over the 1999–2000 period, while average retail price increased by 9 per cent. The strength of the brand over the period was such that it overtook its chief rival in the sector McVities Rich Tea despite establishing a price premium. 'We knew that we had to break out of the price-promotion strategy not least because in a sense we were helping to accelerate the move of the whole sector in that direction. So the "Fudgies" launch really was a watershed for the brand at a time when it looked likely to go into decline. And I'm pleased to say that the net result of that strategy is that the brand has been growing in volume terms since the "Fudgies" campaign at 15 per cent a year', T.C., Marketing Director.

In summary prior to this campaign, there was a concern that Maryland might be losing its saliency. Other biscuit brands were being launched which, on the face of it, seemed more interesting and in many cases enjoyed significant advertising budgets. On the other hand, it was difficult for Maryland to compete single-mindedly on price at the own-label/budget end of the market. The response was to launch a delicious new variant 'Maryland with Fudgie bits' and to focus thinking on two pragmatic objectives, namely, forcing grocery distribution and generating as much free publicity as possible. The 'UFO' campaign which followed was unlike anything ever undertaken by a grocery brand. It resulted in: i) Unprecedented levels of distribution for a new Maryland variant, ii) At least 120 million PR impacts, iii) One-year-on sales increase for the Maryland brand as a whole of some 14 per cent, iv) Brand share increase of just under 10 per cent.

Source: WARC, IPA Effectiveness Awards, 2002, Maryland Cookies, by Mary Kineer

Edited by Natalia Yannopoulou

Discussion Questions

1 What are the strong and weak points in using creative tactics?

2 In which cases would you choose to follow a creative tactic instead of a traditional approach?

3 In which cases combining creative tactics with traditional approaches would be most effective?

4 Looking into examples of brands that have used successful creative tactics, can you identify any commonalities?

FURTHER READING

- A number of researchers have looked at traditional ideas of speech and rhetoric, and their application in creating more effective advertising. Lars Pynt Andersen has done a great deal of work in the area of irony, as reviewed in 'Conceptualizing Television Advertising', in Fleming Hansen and Lars Bech Christensen (eds), *Branding and Advertising* (Copenhagen: Copenhagen Business School Press, 2003), 284–305. Articles appear regularly in the *Journal of Consumer Research* dealing with this area, including recently: Michelle Roehm and Brian Sternthal, 'The Moderating Effect of Knowledge and Resources on the Persuasion Impact of Analogies', *JCR* (Sept. 2001), 257–72; David Mothersbaugh, Bruce Huhmann, and George Franke, 'Combinatory and Separative Effects of Rhetorical Figures on Consumers' Effort and Focus in Ad Processing', *JCR* (Mar. 2002), 589–602; and Edward McQuarrie and David Mick, 'Visual and Verbal Rhetorical Figures under Directed Processing versus Incidental Exposure to Advertising', *JCR* (Mar. 2003), 579–87.

- The use of humour in advertising is another area that receives considerable research effort. Two recent papers include H. Shanker Krishnan and Dipankar Chakravarti, 'A Process Analysis of the Effects of Humorous Advertising Executions on Brand Claims Memory', *Journal of Consumer Psychology*, 13/3 (2003), 230–45, and Thomas Cline, Moses Altsech, and James Kellaris, 'When does Humor Enhance or Inhibit Ad Responses?' *Journal of Advertising*, 32/3 (Fall 2003), 31–46.

- The issue of comparative advertising, and the specific case of the similarity of the benefit claims among competitive brands, is dealt with in Shi Zhang, Frank Kardes, and Maria Cronley, 'Comparative Advertising: Effects of Structural Alignability on Target Brand Evaluations', *Journal of Consumer Psychology*, 12/4 (2002), 303–12.

- Source characteristics are the subject of Joseph Priester and Richard Petty, 'The Influences of Spokesperson Trustworthiness on Message Elaboration, Attitude Strength, and Advertising Effectiveness', *Journal of Consumer Psychology*, 13/4 (2003), 408–21, and Gwen Bachmann Achenriner and Deborah Roedder John, 'Hearing Voices: The Impact of Announcer Speech Characteristics on Consumer Response to Broadcast Advertising', *Journal of Consumer Psychology*, 13/3 (2003), 205–19.

- A number of context factors such as text, complexity, and style for web adverts is discussed in Peter Danaher and Guy Mullarkey, 'Factors Affecting Online Advertising Recall: A Study of Students', *Journal of Advertising Research*, 43/3 (Sept. 2003), 252–67.

NOTES

1   This area was discussed for print adverts in John Rossiter's analysis of Starch scores in his paper 'Predicting Starch Scores', *Journal of Advertising Research*, 21/5 (1980), 63–8.

2   These attention estimates are suggested in J. R. Rossiter and L. Percy, *Advertising Communication and Promotion Management* (New York: McGraw-Hill, 1997). They are based upon a review of a number of empirical studies, including one conducted in South Africa utilizing 9,430 commercials, reported by E. DuPlessis in 'An Advertising Burst as Just a Lot of Drops', *Admap* (July/Aug. 1996), 51–5.

3   The important difference between human evaluative conditioning and classical conditioning is discussed in J. DeHouwer, S. Thomas, and F. Baeyen, 'Associative Learnings of Likes and Dislikes: A Review of 25 Years of Research on Human Evaluative Conditioning', *Psychological Bulletin*, 127/6 (2001), 853–69.

4   Again, Rossiter and Percy, *Advertising Communication and Promotion Management*, summarizes a number of studies that support this rule for print adverts (see esp. ch. 10).

5   Greg Myers, *Words in Ads* (London: Arnold, 1994), 3.

6   See A. J. Wearing, 'The Recall of Sentences of Varying Length', *Australian Journal of Psychology*, 25 (1973), 155–61.

7   John Rossiter and his colleagues have offered a typology of visual elements for gaining attention in J. R. Rossiter, T. Langner, and L. Ang, 'Visual Creativity in Advertising: A Functional Typology', *ANZMAC Proceedings*; electronic document (2003).

8   See J. R. Rossiter, 'The Increase in Magazine Ad Readership', *Journal of Advertising Research*, 28/5 (1988), 35–9.

9   These results are reported in a rather extensive study of over 500 MTV-type commercials with over twenty cuts versus 600 commercials with fewer than twenty cuts by J. MacLachlan and M. Logan, 'Commercial Shot Length in TV Commercials and their Memorability and Persuasiveness', *Journal of Advertising Research*, 33/2 (1993), 7–16.

10   This has been reported by, among others, B. E. Avons and W. A. Phillips, 'Visualization and Memorization as a Function of Display Time and Poststimulus Processing Time', *Journal of Experimental Psychology: Human Learning and Memory*, 6 (1980), 407–42.

11   See S. Oakes, 'Evaluating Empirical Research into Music in Advertising: A Congruity Perspective', *Journal of Advertising Research*, 47/1 (2007), 38–50.

12   Early research on this is reported in R. F. Yalch, 'Memory in a Jingle Jungle: Music as a Mnemonic Device in Communicating Advertising Slogans', *Journal of Applied Psychology*, 76/2 (1991), 268–75, and more recently in D. Allen, 'Effects of Pop Music in Advertising on Attention and Memory', *Journal of Advertising Research*, 46/4 (2006), 434–44.

13   This classic study is reported in R. E. Milliman, 'Using Background Music to Affect the Behaviour of Supermarket Shoppers', *Journal of Marketing*, 46/3 (1982), 86–91.

14   See A. C. North, D. J. Hargreaver, and J. McKendrick , 'The Influence of In-Store Music on Wine Selections', *Journal of Applied Psychology*, 88/2 (1999), 271–6.

15   Because of his work with attitude change, McGuire was frequently asked about the implications of his thinking for advertising. His seminal work is found in G. Lindsey and E. Aronson (eds), *Handbook of Social Psychology*, iii (Reading, Mass.: Addison-Wesley, 1969), 136–314.

16   A. Paivio, in his well-known book *Images and Verbal Processing* (New York: Holt, Rinehart and Winston, 1971), discusses research that found that more frequently used and more familiar words are heard, read, and repeated faster and with fewer errors. Lowenthal, in

'Semantic Features and Communicability of Words of Different Classes', *Psychonomic Science*, 17 (1969), 79–80, found that meaning is easier to grasp with more familiar words.

17 McGuire introduced something he called a two-factor analysis, where low *or* high levels of arousal are less likely to lead to persuasion than some intermediate level. This so-called inverted U-shaped relationship is especially evident when fear appeals are used. A certain level of shock- or anxiety-causing copy or visuals will attract attention, but that very anxiety will inhibit processing of the message. See W. J. McGuire, 'Personality and Attitude Change: An Information-Processing Theory', in A. G. Greenwald *et al.* (eds), *Psychological Foundations of Attitudes* (New York: Academic Press, 1968), 171–96.

18 See M. P. Toglia and W. F. Battig, *Handbook of Semantic Word Norms* (Hillsdale, NJ: Lawrence E. Erlbaum and Associates, 1978).

19 C. C. Jorgensen and W. Kintsch, in 'The Role of Imagery in the Evaluation of Sentences', *Cognitive Psychology*, 4 (1973), 110–16, have shown that high-imagery sentences can be evaluated significantly faster as true or false than can low-imagery sentences. K. Holyoak, in 'The Role of Imagery in the Evaluation of Sentences: Imagery or Semantic Relatedness?', *Journal of Verbal Learning and Verbal Behaviour*, 13 (1974), 163–6, found that sentences rated high in imagery value are significantly easier to understand.

20 See L. Percy, 'Exploring Grammatical Structure and Non-Verbal Communication', in S. Hecker and D. W. Stewart (eds), *Nonverbal Communication in Advertising* (Lexington, Mass.: Lexington Books, 1988), 147–58.

21 See Myers, *Words in Ads*.

22 See e.g. T. Lowrey, 'The Relation between Syntactic Complexity and Advertising Persuasiveness', in J. Sherry and B. Sternthal (eds), *Advances in Consumer Research*, xix (Provo, Utah: Association for Consumer Research, 1991), 270–4.

23 See Myers, *Words in Ads*, 30.

24 Ibid. 47–51.

25 See M. W. Eysenck, *Human Memory: Theory, Research and Individual Difference* (Oxford: Pergamon, 1977).

26 See Myers, *Words in Ads*, 136.

27 W. J. Bryce and R. F. Yalch, 'Hearing versus Seeing: A Comparison of Learning of Spoken and Pictorial Information in Television Advertising', *Journal of Current Issues and Research in Advertising*, 15/1 (1993), 1–20. They make the point that, because of language differences, it obviously makes sense for commercials to be reasonably understandable from only the visual content.

28 John Shearman discusses this idea in a very interesting book, *Only Connect . . . : Art and the Spectator in the Italian Renaissance* (Princeton: Princeton University Press, 1992). It may seem odd to be citing an art history book, but the art history literature can provide important insight into visual communication.

29 The implication of what this means, not only for marketing communication but also for cross-cultural communication, is discussed in a paper by L. Percy, 'Moving beyond Culturally Dependent Responses to Visual Images', presented to the 2nd Conference on the Cultural Dimensions of International Marketing, Odense University, Denmark (1995).

30 See Myers, *Words in Ads*, 146.

31 Ibid.

32 See S. M. Kosslyn, *Images and Mind* (Cambridge, Mass.: Harvard University Press, 1980).

33 Studies by both Rossiter and Percy and Mitchell and Olson have demonstrated the positive impact of larger picture size on evaluative responses and not just memory response. See J. R. Rossiter and L. Percy, 'Visual Communication in Advertising', in R. J. Harris (ed.), *Information Processing Research in Advertising* (Hillsdale, NJ: Lawrence Erlbaum Associates, 1983), 83–126, and A. A. Mitchell and J. C. Olson, 'Are Product Attribute Beliefs the Only Mediator of Advertising Effects on Brand Attitude?', *Journal of Marketing Research*, 18 (1981), 318–32.

34 See R. P. Dooley and L. E. Harkins, 'Functional and Attention-Getting Effects of Colour on Graphic Communications', *Perceptual and Motor Skills*, 31 (1970), 851–4.

35 See G. H. Bower, 'Imagery as a Relational Organizer in Associative Learning', *Journal of Verbal Learning and Verbal Behavior*, 4 (1970), 529–33.

36 This idea of double-coding was originally introduced by Paivio, and is well discussed in A. Paivio, 'A Dual Coding Approach to Perception and Cognition', in H. I. Pick and E. Saltzman (eds), *Modes of Perceiving and Processing Information* (Hillsdale, NJ: Lawrence Erlbaum Associates, 1978).

37 See J. R. Rossiter, 'Visual Imagery: An Application to Advertising', in A. Mitchell (ed.), *Advances in Consumer Research*, ix (Provo, Utah: Association for Consumer Research, 1981), 101–6.

38 See C. J. Brainerd, A. Desrochers, and M. L. Howe, 'Stages of Learning Analysis of Picture-Word Effects in Associative Memory', *Journal of Experimental Psychology: Human Learning and Memory*, 7 (1987), 1–14.

39 These images in Advert 11.2 are from an outdoor poster campaign for H&M that has been tracked over the years by ISI Wissing.

40 A detailed look at how the memory problems described by Schacter in his book *The Seven Sins of Memory* (Boston: Houghton Mifflin Company, 2001) can influence how advertising is processed and what can be done creatively about it may be found in an article by Larry Percy, 'Advertising and the Seven Sins of Memory', *International Journal of Advertising*, forthcoming.

41 This idea is explored in more detail in Rossiter and Percy, *Advertising Communication and Promotion Management*.

42 See J. C. Maloney, 'Curiosity versus Disbelief in Advertising', *Journal of Advertising Research*, 2/2 (1962), 2–8.

43 An interesting case one of the authors was involved with back in the 1970s illustrates how effective a refutational strategy can be. Potato consumption in the USA had been declining for several years, and the National Potato Promotion Board (a potato farmer's cooperative) was obviously concerned. It had been running advertising that extolled the virtues of potatoes, especially their good taste. Unfortunately, while most people did like potatoes, there was a real concern that they were fattening. In effect, when people saw the advertising, they thought, 'yes, potatoes do taste good, but...'. The negative belief that potatoes were fattening overrode the positive taste. Fortunately, potatoes are not fattening, and are lower in calories than other popular carbohydrate side dishes such as rice or noodles. The problem was all the things people added to the potato. Advertising was

Plate XIII Fairy

Even though the headline in this advert comes first, the eye is still drawn initially to the picture, ensuring the desired word–picture sequence for optimum processing. Reproduced with kind permission © Procter & Gamble UK.

Plate XIV Colron

Here we have a very good example of the important ways the visual images used in an advert can help facilitate learning. It is clear you are meant to be outside, observing the 'action', the picture is large, the unique imagery encourages visual elaboration, the use of colour and white space is well proportioned, the product is shown 'in use', and the picture is seen before the words. Reproduced with kind permission © Ronseal Ltd.

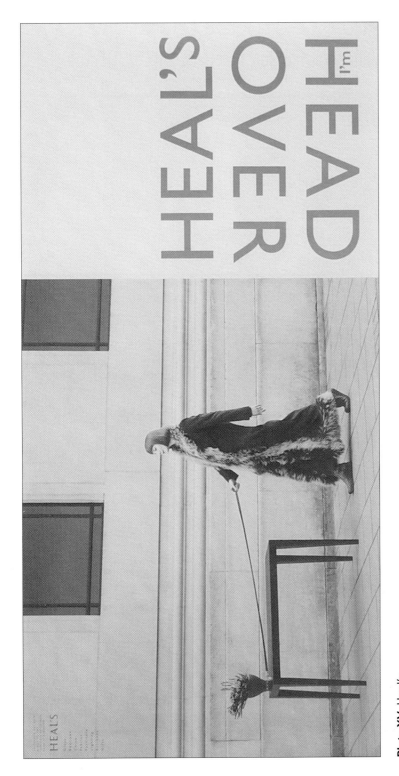

Plate XV Heal's

Consistent with the key creative tactic for transformational brand attitude strategies, this Heal's advert is pure emotion, eliciting a strong positive emotional association for the brand. Reproduced with kind permission © Heal's.

Plate XVI Indian Ocean

Here we see a very good example of how a transformational advert shifts your emotional state from neutral or even dull to a strong positive emotional response. Reproduced with kind permission © Info Associates'.

created using a refutational approach that began with the headline 'You think potatoes are fattening.' But the advert then went on to refute the claim, pointing out all the potatoes' healthy aspects, and finishing with the tag: 'The potato, something good that is good for you.' It worked. Per capita consumption of potatoes not only stopped falling; it increased almost 20 per cent over the three years the campaign ran.

44   This idea of 'liking' an advert can be troubling. On the one hand, there is research that shows the influence on brand preference from ad-liking is not strong: e.g. Jan Stapel, 'Viva Recall, Viva Persuasion', *European Research*, 15 (Nov. 1987), 222–5. On the other hand, Gordon Brown, in 'Monitoring Advertising: Big Stable Brands and Ad Effects. Fresh Thoughts about Why: Perhaps Consistent Promotion Keeps them Big', *Admap*, 27 (May 1981), 32–7, has suggested that ad-liking has a long-term effect. You must look *carefully* at the adverts used in any research on attitude toward the advert. We should only expect a positive effect when dealing with advertising addressing positive motives. This important point has been underscored by Larry Percy in his paper 'Understanding the Mediating Effect of Motivation and Emotion in Advertising Measurement', in *Copy Research: The New Evidence*, Proceedings of the 8th Annual ARF Copy Research Workshop (1991).

45   This study was conducted for a major US brewer by one of the authors.

46   In the casebook edited by C. Baker, *Advertising Works 7* (London: NTC Publications, 1992), there is a detailed discussion of how this type of advertising helped revitalize the Oxo brand. This issue is addressed generally by Marc Weinberger and Harlan Spotts in 'A Situational View of Information Content in TV Advertising in the US and UK', *Journal of Marketing*, 53 (Jan. 1989), 89–94. They show that advertising need not provide information to be effective.

47   Mower's theory was developed in two books: *Learning Theory and Behaviour* (New York: Wiley, 1960) and *Learning Theory and the Symbolic Process* (New York: Wiley, 1960).

48   Hammond's reconceptualization of Mower's work is outlined in 'Conditioned Emotional States', in P. Black (ed.), *Physiological Correlates of Emotion* (New York: Academic Press, 1970).

49   See Larry Percy and John R. Rossiter, 'The Role of Emotion in Processing Advertising', in M. Lynn and J. M. Jackson (eds), *Proceedings of the Society for Consumer Psychology* (Madison: Omnipress, 1991), 54–8.

50   Larry Percy and John R. Rossiter, *Advertising Strategy: A Communication Theory Approach* (New York: Praeger, 1980).

 Visit the Online Resource Centre that accompanies this book for additional resources to support the text: http://www.oxfordtextbooks.co.uk/orc/percy_elliott3e/

13

Creative Execution

 KEY CONCEPTS

1 It is essential that all aspects of a marketing communication campaign have a consistent look and feel that are maintained over time so that they eventually become immediately associated with the brand, facilitating brand awareness and a link with a positive brand benefit.

2 Strategy for a campaign must be clearly communicated to the creative team that develops the actual execution, and this is accomplished with a creative brief that summarizes the important elements of the strategy *as one page*. The creative brief must be agreed to by everyone involved with the campaign *before* work begins on the creative execution.

3 Once the creative executions are developed, it is important to pre-test them using a system that is based upon the communication objectives (and *never* with focus groups).

4 After pre-testing, and any subsequent adjustments to the execution to ensure meeting the communication objectives, the campaign runs and should be tracked in the market over time in order to measure its effectiveness. Tracking helps isolate the effectiveness of a brand's advertising (and promotion) from that of competitors' efforts and other components of the marketing mix in effecting sales.

Many people are involved in the strategic planning and development of a marketing communication campaign, but when it comes to executing the strategy, producing the actual adverts and promotions, this is the job of the 'creatives'. For many, this is really what advertising is all about. But it is important to remember that even the most brilliant creative execution that is *not consistent with the strategy* cannot compete with even an average creative execution that is.

Everything we have been talking about so far in this book has dealt with the necessary tools for developing the right creative strategy for a brand. As we shall see in this chapter, all this work is summarized in a single page, the creative brief. Once the creative idea has been formed and executed, the result will (or should) be tested to ensure it is indeed consistent with the strategy.

Creating Advertising

Who is it that actually generates the creative executions used in marketing communications? Usually what comes to mind are the art directors and copywriters at advertising agencies—the 'creatives'. But we need to remember that a great deal of advertising is actually created by people who do not work for an advertising agency. Many large companies have in-house departments where both the creation and media placement of advertising are handled by the advertiser on its own. Retail stores will frequently employ creative people to generate the many, many adverts they run in daily newspapers. Often small business advertising is created for the advertiser by the media that run it. For example, radio or television stations will develop advertising for a company, and the various 'yellow pages' have creative people who will develop small adverts for use in their books and on-line.

In today's advertising world, and especially in Europe, there has been an interesting trend. Many advertisers no longer use their advertising agency for traditional media planning and buying functions (as we have already seen). Rather, they are turning more and more to specialized media institutes, using their agencies only for the development and execution of creative ideas. But now it would seem that these media institutes are beginning to have a hand in overall strategic planning, and are even advising marketers on their creative product! It is almost as if the media institutes are beginning to 'morph' into traditional full-service advertising agencies. But, regardless of where the advertising is created, two basic functions will be involved: writing the copy and laying out a print advert or developing the visual content of a commercial. With smaller advertisers, the entire creative function may rest with a single individual. At large advertising agencies there may be teams of copywriters and art directors working with production experts and directors to develop and execute a campaign.

Creative executions spring from a creative idea.[1] These creative ideas may come from a variety of sources, and manifest themselves in any number of ways. But, in the end, a creative idea *must be consistent* with the communication strategy and brand position. It is very important that creative thinking does not begin until a creative brief has been agreed upon. It is the creative brief, as we shall see shortly, that helps guide the *direction* the creative execution must take in order to satisfy the strategy. With the creative brief in hand, the creative team assigned to the campaign can go to work.

At its most basic level, a creative execution is simply made up of words and pictures brought together in a creative way to attract and hold the attention of a target audience, and to satisfy the communication objective. We spent a great deal of time discussing the tactics involved with this in Chapter 12. While occasionally you might find an advert with no words or one with no picture, all marketing communication will generally utilize both words and pictures (other than radio, where of course pictures are not possible). Obvious, of course. But this is also why it is so very important for both copywriters and art directors to work closely together in the creation of marketing communication. In fact, in some advertising agencies, creative teams may actually share the same office.

Creative teams, however, are not always completely free to execute an advert in any way they would like. Particularly with corporate or business-to-business advertising, companies may have guidelines where particular requirements for the layout and execution of advertising are given, often as detailed as the type of font that is required. Creatives, with some justification, often feel constrained by such rules. While truly good creative people will always be able to work effectively, regardless of the boundaries, these so-called style books are much too restrictive, and should not be used. The reasoning behind them is usually given as ensuring a consistent look to campaigns. But, as we shall see in the next section, this is not what ensures a consistent 'look and feel' to creative executions.

One of the areas that almost always falls under some advertiser restrictions, however, is the tagline, corporate signature, or logo. It is not unusual for advertisers to specify the size of the logo or tag. We do not endorse this, but at the same time you should never permit any creative licence with the tag or logo itself. Creative people should be involved in the original development of the tagline or logo, but, once established, it should remain consistent in all creative executions until it is changed.

Consistency in Creative Executions

One of the most important aspects of effective creative executions within a marketing communication programme and over time is *consistency*. Within a campaign, all executions must have a consistent look and feel. Whether adverts, promotions, collateral, or even packages, there should be a consistency about them that enables the target audience to recognize it immediately as coming from the brand.

Consistency and Brand Awareness

Consistency over creative executions in a campaign and over time is very important for brand awareness. You will remember from Chapter 8, when we discussed positioning, and Chapter 9, when we talked about brand awareness, the importance of establishing the appropriate link between category need and brand awareness. Consistency in creative executions enables the look and feel conveyed by the execution quickly to establish and reinforce this linkage. When a consistent look and feel to a brand's creative execution have been established, brand awareness will be triggered by the execution itself, without actual reference to the brand name. The brand name will only confirm what has been triggered by the look of the advertising. Look back at the H&M Advert 12.2 for an excellent example.

Another very good example of this was the long-running series of adverts for Silk Cut (a UK tobacco brand). For years their advertising featured little more than some combination of purple silk and a 'cut'. They finally reached the point where they no longer even included the brand name. The consistent imagery of the scarlet silk and 'cut' automatically communicated the brand name. It was almost ironic to see a two-page advert in a magazine with nothing but a wave of scarlet silk and a pair of scissors…and a government health warning about the dangers of tobacco use. Tobacco advertising is now banned in the UK, and the last advert for Silk Cut featured a caricature of a large diva, arms wide and clearly in full voice, wearing a scarlet silk dress with a cut. It was a very clear reference to the old adage: 'It ain't over 'til the fat lady sings.' Well, the fat lady was singing, and advertising for Silk Cut was over.

Actually, a consistent visual or pictorial feel in marketing communication has been found to be a faster trigger for brand identification than the actual brand name or company logo, because memory for visuals is superior to memory for encoded labels or words in general. Interestingly, over half the brain's cortex is used for the processing of visual images.[2] What we are looking for is a general recognition on the part of the target audience that the pictorial or visual execution belongs to the brand. That is what permits variation in the executions. It is not necessary or even desirable for all the creative executions to look the 'same', only that they reflect the same overall look and feel. In fact, if the executions in a campaign are seen as too similar, the campaign will tend to 'wear out' faster. Rather, you want enough variation in the executions so that they remain fresh, and can be extended over time.

For a number of years, Kenco coffee ran advertising similar to the 2003 print adverts shown in Advert 13.1. This provides a good example of what we are talking about. It is freeze-dried coffee, not fresh ground, but the imagery evokes the desired benefit of fresh brewed (something we will be covering next). There is a good deal of variation in the executions, yet they retain the same look and feel.

Consistency and Brand Attitude

Just as with brand awareness, consistency in the look and feel of creative executions is important for brand attitude. We briefly mentioned above the dominance of visual elements in memory. Pictures may be thought of as 'quick shots' into memory. Studies of print adverts with eye-tracking cameras have consistently shown that on average some 70 per cent of the time spent looking at an advert is spent on the picture. As you might imagine, the visual element in advertising is critical to effective communication.

Building upon this understanding of the power of visual elements in effective marketing communication, it is desirable to find an image that the target audience readily associates with a brand's primary or key benefit. This is not as easy as it may seem at first glance. We are not looking for just any image that reflects the brand's benefit, but one that

Advert 13.1 These adverts for Kenco coffee illustrate a consistent look and feel based upon imagery associated with the benefit of fresh-brewed taste. Reproduced by kind permission Kraft Foods™.

is *unique* to the brand. We know from our discussion of positioning in Chapter 8 that we should seek a unique benefit for our brand, and, if that is not possible, at least to execute the benefit claim uniquely. This last is absolutely essential.

Because it is rather easy to identify 'ideal attributes', too often most brands in a category will focus upon the same basic benefit (or set of benefits). Advertisers are likely to fall back on clichés when dealing with a benefit. Truck manufacturers know truck buyers want a 'tough truck', so they all tend to show their truck travelling easily over the roughest terrain, or pulling or carrying incredible loads (or even both!). These clichés then become an image for the category, and do not help any individual 'name plate' (what automobile and truck companies call their brands) communicate that they are 'tougher' than any other.

In developing creative executions, you must be certain that the message and image are compatible with the target audience's schema. Images that are used must be chosen to be consistent with the brand's key benefit, and the linkage to the benefit must be easily made by the target audience. When trying to identify a visual image to correspond with a brand's key benefit, what on the surface may seem appropriate may not in fact be so. A company marketing a very high-involvement product to corporate executives wanted to associate a key benefit of relaxation with its brand. It felt a picture showing a relaxed-looking executive, leaning against a door frame without his suit jacket, holding a newspaper and a cup of coffee, would embody this benefit. But the target audience did not see a man relaxing. What they saw was a man in the morning before work, contemplating the stress of the day to come. Obviously, this was not the imagery the advertiser wished to convey. It is always important to check how your target audience responds to your creative executions. We will be dealing with this in more detail later in the chapter.

An exceptionally good example of finding the right imagery and using it consistently over time to reinforce brand attitude was the long-running campaign in the UK for Oxo beef cubes that we talked about in Chapter 12. Although the campaign finally came to an end in late 1999, it ran for over sixteen years. Beginning in 1983, the advertising featured a family's day-to-day life experiences, centred around mealtime. The campaign featured the same actors over the years, and the scenarios played out in the advertising were designed to tap situations easily identified with the target audience's own family life. In terms of execution, it was a perfect example of what we have described as the critical component of low-involvement, transformational advertising: it was 'real'. The look and feel evolved in keeping with the times as the actor family grew older, but it was always internally consistent and readily identifiable as Oxo advertising. There is ample evidence that this advertising made a significant contribution to the health and growth of the brand.[3]

In summary, every creative execution for a brand must contribute to a consistent look and feel for that brand. While individual messages and executions may (and should) vary, the underlying theme must remain consistent, and the key to this consistent look and feel should be a visual image that is associated in the target audience's mind with the brand's primary benefit. Consistency in creative execution facilitates brand awareness and with the appropriate visual image also facilitates brand attitude. Every exposure of a brand's marketing communication, when seen within the context of a consistent, positive image, helps reinforce a favourable attitude towards the brand. This leads to a more receptive atmosphere for attending to the specific message content of the advertising.

Briefing the Creatives

Before turning our attention specifically to the creative briefing process, let us think about what O'Malley has called a contrasting style between those involved in strategy versus those in creative.[4] He remarks that successful advertising comes from two contrasting styles of problem solving, what psychologists have called convergent versus divergent thinking. Convergent thinking is where you make deductions and draw logical conclusions from information. This is the type of thing we would expect from the strategist, and is inherent in most of what we have been talking about so far in this book. Divergent thinking is when you move outward from specific information to more broadly based generalization. This is the type of thing we expect from creatives. Of course, both types of thinking will be found in each group. But, overall, in our planning we are looking for convergent thinking to uncover the 'hot button' most likely to influence consumer behaviour and divergent thinking to drive creative executions that reflect this in an exciting or memorable way that will help facilitate the effective processing of the message. What we discuss next is how we transfer the fruits of the strategists' convergent thinking to the creatives in order to stimulate their more divergent thinking.

In almost every case, before creatives are asked to begin developing creative ideas, there will be a briefing. This may run from a very loosely written statement of objectives to a rather detailed, formal description of all the information that strategic people feel is important as background in understanding the nature of the consumer and advertised product.

While it is obviously quite important for those working on the creation of advertising to know as much as possible about a brand's market and the people who use the product, there is another, less tangible goal for the creative charge or brief. Creative people are always looking for the big idea, or at least some spark that will ignite the creative juices. The more a creative briefing includes unique and interesting facts about the product, brand, and consumer, the more likely the creatives will be to find that kernel of information that will spark the 'big idea' leading to effective execution. Really innovative briefings are considered so important by many advertising agencies, especially in the UK, that they make a point of spending a great deal of time on *how* they present the briefing. They are likely to go to great lengths in order to present the briefing to the creatives in interesting and exciting ways.

Areas that might be covered in a briefing include such things as:

- market characteristics
- consumer characteristics
- product characteristics
- brand positioning
- competitors' advertising
- communication objectives
- media considerations

Market characteristics. This is usually a background section that discusses what is going on in the market at the time. How big is it? Is it growing? Is it changing? What are the brand shares? Are attitudes changing? It is important that when creative people read this section they come away with a good feel for the market where the advertised product is sold.

Consumer characteristics. We have already spent an entire chapter talking about who makes up the target audience for a brand. This part of the creative briefing will certainly not go into that much detail, but it will provide a vivid portrait of whom we see as the most likely customers for our brand. This description will include not only traditional descriptors such as age, family size, and income, but more qualitative description such as: how they feel about the product, how they go about making choices, the criteria that are important in choice, how they use the product, etc. For transformationally driven decisions, this will also include summaries of their dreams and desires—how the brand will 'transform' them.

Product characteristics. In this section the product itself will be described in detail. What can it do? How is it distributed? What are the specific attributes of the product? Are there real differences between brands? How is it packaged? How is it used?

Brand Positioning. Here you are interested in how the market sees your brand as well as its competition. This is very important information, because the advertising created must be consistent with the brand's current image in the market (as we have just seen in the previous section); unless, of course, the strategy is to change it. But to change the brand's image is a very serious decision, and a very difficult job to accomplish. Generally speaking, radical departures from a brand's current positioning creates uncertainty in the market, and can erode the equity a brand has built over the years.

Competitors' advertising. It is very important to include a review of current and recent competitors' advertising in the charge to the creatives. This provides them with an idea of the general themes and executions that comprise the 'noise' or the environment within which the advertising they create will be seen. This review of competitors' advertising will also ensure that the new advertising which is created is different from their advertising in execution.

Communication objectives. As we learned in Chapter 9, creative work cannot begin until the communication objectives are set. It is the communication objectives that reflect where and how advertising and other forms of marketing communication will fit within the overall marketing plan.

Media considerations. While it is usually not necessary to restrict the creative department in terms of what media they should consider, often it is necessary to request specific media that they may not otherwise have considered. This is particularly true when your model of consumer decision making has identified points within the decision process where such things as point-of-purchase collateral or direct mail might be effective, but also when something other than television or print is desired (for example, outdoor or even radio, which is not often considered).

Other areas may also be covered in the creative briefing, but this outline should provide a guide to some of the more typical kinds of information that will be included. In addition to the creative briefing, a summary document should be provided that acts as the 'blueprint' for the creative executions. This is the creative brief.

The Creative Brief

Most advertising agencies, and many marketers as well (especially of fmcgs), have a specific outline they use for preparing a creative brief. There is no one 'correct' way of preparing a creative brief, but there are certain key areas that should be covered:

- What is the task at hand?
- What are the specific objectives and strategy?
- What, if anything, *must* the executions contain?

Figure 13.1 presents a general outline for a creative brief that addresses these questions. It is important to understand that, even though creative briefs are generally associated only with traditional advertising, they are equally necessary for promotion planning. In fact, a creative brief should be the basis for the development of all marketing communication. The outline that follows includes ten points, and, while specific creative briefs used by advertising agencies and marketers may not look exactly like this, in general these areas will be addressed in their briefs.

Task Definition

The first four areas covered in our outline for a creative brief help you define the task at hand for the creatives. Here is where you are primarily concerned with important insights into the market and target audience. First, we want to identify a *key market observation*. What one point can be made about the market that will help those developing the creative execution understand and believe the brief? Next, what is the *source of business*? Where specifically does the brand expect to get business? This should not be general, but

Brand
Task Definition
Key Market Observation
Source of Business
Consumer Barrier or Insight
Target Audience
Objectives and Strategy
Communication Objectives and Tasks
Brand Attitude Strategy
Benefit Claim and Support
Desired Consumer Response
Execution
Creative Guidelines
Requirements or Mandatory Content

Figure 13.1 Creative Brief

provide a quite specific definition. For example, a creative brief for a luxury sports car might see the source of business as current owners of competitors' luxury cars who are looking for something more exciting. You can see that for a creative brief you are trying to create *images* for the creatives. The third area seeks to provide a specific *consumer barrier or insight*. What one thing do you know about your target audience that would help reach it; or is there something about it that we may need to overcome in order to communicate successfully with it? Finally, you will want to provide a vivid description of the *target audience*. You should provide enough information here so that the creatives can form a true understanding of whom they are to address.

Objectives and Strategy

The next section of the brief contains four points that are primarily concerned with developing the creative execution. Here is where you are laying out the creative objectives and strategy, the positioning, and the key benefits and support, along with the *one benefit* that, if communicated, will achieve your desired objective. First, what are the specific *communication objectives and tasks*? Then, what specifically is the *brand attitude strategy*? Is the decision we are dealing with high or low involvement, positively or negatively motivated? Next, what is the *benefit claim and support*? This is by far the most difficult, and often contentious, area of the creative brief. Here is where the fruits of your positioning work are put into a few words that link the brand to the motivation. The benefit claim takes the benefit, what the consumer wants, and puts it in terms of the emotional response desired. This will be the heart of the creative execution. Finally, you address the *desired consumer response*. You want to provide a brief summary of what you expect to happen if the target audience successfully processes the message.

Execution

The previous two areas covered in our creative brief deal with specific executional factors. Here is where you provide any specific *creative guidelines* that you want to be certain are considered in the execution. For example, this is a place where the look and feel of the brand's advertising may be detailed. The final area covered in the creative brief contains any *requirements or mandatory content*. Often companies have specific requirements for their logos or other layout constraints (although constraining creative layout or production technique is rarely a good idea, as we have mentioned), and these would be detailed here, along with any legal requirements.

Figure 13.2 provides an example of a creative brief for a bank's electronic banking services that follows this outline. Perhaps the most important thing to notice about the brief is its size. It is complete on *one page*. In preparing a creative brief, there are really only two areas where a lot of detail may be needed: the description of the target audience and the *support* for the benefit claim. Otherwise, keep the creative brief to the bare essentials. There will always be plenty of back-up available from the marketing plan and the communication strategy plan if the creatives want more. The key to an effective creative brief is that it is *brief*. This helps ensure that the information provided has been carefully considered.

Product Electronic Banking	Job	Date

Key Market Observations

Potential customers are probably going into branches or using the telephone to conduct business that could be done over the Internet

Source of Business

Current bank checking account/current account customers

Consumer Insight

They are comfortable using the Internet, and are heavy users of ATMs

Target Audience

Loyal and vulnerable, profiled as young and middle-income 'full nest' households with busy lives

Communication Objectives and Tasks

Brand attitude primary objective—to reinforce overall IMC convenience positioning

Brand Attitude Strategy

Low-involvement/informational brand attitude strategy driven by motivation of incomplete satisfaction

Benefit Claim and Support

Telephone banking is more convenient. Support: pay bills almost any time as well as transact basic banking business at any time

Desired Consumer Response

See that telephone banking really is more convenient than branch banking and try

Creative Guidelines

Tie 'inconvenience' of banking to awareness of telephone banking (recall); consider exaggeration in execution

Requirements/Mandatory Content

Requirements legal identifications

Figure 13.2 Creative Brief for a Telephone Banking Service

Ethics and Advertising

This would perhaps be a good place to spend some time considering the issue of ethics and advertising. At root, ethics implies a code of behaviour; but *what* code of behaviour? There are written codes of behaviour throughout the world of advertising. Broadcasters, newspapers, and other media have codes of behaviour for advertisers; advertising trade groups have codes of behaviour for members; government regulators draw up codes of behaviour for advertisers. Is 'unethical behaviour' simply not following such codes of behaviour, or does the issue of ethics and ethical behaviour involve something at a much deeper level?

As Bertrand Russell has put it: 'Ethics is necessary because man's desires conflict. The primary cause of conflict is egoism: most people are more interested in their own welfare than in that of other people.'[5] And of course, advertisers are people, and are therefore likely to be more interested in their own self-interest and the success of their brand than necessarily the good of the consumer.

The real question, however, is not whether or not a manager is more interested in the brand than its customers (which is likely), but whether that leads to behaviour that is harmful to the consumer. This suggests that there are at least two issues with which we must deal. One, what would constitute unethical behaviour on the part of an advertiser; and two, even if the behaviour is unethical, if it does no harm, does it matter? Some people (as we shall see in Chapter 14) consider the use of product placement as unethical because the *intent* is to deceive. Yet there is very little evidence that product placements work.

Dealing with these issues, of course, requires a definition of ethics. Attempts to define ethics have kept philosophers busy since before the time of Socrates. The great break-through by Socrates in defining ethics was the development of ethical rationalism. He argued that ethical truth was *absolute* and demonstrable, much like the truths of geom-etry. Plato took this and injected it into an overarching philosophical system, but his conclusions were criticized by his student Aristotle on realistic grounds. He argued that ethics are not pure science, mathematically demonstrated, as thought by Socrates and Plato. Rather it is the result of practised judgement, or *phrónêsis*. One learns the truth of how to live one's life well not by abstract reasoning but by practical life, and by learning from experience. The Stoics and Epicureans tried to give meaning and direction to an eth-ical life, but without recourse to the traditional mythology of their time.[6]

What these ancient philosophers seem to have been doing was looking at ethics in terms of a study of the nature of the good life and the nature of good itself, which is what informed Christian ethics. But in the Italian Renaissance, the embrace of classical human-ism was often hostile to Christian ethical teachings. Teleological ethical theory was popu-larized by Machiavelli, where the 'end justifies the means', and was also equally a part of Galileo's thinking. They believed that it really didn't matter what you did as long as it led to a positive outcome.[7] This set up a counter-definition to the more traditional deonto-logical view of ethics that one must do the 'right' thing regardless of the outcome.

Philosophers that followed enlarged upon all of this thinking. Locke believed that we learn ethical ideas through our experiences, implying that ethics are wholly relative to experience. For Locke, what we call good is what causes well-being, what we call evil causes pain. This sounds very close to Thomas Hobbes's model of ethical thinking. As Kors has put it: 'The importance of this is dramatic. If our knowledge of ethics in the world is determined by our particular experience, then it would seem that environment determines all. Change the environment, change what causes pain and pleasure, reward and punishment in society, and you change the very thinking in ethical natures of the individuals within it.'[8]

Moving into the nineteenth century, ethics began to be understood in terms of morality. Hume argued that moral judgement is a sentiment of approval or disapproval, which is innate and not based on rational deliberation.[9] Kant's moral theory assumed a moral law within us, and this led to his 'categorical imperative': act only according to that maxim through which you can at the same time will that it should become a universal law for everyone to follow.[10] While scholars disagree about what this is, it seems to be saying that one should follow this no matter who you are or what you might otherwise desire. For example, do not say 'don't lie if you want to be trusted,' but rather say 'don't lie, period.'

In the twentieth century Ayer, one of the leading logical positivists, argued that disputes about ultimate values are pseudo-disputes precisely because they are, in principle, unresolvable.[11] As a result, disputes about ethics are the same as arguments about aesthetics. It is a question of individual preferences. Dewey, an empiricistic rationalist, argues that there are no fixed moral ends. One's ethics guides action in pursuit of an end; it does not in itself determine that end.[12] This leads us back to Aristotle's notion of *phrónêsis*.

The Frankfurt School in the 1930s was the first to see the role of the mass media of culture and communication in the socialization and control of contemporary societies. They argued that Hollywood films, network radio (in the days before television), advertising, magazines, and newspapers were promoting American ideology, just like Nazi Germany and Soviet Russian cultural apparatus. They were among the first to pay particular attention to advertising, packaging, and design, and the 'morality' of such influence. This was the beginning of a merger between philosophy and social science in the development of a critical theory of contemporary society.[13]

The point in looking back at how the issue of ethics has been considered over the centuries is to understand that there has not been, nor is there now, any consensus as to how ethics should be defined. This makes it rather difficult to discuss unethical behaviour in advertising. Does it simply involve intent? Or, does it require a negative consequence of that intent? What if the negative consequence occurs *without* intent on the part of the advertiser? Is that unethical behaviour?

We could perhaps all agree that deliberately misleading in advertising where the consequences are likely to be harmful is wrong; and most would say unethical. This would be especially true of, say, health-related products and drugs, where there are potentially serious side effects. But if the consequences are not harmful, is it unethical? From a Christian moral standpoint, the answer would be yes; but then moral values are not absolute. In a Christian sense, moral merit is concerned solely with acts of will, that is choosing rightly among available alternative courses of action, 'rightly' being defined by Christian doctrine. With other religions, and clearly among those with no religious belief, 'rightly' may be defined in widely differing ways.

Even if we look more broadly at 'community standards', such 'standards' are rarely reflected in the beliefs of everyone, and they change over time (often over short periods of time). For example, in the American Psychiatric Association's first attempt to classify mental illnesses in 1952, homosexuality was defined as a mental illness under paraphilias (the social criteria of undesirable behaviour). It was removed in 1973, and is now considered a lifestyle alternative by the American Psychological Association.[14]

Perhaps the best we can do is strive for the truth in advertising, allowing for a certain degree of puffery (exaggeration that is readily understood as such, for example 'fastest acting ever'). Deliberate lying would be wrong, whether considered 'unethical' or not. Additionally, if an advertiser is aware of facts that could lead to harm, whether or not it actually occurs, there is an obligation to make consumers aware of those facts. Conscious omission would be wrong, again whether considered 'unethical' or not. An exception to this can occur in social marketing where in some cases telling the whole truth could actually cause harm. For example, if people really understood the degree of misdiagnosis by doctors or the actual cure rates for many common medicines and treatments, people could very well lose faith in medicine and not seek any help at all.[15]

As a footnote to this discussion, we are always taken by the fact that academics, consumer advocates, and government regulators are so very concerned that no advertising message 'deceive', even if unintentionally, when there is almost no concern over the overt lying and misleading nature of most political advertising. The consequence of misleading or 'unethical' advertising in the world of commercial speech such as whether or not one detergent actually does clean better than another *pales* to the potential consequences of the lies inherent in most political speech.

In the end, managers need to remember that if their advertising or other marketing activities are not truthful or are misleading, competitors will be quick to point this out, and over the long term consumers are unlikely to continue buying the brand.

Creative Research

With the creative brief in hand, the job of developing the creative execution begins. More often than not, creatives will come up with ideas on their own, although there are a number of research techniques available that can aid this process. If any research is likely to be done at the creative development stage, it will be to explore or screen concepts. Again, there are a number of procedures available to help here as well.[16] The most important thing to remember if you do conduct creative-ideation or concept-screening research is to conduct the research among a sample of the brand's target audience. Once a concept has been agreed upon, one or more test executions will be developed. Actually, the more test executions created, the better, within reasonable constraints of time and cost.[17] While research may not have been involved in the development of the concept, it is *essential* that the test executions be pre-tested. A great deal of money will go into the production and media exposure of the final executions, and you will want to be as certain as possible that the creative execution satisfies the brief, meets the communication objective, and delivers the benefit claim in an understandable manner.

Many agencies and even marketers often do not feel it is necessary to pre-test their creative execution, feeling they can rely upon their experience and knowledge of the brand and market to guide their decision. But, regardless of how experienced or knowledgeable someone is about a brand and market, it is foolish not to pre-test. In fact, one's very experience and knowledge can actually be a handicap in evaluating one's own creative executions. Because managers are so familiar with the brand and the creative execution, they 'see' and process it very differently from how the target audience possibly could. They naturally make connections between the brand and benefit claim *because* of their knowledge (recall our discussion of top-down processing), connections that may not be possible without that knowledge. It just makes sense to pre-test so you are certain of how the target audience will respond to the creative execution.[18]

Pre-Testing Creative Executions

The job of pre-testing creative executions requires original primary research, custom-tailored to reflect the appropriate creative strategy. Relying solely on a standardized pre-testing procedure offered by a research institute or syndicated service may not be appropriate for the execution you are testing. Flexible procedures based on *the brand's advertising communication objectives* provide a much better fit and provide the manager with a better understanding of the execution's potential.[19]

The reason you pre-test creative executions is to improve the chances that the advertising will work as planned when placed in the media. Whether or not it will work depends on three factors:

- the creative content of the executions;
- correct media placement and scheduling;
- competitive advertising activity.

Pre-testing deals only with the creative content of the execution. Tracking a campaign over time evaluates all three factors. Pre-testing a creative execution ensures it is consistent with strategy. It lets you know if the execution is likely to achieve the communication objectives set for the brand, and enables you to predict how it will 'work' in the market. A good pre-testing system also provides the manager with understanding that can be used to revise or improve the execution if necessary. In fact, in a summary of seventy-five top British advertising agencies, the reason given most often for pre-testing was for 'learning' and to improve future campaigns.[20]

Methods Unsuitable for Pre-Testing Creative Executions

Before we begin to examine the best ways of pre-testing creative executions, we want to discuss three methods often used in pre-testing that the manager should avoid: using focus groups to test executions, using advertising recall measures, and using physiological measures.

First, never use focus groups to pre-test creative executions. While focus groups are very helpful for formulating the communication strategy prior to the development of the execution, they are totally inappropriate for pre-testing executions. There are at least two compelling reasons for this. The first problem is that focus groups vastly over-expose the execution compared with how it will be seen in the market. In a group setting, they are thoroughly discussed, a far cry from the 30 seconds or so that a TV advert has to communicate in the real world or the 1–2 seconds that a print or outdoor advert has in which to gain the consumer's attention. The second concern is a validity problem. By their very nature, focus groups encourage group interactions that largely prevent individual reactions to the executions from occurring as they would normally. People process advertising as individuals, even if they are watching TV with others.

Secondly, advertising recall is *not* a valid predictor of communication effectiveness. The most that can be said about recall measures, especially day-after recall (DAR) testing, is that they may be a rough measure of attention to the advertising. But the fundamental flaw is that recall procedures are *advertising*-recall based, not *brand*-recall based. We are looking for *brand*-associated communication effects. *Brand* awareness and *brand* attitude are the fundamental communication objectives, not advertising awareness or attitudes towards the advertising. No *pre-test* measure based upon advertising recall that we are aware of has ever been shown to predict advertising effectiveness, and this is because the media vehicle (as in DAR) or the test situation (as in the case of most syndicated recall measures) is a cue that is irrelevant to the consumer's decision process.

Finally, physiological measures on their own are not particularly effective in pre-testing creative executions. Physiological measures generally measure only attention to an execution. EEG, or 'brain-wave', measures certainly record the fact that something is going on when you are exposed to an execution, but the interpretation of this response in terms of advertising effects is not clear. Eye-tracking techniques have shown some relationship to brand recognition, but not to either brand recall awareness or brand attitude.[21] And new eye-measurement techniques meant to measure emotional response to an execution, while perhaps measuring some level of arousal, do not provide any real diagnostic help.

Pre-test Measures

One of the most important considerations in pre-testing creative executions is the *order* in which the test questions are asked. Basically, you want to order the questions so as not to sensitize or bias later questions. For example, brand purchase intention and brand attitude should be measured before brand benefit beliefs, because measuring the beliefs first could lead a person to form new or revised attitudes or intentions as a result of thinking about the benefit beliefs presented. Brand awareness should be measured on a delayed basis, because, if you measure it immediately after exposure to the test execution, the result is likely to be much higher than it would probably be in the real world, where delays occur between seeing an advert and an opportunity to purchase the brand.

Attention Measures

Print adverts and Internet banner adverts must arrest the reader's attention so that he or she does not continue turning the page or surfing before the message can register. Research has shown that about 50 per cent of all print adverts fail to gain the reader's attention. On the other hand, because radio and television adverts rely upon reflexive attention, an attention measure is not necessary when they are pre-tested.

Eye-tracking experiments by Kroeber-Riel and von Keitz have shown that it takes about 1.75 seconds to process an illustration in a print advert and about 0.25 seconds to process each word in a headline.[22] Since the illustration and headline are the minimum input required if the execution is to communicate anything, when pre-testing print adverts you should compute the time necessary for minimally processing the test execution and then use a timed portfolio test as the first measure in your pre-test. The time spent looking at the test execution should be recorded and compared with the time needed actually to process the picture and headline in order to establish a measure of the number of people likely to pay attention to the execution. The remaining pre-test measures of communication effects should then be corrected for the proportion of attention achieved by the test execution.

Processing Measures

Processing reflects a person's immediate responses to the execution. These responses are transient, so they must be measured immediately following exposure to the test execution. If you were to try to measure them during processing, as some pre-testing procedures do, this would of course disrupt processing and provide a poor measure of the actual effect. An immediate retrospective measurement of reactions to an execution does not affect subsequent brand-related measures. The two types of processing measures that should be taken at this point in the pre-test are acceptance for high-involvement brand attitude, and learning for low-involvement brand attitude.

Acceptance. If the brand decision is high involvement, then, as we have learned, the target audience must *accept* the brand's benefit claims. What matters in high-involvement strategies is the extent to which the consumer willingly agrees with the message. The most valid measure of high-involvement processing is something called cognitive response measurement, which requires post-coding or scoring the test subjects' comments about the message. Mention of the brand should also be recorded, because the comments should reflect opinions about the brand. Failure to mention the brand could indicate a possible brand awareness problem with the execution.

Learning. With low-involvement brand decisions, you are looking for rote learning responses. While learning is also necessary for brand awareness, this cannot be measured until after the other measures are taken. In low-involvement strategies, what counts is the perceived message about the brand. It does not matter whether the target audience fully accepts or is convinced by the message, as long as it is understood correctly. A successfully registered low-involvement attitude shift will show up on the communication effect measures of intention to try the brand (low-involvement informational advertising) or brand attitude image (low-involvement transformational advertising).

Measuring low-involvement attitudinal learning is rather straightforward. It consists of the following type of question: 'In this advert, aside from trying to convince you to try the brand, what do you think the advertiser is trying to *tell* you?' Verbatim playback or accurate paraphrases of the advert-proposed brand benefit (usually there is only one main benefit proposed in low-involvement advertising) are scored as successful learning during processing, with one important qualification. If the brand name has not yet been mentioned, the interviewer should ask: 'What was the brand advertised?' This is because the association to be learned is between the brand (awareness) and the benefit (attitude) and not the benefit in isolation. After the open-ended acceptance measures for high-involvement advert pre-tests or the learning measures for low-involvement ones, for diagnostic purposes you may wish to include some more structured questions.

Communication Effects Measures

On those occasions when category need is a communication objective and you have to remind the prospective buyer of a latent need, you will want to measure *category* purchase intention. If the category need objective is to 'sell' the category, two other measures will be needed: category benefit beliefs, and a delayed measure of category awareness. The addition of a category benefit belief measure is to assess whether in fact the execution generated a perceived interest in the category. The need for a *category awareness* measure is to ensure that, once someone has formed an interest in the category, he or she remembers it. This category-level awareness occurs within the context of competing purchase categories. Once these category measures have been taken, you can then go on to the brand measures.

Brand Purchase Intention Measures. A measure of brand purchase intention is not necessary for low-involvement transformational advertising. The reason is that, in a pre-test situation, it is not reasonable to expect an immediate effect on purchase intention. Instead, the effectiveness of low-involvement transformational advertising should be *inferred* from increases in the brand benefit beliefs, because this is the only reasonable effect that can be expected during the pre-test. Once such advertising is running in the market, you will measure both brand purchase intention and overall brand attitude, because the transformational advertising should have had a sufficient number of exposures to work.

Measures of brand purchase intention must pay attention to the wording of the intention question in terms of 'try' or 'use' and include a time frame for the intention. Paying attention to the wording of questions should go without saying, but too often important distinctions are ignored. For example, with new product categories (and brands), consumers are more willing to state intention to 'try' a brand, which implies less commitment, than they are to state intentions to 'buy' it. The wording of the intention measure should precisely reflect the purchase or purchase-related action objective. The time frame for a brand purchase intention measure is satisfied by making the intention conditional on category need. For example:

- Suppose you were going to add to your investment portfolio. How likely is it that you would consider Alliance & Leicester?

- The next time you buy a candy bar, how likely is it that you will buy Bounty?

Brand Attitude Measures. Next comes the overall measure of brand attitude, except when testing low-involvement transformational executions, as explained above. Measuring brand attitude helps to interpret the ultimate pre-test criterion measure, brand purchase intention given awareness of the brand. For brand purchase intention, we measure how likely someone is to try, buy, or use the brand after exposure to the creative execution. For overall brand attitude, we measure how favourably the brand is evaluated *relative to other brands*, regardless of whether there is interest in buying or considering the brand at the next purchase opportunity. The main thing to remember in a brand attitude measure, as with the intention measure earlier, is to specify the *situation* for which the brand is to be purchased or used. This should directly reflect the purchase motivation. For example, people's attitude toward brands of coffee may differ depending on whether it is for their own breakfast or for serving to guests at a formal dinner. An attitude measure should be situation specific and provide the opportunity to evaluate your brand relative to competing brands when the same question is posed of them.

After this overall measure of brand attitude, you will want a measure of a brand's perceived delivery on the specific benefit or benefits presented in the execution. These benefit claims are there to influence brand attitude, and measuring them serves as a diagnostic method for interpreting the overall brand attitude result. It also serves as the *sole* measure of brand attitude for low-involvement transformational executions. The measures of the brand benefit claim should follow the overall brand attitude rating to avoid contamination. You do not want those evaluating the execution to form a spurious attitude based on benefits suggested in the measures rather than on benefits spontaneously processed from the advertising.

Brand Awareness Measures. Why is the brand awareness measure delayed until the end of the pre-test? Brand awareness is the key communication effect, without which nothing else really matters. It plays a gate-keeping role vis-à-vis the other communication effects, and is critical for purchase of the brand. If the prospective buyer does not recognize or recall the brand, it will not be purchased, no matter how well established or how favourable the other communication effects of the brand are for the consumer.

Only in the special case of direct-response broadcast advertising, such as the 'call or write now' type of adverts that appear on TV or radio, should you measure brand awareness at the beginning of the pre-test. For all other types of advertising, in the real world there will be a delay between advertising exposure and the next purchase decision opportunity. This may range from an hour or so for 'same-day' retail advertising, to a week or more for other products.

Unfortunately, brand awareness measures taken during the pre-testing session itself (or as much as ten minutes later in some syndicated tests of TV commercials) do not provide a reliable measure of a creative execution's ability to generate or increase awareness for the brand. Short-interval measures should never be interpreted as absolute measures of an execution's ability to create or increase brand awareness. This is especially true for recall brand awareness, which declines significantly over time owing to other advertising's competitive interference in memory. The only reliable way to estimate brand awareness is to administer a delayed test. This is obviously more costly and time consuming than attempting to assess brand awareness during the pre-test. But, as you should now realize, to include the measure in the pre-test will be unreliable.

For recall brand awareness, the measure can be taken by phone by calling back those interviewed after an appropriate time interval has elapsed, and asking what brands in the product category they recall and comparing the response with that of a sample that did not see the test execution. For recognition brand awareness, the measure is more difficult, because it requires a personal re-interview in which those interviewed are shown a photograph of brand packages and asked which brands they recognize at a glance. Two-way TV methodologies may eventually facilitate brand recognition measurement, but for now a personal follow-up interview will be required.

Pre-testing Promotion

Promotions too must be pre-tested. The executions that carry the promotion should be evaluated along the lines just discussed. But in addition, particular attention must be paid to an appropriate measure of the likely *success* of the promotion. Unlike with advertising, if a promotion is too successful, it can have a severe impact upon the brand.

The now classic case of Hoover's 1992 promotion illustrates just what can happen if you do not test a promotion. In the UK an offer was made for '2 free flights to the US'—airline tickets worth £400—as a premium for buying any Hoover vacuum cleaner costing more than £100. The promotion was budgeted at £500,000. What consumers quickly did was redefine the promotion as '2 tickets to the US for £100' and set off to buy a new Hoover whether they needed one or not. Demand quickly strained supply and dealers began to increase the price of Hoover models originally priced at less than £100 so they would qualify for the promotions.

It is estimated that over 200,000 people tried to take advantage of this offer. One story has it that a man whose ticket had not arrived in the mail as promised telephoned Hoover customer service for a repairman. When the repairman turned up, the man impounded his van until his tickets were sent. What was to have been a £500,000 promotion ended up costing £48 *million*, and, you can bet, a number of marketing jobs at Hoover. Add to this the bad publicity and the fact that the promotion was *totally unrelated* to Hoover or vacuum cleaners, and this stands as a real marketing disaster.[23] You can (and should) purchase insurance against potential problems and monetary losses associated with promotions, but the best insurance is careful planning and testing.

CHAPTER SUMMARY

We have now considered in detail the creative execution of a communication strategy, emphasizing the importance of consistency related to the brand's primary benefit. We examined the creative briefing process and the content of the creative brief itself. We then talked about the issue of 'ethics' in advertising, and the difficulty in defining just what might constitute 'unethical' advertising. Finally, we discussed creative research, looking at the appropriateness of various pre-testing measures.

QUESTIONS TO CONSIDER

13.1 How does consistency in advertising and all other marketing communication improve the overall effectiveness of a campaign?

13.2 What is the role of consistency in advertising and promotion executions over time?

13.3 Why is a creative brief confined to one page?

13.4 How will an effective creative brief improve an advert?

13.5 What role does, or can, ethics play in advertising?

13.6 Why is it important to pre-test creative executions?

CASE STUDY 13

Nike, Inc.: Air Jordan Campaign

In 1984 Nike Inc., the world's leading designer and marketer of athletic shoes, signed rookie basketball sensation Michael Jordan to promote a line of shoes named in his honour. Faced with faltering sales, powerful competitors, and eroding popularity, Nike sought not only to capture a greater share of the growing basketball shoe segment of the athletic footwear market but also to reinvigorate its tired brand image.

In 1985 Nike launched the first Air Jordan basketball shoes, christened to reflect Jordan's gravity-defying moves on the court and the company's patented 'air' technology contained in the sneaker. To herald the shoe's debut, Nike teamed up with ad agency Wieden & Kennedy to create a print and television campaign that would link Air Jordan to Jordan's magnetic personality. The resulting 'Air Jordan' campaign 'helped turn the company around and changed the face of the athletic shoe industry'. The spot capitalized on the fact that the National Basketball Association (NBA) had banned Jordan from wearing the first Air Jordans designed for him by Nike. Although the underlying issue was the shoe's bold black and red colour scheme, the commercial played up Nike's rebelliousness. Between 1984 and 1986, Nike dedicated $5 million to advertising Air Jordans. In these early years the campaign focused on Jordan's unparalleled athleticism. One 1985 commercial featured Jordan soaring toward the basket. As he dunked the ball, the voice-over queried, 'Who says man was not meant to fly?' In 1987, however, Nike began to chart a new course with innovative 'Air Jordan' ads that infused Jordan—and his namesake shoes—with a dynamic personality. For example, the 'Mike and Spike' ads, which debuted that year, paired Jordan with acclaimed film-maker Spike Lee, who played fast-talking, nerdy, and basketball-obsessed Mars Blackmon (a character Lee had created in his film, *She's Gotta Have It*). Shot in grainy black and white, these commercials relied on offbeat humour to make an impact. In one ad the diminutive Mars was shown hanging from a basketball rim, boasting about his 'serious hang time'. The camera panned to reveal that he was actually standing on Jordan's shoulders. When Jordan grew tired of Mars's chatter, he walked away and returned to dunk a shot in Mars's face. In commercials that ran during the 1992 and 1993 Super Bowls, Jordan teamed up with the Warner Bros. cartoon characters Bugs Bunny, Porky Pig, and Marvin the Martian.

By the early 1990s Air Jordan had transcended its original role as a fairly straightforward marketing effort. Jordan had become a brand unto himself, and the line of shoes and apparel he endorsed became known within Nike as 'Brand Jordan'. By 1996 the Air Jordan sneakers outwardly manifested this evolution. Rather than displaying Nike's signature 'swoosh' logo, they sported their own unique 'Jumpman' icon, a rendering of Jordan in flight. This unprecedented shift reflected the fundamental changes the 'Air Jordan' campaign and Nike's relationship with Jordan effected across the footwear and advertising industries. Advertisers everywhere sought 'the next Jordan', the celebrity spokesperson who could transcend his or her own market niche and become a full-fledged pop icon. Thus even when Jordan announced his retirement from the NBA in 1999, Nike pledged the company's continued fealty to the star and his shoes.

Historical Context

At the time Nike was founded, the athletic shoe market consisted mostly of simple, inexpensive sneakers designed for multisport use. Nike quickly revolutionized the industry. By touting the technological features of its sleek shoes that supposedly aided athletic performance and by linking the Nike brand to celebrity athletes who endorsed the shoes, Nike saw its sales soar. But shifts within the industry during the early 1980s proved costly to Nike. In 1983 the running shoe sector of the athletic footwear market peaked, and the entire industry fragmented as consumers increasingly demanded specialized shoes designed for a particular activity. Nike failed to respond to these changes, while competitors such as Reebok did not.

Target Market

Market research revealed that males between the ages of 15 and 22 purchased 30 per cent of all athletic shoes, and influenced another 10 per cent of sales through word of mouth, although they accounted for a mere 15 per cent of the population. According to the *Wall Street Journal*, American teens were essential to a footwear brand's success, since they bought an average of four pairs of sneakers a year. Jordan's star power helped Nike market the Air Jordan line to young consumers. Jordan's athleticism alone, however, would not be sufficient. As the *Washington Post* reported, an astonishing '60% of Nike's basketball shoes are bought by people who do not play the sport, even recreationally.' Thus Nike strove to create an ultra hip image for the shoes to reach the myriad consumers concerned about image more than performance. While superior athletic performance was part of the image Nike conveyed, the company decided to focus on elements of African American inner-city culture as well. Stylistically, 'Air Jordan' commercials often resembled the music videos so popular among teenagers. 'Spike and Mike' spots featured quick-cutting videoesque images backed by popular hip-hop music. Later ads, most notably 1992's 'Hare Jordan', featured a fusion of cartoon and film. But the core of the 'Air Jordan' advertising was Jordan himself. With his growing celebrity, Jordan crossed all boundaries of race, age, and gender and essentially appealed to everyone.

Competition

When Air Jordan debuted, Nike lagged far behind arch-rival Reebok. Capitalizing on the aerobics craze and the subsequent demand for specialized shoes, Reebok's fortunes rose, while Nike's market share plummeted. But the profound success of Air Jordan threatened Reebok. In 1988 the company launched a massive ad campaign characterized by quirky humour and a pointed message of individualism, The 'Reebok Lets U.B.U.' campaign portrayed such oddities as Reebok-wearing fairy grandmothers and quotes from Ralph Waldo Emerson in hopes of maintaining the company's lead. Despite high praise from ad critics, the 'U.B.U.' campaign failed to impress and the company lost ground to Nike.

Reebok followed with the 'Legends' campaign, which the *Chicago Tribune* described as its 'answer to Nike Air Jordans'. The commercials showed inner-city youths playing basketball. Nevertheless, Nike overtook Reebok in 1989, claiming 26 per cent of the market to Reebok's 22 per cent. In 1990 Reebok introduced its heralded 'Pump' basketball shoes, which featured an inflatable device to help it better fit the wearer's foot. But this innovation failed to help Reebok. Reebok tried again in 1993 when it signed NBA Rookie of the Year Shaquille O'Neal and introduced

Shaq Attack, a product line that debuted with a $10 million flurry of television and print ads. Nike also faced competition from smaller rivals. Asics initiated a $10 million campaign in 1993 for a new line of basketball shoes. Instead of embarking on Reebok's quest to find the next Jordan, Asics used ageing basketball great Isaiah Thomas in a series of unconventional ads. Converse, Adidas, and New Balance all vied for market share as well. Moreover, as Air Jordan basketball shoes became standard garb for America's teens, hip youngsters took to wearing boots and other brown shoes instead of the ubiquitous Nikes.

Marketing Strategy

Nike used a high-profile and massive marketing effort to promote Jordan's shoes. In addition to the multi-million-dollar contracts Nike signed with its superstar endorser, the company selected big-budget media venues to carry its message to the desired audience. In keeping with the performance image of the Air Jordan line, Nike ran 'Air Jordan' commercials during major televised sporting events such as the NBA playoff and all-star games. Moreover, around the start of the basketball season each year, Nike launched an updated version of the Air Jordan shoe. Nike was also careful not to let its 'Air Jordan' advertising get stale. As the campaign continued, the style of the spots shifted from the early focus on Jordan's athletic prowess to the edgy humour and attitude of 'Spike and Mike' and to the more inclusive 'Hare Jordan' ads. These shifts were also intended to prevent the public from tiring of Jordan. Even as his team dominated the NBA, Nike strove to put a human face on him so that he would not lose his effectiveness as a pitchman by becoming too otherworldly In 1997 '9,000 Shots' featured Jordan standing in an empty gym, talking about the 9,000 shots he had missed in his career.

Outcome

From the outset, the 'Air Jordan' campaign was a stunning success. In its first year alone, Air Jordan shoes accounted for $130 million in sales, which according to the *Washington Post*, 'would have made [Nike] the fifth-largest sneaker firm in the world' had Air Jordan 'been its own company'. By 1989 Nike had overtaken Reebok in sales. With 43 per cent of the athletic shoe market in 1996, Nike's rise to the top was triumphant. Air Jordan's significance to Nike quickly transcended a specific line of shoes. Nike developed Jordan's products into a sub-brand—Brand Jordan, with its distinct 'Jumpman' logo. Controlling nearly 75 per cent of the basketball shoe market, Nike planned to expand Brand Jordan beyond the court to encompass a range of lifestyle products. It became clear to Nike just how essential both Brand Jordan and the figure of Jordan were to the company's continued growth. Both times Jordan announced his retirement from professional basketball (in 1993 and 1999), Nike's stock price fell.

Source: From Riggs, Thomas (Editor). GALE BUSINESS STRATEGIES: Encyclopedia of Major Marketing Campaigns, 1E. © 2000 Gale, a part of Cengage Learning, Inc. Reproduced by permission. www. cengage.com/permissions

Edited by Natalia Yannopoulou

Discussion Questions

1 What are the gains and risks for having a consistent advertising message for a long period of time?

2 What would be the best way for the competition to react to such a long-time consistent advertising strategy?

3 What could be a proposed future advertising strategy for Nike?

4 What could be the proposed mix of media selection for a successful long-time consistent advertising strategy?

FURTHER READING

- Perhaps the most important role of the account planner is in briefing the creative team. But how should account planners be evaluated? Margaret Morrison and Eric Haley deal with this in their article 'Account Planners' View on how their Work is and should be Evaluated', *Journal of Advertising*, 32/2 (Summer 2003), 7–16.

- Measuring the effectiveness of advertising was the subject of an insightful doctoral dissertation by Lars Bergkvist, *Advertising Effectiveness Measurement: Intermediate Constructs and Measures*, distributed by EFI, The Economic Research Institute, Stockholm School of Economics (2000).

NOTES

1 While a creative idea of some kind is obviously needed before advertising can be developed, it is probably impossible to describe where a creative idea comes from. Many authors and researchers have tried, and, although there is a general understanding of some of the things that nurture creativity, it is far from complete. A good introduction to the vagaries of creativity is Arthur Koestler's *The Act of Creation* (3rd edn. London: Pan Books, 1966). Creative ideas spring up in different ways with different people. However, successful creative ideas will adhere to some basic guidelines. They will be interesting, unique, and *workable* ideas that enable the creatives working on the advertising to present a brand's positioning engagingly to the target audience. It should also be *extendable*. As Roderick White put it in *Advertising: What it is and How it Works*, 3rd edn. (London: McGraw-Hill, 1993), 51: 'Ideas that can be developed beyond a single campaign into a campaign that will run for years are really worth their weight in gold.'

2 See L. R. Squire and E. R. Kandel, *Memory: From Mind to Molecules* (New York: Scientific American Library, 1999).

3 A detailed case history of the Oxo brand is reported in C. Baker, *Advertising Works 7* (London: NTC Publications, 1992).

4 See D. O'Malley, 'Creative Briefing', in D. Cowley (ed.), *How to Plan Advertising* (London: Cassell, 1987), 77–85.

5 Bertrand Russell, *A History of Western Philosophy* (London: The Folio Society, 2004), 747.

6 These ideas of the Greek philosophers are discussed in Bertrand Russell's *Introduction to the Problems of Philosophy* (Oxford: Oxford University Press, 1959).

7 See E. Cassiner, *The Individual and Cosmos in Renaissance Philosophy* (New York: Dover, 1963).

8 This quote is found in the transcript of a lecture given by Allan Kors in a series on Great Minds of the Western Intellectual Tradition, offered by the Teaching Company (2000), Part 4 of 7, page 47.

9 David Hume, *An Inquiry Concerning the Principles of Morals* (Indianapolis: Hacket, 1987).

10 Kant's philosophy on ethics is discussed in his *Grounding for the Metaphysics of Morals* (Indianapolis: Hacket, 1993).

11 See A. J. Ayer, *Language, Truth, and Logic* (New York: Dover, 1946).

12 See John Dewey, *Reconstruction in Philosophy* (New York: Holt, 1922).

13 For the definitive discussion of the Frankfurt School see Rolf Wiggerhaus, *The Frankfurt School* (Cambridge, Mass.: MIT Press, 1996).

14 See the 1952 and 1973 editions of the American Psychiatric Association's *Diagnostic and Statistical Manual of Mental Disorders* (Washington, DC: American Psychiatric Association).

15 R. M. Greevy, 'Prescription medicine is hit or miss for most', *The Australian* (9 December 2003), 10.

16 See Cowley (ed.), *How to Plan Advertising*, and J. R. Rossiter and L. Percy, *Advertising Communication and Promotion Management* (New York: McGraw-Hill, 1997).

17 See Rossiter and Percy, *Advertising Communication and Promotion Management*.

18 An excellent review of the measures used to evaluate the effectiveness of advertising in the UK and Sweden may be found in two papers by Lars Bergkvist: 'Competing in Advertising Effectiveness: An Analysis of the 1996 British Advertising Effectiveness Award Case Histories', unpublished paper presented at the AEJMC annual convention, New Orleans, 4–7 August 1999; and 'Swedish Awards', unpublished paper presented at the 15th Nordic Conference on Business Studies, Helsinki, Finland, 19–21 August 1999.

19 See L. Percy, 'The Importance of Flexibility in Pre-testing Advertising', *Admap*, 381 (February 1998), 29–31.

20 See M. P. Flandin, E. Martin, and L. P. Simkin, 'Advertising Effectiveness Research: A Survey of Agencies, Clients and Conflicts', *International Journal of Advertising*, 41 (1990), 203–14.

21 See L. Weinblatt, 'New Research Technology for Today and Tomorrow', in *Copy Research* (New York: Advertising Research Foundation, 1985), 180–92, and 'Eye Movement Testing', *Marketing News*, 5 June 1987, 1.

22 See W. Kroeber-Riel, 'Effects of Emotional Pictorial Elements in Ads Analyzed by Means of Eye Movement Monitoring', in T. Kinneau (ed.), *Advances in Consumer Research*, xi (Ann Arbor, Mich.: Association for Consumer Research, 1984), 591–7, and B. von Keitz, 'Eye Movement Research: Do Consumers Use the Information they are Offered?', *European Research*, 16 (1988), 217–24.

23 There are many references to this by-now-infamous Hoover promotion, including an editorial by K. Newman in the *International Journal of Advertising* 15/2 (1993), 94, and 'Hoover and its publicity start dive' in *Marketing* (UK), 8 April 1993, 18.

 Visit the Online Resource Centre that accompanies this book for additional resources to support the text: http://www.oxfordtextbooks.co.uk/orc/percy_elliott3e/

Integrating Advertising and Promotion

14

Sales Promotion and Broader Communication Mix

 KEY CONCEPTS

1 Advertising and promotion may be delivered by a variety of means beyond traditional mass media.

2 Sales promotion techniques, in addition to providing a stimulus for purchase, also provide an opportunity for communicating the brand's benefit.

3 Consumers do not distinguish between incentives that are part of a retail or trade promotion versus those that come directly from the brand, but there is a significant difference from the brand's perspective.

4 Public relations and sponsorships can play a key role in positioning a brand and reinforcing its benefit.

5 Public relations activity directly in support of marketing objectives is known as marketing public relations.

6 Personal selling and trade shows offer unique opportunities for interaction with the target audience when delivering a message.

7 Product placement, while widely used, is open to ethical concerns as well as questions as to its effectiveness.

8 Packaging is an effective but often overlooked means of communicating and reinforcing a brand's benefit.

At this point, the overall strategic planning process is complete, and the creative development set. Now it is time to implement the plan. This will be specifically addressed in the last chapter, but first we want to take a closer look at sales promotion, and also some of the other options available for delivering advertising and promotion that go beyond traditional media. These may or may not be a part of a brand's marketing communication programme, but they are important options to be considered.

Perhaps the most important thing to keep in mind as these are discussed is that when any of these are used, it should be the *same* message, executed with the *same* look and feel, as that delivered through more traditional media. Banners and brochures used at a trade show should focus upon the same key benefit as the brand's advertising; sponsorships and product placements must be consistent with the positioning and key benefit of the brand; sales promotions must be consistent with the brand's advertising. A fashion label that offers traditional clothing styles should not be sponsoring a rock concert; a premium for North Face outdoor gear and apparel should be consistent with their rugged outdoor image. These are all part of the strategic considerations that go into effective advertising and promotion for a brand.

In this chapter we shall be discussing the major sales promotion techniques, and will provide an overview of a number of additional ways of delivering advertising and promotion from the broader communication mix.

Sales Promotion

In our discussion of promotion in earlier chapters we have been underscoring the *strategic* difference between advertising and promotion, and have seen that with promotion, in addition to brand awareness and brand attitude, brand purchase intention is always a communication objective. That is what promotion is all about: immediate action. We have also noted that an incentive is not an absolute requirement for a promotion. Nevertheless, most promotions do indeed include an incentive. They are generally referred to as *sales promotions*, and when defined in this way involve some direct purchasing incentive that is offered for making a specific purchase or taking a specific purchase-related action.[1]

In this section we will be departing somewhat from the strategic discussion of promotion, and will be introducing the specific sales promotion techniques that are used most often when promotion is a part of the communication plan. As we talk about the various sales promotion techniques, you should keep in mind that in reality they are just different ways of *delivering* the promotion, each with their own particular strategic advantages and disadvantages. And in fact, in some cases, a particular sales promotion technique will also be delivering an advertising-like message. For example, samples are a way of delivering a message about the brand as well as an opportunity for trial; coupons deliver a price-off message, and when well executed the key benefit as well. While sales promotions may of course initially be delivered through any part of the communication mix, and this includes such things as personal selling, sponsorships, and other options that we will be discussing later in this chapter, and not just traditional media, after it is delivered the promotion itself may continue to be part of the communication mix. A sample's package continues to deliver an *advertising-like* message: the brand name and key benefit. A coupon that is clipped or saved continues to deliver a message every time it is referred to. It is important for the manager to think about the communication potential of sales promotions beyond their immediate objective of trial or repeat purchase.

Trade Promotion Techniques

There are three basic categories of trade promotion techniques that we will consider: allowance promotions, display material promotions, and trade premiums and incentives. *Allowance promotions* provide the trade with a monetary allowance of some kind in return for buying or promoting a specific quantity of a brand, or for meeting specific purchase or performance requirements. *Display material promotions* usually involve the manufacturer in providing specific display material to be used in featuring the brand, often in conjunction with a trade allowance. *Trade incentives* are special gifts or opportunities to earn or win valuable trips or prizes in return for purchasing specified quantities of the brand or meeting specific sales quotas.

Allowance Promotions

The type of allowance offered to the trade can take many forms: everything from reduced prices across the board, to reduced prices according to purchase volume, to free goods. It is important to point out here that most governments keep a close eye on price allowances to the trade in order to ensure they are equitably applied regardless of the size or type of distributor.

The potential weakness with trade allowances is that there is no real guarantee they will have a positive effect on the customer base. You are hoping to secure a more positive position with the trade. Offering purchase allowances or free goods with certain order levels helps build inventories, which is essential support for customer-based marketing programmes. Performance allowances, one hopes, will at least in part go to merchandising or retail advertising by the trade in support of the brand. Even though there is no guarantee the trade will cooperate, at least to the extent one might wish, consumer, retail, and trade support *must* be integrated in order to maximize your efforts regardless of the cooperation given by the trade in response to the trade promotion.

One way to help improve the likelihood of trade cooperation is to use trade coupons. Although trade coupons are offered to the trade, they are actually to be redeemed by consumers. The difference between a trade coupon and a retail coupon is that with trade coupons the marketer controls the conditions and value of the coupon, not the trade which is generally the case with retail coupons. Trade coupons are a delayed promotion where the trade pays for distributing the coupons to their customers, and is then reimbursed by the marketer after the promotion. The brand's advertising and consumer promotions must be integrated with any trade coupons to ensure a seamless message to the target audience.

Display Material Promotions

Display promotions can be in the form of either a display allowance or actual merchandising material. Perhaps the primary use of display promotions is to help reinforce consumer promotions, although they also play an important role in the introduction of new products and line extensions. Given that many purchase decisions are made at the point of purchase, especially with fmcg brands,[2] display promotions can be an important part of an integrated marketing communication programme. Good display material leads to better attention, especially important for brands driven by recognition awareness.

The use of display promotions has the advantage of generally being implemented quickly when needed, and the ability to support consumer promotion and advertising at the point of purchase. Good in-store merchandising material can also be a good way to effect cross-merchandising, where two different brands are being promoted together. The disadvantage, as with all trade promotions, but especially here, is the need for trade cooperation. Unlike trade allowances or trade premiums and incentives, which we address next, in the case of display promotion, if it does not receive widespread trade support, it will not be effective.

Trade Incentives

This last area of trade promotion is more concerned with individual distribution sources such as wholesale or retail outlets, distributors, brokers, and trade personnel. Incentives can be offered to almost any level of trade, and tend to be very popular. They can be given for reaching specific sales goals, to individuals, departments, or stores. Awards or gifts might be offered to counter personnel for recommending or highlighting your brand, or to staff members who create new or innovative ways to promote the brand. Such incentive programmes can be a big help when introducing a new product or brand extension. They are also an effective way to help move slow products off the shelf.

One of the advantages of trade promotions is that they are relatively inexpensive. Additionally, they can be implemented quickly and easily. However, a disadvantage is that segments of the trade, especially mass merchandisers, have policies against them or regulations that severely limit the type of incentive promotion they will accept.

Retail Promotion Techniques

We will be looking at three general areas of retail promotion techniques, but must remember that the trade promotions just reviewed are also used by retailers. Retail promotions are almost always price related. While they tend to be categorized in terms of specific *price-off* promotions, *point-of-purchase display* promotions, and *retail adverts*, the promotion itself almost always includes a price reduction.

Price-off Promotions

There are many pricing strategies that retailers use in price-off promotions. They must consider concurrent or recent consumer price promotions, inventory balance, and competitive activity. Remember, a retailer is interested in *category* sales. Suppose L'Oréal Paris is running a major price-off promotion in leading French women's magazines such as *marie france* and *Biba* for Kerastase Aqua-Oleun. The cosmetic manager of a major retailer may decide to offer a similar retail promotion for Jacques Dessange or other hair-styling products in order to drive business in the entire category.

Price-off promotions are almost always a part of retail adverts, and frequently a part of retail point-of-purchase displays. But there are also many other ways of implementing a price-off promotion: everything from in-store flyers to 'shelf-talkers', where the price reduction is highlighted at the shelf on a small poster. There is actually some evidence to suggest that different consumers pay attention to different means of presenting price-off promotions, so it is in the retailer's best interest to use several means of conveying a price-off promotion.[3]

Point-of-Purchase Display Promotions

In-store displays are a significant part of retail promotion. Retailers like point-of-purchase display promotions because they are effective. First of all, point-of-purchase displays draw attention to themselves. Shoppers are attracted by newly introduced contrasts or changes to their shopping environment, and will pay attention to discover what it is all about. This can be done with such things as store banners, end-aisle displays, or other stand-alone features. Secondly, point-of-purchase displays are perceived by consumers to be offering a price reduction on the featured product *even if it is not discounted*.[4]

Retail Advert Promotions

When you think of retail adverts, the first things that probably come to mind are newspaper, food, or pharmacy adverts. But, of course, almost any retailer can use retail adverts as promotion, and car dealers, mass merchandisers, shoe stores, and even banks frequently do. Retailers may carry out traditional advertising as well, and we must not confuse the two. Adverts are retail promotions when they feature products and prices, whether discounted or not. Advert 14.1 illustrates a typical retail advert promotion.

Consumer Sales Promotion Techniques

Consumers will not make a distinction between trade promotions delivered at retail outlets, retail promotions, and consumer promotions. If they see a special display in the store or have a coupon or see a price special, they are not concerned with whether it was the brand or the retailer that was responsible. But, from the brand's perspective, there is a world of difference. Consumer promotions are initiated by the brand, not the retailer, and the brand controls the content.

As it happens, consumers tend to have a pretty good idea about how often brands are promoted.[5] This is important to the brand, because it will affect consumer buying strategy for the brand in the light of the perception of the brand's availability on promotion. So, even if you do not have control over retail promotions that include your brand, it is essential that the manager has knowledge of them and includes that knowledge in the promotion strategy. We introduced the six fundamental types of consumer sales promotion in Chapter 5: coupons, refunds and rebates, sampling, loyalty and loading devices, sweepstakes, and premiums (see Table 14.1). While there are many other possibilities—everything from the product itself to unique applications of distribution channels—generally speaking we may think about consumer promotions in terms of these six basic techniques.

Advert 14.1 A retail promotion advert featuring both price advertising and price promotion. Reproduced by kind permission © PC World.

Table 14.1 Six Basic Consumer Sales Promotions

Coupons	Are low cost, and the most common form of promotion
Refunds and Rebates	Offers large price discounts, usually with more expensive products
Sampling	Provides an opportunity to try or use brand at little or no cost
Loyalty and Loading Devices	Encourages repeat purchase or use (loyalty) or changes normal purchasing patterns (loading device)
Sweepstakes	Helps create excitement and reinforces brand image at a relatively low cost
Premiums	Helps facilitate purchase by offering a reward or bonus

Coupons

Because of its relatively low cost, the coupon is the most common form of consumer promotion. While coupons are largely used for fmcgs, there is no reason a brand could not offer higher-value coupons for less frequently purchased products. However, directly discounting the price offers more control with higher-priced, less frequently purchased products.

The redemption rate for coupons can be expected to run between 2 and 5 per cent. The greater the value of the coupon and the longer the time available for redemption, the greater the redemption rate. It is absolutely essential that the expected redemption rate be carefully calculated. Remember that coupons represent a *budgeted* cost, and, if the redemption rate is seriously underestimated, the overall cost of the promotion will exceed the budget. Some of the other cost considerations in budgeting a coupon promotion, beyond the face value of the discount, are such things as additional manufacturing and distribution costs, lost profit, and the resources needed to administer the programme.

Traditionally, coupons are distributed to consumers via print media or direct mail. In magazines or newspapers, coupons may be a part of an advert, as we see in Advert 14.2. This advert for Weight Watchers from Heinz Fat Free Fromage Frais does a good job of integrating a 10p-off coupon within the execution without interfering with the advert's message. But most coupons, especially in newspapers, are delivered as FSIs, those often annoying 'free-standing inserts' of cards, single pages, or booklets, each with a coupon. Sometimes a coupon may be included in or on a package, good for future purchase either of that brand (often called a 'bounce-back coupon') or of a sister brand from the same manufacturer, called 'cross-couponing' or 'cross-ruff couponing'.

Technology is providing innovative new ways to deliver coupons. With today's sophisticated scanner capabilities, companies (and retailers) have the ability to monitor customer behaviour, and offer coupons to consumers at the till. For example, people purchasing Flash anti-bacterial cleaner might be given a coupon for Domestos Germguard to be used the next time they are buying an anti-bacterial cleaner. Asda (acquired by WalMart in 1999) was one of the first grocery retailers in the UK to use this system. Research into

Advert 14.2 A coupon integrated within an advert without interfering with the advert's message. Reproduced by kind permission © H. J. Heinz Co. Ltd. (McCann Erickson).

redemption rates suggests a significant increase from the typical 2–5 per cent up to 6–8 per cent.[6] Additionally, this type of 'checkout' couponing offers the ability to target consumers much more tightly. Another application of technology for delivering coupons uses the Internet. Individual companies and services offering coupons from many companies provide on-line computer-generated coupons. Consumers need only log on, select the coupons they want, and print them out. Unfortunately, this has also made coupon fraud easier. Hackers have found ways to capture on-line images of coupons. They have also found ways to use software to capture and manipulate barcodes that can be used to make more typical-looking coupons, as well as selling CDs with images of newspaper coupons that can be fitted with false barcodes.[7]

Refunds and Rebates

The pendant to coupons for more expensive consumer durable products is refunds and rebates. The primary difference is that with refunds and rebates the price discount is not offered at the point of purchase, but after sending in some proof of purchase to the manufacturer. The face value of a refund or rebate can be either a specific amount or some proportion of the retail price. Again, as with coupons, the request for a refund or rebate will be directly related to its relative value, and must be carefully planned to estimate probable use.

Most refunds and rebates are paid directly to the consumer by the manufacturer, but with very high ticket items a manufacturer's rebate can be assigned to the retailer at the time of purchase. This is not unusual, for example, when car manufacturers offer rebates. Their dealers will apply the rebate directly to the purchase price.

Refunds and rebates are used most often as a temporary sales stimulus or sometimes as a defensive response to competitive activity. The primary strengths of refunds and rebates include the ability to generate interest in high-involvement products, especially those with high price points, and an ability to control price discounts *without* trade interference. The weakness of refunds and rebates is that the reward is delayed, and consumers may not think the effort is worth the discount. To be effective, refunds and rebates must be seen as simple and easy to receive.

Sampling

Sampling provides the target audience with an opportunity actually to try or to use a brand at little or no cost. While most samples are free, specially sized samples are sometimes offered at a significantly reduced price to encourage purchase. The ideal candidates for sampling are products with low trial or products with a demonstrable difference (especially if the advantage is difficult to convey convincingly with advertising).

There are many ways of delivering samples to the target audience, and they come in a variety of forms. There are in-store use or taste tests, distribution of full-size packages of the product or specially sized smaller packages, and even in-house or in-business use of a product for a limited period of time (a good way to 'sample' high-priced, high-involvement products).

Passing out samples in specific locations or offering in-store sampling has the advantage of low distribution cost, but little control over who receives the sample. Direct mail

(a)   (b)

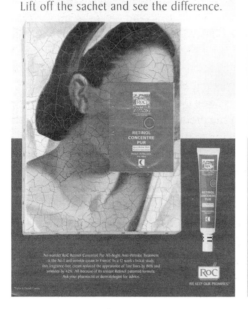

Advert 14.3 (a) A clever advert that includes a sample promotion. Reproduced with kind permission from © Retinol Concentré Pur. (b) Advert 14.3*a* after the sample has been removed, underscoring the benefit of using the brand. Reproduced with kind permission from © Retinol Concentré Pur.

offers more control, but there are obvious limits to what can be sampled (for example, not frozen or other perishable food items). Door-to-door distribution permits sampling of almost anything, but while offering tight control is inefficient and expensive. Certain products such as fragrances can be sampled with 'scratch and sniff' folds in magazines, and, as we see in Advert 14.3, it is even possible to offer small packs of cosmetics in magazines. This sampling promotion is part of a very clever advert that visually underscores the benefit of using Retinol Concentré Pur. In Advert 14.3*a* we see the promotion as it appeared in women's magazines; in Advert 14.3*b* we see the result when the sachet is lifted from the page.

Loyalty and Loading Devices

As the name implies, loyalty promotions are designed to offer a reward to those consumers who are loyal to a brand. The goal is to energize repeat purchase of the brand, and has the advantage of providing an excellent opportunity for developing a strong database of a brand's best customers. The best loyalty promotions utilize *continuity programmes*, where the consumer is required to engage in a continuing behaviour (for example, saving stamps or accumulating some proof of purchase or use) over time in order to qualify for a reward. Perhaps the best-known loyalty promotions are airline frequent flyer programmes and hotel frequent 'stayer' programmes, where customers earn points for staying at a particular hotel chain. This idea has been copied in recent years by a number of different retailers and marketers; it has been used in everything from shopping points for money spent at a retailer to reward programmes for using a specific credit card or telecommunications company. In addition, fmcg companies are increasingly using databases to identify heavy brand-users in order to offer them special programmes or rewards.

Consumer loading devices differ from loyalty programmes in that they do not seek continuity, but rather seek to change a consumer's normal purchasing pattern. These promotions are designed to encourage customers to 'load up' on the brand by purchasing more than they normally do at one time. This is done by using special bonus packs, price packs, and price-offs. *Bonus packs* offer more of the product at the same price, either with a special larger size or an additional package bound to the original. *Price packs* are where a reduced price is printed on the package as part of the label, and *price-offs* are announced at the point of purchase. This can be a very effective and efficient way to encourage brand-switching and as a defensive tactic. For example, if you know a competitor is about to introduce a 'new and improved' version of its brand, offering a loading promotion will in effect reduce the potential market for the competitor's initiative.

Of course, as always there are strengths and weaknesses to loyalty and loading promotions. Bonus packs do create an immediate incentive to buy, but the trade does not like them, because they disrupt normal inventory stocking, and take up additional shelf space without necessarily providing additional profit for the retailer. Price packs and price-offs also offer an immediate inducement to buy, but, unless coupled with advertising or other marketing communications, tend to subsidize regular users more than attracting new tryers or switchers. Continuity programmes certainly energize loyal usage of a brand, but require a long-term commitment by both the consumer and the brand. Because of the long-term nature of loyalty promotions, costs may end up being greater than expected.

Sweepstakes, Games, and Contests

Sweepstakes are a consumer promotion where the winners are chosen by chance and proof of purchase is not required. On the other hand, with *games* and *contests* there is some chance or skill involved, or a demonstration of knowledge, but almost always proof of purchase is required. With contests someone may be asked to answer certain questions or identify pictures related in some way to the brand. Not surprisingly, sweepstakes are more popular than games or contests, being much easier to enter, since no purchase is necessary. Soft drink bottlers and fast-food chains frequently use games as a consumer promotion. You scratch off a square or a card given to you when you purchase food or you look under the cap of a soft drink bottle to see if you have won.

If you are not careful, things can go very wrong with these types of promotions. Smith relates the story of a disastrous game promotion sponsored by Pepsi in the Philippines where the equivalent of £26,000 was offered to anyone finding a bottle top with a specific number.[8] Pepsi paid out £8 *million* before realizing that thousands of winning bottle tops had inadvertently been distributed, and then abruptly stopped paying. According to a report in the trade press, when Pepsi stopped paying there were public demonstrations, its bottling plants were attacked with grenades, its lorries were burned, and its executives hired bodyguards before fleeing the country.[9]

The important thing to remember when using sweepstakes, games, or contests is that they must be *fully integrated* with the brand's other marketing communication, and consistent with the brand's image. A sweepstake where the prize is a trip to an exotic island would be great for a brand like Mars' Bounty chocolate bar, because Bounty has a history of using exotic island imagery in its marketing communication. It would not be appropriate for a skiware brand, where a better prize would be a ski holiday.

Legal requirements are a real concern with sweepstakes, games, and contests. Unlike other consumer promotions, there are usually a number of legal restrictions concerning the wording, rules of compliance, and odds of winning; and these can differ among countries. As one lawyer specializing in these promotions has put it, after you have set your objective and outlined the sweepstake, game, or contest, your next step should be to involve a legal expert. From a legal standpoint, it is the rules of the promotion that are most critical. Even if you have run the same promotion in the past, it is best to check, because even a seemingly insignificant change may mean that a new law applies. This is even more the case as the European Union adds a new level of regulation to the market.

Sweepstakes, games, and contests have the ability to help create excitement about a brand, and this can help reinforce the image of the brand, all at a relatively low cost. But the reward is limited to a small number of people and is delayed.

Premiums

There are many types of premiums, as well as any number of ways of delivering them to the consumer. Using premiums as a consumer promotion helps facilitate purchase, by offering the premium as a reward. Premiums may be free, or require a small payment from the consumer beyond the purchase price of the brand. When the consumer pays something, this is known as a self-liquidating premium because the price asked of the consumer is set to cover the cost of the premium to the brand. Because of the volume-buying power of the company offering the premium, coupled with potential discounts for joint merchandising (after all, the product offered as a premium is being promoted as well), the price to the consumer will be significantly less than he or she would otherwise be required to pay (usually 30–50 per cent of the retail price). The important thing, whether the premium is free or self-liquidating, is that the target audience perceives a real *value* in the offer. Premium promotions have the advantage of creating excitement for a brand, especially if the premium is available at the point of purchase. This, however, can be complicated by the need for more retail space to accommodate the premiums, with no direct return on that space to the retailer. Mail-in requests for premiums with proof of purchase has the advantage of rewarding customers without the need for extra retail space, but the reward is delayed. Regardless of the type of premium, it should be supported by advertising and in-store merchandising, as well as being integrated into the brand's overall marketing communication.

Public Relations and Sponsorships

As with all marketing communications, public relations and sponsorships must be consistent with a brand's overall positioning. The link between the brand and need must be present and clear; and, the key benefit must be communicated. In earlier chapters we have seen that the appropriate brand-need link is critical for establishing brand awareness, and this will only happen if an event or publicity clearly reinforces this link. For example Uncle Ben's rice has used the dual benefit claim 'deliciously healthy in half the time' in its advertising. It would make sense, if they wished to include sponsorships in their communication mix, to look for events or organizations promoting healthier eating; and if using PR, create campaigns for better eating habits, reflecting their key benefit of 'deliciously healthy'.

With most PR and sponsorships it can be difficult to specifically present the key benefit. It must be communicated *indirectly* by the nature of the event or PR campaign,[10] as suggested in the example above. Not only would the link between Uncle Ben's wholegrain rice and the need for healthier eating be made, but sponsoring such events or placing stories, say about quick recipes for healthy meals with Uncle Ben's wholegrain rice, in newspapers or television shows that deal with healthier eating will be likely to associate the brand with both the 'healthy' and 'fast' benefits. The difficulty with such a PR campaign would be getting the brand name mentioned and not just recipes using wholegrain rice.

Public Relations

Most people think about public relations, or PR, as free publicity. There is, of course, nothing free about it. A good PR campaign can be very expensive. It had been estimated, for example, that worldwide some US $10 billion is spent annually on PR.[11] And while it is an important part of the overall communication mix for a brand, most PR practitioners prefer not to think of what they do as part of 'marketing'. They tend to look upon what they do as more concerned with enhancing the image and reputation of an organization. The Institute of Public Relations defines PR as 'the planned and sustained effort to establish and maintain goodwill and mutual understanding between an organization and its publics'. This definition may seem to distance PR from consumers and marketing with its emphasis upon the organization and its problems, but for most companies its most important 'public' is the consumer. While some PR activities are clearly outside the normal strategic planning process for marketing communication, those activities must nonetheless reflect the brand's overall marketing communication objectives.

Public Relations Strategy

Public relations strategy may be thought of as being either *proactive* or *reactive*. *Proactive* public relations involves planned activity that is designed to attract attention to a brand and help build positive brand attitude. *Reactive* public relations occurs when a company experiences negative publicity and must deal with 'damage control'. This is what happens when there are product recalls, for example. In social psychology this is known as impression management, where one is seeking to protect oneself by maximizing positive associations while minimizing negative associations.

Advantages and Disadvantages

There are both advantages and disadvantages to using public relations as part of a brand's marketing communication mix. Compared with traditional forms of marketing PR has the ability to reach highly segmented markets effectively. Because PR messages are not delivered as advertising or promotion, even when placed in traditional media, they avoid the clutter associated with advertising-like messages. And because they are not seen as advertising or promotion, the message is likely to be seen as more credible.

But, there are disadvantages in using public relations. Perhaps the greatest potential problem is the lack of control. It is almost impossible to ensure that a message will be exposed; and if it is, that it will be presented in the way the brand hoped. In addition, because the message is not seen as advertising, it is much more difficult for the target audience to make the desired link between the message and the brand.

Marketing Public Relations

We suggested earlier that many of those involved in public relations do not see their work as part of marketing. However, in the mid-1990s it was estimated that 70 per cent of PR activities were related to marketing.[12] In addressing this, Harris introduced the term Marketing Public Relations (MPR) to describe PR activities in support of marketing objectives. He specifically defined MPR as 'the process of planning, executing, and evaluating programs that encourage purchase and consumer satisfaction through credible communicators of information and impressions that identify companies and their products with the needs, wants, concerns, and interests of consumers'.

This understanding of PR as *marketing* public relations is important for brands that use a source branding strategy. *Source branding* strategies are those where the corporate brand is endorsing the quality of the product, in a sense acting as a guarantor. It is part of the brand name, but the product itself is the star. For example, when Kellogg puts its name on Special K or Frosties, it is alerting the consumer that these products are part of the Kellogg family. Any PR that helps build and nurture Kellogg's image and reputation enhances the image of the Special K and Frosties brands.

Some of the ways in which MPR can contribute to achieving a brand's marketing communication objectives beyond simple publicity is through such activities as media relations, corporate communication, and sponsorships. Maintaining good *media relations* helps to ensure that publicity in the form of press releases and feature stories will be more likely to be used. This requires an ongoing nurturing of editors and journalists. *Corporate communication* includes not only corporate advertising and communications directed to specific target groups, but also things like internal communication and company newsletters. All of this must be informed by the marketing communication strategy. *Sponsorships* and *events* may be initiated as part of MPR, or independently as part of a brand's communication mix, as discussed below.

Buzz Marketing

In many ways one may think about word-of-mouth as a form of PR. Buzz Marketing is the term given to a new trend in word-of-mouth communication for brands that emerged in the mid-2000s. It emerged from an effort to better reach younger consumers who are more and more difficult to reach with traditional media. The idea is to actively enlist the help of ordinary people to talk about specific brands. BZZAgent, a company in the USA, recruits people over the Internet to talk with their friends and family about their client's brands. Those recruited are given free samples of the brand to try, along with an outline of some things they could talk about. In one case these 'bzzagents' (as they are called) were given a sample of a new perfume fragrance and asked to wear it, and then to talk with people about it. While they are encouraged to identify themselves as part of a marketing programme, the 'buzz' that results from talking about the new fragrance has more power than traditional advertising because it is generated among people who know each other.

Brands are also creating buzz by using their websites to encourage entertaining interactions that generate positive word-of-mouth about their brand. Some brands, like BMW, are creating short films for the Internet featuring famous actors and directors and relying on word-of-mouth to build buzz.

Sponsorships and Event Marketing

Sponsorships can play an important role in a brand's overall marketing communication mix. A sponsorship involves a brand providing support for a particular event, organization, cause, or even a specific individual, using its brand name or logo in association with the sponsored activity or individual; and the ability to reference the sponsorship in its other brand marketing communication. This enables a brand to be presented in a favourable environment where it has the potential of benefiting from an existing positive attitude toward the sponsored activity. It is important, however, to be certain the sponsored activity or individual is indeed positively viewed by the brand's target audience.

The difference between a sponsorship and event marketing is that event marketing involves support for a single event rather than an ongoing relationship. For example, if a company supported a concert to raise money for AIDS research, that would be event marketing. If they had an ongoing relationship with the Foundation for AIDS research, that would be a sponsorship. Sponsoring the Olympics is event marketing. In fact, the Olympic Games are one of the biggest examples of event marketing worldwide. But sponsoring an individual Olympic athlete over time would be considered a sponsorship. Worldwide, more sponsorships involve sports than anything else.[13]

While popular, there seems to be very little evidence that sponsorships and event marketing add directly to the bottom line, although they can certainly contribute to brand awareness and brand attitude. As mentioned, the Olympic Games are one of the most sponsored events in the world, yet a number of studies have shown that there is very little positive lift for sponsors.[14] While there may be some lift just prior to and during an event, this is very short-lived.[15]

The key to successful sponsorships and event marketing, assuming no bad publicity, is a reasonable fit between the brand and the sponsored event or individual.[16] There must be an association in memory that can trigger a link between the brand's position, especially its benefit, and what is being sponsored. Octoberfests mean beer and sausage, so a beer or sausage brand would be a good potential sponsor of an Octoberfest event. The positive emotional benefit associated with the Octoberfest should transfer to the sponsor. Tea or biscuits would make no sense. Hellmans Extra Light Mayonnaise ('the lowest fat mayonnaise you can buy') should expect positive carry-over from sponsoring an organization involved in heart research, Häagen-Dazs would not.

The brand manager must look carefully at the fit between the brand and any potential candidate for sponsorship; just as the management of an organization or an event should ask if there is a good fit between them and the brand.[17]

Personal Selling and Trade Shows

Another important area of a brand's marketing communication mix involves personal selling and trade shows. Spending on direct, face-to-face selling in the USA has been estimated at US $500 *billion* annually, a figure that is larger than the spending on all other marketing communication media *combined*. Too often people tend to forget that personal selling is more than direct selling to the trade. It is communication about the brand, and also involves sales to consumers at the retail level. At all levels, personal selling should be fully integrated with the overall marketing communication programme.

One reason personal selling tends to be forgotten is that for many, if not most, fmcg companies sales and marketing are separate functions with separate budgets. Additionally, Dewshap and Jobber point out that for fmcg companies the retailer is the brand for the sales force while the product is the brand for the marketing manager, further complicating things.[18] While it may not be practical to include personal selling as such in the strategic planning process where the functions are divided, the message the sales force is to communicate should and must be consistent with the brand's overall marketing communication. This should go beyond sales support, such things as point-of-purchase merchandising material and sales kits. The sales force should be briefed on the brand's positioning and message in order to inform their discussions with the trade.

We include trade shows and fairs with personal selling because they offer an excellent opportunity for personal interactions between business-to-business and industrial marketers and their customers. For these marketers, trade shows account for a significant part of their marketing communication budget, second only to advertising in business publications.

Personal Selling

Personal selling involves direct contact with consumers, or direct links to retailers or dealers in business-to-business and industrial marketing. The fundamental difference between personal selling and other components of the communication mix is that the messages go *directly* from the marketer to a specific member of the target audience, providing an opportunity for interaction and modification of the basic message to address specific concerns of that individual or company.

With business-to-business and industrial marketers, personal selling may be the primary or only form of marketing communication employed. In such cases the sales message must be developed in the same way as any other marketing communication, carefully positioning the brand and establishing optimum communication objectives, and it must be consistent with the overall positioning and communication objectives for the brand.

Rossiter and Bellman[19] have suggested that the management of personal selling depends upon the type of selling involved, and offer six basic types: regular retail selling, small business selling, trade selling, high-end retail selling, technical selling, and telemarketing.

The first two are described as passive, where the consumer controls the sales exchange. The remaining four are active in the sense that both the consumer and salesperson are involved in controlling the sales exchange. Only the four active types of personal selling are important to marketing communication.

Because of the direct and individual nature of personal selling, it has the advantage of providing an opportunity for customizing the message for each target audience member, and as mentioned above the chance to adapt the message during the interaction between the consumer and salesperson. This means that attention and involvement with the message are likely to be high. Personal selling also has the advantage of being able to demonstrate product benefits that might be difficult or even impossible to convey effectively with other forms of marketing communication.

Unfortunately, the key benefit of flexibility in the message delivered with personal selling leads to its primary disadvantage. Because of the ability to customize and adjust the message, and the fact that there are any number of different salespeople, it is very difficult to ensure message consistency. Another disadvantage is that, relative to other media, personal selling is expensive and has a low reach. Those advantages and disadvantages are summarized in Table 14.2.

Like all marketing communication, brand awareness and brand attitude are communication objectives for personal selling. Additionally, brand purchase intention will also almost always be an objective. The brand awareness objective will be recognition given that the salesperson will generally be calling on the customer rather than the other way around. In personal selling to retailers, and in business-to-business and industrial marketing, the purchase motive will almost always be negative (most likely problem solution or problem avoidance), requiring an informational brand attitude strategy, and the decision high involvement. This makes it essential that salespeople understand their target's *initial attitude* toward the brand because this understanding will be critical for framing message acceptance. The personal, interactive nature of personal selling permits a certain amount of probing to ensure a good understanding of how the target audience sees the brand.

Table 14.2 Advantages and Disadvantages of Personal Selling in Marketing Communication

Advantages	Customized message to each member of the target audience
	Ability to adapt message during the interaction between consumer and salesperson
	Ability to demonstrate product
Disadvantages	Ensuring message consistency is very difficult
	Expensive relative to other media
	Low reach relative to other media

An important consideration follows from this. Even if a brand can deliver its key benefit better than the target audience believes it can, a salesperson should not try to convince them it will. As long as the target is generally positive about the brand, the salesperson should present the benefit at the consumer's level of belief. If when used a product turns out to deliver a benefit better than anticipated, research has shown that overall brand attitude will increase.[20] This happens *because* there was a difference between anticipation and the actual delivery of the benefit.

Before leaving this, there is an important point the manager must keep in mind when using personal selling to the trade. While an informational brand attitude is likely to be appropriate to 'close the sale', it would *not* be appropriate in talking about the *brand* and its benefit if the consumer brand choice decision involved positive motives. The transformational brand attitude used in the brand's marketing communication should be followed.

Trade Shows and Fairs

One might think of trade shows and fairs as falling somewhere between promotion and personal selling. It is not unusual for promotional incentives to be offered in order to encourage attendance at a trade show or fair stand, they are usually advertised in appropriate media, and like personal selling there is direct contact with the target audience at the company's booth. Every industry has a trade show of some kind, and they can be especially important for small businesses unable to afford much (if any) other marketing communication. They play a significant role in the marketing of industrial products, where it has been estimated that trade shows and fairs account for 20 to 25 per cent of their marketing communication budget.[21]

The personal interactions that occur at trade shows and fair booths offer a number of opportunities.[22] For example, they provide a chance to identify and meet new customers, and an opportunity to nurture existing customers. They are an excellent forum for introducing new products, and for demonstrating products. The principle advantage of trade shows and fairs is that all of this can be accomplished within a relatively short period of time, and directly to members of the brand's target audience.

While trade shows and fairs offer a good opportunity for marketers and consumers to meet in a way where the marketer is offering information to interested consumers, there is some debate about their effectiveness. Some studies have shown that they generate awareness and interest leading to sales,[23] but other studies question the value of trade shows and fairs altogether.[24]

Effectiveness here has been defined by some in terms of leads that result in sales,[25] and this reflects how many managers who are heavily involved in trade shows and fairs measure their effectiveness.[26] Yet other researchers[27] have found that the non-selling aspects of trade shows and fairs are highly valued by managers. There does not seem to be a fixed criteria for measuring success, and this complicates any attempt to calculate their cost effectiveness. Also complicating the issue of effectiveness is the tendency of managers to view trade shows and fairs on the own rather than as part of the brand's communication mix.

Product Placement

Including product placement as part of a brand's marketing communication mix has been on the increase for some time. It may be defined as the reference to a brand or its actual inclusion within some context in return for payment or other considerations. That context may be anything from movies and television programmes to video games or even books. Although this is usually referred to as product placement, in reality we are talking about *brand* placement. Nonetheless, we shall follow convention and refer to it as product placement.

There are many people who consider the use of product placement to be unethical. Rossiter and Bellman have gone so far as to say that they regard it as 'ethically contemptible' because there is no guarantee that the audience will understand that an attempt is being made to persuade them.[28] They argue that even if the audience did understand, it is still unethical because the marketer *intends* to deceive. Sutherland complains that even while the use of product placements increase less and less attention is paid to them by regulatory agencies.[29] He also makes the point that product placements distort the perception on what brands are popular (among other things), because people are not likely to make the connection between a brand appearing in, say, a movie or video game, and the fact that it was put there by the marketer.

Product placement was not approved for use in the EU until the mid-2000s, but not all EU countries permit them. Long a controversial issue in the UK, they may not be used there, despite the fact that many US television shows are seen in the UK. Product placement in such programming is identified and pixilated (i.e. digitally blurred out).[30]

In addition to ethical concerns, there is the issue of whether or not product placement is effective. There are few empirical studies of product placement, and those that have been conducted do not tend to find them effective.[31] Despite this, there are many anecdotal stories about their effectiveness. One of the more well-known stories involves the 1986 movie *Top Gun* where Tom Cruise is wearing Rayban Aviator sunglasses. Supposedly this led to a turn-around in the company's financial situation which was in dire straits before the movie's release.[32]

If we assume product placement can be effective, *how* the brand is placed will have an effect upon the likelihood that it will be noticed and impact brand attitude. If a brand is clearly seen being used by a celebrity or is talked about directly by brand name, the potential will obviously be better than if it is simply part of the background.[33] Perhaps the most likely effect from using product placements is raising brand awareness and salience. But to accomplish even this would require *conscious* attention to the placement, and this is problematic.

It is this need for conscious attention that minimizes the potential effectiveness of product placements in effecting brand attitude. While there may be implicit processing of the brand's placement, this will have *no effect* upon brand attitude or behaviour.[34] Again, it is only likely to be the small segment of viewers who actively identify with the celebrity or situation that are likely to attend to the brand. To be effective at a broader level, not only must there be conscious attention, but the placement must stimulate positive associations in memory with the celebrity or the situation within which the brand is shown, and this within the correct emotional context. If this happens, the placement has the potential to contribute to positive brand attitude by creating a sense of personal involvement with what is going on. But as suggested, this is a lot to ask of all but the most highly involved. However, there is an emerging belief among advertising practitioners that product placements will be more effective if accompanied by adverts for the product.[35]

The actual cost of product placement in absolute terms is generally less than other forms of marketing communication, but it is difficult to predict or measure whether or not any positive effect from the placement justifies even the relatively low cost. Regardless, if product placement is to be considered as part of a brand's communication mix it must be used within a context consistent with the brand's positioning.

Packaging

Packaging is often overlooked as part of a brand's communication mix, yet it is a very important part of the brand's marketing communication. While some marketers do appreciate its importance,[36] too often it is underestimated by managers.[37] There are several key emotional and psychological benefits linked to packages.[38] They have the ability to attract attention, enhancing brand awareness; and they have the ability to express the brand's image, reinforcing brand attitude.

Look at Advert 14.4 for Nairn's. Here we see the package not only well integrated into an advert for recognition brand awareness, but the package itself does a good job communicating the brand's benefit of 'oaty goodness'. The strong visual of the biscuits on the package, under the words 'oat biscuit' reinforces the advert's message. Every time you reach for a biscuit, the message is reinforced by the package.

Studies by the Point-of-Purchase Advertising Institute have shown that over 70 per cent of brand decisions in supermarkets are made in the store.[39] A well-designed package will attract attention at the point-of-purchase, which is critical for products where the purchase decision is triggered by brand recognition. If this recognition is linked to the appropriate need in the consumer's mind as a result of its other marketing communication (especially advertising), this aids purchase. The large number package facings in a store mean that the brand's package must be able to cut through competitive clutter, and this means that visual elements of the package must be different from competitors.

Additionally, the 'message' communicated by the package should be consistent with the brand's overall marketing communication strategy. This enables the package to reinforce the brand's image and key benefit. Many products, especially fmcg, are used directly from the package; everything from breakfast cereals to cold remedies, toothpaste to household cleaners. This means that every time the product is used the package offers the brand an opportunity to reinforce its primary benefit, nurturing brand attitude. In a very real sense, a package can operate as post-purchase advertising. Rossiter and Bellman have put this nicely, describing packages as 'take-away or leave behind' communication vehicles.[40]

Oaty goodness

in a biscuit.

WHEAT FREE
NO HYDROGENATED FAT
1.6g FAT, OR LESS, PER BISCUIT
NO ARTIFICIAL COLOURINGS,
FLAVOURINGS OR PRESERVATIVES

Nairn's oat biscuits are full of the goodness of oats. They are as simple, natural and wholesome as possible — but full of flavour. Choose from Mixed Berries, Stem Ginger or Fruit and Spice. So, for a biscuit that's naturally nutritious, treat yourself to something tasty from nairn's.

nairn's, nice 'n natural

For further information call 0131 620 7000, email info@nairns-oatcakes.com or visit www.nairns-oatcakes.com

Advert 14.4 Here we see a package well integrated into an advert for good recognition awareness, and a package that also communicates the benefit on its own. Reproduced with kind permission © Nairn's Oatcakes Limited.

Channels Marketing

'Channels marketing' is a relatively recent term used to describe all levels of marketing communication to the retail trade. It came into being as a result of the increasing importance of trade promotion, coupled with the increasing power of retailers. Basically, it combines co-op advertising with tactical marketing. Co-op advertising has existed for a very long time, and is essentially an agreement between a retailer and a brand to cooperate in part of the brand's marketing communication. The brand offers to produce advertising or promotions that include the retailer's name, and the retailer agrees to participate in funding the advertising or promotion along with the brand. Tactical marketing is a relatively new channel-oriented (that is, distribution) marketing communication system designed to return more control over promotion to the brand and to leverage incremental support for the trade, especially the retailer.

Traditional co-op advertising is generally broad in scope and *passive* in nature. Typically, it is open to a brand's entire retail base, conditioned on sales volume: the more of the brand sold, the more money available for co-op advertising. The adverts and other merchandising material are provided by the brand, but used by the retailer as it wishes. Then, on a periodic basis, the retailer is reimbursed for its expenditures according to the co-op agreement.

With their expanding power, many retailers were treating traditional co-op as a profit centre, diverting funds to offset operating costs. Retailers were also beginning to force brands, as a condition of stocking, to participate in retailer-initiated promotions that often were not consistent or integrated with the brand's overall marketing communication. *Tactical marketing* grew out of the desire on the part of brands to assume more control over the use of their co-op monies.

Tactical marketing, unlike traditional co-op, is always *pro-active*. Programmes are designed for particular retailers, tailored to their specific needs. With the cooperation of the retailer, the brand funds the programme, in accordance with the retailer meeting specific sales goals, and *implements* the programme. The benefit for the brand is *control*. Tactical marketing offers the retailer complete coordination of the programme and production of the materials used, while maintaining control over the content and timing of the advertising and promotions. The pay-off for the retailer is the ability to go beyond the basic print orientation of most traditional co-op programmes (or at best very simple broadcast executions), and the ability to utilize the full marketing communication range of the brand within a plan optimized for each retailer.

CHAPTER SUMMARY

In this chapter we have looked at sales promotion techniques, and at a number of ways other than traditional media in which advertising and promotion may be delivered to a brand's target audience. We reviewed the basic sales promotion techniques associated with trade, retail, and consumer promotion, and discussed their strengths and weaknesses. An understanding of these strengths and weaknesses is what helps the manager to make strategic decisions as to which technique is most appropriate in given situations. Public relations was discussed, and the distinction between PR in general and marketing PR made. Also, where sponsorships, event marketing, personal selling and trade shows fit within a brand's overall marketing communication programme was considered, as was the use of product placement and even packaging.

QUESTIONS TO CONSIDER

14.1   In what ways do sales promotions provide a means of delivering a brand's key benefit? Find good examples of this.

14.2   What are the similarities and differences between trade and retail promotions and consumer sales promotions.

14.3   How can public relations contribute to a brand's overall marketing communication programmes?

14.4   What is the difference between public relations and marketing public relations?

14.5   Identify examples of sponsorships and event marketing; and discuss how they are contributing to the brand attitude.

14.6   Weigh the advantages and disadvantages of personal selling as part of a brand's marketing communication.

14.7   Discuss how trade shows and fairs contribute to a brand's communication objectives.

14.8   Why are product placements seen by some as unethical, and how do you see this issue?

14.9   Find examples of packages that do a good job of communicating the brand's key benefit.

14.10 How does channels marketing differ from co-op?

CASE STUDY 14

Applying First Aid to Insurance Advertising for Norwich Union

Sometimes it can be tough advertising insurance and financial services. It seems that no matter what we do, we are forever faced with the blank-faced cynicism of the focus group and immovable figures on tracking study charts. Contact with the product is infrequent and sporadic—buying a pension, for example, is a once in a lifetime decision, and once the purchase has been made there is little subsequent engagement with the consumer.

This is the story of how the strategic planning team and a client with the vision to see beyond the conventional produced something truly new in financial services advertising. This paper will outline the leadership of planning in:

• Identifying the most motivating 'high ground' in the market in the first place.
• Moving beyond conventional advertising solutions.
• Creating a new sort of advertising for financial services—a form of sponsorship, but unique in its connection to the brand (a Valid Advertising Component).
• Helping to transform the image of Norwich Union more effectively and efficiently than a conventional approach could have, and helping to produce a literally stunning creative result.

We were attempting to create a distinctive identity for Norwich Union in the face of an increasingly competitive environment and a revolution in product distribution. The competition was proliferating, with 'consumer' brands such as Virgin and Direct Line causing the major insurance companies to look again at their marketing, and consumers to demand a higher level of service from the traditional providers. People were no longer willing to be told how best to organize their finances, but were demanding a say in the process themselves. Norwich Union had begun the long road towards establishing a direct *transactional* relationship with customers with the launch of Norwich Union Direct, but the reality was that for most, the relationship with Norwich Union had a gatekeeper—the Independent Financial Adviser (IFA), or the broker, making it extremely difficult to involve the customer in the experience of the Norwich Union brand. In insurance, perhaps more than any other category, buying is an act of faith. Consumers are not interested in the nuts and bolts of the product, and there is no way of knowing how the product will perform until a claim is made. The crucial thing for the consumer is the brand behind the product, not the product itself.

When first appointed to the business in 1994, we worked with Norwich Union to identify a motivating area to own as a brand. Extensive consumer research into Norwich Union's brand values, and those of major competitors, had led us to believe that there was a major opportunity to take the generic need in the market and convey that we offer more than our competitors. A wide consumer vocabulary existed to describe criteria for choosing a company, all of which seemed to be code for one underlying requirement. 'Size', 'reputation', 'track record', and 'consistency' are all *credentials* of a company that offers good protection. 'Reassurance', 'peace of mind', 'trust' all seemed to be *consequences* from a company that has protected you well. *Protection* is the central thought, and no other company owned it as a brand property. Advertising was developed during 1994 and ran during the end of that year and the beginning of 1995. The execution featured different people from around the world, establishing that it was man's basic instinct to protect and claiming that no one protects more of the things that are important to you than Norwich Union. The reaction of focus groups to the advertising was very encouraging, but this approach did not go as far to achieve the transformational results as we had hoped. The issue at hand was not the advertising we had created, but the fact that it was not differentiated in people's minds from other advertising in the sector. We then decided to look beyond conventional advertising, and create something truly different to engage the disinterested consumer. A solution was needed which would be visible and striking, without attracting cynicism. Our research had uncovered a potentially interesting area—the sort of protection which people found most relevant was not that of the insurance company protecting them, but a sort of protection which enabled them to protect themselves, their possessions, and their family. Any solution we produced would have to show that Norwich Union was committed to helping them provide this protection—empowering the consumer, rather than sheltering them. Advertising alone seemed to fail. To really break through, we would have to be seen to put the consumer back in charge. Our communications solution should offer them tangible help in discharging their responsibilities—more of a participation event than an advertisement, but what exactly would this solution consist of? The first question to address would be how to go about achieving a link with the right sort of protection. Sponsorship proved to be a very fertile area for ideas, allowing us to connect the Norwich Union brand with many emotive areas that clearly expressed protection. However, as we gathered suggestions from many different interested parties (Norwich Union staff, Norwich Union's PR agency, and Norwich Union's media agency), it became clear that there was little point in doing something unless we could be clearly seen to be doing it by those whose opinion we sought to change. A solution could of course have been to advertise the fact that we were involved in a sponsorship, a route followed by many other advertisers before us. Our research had already told us that people would immediately see it as empty insurance company boasting.

Insight—The Valid Advertising Component

The planning team now developed the breakthrough insight. The sponsorship had to contain a Valid Advertising Component—broadcast advertising as a seamless part of the sponsorship initiative we developed, rather than just a tool to brag about it. The idea which most seamlessly contained this Valid Advertising Component and created a truly meaningful expression of protection was offering free First Aid training courses to members of the public and advertising their availability.

Creating the Valid Advertising Component?

A clear and inspiring creative briefing was required to ensure that the advertising breathed life into the idea. We had a clear idea of how the advertising would work, and were trying to communicate simply that Norwich Union was offering free First Aid courses to the public. Our single-minded proposition could have been just this fact, but we felt that something more emotive and inspiring was needed to fully achieve our objective of breaking through in this sector. The proposition we developed was designed to make people really think twice about the need to know about First Aid and the inherent importance of the issue. We were attempting to raise the stakes—making First Aid a bigger issue and therefore increasing the credit given to Norwich Union for offering free courses. We looked to capture the moment when knowledge of First Aid would really count, in the proposition 'what would you do if a child you were looking after had just swallowed white spirit?' The proposition had even greater power as the creative team we briefed had children themselves and neither of them knew the correct answer. As a result, they rose to the challenge magnificently, producing an advertising solution which avoided the potential problems with over-dramatizing the gory consequences of not knowing what to do, and focusing on the drama of the crisis itself. The advertising showed a small child drinking opaque white liquid from a child's tea set. This was accompanied by a voice-over setting up the dilemma and then the voices of various members of the public conjecturing about what they would do—'don't let them have anything to drink', 'make the child sick—stick my fingers down it's throat', 'turn them upside down and shake them'. A chilling title showing the answer 'Wrong' or the potential consequences 'This can kill' followed each wrong answer. The voice-over returned to announce that Norwich Union was offering free First Aid courses, and then the tension was resolved by a member of the public giving the correct answer, ('give them a cup of water and take them to hospital in the car') and the child smiling.

So how did it perform?

In September of 1996 the advertising went on air and courses were offered in partnership with St John Ambulance, in our chosen test region of Granada. The results went far beyond our expectations. All of a sudden, studies which typically showed advertising recognition figures of between 40 per cent and 60 per cent in the sector, leapt to more than 80 per cent in our test region, with a lower media spend and a fraction of the production costs. Advertising recorded 94 per cent levels of approval in a sector where the combination of companies and advertising usually leads to cynicism. For the first time we began to see significant increases in association of Norwich Union with the concept of protection. One of the most surprising results was that such a 'soft' brand campaign led to an increase in consideration of Norwich Union products—25 per cent said that the campaign had made them more likely to consider Norwich Union for an insurance policy. Following the success in Granada, the initiative has now been rolled out across the country with all regions covered (apart from London due to logistical problems for St John Ambulance in delivering courses). Clear direction and insight from strategic planning made it possible to create engaging and involving advertising in a traditionally low-interest category. This low-interest category had produced an interesting new type of advertising a sponsorship with a Valid Advertising Component.

Source: 'Applying first aid to insurance advertising', Account Planning Group (UK), Creative Planning Awards, 1997. http://www.apg.org.uk/

Edited by Natalia Yannopoulou

Discussion Questions

1 How could Norwich Union react in the case of a negative event/crisis caused by St John Ambulance? St John Ambulance is solely responsible for the negative event/crisis, which is unrelated with the sponsorship event, but attracts a lot of media attention.

2 Propose an alternative strategy, especially for the London area, using 'other media', such as Public Relations or Product placement.

3 What could have been a second phase for the above campaign for the coming year?

4 Future trends in 'other media' create what kind of opportunities and risks for companies, such as Norwich Union?

FURTHER READING

- An insightful article on managing trade promotion is Jack Kasulis, 'Managing Trade Promotions in the Context of Market Power', *Journal of the Academy of Marketing Science*, 27/3 (Summer 1999), 320–2.

- Some of the problems encountered with pan-European promotions are discussed by Allyson Stewart-Allen in 'Cross-Border Conflicts on European Sales Promotions', *Marketing News*, 33/9 (April 1999), 9.

- More on the strategy of buzz marketing may be found in Gerry Khermouch, 'Buzz Marketing: Suddenly this Stealth Strategy is Hot', *Business Week* (30 July 2001), 50.

- For a good case history on sponsorship, see an article in the 7 November (2005) number of *Brandweek,* 'So you want to be an Olympic Sponsor'. It details the story of Visa's involvement in Olympics sponsorship.

- M. Schell, *Buyer-Approved Selling: Sales Strategies from the Buyer's Side of the Desk* (Vancouver, BC: Marketshare Publications, 2003) offers an interesting perspective of personal selling from the buyer's viewpoint.

- For the classic discussion of the stages involved in personal selling, see A. J. Dubinsky, 'A Factor Analytic Study of the Personal Selling Process', *Journal of Personal Selling & Sales Management,* 1/1 (1980), 26–33.

- A useful guide to event marketing from the Association of National Advertisers, 'Event Marketing: A Management Guide', may be found at http://www.ana.net.

NOTES

1   See L. Percy, *Strategies for Implementing Integrated Marketing Communication* (Lincolnwood, FL: NTC Business Books, 1997), 98.

2   In the USA a 1995 study of consumer buying habits conducted by the P-O-P Advertising Institute found that more than 70 per cent of brand choices are made in the store.

3   See C. M. Henderson, 'Promotion Heterogeneity and Consumer Learning: Refining the Deal-Proneness Construct', in C. T. Allen and D. Roedder John (eds), *Advances in Consumer Research*, xxi (Provo, Ut.: Association for Consumer Research, 1994), 86–94.

4   This is a point made by Rossiter and Percy in a review of several studies dealing with the effect of displays without accompanying price reductions: see *Advertising Communication and Promotion Management* (New York: McGraw-Hill, 1997), 390.

5   See A. Krishna, F. S. Currin, and R. W. Shoemaker, 'Consumer Perceptions of Promotional Activity', *Journal of Marketing*, 55 (1991), 14–16.

6   See Chris Fill, *Marketing Communications: Frameworks, Theories, and Applications* (London: Prentice Hall, 1995), 376.

7   Jack Neff, 'Internet Enabling Coupon Fraud Biz', *Advertising Age*, 20 Oct. 2003, 3, reviews the economic impact of fake coupons generated on the Internet.

8   Paul Smith relates a number of stories of disastrous promotions in his book *Marketing Communications: An Integrated Approach*, 2nd edn. (London: Kogan Page, 1998).

9   This story of the Pepsi Philippine subsidiary promotion was reported in *Precision Marketing*, 26 May 1997.

10   See John Rossiter and Steve Bellman, *Marketing Communication: Theory and Application* (Frenchs Forest, Australia: Pearson Education Australia, 2005), 386.

11   See ibid. 377.

12   The term 'marketing public relations' was introduced by T. Harris in *The Marketers Guide to PR: How Today's Companies are Using the New Public Relations to Gain a Competitive Edge* (New York: John Wiley and Sons, 1993).

13   See T. Meeghan, 'Current Developments and Future Directions in Sports Sponsorship', *International Journal of Advertising*, 17/1 (1998), 3–28.

14   There are a number of studies that have shown little lift resulting from sponsorships, including A. D. Miyazaki and A. G. Morgan's 'Assessing Market Value of Event Sponsoring: Corporate Olympics Sponsorships', *Journal of Advertising Research*, 41/1 (2001), 9–15; J. Crimmins and M. Horn's 'Sponsorship: From Management Ego Trip to Marketing Success', *Journal of Advertising Research*, 36/4 (1996), 11–21; and L. Kinney and S. R. McDaniel's, 'Strategic Implications of Attitude-towards-the-ad in Leveraging Event Sponsorships', *Journal of Sports Management*, 10 (1996), 250–60.

15   This was found in a large-scale study of sponsorship effect from the FIFA 2006 World Cup, and reported by Joe Acaoui in 'Brand Experience in the Pitch: How the Sponsors Fared in the World Cup', *Journal of Advertising Research*, 47/2 (2007), 147–57.

16   See D. T. Y. Poou and G. Prendergast, 'A New Framework for Evaluating Sponsorship Opportunities', *International Journal of Advertising*, 25/4 (2006), 471–88.

17 See K. P. Gwinner and J. Eaton, 'Building Brand Image through Event Sponsorship: The Role of Image Transfer', *Journal of Advertising*, 25/4 (1999), 47–57.

18 See B. Dewshap and D. Jobber, 'The Sales-Marketing Interface in Consumer Packaged-Goods Companies: A Conceptual Framework', *Journal of Personal Selling & Sales Management*, 20/2 (2000), 109–19.

19 See Rossiter and Bellman, *Marketing Communication*, 402.

20 This research is discussed in P. K. Kopalle and J. L. Assuncão, 'When to Indulge in "Puffing": The Role of Consumer Expectations and Brand Goodwill in Determining Advertised and Actual Product Quality', *Managerial Decision Economics,* 21/6 (2000).

21 See S. Gopalakrishna and J. D. Williams, 'Planning and Performance Assessment of Industrial Trade Shows: An Exploratory Study', *International Journal of Research and Marketing*, 9 (1992), 207–24.

22 See D. Shipley, C. Egan, and K. S. Wong, 'Dimensions of trade Show Exhibiting Management', *Journal of Marketing Management*, 9 (1993).

23 See note 21 above.

24 This is discussed in C. M. Sashi and J. Perretty, 'Do Trade Shows Provide Value?', *Industrial Marketing Management*, 21 (1992), 249–53.

25 See A. Sharland and P. Balogh, 'The Value of Non-selling Activities at International Trade Shows', *Industrial Marketing Management,* 25 (1996), 59–66.

26 See J. Blythe and T. Raymer, 'The Evaluation of Non-selling Activities at British Trade Exhibitions: An Exploratory Study', *Marketing Intelligence and Planning*, 14/5 (1996).

27 See note 22 above.

28 See Rossiter and Bellman, *Marketing Communication*, 352.

29 This is argued by Max Sutherland in 'Product Placement: Regulators Gone AWOL', *International Journal of Advertising,* 25 (2006), 107–10.

30 See E. Hall, 'Product placement faces wary welcome in Britain', *Advertising Age*, 8 January (2007), 27.

31 See L. Johnson and C. A. Dodd, 'Placements as Mediators of Brand Salience within UK Cinema Audiences', *Journal of Marketing Communications*, 6 (2000), 141–58.

32 This story is reported by B. R. Fischer in 'Making your Product the Star Attraction', *Promo* (July 1996), 58.

33 See J. R. Semenik, *Promotion & Integrated Marketing Communication* (Cincinnati, Oh.: South-Western, 2002), 398.

34 This point is made by one of the book's authors, Larry Percy, in 'Are Product Placements Effective?', *International Journal of Advertising*, 25 (2006), 112–14.

35 This was reported in the 20 June 2005 number of the *Wall Street Journal*, B1.

36 See D. Walczyk, 'Packaging should be a Critical Element in the Branding Schema', *Marketing News*, 35/23 (2001), 14–17.

37 See P. Southgate, *Total Branding by Design* (London: Kogan Page, 1994).

38 The psychological and emotional benefits associated with packaging are discussed by S. Charearlary in 'An Investigation of the Representation of Brand Image through

Packaging', an MSC Marketing Dissertation from Aston Business School, Aston University, Birmingham.

39 These studies are published by the Point of Purchase Advertising Institute in *An Integrated Look at Integrated Marketing: Uncovering P-O-P: Role as the Last Three Feet in the Marketing Mix* (Washington, DC: Point-of-Purchase Advertising Institute, 2000), 10.

40 See Rossiter and Bellman, *Marketing Communication*, 356.

 Visit the Online Resource Centre that accompanies this book for additional resources to support the text: http://www.oxfordtextbooks.co.uk/orc/ percy_elliott3e/

15

Putting it All Together

 KEY CONCEPTS

1 Integrated Marketing Communication (IMC) is the *planning* and execution of a marketing communication campaign, using a common set of communication objectives and a consistent look and feel to all aspects of the campaign.

2 Advertising and promotion each contribute unique strengths to a campaign. The primary strength of traditional advertising is building long-term positive brand attitudes, that of traditional promotion is creating brand purchase intention for accomplishing short-term tactical brand objectives.

3 If advertising and promotion are used together effectively, the interaction of the short- and long-term effects 'ratchet-up' the overall effectiveness of the campaign.

4 Optimizing the use of advertising and promotion for IMC is facilitated with a Marketing Communication Task Grid, which enables the manager to evaluate various media options for accomplishing specific communication tasks.

5 Once the campaign is running, it is essential that the programme is monitored for both effectiveness and wearout.

6 Unfortunately, implementing truly effective IMC is very difficult because of organizational and, especially, compensation issues. Until a way is found to deal with these issues, it will be hard to convince managers in different areas of marketing communication to yield to others in order to deliver a more effective overall marketing communication programme.

Putting together a marketing communication programme requires a full understanding of the strengths and weaknesses of both traditional advertising and promotion. There are strengths and weaknesses to all aspects of marketing communication, which is why a truly integrated *planning* approach is so important to effective mass communication. Different media have different strengths in different situations. This is one of the things that developing a consumer decision-making model helps isolate. Various target audience roles at different stages of the decision process are better suited to some forms of marketing communication than others. What we want to look at now are the basic ways in which traditional advertising and promotion as we have been discussing them in this book differ in terms of their appropriateness in specific marketing and communication situations. Remember, when we are talking about *traditional* advertising and promotion, we are referring to their basic functions. Traditional advertising is marketing communication used primarily for long-term brand equity *delivered* via such media as print, broadcast, direct mail, and packaging, as opposed to traditional promotion, which is marketing communication used primarily for short-term tactical goals, regardless of whether it is delivered via print, direct mail, point-of-purchase collateral, or broadcast media.

Integrated Marketing Communication (IMC)

One of the most talked-about ideas in marketing during the 1990s was the notion of integrated marketing communication (IMC). And, while marketing managers (especially in the USA[1]) still clearly feel it is a valuable concept, and one that will play an increasingly more important role in their companies, there is unfortunately a great deal of evidence to suggest that *truly* integrated marketing communication is the exception rather than the rule.

There are a great many reasons for this, which we shall deal with at the end of this chapter. One problem is that too often IMC is thought to be nothing more than using several means of delivering a message. If a brand manager uses direct mail, television, and print advertising, along with some promotions and sponsorships, this is likely to be considered an IMC campaign. But simply using a variety of marketing communications does not necessarily mean an *integrated* marketing communication campaign.

Defining Integrated Marketing Communication

If using a variety of marketing communications does not define IMC, what does? You might briefly consider IMC as the *planning* and execution of all types of marketing communication needed for a brand, service, or company in order to satisfy a common set of communication objectives; or, put more simply, to support a single positioning. IMC means *planning*, and the ability to deliver a consistent message, all with a consistent look and feel. The importance of a consistent look and feel was stressed in Chapter 13.

Without planning, it is impossible to have IMC.[2] Centralized strategic planning is the very heart of IMC. The job of a marketing or advertising manager is to use whatever combination of marketing communication options is available to him or her in order to achieve the desired communication objective. But the use of these options must be *centrally planned and coordinated*, utilizing a systematic strategic planning process. In a very real sense this book has provided a detailed description and understanding of the tools involved in planning an effective IMC campaign. Chapters 6 to 10 laid out the necessary strategic planning process.

In our example above, if a brand manager uses a direct mail programme that is not tied into the advertising, that does not have the same 'look and feel', that is not developed from the same umbrella creative brief, it is not a part of an integrated campaign. If the promotions are not extensions of the advertising's message, they are not a part of an IMC campaign. If a sponsorship has little connection with the brand and its advertising, it is not part of an integrated campaign. In fact, it is quite possible to have an IMC campaign that utilizes *only* direct mail or *only* advertising or *only* some promotion, or *just* a sponsorship. How? If the manager went through a thorough strategic communications planning process and came to the decision that only one form of marketing communication was required to meet the brand's marketing communication objectives effectively, then the result is indeed an IMC campaign. Why? Again, because IMC is in the *planning*. All possible options were considered, even if only one was needed.

Traditional Advertising and Promotion in IMC

We must never forget that *all* forms of marketing communication may be considered in IMC planning: everything from product packaging to store signs to more familiar forms of advertising and promotion, and, of course, the Internet and other new media. But, from a practical standpoint, it is easier to talk about marketing communication options in the traditional terms of advertising and promotion, our long-term strategic and short-term tactical marketing communication, as we have done throughout this book.

As we saw in the first chapter, to understand the fundamental distinction between traditional forms of advertising and promotion, we need only look at the Latin roots of the two words. You will remember that the Latin root of advertising is *advertere*, which may be roughly translated as 'to turn towards'; and the Latin root of promotion is *promovere*, which may be roughly translated as 'to move ahead'. This summarizes nicely the difference between the communication contribution of each: advertising contributes to long-term attitude while promotion contributes to short-term action.

We have emphasized, and will continue to emphasize, that IMC is all about planning. The word 'integrate' comes from the Latin verb *integrare*, and is defined by the *Oxford Dictionary of Current English* as 'combine [parts] into a whole'. In IMC planning, we are looking at all our available options in terms of their ability to satisfy the communication objectives of our brand. The parts that are 'combined' are various forms of traditional advertising and promotion, and the 'whole' is a consistent marketing communication programme.

You may be wondering why we have been using the adjective 'traditional' throughout this book in referring to advertising and promotion. This is to remind us of the *strategic* roles each plays in planning marketing communication. But in today's world of marketing communication it is often not easy to tell an advertising execution from a promotion execution. Television commercials include direct response toll-free numbers or ask consumers to look for coupons in newspapers or magazines, and actually show the coupon. FSIs (those 'free-standing inserts' that clutter up Sunday newspapers and other print media), which are traditional promotion vehicles for delivering coupons, are often very like adverts in their appearance.

In the past there was a rather clear-cut difference between advertising and promotion media. Advertising was delivered via 'measured media' in such things as television, radio, newspaper, magazines, and outdoor. Today, however, it is not unusual to find advertising messages being delivered through direct marketing and channels marketing (trade-oriented marketing programmes similar to 'co-op' where the marketer and the retailer cooperate on marketing communication programmes, and discussed in Chapter 14), which in the past were used only for promotional messages. In addressing this issue of traditional advertising versus promotion, Rossiter and Percy[3] have made two important points. Talking about the increase in the marketing monies going into promotion relative to advertising in recent years, they point out that, in spite of this swing, there has nevertheless been an *increase*, not a decrease, in the use of general advertising media because of an increase in the number of media options available for advertising (as we mentioned above). They also note that most of this growth in promotion spending, apart from all-but-required promotions to the trade, has been *additional* spending, and most of this increase has gone into promotions that look more like adverts.

A second point they make is very important. Familiar forms of promotion (things like sweepstakes, coupons, and samples) are not growing. What is growing is the use of promotion-oriented messages that are very much like advertising. As they point out, the fastest-growing forms of marketing communication are direct mail and telemarketing, which have traditionally been thought of as 'promotion' rather than 'advertising'. But both direct mail and telemarketing are as much 'advertising', in the traditional sense of 'turning towards' (for example, in terms of building brand awareness and brand equity), as they are 'promotion', in the traditional sense of 'moving ahead' some short-term action objective such as sales. As we have already discussed, even FSIs, which are by far the most widely used way of delivering coupons, are more and more like adverts in how they are being used to help build awareness and brand equity at the same time as they offer a coupon.

As the old distinction between advertising and promotion becomes more blurred, thinking in terms of IMC is all the more important. What has in the past been thought of as traditional 'advertising skills' now play a critical role across the board with IMC. Planning an effective marketing communication programme with IMC requires a manager to address the creative and media questions that have always been addressed with traditional advertising. These same principles are simply being applied to a wider range of options.

Optimizing the Communication Objectives

One of the fundamental decisions a manager will be charged with is how to use traditional advertising and promotion in order to meet specific communication objectives in planning an IMC programme. Depending upon the communication effect, advertising and promotion will have different strengths. For marketing communication to be effective, it is important to understand the relative strengths and weaknesses of traditional advertising and promotion in contributing to the four basic communication effects. These relative strengths and weaknesses are discussed below.[4]

Category need. Neither advertising nor promotion is especially strong in stimulating category need. Category need generally springs from some felt need, the result of a particular consumer motivation. Advertising would have a hard time trying to *create* a motivation. Its strength would be in positioning a category so that it is seen as satisfying an existing motivation. Promotions have the ability to *accelerate* category need, but again are not likely actually to generate category need. As a result, neither advertising nor promotion is likely to have a major impact upon creating category need. (In fact, this is a case where publicity can make an important contribution.)

Brand awareness. Brand awareness is a traditional strength of both advertising and promotion. However, the manager must remember to consider what type of awareness is involved. While advertising can deal effectively with both recognition and recall brand awareness, promotions are likely to be more effective for recognition brand awareness.

Brand attitude. Here we have the traditional strength of advertising. By its very nature it offers the message flexibility that is so very well suited for brand attitude objectives. But good promotions should also work on brand attitude, as we saw in Chapter 14. If proper attention is paid to how a promotion is executed (especially in terms of the words and images in the message) it will be able to contribute something to brand attitude. Nevertheless, advertising is still the strongest contributor to brand attitude communication effects.

Brand purchase intention. This is the traditional strength of promotion. Because of their generally short-term, tactical nature, promotions are geared to immediate action on the part of the consumer. Advertising can contribute to brand purchase intention, but, if it is truly an advertisement, and not a hybrid advertising message that includes a promotion, it is unlikely to make as strong a contribution.

The relative strengths of traditional advertising versus promotion are summarized in Fig. 15.1.

Marketing Considerations Affecting Advertising or Promotion Emphasis

As we can see, the relative strengths of advertising and promotion are directly related to communication effects. But, apart from this, perhaps the next most important guide to the relative emphasis placed upon the use of traditional advertising versus promotion in marketing a product is where the product falls in the product life cycle.[5]

Product Life Cycle Influence upon Relative Emphasis

The product life cycle is generally presented in four parts, as shown in Fig. 15.2. There is an introductory phase, followed by a period of growth. After a certain point the product reaches maturity, and in the long run most products will decline. One of the key determinants of the shape of this curve is the effectiveness of the overall marketing effort. Ideally,

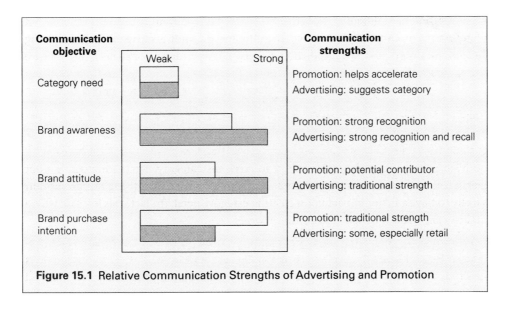

Figure 15.1 Relative Communication Strengths of Advertising and Promotion

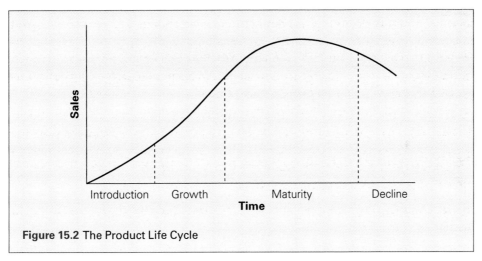

Figure 15.2 The Product Life Cycle

a company would like to accelerate the early stages of the cycle, quickly introducing the brand and growing to a position of strength in the market. At this point it is possible to scale back marketing expenditures, while at the same time experiencing manufacturing efficiencies. This is the period of greatest profit from the brand, and every effort is made to prolong this period before the forces of the ever-changing market eventually push the brand into decline.[6]

Where do advertising and promotion fit in relation to the various stages a brand experiences over its life? If you were to ask yourself where you would probably need to spend the most marketing monies over the life of a product, the obvious answer is during its introductory phase. This is the time when you must make potential consumers aware of the new brand, and teach them something about it in order to interest them in trying it.

A very high level of spending is required here, for both advertising and promotion. The high advertising expenditure goes into helping make people aware that the brand exists and just exactly what kind of product it is. The high expenditure for promotion is needed to help make the target audience aware of the brand, and to induce it to try it. Both the advertising and promotion efforts must be carefully integrated here in order to provide the consistent image we talked about in the previous chapter.

As the brand moves from the introductory stage into the growth stage, the proper distribution of advertising versus promotion expenditure will depend upon the nature of the product itself, or upon the marketing strategy undertaken for the brand. If the new product is a leader in the category or has a readily apparent difference that makes it more desirable than competitive brands, you will want to spend heavily on advertising. Why? Because with advertising you are able to underscore your competitive advantage and maintain high levels of awareness for the brand. Promotions really do not make a lot of sense here, since potential consumers should be interested in trying your brand because of the benefits associated with it, not because of some incentive.

On the other hand, if there is really not much to differentiate your brand from others in the category, you will probably spend less on advertising because you are counting on competitors' advertising to help maintain interest in the category. But, if you adopt this strategy, you must invest in promotional expenditures in order to entice consumers to try or switch to your brand once the category need has been established and maintained by the overall advertising expenditures in the category. However, you must be *very* careful not to overuse promotions to the point where your target audience anticipates them, effectively lowering the brand's price point. In the growth stage of a product's life cycle, you can see that the relative roles of advertising and promotion will differ, depending upon the nature of the product. This same situation occurs when a product reaches maturity, only in this case the difference in expenditure will vary as a function of brand loyalty. If you enjoy a high degree of brand loyalty, it makes very little sense to spend much money on promotion, since all you would be doing, in effect, is lowering the price of your product because most of your users would be buying the brand anyway. However, if there is very little brand loyalty in the category, with a great deal of switching among brands, you will spend less on advertising but more on promotion. In this case advertising is primarily used to maintain awareness for the brand, while promotion is used to attract and hold customers.

Finally, once a product begins to decline, both advertising and promotion spending should drop too as the marketing manager begins to phase out support for the brand. Soon there will be no spending at all on advertising, and only minimal spending on promotion to the trade (not the consumer) in order to maintain distribution for the product until the company has used up its inventory of the brand. All these relationships between the amount spent on advertising versus promotion during different stages of the product life cycle are summarized in Table 15.1.

Additional Marketing Considerations Affecting Relative Emphasis

In addition to the inherent strengths of advertising and promotion as they relate to communication effects, various characteristics in the market also suggest emphasizing either

Table 15.1 Relating Advertising and Promotion to the Product Life Cycle

Product Life Cycle Stage	Utilizing Advertising	Utilizing Promotion
Introduction	Drive up awareness	Generate initial trial
Growth		
Differentiated brand	Underscore brand's advantage	Unnecessary
Undifferentiated brand	Rely upon category spending to maintain interest	Encourage switching to brand
Maturity		
High brand loyalty	Maintain loyalty	Avoid because it effectively lowers price point
Low brand loyalty	Maintain brand awareness	Use to attract and hold customers
Decline	Unnecessary	Maintain distribution until inventory is gone

Table 15.2 Advertising versus Promotion Emphasis under Specific Market Considerations

Market Consideration	Emphasis
Product differentiation	Advertising
Strong market position	Advertising
Poor market performance	Promotion
Competitive activity	Respond accordingly

advertising or promotion. These market characteristics may be grouped into four categories, and are reviewed below (see Table 15.2).

Product Differentiation

Generally speaking, if a brand has a positively perceived difference over its competitors, there should be an emphasis on advertising in its marketing communication programme. Two potential differences to consider are quality and price. If you have a brand that consumers see as high quality, you will be likely to spend more on advertising in order to communicate its quality benefits and support its 'quality image', reinforcing positive brand equity. If your brand is seen as lower quality, you will tend to spend more on promotion in order to persuade people to 'trade down'. Quality generally relates to price, so you will tend to find high-priced brands spending more on advertising in order to build and sustain a strong brand equity to justify their higher price. Lower-priced brands generally spend more on promotion, and usually price promotion, in order to appear to offer consumers a better value. Price promotion could certainly help tactically in the short term, but it will not help justify a higher price in the long term.

If your brand is seen by consumers to have special benefits not found in other brands in the category, you will be more likely to spend money on advertising in order to inform your target audience about unique benefits associated with the brand. On the other hand, 'commodity' brands are thought of as similar and as a result tend to compete more on a promotion basis. Brands can be differentiated on the basis of obvious benefits, such as taste, but also on the basis of attributes that the consumer never really sees, such as special whitening ingredients in a detergent or the presence or absence of caffeine in colas. As long as a brand is perceived as different, advertising can have a greater effect than promotion.

Products that have a real risk associated with them, not just high-priced brands or ones with perceived psychological risk (that is, high involvement), tend to employ advertising to reassure consumers that they are making a safe choice. Such potentially high-risk products—for example, those needed for very serious health problems—are unlikely to use promotion.

Strong Market Position

If a brand has a strong market position, based upon either a high market share or frequent purchase, advertising should be emphasized over promotion. The key again is advertising's ability to help build and reinforce a positive brand attitude, especially in a market where there may be a lot of switching behaviour. Promotion, of course, can be used tactically, but to sustain a strong position in the market requires an advertising emphasis.

Poor Market Performance

If a brand is having problems in the market, promotion should be emphasized over advertising because of its more immediate impact. This emphasis makes sense at both the consumer and the trade levels when a brand is in need of a 'quick fix'. It is assumed, of course, that there is not an inherent product problem, or other serious marketing mix problem, because promotion will not provide a long-term cure.

Competitive Activity

A final and obvious factor in the relative expenditure of marketing monies for advertising versus promotion is the activity of your competitors. Suppose a direct competitor increases its advertising spending. If you are to maintain your relative position in the market, it will probably be necessary for you to increase your advertising spending. Likewise, if your major competitor turns to heavy use of promotion, it will probably be necessary for you to increase your promotion spending at least somewhat as well, in order to minimize the likelihood of people switching from your brand as a result of your competitor's promotions. Then again, this may not be in your brand's best interest. It is important to study each situation carefully and respond accordingly.

As we shall see in the next section, one of the advantages of a good marketing communication programme that effectively utilizes the strengths of both advertising and promotion is that strong brand equity can help minimize the effect of a competitor's promotions. And again we caution that you must guard against falling into the trap of regularly using promotions, effectively telling your target audience to make their choice on price. Another area to consider is the strength of private labels in your brand's category. If there is a strong private label presence in the market, it makes sense to emphasize advertising and not try to compete on price with promotion.

It should be clear now that in marketing a brand you must make strategic use of both advertising and promotion. You should not think in terms of advertising versus promotion, but rather whether advertising *or* promotion is most likely to satisfy a communication objective, and whether or not certain market conditions suggest *emphasizing* either advertising or promotion. These are not unrelated. The market conditions discussed above will suggest the need for a particular communication effect, which will guide the selection of the communication objectives.

So we can see that depending upon the desired communication effect (which could be a function of more than the market characteristics just discussed) there will be advantages to emphasizing either advertising or promotion. It is not enough to regard advertising and promotion as independent parts of the marketing communication mix. Rather, traditional advertising and promotion each have special characteristics that make them more or less appropriate to achieve particular marketing and communication ends. The decisions as to where you place your emphasis will be a function of specific circumstances in the market.

While it is certainly possible to use only advertising or only promotion since both are able to produce each of the four basic communication effects, this is generally not desirable. The best course is an integrated marketing communication programme that builds upon the individual strengths of advertising and promotion, and the advantage of using them together, which is discussed next.

Advantages of Using Advertising and Promotion Together

There is no doubt that using advertising and promotion together offers real advantages over using advertising or promotion alone. Nevertheless, while a brand's marketing communication profits from using advertising and promotion together, for most brands traditional advertising will almost always be more important. This stems primarily from advertising's brand attitude strength, and the fact that brand attitude should be the central communication effect for all brand marketing communication. This may seem surprising given the fact that traditional advertising receives only about one-third of all marketing communication spending. Unfortunately, too often brands get caught up in short-term competitive marketing and rely too heavily upon promotion.

What makes using advertising and promotion *together* so strong is the interaction between the long-term effects of brand attitude on building brand equity, and the tactical advantages of promotion. Without a strong brand attitude, promotion effectiveness suffers. When advertising has been effective in generating a strong brand attitude, all the brand's uses of promotion become that much more effective. There are two principal reasons for this:

- When a strong positive brand attitude is developed through advertising it means that when a brand does use promotion the target audience will see the promotion as a better value, and

- The strong positive brand attitude also means that when a brand's competitors use promotion, the brand's target audience will be less likely to respond.

The logic here is straightforward. If consumers have a strong positive attitude towards a brand, they will be less likely to switch simply because of a competitor's promotion; and when a brand consumers like does offer a promotion of its own, they will be that much more pleased. Additionally, a promotion in that light will also tend to reinforce consumers' already held positive brand attitude.[7]

There is another thing to consider here. What we have been discussing are the reasons why advertising and promotion work so well together in terms of communication effects. You might well be thinking that, if advertising does such a great job building brand attitude and brand equity, and tends to immunize your target audience against competitive promotions, why promote at all? The reason is simple. Even with a positive brand attitude, most consumers will occasionally switch brands. If they were always loyal to your brand, there would be no need to promote. But most consumers tend to use more than one brand in a category, at least on occasion. That is why some promotion will almost always be needed for tactical support of the brand. We want to maintain as large a share of our customer's purchases as possible, and the effective use of promotion helps accomplish this task. While advertising is of critical importance to a brand, because without advertising it is very difficult to maintain strong brand equity, the overall strength of a brand is increased when it is used along with promotion. When advertising and promotion are used together, the overall communication effects are stronger.

The Ratchet Effect

A good explanation of how this mutual reinforcement between advertising and promotion works has been offered by Bill Moran, a marketing consultant. He calls his explanation a 'ratchet effect' and it reflects the discussion we have been having.[8]

One of the behavioural consequences of most promotions is that they 'steal' purchases, either by moving forward a purchase by a consumer who would eventually be buying the brand anyway, or by taking a regular purchase away from a competitor. As just discussed, one of the reasons for a brand to promote, even when it enjoys a strong positive brand attitude, is to maximize the brand's purchase by the occasional brand-switcher. As a result, when a brand promotes, it should generate more sales than usual. But our objective is to increase sales not temporarily (except for an occasional short-term tactical reason), but *permanently*. Without advertising, after the promotional period sales will drop below average levels for a while, then slowly return to normal as consumers return to their regular purchase patterns.

This is where advertising comes in. When advertising is used together with promotion, the effect of a promotion within or following a period of advertising is to stimulate the overall growth rate for the brand faster than with advertising alone. This is what is meant by a 'ratchet effect'. A well-conceived promotion, one that also addresses brand attitude, helps to reinforce the positive brand attitude of regular users. The occasional user of a brand who is attracted by the promotion will be more likely to stay with the brand, buying it more often after the promotion because of the effect of the advertising that ran along with or after the promotion, building upon the advertising-driven brand attitude that existed prior to the promotion. As this cycle continues, the regular base of consumers grows, 'ratcheting up' with each advertising-promotion cycle.

You can see how this happens by looking at the charts in Fig. 15.3. When only promotions are used, a brand experiences a short-term spike in sales, followed by a steady decline until sales return to relative equilibrium and normal purchase cycles resume.

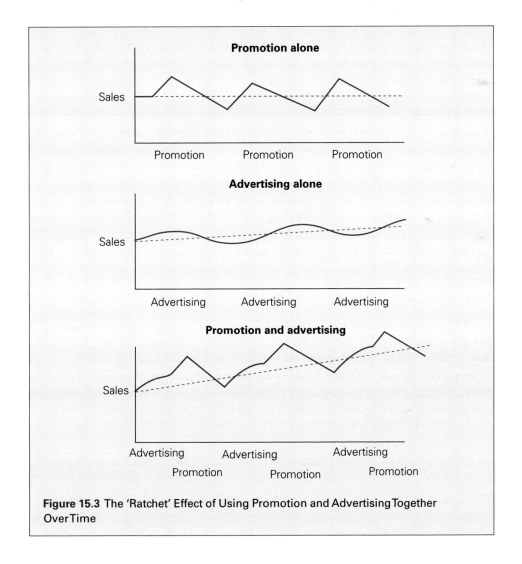

Figure 15.3 The 'Ratchet' Effect of Using Promotion and Advertising Together Over Time

Unless the promotion attracts new *loyal* users, the promotion will not have added incremental business. Over time, nothing has been gained. When only advertising is used, we see that sales generally build steadily if not dramatically over time as the effect of positive brand attitude develops more interest in the brand. But, when advertising and promotion are used *together*, we experience Moran's ratchet effect. Promotion accelerates purchase, but ongoing advertising helps sustain and build a customer base so that over time the overall effect on sales is greater than when advertising is used alone.[9]

Moran has suggested that this ratchet effect can be explained in terms of two kinds of demand elasticity: 'upside' and 'downside' elasticity. These are important considerations in communication planning, because they help focus a manager's thinking on *how* the relationship between advertising and promotion that we have been talking about influences sales, and not simply on the overall price elasticity of a brand. These notions of upside and downside elasticity relate to a brand's pricing strategy as well as *competitor brand* pricing strategy. When prices are cut, either directly or via promotion (our interest here) and sales go up, we have upside elasticity; when sales decline as a result of a price increase, we have downside elasticity. It is important for the manager to remember that, when competitors aggressively promote, they in effect 'raise' the price of our brand.

As this discussion should make clear, the best defence against an aggressive promotion campaign by a brand's competitors is *not* necessarily to match their promotion spending, but to maintain a strong advertising presence to ensure a strong brand equity, while promoting *tactically* as necessary. Effective advertising stimulates high upside and low downside elasticity by building and maintaining strong brand equity through positive brand attitude.

Once again we are back to the importance of understanding communication effects and which communication effects are necessary for the effective marketing of our brand. And at the heart of this understanding is how to deal with the important and essential communication objective of brand attitude.

Now that we understand how best to use advertising and promotion in IMC, it is time to consider how we put together an effective IMC programme.

Marketing Communication Task Grid

Thinking back to the strategic planning process, the first four steps identified the target audience, provided an understanding of how it made purchase decisions, the best positioning for the brand in its marketing communication, and the overall communication strategy. The last step involved optimizing the media strategy, and selecting the best available communication options to deliver the message.

In putting together an IMC programme, a manager will be confronted with a wide range of potential ways to meet the brand's communication objectives. How is it possible to ensure the best allocation of what are almost always limited resources to spend on marketing communication? Rarely will the manager have enough money to do everything desired. This means setting priorities, and a good way to do this is with a Marketing Communication Task Grid.

Decision Stages	Communication Tasks	Target Audience	Where and When	Marketing Communication Options
List appropriate decision stages	List specific results desired in terms of communication effects at each stage	Determine primary target audience group to reach at each stage	Determine best way to reach primary target audience group at each stage	List best marketing communication options for accomplishing the communication tasks at each stage

Figure 15.4 Marketing Communication Task Grid

Basically a Marketing Communication Task Grid looks at the decision stages that consumers go through in making choices, and for each stage details the communication tasks required and the target audience to be addressed. Then, for each stage it asks the manager to think through 'where and when' to reach the target audience for maximum effect, and the various marketing communication options available to accomplish this task (see Fig. 15.4).

Utilizing the generic decision stages we talked about in Chapter 7, let us consider how the manager can use the task grid. The first stage in most decisions will be some form of need arousal, after which a brand is selected, purchased, and used. Using these decision stages, how will the manager apply the task grid? For each of these four decision stages, the manager will list the *specific* results desired from the appropriate communication effects serving as communication objectives. Next, again for each of the decision stages, the target audience *at that stage of the decision process* will be detailed. Then the manager must decide the best way of reaching the target audience and the best marketing communication option to do the job, again for each stage of the decision process.

As an example, consider the initial decision stage, need arousal. One obviously needs to stimulate brand awareness and a certain level of brand attitude. But what kind of awareness, and do we need simply to raise or to maintain the awareness? In terms of brand attitude, must we teach the target audience something new about the brand; do we need to create interest, stimulate enquiry, give potential consumers a good feeling, or underscore a unique feature? As you can see, in detailing the specific results we want from the communication, we are going well beyond just the communication effect we are seeking, and thinking through what we want to happen as a result of meeting our brand awareness and brand attitude communication objective.

Next, what specific members of the target audience are we to reach at this need-arousal stage? Most likely it will be those playing the initiator or influencer role, but this information will come from your understanding of consumer decision making. Which of the possible multiple influencers should be the primary target audience; will we need or want secondary or even tertiary target audiences at this stage; if so, can we afford them?

For most fmcgs, the best way of reaching the target audience will probably be *prior* to purchase in order to build or sustain brand salience (a 'presence' of the brand in the consumer's considered set) and attitude, but also perhaps at the point of purchase for stimulating impulse purchases. In stimulating need arousal for most business-oriented products, the best way to reach the initiators and influencers would most likely be at their place of business.

Questions for the manager to ask, once these issues have been addressed, should deal with identifying the best marketing communication options to effect the desired need arousal (the decision stage we are talking about in this example). What media will best sustain awareness consistent with the brand awareness strategy? Should print advertising, billboards, or coupons be used? What about the Internet? Would it make sense? Will a direct mail campaign aimed at the initiators and influencers of a business decision be best, or would targeted trade magazines make more sense?

In addition to dealing with possible communication options at a general media level, specific media should also be addressed. The point of the Marketing Communication Task Grid is to help *focus* the manager's thinking to optimize the best choice of available communication options. If money were no object, you could proceed to implement everything suggested by the Marketing Communication Task Grid. Unfortunately, as already pointed out, that is almost never the case. Rather, realistic budget considerations will require the manager to determine the best mix of communication tasks that can be accomplished with available resources.

We have dealt only with the first decision stage in this example. These same questions will need to be addressed for *each stage* in the decision process. Once a Marketing Communication Task Grid has been completed, with its list of potential marketing communication options for the various communications tasks associated with each decision stage, the manager must give thought to the *specific* marketing communication media that can be accommodated within the media budget. The work done in completing a Marketing Communication Task Grid provides the manager with an opportunity to review objectively what might be done to exert a positive influence on each stage of the decision process. It does not necessarily provide 'the answer', but it does provide a summary of our best understanding of what should be done to optimize a marketing communication programme.

Matching Marketing Communication Media to Communication Effects

So far we have been looking at media rather generally in terms of communication options. But we must deal specifically with the appropriateness of particular marketing

Table 15.3 Considerations in Matching Media with Communication Objectives

Visual Content	Critical for recognition brand awareness and transformational brand attitude
Time to Process Message	Important for high-involvement informational brand attitude
Frequency	Higher frequency is needed for recall brand awareness and low-involvement transformational brand attitude

communication options for specific communication effects, as you will remember from the chapter on media. Direct mail may be a good way of reaching a certain target audience, but is it a good way of delivering the creative message needed to satisfy the communication objective involved? Television advertising offers broad reach, but is it suited to the communication effect you are looking for? As we know, certain traditional advertising and promotion media will be more or less appropriate for specific communication objectives.

Because brand awareness and brand attitude are always communication objectives, let us focus on them. Let us review the three important considerations the manager must look at when considering marketing communication options in order to ensure a proper match with the communication task and objective that were introduced in Chapter 10 (see Table 15.3). The first is *visual content*. To what extent does a particular option facilitate visual communication? This is critical, for example, when brand recognition is required for brand awareness.

Secondly, how much *time* is available for the target audience to *process the message*? In some cases, for example, when the brand attitude objective involves a high-involvement, informational strategy, which is the case for most consumer durable products (televisions, home computers) and many business purchase decisions, the target audience will need time to process the message in order to learn enough about the brand. In other cases, such as with most fmcg products, only a brief exposure time is necessary. When more processing time is necessary, broadcast media such as television and radio will not do, but they will be very appropriate when only a short time is needed for processing.

The third consideration is *frequency*. Some marketing communication options, such as broadcasting and newspapers, offer the potential of high frequency. In other words, the creative message can be presented frequently to the target audience. Think of how many commercials for a particular brand you see during the broadcast of a football match. Other media options, for example, direct mail or monthly magazines, are much more restricted in terms of frequency. True, a brand could have multiple insertions in a single magazine, but, because of the narrow reach of magazines compared to something like television, this will not usually be a very efficient way of obtaining higher frequency for your creative message. When the brand awareness objective is recall, higher frequency is required than when it is recognition. When the brand attitude objective involves a low-involvement, transformational strategy, again we need more frequency. The Marketing Communication Task Grid makes it possible to come to more efficient and effective decisions as to how to implement a marketing communication campaign.

Table 15.4 Primary Media for Recognition Brand Awareness and Appropriate Brand Attitude Strategy

Low-Involvement, Informational	• Television • Print • Posters • Sponsorships
Low-Involvement, Transformational	• Television • Newspapers (if four-colour available) • Posters • Sponsorships
High-Involvement, Informational	• Television (using 60-second or longer commercials, e.g. on cable) • Print • Direct response
High-Involvement, Transformational	• Television • Print • Posters • Sponsorships • Direct response

Primary Media

Media that satisfy those three criteria in terms of the appropriate communication objectives are called *primary* media. These are marketing communication options you look to first in putting together an IMC programme. Primary media must be capable of delivering the appropriate brand awareness *and* brand attitude communication objectives (as we discussed in Chapter 10), as well as category need and brand purchase intention if appropriate. Primary media for *recognition* brand awareness and brand attitude must first of all be able to present the brand as it will be confronted at the point of purchase, and then satisfy the processing requirements of the brand attitude strategy involved (see Table 15.4). Since most media will work for recall brand awareness, as long as a few possible cautions are taken into account with print media (especially with magazines as discussed in Chapter 10), the primary media selected will be mediated only by brand attitude strategy communications (see Table 15.5).

Just because a particular medium should not be considered as a primary medium does not necessarily mean it should not be used at all. Often it makes sense to use a medium

Table 15.5 Primary Media for Recall Brand Awareness and Appropriate Brand Attitude Strategy

Low-Involvement, Informational	• Television • Radio • Newspapers • Magazines (with attention to frequency) • Sponsorships
Low-Involvement, Transformational	• Television • Newspapers (if four-colour available) • Magazines (with attention to frequency) • Sponsorships
High-Involvement, Informational	• Television (using 60-second or longer commercials, e.g. on cable) • Newspapers • Magazines (with attention to frequency)
High-Involvement, Transformational	• Television • Newspapers (if four-colour available) • Magazines (with attention to frequency) • Sponsorships

because it helps enhance the delivery of a communication objective, even if it is not appropriate for all the core communication objectives. In these cases the additional medium could be used to help boost a particular objective. This is especially true for brand awareness. There may also be certain situations where the manager may need to use a less-than-ideal medium because it reaches a part of the target audience that is not effectively covered, in terms of either reach or frequency, by the primary media.

The primary media presented in Tables 15.4 and 15.5 reflect what is necessary to achieve the two primary communication objectives effectively. But when dealing with certain types of advertising, there may be specific concerns that suggest particular media are more or less appropriate. To illustrate, we will consider the cases of retail, business-to-business, and corporate image advertising.

Retail Advertising
In the case of retail advertising, it is almost always *local* regardless of the number of stores a chain may have, because any one store is only likely to draw customers from around its location. Additionally, most retail advertising must concern itself not only

with promoting the image of the store, but also with the products it carries. This can make for a rather complex mix of communication problems. In the end, local media are what one should consider, with the type consistent with the requirements of the core communication objectives of brand awareness and brand attitude as well as, in all cases, brand purchase intention. Local television, newspapers, outdoor, direct mail, and, where appropriate, local radio could be considered.

Business-to-Business Advertising

Media options for business-to-business advertising are generally a function of the target audience's size and the roles people in the target audience are playing in the decision process. When target audiences are small, when there are really only a limited number of decision makers, general advertising does not really make sense. Here, most marketing communication will be handled via sales calls, and the only media involved will be collateral (brochures and catalogues) and possibly direct mail. With a somewhat larger target audience, where it begins to make sense to use print media, trade publications and direct mail are appropriate, and in some cases targeted use of the Internet. The key here is to be certain to identify the different roles played by different segments of the target audience. With somewhat larger target audiences it is likely that there will be both important but lower-level decision makers as well as senior management to consider. With larger target audiences, trade publications and more general business magazines with broader reach are appropriate, as well as the tactical use of direct mail and the Internet.

Corporate Image Advertising

You will remember from Chapter 9 that corporate image advertising almost always involves a transformational brand attitude strategy. A manager must keep this in mind when considering media for corporate image advertising. And, just as with business-to-business advertising, the size of the company will dictate media options to consider. With many small companies, image advertising as such may not make any sense. However, local sponsorships would be appropriate, and any product-related advertising could include a certain degree of corporate image messaging as part of the brand attitude strategy.

Larger companies should utilize the primary media associated with recognition brand awareness and transformational brand attitude strategies as appropriate. In addition, event marketing and sponsorships (that are compatible with the image sought) could also work. But, if the target audience is small or specialized—for example, when directly addressing financial analysts—special interest publications, direct mail, or the Internet might be considered. It should also not be overlooked that, regardless of the size of a company, effective public relations should be *integrated* with any corporate image advertising; and the annual report is always a part of corporate image advertising.

The point here is that, when selecting specific media to use from the options listed in the Marketing Communications Task Grid, the manager must look first to the appropriate primary media, but also take into account any unique consideration specific to the brand's target audience.

Advantages of the Marketing Communication Task Grid

For each important stage of the decision process involved in choosing a product or service, the Marketing Communication Task Grid provides an opportunity to summarize:

- what we want to accomplish with our marketing communication at that stage in the decision process,
- whom we want to reach with our marketing communication at that stage,
- how we can best reach them at that stage, and
- the best media available to accomplish the task.

By now you should be able to see the potential this has for IMC strategy, and putting together an effective IMC programme. In effect, the Marketing Communication Task Grid provides a single source for reviewing all the ways it is possible positively to affect the decision to purchase a brand or use a service.

Rarely would you be able to implement all the possibilities suggested from the Marketing Communication Task Grid, but it will certainly inform your thinking as you integrate the available options into an optimum strategic plan. It also will remind you of the need to be consistent in the look and feel of the message and execution, *regardless* of the marketing communication options selected to meet the communication tasks needed for positively effecting specific steps in the decision process.

With IMC we are setting communication objectives and selecting media to maximize our ability to reach our target market effectively. Unlike in the past, when managers considered various ways of using traditional advertising messages, and independently considered using some form of traditional promotion, the planning and execution of all marketing communication must be *integrated*.

Monitoring the Campaign

The campaign is now ready to run, but the manager's job is not done. The ongoing advertising and other marketing communication must be monitored both for effectiveness and wearout.

Campaign Tracking

A carefully considered pre-test as discussed in Chapter 13 should help ensure that the creative execution will deliver the desired message effectively, assuming it has proper exposure among the target audience and proper attention is paid to the advertising. Whether or not the advertising works, however, is another question.[10]

Once the finished executions have been placed and are running in the market, to be certain they are actually working requires *tracking*. Tracking a campaign is a good idea, even if every indicator you have suggests the advertising is working well. Without tracking you can never be sure if it is the *advertising* that is causally responsible for sales or usage in the market, or whether other factors in the marketing mix, such as competitors' activity or even unusual market conditions, are mediating sales. Tracking can be expensive, but it is money well spent.

For tracking to be successful you must measure not only responses to your own advertising and other marketing communication (such as promotions or direct marketing activity), but responses to your competitors as well. Unlike pre-testing, when we are concerned only with specific executions, now we are concerned with how executions perform within the overall context of the market. This means that we must also measure not only our brand and competitors' brand advertising, but any marketing activity that might influence target audience behaviour. This includes such things as promotions, your brand and competitors' media spending, and even trade activity. For example, your advertising may be communicating very well, but, if your competitor has just secured a special trade promotion for its brand, this could seriously affect overall market share.

There are basically four ways to track advertising campaigns. Some marketers simply monitor sales activity, correlating it with known advertising and promotion spending for their brand versus competitors. The problem here, of course, is that you are assuming the advertising is *directly* responsible for any observed sales results. This can lead to serious misinterpretations because you simply cannot know what may be causing the activity observed in the market.

Another way of tracking advertising is to utilize a panel of consumers who are questioned about their purchases and recall of advertising. This does have the advantage of measuring causality at the individual level, but it has its own problems. Using a panel of consumers may sensitize those participating and influence their purchase behaviour over time. The most common way of tracking the effectiveness of a campaign is to take a series of measures over time, 'tracking' the results. With waves of interviews, a benchmark is established prior to a campaign and additional measures are taken at various points in time. These measures generally correspond to the end of major periods of advertising, providing a 'before-after' comparison. The biggest problem with taking periodic measures is that you do not know what is going on between the measurements.

Look at Fig. 15.5. If this represented what was actually going on in the market, periodic measures would significantly underestimate the effectiveness of the advertising campaign. What the graph suggests is that it takes a while for the advertising effect to build, and by taking a measure at the end of the advertising flight you are missing the true effect of the campaign. Figure 15.6 illustrates another possible scenario. By measuring the results at the end of the advertising flight, in this case you completely miss the advertising's effect, and in fact show no effect at all!

The best way to track advertising is with *continuous tracking*. Continuous tracking utilizes ongoing interviewing of small samples of consumers, 'rolling' the results, with moving averages for weekly, fortnightly, or four-week periods. This permits a relatively continuous measure of what is going on in the market, offering a sensitive measure of actual advertising effects. Because the measures are ongoing, it is possible to read the result for any period, at any time. This provides the manager with a powerful diagnostic tool, and avoids the danger inherent in other methods of misreading the effects of a campaign.

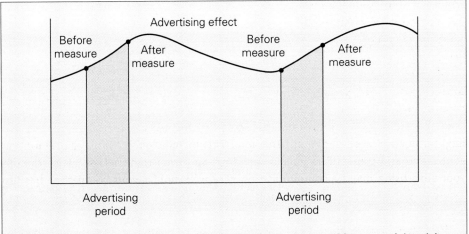

Figure 15.5 Potential Problem with Before-After Effectiveness Measures: Advertising Effects Continue to Build after the End of the Advertising Period

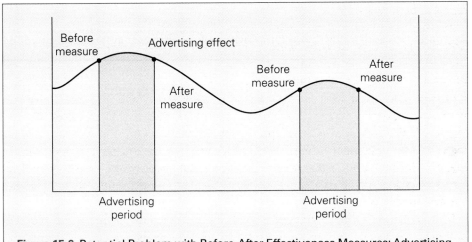

Figure 15.6 Potential Problem with Before-After Effectiveness Measures: Advertising Effects Peak before the End of the Advertising Period

Of course, even with continuous tracking, the results will only be as good as your measures and analysis. The measures used in tracking a campaign reflect the four stages of the communication response sequence introduced in Chapter 4: exposure, processing, communication effects, and target audience action. In tracking a marketing communication campaign, the manager is not only interested in the 'results' (i.e. the target audience action), but also with each step that led to that result. It is only by looking at the entire sequence that one is able to *understand* the result, and to be in a position to correct any aspect of the campaign that is not working as planned.

Exposure Measures

Exposing the message is the job of media, so measures of exposure reflect the media plan, and may be measured in several ways. Perhaps the most frequently used measure is GRP (gross rating points), within the time period being addressed. This will include the audience figures for all of the media vehicles used during that period. A better measure would be some kind of estimate of the *minimum effective* reach, or the number of people exposed to the campaign during that period at the minimum level of frequency required for the advertising to be effective.

Measures of exposure are usually related to sales, but may also be looked at in relation to measures of the other steps in the communication response sequence. This can be especially useful when compared with specific communication effects such as increases in brand awareness or shifts in brand attitude.

Processing Measures

As discussed in Chapter 11, there are four stages involved in the processing of an advert or promotion: attention, learning, acceptance (for high-involvement decisions), and emotion. While it is impossible to actually measure processing when it occurs, in campaign tracking indirect measures are used. For attention, this usually means some measure of recognition or recall of the campaign, which would suggest that at least some attention was paid, and some level of learning achieved. If it is a high-involvement category, acceptance is inferred by appropriate measures of communication effects. If the campaign is remembered, it is possible to ask about any emotion associated with it.

Campaign recognition is generally measured by showing a member of the target audience the advertising or promotion from a campaign and asking if they remember seeing (or hearing it if radio). Recall of the campaign is measured by asking if they remembered seeing (or hearing) any advertising or promotion for the brand. If they do, they are asked to describe it. Only if the description matches the actual content of the executions is it considered an indication of processing.

A more rigorous variation of this, pioneered by Market Mind, is to prompt with the category, not the brand. A category cue asks for what advertising or promotion the target audience remembers seeing for the category, and to describe it. If the brand is not mentioned in the description, they are asked what brand it was for. This provides a very sensitive measure of how well the components of the campaign were processed, both in relation to category need as well as its link to the brand, and the salience of the outcome of the processing.[11]

Communication Effects

Basically, in measuring the communication effects of a campaign one uses the same measures as those used for communication effects in the pre-test. The only difference is in the order in which the questions are asked. You will recall that when we discussed pre-testing in Chapter 13 we made a point of how important the order of questioning is. While brand awareness measures are at the end or even delayed in a pre-test, they are measured first in tracking a campaign. This is because the brand must be either recognized or recalled first before it can be purchased.

Target Audience Action

In a tracking study, the measure of target audience action is asking what items were purchased during the tracking period, or what action was taken if the objective was something else such as going to a concert, calling an investment banker, visiting a trade fair, sending for 'more information'; or in social marketing, making the desired behavioural change. For fmcg products, marketers will also use retail scanner data.

Campaign Wearout

What we mean by 'wearout' is that the current campaign is not performing up to expectation, in the *absence* of external causes (such things as poor distribution or changes in market dynamics). If there are external factors that are adversely affecting the expected results of an advertising and promotion campaign, this would call for a careful review of both the marketing and advertising *strategy*. Otherwise, the manager must look to the campaign itself. This means either the media plan or the executions, reflecting the first two steps of the communication response sequence. Problems with the media plan would directly affect exposure and the opportunity to process the messages; problems with the execution would reduce the likelihood of successfully processing the message.

The first step is to check for problems with the media plan. The manager should determine if the plan is still delivering the necessary reach to be effective. This will require a careful examination of the specific vehicles being used, or specific programmes in broadcast, for target audience delivery. Tracking measures of advertising and promotion recognition and frequency can help provide a check on whether the required minimum effective frequency is being obtained, the frequency level required for successful processing. If the media plan checks out, attention must then turn to the executions being used. Even though pre-tests of the executions indicated they 'worked', over time there is the possibility of processing wearout. This may occur at any stage of processing: attention, learning, acceptance, or with the emotional responses associated with them.

A common cause of processing wearout occurs after an advert has been exposed several times, as a result of *diminished attention*.[12] This is especially true of print advertising where attention may be easily diverted. To help prevent this, one can use a number of variations of the execution (always with the same consistent look and feel).

Processing wearout may also occur when learning is *interfered* with by better or increased numbers of executions for competitive brands. A change in competitive executional content or emphasis, or a change in media schedule, could interfere with the processing of a brand's message.[13] Interference can also result from a brand's own advertising, when new executions are introduced into a campaign. Carry-over from existing or previous advertising, especially when there is not a consistent look and feel, can interfere with the building of new associations in memory for weeks, or even months.

Overexposure, especially with broadcast, can lead to *attitudinal* wearout, which will affect the acceptance of a message. In fact, overexposure can even lead to a negative response to a brand's advertising, this can happen as counter-arguing increases with multiple exposures, leading to a rejection of the message.[14]

Problems in Implementing IMC

We mentioned earlier that, although most managers agree that IMC is the best way to approach their company's marketing communication needs, in reality true integrated planning for marketing communication is rare. Why should this be the case given such general acceptance of its value? Unfortunately, there are a number of potential roadblocks to the implementation of IMC.[15] Perhaps the single biggest problem involves the decision-making structure of most companies. The structure or organizational make-up of a company, and the way managers think or approach marketing questions, often create problems in trying to implement IMC programmes. While the decision-making structure is by far the biggest problem, there are at least three other areas that can cause problems: managers' perceptions of IMC, compensation considerations, and current marketing trends (see Table 15.6).

The Decision-Making Structure

IMC requires a central planning expertise in marketing communication. However, with widely dispersed resources, individual manager relationships with marketing

Table 15.6 Problems in Implementing IMC

Decision-Making Structure	• Organizational structure too often is not conducive to sharing information
	• Too often marketing communication has a low priority, and is peopled by specialists with a narrow focus
	• Organization character inhibits a common culture
Manager Perceptions of IMC	• Resistance to change and politics associated with power inhibit sharing
Compensation	• Worries about position and salaries in a re-structured IMC-oriented group
	• Compensation is based upon individual budgets, not contribution to total good
Trends in Marketing	• Belief company already implements IMC
	• Niche and micromarketing are thought not to need common themes

communication agencies and vendors, and (critically) a lack of incentive to cooperate, it is no wonder there are problems when it comes to trying to develop and implement IMC.

A number of aspects of a company's decision-making structure contribute to these problems. Basically they reflect organizational structure and what we might call organizational character, or the way an organization 'thinks'.

Organizational Structure

We have noted that there is broad agreement among marketing managers over the need for IMC, but the very organizational structure of many companies stands in the way of effective implementation. At the heart of this problem is an organization's ability to manage the interrelationships among information and materials between the various agencies and vendors involved in developing and creating marketing communication. There are a number of specific structural factors that can make this difficult.

The Low Standing of Marketing Communication in an Organization

Unfortunately, for too many companies, marketing communication has a very low priority within the organization. For many in top management, spending money on marketing communication is seen as a luxury that can be afforded only when everything else is going well. One of the fastest ways for a company to send a lot of money to the bottom line is not to spend budgeted marketing communication money. When companies frequently employ this tactic, it is not surprising that those most responsible for marketing communication occupy lower-level positions within the organization.

Specialization

To manage IMC effectively, those in charge should ideally be marketing communication generalists. Unfortunately, there are very few people like this holding marketing communication positions. In fact, what you are most likely to find are people specializing in particular areas; and, even more problematic, these specialists rarely talk with each other. They have their own budgets and their own suppliers, and jealously guard the areas they control.

Given the narrow focus and understanding of such specialists, it is very difficult to bring them together in the first place, let alone expect them to have the broad understanding and appreciation of the many marketing communication options necessary for effective IMC planning. But, even if they did have this understanding, getting them to give up control, especially when it is unlikely to be financially advantageous (which we shall discuss more specifically later), is a lot to ask. Yet this is precisely what is necessary if IMC is to work.

How the Organization Thinks

In addition to the problems inherent in the way most marketing departments are structured, there are less tangible aspects of an organization's thinking and behaviour that also pose problems for implementing IMC. Because of the structural barriers we have just been talking about that can impede the flow of information, it is very difficult for an entire company to share a common understanding of that company's marketing communication.

But it is very important for everyone working at a company to understand and communicate the image being projected by the company's marketing communication. Anyone who has any contact with customers must reflect this image. This means store clerks, sales force, telephone operators, receptionists—all are a part of a company's marketing communication, and hence in many ways are IMC 'media'. Unfortunately, all too often only those directly involved with the marketing communication programme are familiar with it, and this can be a serious problem.

Manager Perceptions of IMC

How managers perceive IMC is something that can hinder its effective implementation. Managers with different backgrounds or different marketing communications specialities, either within the company organization or at marketing communication agencies or vendors, are likely to have different perceptions of what constitutes integrated marketing communication and what roles different people should play in the planning and implementation of IMC.

Resistance to Change

Different perceptions of IMC will certainly influence its effective implementation. But even more troubling is the natural resistance to change that the idea of IMC is likely to trigger, making it difficult if not impossible to implement even though IMC's benefits are generally accepted.

Perhaps the most serious problem associated with this is a fear that the manager responsible for IMC planning will not fully appreciate someone else's area of expertise. This is compounded when advertising takes the lead (which it should in most cases), because of long-held feelings that advertising managers simply do not understand or even consider other means of marketing communication (which, unfortunately, is all too often the case). This is aggravated by the conflict, for example, between the short-term tactical experience of those working in promotion and the longer-term thinking of advertising managers.

Politics and Power

Another way of looking at this tendency to resist change is in terms of both intra-organizational and inter-organizational politics. It does not matter if the motivation is individual self-interest or an actual belief by managers or employees in the superiority of their way of doing things: the result is the same. People, departments, and organizations want power and the rewards that go with it. Too often managers and their staff believe they will be giving up too much personal responsibility if they are part of more broadly based IMC planning. Compensation (which is discussed next) is only one part of the problem. When lines of responsibility are blurred, it is easy for individuals to feel that their prestige and position, in many cases hard won, is threatened. This can be very difficult to overcome.

Compensation

While compensation issues are less of a direct problem with companies than with agencies and vendors working in marketing communication, they can still be a problem. When managers are worried about the importance of their positions in a realigned IMC-oriented marketing communication group, this leads quite naturally to worries about salaries and promotion, which lessens interest in IMC.

But the real concern about compensation is with agencies and vendors involved in the marketing communication needs of the company. Management at agencies working in the marketing communication field are traditionally rewarded on the basis of the total size of their business with companies. This means they are very unlikely to suggest to their clients that they might be better off spending more of their money on some other form of marketing communication.

Somehow these managers must be compensated in terms of their contributions rather than of how much is spent on their particular speciality. Without such a scheme, effective IMC is impossible because those managing one type of marketing communication will be more concerned with 'selling' it, not with how their speciality will best contribute to an overall IMC programme.

Trends in Marketing

Surprisingly, several trends in marketing have also created problems for effectively implementing IMC. Perhaps the most perplexing is the trend towards IMC! When many managers are asked about IMC, they are likely to report that their company is indeed implementing it. But this is unlikely, at least in the way we have been discussing it. If a company is in fact implementing IMC in some limited way, or feels that it is, this makes it very difficult to get managers to think in different ways, or to acknowledge that they still have a way to go before they are effectively implementing IMC. One recent trend in marketing is niche or micro-marketing, an increasingly popular way of addressing complicated markets. One of the problems here is that too often managers feel that each segment or niche requires its own distinct communication programme. But, if a single *brand* is involved, the most effective course is still likely to be one IMC programme. The *executions* will not necessarily be the same, but the overall look and feel must be if you are to maximize the impact of your communication expenditure. Even if it may be better to position a brand differently to different segments under certain circumstances, within each segment you should still be approaching the strategic development of the communications within the same IMC framework.

CHAPTER SUMMARY

In this chapter we have seen how the notion of Integrated Marketing Communication (IMC) defines how effective marketing communication programmes are developed. And importantly, we have seen that IMC is defined in terms of *planning*, the strategic planning process that is at the heart of this book. We then looked at the differences between traditional advertising and promotion, and how they can be integrated for optimal effect. We outlined their relative strengths and weaknesses in relation to the four basic communication effects, and then went on to discuss the way in which a product's position in the product life cycle can guide the relative emphasis placed on traditional advertising versus promotion. We examined the ratchet effect of combined advertising and promotion activity, but suggested that, although advertising and promotion used together offer real advantages over using only one or the other, the emphasis should almost always be on using advertising, because of its ability to build brand attitude strength. We went on to discuss integrated marketing communications and related it to the use of the Marketing Communication Task Grid, emphasizing the need for all communications to be driven by strategy. As part of the Marketing Communication Task Grid we considered the primary media needed for achieving the desired communication effect, and addressed additional media options for specific cases. Then, we looked at the importance of tracking the campaign. Finally, we discussed barriers to the implementation of effective IMC.

QUESTIONS TO CONSIDER

15.1 How would you define Integrated Marketing Communication?

15.2 What are the roles of advertising and promotion in IMC?

15.3 In what way do advertising and promotion each contribute to an effective overall campaign?

15.4 How can a Marketing Communication Task Grid help the manager in putting together an IMC programme?

15.5 What are primary media, and how do they differ in terms of brand awareness and brand attitude strategy?

15.6 How would you approach selecting primary media for non-consumer advertising?

15.7 Why is it important to track advertising over time?

15.8 Why is it so difficult to implement IMC successfully?

CASE STUDY 15

VisitScotland—How the Adventure Sport Campaign Created a Step-Change for Brand Scotland

This paper will demonstrate how VisitScotland built a successful Adventure Sports brand through TV, PR, and Events, extending its brand portfolio effectively. *'In early 2003, the adventure sports market in Scotland was highly fragmented made up of hundreds of small, independently run businesses competing with each other rather than for Scotland. No umbrella official body existed and VisitScotland, seeing the huge potential of developing an adventure sports brand.'*

The majority of activity holidays taken by the British are within the UK and short break takers are looking for new destinations closer to home. Scotland, with its beautiful natural environment, space, and proximity to England is ideally placed to capitalize on these trends. The UK adventure visitor is also a younger, more lucrative proposition than the average UK visitor to Scotland as they spend more and stay longer. Therefore, they are worth going after. Therefore Adventure Sport presented such a great opportunity for growth and destination image enhancement that it was immediately elevated to one of the key product pillars supporting Brand Scotland. *'It was clear from the findings that Scotland offered massive potential for Adventure Sports, having identified a young, new, keen audience in the UK who love the idea of Scotland as an adventure activity destination. It earmarked Mountain Biking, surfing and sea kayaking as well as adrenaline sports as key development areas for Scotland.'*

This was the green light for VisitScotland to invest significantly in developing the Adventure Sports 'brand strand'. Scotland's Adventure Sports brand positioning was designed with the aim of becoming 'Europe's Adventure Capital'. The real opportunity was not only to develop a lucrative Adventure Sports brand strand for Scotland, but to also use this strand to force a fresh re-evaluation of Scotland as a destination as a whole.

The core objectives were therefore:

- To reposition Brand Scotland in the UK to a younger, short-break taker as a more diverse, contemporary, and compelling destination with the use of Adventure Sports.
- To build awareness of Scotland as a World Class Adventure Sports destination.

Three key Strategic Activity Pillars for Adventure Sports were developed. A combination of new TV, staging world class events (and the PR spin off from these), and a new web-site formed the backbone of the activity.

1. TV

The aim of the ad was to build greater awareness of Scotland as a diverse, exciting destination amongst younger people, offering a variety of activities. As a result, the new Adventure ad rapidly built 'Recognition', with a 48 per cent increase. The ad also successfully communicated that Scotland has 'lots of activities to do'. Moreover, the ad had a very positive impact on Scotland's brand imagery amongst those who'd never been to Scotland. Very importantly, the ad challenges how people 'feel about Scotland' and it makes them feel more positive. Finally, the ad did specifically have a greater impact on younger people not loyal in any way to Scotland. Clearly, VisitScotland had achieved their key Brand Development Objective of changing perceptions of Brand Scotland through Adventure Sports amongst a younger market.

2. Events/PR

The second Strategic Activity Pillar of Adventure sport was to have a strong presence at all major adventure sporting events in Scotland and to gain as much PR coverage as possible from these events. It was specifically at the phenomenally successful Mountain Bike World Cup at Fort William in 2004 that VisitScotland really articulated a new, more dynamic side to Scotland's persona by creating a highly impactful and fun ambient campaign. The idea was to have a VisitScotland open top bus—the most striking object at the event which managed to outdo even Red Bull in the impact stakes—sporting a 6 ft mountain bike rider perched on top with the strapline 'Maniacs wanted, apply within'. In addition, a blow-up poster in the shape of an air bag was sited right next to the finish line, the message reading: 'With over 40 adventure sports from the mildly exhilarating to the downright scary, you might need one. Live it. VisitScotland.'

As a result, visitor numbers to the event went up dramatically by 17.5 per cent year on year. The TV coverage and PR VisitScotland generated for Scotland by the event was fantastic and key in establishing Scotland as one of the top mountain bike destinations in Europe as the event was broadcast throughout the world. Thus, Scotland is now hosting the Mountain Bike World Cup Final in September 2005 and the Mountain Bike World Championships in 2007—the 'Olympics' of the mountain bike world. Finally, the highly respected International Mountain Bicycling Association declared Scotland one of the top five places to go on the planet for mountain biking and, in late 2004, it was voted Number One in the world under the 'People's Choice' category which is determined by the highest combined grades in an on-line poll of mountain bikers. Scotland not only beat America and Australia to get these amazing accolades, but the Welsh, who have also been working hard to develop their Mountain Biking brand.

In terms of PR, the VisitScotland team had carefully cultivated a strong relationship with key sports journalists over 2003/2004—and the press coverage and support has been truly excellent, the equivalent of a staggering £91,000 in paid-for media terms.

The Scottish journalists particularly have been extremely important in promoting a positive side of Adventure sports in Scotland and the destination as a whole. *'Change does appear to be in the air. And it seems that, from the Scottish Parliament to the 17,000 people who attended this year's Mountain Bike World Cup, to the development of the Glencoe Ski resort as a year-round adventure centre, Scotland's claim to be recognised as a world-class adventure sports destination becomes ever more credible.'*

3. Information/Web

This final Strategic Activity Pillar is critical because the adventure sport industry in Scotland is so fragmented that easy to find, good quality information for Scotland had been elusive. VisitScotland knew that its key market for adventure sports—20- to 40-year-old 'urban adventurers'—are huge web users and utilize the web 80 per cent of the time to find out destination information. Therefore, the Adventure Sports web-site would be the key portal for quick information about Scotland for this market. The aim was to make the new site the definitive site for all adventure sports in Scotland as part of the VisitScotland brand. The brief said: *'It has to be inspiring but not "frightening" It has to have "wow" factor images to evoke the response "I didn't know you could do that in Scotland". It is about building awareness of the array of sports, providing them with the necessary information and converting it into a trip to Scotland. It is crucial that it is funky, cool and stylish.'* The dynamic new site emerged in September 2004 as VisitScotland.com/adventure, featuring over 60 adventure operators keen to work in partnership with VisitScotland. Even though only launched in September 2004, the web results are already very encouraging.

VisitScotland also collaborated with *The List* magazine to produce an 'Adventure Sports Guide to Scotland'. This was distributed to hostels, bars, outdoor-related companies and events in Scotland and was the first ever all-inclusive adventure sports brochure produced by Scotland. A highly successful 'Adventure Pass' was also created by VisitScotland which showed a 330 per cent increase in demand over 2003/04.

But how did the adventure industry itself feel by the end of 2004?

VisitScotland commissioned an on-line survey with the industry in December 2004. The results are very encouraging.

Operators report that 2004 has been a better year than 2003. They also report that their annual turnover has increased. And that customer numbers have gone up too.

Finally and with regards to ROI, the most recent data, as measured by the United Kingdom Tourism Survey, showed an increase in visitor spend on adventure tourism in Scotland of £39 million generated from 100,000 more trips between 2002 and 2003. VisitScotland's budget in 2003 was £714,000, equating to an approximate ROI of £54 for every £1 spent—way above the target of 1:12 set by the Scottish Executive.

This evidence vindicates VisitScotland's decision to invest in the Adventure Sports Brand.

This paper has demonstrated that VisitScotland's brand development vision has created a brand extension success story using a combined advertising, PR, and Events strategy. Due to VisitScotland's insight and bravery as a marketing organization, the destination is now being seen in a fresh light and as a 'World Class' Adventure destination.

Source: WARC, Institute of Practitioners in Advertising, Scottish IPA Effectiveness Awards, 2005, 'Visit Scotland—How The Adventure Sport Campaign Created A Step-Change for Brand Scotland', by Ruth Lees

Edited by Natalia Yannopoulou

Discussion Questions

1 What was in this case the key element for having a successful planning and implementation of IMC?

2 What would be a proposed strategy for the coming years for VisitScotland?

3 What are the elements that should be taken under consideration when deciding to implement IMC?

4 How should they go about deciding on the best IMC combination?

FURTHER READING

- In a paper that looks at the relationship between IMC and performance, 'IMC-Performance Relationship: Further Insight and Evidence from the Australian marketplace', *International Journal of Advertising*, 22/2 (2003), 227–48, Mike Reid finds a positive relationship between IMC and brand-related performance.

- Although the concept of IMC has been around now for over a decade, there continues to be a sense in the marketing and communication literature that it reflects the 'future'. Two papers by J. P. Cornelissen are typical: 'Integration in Communication Management: Conceptual and Methodological Considerations', *Journal of Marketing Management*, 16 (2000), and 'Integrated Marketing Communications and the Language of Market Development', *International Journal of Advertising*, 20/4 (2001).

- In an interesting paper, George Lowe, 'Correlates of Integrated Marketing Communication', *Journal of Advertising Research* (Jan./Feb. 2000), a number of factors are identified that are related to the degree of integration on a firm's marketing communication activity.

- An overall look at how advertising contributes to brand success may be found in a collection of twenty essays edited by Leslie Butterfield, *Advalue: Twenty Ways Advertising Works for Business* (Oxford: Butterworth-Heinemann, 2003).

NOTES

1 A number of US studies conducted in the early 1990s that researched marketing managers' opinions of integrated marketing communication all suggested a positive response to the idea. A study reported by C. E. Caywood, D. E. Schultz, and P. Wang, *Integrated Marketing Communication: A Survey of National Consumer Goods* (Evanston, Ill.: Department of Integrated Advertising Marketing Communications, Northwestern University, 1991), found that senior marketing executives of major fmcg advertisers believed IMC to be a sound idea with real value to their company; and two-thirds said they now practised IMC. In another study reported by T. R. Duncan and S. E. Everett, 'Client Perceptions of Integrated Marketing Communication', *Journal of Advertising Research* (May/June 1993), 30–9, communications and marketing managers overwhelmingly reported feeling that IMC was 'very valuable'.

2   A useful discussion of the need for planning in IMC can be found in L. Percy, *Strategies for Implementing Integrated Marketing Communication* (Lincolnwood, Ill.: NTC Business Books, 1997), and J. Moore and E. Thorson, 'Strategic Planning for Integrated Marketing Communications Programmes: An Approach to Moving from Chaotic towards Systematic', in E. Thorson and J. Moore (eds), *Integrated Communication* (Mahwah, NJ: Lawrence Erlbaum Associates, 1966), 135–52.

3   J. R. Rossiter and L. Percy, *Advertising Communication and Promotion Management* (New York: McGraw-Hill, 1997).

4   When J. R. Rossiter and L. Percy first introduced their notion of communication effects in *Advertising and Promotion Management* (New York: McGraw-Hill, 1987), they also went into considerable detail discussing the relative strength of advertising and promotion in generating those effects.

5   See R. A. Strang, *The Practical Planning Process* (New York: Praeger, 1980).

6   Lodish and others have found that advertising elasticities are dynamic, and decrease during the product life cycle. See L. M. Lodish *et al.*, 'How Advertising Works: A Meta-Analysis of 389 Real World Split Cable TV Advertising Experiments', *Journal of Marketing Research*, 32 (May 1995), 125–39.

7   A number of case histories supporting the idea that effective advertising leads to better promotions are discussed by W. T. Moran in a paper presented to the Association of National Advertisers' research workshop in New York on 9 Dec. 1981. This paper was summarized in 'Use Sales Promotion Yardstick ANA Told', *Advertising Age*, 14 Dec. 1981, 12.

8   See W. T. Moran, 'Insights from Pricing Research', in E. B. Bailey (ed.), *Pricing Practices and Strategies* (New York: The Conference Board, 1978), 7–13.

9   There is a great deal of empirical research that supports this notion. Lodish and his colleagues have found that short-term effects in marketing communication are necessary for long-term effects, as they point out in 'A Summary of Fifty-Five In-Market Experimental Estimates of the Long-Term Effects of Advertising', *Marketing Science*, 14 (1995), 6133–40. A more specific conclusion has been reached by John Philip Jones, who notes that short-term promotional effects are longer than advertising effects, and that short-term advertising effects diminish rapidly. See his 'Exposure Effects under a Microscope', *Admap*, 30 (Feb. 1995), 28–31, and *When Ads Work* (New York: Lexington Books, 1995).

10   An excellent review of advertising effectiveness testing may be found in a paper by Flemming Hansen, 'Testing Communication Effects', to appear in the *Handbook of Marketing and Opinion Research*, ed. Colin McDonald for ESOMAR. Also J. P. Jones (ed.), *How Advertising Works* (Thousand Oaks, Calif.: Sage, 1998), provides a number of informative chapters on research in advertising.

11   The Market Mind tracking system was developed by Max Sutherland, and his book with Alice Sylvester *Advertising and the Mind of the Consumer* (Sydney: Allen and Unwin, 2000) offers a good introduction to continuous tracking, along with extensive examples.

12   See C. S. Craig, B. Sternthal, and C. Leavill, 'Advertising Wearout: An Experimental Analysis', *Journal of Marketing Research*, 13/4 (1976), 365–72.

13   Dramatic interference effects were demonstrated in another early study by L. A. Lo Sciuto, L. H. Strassman, and W. D. Wells, 'Advertising Weight and the Reward Value of the Brand', *Journal of Advertising Research*, 7/2 (1976), 34–8.

14 With multiple exposures counter-arguing can occur that leads to negative attitudes and rejection of the message. See B. J. Calder and B. Sternthal, 'Television Commercial Wearout: An Information Processing View', *Journal of Marketing Research*, 17/2 (1980), 173–86.

15 A more in-depth discussion of potential problems in implementing IMC may be found in two papers in E. Thorson and J. Moore (eds), *Integrated Communication* (Mahwah, NJ: Lawrence Erlbaum Associates, 1996); D. Prensky, J. A. McCarty, and J. Lucas, 'Integrated Marketing Communication: An Organizational Perspective', 167–84; and L. A. Petrison and P. Wang, 'Integrated Marketing Communication: Examining, Planning, and Executional Considerations', 153–65.

 Visit the Online Resource Centre that accompanies this book for additional resources to support the text: http://www.oxfordtextbooks.co.uk/orc/ percy_elliott3e/

GLOSSARY

acceptance   believing a message; necessary to forming positive brand attitude when there is perceived risk in a purchase decision (high-involvement brand attitude strategies)

affect   in cognitive psychology, this is the evaluative dimension of attitude (favourable or unfavourable)

affect programme theory   the coordinated set of changes that constitute an emotional response, including physiological, behavioural, and subjective feelings

assimilation-contrast theory   the idea advanced by Sherif and Hovland in the 1960s that a person's current position serves as a point of reference in relation to an attempt to persuade, assimilating positions close to his or her own and contrasting (or rejecting) positions discrepant from his or her own

attention   partly an automatic process, and central to perception and consciousness, it is the first step in processing a message

attitude   a relative concept, described by Fishbein and Ajzen as 'a learned predisposition to respond in a consistently favourable or unfavourable manner with respect to a given object'

attributes   objective characteristics of something—for example, a brand

automatic processing   what psychologists call processing of information that guides behaviour, but without conscious awareness, and without interfering with other conscious activity that may be going on at the same time: for example, driving slowly down a street (automatic processing) while looking for a specific address (conscious processing)

behavioural sequence model (BSM)   a way of looking at how consumers make decisions in a product category, establishing first the stages they go through, then for each stage who are involved and the roles they play, where that stage occurs, the timing, and how

benefit   for a brand, the answer to the question 'What does it offer?', described in terms of attributes, subjective characteristics, or emotions

benefit focus   how the benefit claim in a message is made, positioning a brand consistent with the underlying motivation driving behaviour in the category

brand attitude   a necessary communication objective reflecting the link between the brand and its benefit

brand awareness   a necessary communication objective reflecting the link in memory between the brand and the need it fulfils (category need)

brand awareness strategy   how brand awareness is used by consumers in the actual purchase decision, either by recognizing the brand at the point of purchase, or recalling it when the need occurs

brand attitude strategy   one of four strategic directions reflecting the degree of perceived risk in the purchase decision (low versus high involvement) and the underlying motivation driving behaviour in the category (positive versus negative)

brand equity   the perceived assets and liabilities associated with a brand, as reflected in people's attitude towards it, that add to or detract from its value in their mind

brand purchase intention   a desirable communication effect, and necessary communication objective for promotion, reflecting a positive disposition to purchase after processing a message

bottom-up processing   response to a stimulus directly in terms of what is seen or experienced

category need   an essential communication effect that becomes a communication objective either when there is a diminished perceived need for a product, or when the need must be established—for example, with new product introductions

central positioning   where a brand is seen as able to deliver all the main benefits associated with the category, and in effect defines the category (usually a successful pioneer brand or the market leader)

cognitive   in cognitive psychology this is the component of attitude that involves perceptual responses and beliefs about something (knowledge and assumption)

cognitive response theory   relating existing knowledge and assumptions (cognitions) to new information—for example, when exposed to an advert, in order to generate message-relevant associations

communication effect   one of four likely responses to a message: category need, brand awareness, brand attitude, or brand purchase intention

communication objective   the desired communication effect, which must always include brand awareness and brand attitude for any marketing communication, and brand purchase intention for promotion

communication response sequence   the sequence of steps necessary for the success of marketing communication: exposure to the message, processing of the message, achievement of the desired communication effect, and target audience action

communication strategy   the selection of appropriate communication objectives, and the identification of the specific brand awareness and brand attitude strategy consistent with behaviour in the category

conative   in cognitive psychology this is the component of attitude that involves actual behaviour

creative brief   a one-page document that outlines the strategic direction for creative development, covering the specific task at hand, the communication objectives and strategy, and any elements that the executions must contain

cross-elasticity   a way of defining markets in terms of price relationships between brands, where a change in price for one brand brings about a change in price for another brand

decision roles   whether a person is involved as an initiator, influencer, decider, purchaser, or user in the decision to buy or use a product or service

declarative memory   what we 'know we know' and can easily state in words

differentiated positioning   a positioning based upon a benefit that gives a brand an advantage over other brands in the consumer's mind

direct marketing   utilizing a database specifically to target consumers, bypassing traditional channels of distribution

emotion   incidents of coordinated changes in several areas, including what has been called the 'reaction triad' of physiological arousal, motor expression, and subjective feeling, in response to either an internal or an external event of significant importance to an individual

emotional authenticity   necessary for all advertising addressing positive motives (transformational brand attitude strategies), where the creative execution is seen as 'real' and not posed or artificial

encoding specificity   an idea advanced by Endell Tulvincy suggesting that to retrieve something successfully from memory requires a match between how the information was originally encoded and the information available when trying to retrieve the memory

episodic memory   memories of a single event, and part of declarative memory

ethos   following Aristotle, persuasion based upon an appeal that concentrates upon the source of the message rather than the source itself

excitatory behaviour   from classical conditioning, it is related to the underlying motivation that initiates an emotional sequence in the processing of a message

expectancy value   perhaps the most widely used model of attitude (generally attributed to Martin Fishbein), it posits that one's attitude is a summary of everything believed about something weighted by the importance attached to those beliefs

explicit memory   the conscious recall of information that is recognized as coming from memory

frequency   the number of times an individual in a target audience is exposed to a campaign in a specific time period

goals   an objective (which is a broad aim or desired outcome) made specific in terms of time and degree—for example, increasing sales 20 per cent over the next year

gross rating point (GRP)   the product of reach time frequency in a media schedule

hierarchal partitioning   a way of looking at markets by determining the order in which consumers consider the characteristic of a product in the decisions they make

implicit memory   the unconscious impact of recent experiences on behaviour

informational brand attitude strategy   communication strategy for building positive brand attitude when the underlying motivation driving behaviour in the category is negative (for example, problem solution or problem avoidance)

information processing paradigm   a model proposed by William J. McGuire to define the steps necessary for communication to change attitude: the message must be presented, attended to, comprehended, and yielded to, and that intention retained and acted upon

inhibitory behaviour   from classical conditioning, it is related to the motivation and emotion associated with the end state in processing a message

integrated marketing communication (IMC)   the planning and execution of all types of advertising and promotion (that is, any marketing communication) for a brand, service, or company in order to meet a common set of communication objectives in support of a single positioning

involvement   the perceived risk associated with a purchase or usage decision, measured dichotomously as high (risk attached) or low (no risk attached)

learning   an essential stage in the processing of all messages, it is the rote acquisition of some part of a message's content, and can occur without conscious effort

limbic system   an area in the forebrain traditionally considered critical for emotion, and where innate responses required for survival as a species are thought to originate

logos   following Aristotle, persuasion that uses an appeal to logical arguments that requires one to draw one's own conclusion based upon the argument presented

long-term potentiation (LTP)   the neurological basis of learning, it is the process of stimulating a dendritic spine repeatedly, leaving it more responsive to new input of the same type

marketing plan   a general term used to describe the overall plan for marketing a brand, which outlines goals and objectives for the brand, and how to reach them

memory   studied by philosophers, writers, and scientists for hundreds of years, it is the reflection of an accumulation of all of our experiences, and is (as described by Howard Eschenbaum) 'who we are'.

mere exposure   described by Zajonc and his colleagues, it represents an example of unconscious affective memory, independent of declarative memory, where a slight preference is expressed for familiar items even when they are not explicitly remembered

motivation   the innate or acquired drive that stimulates behaviour, and that may be negatively originated to solve or avoid a problem (for example) or positively originate for sensory gratification or social approval

new media   a general term covering non-traditional ways of delivering advertising or promotion messages, anything from text messaging to the Internet

non-declarative emotional memory   centred in the amygdala, it is where emotional associations and experiences are stored out of consciousness, but nevertheless inform conscious processing

objective   a broad or general description of a desired outcome

objective characteristic   specific attributes or features of a brand or product such as alcoholic content in beer or memory capacity in a computer

partitioning   a way of looking at markets in terms of how consumers categorize products in relationship to perceived characteristics of the category

pathos   following Aristotle, persuasion that uses appeals that involve feelings, values, or emotions

perceptions   in both a colloquial and neuro-psychological sense, what your mind tells you something is

positioning   in terms of marketing communication, locating a brand in the target audience's mind relative to competitors in terms of benefits

primary emotion   following Damasio, universal emotions that are located in the limbic system and are triggered directly by sensory input without the mediation of higher brain centres: happiness, sadness, fear, anger, surprise, and disgust

primary media   the key media in a campaign that provide the most effective media for achieving all a brand's communication objectives

processing   the immediate response to elements in an advert or promotion: attention, learning, emotion, and (for high-involvement purchase decisions) acceptance

product benefit-oriented positioning   positioning a brand in marketing communication where the product is the hero and is defined in terms of specific benefits, not the user

product life cycle   traditional marketing understanding of the progress of a brand or product over time, moving through four stages: introduction, growth, maturity, and decline

psycho-graphics   term used to describe various target audience characteristics such as 'feelings' and other non-demographic variables

psycho-linguistics   the study of how verbal content of a message is processed, and what is needed for effective communication

ratchet effect   following William Moran, the idea that using advertising and promotion together in an appropriate way enables promotions to help 'ratchet up' the overall effect of advertising

reach   the percentage of a target audience that has an opportunity for exposure to a campaign in a given time period

recall brand awareness   where the category need stimulates the recall of a brand that will satisfy that need

recognition brand awareness   when a brand is recognized at the point of purchase, and that recognition reminds the consumer of a need for the product

reflexive attention   unconscious attention that occurs automatically, and associated with bottom-up processing

schemata   following Bartlett, a way of organizing in memory past experiences so that in remembering one constructs or infers the probable components of a memory and the order in which they occur

secondary emotions   following Damasio, emotions that are acquired such as embarrassment, jealousy, guilt, or pride and that are triggered by things one has been sensitized to through experience

selective attention   voluntary attention that occurs consciously, and associated with top-down processing

semantic memory   everything one knows, not connected to any specific experience where it was acquired (unlike episodic memory), and part of declarative memory

segmentation   identifying niches or subgroups within a market, generally with the aim of more targeted communication

sequential planning   a planning process where the order in which the steps taken are critical to the result, such as the strategic planning process for advertising and other marketing communication

strategy   in the broadest sense, a specific way in which something is to be done

strategic planning   the specific process used to accomplish a task, such as the five steps necessary to develop an effective advertising campaign

synapses   the gap between two neurons, over which impulses lead to learning

tactic   specific details or parts of a strategy, and how it can be implemented

target audience   that portion of a market identified to receive messages in the form of advertising or promotion

top-down processing   the use of knowledge and assumptions in the processing of any stimulus, beyond simple sensory input (bottom-up processing)

transformational brand attitude strategy   communication strategy for building positive brand attitude when the underlying motivation driving behaviour in the category is positive (for example, sensory gratification or social approval)

user-oriented positioning   while utilizing brand benefits, the message is specifically addressing the user of the brand, not the product

visual imagery   the images stimulated in the 'mind's eye' either by something concrete such as an advert or by a memory

working memory   temporary storage of information while one is working with it or attending to it

■ INDEX